THE AMERICAN EARTHQUAKE

THE AMERICAN EARTHQUAKE

A DOCUMENTARY OF THE
TWENTIES AND THIRTIES
BY
Edmund Wilson

OCTAGON BOOKS

A DIVISION OF FARRAR, STRAUS AND GIROUX

New York   1980

Copyright © 1958 by Edmund Wilson

Reprinted 1971
by special arrangement with Doubleday & Company, Inc.

Second Octagon printing 1975
Third Octagon printing 1980

OCTAGON BOOKS
A DIVISION OF FARRAR, STRAUS & GIROUX, INC.
19 Union Square West
New York, N.Y. 10003

LIBRARY OF CONGRESS CATALOG CARD NUMBER: 78-139823
ISBN 0-374-98649-5

Manufactured by Braun-Brumfield, Inc.
Ann Arbor, Michigan
Printed in the United States of America

CONTENTS

I. THE FOLLIES
1923–1928

II. THE EARTHQUAKE
OCTOBER 1930–OCTOBER 1931

III.   DAWN OF THE NEW DEAL
1932–1934

THE MATERIAL IN THIS VOLUME, a selection from my non-literary articles written during the twenties and thirties, runs more or less parallel to the literary material collected in my earlier volume, *The Shores of Light,* a selection of articles on books written in the same period. The pieces in the first of the three sections have never been reprinted before; the pieces in the second section were reprinted in a book called *The American Jitters* (in England, *Devil Take the Hindmost*), published in 1932; and most of the pieces in the third —though a few have not been printed or collected before— in *Travels in Two Democracies,* published in 1936. Most of this material is simple reporting, as accurate as I could make it—though Miss Dabney in *Red Cross and County Agent* is more or less a composite type. The purely satirical sketches will be readily recognized. Four narratives—*After the Game, Reunion, The Men from Rumpelmayer's* and *What to Do Till the Doctor Comes*—though told in the first person, are fiction. All the pieces have been revised, and in some cases much rewritten. The dating of the items in the first section refers to magazine publication; in the third, by month and year or merely by year, to the time of the occurrence of the event reported. In the second, a dating by publication would result in a false chronology, and, since only a little more than a year is covered, the month or season is usually clear.

I did not visit Soviet Russia till 1935, a year after the last of these sketches was written. I was still in the earlier phases of what was to become later on a fairly intensive study of Marxism, and I find that—though the class war was very much a reality in the United States during the thirties—I too eagerly drew Marxist morals from the phenomena I went out to explore. The more shallow or nagging of these I have been happy to lop away, but I have not, beyond this, made any attempt to correct my point of view of that time. The class conflict, as I say, was perfectly real, as well as the catastrophic breakdown of the uncontrolled competitive system, and my confidence in the Soviet Union to put into practice its Leninist ideals was implied in my whole attitude toward what was going on at home. I realize, however, that, for anyone who did not live through those years, it is hard to imagine them accurately and, in consequence, to understand the direction that the interests and activities of American liberals took. Certain reviews of the admirable first volume of Mr. Arthur M. Schlesinger, Jr.'s *The Age of Roosevelt: The Crisis of the Old Order, 1919–1933*—which supplies an historical background for this fragmentary panorama—illustrate how difficult it is for persons who were born too late to have memories of the depression to believe that it really occurred, that between 1929 and 1933 the whole structure of American society seemed actually to be going to pieces. And I am also aware that, for the period of the boom, it may be as difficult to understand why, in 1925, for example, I should have watched with a certain emotion the trial of Dorothy Perkins as why later, in 1930, I should have been so much stirred by the spectacle of William Z. Foster appearing before the Fish Committee. But I have mostly depended on my chronicle to tell its own story.

The greater part of this material originally appeared in the *New Republic,* though a few of the pieces included came out in other magazines: the *Dial,* the *New Yorker, Scribner's Magazine, Common Sense* and the *Modern Monthly. Return from Louisiana* is reprinted from my *Note-Books of Night.*

Acknowledgments should be made to the Macmillan Company for permission to reprint the poem by Thomas Hardy.

I
THE FOLLIES

1923–1928

"ON THIS SITE WILL BE ERECTED"

WALKING IN Varick Street, I find that I am sometimes haunted by the image of St. John's Chapel. When I last saw it, between the Sixth Avenue El and the freightyards of the Central Railroad, it presented, with its fine proportions and the dignity of its brown façade, a solitary architectural visage among the faceless constructions that outbulked it. There was still a placard on the door which said, "Seats Free. St. John's Chapel. Trinity Parish"; but the steps and the floor of the portico had already been taken down to make room for the new subway, and the pillars lifted tarnished foliation straight from the dirt of the road. Many of the small square panes had been broken in the round-arched windows; the clock in the spire had lost its hands, and its face was obliterated. The old spire itself, with its multiplied tiers, was beginning to lurch a little, like the mast of a sinking ship. And now, indeed, the office buildings, the freightyards and the factories have closed over it and swallowed it up, imposing a monotony as blank as the sea.

———

One notes with a certain curiosity the survival on West Fourteenth Street, just opposite Hearn's department store, of a very large old brownstone mansion which, in spite of its dismal and rubbishy color, still exhibits a striking magnificence. The basement, with its iron-grated windows, is not, like most basements, buried, but rises above the pavement so that the front door looks down on the street from a haughty and impressive height; dark panels carved with rosettes and garlands are deeply framed in an elaborate doorway of fluted

acanthus-wreathed columns and a stone pediment with ornamental scrolls; and, on either side, two tall windows, capped
with similar pediments—very grand like a French *hôtel*—open
on a gray stone-railed balcony. One sees the long folding
blinds inside—white panels with a fine thread of gold—still
elegant and clean, since protected from the sordidness of today's Fourteenth Street. There is also a yard—very large for
New York—which extends to the street behind and is guarded
in front by a high-paled brown fence; and here one sometimes sees an old man who works about the lawn and the
stables. He is decrepit and, though obviously respectable, has
come to look rubbishy like everything else. The low stable—
to which leads a driveway fenced off from the lawn by a
wrought-iron hedge—has a frieze of pigeonholes, in which
there are still a few pigeons, and old-fashioned hairpin-
shaped doors, which, when open, reveal ancient carriages
dating from some period when the city was half a provincial
town. The lawn has gone partially bald, and most of the iris
plants which the old man still tries to tend are bedded in
hard barren earth. On the other side of the house from the
stable the yard is a narrow strip, walled in by the beginning
of a block of shops, and here there is no grass at all, but only
bare dirt strewn with paper and glass, in which stand thin
skeletons of trees that lean like overgrown weeds. Two brown
oriel windows protrude toward these trees, and one can imagine a family of nice city children looking down from the
security of their window-seats into the rainy April yard.
But no children look out of these windows now, nor even
any comfortable old people. The high flight of steps to the
august front door has been encased in a wall of stone, which
reaches from the walk to the sill: it is as if the family had
pulled up their drawbridge, locked their doors, closed their
blinds and quietly died out in the dark.

————

In Brooklyn, in the neighborhood of Henry Street, the
pleasant red and pink brick houses still worthily represent
the generation of Henry Ward Beecher; but an eternal Sun-

day is on them now; they seem sunk in a final silence. In the streets one may catch a glimpse of a solitary well-dressed old gentleman moving slowly a long way off; but in general the respectable have disappeared and only the vulgar survive. The empty quiet is broken by the shouts of shrill Italian children and by incessant mechanical pianos in dingy apartment houses, accompanied by human voices that seem almost as mechanical as they. At night, along unlighted streets, one gives a wide berth to drunkards that sprawl out across the pavement from the shadow of darkened doors; and I have known a dead horse to be left in the road—two blocks from the principal post office and not much more from the Borough Hall—with no effort made to remove it, for nearly three weeks. In the summer, warm sickening fumes from a factory that makes cheap chocolate give a stagnancy of swamps to the heavy air. In the evening, an old woman steals through the streets, softly calling to cats, which she poisons and which die slowly of gripes in the areas of decorous houses from which the families have moved away.

———

So much for the dead and the dying; in the newer part of town, the East Forties, looking down from a high upper window, one takes account of the monstrous carcass of the Grand Central Station and Palace, with its myriad skylights and its zinc-livid roofs, stretched out like a segmented seaworm that is almost unrecognizable as a form of life. Beyond it rise the upright rectangles of drab or raw yellow brick—yellows devoid of brilliance, browns that are never rich—perforated, as if by a perforating machine, with rows of rectangular windows; the stiff black fingers of factories; blunt truncated meaningless towers; a broken scrambling of flat roofs and sharp angles which is yet a compact fitting-in; and then the lead-silver river strung across with its skeletal bridge. In the middle distance, the sky itself seems to be overdisplaced—like a pool in which a large safe has been dropped—by a disagreeably colored hotel, brownish yellow like a bronchial trochee and so immense that its cubic acres seem to weigh down the very island, almost to make it sag. A flock of pigeons that fly below have the look, in the dull light, of wastepaper blown by the wind.

————

Sitting indoors in New York by day, one becomes aware of mysterious noises: the drilling of granite teeth, the cackling of mechanical birds, the thudding of Cyclopean iron doors; accelerating avalanches of brick, the collapse of deserted warehouses; explosives that cause no excitement, pistol shots that are quite without consequence. Nor does one care to find out what these noises are. One goes on with whatever one is doing, incurious and wholly indifferent.

May 20, 1925

THE PEOPLE AGAINST DOROTHY PERKINS

DOROTHY PERKINS was born and lived all her life at 26 Jane Street, between Greenwich and Eighth Avenues—one of those dingy red brick apartment houses characteristic of the lower West Side, with dark stairs, narrow halls and narrow windows, the latter obscured by black old-fashioned blinds of which many of the slats are missing. Her mother is an Irishwoman; her father is a carpenter whose addiction to drink has interfered with the practice of his trade. Dorothy went through public school, took a two months' course at a business school, and in September, 1923, when she was fifteen years old, got a job as a telephone operator. She was a pretty, quick-witted red-haired girl, slight of figure but tense and strong-willed and reputed to have a bad temper. When she was asked, in the course of the questioning, why she had taken the revolver from her aunt's house, she replied that she had done it on impulse, and when it was inquired whether she "always acted on impulse," she replied that "when she wanted a thing she usually got it." Her pastor described her in a letter to the judge as a "wayward" girl who "disregarded the tenets of the religion in which she was born" and "would not follow moral teaching." In August of 1923 she began a love affair with a truckdriver of thirty-five known as Mickey Connors, who had a flat on the floor below her parents and often came to dinner with them. She used to run errands for him, and one day he asked her into his room and offered her a drink which he said was soda water but which turned out to be a highball. He appears to have threatened and maltreated her, and she seems to have loved him fiercely. He had twice done time in jail, once for robbing the mails.

They broke off at the end of nine months, for reasons which do not appear, and Connors, a month afterwards, married a woman who had just been released on parole from a sentence for grand larceny. Connors moved up to 126th Street; and Dorothy began going about with a young brakeman on the Pennsylvania Railroad named Templeton, who had fallen in love with her and wanted to marry her. She had told him about Mickey Connors, but that had not made any difference. In the second week of February, 1925, Mickey Connors left his wife and came back again to Greenwich Village, taking a room in a house on Greenwich Street where an aunt of Dorothy's lived. At about the same time, Dorothy, going to the theater one evening with Templeton and some of their friends, showed them a revolver which she said she had taken from the house of an aunt in the country. They asked her what she was going to do with it, and she replied that she was "the blond-haired bandit." "Don't you know if you carry that gun," said Templeton, "you'll get us both into trouble?" Dorothy is said to have answered that she needed it to protect herself against Mrs. Connors. On the night of February 13, Dorothy went with Mickey Connors to the Fourteenth Street Armory to attend a review of the Ninth Coast Artillery Regiment, of which both her father and Templeton were members. They ran into Templeton there, and he asked her to come to his company room, where there were dancing and refreshments, but Dorothy said she did not want to, and Templeton became very angry: "If you want to see me any time," he challenged Connors, "I'm right here in Company F!"

The next night, the Perkins family gave a party in celebration of Mr. Perkins' birthday, which fell on St. Valentine's Day. Templeton called up early in the evening and asked if Dorothy would mind his coming, in spite of what had happened the day before, and she told him to come along. She then went out to Greenwich Street, where Connors lived, for the purpose, as she testified, of looking in on her aunt's baby, but according to the prosecution in order to urge Connors to come to the party—he is said to have protested that he had not shaved and she to have offered to get

him a razor. This was about half past ten, and when Dorothy
got back home, the party was well under way. Everybody
was drinking and dancing—the pianola was playing. Templeton was there with his brother and some of their friends,
all of whom had been drinking before they came; and as
soon as Dorothy appeared, there was a movement to leave
her and Templeton together and allow them to make up their
quarrel. When Dorothy and he were alone, Templeton demanded of her why she kept on going with Connors, and
she replied "because she wanted to." "Is it all over between
us, then?" he asked. "If you want to take it that way," she
answered. "As things stand now, Tommy, you and I can
never be happy. I could never be happy with one man while
I was thinking of another." He said, "I'd give my two arms
and my two legs, I'd give my life for you, Dorothy! But if
we can't be sweethearts, let's be friends anyway." "We'll have
a drink on it," she said. At this moment, Dorothy's father
interrupted the conversation: "What do you want with a
bum like Connors," he cried, "when you have a nice fellow
like Tommy? If Mickey Connors comes up here tonight, he'll
go down with bullets in him!" "Last night when you were
perfectly sober," she said, "you invited him yourself at the
armory!" "I've changed my mind since," said her father.
"That's a woman's privilege," said Dorothy.

Dorothy went to her bureau and took the revolver out:
she was afraid, she says, her father would get hold of it. He
was supply sergeant at the armory and had had one that he
was entitled to carry, but his family had taken it away from
him for fear he would shoot it off in the house. At any rate,
Dorothy went out of doors and, according to her testimony,
walked up Jane Street with the intention of getting rid of
the gun, but finally came back to the house without having
done anything with it: she had had four glasses of gin and
one of Scotch. There is a presumption, however, that she
went to Connors and tried again to make him come to the
party. When she returned, she found Templeton and her father standing together in the hallway: they were calling
Mickey Connors abusive names. "Keep Mickey's name out of
your mouths!" said Dorothy. Mr. Perkins, who was by that

time quite drunk, turned upon her and began to curse her for a slut and a loose woman. "You're to blame for all this, Tommy," she said, "having my father fight with me!" "Mickey Connors is yellow!" cried Templeton, "he's got a rod [a gun] and he's afraid to use it!" "I'll show you," cried Dorothy, pulling out her own gun, "whether my friends are yellow!" "I'll kill you, you———!" shouted her father, raising his hand to strike her. Dorothy fired the revolver, piercing her father's coat and wounding Templeton in the heart. He fell to the ground, said, "She's got me!" She threw herself upon his body and screamed, "Oh, I didn't mean to!" They bathed him with whisky but found he was dead. A scene of confusion and panic followed. Mr. Perkins fell upon Dorothy again: "I'll put you where you put him!" he shouted, and when Mrs. Perkins attempted to restrain him, he seized her by the throat and threw her against the wall. Dorothy finally escaped to her aunt's. When her uncle heard what had happened, he went downstairs and told Mickey Connors, and Mickey returned at once to his lodging in 126th Street. Dorothy was arrested in the early morning and cross-examined by policemen and detectives: she gave an account of what had occurred which is substantially the one I have followed.

She was confined in Jefferson Market Jail, and her case did not come up till June. In the meantime, Mickey Connors had been sentenced to six months in the workhouse for "assaulting" his wife. Dorothy wrote him a letter, in which, according to her own account, she begged him to keep his wife from spreading scandal about her; and then, when she had no reply, wrote him again to ask if he had got the first letter. She smuggled both these letters out of jail by women prisoners who were being discharged, but the second one was intercepted and later produced at the trial: it was signed "Lots of Love. Dot."

The Perkinses had no money and so were unable to retain the kind of criminal lawyer who could perhaps have got Dorothy acquitted. The attorney for the defense was Mr. Sidney Lash, who took no fee for his services and told the jury, in the course of his summing-up, that he had undertaken the case as a friend of the Ninth Regiment, in which he himself had served. It may be that the prospect of scoring a success in what promised to be a sensational trial may have also counted for something with Mr. Lash. But from my observation of him in the courtroom, I should say that Mr. Lash, who is Jewish, is both intelligent and generous enough to have defended Dorothy for her own sake. During the final days of the trial, he seemed as harrowed and anxious as the defendant herself. In any case, he prepared a defense which repudiated Dorothy's story taken down the night of the shooting, on the ground that she had been hysterical and intimidated by the police, and substituted for it a different account, to which Mrs. Perkins and other members of the family as well as Dorothy herself swore on the witness stand. According to this version, Mr. Perkins had seized Dorothy by the hand as soon as he saw the revolver, and, while he and Mrs. Perkins were struggling with her, it had gone off accidentally without its being possible to know who had pulled the trigger. The defense also sought to establish that Dorothy had taken the revolver merely because Templeton had offered to give her shooting lessons.

At first sight, it may seem rather improbable that a jury could be induced to convict a seventeen-year-old girl—especially so attractive a one as Dorothy Perkins—under the circumstances I have described. As I write, the State's attorney in the case of Olympia Macri, who shot her lover as he was coming out of a moving-picture theater and who was acquitted by eleven of her jurors, is moving for a change of venue on the grounds that public opinion in New Haven is so thoroughly prejudiced in her favor that a fair trial there will be impossible. But in Dorothy Perkins' case there appeared certain special elements which inevitably worked against her. For, not only is this snub-nosed gamine the sort of girl that men fall badly in love with, she has also the fiery spirit, the instinct of independence, which is equally sure to enrage them. Judge, jury and prosecutor alike were evidently agreed from the first moment they saw her that Dorothy was a "bad" girl; not only did they strongly resent her, they were perhaps even a little frightened by her. As one saw her in court at the trial, in the setting of the flaccid clothes and the unfocused American faces of the newspaper reporters, the spectators and the representatives of the law, beneath the massive trappings of the courtroom—the yellow panels, the plaster columns, the snarling copies of heraldic lions which have lost the conviction of the originals, the hemispherical wrought-iron chandelier like a gigantic old-fashioned mouse-trap and the Stars and Stripes over the judge's desk, hanging crooked and nearly black, as if tarnished by decades of fumes from the cases of the criminal courts—her hair of red-gold and her pale little face, her slim figure in its plain black dress, seemed to burn the assemblage at a single point with an intensity of passionate life. On the stand, drooping forward like some creamy flower on the strong little stem of her neck, confronting the prosecutor with shadowed eyes, she met a whole day's severe cross-examination on an obviously fictitious story with extraordinary readiness, bravery, endurance, ingenuity and precision. Her answers were low-voiced but direct; her gestures were few but definite—usually to brush back her bobbed hair. She had collapsed the day before after Connors had been put on the stand, and when the prosecutor made her stand up to show how the revolver had been held—her long adolescent's arms like broom handles making awkward angles against her black dress—and told her to pull the trigger, she turned to the judge and evenly asked him if she could have a few minutes' recess so that she shouldn't hold up the proceedings again. This was granted; she soon reappeared, and the questioning was continued.

But Dorothy's coolness had apparently no virtue to influence the jurors in her favor. "She's a cold little proposition!" said one man in the audience to his neighbor, "A cold little proposition!" Nor was Mr. Lash, it appeared, the man to succeed in moving them. In the first place, they had the example of the attitude of the Court, who had adopted toward the defense rather a markedly rigorous attitude: Judge McIntyre, so far as I remember, overruled, during the last three days of the trial, all of Mr. Lash's objections at the same time that he almost invariably found reason to sustain those of his adversary. As for the District Attorney himself, his well-bred irony at the expense of Mr. Lash was an effective forensic performance. Criminal lawyers are like actors: they have to capture the attention of an audience, and each has a characteristic set of tricks designed to appeal to the ordinary man. Mr. McDonald's game is gentlemanliness and affability, and, in the atmosphere of the Criminal Courts, he has no difficulty in conveying this impression. He is a good-looking man, clean-shaven and well set up, with a robust and commanding presence, who comes into court every morning in a different and beautifully pressed suit; in the courtroom, he is everybody's friend. He talks intimately with the judge, he makes the exiled jurymen feel at home, he smiles charmingly at the women reporters and puts his hand on the shoulders of the men reporters. When bullying witnesses, he brings into play a strikingly cultivated accent: he will say, for example, exquisitely, "What time in the morning were you theah?" and "So you wanted to be a shootah, did you?"

The fascination of Mr. McDonald seemed, indeed, to prove so overpowering that Mr. Lash, when he came to his summing-up, felt obliged to warn the jury against it: the District Attorney, he said, was the fortunate possessor of a "suave manner" and a "pleasing personality," and he confessed that he found himself at a disadvantage by reason of his less prepossessing presence, but hoped that this fact in itself would not prejudice them in favor of the prosecution. Then, with paroxysms of cumulative rhetoric, with salaaming gestures that almost bent him double, in a speech which contained some specious appeals and at least one passage of brilliance, he spoke of the flag of the "old Ninth Regiment," from which he had pledged himself to remove the stain and reminded the jurors that Our Lord had forgiven the woman taken in adultery. I do not know whether the jury believed in the passion of Mr. Lash's patriotism; but if they held the same opinions as a lady in the audience whom I afterwards heard discussing the speech, they must have rejected his Christianity: "I don't like a Jew like him," said this lady— one of the women reporters, I think—"bringing in the Christian Jesus!" While the lawyer for the defense was summing up, the debonair District Attorney strayed carelessly about the room, joking quietly with the reporters—apparently about the defense—and effectively diverting attention from one of the most desperate of Mr. Lash's exhortations by leaving the room by a circuitous route which enabled him to converse with a great many people and to linger for a parting pleasantry with one of the attendants at the gate. Judge McIntyre, who seems to have developed through long occupation of the Bench the kind of mountainous sedentary figure which is most imposing in a judge's gown, and who chewed something—whether gum or tobacco—throughout the later sessions, at one point walked to the window and, with an owlish gaze behind round spectacles, stared out into Lafayette Street. He said finally, "You have been talking two hours and a half: I will give you fifteen minutes more."

When the prosecutor, however, began his speech, Judge McIntyre turned his chair around and listened with respectful attention. Mr. McDonald, it should be said in justice to him, did not overdo the prosecution. The State had not been able to produce a single witness who had actually seen the shot fired, but it was only necessary for the District Attorney to read from Dorothy's first statement to make plain the discrepancies between it and the second and the superior plausibility of the first. He recommended a verdict of manslaughter and suggested a reformatory sentence. The most that he sought to establish was that Dorothy had fired the shot herself when she was drunk and in a fury, that she had been "mad enough to kill either her father or Templeton." He went on, nevertheless, to point out to the jury that the girl was given up to lies and deception, adducing as proof of this that she had smuggled her letters out of prison, "trying to get round the law!", that she had given her name as Connors at the telephone exchange and had introduced Mickey to the girls there as her brother, and finally that, just now in court, she had supported a tissue of lies with a cunning almost diabolic. Dorothy had, however, made one fatal slip in her long cross-examination—she had said, "It was when my father had hold of me that I shot the pistol," afterwards correcting herself; and of this the State was able to make telling use. Finally, the District Attorney read the jury a passage from an editorial that had recently appeared in the *Daily News:* it was complained that "the administration of the criminal law in New York, especially where women were concerned, had become a scandal and a byword"; and at this point Mr. Lash objected. Judge McIntyre, however, retorted that the District Attorney was well within his rights, adding that the Court found itself in perfect agreement with the statement which the prosecutor had read. Mr. Lash, in the last ditch of repressed resentment, replied unexpectedly that he continued to object, not only to the prosecutor's statement, but also to the attitude of the Court.

When the summings-up were over, Judge McIntyre charged the jury to allow no considerations of the defendant's sex or youth to interfere with the justice of their verdict, and the jurors withdrew to deliberate. In the course of these deliberations, it turned out that four of the twelve citizens— all married and all fathers of children—were in favor of finding Dorothy guilty of murder in the first degree and having her electrocuted. A compromise was arrived at, however, on manslaughter in the first degree. One man suggested a recommendation to mercy, but the others rejected this. The verdict was delivered about midnight. The judge summoned Dorothy to the bar and fixed his eyes upon her a moment. Then he motioned for the attendants to stand behind her. When she saw him signal to the attendants, she knew that she had lost. He then asked the jury for their verdict, and the foreman delivered it. Dorothy collapsed, and the attendants caught her; Mr. Lash began slapping her wrists and did what he could to comfort her. "In view of the defendant's condition," said the judge, "I'll defer sentence till next Monday morning." They carried her out, moaning for her mother, who was waiting outside in the hall but was not allowed to see her. Dorothy was really not unconscious, she explained to reporters afterwards: she remembered hearing the clock chime midnight in the tower of the Tombs prison. The judge thanked the jury for their verdict and told them that "women had a tendency to shoot men and then come into court and depend on the sympathy of men jurors to free them—this may stop women shooting men," he added. He said also that "speaking in a general way, the trouble with the situation was nowadays that the crimes were committed by the younger set."

On Monday Dorothy received her sentence. And on that occasion Judge McIntyre amplified the thought which he had expressed at the previous session. "Women have done too much killing," he said, "and weaklings in the jury box have set them free. It seems to me that women pick the counties in which to do their killing. Nassau, for instance, then Kings, and now here in New York. It's not going to go with me! . . . In the first place, I want to say to this defendant that I feel very very sorry for you. It is to be regretted that you stand here in the position you do, but you committed a heinous wrong. You lived a very bad life. I have received many letters concerning you. Very few sympathize with you. . . . You had from very early life meretricious relations with a married man. I regard him as a beast." He then brought forward a piece of information which, if it had been in the possession of the Court all along, might have been supposed to influence it in the direction of more rather than of less leniency, and which might have provided, in any case, an explanation of Dorothy's loyalty to Connors— so caustically denounced by the prosecution—that would have been easily comprehensible to the jury. "I have been told that the child in your aunt's house is your child." Dorothy shook her head in denial. "You are a girl, it is true, but women are not exculpated because of their sex. When a woman is bad," here he fixed the ladies in the courtroom, "she is as bad as a mortal being can be, more vicious than a man many times over. . . . I do not want to be hard on you, but I've got to punish you, and, while doing so, I want to say that you have my heartfelt sorrow. I want to add that I am not going to give you the severest penalty provided by the law. . . . The sentence of the Court is that you be confined in Auburn Prison for a minimum term of five years and a maximum period of fifteen years. Take her away."

July 15, 1925

"IT'S GREAT TO BE A NEW YORKER!"

TELEPHONE CALL AT 7: Cushman Corset Company? No; you have the wrong number! Gray winter. The crowded mailbox: Tannenbaum, Ladies' Tailor; A Good Bond Investment; You Will Want the Digest of Digests, with a Set of Kipling Free; landlord's complaint that tenants below are annoyed by sound of typewriter; letter delivered to wrong address. Iceman at wrong door. Telephone: Excuse it please! Newspaper: Collins Found Dead After Seventeen Days; Seven-Cent Fare is I. R. T. Plan. Telephone: too late—there's no one on the wire now. Genial Heywood Broun prefers Kaufman and Connelly to Shakespeare. Breakfast. Telephone: I have been trying to get you for a little party tonight. Breakfast. Somebody to see you: I don't want you to buy anything, I just want you to vote for me; I'm working for a scholarship; I want you to subscribe to the *American Farm Woman* for five years. Breakfast.

The cold taste of winter in the vestibule. Gray winter, gray paves. Old man who wants the price of a meal. A fire. The bus stops at even numbers only: 10 instead of 9; 61,800,977 passengers used these buses in the past 12 months. The number carried INSIDE was 42,024,664; all multiples of 2; 8 instead of 9, instead of 10—walk back one block. Old servant's bedroom on Ninth Street, turned into four-room apartment; two rooms without air, two rooms without air or light; a lovely old house; there is a kitchenette in the clothes closet; would they mind the typewriter? Oh, no; the partitions are very thick—see?—the house has all been done over; Mr. Hicks is the agent; $2,000 a year.

Crosstown car: they don't stop here; they do stop but when they stop it is when the whole traffic stops—a guard of taxis hedges them that keeps people from getting in; a narrow slip;

will they let down the step? a nickel for the glass trap; we don't transfer to Lexington Avenue. Lexington Avenue. Lofts to let; life in a loft—a blank life. Five rooms above Finck the Furrier; warm blast of a million wet cats; a kitchen that opens into the bathroom; you can serve your meals in the hall; this is where the roaches breed—I can smell their leafy smell; gas-heaters asphyxiate—it's all right if you put a little water over it; sign a lease to boil three hundred and sixty-five days of water over a gas radiator; there is a star-headed rivet in that brick wall that strikes an aesthetic note; $2,500.

Lunch: tables all taken—sit down opposite lady with glasses; the regular lunch; are my plates in your way? I see the salad on the brink; with salad a dollar ten—without salad a dollar; the tip a tenth of the check—a tenth of a dollar ten— eleven cents—a dollar eleven—a dollar and a quarter. It is a gray day. The steep El steps: Walk on Air Roach's Rubber Heels, Walk on Air Roach's Rubber Heels, Walk on Air Roach's Rubber Heels; we obstruct one another going up these steps—there! I have stepped on you—sorry!—just as I thought I was going to do; the automatic gate; the nickel clicks—will it stick? Take the Air Line! Read the Furriers' Sign; Hotels for Gents. The long straight uptown distances. This is going to be expensive—the elevator's wrought-iron cage; luxurious purple carpet, luxurious orange lights; The Fenimore; there is a shower, you see—yes; but no curtains— no; but there are curtain rings to hang them on, you see. Yes: I see; do those grates burn? You could have the plaster taken out and use them; they've just been sealed up with plaster; but I don't think you'll need any more heat—we've never had any complaints about the heat—in fact, some ten- ants say there's too much heat. Would he be willing to take a one-year lease?—$5,000.

Eighty-three—I must get it at 82, instead of at 83. A nar- row squeeze to a narrow seat; A Good Bond Investment; 61,800,977 passengers used these buses in the last 12 months; the dime-snatching slot; block by block—we are embedded in taxis; a fire. It is a longer walk to 159 West Eleventh Street than you are likely to think. Four- and Five-Room Apartments: the superintendent goes away after 5. An old man who wants the price of a meal. Home again: rush up the stairs—the telephone is ringing: Is this Murdock and Kruger?—No; you have the wrong number. The gasman to look at the meter. A man who says I wrote to ask about a trip to the West Indies; No: those are not my initials. A confidential bootlegger. Alone at last; don't go near that typewriter case!—that's where the bills are hidden. The bath: there is hot water but it is brown and has a sandy sediment. The telephone: Do you know where Frank is? We want him to come, too. I'll look it up—I'll try to get him. They have crushed the absorptive properties out of this towel—and see! here is a hole. A fire; every fire is a triumph—a triumph over traffic—they have gone to save Finck the Furrier, who now has a fire in his loft. Hello: is Frank there? Isn't this Atwater 8965? Give me Atwater 8965: Walter, do you know where Frank is? You might try Circle 9200, Extension 12. Is this Circle 9200, Extension 12? Is Mr. Merriwell there? Mr. Merriwell has gone to the Coast.

It is either 53 East 56 or 56 East 53. No; then it is 56 East 53. I can hear the victrola through the door; the faster you play it, the higher the pitch. Frank has gone out to the Coast. Thank you. The gin is bad in itself but it is the orange juice that makes it sickening. My affability is insincere. I have been looking for an apartment but they are all so expensive. Yes, they are all terribly expensive. Thank you. This is the very worst stage—when there is nothing but melted ice. When it is running down, the pitch becomes lower. Have you seen *The Guardsman?* It is wonderful. No; but I saw *The Swan*—I thought it was wonderful. Thank you. Yes; we have fallen for the crossword puzzles. There! I have asked them to dinner—that's a mistake. I must leave the place at once before I do anything ridiculous. I'm afraid I must go now. I wanted to get away before the buses stopped running. I will catch it at 54; 61,800,977 passengers used these buses in the past 12 months; A Good Bond Investment. I am sorry I asked them to dinner—I am sorry I said *The Swan* was well acted; but then one is really obliged to make some pretense of enthusiasm—even if one doesn't feel it.

March 11, 1925

NIGHT CLUBS

I

TEXAS GUINAN'S: *Now this little girl isn't much of a singer —I mean, singer. She learned singing in a correspondence school, and she missed a coupla letters. But she's the nicest little girl in the whole show! Now I wantcha all to give this little girl a nice great big hand!* Everybody applauds: they are forced to. In the windowless compact room, under the great glowing peony of the ceiling that melts from pink through deep rose to orange, swollen and hypnotic to drunken eyes, among green and red carnation panels that frame bogus señoritas, this formidable woman, with her pearls, her prodigious glittering bosom, her abundant and beautifully bleached yellow coiffure, her bear-trap of shining white teeth, her broad back that looks coarse and raw behind its green velvet grating, the full-blown peony as big as a cabbage exploding on her broad green thigh, not merely lords it over her little girls, chucking them under the chin, goading them to special efforts, jacking them up during their dull moments—*This little girl is new: give her a hand!*—fore-stalling outcry against their deficiencies—*You girls sound like Charlie Schwab's backyard!*—but dominates the audience, drills their applause, summons the languid to attention, deals immediately with tact but authority with disorderly inter-ruptions, makes short work of disapproval or dissent, drives everybody and everything along through an evening of enter-tainment without gaiety, of speed without recreation, stimu-lating, directing, controlling, in a race with the excitement she has roused. As the night is stretched later and later, this excitement becomes more and more violent: by four, there is likely to be a fight. Jealousies, desperations, stepped up with doses of Scotch, break through the pressure that has kept them in check. But Texas knows how to deal with them: the brawlers are summarily torn up by the roots and quietly put through into the street, with the ruthlessness and despatch of a Renaissance prince making away with a dangerous enemy.

II

CLUB ALABAM: The Alabam is more open, easier and more leisurely than Texas Guinan's. There is a long and quite ample dance-floor lined with tables sufficiently far apart—red and white checkered tablecloths under imitation palms. The entertainment is elaborate and extremely good—I particularly like the posed evolutions of the high-yellow girls in their towering pink plumes. The chief feature of the show is Johnny Hudgins, the Negro jazz dancer and pantomimist. Johnny Hudgins, who has appeared much in vaudeville, seems to have earned the reputation among the Negroes themselves of being the most considerable colored comedian since the late Bert Williams. He is unquestionably, in his line, a remarkable artist. What is most striking is the simplicity of his material. He neither sings nor tells any jokes nor does he work anything up with a partner. One of his most effective acts is a pantomime of singing a pathetic song with intense single-mindedness and naïveté while a cornet supplies the bleating of a tremulous tenor voice. Another is a dance with an invisible girl: nothing he does is better than the bad few moments he passes when he has been cut in on and has lost her, and is left alone on the dance-floor dodging imaginary couples—disappointed, bewildered, gaping.

Johnny Hudgins' great distinction lies in his restraint and economy, and in his fine sense of musical rhythm. All that he does—his stumblings on the dance-floor, his tossing flowers to the audience from his hat, his sudden plunge from his sobbing solo into a spasm of Charleston steps—is part of a jazz dance. No clown has ever worked more freely in stricter observance of beat.

III

THE TRIANGLE: The Triangle is not quite a night club but then it is more like a night club than a theater. Though it put on *Uncle Tom's Cabin* last winter, its present show is a Greenwich Village cabaret. Of all the small Village places of entertainment, the Triangle is undoubtedly the smallest. Accessible by a long and narrow flight of stairs which takes you far below the Eleventh Street pavement, it consists of a room filled with gray wooden tables and decorated with newspaper clippings, and a stage without footlights on the same level—so that in acts in which the set includes tables and chairs, late arrivals are likely to walk into the performance and sit down among the actors under the impression that they are taking their seats. The man who manipulates the spotlight has to do it from the first row of the audience, and a spectator situated next to him, if restless, may jog his elbow and make him drop his gelatine slide, thus robbing the prima donna of her moonlight and exposing her to a hard white glare. Visitors in search of the smoking room are obliged to pass back-stage among the actors.

The show includes odds and ends of jokes, a lady dressed up as a Pierrot and a deep-sea chanty sung in nautical costume by a chorus of refined young fellows who can never have been to sea. It is called *The Diverted Village* and announced as "a satire" on our Latin Quarter, but it has no more appropriateness to anything here than if the producers were living in Flatbush. One feels a little, in fact, that the Triangle is a sign of the decay of the Village. From groups of this kind below Twelfth Street there has in the past come a good deal that is interesting, and one still feels a certain satisfaction in realizing that they can continue to operate. There may be a spark of life in the Triangle—as there is perhaps in the Cherry Lane Theater, too. But how different from the old Provincetown Players and the old Golden Eagle restaurant—scarcely more cramped or more sordid: those were at least not poor in wit and imagination. They are supposed to serve refreshments at the Triangle, but I did not see anybody order anything; a girl who sold cigarettes was also trying to sell pictures of herself and a caricaturist was making caricatures, but nobody seemed to buy them. It was certainly with a quite different verve that Tiny Tim in the old days used to unload at preposterous prices his packages of bad candy—he is now said to be living on the profits in a handsome house in the East Eighties and to have bought a summer cottage at Great Neck. It is the landlords who are spoiling the Village: in making life there expensive and respectable, they are discouraging the clever people who do not have much to live on and are causing the younger Bohemians who still sometimes try to get a foothold to feel rather out of place and self-conscious.

September 9, 1925

ALICE LLOYD AND FARFARIELLO

MISS ALICE LLOYD, the music hall singer, has been appearing at the Palace. Though always somewhat overshadowed by her more famous sister Marie, Alice Lloyd has had her own reputation. She was prettier and less coarse than Marie; and she diversified flirtatious young-girl songs, such as *May, May, May—She Lives in Mayfair so Gay*, with pathetic cockney plaints such as *Never Introduce Your Bloke to Your Lady-Friend*. It is agreeable to hear her again—and all the more because she now brings with her some of the best of Marie's old songs, the rights to which were bequeathed her by her sister.

Marie Lloyd was one of the most memorable of the music hall performers of her generation. She was not a success in New York: on the occasion of her first visit, fifteen or twenty years ago, she was denounced by a newspaper critic in some such language as "a combination of French salacity with English vulgarity"; and when she tried to visit us again, during the War, she suffered the same fate as Gorki and was at first not allowed to land. But in London her position was supreme. As Mr. T. S. Eliot wrote in the *Dial* on the occasion of her death, "whereas other comedians amuse their audience as much and sometimes more than Marie Lloyd, no other comedian succeeded so well in giving expression to the life of that audience, in raising it to a kind of art. It was, I think, this capacity for expressing the soul of the people that made Marie Lloyd unique and that made her audience, even when they joined in the chorus, not so much hilarious as happy." Her cockney characterizations were wonderful. They were not the impersonations of a virtuoso like Albert Chevalier, who incorporates himself so completely in the dialect and make-up of his role that we lose sight of a basic personality. Marie Lloyd was primarily herself and always remained unmistakable through the variety of ages and conditions which she assumed in her various songs and which sounded the different keys of her instrument. This instrument was certainly as vulgar as Marie's grinning mouth of English horse teeth and yet as fine as the artistic instinct which enabled her to appreciate their value.

It is interesting to compare *Good Old Iron*, a song which Alice Lloyd has been singing at the Palace and which must, I think, be one of Marie's, with the somewhat similar number—"Although they used to call me Gladstone's Pet, There's life in the old girl yet!"—performed with so much success by Miss Beatrice Lillie in Charlot's Revue. Funny as Miss Lillie is, she does not succeed, or try to succeed, in making her superannuated comic opera star into a three-dimensional human being: her effectiveness, indeed, depends to a great extent on the mere business of the rest of the company, who are supposed to be helping the old lady out. Nor—what is also to the point here—did Miss Lillie really do very much with the waitress in the restaurant scene: she did not even "live" the role sufficiently to keep up its cockney accent; whereas either Marie or Alice Lloyd would have fallen into the accent with the character, and the main strength of the character would have lain, not in its jokes, but in its humanity. Good Old Iron is a lady of pleasure who has seen her best days.—"Of course, I can't deny I may have lost a pound or two—lost me purse—lost me way—but what is that to you?" With her prunellas, her little parasol and her high-necked black gown of the nineties, she would be distressing or gruesome if it were not for her unwithered good humor and her indomitable British spirit: "Come on, fellows! Take a chahnce! Have a dip in the lucky bag!—

> *Good old iron! Never was known to rust!*
> *Never was known to rust!*
> *A little fruity on the crust!*
> *I'm no chicken—but everything's complete.*

The fellows think I'm no good becuz
I'm not so plump as I useta wuz.
But don't forget, the closer the bone—the
sweeter the meat!

————

The English-speaking stage in America has had, so far as I know, no great singing comedian of this type—no Chevalier, no Harry Lauder, no Marie Lloyd, no Yvette Guilbert. Fanny Brice, with her less robust gift, is, I suppose, our nearest approach to it. But the Italian-speaking theater does possess a distinguished impersonator in the old music hall tradition. This performer is Farfariello, an Italian who has lived in the United States for now nearly thirty years. He is a favorite of Italian audiences and has appeared all over the country, wherever the Italians possess a stage. His reputation is thus rigorously limited; but within his own field he is brilliant, a genuinely creative talent. Farfariello originates all his own ideas, writes all his own songs and even makes his own wigs. He gives the impression of amusing himself much with his work, for he has brought to it much intelligence and much sympathetic insight into the lives of his fellow immigrants. He has invented a repertoire of characterizations so enormous that he is able in his present engagement at the Fugazy Theater on Houston Street to sing a different set of songs every week. One is astonished by the immense variety of types—young and old, male and female, of all conditions and occupations—which this repertoire now includes, and by his skill in differentiating them from one another. The little girl from the public school whose attainments in American history are confined to a dubious statement about George Washington but who has acquired a large repertoire of jazz songs which she can and does sing from beginning to end; the man who has got drunk at the Fiesta di San Antonio and attempts to tell about it; the comfortable barrel-shaped matron who refuses to exchange her native costume for the short skirts of the Americanized women, challenging them to show her an Americanized wife who has produced such quantities of children; the watchman; the old woman; the orchestra leader; the opera tenor—they have evidently all been studied from life; each has its own accents and gestures. Most charming perhaps of all those I have seen is the stupid but great-spirited fellow who has tried to take out naturalization papers; all went well till it came to the point where he had to renounce his Italian citizenship; understanding this as an order to deny his Italian birth, he has protested indignantly, shouting, "Eviva l'Italia!"—whereupon they put him out. He is tremendously excited and expresses his emotions at the prospect of repudiating Italy—he enumerates her provinces and peoples—carefully including the Sicilians, who, he explains, are Italians, too—and, particularly, his local compatriots of the little town from which he comes. His voice breaks, he sobs at the thought of the glories he has been asked to betray. These are, as I have said, not parts which have been written to order for Farfariello; they are people he himself has imagined, people whom he intimately knows and whom he compels his audience to recognize.

October 21, 1925

THE GREATEST SHOW ON EARTH

AT THE BUGLE, the doors are thrown open and the drum-major, coated in yellow, strutting with baton and shako, leads in the fantastic parade. Behind him roll the golden floats; the green dragons and scarlet sphinxes; Cleopatra jolted on her elephant, Cinderella trotting to ponies; big-headed Chinese *magots* in high green steeple-hats; comely jockeys, men and girls, in pink and green, with pink-and-green-garlanded hurdles; camels, stepping disdainfully, caparisoned in gold and crimson, wobbling limp humps.—Once off stage, beyond the exit doors, the hurdles are slapped away; the girls have to dodge the horses, who have been excited by the lights and music; the elephants are made to kneel, and their trappings are unharnessed in haste; the clowns undo their monstrous bodies; Cleopatra grins at her maids.

The band, appearing aloft in its box, now possesses the house with loud volume, sets all pumping to a fast and emphatic waltz. Wide red carpets are stretched on the yellow floor under the firmament of yellow planets. Trapeze-performers mount their bars. All in white, symmetrically posted, they inhabit the vast diagram of ropes designed like some impossible geometry in the void of the upper light: swimming in the void of the waltz, they swing and swoop—they fly to each other's hands—they fall in soft nets. Outside, in the meantime, the elephants are being lined up for their entrance by a little sturdy determined man, whose impassivity and whose large heavy head are themselves somewhat pachydermatous. He herds them with a rod behind the ear. One elephant, nervously, with a tentative trunk, feels at a bystander's shoe.—Coming off, two trapeze performers—a man and woman, heroic and blond—exchange a kiss as they part, on their way to their dressing rooms.

One notices a sign which says: "DOCTOR. KEEP AWAY FROM THIS DOOR." Clowns are mounting their stilts, loading on their false scalps and slapsticks, hauling down gigantic false female bodies.—A contortionist—in preliminary practice—curls himself on a table like a dying spider.—Girls, who have been talking on a blue circus truck and who wear street clothes as other women do kimonos, hurry away to change.—Mme. Pallenberg's bears wallop off, much delighted to be done with their roller-skating and cycling, dragging attendants on their leashes.—Applause: the broad white horse of May Wirth rounds the ring at a slow lope. Running, with her little girl's bow at her ear, her arms held down to her sides like a girl's, she jumps to a perch on the horse's round back, slides down and jumps again. Then, with deliberate ease, slow like the slowed-up music, slow like the loping horse, she flips backwards on the horse's back, over and over. She is an organism perfectly developed, accurately, effortlessly adjusted, to maintain her balance on a moving horse.

The dwarfs assume glaring false heads of the Yonghy-Bonghy-Bo. Crossword puzzles; a skeleton; a doctor with a giant stork. The clowns start their catastrophic motor.—The sea lions are waiting in their red barred box, uttering strangulated roars. The trainer slips them fish: *Now get over, you big bum, and let Pearl have some!—Come on, Pearl, here go.—Cut it out, you big hog!—Come on, Pearl, don't be scared.*—One Weary Willy, left alone when the other clowns have cleared the scene, sways on a towering stack of tables: he rocks first backward, then forward, each time tipping further and further—almost it topples, then topples—as the chair falls backwards under him, he rights himself adroitly in the air and neatly alights on his feet as the tower crumbles to tables.—The girl acrobats, slender and dark, in green bodices and salmon tights, slip into their blunt gold mules: they know just where they are going, and they go there straight: they do not need to lean against anything.—From the arena, the music has intensified to the sinister dry buzz and bump of the difficult tight-wire somersault.—The tall dog-trainer in the brown frock coat takes a twist at his waxed mustache while his brindled gigantic police dog crouches blinking behind him. A little cowgirl with butterfly bows on her shoes has to haul up her horse, which is wild to dash on.—Mlle. Leitzel, in a high-pitched nervous voice, cries, *Where are my flowers?* to her maid.—In three rings, equilibrists lean out from white masts, each based on the box of a companion's chest.

Then the darkened arena heaves to a dark and sonorous waltz. Mlle. Leitzel, costumed in silver, concentrated by white blades of light, walks the length of the driveway alone. The darkened audience roars with applause. She mounts her rope, still focused in silver, swinging her body over and over, lingering in rhythm to the languor of the waltz. Near the top, she clamps the rope between her thighs and stretches her small body out, reclining high in space, making poses and throwing them away. She is the freest, least self-conscious of performers, and the performer most distinguished by style. She descends; she bows: the arena resounds with the ringmaster's hollow bellow. Now catching the end of the rope with one hand, she ascends, as the rope is pulled up in a smooth unbroken flight. The music has turned somber, ominous. By one bare arm, hanging at the rope-end, she begins to thrash about in the air. Higher, higher—she flings her body above her shoulder, she flings it over her shoulder. Her bronze-brown hair, shaken loose as she tosses, is wrenched to and fro. Her efforts are terrific, have a bacchante's violence. Over and over—at last she slows down. She is lowered; she receives her applause. Then, walking not quite straight on her little feet, but alone as she entered, she leaves the arena, bowing right and left to the roar. Once outside, she sinks into a chair, and her brow is wrung with agony. She gasps; her great bright black eyes stare. People come around her with compliments. They smile, but she can hardly answer them.—All five rings now are turning with horses—glossy flanks and slender elegant legs—performing the figures of the grand manège, nodding black or white cockades.—Mlle. Leitzel now smiles at last and begins to talk again. She clasps her cloak with one little hand—the hand that supported her above the arena: one sees that the fingers are finely shaped and the fingernails carefully tended.

The dingy city audience, when the show is over, sifts away down the aisles and the stairways. They do not envy the circus performers. They realize that there is really no more sense in learning to do what Mlle. Leitzel does than in acquiring the ability to land on your feet after balancing on a tower of tables. But one cannot help having a feeling of mingled abashment and pride at the spectacle of any human aptitude carried to its extreme unpredictable li·• it. Most of us have been content with such a modest cultivation of our aptitudes. Or even if we have been led or driven to push our powers to the point of risk, we have not enjoyed the stimulus of the circus band, the glory of the crash of applause. So the audience goes home to Harlem, to Central Park West, to the Bronx, to Flatbush, to Lexington Avenue, to the commuting-distance out-of-town suburbs, and these prodigies slip out of their minds. Only the younger children will imagine being bareback riders or masters of the flying rings, and they will soon put such fantasies out of their minds.

May 13, 1925

THE FINALE AT THE FOLLIES

Dress Rehearsal

IN THE DUSK of the darkened house, the Tiller girls link
in a swinging line, practicing their steps and humming their
refrain: alone in the dark, without orchestra, their voices
sound girlish and soft. *Finale!* They troop to the back. The
little waitresses in lavender come off—the pale green and
lavender set folds away with large leisure and ease. An incisive New York voice—Florenz Ziegfeld, who is standing at
the front of the house: *You've got to get those stockings right!*
Their garters are out of alignment. *There's nothing to the
costume but the stockings!* A rustle of laughter. *Darn right!*
A Spanish mission has been unfolded—behind it, a backdrop of bright orange sandstone and bright purple cactus. A
tall girl with a flopping sombrero mounts a pedestal and begins to pose. *All right: let's go!* The Tenor takes the stage:
*Although I stand here singing, A rope I should be swinging,
But I've really got to get it off my chest!* The show girls—
white, green, white, white, black, orange; purple, green,
orange, black, white, green. *You've got two white ones together! Put somebody between them. You go over on the
end, Gladys. Now, begin again!* The girl who is doing the
Circassian slave in the number *The Pearl of the East,* soft-
molded in a fawn-colored robe under which she is almost
nude, pale hair smoothed close to her calm little head to
accommodate the flooding yellow wig, moves softly down
the house toward a friend. The show girls come in again:
one is missing. *Who died?* She appears. *Now do that over.*
In the wide space behind the backdrop, a great long-legged
loose-legged girl is throwing herself about like a colt; a man
holds up his gray hat for her; smiling, amiable, superb, she
kicks it; then he sets out to sketch her. *Now, what's the matter*

with the light? Keep the light off the scenery! The electrical lighting apparatus with military urgency is rushed to the wings. *Look out!* the smart nasal voice of the liveliest girl in a small town, *You'll get killed like that some day! I suppose you've come to make some more sketches. Yes? Well, you can't sketch them when they're leaping around like that!— I want to look before they leap.* She is gone. *I don't think she got that.—Say, do they ever get anything?* The lighting uncomfortably wavers from a warm orange to a cold pink. *Say: the girls are all right. It's the lights!—I know it: I'm explaining to the girls about the lights!*

The ponies are trooping downstairs with the pink legs and arms of the South Seas. *Come on, dumbbell!*—one reaches back for the hand of the girl behind her. A toe dancer sits rubbing her feet, strapping on her silk shoes. Another stands on one white leg, lifting the other straight up before her— hugging it, she leans against the scenery; with young intent eyes she watches the show. *You'll find it rough but gentle, Romantic, sentimental, Though I'm not a butter and egg man from the West! I would LIKE to corRAL*—The Tiller girls burst in, in a line—orange leggings and orange sombreros. *No: they don't come in yet.* The music of the orchestra stops: their voices sound girlish and foolish. *You don't come in on the beginning of the refrain: you come in on the second half of the refrain.* He sings the verse and half the refrain. *You come in on the second half of the refrain. Now do it over!* The girl on the pedestal, bored, breaks her pose and performs a shimmy step. The toe dancer drops her upright leg and lifts the other leg up, nursing it as she watches. *No brains! no beauty! no personality! Can't sing— can't dance—can't act!—stand 'em on their heads and they're all alike—you know!—Who's fucking her?—I don't know— but she's got a built-in radio in her apartment—so she says. —You still here? Still sketching, eh? Say: the doorman has orders not to let in any more synthetic men—what I call synthetic men. I've got to go on again! So long!* Will Rogers mounts the block, about which the Tiller girls are wheeling. *Say: he's going to whirl the lasso around the whole thing. Yeah: he's clever!* They crowd the wings. Behind them waits the Negro wardrobe woman, patient with a shade of sullenness—knowing herself handsome in another kind, she bides there, blinking at all that white beauty, those openeyed confident white girls in their paradise of bright dresses: turquoise skirts and canary cloaks, pink bodies hung with dark green leaves, tall white flowerlike stalks that burst into purple and orange—all of them excited by the costumes and the music, proud to have been picked by Ziegfeld, happy to look like the covers of popular magazines—brown-eyed, clearskinned, straight-browed, straight-backed.—A touch of the hand in passing: *Tomorrow at 11 o'clock?* The thin girl comic, a little strained: *How long has this been going on?* The curtains close. *No: listen here! The second time you close in—the second time! The curtains close: you're turning. They open: you're still turning. They close again: you close in and you stop! Now, go through it again from the beginning!*

The Tenor takes the stage: *Although I stand here singing, A rope I should be swinging, But I've really got to get it off my chest!* The towering shapes of the show girls, blooming in their enormous sombreros: black, white, green, white, orange, white; purple, green, orange, black, white, green. *You'll find it rough but gentle, Romantic, sentimental, Though I'm not a butter and egg man from the West!* The show girls droop away. *I would LIKE to corRAL, A very merry necessary little gal!* At the signal, the Tiller girls enter: white with orange leggings and sombreros, white with purple leggings and sombreros. They make a swinging line: all together, with the strong urgent beats of their kicking they send home the strong beats of the music. *I would LIKE to corRAL!* They crack their whips all together. Will Rogers mounts the pedestal: the tall girl drops to a sitting pose, hugging one knee, hanging the other. The Tiller girls circle about the pedestal, two rings, one inside the other and turning in opposite directions. He drops his lariat down about them, making it whirl in the opposite direction to the outer circle of girls. *I would LIKE to corRAL!* The beat has mastered everything; it pounds fast in a crash of orange. For two minutes, in wheeling speed, focused in the green-gilt proscenium frame, they concentrate the pulse of the city. The bronze gilded curtains close on the girls and the turning lariat. They open: the rings are still turning. They close, as the circles draw in and halt.

March 25, 1925

ON AND OFF BROADWAY

Shakespeare by Arthur Hopkins

NEITHER *Romeo and Juliet* nor *Hamlet* will be running when these notes appear, but it is perhaps still worth while to say something in general about Mr. Arthur Hopkins' productions of Shakespeare. We have now had four of these, and on the whole they have been pretty bad. The trouble is that Mr. Hopkins is not, in the true sense, a producer. He has the taste to select good plays and the courage to put them on, but not the sort of genius really to make anything of them. He seems to expect them to produce themselves. You have the feeling that no unifying creative force has ever been brought to bear on the material; that Mr. Robert Edmond Jones has been allowed to follow his own inclinations and the various Barrymores theirs, and the rest of the members of the cast to do pretty much as they pleased. There never seems to be any coherent concerted idea as to what a given play is about.

In so far as these productions have in common any feature which is identifiable as contributed by Mr. Hopkins, it is a tendency toward the natural, the casual—the kind of thing that was so charming and refreshing when we first had it in the Clare Kummer comedies, but which is hopelessly inappropriate to Shakespeare. For Shakespeare, after all, is poetic drama and should be acted like poetic drama, not an understated tragedy by Galsworthy. There is an element of declamation in Shakespeare which has to be accepted and handled; it requires a different convention from Clare Kummer. But Mr. Hopkins tries to play down *Hamlet* till it sounds like the staccato dialogue of *Loyalties*. He has accomplished the depressing feat of completely stripping Shakespeare of music. The tremendous rhythm of English blank verse is reduced to a colloquial flatness. Mr. Winthrop Ames, in *Will Shakespeare,* has actually made the blank verse of Clemence Dane, completely uninteresting in itself, a good deal more effective on the stage than Mr. Arthur Hopkins' version of the greatest blank verse ever written. In *Will Shakespeare,* the movement of the verse does carry the whole performance; the speakers catch it up from one another. In *Romeo and Juliet* it is broken into a thousand bits.

March, 1923

––––

The Moscow Art Theater

To say that the Moscow Art Theater, which has brought its repertoire to New York, is a "Naturalistic" theater may give rise to a misunderstanding. Since the advent in the theater of Expressionism, we have been tending to make a bugbear of Naturalism, to associate it with everything in the drama that is labored, prosaic and dreary. We think at once of *Hindle Wakes* and *The Weavers*—not that the latter is dreary—all that theater of the proletariat and industrial middle class that has corresponded to the novels of Zola, of Arnold Bennett and Dreiser. Now, the Art Theater represents something quite different from this: it represents the higher reaches of the realistic movement. It has been perhaps the most brilliant exploit in an attempt to bring on to the stage the art that has been practised, not by the men I have mentioned, but by the school of Flaubert and Turgenev, Henry James and Anatole France—that is, by the school which went beyond notation, beyond merely reproducing the surface of life, and, accepting the convention of plausibility, aimed to produce something not merely persuasive, but beautiful, valid as a work of art.

It is this difficult aesthetic ideal which the Russians have realized in the theater. They are as subtle, as selective, as full of glamor as any of the great novelists I have mentioned above. They present so convincing a surface that, by the time we walk out of the theater, we can scarcely believe that we have not been actual visitors in an old-regime Russian household, that we have not sat watching the family go about its intimate business; but they succeed at the same time in creating a whole set of artistic values to which we are hardly accustomed in the Naturalistic theater: the beauty and poignancy of an atmosphere, of an idea, a person, a moment are caught and put before us without emphasis, without anything which we recognize as theatrical, but with the brightness of the highest art. In *The Cherry Orchard,* for example, not only is a complex of social relations presented with impressive exactitude, but the cherry orchard itself, the kind of beauty which Mme. Ranevskaya represents, the charm that hangs about this Russian gentry even in its pre-revolutionary decay are somehow conveyed from the stage in such a way that their futility is moving, their ineptitude touched with the tragedy of every human failure.

It is true that the Moscow Art Theater may sometimes seem a little too smooth. Isn't life itself a little more violent and a little more unexpected, than anything to be seen on their stage—even in Gorky's *The Lower Depths?* But it seems to be inevitable for this form of art to eliminate the surprising and the violent. There are no earthquakes in Henry James; and in Flaubert—in his fiction, at least, which deals with contemporary subjects—even a revolution is never allowed to be shattering. This is the art of a steady underemphasis and of effects that are slowly unfolded.

March, 1923

————

The Follies as an Institution

It MAY SEEM rather late at this time to be writing about the current Ziegfeld Follies—almost now at the end of its season —but the Follies is a permanent institution and comments on it are always in order. Mr. Ziegfeld has now "Glorified the

American Girl" in a very real sense. He has studied, with shrewd intelligence, the American ideal of womanhood and succeeded in putting it on the stage. In general, Ziegfeld's girls have not only the Anglo-Saxon straightness—straight backs, straight brows and straight noses—but also the peculiar frigidity and purity, the frank high-school-girlishness which Americans like. He does not aim to make them, from the moment they appear, as sexually attractive as possible, as the Folies Bergères, for example, does. He appeals to American idealism, and then, when the male is intent on his chaste and dewy-eyed vision, he gratifies him on this plane by discreetly disrobing his goddess. He tries, furthermore, to represent, in the maneuvers of his well-trained choruses, not the movement and abandon of emotion, but what the American male really regards as beautiful: the efficiency of mechanical movement. The ballet at the Ziegfeld Follies is becoming more and more like military drill: to watch a row of well-grown girls descend a high flight of stairs in a deliberate and rigid goose-step is far from my idea of what ballet ought to be; it is too much like watching setting-up exercises.

Yet there is still something wonderful about the *Follies*. It exhibits the persistent vitality as well as the stupidity of an institution. Among those green peacocks and gilded panels, in the luxurious haze of the New Amsterdam, there is realized a glittering vision which rises straight out of the soul of New York. The Follies is such fantasy, such harlequinade as the busy well-to-do New Yorker has been able to make of his life. Expensive, punctual, stiff, it moves with the speed of an express train. It has in it something of Riverside Drive, of the Plaza, of Scott Fitzgerald's novels—though it radically differs from these latter in being almost devoid of wit. In spite of the by no means mediocre efforts of Will Rogers and Ring Lardner, in spite of Mr. Tynan's impersonation of Belasco, there is still something formal about the jokes in the Follies: a signal is given from the stage, and the audience responds like a shot. The actor who made the joke is as cold as the American Beauties drilling on the Grand Staircase, and there is no trace of mirth in the metallic laughter set in motion by the stimulus from the stage. I personally was much entertained, a couple of weeks ago, by a skit called *Koo-Koo Nell, the Pride of the Depot,* but the last time I saw the show, it turned out that *Koo-Koo Nell* had been discontinued. There had been substituted a deafening farce of the Jarr Family school—one of those domestic scenes in which husband, wife and children break dishes and bawl at one another. As each cartridge of abuse is exploded, the audience lets off its automatic roar. I am told that *Koo-Koo Nell* was taken off because there were "no laughs in it."

Yet, as I say, there is a splendor about the Follies. It has, in its way, both distinction and intensity. At the New Amsterdam, the girls are always young—the *mise en scène* nearly always beautiful. And there is always one first-rate performer. Just now it is Gilda Gray. She is not the official American Girl; she embodies a different ideal: an ideal which was probably created by the vibrant and abandoned Eva Tanguay and which has produced the jazz baby of the years since the war who now rivals the magazine cover. She is the obverse of Mary Eaton—she is the semi-bacchante of Main Street.

April, 1923

————

An Early Theater Guild Production

Roger Bloomer, by John Howard Lawson—in spite of occasional gleams of wit or beauty—fails chiefly, it seems to me, for two reasons. In the first place, it is the tragedy of adolescence written from the point of view of the adolescent—that is, we have to accept the boy in his teens as a helpless and pathetic martyr and everybody else as a beast. And, in the second place, it collapses inward by reason of the feebleness of the central character. You cannot have much of a drama with a protagonist who is always passive. Roger Bloomer never reacts upon the circumstances about him; he is always acted upon by them. We hear much about a "struggle," but we never see the struggle take place. Roger's positive deeds are limited to his running away from home and then, after submitting for years to the insults of a villainous Yale man, to finally challenging this sadist to a fight which never seems to come to anything. In the end, it is not Roger Bloomer's own will, of which we also hear a good deal, but his father's intervention and money which save him from the mess in which he finds himself. My point is not that there may not exist such tragic adolescents as Roger, but that it would take an extreme virtuosity to make one provide motive power for drama.

April, 1923

———

A Greenwich Village Production

I UNFORTUNATELY missed the first act of *Sandro Botticelli* but from the program and what I saw afterwards, I know it must have gone much like this:

LEONARDO DA VINCI. What ails our friend Botticelli? He seems silent and distracted to-day—this day of all days, the birthday of Lorenzo the Magnificent, when the people are dancing in the streets like cicadas after rain.

FRA LIPPO LIPPI. They say he is enamored of Giuliano's mistress, the beautiful Simonetta. But look, here comes Lorenzo himself with the learned Poliziano!

LORENZO DE' MEDICI. Ha, our incomparable Leonardo! How goes the Mona Lisa and what are your latest experiments in engineering?

POLIZIANO. Gentlemen, I must confess it. I have turned another little canzone to Simonetta. *Per Bacco,* I cannot find it in my heart to keep away from the subject. (*All laugh.*)

FRA LIPPO LIPPI. No more can our friend Botticelli! (*All laugh.*)

BOTTICELLI (*joining them*). Greeting, good Master Leonardo and Your Most Excellent Highness Lord Lorenzo. Is

it not a day for men and for angels, for music, for flowers—
LEONARDO. And for lovers? (*All laugh.*)

POLIZIANO. All Florence is laughing in the sun. Come, let us taste some of our host's good wine.

Exeunt omnes—except Botticelli, who hides behind a potted rosebush to watch Eva Le Gallienne make her entrance.

May, 1923

————

Guitry without the Guitrys

THE AMERICAN VERSION OF *Le Comédien*—produced by Mr. Belasco—only provides another proof that the Guitry plays without the Guitrys never really come off. This seems to be especially true of the plays written by Sacha for the elder Guitry: they contain a larger admixture of seriousness, and straight drama is not Sacha's best vein. Lucien Guitry—who is a great actor—can make any rôle distinguished, but when one of these plays is done without him, it is seen to be a flimsy scaffolding with nothing to be built around. And yet it is these pieces intended as vehicles for the genius of the elder Guitry that are usually done in New York. Those that are mainly ironic are likely to be turned, on our stage, into straight romantic comedies. *The Grand Duke* I know from having seen it in Paris, *The Comedian* I suspect, to have been written in a spirit of farce—though with occasional moments of feeling—that verges on the Gilbert and Sullivan. But where Sacha has written and Lucien played an objectively seen comic figure of a French actor or a Russian Grand Duke, our own Lionel Atwill gives us an old-fashioned leading man, who would be more at home in Pinero's drawing rooms than in the comedy of the boulevards. It is irony which makes Sacha amusing. Robbed of irony, he is mostly banal.

It is in the plays which Sacha Guitry writes primarily for himself that this irony appears in its purest form and in

which his great talent finds its happiest expression. These
have at worst a decorous kind of silliness that is reminiscent
of William Collier, whom Guitry in some ways suggests. (He
has the same slight habitual embarrassment in situations
which are just a little too much for him or in which it is
becoming more difficult for him to conceal that he is playing
a false rôle. I remember a scene in which somebody asks him
what he got out of going to Aix-les-Bains: he answers,
"*Beaucoup de bain,*" and then hastily adds in his worried way,
"*Heu . . . je veux dire, beaucoup de bien*"—which is pure
William Collier. But beyond this polite vein of gagging, he
is capable of a rather high comedy. The scenes that Sacha
writes for himself and his wife, Yvonne Printemps, are
masterpieces of their kind. Though he lacks the point of
view at the center of his work which would make him another Molière (to whom someone once compared him),
though his comedies do not lead us, as the best French comedies do, to a bitter or a balanced judgment, he does manage
to strike off passages which are quite in the Molière tradition. The scenes between lovers, for example, have often
a real comic truth; and there hangs always over his silliest
dialogue a wing of philosophic wit which gives its touch to
almost everything he writes. Furthermore, there are his wonderful Parisiennes, drawn with affection and gusto: the
flapper in *The Grand Duke,* the little music-hall singer in
L'Illusioniste, the unfaithful and wide-eyed wife in *Le Mari,
la Femme et l'Amant.* They are gauche, naïve, witty, adora-
ble, like Printemps, who plays them, herself. They seem
facets of her own personality.

June, 1923

Late Pinero and Early Cornell

MR. PINERO's *The Enchanted Cottage* is a fantasy without
much imagination. Instead, you have soft music, red fire and

old-fashioned masquerade costumes. When enchantment has descended as a curtain of gauze, you are startled by sudden flashes of a blinding violet light which you mistake at first for short circuits; but it is only William Brady's idea of a star dust of fairy fire. At the end, there is a phantom child which suggests the old illustrated songs. Miss Katharine Cornell is quite good as the inhibited spinster of the first act, but in the later more lively ones her vivacity seems to cost an effort.

June, 1923

————

Philip Barry and Clyde Fitch

You and I by Philip Barry is a partially interesting attempt to deal with a serious theme and to study an authentic milieu. But the idea is not carried out in the serious way it deserves. A prime weakness of Mr. Barry is that he takes the inhabitants of his country house for clever and cultivated people when they are actually half-baked provincials. You think that he is going to approach them in a critical, an ironic spirit; then you discover that he shares their own point of view, that he takes their own view of themselves. He is impressed by their suburban luxuries and ravished by their mediocre wit—a wit which, like their curtains of flowered chintz and their little electric wall-lamps, is a rather pathetic device for enlivening the banality of their lives. Let us, however, accept Mr. Barry's world. The trouble is that, even when we have done so, we find that he fails to deal with the problem with which he sets out. His situations are purely contrived. How are we to believe in his heroine, who loves her young man so much that she is willing to give him up in order that he may not be taxed with the burden of having to support her but may follow his architectural dreams, yet never offers to share his struggles, to assist him with her $2,000 a year? Or in the father who has chosen to smother his own artistic ambitions and go in for a career of money-making, yet allows his son to do the same thing just at the moment when he himself is most keenly feeling his own futility; who has risen to be one of the top executives in a highly successful soap company yet is unable to take a year's vacation without running the risk of losing his job? I do not know whether it was due to the presence in the cast of that fine actor Mr. Ferdinand Gottschalk—brought to this country by Clyde Fitch for *The Climbers*—but the whole thing reminded me a little of the comedies of Clyde Fitch. Fitch was par excellence the virtuoso of American externals: the appliances, the furnishings, the baggage of the early nineteen hundreds. His true gift was in playing with these. When I think of his plays, I remember the scenes in which people are kept awake by the banging of steam radiators, in which, with embarrassing results, they turn on the wrong electric lights or try to eat ornamental wax oranges, in which the gentlemen, at the end of the dinner, all have to dive under the table to retrieve the objects that the ladies have dropped. I think of characters who, in lighter moments, speak in the accents of life but who invariably, in passages that demand emotion, talk the language of the melodramatic theater of fifty years ago. When Clyde Fitch was on the surface, he was excellent. He was a master of the "line"* and the "property," but when he was serious, he was almost always dreadful: his situations were wholly for and from the stage. Mr. Barry has cultivated a shimmer of "line" rather than a jugglery of "properties": our interiors are not quite so cluttered as they were in Clyde Fitch's day; but his gift is not unlike Clyde Fitch's. Let him beware, as he hopes to be an artist, of resorting to the same ancient tricks.

July, 1923

———

Animals at the Circus

AT THE CIRCUS you saw beautiful horses and beautiful human beings—which is much. For the rest, I do not mind

* In those days, a "line" was a "line of talk"; in college and débutante slang, a way of being amusing.

having dogs and seals, and even horses and elephants, trained to do circus tricks; but I do object to exhibitions of sulky lions and tigers badgered into sitting on stools and jumping over one another. Lions and tigers, like domestic cats, have no feeling for human games; they cannot enter into the spirit of the thing. Where a seal will dance about on a springboard and eagerly bark for fish, a lion, a tiger or a leopard has to be goaded with the cracks of a whip and a revolver fired off in its face. Nor are the beasts that are made to perform the only ones that suffer at the circus. I saw also a red-eyed hippopotamus in a cage half as wide as its own length, in which, I suppose, it had been hauled by train from Bridge-port to New York and was soon to be dragged from New York to a series of other cities. It gazed wildly from its meager bath with the frightened innocence of cows and steers packed into cattle-trains, and when one of the hands slammed a trunk behind it, it started like a nervous woman. I pity this hippopotamus and wish it were back in its native river.

July, 1923

———

Herbert Williams

AMATEURS of the slapstick arts who go in for Charlie Chaplin and Joe Cook should not fail to see the vaudeville act billed as Williams and Wolfus. Herbert Williams is a clown of a high order, with a curious fantasy of his own. A respectable and serious character, he is doomed to disappointment and failure. When he comes on, there is no spotlight, and he has to shout to the electrician. He desires to sing a song, but his voice is not quite strong enough, and when he does get it more or less under way, his silk hat begins slipping off toward the back of his egg-shaped bald head. Then he is flustered by the orchestra leader, who turns out to be a malignant demon: instead of keeping time with his baton, he begins twirling it about like a drum major and otherwise behaving in a distracting manner. The singer finally snatches the stick away and bashes him over the head, but the baton only bends in two, and the demon remains unscathed. There is nothing for the poor man to do but politely to hand it back as he touchingly confides to the audience in his low inadequate voice, "This is very embarrassing for me!" His fiascos have the quality of a bad dream—or of a French Dadaist drama. I suppose it will be only a question of time before someone puts him into a revue.

July, 1923

―――

Bert Savoy and Eddie Cantor of the Follies

THE "NEW EDITION" of the Ziegfeld Follies is a considerable improvement on the old—it is, in fact, one of the very best Follies I remember. The new acts that have been substituted for old ones are not only, in general, more interesting; they also fit into the Follies better: you have, in almost every case, a fast-moving dynamic act in place of a slow or vague one. Instead of Ring Lardner's rather casual Rip Van Winkle sketch, there is a terrific team of rube dancers, and Will Rogers with his halting drawl has been replaced by the machine-like energy of Eddie Cantor. Ann Pennington has also been added, so that, with Cantor and Gilda Gray, you have now perhaps the three highest-pressure performers in the city all on the same stage. The tempo of the show is now uniform, and it is the same as that of the life outside. This is New York in terms of entertainment—the expression of nervous intensity to the tune of harsh and complicated harmonies. When, afterwards, you take the subway home, it speeds you to your goal with a crash, like a fast song by Eddie Cantor; and in the roar of the nocturnal city, driven rhythmically for all its confusion, you can catch hoarse echoes of Gilda Gray and her incomparable *Come Along!*

One instrument in the Follies' jazz orchestra has suddenly and sadly been silenced: Bert Savoy is dead.* But the char-

---

* He was killed by a stroke of lightning on the beach at Coney Island. It was said at the time in New York that, in view of the field for punishment presented by the city then, the Almighty had picked a poor object for so drastic a retribution.

acter he created will never be forgotten by those who saw it. When Bert Savoy would come reeling on the stage, a gigantic red-haired harlot, swaying her enormous hat, reeking with the corrosive cocktails and the malodorous gossip of the West Fifties, one felt oneself in the presence of the vast vulgarity of New York incarnate and almost heroic. And now we have heard the last of the wisecracks of Margy the girl-friend, and the thought is truly a sad one. Yet still, in the brash city nights, between the Montmartre and Reisen-weber's, we may sometimes be haunted by the accents of a gasping raucous voice, shamelessly brassy, obscene, but in a tremor of female excitement: "I'm so glad you asked me that, dearie! You don't know the half of it, dearie! You don't know the half of it, dearie!"

August, 1923

—————

Why not Restoration Comedy?

ONCE OR TWICE every year in New York, there is a solemn and pretentious revival of Sheridan. We have had this year both *The Rivals* and *The School for Scandal*. Might it not, for a change, be a good idea to do Wycherley or Congreve instead? The comedy of the Restoration was a good deal more interesting artistically—if a little less easy to act—than the comedy of the late eighteenth century. In *The Critic*, Sheridan himself confesses the relative tameness of the comedy of his own day, made mawkish by the importation of the *comédie larmoyante*, and what is most vivid in his comedies is surely the part that comes nearest to the vein of Restoration comedy. But Sheridan, in vindicating morality out of defer-ence to the new middle class, had to sacrifice a good deal of the style and force which, in the case of his predecessors, had derived from their aristocratic point of view, their thorough-going worldliness, their cynicism. Actually, *The School for Scandal* is little more than a domesticated version of Wycher-ley's *The Country Wife*, with the difference that in Wycher-

ley's play the Joseph Surface character is the hero instead of
the villain. As it is, in the later comedy he remains its most
amusing figure and expounds his point of view more persua-
sively than accords with the vindication of the latter-day
morality. In Wycherley, the rustic Mrs. Pinchwife drops like
a piece of ripe fruit into the lap of the city gallant, as Lady
Teazle would certainly have done if Sheridan had gone
through with his comic logic. If Joseph Surface is less attractive than the heroes of the Restoration, it is not merely because he has been cast as villain, but because he must become
a hypocrite as well as a voluptuary. The reduction of the
rake to hypocrisy breaks the back of the Congreve tradition,
which was never to rise again quite to Congreve's intensity
and brilliance. Even Maugham and Oscar Wilde have had
to compound with the domestic virtues.

But what could be more exhilarating—for an evening or
two at least—than these husbands and wives who are never
faithful, these young suitors whose intentions are never honest, these beautiful young coquettes whose desire is never to
marry? What could be more bracing, in its way, than this
contact with that brilliant world, in which our most primitive instincts are subjected to a subtle scrutiny and ex-
pounded in a polished style, in which no confusion of "spirit"
dims the gulf between mind and body, in which the relations of the sexes are befogged by no romantic emotion
either savage or sentimental?

New York has now surely become sufficiently wicked to
enjoy these remarkable pieces. The Phoenix Society in London has recently revived *Love for Love*. Why may we not
do the same? For Sheridan has become rather tiresome. He
was never quite first-rate at best.

October, 1923

————

Henri Becque as Good-Will Ambassador

MME. SIMONE, during her last week in New York, performed
those two admirable comedies, *La Parisienne* and *Amour-*

euse. The former of these, on the opening night, was diversified by a scene of broad humor in a vein quite different from Becque's. The curtain, after falling on the second act, immediately rose again to disclose a white-tied committee—from one of those organizations that try to promote good reations between France and us—presenting Mme. Simone with the largest and clumsiest bunch of flowers I have ever seen on such an occasion. An old gentleman who stated that he was a former singer stepped forward and intoned a salutation in the grand manner of French oratory. He was followed by another Frenchman, who delivered an interminable address in very inadequate English, congratulating France and America on having been able to establish their "friendshipness," not merely through the visit of Mme. Simone, but also through the mediation of the American moving-picture industry, which had given us splendid productions of such masterpieces of French culture as *The Two Orphans, The Three Musketeers* and *The Hunchback of Notre Dame.* Mme. Simone replied with a little speech of thanks in surprisingly perfect English, and the orchestra, uncertainly faltering, launched forth upon the *Marseillaise.* Everybody had to stand up, and one gentleman sang the words in an intermittent way, like an imperfectly tuned-in radio. When the *Marseillaise* was finished, the audience tried to sit down, but the orchestra proceeded to *The Star-Spangled Banner* and, losing the thread about half way through, struck off some rather acrid passages suggestive of Schoenberg's *Pierrot Lunaire.* The gentleman continued to sing; the committee stood about the enormous bouquet, which they had upended on the stage like a rhododendron bush. And finally the curtain came down to a mixture of applause and laughter. This kind of thing—of which the Gémier run also had its share—especially becomes a nuisance in connection with literature and the theater. One resents having Becque and Molière made the agents of official propaganda. How can *La Parisienne,* that tour de force of sexual sang-froid, be made to promote the interests of present French foreign policy?

February, 1925

J. P. McEvoy in the Ziegfeld Follies

ONE FINDS in the new Ziegfeld Follies what one would never have thought to see there: an element of systematic satire. Mr. Ziegfeld has incorporated in his "new edition," along with the conventional Follies numbers, a series of sketches from *The Comic Supplement,* an entertainment by J. P. McEvoy, which was tried out by Mr. Ziegfeld in Newark but not in its entirety brought to New York. Mr. McEvoy is the author of *The Potters,* a caricaturist of the school of Sinclair Lewis; and his *Comic Supplement,* enlivened though it is by the bright costumes of Norman Bel-Geddes and partially humanized by such persons as Ray Dooley and W. C. Fields, is as harsh in intention, as mirthless, as his hideous realistic comedy. Mr. McEvoy, by rewriting as if it were actual what in the funny papers is conventionally grotesque, produces something that is almost intolerable. You have a picnic with vandalistic picnickers camping on the lawn of a private house: they steal flowers, wreck everything in sight and finally break into the house and carry away the furniture; or a man tries to sleep on the back porch, but the chain-swing in which he is lying is continually slipping down, and he is driven nearly insane by being disturbed every other minute by the iceman, the milkman, the baby or the recurrent family quarrels. When Mr. McEvoy tries his hand at a spooning scene, he so emphasizes the banalities of the lovers that not even the grace of Vivienne Segal and a charming set of purple and green can make them appear sympathetic. Mr. McEvoy is obviously one who has suffered in a most acute way from the commonness and ugliness of American life and who has not, as an artist, got much beyond this. The remarkable thing, however, is that a writer of this kind, at the present time, should have become, not only the author of a popular satirical comedy but a collaborator in the Follies, where the humor in the past has, in general, been mechanical and commonplace. Can it be that the audiences of the Follies have their nerves on edge like Mr. McEvoy's, that the demand to have their dissatisfaction vicariously expressed in this way has actually made itself felt even in the Ziegfeld box office?

April 8, 1925

––––

Can New York Stage a Serious Play?

THERE WERE a number of reasons why Wedekind's *Erdgeist,* produced in New York as *The Loves of Lulu,* should have failed so completely of effectiveness. For one thing, it was inadequately acted; and, for another, the translation was so bad as to make it partly incomprehensible—I doubt whether even the actors always knew what was supposed to be going on. But assuming even a bad translation and a company as indifferent as this one, it is conceivable that something could have been done with it by playing it for melodrama. What was fatal was the inert direction. Frank Wedekind's plays are hysterical, tense; they should be tensely and hysterically played; but what one got at the Forty-ninth Street Theater were suicides, murders and storms of passion performed like slowed-up moving pictures. The result of this was sometimes comic: scenes of consternation and violence, such as the suicide of the young artist at the end of the third act, were so lackadaisically dealt with that they seemed to be completely meaningless and only made the audience laugh.

The Loves of Lulu, however, was scarcely a worse fiasco than a good many other plays with better texts and better actors that have lately been seen in our serious theater. The fundamental weakness of that theater is its vagueness and its lack of energy. One does not, of course, wish to belittle such producers as Mr. Arthur Hopkins, the Theater Guild, the Neighborhood Playhouse and the Provincetown Players: it is mainly to their taste and intelligence that we are indebted for most of what is worth seeing. But their productions are let down by a listlessness which causes some of their best plays to miss fire. A conspicuous victim this season was James Joyce's play *Exiles* at the Neighborhood Playhouse.

Joyce no doubt has his deficiencies as a dramatist, but from the Neighborhood production of *Exiles* it was difficult to tell how serious these deficiencies were: the slowness and dreariness with which it was performed would have made any play seem boring. In reading the text, one had felt, from the brevity and precision of most of the speeches, that they were meant to be delivered rather briskly; but at the Neighborhood the actors paused so long between their lines that one's attention was likely to wander—a fatal disaster for a play like *Exiles,* which provides so few theatrical baits. But even *Processional,** which provides so many, seemed to suffer from a lack of vitality. *Processional,* I take it, was supposed to have been run off with the emphasis and swiftness of a vaudeville show; but certainly the performance I saw—a matinee, to be sure—had nothing of this headlong quality. Nor did *What Price Glory,* for all its great merits, seem vigorously organized: it was only when one went to the text that one felt that the authors had tried to convey the agitation and pressure of war. It is partly, no doubt, this kind of thing that makes it possible for a critic like Mr. Gilbert Seldes to remain under the illusion that the musical shows are intrinsically more impressive than the serious plays: they, at least, like the moving pictures, tend to stimulate the attention of the spectator instead of lagging behind it. What is the good of talking pretentiously about "rhythm" if you do not teach the actors to take up their cues?

There is, however, perhaps another factor involved in our dragging performances. Foreigners visiting the United States are struck by the slowness of American speech, as we are likely to get the impression that all Europeans—including the English—speak with excessive rapidity. And the truth is that Americans still drawl—in the city as well as in the country: not even New York, unlike Paris or London, has a language of the quick intelligence. Compare an English company playing Galsworthy or a French company playing anything with the American productions I have mentioned above. One of the things that our theater most needs is a training in preci-

* By John Howard Lawson.

sion and speed in the delivery of lines. The lack of this tends to make Shakespeare—or any classical dramatist—all but impossible in America. We are doing away at last with the shifting of elaborate sets which used to take up so much time in the old-fashioned Shakespearean productions and to necessitate such sweeping cuts; but we still cannot manage the lines fast enough to get through more than a much abridged version of the play. Now, Shakespeare composed on a five-act scale and does not justify himself dramatically on any other. (This is the reason why the newspaper critics so often describe Shakespeare as an incompetent dramatist: unfamiliar with the printed plays, they conclude, not unnaturally, from the medley of selections presented to them on the stage that the author was a careless artist, devoid of any sense of proportion.) The Elizabethans carried off their five-act plays by going through them very rapidly, with almost no business and no intermissions. The plays were constructed with subplots which alternated with the main action and served the double purpose of allowing the actors to rest and refreshing the attention of the audience. Shakespeare was written to be played in this way and could be played in this way still—with two short intermissions, perhaps—if American actors could be found to read long stretches of blank verse fast enough. In some ways, the most enjoyable Shakespeare that the present writer has ever seen was *The Tempest* as given at the Century Theater nine or ten years ago. The whole text was played straight through with one set and very brief breaks.

May 27, 1925

————

American Jazz Ballet

Sooner and Later at the Neighborhood Playhouse was a "dance satire" by Irene Lewisohn, with music by Emerson Whithorne. Like John Alden Carpenter's Krazy Kat ballet and Cole Porter's *Within the Quota, Sooner and Later* represents an attempt to write a ballet on an American theme using authentic American material. All of these recent efforts to create a native ballet have been interesting. It may be true that our popular humor—which Mr. Carpenter here exploited—our popular music—which Mr. Porter has laid under contribution—and our Indian dances—which Mr. Whithorne makes the foundation for the first section of *Sooner and Later* —contain seeds of a new kind of entertainment different both from our musical shows and from the European ballet. *Sooner and Later* was planned more ambitiously than either of its predecessors. But, more elaborate, it was also more difficult, and it turned out, on the whole, less satisfactory than either. *Krazy Kat* and *Within the Quota,* though they scarcely pretended to be more than trifles, had a certain finish and point, whereas *Sooner and Later* suffers from a certain effect of aimlessness, of being too loosely strung together. The first section of this ballet is supposed to represent the primitive America of the Indians; the second, the New York of today, mechanical, weary and arid; and the third, the scientifically developed, the "crystallized" world of the future. But the significance of the "satire" was hardly clear; what was supposed to be the point of the contrast? None the less, if not quite an artistic success, *Sooner and Later* was entertaining and worth the Neighborhood Playhouse's trouble. The ritual of the Indians was effective, as was also the ironical rendering of the monotony and fatigue of New York; and in the sublimated final section, there was a most amusing use of the color organ, which was made to perform a sex drama in purely abstract terms.

If anyone could write jazz ballet, it might perhaps be George Gershwin. With Gershwin, the idiom of popular music is a natural mode of expression, the medium in which he has always worked—not, as with Whithorne or Carpenter, a language deliberately adopted and overlaid on an academic training. That Gershwin has musical ambitions beyond his accustomed vein is proved by his *Rhapsody in Blue.* What has become of that all-American opera about Carmen the cigar-store girl which he was reported to be writing with Ring Lardner?

May 27, 1925

The New Jersey Ferry

THE RIVER is oily gray; downtown is a dull gray wall. A railroad barge, pushed by a tug, conveys used discolored freight cars, all labeled Wabash and Reading. The dull gray and yellow skies are tightening, distended with thunder. When they burst, they must strew larger, louder, more exciting, more extraordinary names.

July 22, 1925

The New Chaplin Comedy

THE FUNDAMENTAL DEVICE of American moving-picture humor is what is technically known as the "gag." A gag is a comic trick, the equivalent in cinema action of the spoken gag of the stage. When Buster Keaton on a runaway motorcycle knocks the ladder out from under a house painter and goes off with the bucket of paint on his head, or when a clothesline, strung between two houses, on which Harold Lloyd is escaping, is cut at one end by an enemy and Harold, still clinging to it, swings into a room below where a séance of spiritualists are awaiting a materialization, this is a movie gag. Inventing such tricks is today one of the principal professions of the film industry. In Hollywood, the gag-writers of the comic stars are among the most influential and the most envied members of the community; for without them the stars would be nothing. There are moments when Buster Keaton gives evidence of a skill at pantomime which his producers do nothing to cultivate; but one may say of these comics in general that they hardly need to be actors any more than Baby Peggy, Rin-Tin-Tin, Strongheart or Silver King.

The one performer of Hollywood who has succeeded in doing anything distinguished with this primitive machinery of gags is, of course, Charlie Chaplin. In the first place, he is, I believe, the only comic star in the movies who does not employ a gag-writer: he makes everything up himself; so that, instead of the stereotyped humor of even the best of his competitors, most of whose tricks could be interchanged among them without anyone's knowing the difference, he gives us jokes that, however crude, have an unmistakable quality of personal fancy. Furthermore, he has made it a practice to use his gags as points of departure for genuine comic situations. Thus in his latest picture, *The Gold Rush*, there is a cabin—with Charlie and his partner in it—which is blown to the edge of a cliff while the occupants are asleep. This in itself is a gag like another: for any other screen comedian it would have been enough to startle the audience by showing them the little shack rocking on the dangerous brink and then, by acrobatics and trick photography, to follow this with similar shudders. But Chaplin, given his gag, the same kind of thing as Lloyd's clothesline, proceeds to transport his audience in a way of which Lloyd would be incapable, by developing it with steady logic and vivid imagination. Charlie and his companion wake up: the panes of the shack are frosted; they do not realize what has happened; Charlie sets out to get breakfast, but whenever he moves to the side of the room where his heavy companion is lying—the side hanging over the abyss—the house begins to tip. He puts this down, however, to dizziness—he has been drunk the night before—and goes resolutely about his business. But when his companion —the gigantic Mack Swain—gets up and begins to move around, the phenomenon is aggravated: "Do you have an illusion that the floor is tipping?"—"Ah, you notice that, too, do you?" They jump on it to see if it is standing solid; but as Charlie is jumping on the overhanging side while Swain is holding it down on the other, they do not at once find out what is wrong, and it is some time before the fatal combination—both men on the projecting side—almost sends them over the cliff. They rush back to the safe side of the room, and Charlie goes to the door—which has been frozen tight in the night—to see what is going on: after a struggle, it suddenly flies open, and he falls out into the void, only saving himself by a clutch at the sill. His companion rushes down to save him, but by the time he has pulled him in, their double weight has set the cabin sliding: it is anchored now only by a rope which has caught fast to something not far from the cliff. Charlie and his companion, abject on their bellies, try to crawl up the terrible floor, now at an angle of sixty degrees. At first, though the eyes of his companion are popping, Charlie remains cool and sensible. "Just go easy! A little at a time." But no matter how little they attempt, every movement makes the cabin slip. And so on, through a long passage of pantomime.

Conversely, however, the gag is sometimes resorted to by Chaplin to break up the non-farcical sequences—ironic or even pathetic—that are becoming more frequent in his comedies. Thus the love story in *The Gold Rush* is, on the whole, treated seriously, but from time to time enlivened by such low comedy incidents as that in which Charlie accidentally saturates his bandaged foot with kerosene and then has it set on fire by a match dropped by one of the ladies. In these sequences, it sometimes happens—as in parts of *The Pilgrim,* his previous film—that such gags in the straight situations produce a jarring effect. They seem to be introduced in order to hold Chaplin's old public, who expects their full allowance of "belly laughs." He has never dared desert this public, who first saw him in the Mack Sennett comedies and who still go to him for the same sort of entertainment that they find in Fox and Christie comedies. Yet in proportion as his reputation has grown with the sophisticated audience and the critics, his popularity has hardly gained—it has not even, perhaps, held its own—with this original popular audience, who do not seem to feel any difference between Chaplin himself, on the one hand, and his imitators and rivals, on the other. They seem, in fact, to be coming to prefer the latter. Buster Keaton and Harold Lloyd have, in a sense, carried gagging far beyond Charlie Chaplin. Their films have more smartness and speed; they cultivate more frightening mechanical devices. With their motorcars, their motorcycles, their motorboats, their airplanes, their railroad trains, their vertiginous scaling of skyscrapers and their shattering cataclysmic collisions, they have progressed a long way beyond Chaplin, who has made no attempt to keep up with them, but continues with the cheap trappings and the relatively simple tricks of the old custard-pie comedy. For Chaplin is even more old-fashioned than the old-fashioned Mack Sennett movies; he is as old-fashioned as Karno's Early Birds, the unusual music-hall turn in which he originally appeared and which was at least a school for actors, not for athletes.

What turn Charlie Chaplin's career will take is, therefore, still a curious problem. He is himself, I believe, acutely aware of the anomaly of his position. In the films, he seems hardly likely to play an important role in the artistic development of the future. His gift is primarily the actor's, not the director's or artist's. All the photographic, the plastic development of the movies, which is at present making such remarkable advances, seems not to interest Chaplin. His pictures are still in this respect nearly as raw as *Tilly's Punctured Romance* or any other primitive comedy, and it is only when the subject is sordid—as in *Pay Day*, with its crowded city streetcars taking people home after work and its suffocating slatternly city flat—that the *mise en scène* in Chaplin's comedies contributes in any way to their effectiveness. The much-praised *A Woman of Paris* was handicapped particularly, it seemed to me—since it did not have Chaplin as the central figure—by this visual lack of taste. It was intended as an attractive, a serious picture, yet, for all the intelligence he brought to directing it, he allowed it to go out as if naked in its flat light and putty make-up. He is jealous of his independence in this as in other matters. He is very unlikely to allow himself to be written for, directed or even advised. If he is not carrying along his old public, he will unquestionably in time have to give it up; but whether he will then simply retire from the screen or try something altogether different, it is impossible to predict. In the meantime, it may be that his present series of pictures—*The Kid, The Pilgrim* and *The Gold Rush*—with their gags and their overtones of tragedy, their adventures half-absurd, half-realistic, their mythical hero, now a figure of poetry, now a type out of the comic strips, represents the height of Chaplin's achievement. He could scarcely, in any field, surpass the best moments of these pictures. The opening of *The Gold Rush* is such a moment. Charlie is a lone adventurer, straggling along after a party of prospectors among the frozen hills: he twirls his cane a little to keep his spirits up. On his way through a narrow mountain pass, a bear emerges and follows him. Any ordinary movie comedian, given the opportunity of using a bear, would, of course, have had it chasing him about for as long as he could work up gags for it. But Charlie does not know that the bear is there: he keeps on, twirling his cane. Presently the beast withdraws, and only then does Charlie think he hears something: he turns around, but there is nothing there. And he sets off again, still fearless, toward the dreadful ordeals that await him.

September 2, 1925

1957. Years later, on visits to London, I went to the Christmas pantomime and realized that the bear of *The Gold Rush* was one of the many things that Charlie Chaplin had borrowed from the British popular theater. There is always, in the pantomime, a scene in which the comedians are lost in a forest, and there used to be always a bear—though in the winter of '53–'54 a space man was substituted—which is following them but hides when they look around. Eventually, however, they must face the bear: it was Chaplin's original touch never to allow the traveler to see the bear at all. In the meantime, the pantomimist Chaplin—contrary to my expectations of 1925—had quite sloughed off the old vagabond and emerged on the speaking screen in characterizations wholly new: the contemporary Bluebeard of *Monsieur Verdoux* and the old music-hall comedian of *Limelight*. Though the last of these takes us back to the music hall, it is no longer to the music-hall devices as material for Hollywood comedy. Chaplin has outgrown these, and he now recreates the music hall, makes it one of the subjects of a work of art. The sequences in which Chaplin's hero is seen in his professional act, have something poetic, daemonic. They are among the high points of Chaplin's career. As funny as any of his earlier scenes, they are also intensely emotional. The clown with a breaking heart is as ancient as any of the stock situations which Chaplin has never hesitated to exploit; but the result is, as usual, astonishing: the nightmare of the dead-pan accompanist, whose music keeps slipping off the stand while the comedian diverts the audience by primitive clowning tricks that are at once unashamed and embarrassing; the sudden and mad climax in which the aging comic produces a small violin and fiddles feverishly till he falls into the orchestra. The accompanist here is Buster Keaton, who had passed into eclipse in Hollywood but was invited by Chaplin to take part in this film and is perfect in the uncanny atmosphere of this music hall of Hell. Not long afterwards— in February, 1954—I saw Buster Keaton perform at the Cirque Médrano in Paris, and was confirmed in my opinion of twenty-eight years before that Hollywood had not made the best of him. He is a pantomime clown of the first order, and his act at the Cirque Médrano—a presser's boy, morose and detached, attempting to deliver a dress suit while the circus is going on—seemed to me the best thing I had seen him do. His loss of reputation in the United States and his appearance in an engagement abroad is only another example of the perversion and waste of talent for which Hollywood has been responsible. Who could ever, in 1925, have believed that Charlie Chaplin would escape from it—having always been his own manager—and take his place among his age's first artists? But see my later note on this subject.

––––––

An American Caligari

ONE HAS LATELY NOTED signs of a new sophistication on the part of our moving-picture directors—in certain of the films, for example, of Tod Browning and Allan Dwan. One imagines that, bored by the manufacture of stupid routine films, they have yielded at last to the temptation to smuggle into some of their trade goods a little superior workmanship, a little real characterization and a few sequences independent of captions. One of Tod Browning's recent products, a picture called *The Unholy Three,* is an attempt at a macabre fantasy in the vein of the German film, *The Cabinet of Dr. Caligari;* and, since *Caligari,* for all its excellences, was never very popular here and since Mr. Browning has here refrained from sweetening his macabre and ironic story with any of the conventional romantic values without which successful films are supposed to be impossible in America, this picture ought to be counted to him for righteousness. *The Unholy Three,* to be sure, does not have the scenic and photographic interest of *Dr. Caligari,* and toward the end it rather misses its climax; but, with its parrots that cannot talk, its misanthropic midget, its infernal scene around the Christmas tree, in which the tranquil benevolence of a family circle serves as a mask for the murderers, it is almost comparable to the German picture. What I admire especially is the way in which the director has understood that occurrences so grotesque can only be accepted seriously when they have been quite taken out of the actual world. Mr. Browning does not have the resource, as did the maker of *Caligari,* of a madman's imagination to which to attribute his impossible story, but he is careful to close it in from any suggestion of a recognizable environment: we believe in the behavior of his characters, no matter how fantastic this is, because the world of natural behavior has been completely excluded.

The Unholy Three is very well acted by Miss Mae Busch and Mr. Lon Chaney. The reputation of Mr. Chaney is unique and of a singular kind. Ever since his appearance in the title role of *The Hunchback of Notre Dame,* he has been famous as a virtuoso of sinister make-ups. Indeed, he has passed into a legend and become the hero of such current popular jokes as, "Hey! don't eat that lobster!—or don't kill that tarantula!—it may be Lon Chaney!" Mr. Chaney's most spectacular appearance this fall has been in *The Phantom of the Opera,* an ingenious and entertaining detective story, which does not, however, offer the smallest opportunity for acting and which, besides, imposes upon him a mask so deforming and complicated as to render him incapable of any play of expression even if this were expected of him. But his real success has been scored as the ventriloquist in *The Unholy Three,* not only in his disguise of the kindly old lady, in which he manages to be five times as frightful as in the bugaboo role of the Phantom, but also in the close-up pantomime of the ventriloquist in his own character. Lon Chaney may, in fact, have it in him to become a sort of Mansfield of the moving pictures, and nothing could be more characteristic of American producers of "feature films" than the fact that Carl Laemmle, in *The Phantom of the Opera,* after two years of great preparations, involving undoubtedly immense expense, has presented his most advertised favorite in a role which gives him no chance at all to distinguish himself as an actor.

September 23, 1925

————

Enlightenment through the Films

THE FILM about Evolution which was shown in New York last summer reminded one of the great possibilities of the cinema for scientific exposition. Here one witnessed the genesis of the solar system through a monstrous collision in the heavens; the hydrogen geysers of the sun, the boiling surface of the earth; the solidification of the earth's crust, the gradual emergence of the mountains; then the huge race of dinosaurs, feeding and fighting in their marshes, their extinction under the glaciers of an ice age. One was also shown the origins of life, the division, as if by magic, of a single-celled protozoön; beautiful photographs of mastigophora whipping themselves about and silvery cilia-fringed paramecia; a variety of curious animals demonstrating adaptation to environment: anteaters, devil's walking-sticks; then a selection of anthropoid apes, and, finally, some primitive human tribes. When I saw this film, I was much impressed by its possible educational value. If the picture could only, I thought, be shown in Dayton, Tennessee, the inhabitants of that backward region might be shaken in their literal faith in the account of creation in Genesis. I paid a visit, however, soon afterwards to a Biblical picture, *The Wanderer,* and there found a representation, just as plausible and just as impressive, of the fall of the Scriptural Babylon, with its palaces, princes and priests, condemned by an angry Jehovah; I beheld the idol of Istar split apart by a thunderbolt and the gigantic finger of God writing, in the Chaldaic of the Book of Daniel, its warning on Belshazzar's wall.

November 11, 1925

—————

Current Fashions

THE PEOPLE who make women's hosiery must be employing poets. I quote from an advertisement: Peach—beige—pearl—beach—suede—silver—cinder—rose taupe—African brown—russet—blonde satin—blush—Airedale—cork—shell pink—pebble—skynn—lark—tan—cordovan—mauve—muffin—nude —buck—gold—fawn—racquet—sandalwood—oriental pearl—tanbark—log cabin—oakwood—gunmetal. And from another: Mauve gray—rose nutmeg—peach nude—sauterne—orange nude—blush pink—natural.

—————

In the billiard parlors of Waterbury and Scranton, young men are wearing the blue shirts and the white-rimmed gray hats of the Prince of Wales; and in the back streets of Newark and Schenectady, little girls in the green hats of Michael Arlen are dancing the Charleston on the pavement.

November 11, 1925

Chaplin and His Comic Rivals

IT WAS ASSERTED by the present critic, when *The Gold Rush*
appeared last August, that moving-picture comedy was dominated by the school of Buster Keaton and Harold Lloyd, by
the exploitation of elaborate "gags." I prophesied that Chaplin, with his finer psychology and his less spectacular farce,
would not be able to hold his popularity against it. What has
happened is the reverse of what I predicted. *The Gold Rush*
has had a conspicuous success; and, so far from playing Chaplin off the screen, Buster Keaton and Harold Lloyd have
taken to imitating him. What is striking in their new films
is the reduction of the number of gags and the attempt to
fill their place with straight drama. Lloyd and Keaton, or
their producers, have tried to follow Chaplin's example by
allowing their comic characters to become partly credible as
human beings: they have gone in for wistfulness and pathos.
In the case of Harold Lloyd, the effect of this attempt is not
particularly happy. Lloyd has never been a very good actor;
he is a dummy for comic devices. We cannot be very much
moved by the scene in his new film, *The Freshman,* in which
it breaks upon him at last that, instead of being a hero to his
fellow students, he has in reality been serving as their butt;
nor when, entering the big game at the last moment, he wins
with a miraculous touchdown. But Buster Keaton is an able
pantomimist; his sullen and sensitive face commands a certain sympathy. We are, therefore, not entirely unresponsive
to his newest picture, *Go West.* Here he figures as a friendless boy on a remote Western ranch, who conceives an attach-
ment for a cow. He has taken a stone out of the cow's foot
and the cow has, in turn, defended him—in the manner of
Androcles and the Lion—against the attack of an angry bull.
When she is finally sent off to the slaughterhouse, he opens
up the cars and lets out the whole herd. We may foresee
a danger, however, that if the movie comedians continue in
their present policy of playing for tears instead of laughs,
they may, not excluding Chaplin, merely succeed in becoming maudlin. Buster Keaton's dumb solemnity was more

touching, perhaps, in his old comic films than in this new sentimental one.

December 16, 1925

—————

A German Director in Hollywood

THE FILM made by Ernst Lubitsch from *Lady Winder-mere's Fan* is not easily recognizable as a version of Oscar Wilde's comedy. For the plot is the only thing that Lubitsch has taken from Wilde, and the plot of *Lady Windermere's Fan* is something to which no one has ever paid much attention. In itself, it is old-fashioned, banal and even rather cheap, and it is, therefore, ideal from the point of view of the Hollywood producer. Mr. Lubitsch has brushed off the sparkle of wit and cleared away the atmosphere of cynicism which formerly obscured and made tolerable this highly conventional comedy; but he has clothed it in such beautiful photography and directed it with so much resourcefulness that he has turned out a very attractive film. The silver and gray London streets, the white-gowned or black-morning-coated figures, standing in high-ceilinged rooms or looking out of long-curtained windows, are in his most distinguished manner; and his theatrical ingenuity, his great knack of shooting commonplace incidents from inobvious and revelatory angles, though less amusing than in *Kiss Me Again*, is at least as effective as ever.

At one of the early showings of *Lady Windermere's Fan*, one was given a demonstration of another phase of Lubitsch's genius—his ability to induce his actors to embody his own ideas. The actress who played Mrs. Erlynne, Miss Irene Rich, appeared on the stage in person and made a little speech. In her role of the clever adventuress, Miss Rich had been notably successful—smart, slender, brunette and lovely, with a charming air of sweetness and frankness which did not conceal, however, the exercise of a calculated tact, the product of much worldly experience. But in person, Miss

Irene Rich turned out to be something quite different—a wholesome strapping girl from the Coast, as blond as a Pacific peach and as well-grown as a sequoia tree, who has never, it appears, hitherto played anything other than rôles of betrayed and abandoned wives. That Lubitsch should have seen her possibilities as Oscar Wilde's Mrs. Erlynne and enabled her to realize them successfully is a proof of the cardinal difference that an intelligent director may make to the acting of the moving pictures. This is perhaps even more important in the films than on the speaking stage, since, in the former, the actor has no audience but only the director to play to, and the relation between actor and director is closer and more direct. The effect of certain directors on their actors is, in fact, said to be almost hypnotic. Who knows but that a certain proportion of the Hollywood pretty girls as well as of the Hollywood male popinjays might be turned into respectable performers taking part in attractive films if there were only enough German directors imported to mesmerize them?

March 24, 1926

————

The Follies in New Quarters

THE FOLLIES have moved from the New Amsterdam Theater and now go under a different name. I find it a little sad to see the great framed display of the photographs of former Follies girls simply propped up in the corridor that leads to the Globe, their new home, like the posters of a traveling vaudeville act, instead of hung just above the staircase of the spacious New Amsterdam, where they gave the effect of a gallery of the more illustrious graduates of some rather smart college. Yet the Ziegfeld show itself remains the best thing of its kind in New York: Edna Leedom, the Amazonian but amiable 100 per cent American blonde grinding out the wisecracks of her songs from between a wide set of white teeth, which have the same expensive glitter as her diamonds;

James Barton, with his fixed ginny stare and his partially paralyzed fingers, passing through the grisly stages of his disquieting drunken act; the sumptuous Greta Nissen, in a preposterous oriental pantomime, in the course of which, as a female Bluebeard, with a complacent Scandinavian smile, she slowly decapitates her lovers and shoves their heads out the door with her foot; the droll and slow dialogue of Moran and Mack ("What are goofus feathers?" "They're—so—soft!"); a rowdy little Charleston-dancer called Mary Jane; Claire Luce, the pale moonbeam blonde, suspended in a revolving silver globe which sprays a dance of lightmotes on the backdrop, while the show girls weight down the eye with a parade of white peacock-feather headdresses, each outdazzling and outtowering the last. The only features of which I complain are the increasing sourness and dulness of E. P. McEvoy's sketches and the fact that W. C. Fields—who, besides, used somewhat to sweeten these latter—was not there to dance with Ray Dooley.

July 28, 1926

————

Book Galleries and Book Shops

AT THE TIME when Brentano's book shop, stranded below Twenty-third Street among the rising tide of textiles, announced its intention of moving uptown, one was troubled by the anticipation of another Fifth Avenue book palace, pretentious but unsatisfactory.

These fears have been proved vain. One finds in the new Brentano's the same admirable features as in the old: the varied and enormous stock, the easily accessible galleries, the comprehensive foreign departments, with clerks who are at home in the languages of the literatures to which they are accredited, and the fascinating display, in the basement, of the tables of periodicals from all over the Western world. It is quite free from that uptown atmosphere which, in the case of certain other book shops, has rendered their new quarters a little oppressive: the vastness and glitter of a Scribner's, the solemnity and darkness of a Dutton's. Though somewhat more luxurious than the old Brentano's, its interior decorations are of rather a genial kind. The principal motif here is a garland of acorns and oakleaves, which, against the brown woodwork and white ceilings, appears in several combinations of pink, brown and green, like the holly designs on the boxes in which Christmas presents come; and, going down to the basement by the staircase, one is confronted by a genial mural which depicts the new shop itself and in which, against the mountainous background of a customer in a red dress looking at books on the counter, a lady of a different type, with blue eyes and pale blond hair, a little wasted in figure, a little haggard from too much reading, holds aloft—in high exaltation—a book which, it would seem, after passionate search and beyond all expectation, she has just found on Brentano's inexhaustible shelves, while, looking up from the lefthand corner, a small girl in a coat with big buttons is a sympathetic witness of her triumph. This picture, in execution, reminds one a little of the crude cartoons of prestidigitators, snake-charmers and strong men that are displayed before the sideshows of circuses; and it also has something akin to the old-fashioned hand-painted signs of which very few specimens now survive in New York: the advertisement for rented dress suits at Sixth Avenue and Forty-third Street, the dog on lower Fifth Avenue which is viciously ripping the trousers of a gentleman of the eighties (who will subsequently have them mended by the tailor on the second floor), and the pink pigs that sometimes appear on the delivery wagons of downtown butchers. The lady who has just found the book is, like these, a little ridiculous, but one knows that she will become familiar, and that one will feel for her a sort of affection that one cannot feel for printed advertisements. She is unique: we have to go to Brentano's to see her; we shall not find her reproduced on the subway, in magazines, on the signboards along the railroad. She is frankly a sign for a shop, and thus symbolizes the spirit of Brentano's, which has not been ashamed to remain an old-fashioned New York book shop at the service of the general public, selling all kinds of books to all kinds of people. The other big booksellers in this part of town have been tending in a different direction. One gets the impression that their wares are to be taken as articles of luxury rather than as intellectual currency. They go in for eighteenth-century editions bought up by their scouts in England, regilded and polished in America and sold at six or eight times the original price, and for green, red or blue morocco "library sets" bound so stiffly that it is impossible to open them and containing the collected works of such in any case unreadable authors as Ik Marvel, S. Weir Mitchell and Henry Van Dyke.

The most blighting influence on the book shops has, however, been the recent traffic in first editions and other rarities. The inflation in the price of such things is said to be an American achievement, mainly due to Dr. Rosenbach, the dean of the trade, who has sent the price of rare books rocketing in Europe as well as America. In any case, today in New York, there are book galleries just as there are art galleries. About Rosenbach's establishment on Madison Avenue there have grown up a whole cluster of minor ones, the most ambitious of which aim to emulate it in getting away from the ordinary procedure of a book shop and imitating an elegant private house. These are equipped with wrought-iron doors, an atmosphere of muffling carpets and hushed money-conscious voices, and sets of dark high-backed chairs invoking the Renaissance. But the general bookdealers, also, are developing rare book departments, with safety deposit vaults to which one is admitted with difficulty and in which are kept Beardsley's erotic drawings, seventeenth-century Puritan tracts and first editions of Thomas Hardy. The types that preside over all this are similar to those in the art galleries: ceremoniously upholstered young Jews, plump and with soft white hands; aloof and relentless Britishers with a keen scent for American snobbery; old gentlemen with eyeglasses and ragged mustaches, who seem to live in a state of morose trepidation for fear somebody will ask them for a copy of *Gentlemen Prefer Blondes*.

The galleries that deal in pictures have perhaps a little

more justification. There can be only one original of every painting. But this is not true of literature. There is no special virtue in first editions: one would usually prefer to read a later one in which the printing is up to date, the paper has not faded and the author has corrected the errors. All this trade is as deeply boring to people who are interested in literature as it seems to be fascinating to those others who, incapable of literary culture, try to buy the distinction of letters by paying unusual prices for bibliographical rarities. I do not deny that there is an art of the bookmaker: there have been books that were beautifully designed, as well, of course, as books that have fine illustrations. But the values of our New York dealers are mostly not aesthetic ones. It may be necessary for a critic or a student—unless he has within reach a large library—to accumulate a considerable number of books; but it is doubtful whether any first-rate man of letters has ever gone in for collecting books except on some special subject in which he might happen to be interested. A well-known American writer* once told me that, at a time in his earlier days when he did most of his reading on streetcars, he had the habit of lightening the volumes by tearing out the sections he had read and throwing them away at the end of the trip. I shall not reveal his name, for I know how much pain it would give to the collectors of his first editions; but I can assure them that it is easier for a camel to pass through the eye of a needle than for a collector of first editions to enter the Kingdom of Literature.

August 4, 1926

––––

Broadway in August

AUGUST ON BROADWAY is all but opaque: it resembles that hour of morning when all the stars have faded and the dawn has not yet appeared. The people are submerged in the

* 1957. Sherwood Anderson.

grayish haze that seems volatilized by the heat from the asphalt and hushed by the oppression of summer which mutes the very taxis and trucks. They swarm to the open street counters, where imitation orange juice is sold, and, for refuge from the tepid air, seek refrigerated movie-houses, where films of incredible dulness are shown. The Winter Garden floats a yellow balloon with a great streaming pennant attached, like the race track of a county fair. The girls in the dance halls perspire and swim round and round like goldfish.

The Vitaphone, that new combination of phonograph and moving picture, which is being exhibited as a prelude to the Barrymore *Don Juan,* is astonishingly synchronized and very distinct and loud. It is almost, in fact, a little too loud: the giant figures have giant voices—voices which, from being distended, sound hollow and rather lifeless. The world of the moving pictures, which no one mistakes for real, has achieved a life of its own, which partly depends on its silence, on running off, with speed and no uproar, events which, if put on the stage, would involve an immense amount of pother. The films are an abstraction of movement, as music is of sound. But when voices are added to the creatures of the screen, we become more conscious rather than less that what we are watching are only shadows. As Mr. Will H. Hays pointed out, in an introductory Vitaphone appearance, this invention will make it possible for the people of "every hamlet" to listen to "symphonic orchestration"—and not merely to listen to the music, but also, at the same time, to pore upon a close-up of the orchestra. Now all the American provincial towns which have never in their whole histories got up enough musical enthusiasm to organize a choral society or an amateur orchestra will be—as the audience at the Warner are—in a position to hear and see and marvel at the swollen and savorless phantoms of Mischa Elman playing Dvořák's *Humoresque,* of Martinelli singing *Pagliacci* and of Zimbalist and Harold Bauer performing a theme and variations.

As for the Hollywood version of *Don Juan,* it differs strikingly from those of Byron, Mozart and Molière. The

older Don Juan (John Barrymore doubling as his own father) is a high-minded Spanish nobleman embittered by his
wife's infidelity. As a result of his disillusionment, he goes
in for Babylonian revelries that recall the huge Biblical films
produced by D. W. Griffith. This sets a bad example to John
Barrymore the son and destroys the latter's respect for women.
The unfavorable impression is intensified when the father
is stabbed by one of his favorites. The young man now sets
out systematically on a career of coldblooded seduction. Arriving in Rome, he attracts at once the attention of Lucrezia
Borgia, who makes passionate advances to him; but, knowing
her reputation, he firmly repulses her charms, and he rescues
the Duke della Varnese, the father of Mary Astor, a beautiful American girl, from being poisoned at a Borgia banquet.
He falls in love with this beautiful American, and, by driving him out of her bedroom, she restores his faith in the
honor of women. When an attempt is made by the Borgias
to marry her against her will to one of their wicked noble-
men, John Barrymore–Don Juan, in his blond wig, dashes
into the bridal chamber, kills the nobleman in single combat,
escapes from the Castel di Sant' Angelo by diving under the
Tiber, and carries off Mary Astor on horseback while cutting
down an armed pursuit of six or eight horsemen.

The Warner Theater is decorated with a gigantic apotheosis of John Barrymore kissing a girl in the clouds; programs
in three colors are sold as you go in; and outside there are
magic pictures, on which blue and red lights are flashed, so
contrived that, when the blue goes on, it reveals naked female figures that are invisible under the red. In the lobby,
a painting of Barrymore, flanked by Earl Carroll nymphs
about half the size of the star, is illuminated day and night
by a lighting that changes color like the galaxies of Fourth
of July rockets. The ushers are dressed in high ruffed collars
and long bell-skirted gowns designed to transport the visitor
into the atmosphere of the fifteenth century. They must be
extremely hot.

September, 1926

Vantine's in Five Floors

VANTINE'S, in moving uptown, has, like several other attractive shops, lost a good deal of its fascination. The curse of the Fifties has fallen on it. To wander about in the old Vantine's gave a taste of the Arabian Nights. I do not remember using elevators: it was by staircases that one made one's way among galleries, tearooms and basements, and one never knew what one was going to find. There were gem-studded vanity boxes, red lacquered canisters of tea, copper and white-gold neckties, Japanesy stone rabbits for gardens, brilliantly embroidered slippers, candied fruits so beautifully finished that one might almost mistake them for ornaments, incense, obese Chinese statues, chop suey sets, sumptuous rugs—variety, richness, confusion. But today all these interesting objects have been systematically classified and sorted out. There are five well-organized floors, accessible only by elevator, with a segregated department on each. One sees clearly that the rabbits, the rugs, the slippers and the other things are not the figments of an oriental fantasy: they are so many imported commodities; and one thinks about poorly paid girls sugaring and packing the candied fruits, of companies that turn out stone rabbits; one wonders about the rugs: are they woven by handlooms or machinery? For each of these products, one realizes, there must exist a well-established demand; and one gets the impression that oddities for which the demand is uncertain have been rigorously eliminated here. It is, at any rate, not possible this season to find in the new Vantine's those elegant cigarette-holders in the form of coiling snakes, bright blue, red or orange with speckles of black, and ruby or amethyst eyes.

January 5, 1927

————

"Broadway"

To ONE who has not seen *Broadway* acted, the published text reads extremely well. The play is supposed to be the product of a collaboration between two writers, George Abbott and Philip Dunning; but the writing has an evenness and sureness which suggests that, though the plot may have been cooked up in conference, the dialogue is the work of one hand. Indeed, from the literary point of view, *Broadway* has a certain distinction. It is written entirely in New York slang, but the language has flavor and color, and there is no attempt to work up gags merely for the purpose of getting laughs: the wisecracks are provided quite naturally by the characters and the situations. Each character has a vein of his own. The cabaret girls are wonderful; the song-and-dance man is almost as good as one of Ring Lardner's creations; and even the heroine is plausible, quite free from sentimentality, a little like a younger Lorelei Lee acting in good faith. One wonders whether it might not have been possible, with such a turn for character and dialogue, for the author to have written a serious play almost as easily as a melodrama. A melodrama, however, *Broadway* remains: the villain is shot by a spirited girl with a just grievance against him; and the hero, though a comic hero, wins the love of the virtuous heroine. With the materials at their disposal the authors might perhaps have produced a vividly colored nightmare like Wedekind's *Lulu;* but they have aimed at nothing more pretentious than a sure-fire theatrical success. One had a somewhat similar impression in connection with *The Shanghai Gesture,* which displayed a good deal of imagination and a certain amount of literary ability. One thinks sadly, in the case of such melodramas, of our dreary Expressionist plays, whose authors make a desperate effort, by loud noise and novel tricks, to find a contact with vulgar American life. What these are obliged to strain for is precisely what the authors of *Broadway* and *The Shanghai Gesture* have at their command in abundance. T. S. Eliot has published in the *Criterion* two instalments of a hard-boiled drama in verse called *Wanna Go Home, Baby?* It is written in a vernacular—part English and part American—which Mr. Eliot appears to have acquired in somewhat the same fashion as Sanskrit. The songs which he invents for his characters are echoes of American ragtime of the vintage of almost twenty years ago.

With the resources of the authors of *Broadway*, what might not a real poet achieve?

March 2, 1927

————

The Ziegfeld Theater

THE NEW Ziegfeld Theater is a curious affair, quite unlike anything else in New York. The house itself is oval, and it seems a little smooth and bare, if one enters it with still living memories of the luxury of peacocks and panels, the rich haze of the old New Amsterdam. The proscenium arch is a dull smooth gilt, with rather broad columnar ruchings; the ceiling and the convex walls have been decorated by Joseph Urban with a continuous green-and-purple mural that glitters with gilt dandelion-leaf tinsel and is animated by slender male figures, mysterious and somewhat Wagnerian, attended by gamboling gazelles. The show is no longer a Follies but a commonplace musical comedy. Miss Ada May, among the principals, is the only first-rate performer: a very engaging dancer, whose whining and nasal voice is nevertheless seductive. Mr. Ziegfeld appears to have scanted himself in a fashion unusual with him by sometimes allowing the chorus to appear without change of costume; but this does not matter, since both costumes and dancing are up to the best Ziegfeld standard. The Albertina Rasch Dancers and the ensemble—with its typically Ziegfeldian Americanization of the Germanic beauty and energy of Elsie Behrens—are enough in themselves to make the spectacle worth while. The real inauguration of the theater will, however, one hopes, take place later on with a new 1927 Follies.

March 2, 1927

1957. There was a new Follies that August; but only one more after that, in 1931. In spite of the success of *Show*

Boat in 1928, Florenz Ziegfeld did not survive the depression. He went bankrupt, and in 1932 he died.

————

The Lexicon of Prohibition

THE FOLLOWING is a partial list of words denoting drunkenness now in common use in the United States. They have been arranged, as far as possible, in order of the degrees of intensity of the conditions which they represent, beginning with the mildest stages and progressing to the more disastrous.

lit
squiffy
oiled
lubricated
owled
edged
jingled
piffed
piped
sloppy
woozy
happy
half-screwed
half-cocked
half-shot
half seas over
fried
stewed
boiled
zozzled
sprung
scrooched
jazzed
jagged
canned
corked
corned
potted
hooted
slopped
tanked
stinko
blind
stiff
under the table
tight
full
wet
high
horseback
liquored
pickled
ginned
shicker (Yiddish)
spifflicated
primed
organized
featured

pie-eyed
cock-eyed
wall-eyed
glassy-eyed
bleary-eyed
hoary-eyed
over the Bay
four sheets in the wind
crocked
loaded
leaping
screeching
lathered
plastered
soused
bloated
polluted
saturated
full as a tick
loaded for bear
loaded to the muzzle
loaded to the plimsoll
    mark
wapsed down
paralyzed
ossified
out like a light
passed out cold
embalmed
buried
blotto

lit up like the sky
lit up like the Commonwealth
lit up like a Christmas tree
lit up like a store window
lit up like a church
fried to the hat
slopped to the ears
stewed to the gills
boiled as an owl
to have a bun on
to have a slant on
to have a skate on
to have a snootful
to have a skinful
to draw a blank
to pull a shut-eye
to pull a Daniel Boone
to have a rubber drink
to have a hangover
to have a head
to have the jumps
to have the shakes
to have the zings
to have the heeby-
    jeebies
to have the screaming-
    meemies
to have the whoops and
    jingles
to burn with a low blue
    flame

Some of these, such as *loaded* and *full,* are a little old-fashioned now; but they are still understood. Others, such as *cock-eyed* and *oiled,* which are included in the *Drinker's Dictionary* compiled by Benjamin Franklin (and containing two hundred and twenty-eight terms) seem to be enjoying a new popularity. It is interesting to note that one hears nowadays less often of people going on *sprees, toots, tears, jags, bats, brannigans* or *benders*. All these terms suggest, not merely extreme drunkenness, but also an exceptional occurrence, a breaking away by t¹ e drinker from the conditions of his normal life. It is possible that their partial disappearance is mainly to be accounted for by the fact that this kind of fierce protracted drinking has now become universal, an accepted feature of social life instead of a disreputable escapade. On the other hand, the vocabulary of social drinking, as exemplified by this list, seems to have become especially rich: one gets the impression that more nuances are nowadays discriminated than was the case before Prohibition. Thus, *fried, stewed* and *boiled* all convey distinctly different ideas; and *cock-eyed, plastered, owled, embalmed* and *ossified* evoke quite different images. *Wapsed down* is a rural expression originally applied to crops that have been laid low by a storm; *featured* is a theatrical word, which here refers to a stage at which the social drinker is inspired to believe strongly in his ability to sing a song, to tell a funny story or to execute a dance; *organized* is properly applied to a condition of thorough preparation for a more or less formidable evening; and *blotto*, of English origin, denotes a state of blank bedazement.

March 9, 1927

————

Emil Jannings' American Film

THE FIRST FILM made by Paramount with Emil Jannings has the title *The Way of All Flesh*. But this title is a Hollywood come-on: the picture is not voluptuous. It follows what seems to have become the standard formula for tragedy in the German films: the moral collapse and downfall of a large, honest, thickset, God-fearing, elderly, simple German. These pictures have sometimes been moving—Jannings' *The Last Laugh;* sometimes dreary—Werner Kraus's *Shattered*. It has remained for the Hollywood producer to make them completely absurd.

August Schilling of *The Way of All Flesh* is a Milwaukee German-American, the cashier of a bank, the father of a family. We see him first in his home, with his six children, his serious German wife: his magnificent beard, his elastic-sided prunellas, his dignified embonpoint; we see him waking up his children, putting them through their setting-up exercises, overseeing their piano and violin practice, pretending to punish them severely but secretly letting them off. Then we see him at his work in the bank, obsequious to his employer, stern but sympathetic with subordinates, full of naïve self-importance and incorruptible conscience. In all this part of the picture, Emil Jannings is splendid: it is perhaps the most effective sequence I have ever seen him do. From the placid bourgeois life of Schilling, he extracts the same sort of poetry that Arnold Bennett derives from the Five Towns. The character he here creates is borrowed from the doorman of *The Last Laugh,* but it is much more completely elaborated and even, perhaps, more interesting.

Unfortunately, the concoctors of *The Way of All Flesh* have attempted to combine the most successful features of *The Last Laugh, Variety* and *Stella Dallas* in one immense super-heartbreaker. The character described above, studied by Jannings so lovingly and carefully, only remains a consistent creation until Schilling boards the train for Chicago, where he has been sent to sell bonds for his bank. On the journey he is made to fall in with a siren, who catches a glimpse of the bonds, picks him up, gets him drunk, induces him to shave off his beard and finally steals the bonds. We watch all this with growing uneasiness. It is unlikely in the last degree that so conscientious a fellow as Schilling would so carelessly have handled the bonds as almost to drop them out of his pocketbook. It is furthermore inconceivable that he would readily have shaved off his beard, of which he is supposed to be inordinately proud and which has inspired the profound respect of his family and his business subordinates, for the whim of a shoddy baggage whom he has met by chance on a train. But it is plain that the producer is aiming to draw on the same source of pathos that was exploited in *The Last Laugh* by the episode of the doorkeeper's uniform.

When Schilling discovers that the bonds have been stolen, he follows the girl to a dive, makes her a furious scene and is beaten up by the proprietor, who drags him out and leaves him on a railroad track. Schilling, however, comes to, gets the better of the thug in a tussle and throws him under the oncoming train. Bewildered and despairing, he wanders away. A few days later, he reads that his body has been found on the track and that he died in a struggle with someone who was trying to steal the bonds. Rather than reveal the truth, he will never now go home again. Years pass: his children grow up; his son becomes a famous violinist. Schilling is a vagrant old man, reduced to peddling chestnuts in the street. In the end, he looks in through a window on his family, who are celebrating Christmas—*Stella Dallas*—then turns away into the snowstorm.

It is, of course, extremely improbable that Schilling's devoted wife would have mistaken for the remains of her husband the body and clothes of the gangster; but what is even harder to swallow is the senseless transformation of Schilling. Jannings, without his beard, is obliged to play a different character—a character like the showman in *Variety*.

The director, Victor Fleming, has been admirable. The minor roles—even to the people in the bank—are amazingly well cast and acted. But the bad taste of Hollywood prevails. The producers have been so leery of launching the European Jannings without ballast of American hokum that they have wasted first-rate ability on a maudlin and nonsensical film.

August 3, 1927

————

The Crushing of Washington Square

RETURNING TO NEW YORK at the end of the summer, one was shocked to find Washington Square completely transformed since the spring. The big red houses of the north and west sides had already been gutted of their grandeurs and crammed with economized cells, the cubbyholes of modern apartments, and the sooty peeling fronts of the south side, with their air of romance and mystery, had already been replaced by fresh arty grays and pinks. The Brevoort had already, as someone has said,* had its face lifted, and looked worse for the operation. Already last spring one was finding whole blocks of familiar shops, delicatessen stores and old saloons snatched away without warning from under one, so that they seemed to be losing their shapes as well as their personalities. And now, in the short months of summer, there have been erected on lower Fifth Avenue two monstrous apartment houses—one just south of the Brevoort Hotel and the other between Tenth and Eleventh Streets. They loom over the Village like mountains, and they have suddenly changed its proportions. Their effect is to crush, in Washington Arch and in the row of red façades behind it, whatever these had formerly kept of chaste elegance and decorous pride. The whole Village seems now merely a base for these cubic apartment buildings. Such good quality as still lingered here along with the low roofs of the provincial town has thus been rendered insignificant: it is impossible to get away from these huge coarse and swollen mounds—blunt, clumsy, bleaching the sunlight with their dismal pale yellow sides and stamping down both the old formal square and the newer Bohemian refuge.

October 12, 1927

* Edna St. Vincent Millay.

GEORGE BELLOWS

THERE EMERGED about ten years ago a school of American artists who broke away from the older conventions not only by tackling directly the more vulgar aspects of American life but also by trying to treat them in an idiom appropriate to the subject. The artist began audaciously to represent the American city in terms of its own crudeness, and the writer to describe the people in their own half-literate language. What is especially characteristic of this school and what distinguishes its departure from its predecessors is the frank acceptance by its exponents of the ugliness of their material at the same time that they confess their appetite for it. We had not lacked, in the past, for either corrosive critics or enthusiastic prophets: what was new was the combination with an attitude of savage cynicism of an intimate knowledge and insight. Carl Sandburg was the poet of this movement; Leo Ornstein its composer; Sinclair Lewis its novelist; H. L. Mencken its satirist; Eugene O'Neill its dramatist; and the *Liberator* its magazine. George Bellows, who died last January, was in the same way preëminently its painter.

A memorial exhibition of Bellows' work is now at the Metropolitan, and one can see how it all runs true to the gamut of this generation. The followers of Whistler and Sargent had as a rule aimed at delicacy or smartness; but as the earliest of Bellows' portraits already belongs to a different world from that of a portrait by Alexander, so a New England group by Bellows has nothing in common with a New England group by Charles Hawthorne or a New York street by Bellows with a New York street by Pennell. The awkward contours and muddy colors of contemporary industrial America are present in every canvas of Bellows. Instead of following the usual practice of traditional portrait painters in attempting to make their sitters look distinguished, the effect of George Bellows' treatment of even the most charming of his is somehow to make them seem homely; and even the freest of his out-of-door pieces seem dulled by the smoke of the city. He gives an effect of intensifying his colors without really making them brighter; the most violent of his greens and purples are garish rather than brilliant; and his *June Day*, his *Polo at Lakewood* and the summer mountains of his *Picnic* seem all to be threatened by the same turbid cloud which lowers at the back of his *Approach to the Bridge*—where, behind the bald and lumpy waste, the livid street lights, the solitary dray, the fragmentary stretch of cheap shops and the skeleton of the bridge, this looms with the density and darkness, as it were, of the city swarm. Not among the mirrors of northern lakes does his palette find its proper harmony, but in the dirty green waters of the Hudson, hemmed in by its railroad tracks and churned by its nudging tugs, infested with ungainly adolescents bathing in the brassy sun.

It may be that Bellows shared, also, with a number of these other artists a certain technical untidiness and a certain unsteadiness of grasp. These men were all working with material, and working from a point of view, for which we had no tradition in the United States. They do not always seem to know what they want to do, whether their pictures are to be biting pieces of journalism or perdurable works of art. They seem sometimes to lack adequate training, sometimes artistic intensity.

Reflections of this kind suggest themselves in connection with these ·pictures of Bellows—though one must not be severe toward an artist who died at the age of forty-two and whose work shows a steady development. One can see how he fortified his structure and steadied his uncertain hand. His earlier paintings—for all their dash—seem sometimes hasty and a little thin, with the thinness of his master Robert Henri. The satiric lithographs, of which the first, the *Prayer Meeting*, was made in 1916, seem to have derived most from the Goya of the *Caprichos* and *Proverbios*. Goya here depends less on drawing than on boldly handled masses of light and shade: he flattens out and distorts; he leaves many things rough and vague that we should ordinarily expect to be clear. So George Bellows, though quite successful in manipulating Goyesque masses, did not profit, in imitating Goya, from the point of view of sureness of line. Both his lithographs and his painting of this earlier period seem full of inaccuracies and lapses.

But as the painter progresses, he sets himself to remedy this deficiency. Compare the late prize-fight painting called *Ringside Seats* or the Dempsey and Firpo picture with the earlier painting of Sharkey's; or compare the John L. Sullivan of 1923 with the lithograph on the same subject of a much earlier date. The outlines now come into focus; the shapes are now neat and compact. The effect of the whole picture is surer. It is only occasionally here that one comes to regret a new influence, the influence of Rockwell Kent. No doubt it was the clearness of Rockwell Kent that made it easy for George Bellows to take his stamp. Bellows passed, toward the end of his life, through a veritable Rockwell Kent period, in the course of which he produced an enormous number of Kentian drawings and lithographs. Fortunately, few of these are included in the selection at the Metropolitan. There are only two of the lithographs: *The Return to Life* and *The Journey of Youth;* but one recognizes also Kent's influence in those paintings in which the figures show a tendency to stiffen into systems of hollow stovepipes or to take on the wooden aspect of long-legged marionettes.

Yet Bellows was always able to tincture with a sharper flavor the insipidity of Rockwell Kent, as he had stained with a stronger reality what in Henri was superficial. And, at his best, in his river-fronts and prize-fights, he has left us what are so far surely the happiest exploits in painting by an American artist who confronts his environment in all its angularity and rawness and, unable still quite to decide from precisely what direction to approach it or by what molds it may be transmitted, envisaging it at last—not as something which the artist may not acknowledge—but as a matrix of precious metal.

October 28, 1925

THE STIEGLITZ EXHIBITION

IN MISS GEORGIA O'KEEFFE America seems definitely to have produced a woman painter comparable to her best women novelists and poets. Her new paintings in the Stieglitz exhibition at the Anderson Galleries are astonishing even to those who two years ago were astonished by her first exhibition; and they seem to represent a more considerable development for the period of the past year than last spring's exhibition did for that of the year before. For one thing, she has gone in for larger canvases; she has passed from close-rolled white lilies to enormous yellow lilies and wide-open purple petunias. Yet although she has allowed her art to expand in this decorative gorgeousness, she has at the same time lost nothing in intensity—that peculiarly feminine intensity which has galvanized all her work and which, as a rule, seems to manifest itself in such a different way from the masculine. Male artists, in communicating this quality, seem usually not merely to impart it to the representation of external objects but also, in the work of art, to produce an external object—that is, something detachable from themselves; whereas women imbue the objects they represent with so immediate a personal emotion that they absorb the subject into themselves. Where the masculine mind may have freer range and the works it produces lead a life of their own, women artists have a way of appearing to wear their most brilliant productions—however objective in form—like those other artistic expressions, their clothes. So the razor-like scroll-edges of Miss O'Keeffe's autumn leaves make themselves directly felt as the sharpness of a personality; and the dark green stalks of one of her corn paintings have become so charged with her personal current and fused by her personal heat that they seem to us not a picture at all but a kind of dynamo of feeling, along which the fierce white line strikes like an electric spark. This last picture, in its force and solidity, seems to me one of her most successful.

One finds also among these new paintings remarkable effects of fluidity and vagueness: her white birches are mistier than last year, and she has found a new subject in the shifting of water over the pebbly bottom of a lake. She combines in other canvases the blurred with the sharp in such a way as to produce violent dissonances; and dissonance is one of the features of the work of this exhibition. Miss O'Keeffe seems to be bent on bringing together elements of which one would say that they could not coexist in one picture—not only vagueness and edge, but mutually repellent colors. In some pictures, which seem less successful, this gives the impression of a fault of taste. Thus she will paint a red leaf against a green background in such a way as to give a harmony in bronze, but on the green leaf a neutral brownish leaf which jars with the other colors and seems irreconcilable with them. Again, in *Red to Black,* one of her most elaborate pictures, there appears above a rich foundation of flesh-like folds—occupying half the canvas and in her vividest vein of red—a stratum of black, not intense, as the eye expects after the intense red, but discomfitingly washy and dim, and above this a light superstructure of sketchily outlined hills, whose pinks and lavenders seem quite out of key with the deep reds and purples below; the effect is of an overweighted and inartistically feathered shuttlecock too heavily dragged to earth. Yet it seems plain from other pictures that these anomalies are deliberate and significant, and we recognize them as analogous to the dissonances of modern music and poetry. A sunken tree trunk is seen in the water, blurred brown under turbid green—but there floats above it a single leaf of blue-silver as livid and bright as the mercury tubes in photographers' windows and so distinctly outlined that it almost seems impossible for the eye, without changing focus, to take in both leaf and log. Again, from a preliminary study of a plain white house with an open door, set in greenery and lilac bushes, she develops an abstract picture (*The Flag*

Pole) in which the actual outlines of the house have all but melted away in the exquisite green and lavender mist, while the rectangle of the doorway, dark before, has intensified itself to a black opacity and a strict geometrical exactitude, which cause it to seem projected from the plane of the picture itself and to hang in the air before it. One finds oneself fascinated by these discords at the same time that one is shocked by them: one stares at them, trying to eliminate or to soften the repulsion between opposites—the harsh rectangle and the aura of springtime, the dim lake and the incandescent leaf.

Georgia O'Keeffe quite outblazes the other painters in the exhibition—John Marin, Marsden Hartley, Arthur Dove and Charles Demuth—but it is hardly possible to compare her with them even in those pictures which are closest to hers: the white-silver and black storm clouds of Dove. If the art of women and the art of men seem to present fundamental differences, they sometimes seem incommensurable. The water colors of Mr. Marin are masculine masterpieces: they represent the investiture of nature with the qualities of a distinguished temperament: some of the Maine seascapes, with their greens and blues and white sails, with their combination of dryness and freshness, are among the finest Marins I remember. Mr. Marsden Hartley appears with his characteristic repertoire of plain plates and bottles and fishes, which he embrowns or dully empurples with his characteristic sullen felicity.

Mr. Stieglitz celebrates with this exhibition the twentieth anniversary of the opening of 291 Fifth Avenue, the small gallery with which the careers of most of the painters here shown have so intimately been associated. He exhibits, also, new examples of his own amazing genius for making of the camera an instrument of the artist's sensibility—a genius of a sort so unusual that between the productions of Stieglitz and the photographs of the ablest of his rivals there seems to lie a difference not merely of degree but almost of kind. Mr. Stieglitz, in pushing his mastery of the camera further and further from mechanical reproduction and closer to the freedom of plastic art, has lately left the earth altogether and taken to the shifting clouds, where he seems to have found a material of maximum variability. The textures and shapes of the sky are infinitely irregular and strange, and they never are twice the same—so that the artist can have practically whatever he likes; and the person who looks at the picture is never distracted from the artist's intention by recognizing familiar objects, familiar subjects of photographs. One finds effects of a feathery softness or of a solidity almost marmoreal. Certain of these prints, I suppose, are among the artist's chief triumphs. Especially impressive are cloud-masses—somber and grand in their darkness—which lift themselves as if in grief.

March 18, 1925

1957. Alfred Stieglitz was something of a mesmerist. Since the opening in 1905 of "291 Fifth Avenue," an attic kept warm by an iron stove, he had been delivering a monologue, a kind of impalpable net in which visitors and disciples were caught from the moment they came within earshot. It was impossible to interrupt or to change the direction of this monologue, the tone of which was rather casual and which wandered from subject to subject but which never for a second slackened—the ribbon of talk was as strong as a cable— and which influenced the mind of the listener in a way that was not accidental. On the occasion recorded above, he was expecting me and took me in hand at once. He gave me a program of the exhibition, then saw that it was slightly smudged, took it away and gave me another. "I'm sure you're like me," he said."You like to have that kind of thing clean." This and the program itself were characteristic of him—the Germanic love of neatness, good craftsmanship. We now passed from picture to picture, and his somewhat nasal voice, interrupted at that time by sniffles, droned and drawled along but never relinquished its dominance. He was then sixty-one years old, with wiry gray hair, nickel spectacles and a wiry white toothbrush mustache; he may have worn, as he sometimes did, a pepper-and-salt suit. He had been trained as a mechanical engineer and had arrived at photography by way of chemistry, and there was more in his outward appearance of the expert "technician" than the artist. Still less did he give the impression of the dedicated spiritual teacher. Yet a spiritual teacher was what he was. I had been prompted by one of his disciples to see in his darkened skies the emotions with which I associate them; and when I talked about my visit later with an acquaintance who had also gone as critic to one of the Stieglitz exhibitions: "Yes," he agreed, "when I came away, I couldn't help wondering a little whether it hadn't been a case of the innocent young serpent being swallowed by the wily old dove." My admiration for these artists was genuine, but if I had not been subjected to Stieglitz's spell, I might perhaps have discussed them in different terms. I note that there were pictures by Charles Demuth, and I do not now remember what they were; yet Demuth—as I realize today—interests me more than Marin, whose reputation I now suspect Stieglitz of having rather unduly inflated, and I might have discovered this if I had been left alone with the pictures. If Stieglitz played Demuth down, it was undoubtedly for the reason that he did not belong to the inner group of the artists whom he had himself introduced and to promoting whose reputations he had so jealously devoted his energies that any mention of an artist quite outside this group brought a quick and expulsive response: he was either not at all the real thing or had been ruined by a craving for worldly success.

Yet Stieglitz commanded respect. To think that he had been working for "modern" art—in an age of convention and commerce—since the time when I was ten years old! And it touches me today to think of him running counter to the pressures of that era and trying to make beauty of—in Paul Rosenfeld's words—the "strange brazen human emptiness" of the city in which I then lived and of which, as will be plain from these pages, I was irked by the recent overbuilding and increasing unsightliness. I could remember when New York was as bracing, as electrical and full of light, as San Francisco had been; when the Flat Iron Building was a wonder, the tallest thing on the skyline. Alfred Stieglitz—born in Hoboken across the river, educated in New York and Berlin—had modulated into photography from that practical mechanical field in which his father had rightly believed the future of American enterprise lay; had set up his little bird-refuge for artists on a lower-roofed and clearer Fifth Avenue; had lived through the vertical expansion of the vast real-estate speculation; and now, shuffling and coughing in his uptown gallery, was maintaining his old intransigent attitude at the same time that he was able to enjoy the success of his protégés and his own prestige as a prophet.

STRAVINSKY

THE PERFORMANCE of *Petrushka* at the Metropolitan, though brilliantly designed and admirably danced, seemed to excite, on the opening night, only a rather perfunctory applause. The composer appeared for a bow, and the clapping was politely prolonged, but one felt that it lacked spontaneity—especially when one heard the salvos which greeted *Pagliacci* afterwards. The occasion thus unfortunately contributed to the somewhat unsatisfactory impression produced by Mr. Stravinsky's visit. In this case, the blame is no doubt to be laid on the stupidity and torpor of the regular opera subscribers, many of whom did not arrive in their seats till the ballet was nearly over and who gave no signs of acknowledging the honor of having before them one of the most distinguished of living composers. The disappointing effect of the Philharmonic concerts may be partly ascribed to a similar disaffection on the part of the concert patrons and partly to the fact that Stravinsky turns out to conduct his own works on the whole rather less vigorously and vividly than we have been accustomed to hearing them conducted by others. But the really fatal feature of the visit was probably the comparative failure—with the critics and public both—of the two new Stravinsky pieces: the Octet and the Piano Concerto, which were here given their first performance.

The writer has heard only the Piano Concerto and has, in any case, no competence as a music critic; but there seems to appear in these works a tendency plainly recognizable as analogous to a certain current tendency in poetry and fiction: the artist, in dissatisfaction with the emotions and materials of his own time, attempts to supply their deficiencies by falling back on the forms of the past, as if by reproducing the form he could summon the inspiration. Stravinsky had already had recourse to the eighteenth century in his *Pulcinella* suite, also played here: a rescoring of Pergolesi. And in his new Octet and Concerto he echoes Handel and Bach: in the latter, the Bachesque development is finally broken up by momentary ragtime rhythms and fragments of sarcastic parody, just as Eliot interrupts his Elizabethan blank verse with bar talk and popular songs. It seems evident that Stravinsky, for the moment at least, is suffering from an undernourishment of the artistic imagination and that he has come to be convinced of the inadequacy of the food the modern world supplies. "The material of Bach's day," he told Mr. Paul Rosenfeld in an interview published in the *Dial,* "was, let us say, the size of this hall. The material of our day"—he lifted his cane—"is about the size of this." In any case, his new compositions so far failed to please the critics that these sometimes even gave the impression that his old ones had been overrated. Among the newspaper critics, Lawrence Gilman was, so far as I know, alone in keeping the fact of Stravinsky's genius squarely before the public.

Yet, admitting that these works of Stravinsky may exemplify the aridity and the fragmentary character toward which modern music seems tending, one has only to compare this composer with even the most eminent of his contemporaries to realize a difference between him and them. The recent concert of the International Composers' Guild gives an excellent occasion for comparison: the interesting program of this concert included work of four characteristic moderns—Arnold Schönberg, Erik Satie, Henry Eichheim and Edgar Varèse—all quite different from one another. Yet each, in his different way, conveyed to the present writer an unmistakable impression of bankruptcy. Of these four composers, one—Varèse—is attempting to write the music of pure abstraction—the "geometry of sound," as he calls it—and he names his composition after the calculus. "For me," he says, "there is more musical fertility in the contemplation of the stars—preferably through a telescope—and the high poetry of certain mathematical expositions than in the most sublime gossip of human passions." Another—Henry Eichheim—has resolved to abandon the conventions of European music and to master the idiom of the Orient: "I have in my notebooks," he tells us, "more than two thousand themes collected in the Far East." A third, Erik Satie, is content with little parodies—ironic rather than gay—lasting only half a minute each. And Schönberg, the fourth, working still with the conventional material of romantic music—that is, with the personal emotions—only shows us how little is left: a lament and a sifting of ashes. One felt about all these composers that, in spite of their courage and skill, their material was indeed, inescapably, only the size of their canes and that ingenious attempts to enlarge it had not taken the place of organic growth. One felt that one blast of Stravinsky—even from the Piano Concerto—would have been enough to blow them all away.

For Stravinsky is one of the few modern artists who have really made effective use of the material supplied by their time. Two elements in particular which modern musicians have made much ado about exploiting have been utilized by Stravinsky more naturally and successfully than by anyone else: I refer to machinery and jazz. His interest in mechanical effects does not seem the same self-conscious effort to put modern machines into music which has produced Honegger's locomotive or Varèse's symphonies of street sounds. The mechanical bird of *Le Rossignol*, the mechanical puppets of *Petruskha*, these are merely the properties of fairy tales, which Stravinsky has chosen to emphasize. And in the same way, Stravinsky's jazz does not give the same impression as that of, say, Darius Milhaud—of a systematic use of themes that have been gathered from American phonograph records: it seems an original rhythm heard first in the composer's own head. You will recognize Russian folk songs in Stravinsky but not Gershwin or Irving Berlin; yet the folk songs will have been energized and syncopated by Stravinsky's own personal pulse into something analogous to jazz: the village band in *Renard* is Russian and supposed to skip its notes by accident but its rousing and elliptic effect, not in the least reminiscent of Paul Whiteman, seems to arise from a similar impulse to that which has produced popular jazz. The work of this composer which has most stimulated its hearers to talk about both jazz and machinery—*Le Sacre du Printemps* —has ostensibly nothing to do with either but presents a fertility rite of prehistoric Russia. It has been the glory of Stravinsky actually to achieve, in works of art of compelling emotion and imagination, that musical expression of the *Zeitgeist* which, in the case of so many of his contemporaries, has remained largely theoretical.

This emotion, this imagination, have a flavor unmistakably personal: one could not even mistake a scenario of Stravinsky's for a scenario of anyone else's. *Petrushka, Renard, L'Histoire du Soldat*—all these stories run true to a cynicism, invigorating rather than dispiriting, which gives its sharp edge to his music. It was characteristic of him that when he chose, in his earlier days, a subject for a fairy-tale ballet, he should have produced something more disquieting than Chaikovsky's sweet sleeping princess or Rimsky-Korsakov's sleepy old king: the electrical *Fire Bird,* with its shimmering visitations, the bristling enchanter Koshchei, with his talons and his untrimmed beard, who can only be put beyond mischief by the breaking of the egg which contains his life. The rind of Stravinsky is thorny, but inside is a sound core. The wholehearted blare of the village band balances the rasping of *Renard,* as the dryness of the puppets in *Petrushka* is offset by the gaiety of the street fair; and the puppet, at the end of the *Petrushka,* proves to have possessed a soul, as we feel that the love which is forfeited by the hero of *L'Histoire du Soldat* and the art which he sells to the Devil have been articles of real value.

What is important, of course, however, is the musical treatment of these fables. That Stravinsky was influenced by Wagner is evident from the early *Scherzo Fantastique,* full of Wagnerian themes, which was played at one of his concerts here; but, unlike that other dramatizer Richard Strauss, he did not pursue the Wagnerian formula. Where Strauss took to composing "tone poems," which are more like musical novels, in which every detail of the story is given its explicit equivalent, Stravinsky tended rather to large musical ideas, which, though appropriately connected with their fables, have a vivid and complete existence independent of dramatic incident. A good deal of Richard Strauss is either what the program says it is or nothing; but Stravinsky's *Le Sacre du Printemps* produces its astonishing effect whether we know what is supposed to be happening or not. "I have not the same feeling," Stravinsky explained in the interview quoted above, "against what is purely anecdotal as against what is either picturesque or literary. I feel there is a difference, and I am perfectly willing to acknowledge that certain bits of the *Sacre* have an anecdotal interest. But not picturesque."

Stravinsky, nevertheless, seems preëminently a dramatic composer. With him the ballet, under Diaghilev, has been brought to what is probably so far its highest point of artistic importance. And one is almost tempted to believe that, if his new works seem less effective than his ballets and cantatas have led us to expect, this may have something to do with their not having been written for the stage. On the other hand, his exile from Russia, his divorce from the Russian material upon which most of his best work has been based, may in the long run have had the result of making his vein run dry. In any case, he does not strike one as an artist who is likely to go bankrupt: it is hard to imagine the fading of so deeply stained a personality or the permanent lapsing of such energy. Acrid, spasmodic, irritable though Igor Stravinsky is, he yet gives an impression of robustness; feeling the pressure and strain of the age, he is nonetheless not hysterical. He does not yield to the rhythms of the machines and attempt to compete with them, to reproduce them: he opposes to them rhythms of his own, the rhythms of titanic dances. His powerhouse is all his own, and he is in a different line of business. He is the artist, not as victim, but as master.

April 1, 1925

The music of Stravinsky's ballet *Les Noces* has been heard for the first time in America, under the auspices of the International Composers' Guild. There was no dancing and hardly any action, but it proved to be tremendously effective. Leopold Stokowski conducted; and the four pianos, stripped to their metal ribs, were played by Germaine Taillefaire, Alfredo Casella, Georges Enesco and Carlos Salzedo. The whole score was twice done, and between its two performances—which reared themselves like colossal peasant statues, crude-featured, square-fingered, square-footed—the Casella Concerto for String Quartet, with its pedantries and its honey spread thin, seemed to dwindle to almost nothing. In *Les Noces,* Stravinsky's subject is simple, and he has made no attempt, in the theatrical sense, to get a drama out of it. He has presented merely a Russian country wedding, a wedding reduced to its primary elements. First we have the bridesmaids, at the bride's house, braiding the bride's hair; then we have the friends of the groom, at the groom's house, sending him off; then the departure of the bride to be married, and the mothers of the couple left behind in the house after the rest have gone; then the wedding celebration, at which many of the guests get drunk and rally the bride and groom; and, finally, the putting of the couple to bed. But Stravinsky has energized these homely events with such a terrific vitality, given voice with such pounding vigor to the pungent naïvetés of his libretto (also written by himself) that he is able to produce upon us the arresting, the absorbing, almost the shocking effect which is the result of any powerful revelation of the impulses that animate the natural man. Stravinsky is at once cruel and genial, at once solemn and ribald, and in carrying us above, or below, the obvious realms of sentiment or irony, he communicates an exhilaration as impossible to the jazz orchestra as to the most accomplished modern composer of defeat and disintegration. It is the ruthless exhilaration of moving with the force of life, which creates, just as it kills, in spite of anything we may think about it. Stravinsky has been described as a poet of machinery; but, for almost all his most successful compositions, he has gone to the folk tales of peasants or the rites of primitive peoples.

It would, however, be unfair to contrast *Les Noces*—first conceived about 1912 and completed in 1917—with the music which has been written since the war. It is particularly interesting, however, to compare *Les Noces* with another and more recent work by another Russian composer ten years younger than Stravinsky. Arthur Lourié's Sonata for Violin and Double Bass, which was played at an earlier concert of the International Composers' Guild, proved too dreary, too disjointed and too flaccid even for an *avant garde* audience that was respectful toward the later Schönberg: the stumblings and mopings of M. Lourié provoked unaccustomed laughter. Yet the Sonata has its interest as a symptom: as an example of emotional exhaustion, it would seem to be hard to match, and we cannot but associate its deficiencies with the condition of post-war Europe. M. Lourié was formerly the head of the Soviet Music Commission organized by Lunacharsky, but he left Russia in 1921. It is possible that M. Lourié would not be a first-rate composer even under the most favorable conditions; but, in a period of vigorous artistic life, the lesser artist has his dignity and even his charm: though he may not be conspicuously original, he can continue in his devotion to his art and in the forms he has learned from his masters. But where the masters themselves are harried, depleted of their normal vitality, the pupils may become most depressing. In the final movement of his Sonata, M. Lourié introduces what one takes to be a peasant dance or a folk song of some sort. I do not know whether the composer intended it to sound as flat and as lame as it does or whether he desired to redeem his earlier moods of despondency with a few moments of sweetness and cheer. But, in any case, his dance from old Russia is already a dance of the dead. The barbaric health and rustic richness of Stravinksy's village wedding go back to a civilization which, though harsh, had still its strength and its force. Not even perhaps Stravinsky himself would be able to recover them now.

March 10, 1926

1957. Since revising this, I have been playing on the phonograph my records of the Octet for Wind Instruments, which I missed in 1925, and have been struck by its pulsing high spirits, and the irrelevance of the complaints, at the time it was first heard, that the composer was archaizing. It is likely to be one of the signs of the career of a great artist that each of his successive works should prove for his admirers as well as for his critics not at all what they had been expecting, and cause them to raise cries of falling-off. Besides having listened in the theater to most of the ballets and cantatas composed since these articles were written, I have stocked myself, through these years, with records of Stravinsky's less spectacular—that is, non-theatrical—pieces, which one does not often hear performed but which impress one more the more one hears them, and I have come to respect and prize him even more highly than I did thirty years ago when he was still a novel excitement. His intensity and variety, his persistence and craftsmanship, continue to delight and to fortify the worker in any craft. He has triumphed over exile and displacement, the disruptions of Russia and Europe, the temptations, on the one hand, of patronage and, on the other, of popular applause. In the shrunken conditions of the musical art, he has managed to maintain his stature, and I understand better today the conclusion of his remark to Paul Rosenfeld which I dropped off in 1925 when I quoted from his talk with Stravinsky: after pointing out the discrepancy in magnitude between the modern material and Bach's, he had added, "But I feel we in our day are working with our material in the spirit of Bach, the constructive spirit, and I feel that what we give, though it is perhaps smaller in comparison, is in its concentration and economy an equivalent for the immense structures of Bach."

In youth, we admire the heroes, the affirmers, the "lords of life." Later on, when we have had some experience of the difficulty of practicing an art, of surviving to grow old in its practice, when we have seen how many entrants drop out, we must honor any entrant who finishes. I felt much more regard for Arthur Lourié when I heard, at a Tanglewood festival in the summer of 1948, a chamber concerto of his: a wavering outline—fastidiously traced with an art that was fragile and faint—like the thread of a twilight revery.

THE PROBLEM OF THE HIGHER JAZZ

THE EFFORTS of popular jazz and serious musical art to effect an harmonious union continue from both directions. This problem has constituted, in fact, perhaps the main source of interest of the new music of the season.

You have, on the one hand, the *Jazzberries* of Louis Gruenberg and the Piano Concerto of Arthur Honegger—both played under the auspices of the League of Composers—which apply to the popular rhythms the elegant selective formulae of modern impressionism, and which, fracturing them and shaving them down, have robbed them of a good deal of their power. On the other hand, there is Mr. George Gershwin, who, parallel with his regular business of turning out musical comedies, has proceeded, from the direction of Broadway, with his assault on the concert hall. The writer missed one capital piece, the new Gershwin Piano Concerto, which was played by the New York Symphony Society; but he found the Gershwin one-act opera, *135th Street,* one of the most interesting features of Paul Whiteman's recent concert in Carnegie Hall. This opera was first produced three years ago in George White's *Scandals,* and its origin probably explains the disappointment we are bound to feel in it —if we expect to be moved by drama—when we see it on a more pretentious stage; for it does not seem to take a clear line as either burlesque or tragedy. The scene is a Negro joint in Harlem: one of the girls is in love with a professional gambler; the latter announces to the proprietor, though not in the presence of his sweetheart, that he is going to visit his dear old mammy, whom he has not seen in years. The café fills up with people; the girl and her lover are together; the latter receives a telegram and suddenly leaves the room, refusing to divulge its contents to his jealous companion; interested parties induce her to believe that the message is from another woman, and when her lover returns, she shoots him. He dies; but not before he has cleared himself by giving her the telegram; it says, "It is no use to come. Your mammy has been dead three years." Mr. Gershwin's music, however, evidently aims at a certain dignity: a prologue which derives from *Pagliacci* introduces a melodramatic score of which most of the setting of the action is cast in the conventional accents of modern Italian opera. This setting cements together a succession of separate "numbers" in a vein of sophisticated jazz—a mammy song, a love song, a "blues." And here again the blend does not jell: the mixture of the Follies and the Met seems mechanical and unsatisfactory. In the case of the composers mentioned above, their alien technique and spirit had the effect of blighting the jazz. In the case of Mr. Gershwin, the jazz idiom itself, his natural vehicle of expression, does not lack vivacity or color—especially in such passages as the prelude, where he elicits disturbing effects from the characteristic voices of the jazz orchestra. But it gives the impression of emerging in blocks from a background of conventional opera which has nothing in common with it and which, beside the vitality of the jazz, tends to look like a tawdry imposture.

More artistically satisfactory than any of these compositions was Aaron Copland's *Music for the Theater,* played at one of the League of Composers concerts. There are traces of Stravinsky in Mr. Copland; but he is not an imitator of Stravinsky. His musical personality is quite his own, and he has his own idiom for rendering in interesting musical form that excitement in the air of our time which gets its popular expression in jazz. His vitality is as spontaneous as his culture is genuine. And there is probably more musical drama in his untitled and unannotated *Music for the Theater* than in the whole of Gershwin's opera.

The career of Mr. Paul Whiteman, at whose concerts in Carnegie Hall the Gershwin opera was sung, is itself a curious episode in the artistic development of jazz. Mr. Whiteman, as everyone knows, was formerly the leader of the most popular hotel dance orchestra in the United States. Now he occupies a different position: he gives concerts and appears in vaudeville; his orchestra has become an entertainment, an artistic performance, in itself. In sitting through a whole evening of Whiteman, we cannot always rid ourselves of the feeling—which obtrudes itself also, and to a greater degree, in the case of Vincent Lopez—that we might enjoy the music more if we were eating and talking while we listened to it. But, on the other hand, Paul Whiteman's orchestra would today be out of place in a hotel; and I do not know whether it is any use for dancing. No up-to-date French composer could deprive Charleston music more effectively of the qualities which make people dance the Charleston to it than, in reducing it to an abstract pattern, has been done by Mr. Whiteman. He has refined and disciplined his orchestra to a point at which, one would think, his old clientele of dancers and diners could only be embarrassed by it. Not, however, that his virtuosity is not sometimes rather freakish than exquisite. Among the features of Mr. Whiteman's recent concerts was a pair of stunt pianists who played the same compositions on two different pianos in exact synchronization and with the effect of automatic piano players; and a man who performed a duet on a cornet and a clarinet, rendered *Pop Goes the Weasel* on a violin held in sixty-five different positions and finally got *Hiawatha* out of an old bicycle pump. But Whiteman has drilled his musicians to better artistic purpose. When we hear him address the audience, as he did at Carnegie Hall, we realize how much his orchestra shows the imprint of his own personality. Whiteman's voice has precisely the qualities of one of his own muted trombones: he speaks with a hard Western r, but his phrases have a precision and economy, a sharp edge and a metallic resonance. And this is the character that his instruments take on when they farthest depart from their function of playing for other people to dance: a little dry, a little deliberate, a little lacking in lyric ecstasy, but very fastidious and elegant, and stamped with the ideal of perfection.

Mr. Deems Taylor has hitherto been rather conspicuous for his avoidance of the universal fashion. In his *Circus Day,* which was played at the Whiteman concerts, he has, to be sure, made some use of jazz material; but he stands quite outside the developments I have been discussing above. It is as plain from his own compositions as it was from his musical criticism that the problems and the struggles of contemporary music do not really interest him. I did not care much for his *Jurgen,* a symphonic poem played earlier in the season by the New York Symphony Society. It had a syrupiness and an insipidity which, it is true, are characteristic of Cabell, but it failed to catch the sinister malaise, the real note of natural magic, which are also to be found in the novel. That Mr. Taylor desired to capture at least the former of these elements his program notes seem to show; but, to this auditor at least, he failed to evoke either Mother Sereda or Koshchei the Deathless. He is, one feels, too easygoing, too amiable, to be troubled by the unknown quantities which these symbols represent; he leaves out the disturbing elements of *Jurgen,* as he did, in his Alice suite, those of *Through the Looking Glass.*

But he has chosen in *Circus Day* as goodnatured and innocent a subject as possible, and he has produced a descriptive piece that is jolly, ingenious and charming. With much cleverness in finding equivalents for clowns, jugglers, roaring lions and other features of the old-fashioned circus, he has combined a taste which restrains him from overdoing grotesque effects and sacrificing music to cleverness. *Circus Day* was perhaps, on the whole, the most felicitous number of the Whiteman concerts.

January 13, 1926

MOSCOW, ATHENS AND PARIS

"Lysistrata"

WHEN THE MOSCOW ART THEATER first came to New York, three seasons ago, the Russian comedies in their repertoire proved to be their least popular productions. There is something harsh in Russian humor which we westerners find unsympathetic. Compare the serious long plays of Chekhov, by which we are completely enchanted, with his ferocious one-act farces, which make us shudder. Now, something of this shocking harshness is to be found in the comedy of Greece: what fascinates us in the Greeks and what makes their literature so different not only from our own but even from that of Rome, which seems in comparison modern, is the piquancy of a high culture still rooted in primitive conditions. The comedies of Aristophanes were performed at Dionysiac festivals which a producer of modern French farces would consider impossibly obscene; and their mockery was edged with a cruelty which even the audience of a modern German satirist might at moments find rather strong. Yet Aristophanes, in his own Attic world, was neither obscene nor bitter. He can rise from either ribaldry or jeering to a lyric exhilaration that, in its airiness is almost Shelleyan, or to a delight in the play of intelligence which makes his denunciations—against war and Athenian demagoguery—exhilarating and liberating, too. It is characteristic of him, as distinguished from such modern equivalents as Anatole France or Shaw, that we should feel in him no opposition between these free flights of the mind and the crudities of the natural man.

For this reason, the Russians, who have been closer to the earth and further from the industrialized world than any other great Western people, at the same time that they have brought their theater to a perfection that is probably unique, prove to be particularly happy as performers of Aristophanes. The Irish Players, perhaps, in their period of *The Playboy of the Western World,* might have had some such success with *Lysistrata.* But, as one watches the current production by the Musical Studio of the Moscow Art Theater, one wonders who else could have furnished such a fusion of efficiency and intelligence with animal spirits and natural directness. I have never seen a Greek play brought so vigorously to life on the stage: while it lasts, the Peloponnesian War, the civic life of Athens, become for us quite immediate, yet at the same time vividly alien, with the strangeness of remote times and peoples. Some part of this strangeness, no doubt, is due to the fact that it is not merely the Greeks but the Russians who are foreign to America; so that the "papapapaxes!" and the "alalas!" sound considerably more convincing in the mouths of the Moscow actors than they would in those of familiar members of the Actors' Equity Association. But those who saw the Russian productions of *An Enemy of the People* and Goldoni's *La Locandiera,* with their careful differentiation between eighteenth-century Italy and modern provincial Norway, will recognize in the *Lysistrata* the pains that have been taken here, too, not merely to achieve an accuracy of archaeological detail, but, working with material derived from research, to produce a tempo, a color, a tone appropriate to Aristophanes.

The scenery and the action are conventionalized, but conventionalized in such a way as to bring out the play's actuality and to give freer scope to its life. Only, perhaps, in the case of the grotto of Pan—a compartment in an open scaffolding—do we feel that the proper balance between realism and convention has not been preserved. The Acropolis is represented by three groups of tapering, white fluted columns, supporting broken arcs, of which the middle group stands highest and is approached by winding steps. On these stairs, the Athenian women, with their brown legs and earth-red mantles, are outlined, as if in clear air, against the deep bright blue sky of Greece. Nothing could be more different from the choruses of women we are used to in the modern productions of Greek tragedies. In their contrast with the chorus of old men, headed by the City Magistrate, who have come to dislodge them from the citadel, they loom as a magnificent embodiment of female natural energy and robust female strength; they are precisely what the Greeks called them, "citizenesses." Not even in their Corybantic moments of dancing and cymbal-clashing are we reminded of a theatrical production. The old men are caricatured, but in an unfamiliar fashion: they have thin fishbone-like noses, high chirruping effeminate voices and helmets which suggest at once decrepitude and obsolescence. The women pour water on them from earthenware jars and finally put them to rout in a hand-to-hand contest. Lysistrata, superbly played by Mme. Belyakova, is seen, at the rise of the curtain, alone at the top of the stairway, and thereafter dominates the scene. With her stature, her deliberate step and her long greenish-gray robe, she has the dignity, the magistral presence, of an heroic figure of tragedy or even of an ancient goddess. But her rich brassy hair is stained with the color of the earth, again; and she talks to her sister insurgents, not as a preceptor, a Princess Ida, but as a woman to other women. She can back her audacious project with the vigor of the common life. Such qualities—the stamina and flavor of a weather-seasoned active race—have been what has always been lacking in our own attempts to put on Greek plays. It is only these actors from the barbarous steppes who have been able to bring them to us. Among the crowd of Athenian women as we see them in the Russian *Lysistrata,* we might well, if the action of the play had taken place a little earlier, imagine we could catch a glimpse of the female greengrocer who gave birth to Euripides or the midwife who was Socrates' mother.

January 6, 1926

———

Opéra Comique

THE SECOND TWO BILLS of the Musical Studio of the Moscow Art Theater—Offenbach's *La Périchole* and Lecocq's *La*

Fille de Madame Angot—were by no means so successful as the *Lysistrata*. For one thing, being true opera, they require to be sung throughout; and the young Russians have turned out to be somewhat less remarkable as singers than as actors. What is more fatal, however, is the fact that the Russian genius, so well suited to Aristophanes, proves a little too heavy and harsh for this sort of light French comedy. What the Art Theater has done to these operas is unexpected and very curious. In the first place, they have rewritten them in such a way as to turn them into serious dramas—thus imposing upon the original material a load which it can hardly bear. In the French *Madame Angot*, it appears, Ange Pitou, when Clairette has thrown him over, consoles himself with Lange, the actress; in the Russian version, however, he detaches himself from both complications and passes on to higher things: "the dénouement," explains Mihail Galperin, the arranger of the new libretto, "is a symbolical apologia for poetry, free and unfettered by earthly laws." Into *La Périchole* the adapters have injected a new element of political drama by transforming the young street singer and her lover from Spaniards into native Peruvians, who may thus be made butts of oppression for the Spanish army of occupation. The light impudence of *La Périchole* becomes imbued with emotion, with revolutionary implications; and the melodrama does not mix well with the old situations and lines which still belong to *opéra bouffe*. Having thus revolutionized the libretti, the Russians stage them quite realistically: the only attempts at a comic convention are in the direction of Hogarthian caricature. Thus the comic Spanish dukes and viceroys of *La Périchole* are characterized by the actors with all the detailed make-up, the carefully sustained physical infirmities and the idiosyncratic mannerisms of decayed Chekhovian aristocrats impersonated by Stanislavsky.

In *Carmen*, however, the Russians have a subject which is perhaps really capable of being benefited by their treatment. One has always felt that Bizet's opera fell far short, in dramatic dignity, of Mérimée's story; and the Russians, in rewriting the libretto and rearranging the score, are only restoring to the theme its original tragic force. The result, however, is not Mérimée any more than it is Meilhac and Halévy: it is something more somber than either. The whole action, as in *Lysistrata,* is played against the background of a single set—a towering system of arches, walls and galleries, which serves for both interiors and street scenes. From these galleries a company of Spanish women perform the function of chorus, commenting on the action of the tragedy from a point of view outside it and detached from it; while, on the rusty rufous walls behind them, the light, with the progress of the drama, is appropriately made to vary from the baking red of the southern sun to the dull dark stain of dried blood. Below this, the tragedy is concentrated in a succession of realistic scenes, which, disembarrassed of the trappings of opera, proceed straight to their inevitable catastrophe. This Carmen is no longer a pert soubrette; this Don José is a heavy peasant; Micaela has entirely disappeared; and for the smart comic-opera café of Act Two of the original version has been substituted a sordid den presided over by a shapeless old woman who has been copied from the caricatures of Goya.

January 20, 1926

THOUGHTS ON LEAVING NEW YORK FOR
NEW ORLEANS

AT THE AQUARIUM, a tropical booby bird, imprisoned in a small tank, is shivering with the cold.

Horses are slipping in downtown streets and cutting their knees on the ice.

The boys in the office of the *Daily Graphic* are hot on the trail of Earl Carroll's orgy; the boys in the office of the *Herald Tribune* are hot on the trail of the Countess Cathcart.

Young lawyers in the District Attorney's office are forswearing the use of alcohol in order that they may act as *agents provocateurs* in fashionable bootlegging night clubs. Young lawyers in private firms are protecting the interests of the Consolidated Gas Company.

Young men in bond-selling houses are worrying for fear they may not have enough self-confidence to put over the sale of their bonds.

Typists are looking forward to the moment when they can go to the water-cooler.

Gray snow, which matches the sky, is falling.

The students at New York University are making a loyal effort to pretend that Washington Square is their campus.

At a dance in Webster Hall, the waiters are picking the pockets of a fat Greenwich Village bookdealer who has come in a pirate costume.

Young poets, who cannot afford night clubs, are writing poems on the hollowness of modern life.

The Brevoort and the Lafayette are being unattractively renovated in the style of the lavatory of the Pennsylvania Station.

The gray snow, as soon as it has fallen, begins rising in

exhalations, and many people come down with bronchitis, tonsilitis, pneumonia, pleurisy, influenza and tuberculosis.

Clothing stores on Fourteenth Street are selling out their entire stock.

In the textile district, the textile workers are pumped in early in the morning, in and out at the lunch hour and out at the end of the day.

Furniture imprisoned in the fortress of the Manhattan Storage Company is running up enormous bills.

In drug-stores, miscellaneous women, as they wait to use the telephone booths, are buying banana-nut sundaes and listening to phonograph records of Ukulele Ike.

At the Grand Central Palace there is a big Bathroom Fixture Exhibition.

At the Algonquin, when a popular dramatic critic says, "I'm going to South America," an eminent humorist will flash, "Going in for the big Honduras contest?"

At the Opera, they are working on the revival of a long-forgotten opera by Meyerbeer.

Highbrow theaters are straining every nerve to discover another Michael Arlen.

People are waiting in line in the cold to see the new Gloria Swanson picture.

Popular actors in the West Fifties are endeavoring to seduce young actresses by showing them oil portraits of themselves; the young actresses are extorting contracts before they consent to yield.

The hostesses and hosts of night clubs are working on quaint accents and wisecracks which will make it seem worthwhile to their clientele to pay their exorbitant cover charges.

Antique stores on Madison Avenue are selling pairs of faked china dogs for sixty-five dollars apiece.

On Park Avenue, above the Grand Central, many people —at a very high cost—believe they are living in style.

People on Lexington Avenue are wishing that they lived in a more cheerful street.

At the concerts of modern music, the ladies wear auburn sideboards and corpse-white toques.

At the concerts of the Philadelphia orchestra, Mr. Stokow ski wears a handsome dress suit.

Big theatrical men with their mistresses, both shaped like well-stuffed ottomans, are eating sandwiches at sandwich palaces.

Detectives and tarts in collusion are framing victims in the upper Forties.

Smart book-stores on the side streets in the Forties are disposing of first editions of Joseph Hergesheimer for seven dollars apiece.

The art galleries are lined with carpets, like Campbell's Funeral Church.

Bishop Manning has made public statements on the importance of Christian faith.

People suffering from exhaustion, despondency and acute self-dissatisfaction are being treated by expensive specialists for dental trouble, mastoiditis, astigmatism, inflammatory rheumatism, ophthalmic goiter and fallen arches, then finally turned over to analysts.

People coming home late at night in the upper East Eighties and Nineties are compelled to struggle with three Yale locks in order to get into apartments which they will subsequently find have been robbed.

Corner drug-stores will supply bad gin to people who are well enough known to them.

Students at Columbia University are electing courses in Collective Bargaining, The History of Modern Thought and Problems of Abnormal Psychology.

In Harlem, the whites come to visit the Negroes in the hope of enjoying among them a little color and warmth; and the Negroes are making an effort to live as much as possible like the whites.

March 17, 1926

ALL GOD'S CHILLUN

A Cotton-Mill Owner

ONE SUMMER when I was down in New Orleans, I had a little tug fitted up and I lived in her all summer. I'd go on shore in the daytime and I'd go back to the boat in the evening and sometimes I'd hail somebody from the shore and invite them on board for dinner, and other times I'd just sit out on deck and watch the shore and think. And at night I'd anchor in the bayous. New Orleans was nice in those days. I had niggers to work for me. One day one of the niggers discovered he was free and that he didn't have to work —so I paid him five dollars a month after that. He was my favorite nigger and the softest-spoken faithfulest nigger I ever knew. After I left, he got into trouble—he went to work in a factory and while he was working in the factory, he got into a quarrel with another nigger and he hit him with a club and killed him and he got sent to jail. Well, first he wrote to a man that he'd worked for once and he asked him to recommend clemency to the governor of the prison. The man sent him the note all right but, when he got there and delivered it to the governor, it turned out that, instead of recommending clemency, the man had recommended that the governor give the nigger forty stripes for a debt that he owed the man. So they gave him the forty stripes, and all he said, when they got through, was, "Well, Mistah Ferguson sure do collect his debts!" Then he wrote me a letter—I remember it began, "Kind Captin"—and when I came back there the next spring, I went around to see him. There he was, expecting to get hanged, but it didn't seem to weigh on him much. I suppose he forgot about it most of the time: he seemed just as cheerful as ever. I got him let out after two months, and I took him back into my service, and he worked

for me again all summer. And he was the faithfulest politest
nigger I ever had.

A Steamboat Captain

WHEN WE PAY 'EM on the last day of the trip, we have to
hold out a dollar on 'em. And that's known as "tie-up money,"
because it's to make 'em tie up the boat. As soon as they get
paid, they sit right down and they begin to play a game
called Skid—that's the fastest game there is—there's a bet on
every turn of the cards. At the end of half an hour, one nigger's got all the money and all the other ones have got is the
dollar that they get for tyin'-up. And the nigger that won all
the money goes to a nigger sportin' house that night and he
gets it all stolen from him. No: if we paid 'em all at once,
they'd just jump ashore and leave us—wouldn't take that extra trouble. They won't take no trouble they don't have to.
Now, for instance, there's one kind of cargo that the niggers
don't like to unload and you can't get 'em to do it. It's a kind
of fertilizer that's got some kind of acid in it and when they
carry it on their shoulders the acid eats through the sack and
it makes welts on their shoulders. Well, one trip we had a
cargo of this fertilizer, and we wouldn't let the niggers look
at it to see what it was, so that they couldn't tell the niggers
on land when we came to have it unloaded. But the niggers
on shore got suspicious when they couldn't find out what
it was from the niggers on the boat, and they sent one nigger
on board tó investigate. They knew that, if they undertook
to land and then didn't do the job, we could have had the
law on 'em. Well, this scout took one peek at the cargo and
he knew he had to give the warnin', but he knew that if he
told 'em what it was, we'd beat him up on the boat. So he
just stood and looked at the boat and he didn't say anything
for a minute—the niggers on the shore were all waitin' to
see whether they should come aboard. He just stood and
looked, and finally he read the name *Peerless* on the pilot-
house. And then he said, just as loud as he could, so that

the niggers on shore could hear him: "*Peerless!* This ain't no *Peerless!* This is the *Lusitania!*"

Another trip, they broached the cargo. I began to smell a smell of roastin' and I began to get suspicious—we had a cargo of yams. I went down to look at the cargo and the barrels looked all right with the tarpaulin across the top, but when I came to look underneath, some of the barrels were half-empty—they'd stuck stones and rags inside to make the top layer come level. Well, I lined the niggers up on deck and I said to 'em, "Now, you black bastards! I'm gonta find out who broached that cargo if I have to knock you all dead!" And I began to knock 'em down with a club, just as they were lined up there, one after the other. I hadn't gone very far—I hadn't knocked down more'n about five—when the next nigger spoke up just as I was about to hit him and he said, "Don't hit me, boss, I'll tell!" And so he told, and the ones that done it got a beatin'. What happened to the one that told? Oh, that was funny! They killed *him!*

A New Orleanian

IT'S VERY EXCITIN' when the river rises and we're afraid the levee's goin' to break—there's a great feelin' of danger in the air. It makes you feel so queer: you look up and see the boats floatin' above the level of the streets. If the levee ever broke by the city, New Orleans would be gone—wouldn't be a thing left of it! They don't print it in the papers, but when they're afraid the levee's goin' to break, they have a thousand men mobilized, ready night and day with sandbags. And when it does break, like it did at Poydras just a few years ago, all the doctors and the lawyers and everybody turn out, just like it was a war. I went up to the Poydras crevasse in a motor-boat and the houses were ten feet under water. In one house, the niggers had gone up on the roof and they were calmly cookin' fish up there. They'd moved the stove up on the roof and one of the boys was holdin' it in place so that it wouldn't slide down the slope, and another was tearin' up shingles and feedin' 'em into the stove for fuel. And the ol' mammy

was cookin' the fish—I don't know where they got the fish
—caught 'em most probably. I saw another nigger in another
house sittin' on a board out the window and playin' a guitar.
I came up alongside in the motorboat and told him to jump
in, but he was just beginnin' to sing and he didn't pay any
attention to me. I said, "Come on! You better jump on in!
Don't you want to be taken to land?" But he just shook his
head and smiled and went on playin' his guitar.

April 7, 1926

1957. The second of these stories was relayed to me by
Sherwood Anderson—who was at that time living in New
Orleans—from his Mississippi steamboating days. He liked to
talk about his memories of these. He had had a mulatto
mistress, with whom he liked to travel and whom he made
sound very attractive. I urged him to write all this; but I
realized that something prevented him from writing the stories he told or writing anything in the way he talked. His
ideal of literature seemed partly to have been derived from
his training as a composer of advertising copy: he liked to
make simple statements and to emphasize them by repetition
—often to the ennui of his readers; and partly from the *Dial*
and the Stieglitz group and other writers whom he had met
when he came to New York and who had encouraged him
to take himself seriously. All these persons were city-bred, and
they had had no such experience of the common life as that
from which Sherwood Anderson had gleaned his Mississippi
stories. For most of them, the practice of literature was a
formal affair for which one dressed, or even a kind of sacrament for which one put on priestly robes. It is true that he
came to the defense of Mark Twain when Van Wyck Brooks
was taking him to task for falling short of the writer's high
rôle, and that he felt, as he wrote to Brooks, that his own
story *I'm a Fool* was in the vein of *Huckleberry Finn*. But
this story and its companion piece *I Want to Know Why* are
exceptional in Anderson's work. He preferred to develop in a
void those dreamlike and humorless fables in which people
almost never talk like the kind of provincial Americans
among whom the author had spent most of his life; and it

rarely occurred to Anderson to exploit for the purposes of his fiction the immense amount of material—anecdotes, adventures, queer characters—which, for purposes of conversation, he had always so entertainingly on tap. I wrote down the above story as nearly as possible in his own words soon after he had told it to me. Compare it with the style and the method of the stories that Anderson published.

THE OLD CONVIVIALITY AND THE NEW
New Orleans

I

"How 'BOUT YUH?" says the boy from the city desk, running
into friends on Canal Street. "Which way yuh goin'? Come
on along an' get a drink. I'm just goin' to stop into the Red
Crescent and have a couple o' drinks before I go home." "I'm
on the wagon now, Charley," says the artist; the Tulane student has to work. Inside the bar, the white-coated mulatto
boy serves them all around. "Before you drink any o' that,"
says the bartender, "I just want you to taste this." He brings
out a brown whisky bottle and pours a little in a small glass.
"This here's the real thing," he announces. "First real stuff
I've seen in a year! Just taste it!" "That's the real thing, all
right!" Charley meets him with enthusiasm. The artist orders
another round. "This stuff is all right, though," says the student. "Won't do you any harm, anyway!" "I'd be dead, if it
did!" says the bartender. "It's just straight Cuban alcohol,
with a little caramel flavoring." The artist, contemplating the
bartender through the crystal of those two late drinks, sees
him glow with benevolent radiance: the old-fashioned type!
he reflects, the barrel girth, the tight ruddy skin, the distinguished silver hairs: he won't lie about bad whisky! "Look
at that bead!" the bartender exclaims. "See how it lasts! Look
at that! Ever see any bead like that around town?" To Charley, the bead seems as durable and as precious as a jewel.
The student stares at a picture of a race-horse, unglazed and
yellow with age: what a beautiful creature a horse is! what
a magnificent occasion the Derby!—he wonders whether he
has made a mistake in going to college instead of following
the races in his youth, as Sherwood Anderson did. "No: never
bothered me yet," says the bartender in answer to a question
from Charley. "Be funny if they did come in here and see

everything right out like it is—just like an old-time bar: whisky open on the counter—jug o' this other stuff—couple o' cases o' beer! They'd say: 'Guess you ain't heard about Prohibition!—didn't know that law had been passed!' " Everybody laughs; the student orders another round.

A long-legged gawky Negro carrying a guitar comes into the bar from the street. "Let's have a little music!" says Charley. "I gotta sit down to play," says the Negro. "Come inside, boys," says the bartender. "Come inside and make yourselves comfortable!" Inside, they draw the chairs in a circle, and the Negro begins to strum:

> Down in New Orleans—dance that's new!
> Men can do it an' the women, too!
> Oh, shake that thing! Won't you shake that thing!
> I'm sick and tired tellin' you to shake that thing!

"Bring him a drink!" orders Charley, nodding in the direction of the guitarist, as the boy serves another round. At a word from the waiter, the bartender goes out and brings back an enormous man with a fixed glare and a wooden leg. "That's a detective," whispers Charley to the artist. The detective sweeps the room with a glance, then sits down and swallows a drink.

> Old Uncle Joe, the Jelly-Roll King!
> Got a hump in his back from shakin' that thing!

Everybody laughs loudly; the detective smiles; he recognizes Charley and nods. "How 'bout yuh?" says Charley; "How about yuh?" says the detective. "What raciness! what wit!" reflects the student. "How unabashedly Dionysian in the face of the white man's conventions!" "Bring another round—on the house," the bartender orders the waiter. "That's a swell picture!" says Charley, looking up at a tarnished landscape in the foreground of which oriental beauties are lolling on tiger skins. "Don't see many like that any more!" "Wouldn't take a hundred and fifty dollars for it!" replies the bartender. "Gettin' piped himself!" whispers Charley.

"Story for yuh over on Royal Street tonight," says the detective confidentially to Charley. "Organ-grinder's monkey got away and got into Betty Johnson's." Charley laughs extravagantly. "All the girls came out on the galleries and began to holler bloody murder. Couldn'ta carried on worse if the place had been on fire. A policeman had to go in an' ketch the monkey an' quiet him down!" "What a jolly place New Orleans is," thinks Charley as he whoops with laughter, "where the police reassure the whores! It's a real Catholic city!" "That bottle," the artist proclaims, "is the most beautiful thing of its kind I have ever seen: it has significant form. I bought a pair of Empire vases at an auction today, and I give you my word of honor, as an ornament, I would rather have that bottle!" "Make you a present of it," says the bartender, who has overheard him across the room. "That's real ol' French brandy." He comes forward, proffering the bottle with the expansive and casual air of a rich plantation-owner.

"Can you remember the *Barrel-House Blues?*" "Yeah; I cain remember dat one," says the Negro, drooping heavily over his guitar. "Lemme have another drink an' I'll try and sing it." "Bring *him* another drink," orders Charley, and adds to the company at large, "I can sing *Sweet Adeline!*" "We'll take your word for it," says the artist. "Go ahead and sing it then," says the student. "The tenor is all I can sing: I've got to have another voice." "I kin sing the bass," says the detective. "Go ahead and play the accompaniment," Charley commands, beaming. "Do you know *Sweet Adeline?*" "Yass: I know dat one," says the Negro. They go through it, in imperfect synchronization and with a gap between tenor and bass. "That's not *Sweet Adeline,*" says Charley, with intense professionalism. "That's the same accompaniment you were playing before!" "I couldn't jes' remember it at first. Start again an' I'll play it right." He puts his hat down on the floor, and they fling coins with the gestures of princes. "I can sing a baritone," says the student, who, in his mind, has been trying out his voice and is very well satisfied with it. "Well, hadn't we ought to make it a quartet then?" the bartender urges. "I used to sing that song once." The guitarist, struggling against torpor, pulls himself together in his chair and strikes a few inappropriate chords. Then the quartet bursts on the room:

> *Sweet Adeline!—Sweet Adeline!*
> *Say you'll be mine!—Say you'll be mine!* . . .

II

JUST BEFORE the weekly luncheon of the Kittiwake Club, the Reverend Kendricks comes over to the President: "We've got to throw some more pep into these lunches," declares the fighting pastor. "There hasn't been a spark of life in them lately! Half the members act like they were strangers to each other; they sit around like they were in a restaurant. If we don't want to be considered just a charitable home for leftovers from the Rotary, we've got to take a brace!" His black eyes, his sharp nose and his jaw of snapping white teeth bite fiercely into the President, whose round spectacles and egg-shaped head seem to melt and disintegrate before the pastor's attack. Mr. Evans is the proprietor of the third largest clothing store in New Orleans. "Another thing," continues the Reverend Kendricks. "You mustn't let Peterson talk about the trip to Mississippi. He's peeved with the way they were treated—whether rightly or wrongly I don't know. But, in any event, he's all primed to make himself nasty about it—and if the Kittiwake stands for brotherhood, any reflections on brother Kittiwakes are contrary to the Kittiwake spirit!" "I've asked him to speak already," the President helplessly answers. "Well, just leave him out," says the pastor.

The tables are nearly filled; the waiters bring on the soup. Mr. Evans sits in front of the American flag, spread out on the wall behind him. He swallows a few spoonfuls of soup, then, mindful of their schedule, stands up: "Now, to see who wins the attendance competition, will those with red badges please rise." When the reds have risen, the whites rise, interrupting their gumbo soup. While the soup plates are being removed, the Reverend Kendricks springs to his feet: "Now, we'll sing Number Seven in the songbook, and I want you to put some pep into it!" The Brothers sing *Auld Lang Syne* as fast and as hard as they can: when they have finished, their minced chicken is before them and even a little cold. Mr. Evans rises again: "Mr. Zeismann will now address us—" "Fine the President!" cries a voice with a sharp laugh; "Yes: that'll be a dime!" "I mean to say, *Brother* Zeismann will now address us on business methods in the shrimp-packing industry." Brother Zeismann, who takes such things seriously, reads aloud in an inaudible voice a paper which he has carefully prepared. Some of the younger members become restive and grumble among themselves: the paper so far overruns the minced chicken that, by the time Brother Zeismann has finished, the Reverend Kendricks has only time for two stanzas of a comic song.

Brother Evans begins in some embarrassment: "I have asked Mr.—Brother Peterson to talk on his trip to Gulfport last week——" "I want to move," cracks the Reverend Kendricks, "that no public report be made: it has no place at a Kittiwake luncheon. Let Brother Peterson make a report to the officers, if it is desired, at some other time." "I move that a report be made here!" says a Brother who has been on the trip and who does not like the Reverend Kendricks. Somebody else seconds the motion; a vote is taken, and the ayes have it. "Some of the Brothers were surprised," says Brother Peterson, after a few preliminary remarks, standing at ease with his hands in his pockets, "at what happened to us up there. But I wasn't surprised: I'd been to Mississippi before. In the first place, they put us up in a little hotel that stood right beside the jailhouse: we wouldn'ta minded that so much if the rooms had only been clean: I expect the prisoners were better off than we were. Then, at the meeting, they didn't introduce us and they didn't say nothing to us: a Mississippi proposition was handled from soup to nuts! We had a little table to ourselves, and it was 'way off on one side; and, after the dinner, we just filed out—like a football team! As I say, some of the Brothers were surprised; but I'd been up to Gulfport before, and the last time I went I got shot. I've got the bullet-hole in my arm now! So I knew what to expect, and we got what I expected. In other words, the whole thing can be summed up in a single word, and that word is Rotten!" The Reverend Kendricks checks the laughter by leaping into another song. "Now, we'll sing a new song," he shouts. "The new Kittiwake song—written by Brother Benziger!" He drives them through it with spiteful force. At last they subside to eat chocolate pie with a lump of meringue on top. But the Reverend Kendricks has seen his chance: "What about these pie-eaters here?" he cries. "Couldn't wait to get at their pie! How 'bout a little duet from these pie-eaters?" The two Brothers who had begun on their pie before the Kittiwake song was finished respond with a foolish smile: one is the man who seconded the motion. "It's not a joke—not a bit of it!" insists the Reverend Kendricks grimly. "Come on, you, Buzz!" He leans over and glares at the celluloid buttons which indicate their nicknames, "And you, Doc! Let's hear how you can sing! Come on: stand up and sing!" At his command, the two men stand up; he herds them to the middle of the room; their faces turn red. "Come on," cries the Reverend Kendricks, "let's hear you sing it through!" He leads them triumphantly:

New Orleans, New Orleans! You're such a grand old town!
We're proud to say it now! We'd say it anyhow!
New Orleans, New Orleans! We'll spread your name around!
We'll tell the world with flags unfurled,
  We're all for you!

                                                    May 12, 1926

RETURN FROM LOUISIANA

ONE IS GLAD to come back to the gray New York air, the cold faces, the colorless buildings
even from green-shuttered houses wreathed with old wrought-iron balconies—acorn scrolleries and daisy garlands and cupids netted in webs—where the stitchery of green creepers delicately interweaves and feathers the filigree of iron lace and among which, after rain, on March mornings, one can catch the faint perfume of greenery like the scent of maidenhair fern; from the damp days that draw from old walls that rich toasted smoky smell, the emanation of soft coal and masonry; from the warm days of sun that release in the streets the brightness of girls in light dresses—absinthe-greens and sky-blues and shrimp-pinks—like the variety of hues of an aviary; from French alleys of slender-limbed water oaks lit with leaves of a translucent green-yellow; from stems of yellow-green glasses, out of which, from pearl-green and ice-crystal, one imbibes an iridescent exhilaration; from the music of the Charleston in the streets, heard and lost in the warm March air, running lightly in the head of the city; from fresh fragrance of raw sugar on the docks, as if of a kind of honey that has been purged of its amber smell and refined to the shadow of something white; from wooden lace of old riverboats, from Doric columns and slim pilasters, from incredibly ornate old bank buildings with barley-sugar twisted pillars; from good beer on draught in old-fashioned bars and gravy-dropping pot-roast sandwiches; from restaurants where crayfish soup is served as piping hot as the deviled half-crayfish, in its brown, flashes a vivid scarlet, and so rankly aromatic that it tastes like the smell of stables; from restaurants where white halves of broilers or

morsels of pompano, cooked with mushrooms in envelopes of paper and crisply embrowned from the oven, are elegantly sliced open by waiters with black-handled knives of thin steel; from the palaces, the squares, the old convents; from the city that floats in the water with the shipping at the end of its street-vistas; from the life that floats with the city, the life without roof or walls; from those tones of exquisite sweetness: the high shivering cries of riverboats; the fine urban diphthong of *er* that verges like our own on *oi* but vowels the stops of a softer speech; the tangle of Negro children's voices, incessant as the song of birds, that play all about the house toward noon on a sunny day; the light tingle of a double-tine when Saint Louis tells the quarter-hours; the vibration of some steamboat-blown peal that beats as it dies in the air; from the cadences everywhere of fronds, forever drooping gracefully, loosely: the green spray of ferns and the white frothing-over of garden-urns studded with rams' heads, the gray dripping moss of live-oaks, the slack wreathing of lantana trailers that flower in heliotrope about tombs where the thin splitting panels reveal a debris of bones; from that cadence—easy, lovely, loosely falling—like the name Louisiana itself—

even from all these, from the city where life is most fastidiously dressed, from the city where it seems enjoyed most freely, we pass to this other city where it is perhaps most intensely felt.

Back there the old gulf-port no longer pumps blood for the exploits of a powerful race. Our harbor draws us back into an organism that shakes with a rapider pulse, an organism still expanding. And, for all the confusion and the harshness, we find here, in a sense, relief.

Do we not stand, in this northern port, at the farthest post of history and look out on the newest horizons? Do we not get the latest news and explore the extreme possibilities? Do we not, between the office and the night-club, in the excitement of winning and spending, and slightly poisoned by the absorption of bad alcohol, succeed in experiencing sensations which humanity has never yet known? May we not, under this pressure, in constant collision, be proud at least of striking off flashes of a novel repercussion and color?

Yet we remember the plantation-houses with their wide eighteenth-century gardens, their white columns and high-poised balconies; their furniture: the wardrobes and beds that seem designed for a race of giants; the tall silver candlesticks like tulips that flower in crystal bells and the flower-chased crystal *cylindres*, tall ornaments for lofty mantels; great greenish-blue celestial and terrestrial globes, mounted on mahogany stands, that make the universe more majestic and that lend man himself more stature; allegory-encrusted clocks, displayed under bubbles of glass, that invest human efforts with meaning; luster-showers, forever suspended in the cloudbursts of glass-diamond gouts, which fix the profusion and splendor of the impulse that squanders its treasure and that offers it to kinfolk and friends. All these are the equivalents of the steel of our girders, the vaults of our railroad stations, the marmoreal contours of our bathrooms. They are an allotropic form of money acquired through exploitation. And did the infamous Mme. Lalauré, who kept her slaves chained in cells and starved them, commit a worse crime against our common humanity than the barbarous commercial enterprise which has produced the office-buildings and the subways and which has mechanized the people that live in them? Do we show ourselves less cruel in our dull way than they did in their dramatic one? And who will buy our old phonographs in antique-shops when our property and power are gone? Who will raise funds to rescue our old apartments? Who will envy our shortness and quickness when they find them surviving in the manners of some relic of our long-decayed race, then fallen from its classical efficiency, as we are charmed by the manners and the speech of the South, even when the man who inherits them has no longer personality or possessions?

—Muddy breadth of the Mississippi, dun cement of the foursquare cathedral, thick forest of slate-lilac and chocolate angles of the shoved-down roofs of the town. Coarse stalks of banana-plants, dark green glossy leaves of magnolias, straight stocky palms that expand in stiff bristling tignasses of tresses, dull green shaggy grass under shade-trees, dull gray crustaceous claws of cactus-clumps. The gray waters that spread out to the Gulf where the shrimp-fishers perch like sea-birds, hardly sheltered by flimsy shanties and living with the tides and the mud;

the horrible stink from the broken closet in which a condom floated; the dirty green wall broken through and showing the plaster and laths, scribbled with dates and names; the pulp magazine on the couch and the picture of Christ in the room below. *Want your ass again? When you jazz last?—Goddam, that's a pretty dress!* Her hair was reddish and bobbed, her eyes were round, brown and pretty, and she would pucker up her mouth half-open—she was creamy and firm like a new blancmange or the plasm of life in the mud.

April 28, 1926

AFTER THE GAME

Princeton and Yale Ten Years Ago*

You SEE IN ME an Athenian who has just returned from Sparta!—No: I really had a darn good time.—Well, Bill Trotter and I went over to Arthur's rooms the first thing after the game, and in some ways I thought he'd changed a good deal. He seemed frightfully nervous and exhausted; and he's more serious-minded than ever—excruciatingly so. He greeted us with heavy politeness about Princeton's losing the game. "You did some brilliant work in the last half," he said. "It was a pity you couldn't have scored then." You remember how he used to be found in the library when St. Matthew's was playing Kendall? Then I complimented him on his translation of the Sophoclean ode in the *Lit*. "But I'm surprised," I said, "after what you told me once about *Tess of the D'Urbervilles* that you should have any use for such a pessimist." "Oh, there is certainly nothing in common between Sophocles and Hardy," he said. "Modern writers like Hardy and Ibsen merely vituperate against the world and futilely abuse God for injustice, whereas Sophocles makes it plain that *Oedipus* has broken the moral law and that his punishment is quite just. That is why *Oedipus* is a great tragedy whereas *Tess of the D'Urbervilles* is a purposeless assault on our emotions." "But in *Oedipus Coloneus*," I said, "Sophocles makes *Oedipus* become aware of the fundamental injustice of his punishment. Such thoroughgoing expressions of pessimism as one finds in the second *Oedipus* are hardly to be found elsewhere in literature. Surely no one has outdone Sophocles in griping about the worthlessness of human life: 'Not to be born is best; but, once born, the next best thing

* That is, ten years earlier than 1925, when this monologue was written.

is to die as quickly as possible.'" Then he confessed that he hadn't read *Oedipus Coloneus* but had merely translated the ode on Athens—implying, of course, that if he *had* read it, he would have found that my view of it was quite unsound. "I have so little time for Greek," he said. "Outside my Plato course, I find it possible to spend only about thirty-five minutes in the Classical Library in the late afternoon, between the time when I come in from track and the time when I go to dinner. I envy you Princetonians with your more ample leisure." "Why on earth do you go in for track?" I asked him. And then he explained that he thought that, if you wanted to be an all-around man, you ought to cultivate some form of athletics—he's actually taken up pole-vaulting: isn't that a ghastly thought? I can imagine him gritting his teeth when he doesn't get over the bar and drops. And he writes for the *Lit,* debates, sings in the choir and the glee club, and intends to go out for the Dramat. Bill Trotter mumbled something about, "Idea 'd never occur to me!" "What idea?" Arthur demanded. "Idea being an all-around man," said Bill. "Really, Bill," Arthur said, "every time I see you, you have become more unintelligible. I hope Princeton isn't doing that to you. You know what the Harvard men are like: you can hardly understand them at all." "Not Princeton," mumbled Bill. "Mere decay of the moral fiber."

Then Ed Haynes came in—Arthur is still rooming with Ed—beaming from ear to ear and a little bit lit. "Well, men!" he said, "I'm right on the crest! And before the evening is over I'm gonta be still higher. I'm gonta be drunk tonight!" "You're drunk already," Arthur said grimly. "Oh, say not so, Duchess!" said Ed. And then he said, "Have you heard about Prexy Hadley's latest prank? He went by Anson Phelps Stokes's office the other day and called out for him to stick his head out. 'What's the matter?' said Anson. 'There's a window open in Woodbridge!' replied the President of Yale. 'Bless my soul!' exclaimed the Secretary. 'Which window is it?' 'The one you've got your goddam head out of!' was the President's unexpected reply. And now, Men of Yale"—he began. "But I forget we are not all Yale men here. No: an older—I might almost say a more sacred—tie unites us. Old

Fellows of St. Matthew's School!—journeying along diverse
roads on the great ocean of life, yet always welded together
by the memory of the old school water-tower!" And then
he began to give an impersonation of Weeping Fred Hotchkiss: "I see a bare and unlighted room on the topmost
story of a tenement. I see a man and a woman huddled there
about a guttering candle. Their seventeen children—all under the age of three—are clamoring for food. A package has
arrived. What is in it? They carry it to the failing light. At
first, they think there must be a mistake. It must have come
to the wrong address. But no! there is a card: it says, 'From
the students of St. Matthew's School—bought by voluntary
contributions.' And inside is a ripe grape. And I see the joy
that fills that humble room—I see the smile that lights the
mother's face as she turns to the children about her,"—here
his voice begins to break, don't you know?—"and says, 'Children, the boys—of St. Matthew's School have sent you this
ripe grape!' " Then he did the Performing Seal, and he was
going to give us the Transformation Scene from *Dr. Jekyll
and Mr. Hyde*—he said, "I've got a new ending where the
United States Marines come in! I defeat the Forces of Evil!"
I told Arthur I was glad to hear that they'd got this unpleasant tragedy all straightened out at Yale. Ed has improved his
line: he's hilarious—and he looks so funny in his New Haven
clothes—you know these dark sheet-iron clothes that they all
seem to wear—with his dip—they all wear dips—jammed
down over his spectacles, so that he's more like a frog than
ever. But Arthur shut him off. He doesn't approve of Ed's
buffoonery. When they were first at college, it seems, Arthur
made Ed go out for Dwight Hall, then afterwards when religion didn't seem to take, he had him heel the *News,* and Ed
got on—through Arthur's so useful alliance with Huntington
Barnes, I imagine. But the night we were there was precisely
the night of Ed's moral collapse. He asked us to come out
and have dinner with him and go to the show at the Hype.
Arthur wouldn't come—he said he had some kind of committee meeting—and he said to Ed quietly but searchingly,
"Do you think you can afford to do this?" "Yes, Duchess,"
replied Ed. "I can—by a strange coincidence! I won some

money on the game." "I mean, don't you have a lot to do?" said Arthur. "I got by on that chemistry test," said Ed, "so I think I'm entitled to celebrate!"

We had some drinks and went to Mory's—which was in a great state of drunken confusion and absolutely deafening. It was full of old grads and people, greeting each other with terrific impact. After that, we went on to the Hype, where one of the most tremendous brawls that I've ever seen was staged. In the first place, the curtain was late going up, and the audience demonstrated loudly. At first they just stamped and sang songs, but gradually they grew more bitter. At last, a man came out and announced that Gertrude Hoffman would not be able to appear. This of course was a disappointment—they'd been hoping to see her dance in the nude —and a shout of disgust arose. Then finally the curtain went up on a lunch-hour act of acrobats, which everybody of course horsed. The climax of the act was one of those stunts where they all pile up on one another. Somebody began shushing the audience, and then when there was comparative silence and the acrobats had just made their pyramid, Ed Haynes, who was sitting in a box, said, "Hup!"—and the acrobats mistook it for their own signal and all came down on their necks. Everybody was delighted. The acrobats tried it again, but were rattled. Ed said "Hup" at the wrong moment again, and they nearly didn't make it. When they went off, the chief acrobat came up to our box and said to Ed, "I could keell you!" The curtain came down, and there was another long wait. Then Ed's friends began to urge him to go up on the stage and do something to entertain the audience. When he appeared, there was tremendous applause. He said, "I'm going to give you the Transformation Scene from *Dr. Jekyll and Mr. Hyde*. But I don't want any of the ladies to be nervous when they see me turn into Hyde. I've created a new ending where the United States Marines come in." But he never got any further than the first line: "I have r-r-ransacked London in vain for the drug that has been the cause of all muh misery!" The curtain went up behind him, and he found himself in one of these interior sets for a typical vaudeville skit—with a telephone on the table, don't you know? He went straight over to the table, sat down, took up the receiver and said, "Hello, is this Police Headquarters? Detective O'Brien speaking—" But before he got any further, an actor in a dress suit and silk hat came in. Ed got up and shook hands with him warmly and said, "Good evening, Count! Welcome to the Taft lavatory!" Then the manager or somebody came out and tried to put Ed off the stage. Ed wanted to remonstrate with him, but the man pushed him along backwards, and finally he fell into the orchestra. When he got up he was sore as a crab and tried to get back on the stage. The audience, in the meantime, had been going wild, and when they saw Ed crash into the woodwind, they began to rush the stage. Then the management brought out a hose and turned it on the students—which, of course, only made them more furious. Finally the police were called in, but before it was over the theater was wrecked: the set was all torn to pieces. A man who had been sitting in the box with us threw a chair into the big drum. They do those things on a big scale at Yale.

We got Ed out of the theater, though he wanted to beat up on the management and kept insisting that he would sue them for breaking his spectacles, and we went back to Ed's and Arthur's rooms—they had offered to put us up—where we found Arthur very much agitated over the rumors of the riot he had heard. We tried to tell him how funny Ed had been, but it only made him grim and depressed. The thing is, that even though they're Juniors, they're always afraid of getting in wrong: Arthur was afraid that Ed had gummed his chances for Bones or something. Arthur, I think, has got his own future pretty well secured. The chairmanship of the *Lit,* it seems, is the object of a competition—the contributor who gets most manuscripts printed wins it. And Arthur has written a sequence of something like twenty-eight sonnets all about the Yale campus, Yale brotherhood, Yale ideals, etc. —each of which counts as a separate manuscript. So he has the *Lit* chairmanship cinched, and the chairman of the *Lit,* I gather, is elected automatically to one of the senior societies. But he's been worried about Ed—who, it seems, has been running it out a good deal lately. After we had gone to bed—

they in their bedrooms and Bill and I on the window-seat and couch—about three o'clock in the morning we heard Ed get up again and go into Arthur's room, and they had a long conversation which we couldn't help overhearing. Ed was still more or less drunk, but he'd begun to worry, too. "I suppose I made a damn ass of myself," he said, and then he went on to tell Arthur how much he thought of his character and how much his influence had meant to him and how terribly he felt at doing anything that could bring discredit on Yale. "I was drunk," he said, "and when I'm drunk I always want to play the clown, but you mustn't think, Art, that, under it all, I could be satisfied with cheap success, just with making people laugh, or that these years at Yale haven't meant more to me than just drinking and buffooning and parties." It was sort of embarrassing. If it had taken place at Princeton, we would just have yelled to tuck it in; but there was something sort of religious about it. Bill Trotter lay there muttering, "My God! This is killing me! Little more of this and I'll break down and cry like a child!" But finally we heard Arthur say, "Well, don't worry about it now any more. Go back and try to go to sleep. I understand that the real rowdyism was all started by the Sheff men."

November 25, 1925

REUNION

We were sitting around at the club the second day of Reunion. We ought to have been at the game, and I was surprised to see so many people leave it. In my own case, I no longer enjoy watching baseball as much as I once did, and after marching onto the field with my class, I went back to the club again with the intention of reading *Manhattan Transfer:* the first fifty pages had been wonderful—much better, I thought, than *Three Soldiers.* How boldly and ably Dos Passos had gone ahead from the bitterness of the end of the war to a critique of capitalist society! I didn't get very far, however: several other people soon joined me, and before the game was over the lounge was full. When a newcomer would join our company, we would reproach him for his lack of loyalty; and when we demanded, "Why aren't you at the game?" he would answer simply, "What game?" or "We seemed to be dropping the ball so much, and I always find that so depressing." I had never gone in for "college spirit" myself, but I was sorry to see the others so demoralized. We were all more or less drunk: the gin bottles stood around foursquare on the big mission tables and the mantelpiece like some austere and monumental motif of the university architecture. I commiserated with one man on the difficulty of getting anything decent to drink in Columbus; and from another I listened to a long encomium on the golf and good sense of his wife, which made me think he was becoming dissatisfied with her. Clark Wilder presently appeared. "How's the game going?" somebody asked. "Heigho! lackaday! Here today—gone tomorrow!" said Clark; and then added, "It won't be long now!" This was a formula he had been featuring all through the Reunion—an occasion to

which he had brought the remarkable endurance and forti-
tude which had distinguished his record in the Argonne (it
had rather astonished his friends that Clark should have
turned out a war hero). Though his consumption of alcohol
was heavy, his superb form was never affected: he always
knew what he was doing and he never did anything disgraceful; his great frame was usually conspicuous in the front
rank of any parade, and whenever a speech was called for,
Clark would be seen on his feet, speaking vigorously, coher-
ently and nonsensically. When he was completely overcome
with liquor, he would simply lie down and go to sleep,
wherever he happened to be, and then wake up as stout as
ever. When he arrived among us now, we all took another
drink, and our lounging conversation, with its laughter at
the end of pauses, in the wide and somber room where the
afternoon sun sank its shafts, began to give somewhat the
impression of a slowed-up moving picture. I asked Clark what
he was doing, and he told me he was working in a broker's
office. "Ah, well!" he said, "it won't be long now!"

At last, after one of his most amusing speeches, delivered
a little thickly, he suddenly stretched out and went to sleep.
A comparative silence ensued; and I presently dozed off myself. I was vaguely aware of more people coming in after the
game, but I didn't wake up to ask who had won. When I did
wake up, I found Newt Graves sitting in the leather chair
next to mine. I was glad to see Newt again: I hadn't seen
him for years. He began to ask me questions at once, with an
eagerness I thought slightly unnatural, about what I had
been doing since the War. I told him that I had a job, but
that I had not yet got around to the long Dantesque poem
which I was contemplating at the time I graduated. "In the
Army," he said, "I used to yearn terribly for quiet and leisure
to work. I could almost have wept about it." I thought he
was a little drunk, too. "Just to get up in the morning and
to know that you'd be there till evening! I bought a copy of
Dürer's St. Jerome in a print-shop at Nancy, and I used
to carry it around with me. It would never have occurred to
me to envy St. Jerome before I was in the Army, but the
sight of that solid old man sitting there in that clean solid

room, with its thick walls and heavy beams, while the sun of a whole long day was moving the panes of light across his desk and the floor, and with a lion, which apparently he kept as a pet, contentedly dozing beside him, used really to affect me deeply. No privacy! no peace! no security! I worked in a flimsy little office that was finally blown to splinters by a shell, and as for domesticating lions, I sometimes used to get the feeling that we were all wild animals ourselves! One never had a moment for one's own thoughts. One got so used to the conditions of war that the ordinary pursuits of peace came to seem out of bounds, illegal, contrary to duty—the conditions of peacetime seemed incredible. How wonderful to write a book, to follow a line of study, to talk with one's friends in the evening about books and ideas and the affairs of the world! By the time one got out of college—after four more or less passive years—one had wanted more action and excitement; but by the end of a year of war, one had had quite enough of that. One realized that, left to itself, humanity was a raving madhouse, and that it was only by long effort that any order could be brought into it at all—that even duckboards could be laid in the mud. But such patience and effort as were needed, how sweet they seemed to me then!"

I wondered what was on his mind: his tone was not the tone of disillusionment, but had the accents of the freshest enthusiasm, and I hardly knew how to meet it. I tried to find out what had happened to him, but all his answers baffled me.

"I know," I said at last—obviously enough, it seemed to me, yet he would not take it as obvious. "But I suppose that the peace that we got, instead of giving us something to go on, only left us more or less demoralized, so that we didn't know precisely what to lean on in order to start on our patient effort."

He looked at me quickly and said, "Well, I live now so far away that I know very little of what's going on. But things were so bad during the war that it seemed as if, as soon as it ended, they must take a violent turn for the better. I kept feeling more and more strongly that humanity couldn't stand it much longer, that when we finally woke up from that nightmare, there would be such a reaction toward peace, toward supernational arbitration, as had never been known in history. At first, I kept looking forward to an ultimate triumph of liberalism; then, later on, I was ready to say with Lenin and the Bolsheviks that, if the governments of a capitalist Europe were unable to put a stop to a war which was wrecking the whole of their society and of which all parties were desperately sick but which seemed now to be carrying them down with the uncontrollable momentum of an avalanche, then it was time to sabotage this horror and take a stand for a new society that would be founded on different assumptions. I was coming more and more to expect that there'd be general revolution in Europe. In any case, it seemed to me impossible that one could ever live indifferently or trivially again. If one survived, one would have the advantage of having received a profound revelation as to what was important in life and what was not, of seeing clearly one's only course and of pursuing it unfalteringly and fearlessly."

He spoke hopefully. He must, I thought, have been living very much out of touch with the world to speak in that way of the end of the war; and in his mouth the word "humanity" seemed dated.

"Yes," I answered, "one didn't take it into account that Europe was exhausting all its energy, and that it was bound to be left too weak to do anything very effective in the direction of a new order; and we who were in Europe during the war forgot that the United States was too remote and too ignorant to contribute much toward rescuing Europe. And, besides that, not only the possibility, but even the desirability, of a really drastic revolution began, in the long run, to seem dubious. One even came eventually to doubt whether it was possible to solve all our difficulties by the machinery of legislation: by a socialist state or a league of nations. Our experience of the Army, I am sure, was to modify our whole point of view but not in the way we expected. In the Army we were principally conscious of a desperate thirst for freedom, which made us sympathize with everybody else who had been deprived of freedom—political prisoners, disfranchised citi-

zens, dissatisfied laborers, oppressed nationalities. Yet the
Army, in the long run, also gave us a lower opinion of the
human race. Hitherto, we had been in the habit of looking
somewhere—to some powerful institution or group—for the
enforcement of justice and reason. We may have thought
ourselves skeptical and worldly wise by the time we got out
of college, yet we still could not help believing, as we had
done in the days of our childhood, that the judges could settle disputes, that the doctors could cure diseases, that the
clergy could preserve Christianity, and that the government
could maintain order. We had, further, a sort of confidence
in the instincts of the common man. Then, afterwards, confronted by the chaos of the war, the professions and the government seemed futile. No one who has ever watched an
army doctor trying to deal with a flu epidemic will ever get
over his impression of the miserable impotence of the human
race at the mercy of multiplying bacteria. And as for the
common man, to live with him and to work with him is to
learn to get on with him and like him; one can even feel
the deepest solidarity with him. But, although one may hate
army discipline and recognize that soldiering is one job in
the world that almost nobody does willingly, it is impossible,
if you have ever had experience of serving in a military unit,
to imagine effective action being taken by any large number
of men unless they have a group of directors empowered to
dragoon and to punish the rest. So that young men who went
into the Army with Kropotkin under their arms not infrequently came out with a feeling that there was something
to be said for Mussolini.

"But what changed one's ideas most of all was an eventual
realization of one's own fatal human inadequacy, one's capacity for becoming demoralized. It is easy enough for young college men to have a good opinion of themselves, but, in a
sense, it is perhaps impossible for the non-professional soldiers to do so. I don't merely mean the periods of nervous
strain, though many people have never really got over them:
a good deal of our modern instability is, I am sure, a result of
the war. But to have had to admit to oneself one's possibilities for cowardice, for brutality, for bestiality, to have had it

brought home to one how easy it is to shirk duties, to abuse a position of power—is enough to give one pause, don't you think?, in making any sanguine assumptions about progress in the ordering of human affairs. How many, do you suppose, in this room have more even than the blood of the enemy buried in their memories of the war? How many may know that they have wasted the lives for which they took responsibility?—aviators who will never cease to reproach themselves with not having given proper instruction to one of their pupils who came to grief; doctors and orderlies who, through negligence, have allowed their patients to die; commanders of companies who have misunderstood their orders and led their troops into unnecessary danger—or that idiotic company commander who suffocated half his men by sending them back to check up into a shack that had been bombed with gas! Colonel Whittlesey, who, in spite of his glory, was tormented by the thought of the blunder that had cost his detachment their lives, finally committed suicide. To learn to think ill of oneself is to learn to think ill of the world. It's no wonder if, since the war, we find we have lost our faith in the theories of perfectibility which assume a natural goodness and a natural common sense on the part of the ordinary person—if, indeed, we become reactionaries and read pessimistic classical writers instead of hopeful romantic ones and, taking refuge in such battered old fortresses as our race has been able to defend, unexpectedly align ourselves on the side of tradition and authority!"

There is nothing like a little gin to bring out an eloquent moralist. Newt smiled a little disappointedly. "Well," he said, "there are certain compensations, it seems, about being in my situation." I was just about to ask him what he meant, what his situation was, when Clark Wilder came to with a bang. "Well, thanks for the buggy ride!" he announced, with his hoarse deliberate laugh. "Here today and gone tomorrow—if *any!*—if *any!*" he added, delighted with his new variation. Everybody laughed at this, and we all had another drink. When I looked around, Newt was gone. I asked Clark what Newt Graves was doing now. "Newt Graves is dead," said Clark. "He was killed in the War." "But I saw him here just now," I insisted. Clark laughed his slow drunken laugh: "Ideal reunion," he said. "Not only see classmates who are still alive, but get drunk enough to see classmates who are dead!" "He was adjutant in my outfit," he added, "and his office was hit by a shell. I missed him because after he was killed, there was nobody at Toul I could talk to."

April 27, 1927

THE MEN FROM RUMPELMAYER'S

I WOKE UP in a country club. When I got out of bed, it was rather late, and there was a tennis match going on below my window. I saw the dimmed and mist-dampened tennis courts, from which the sounds of the game came subdued and sparse. Slender Boston girls, in gray or brown coats, stood with their backs to me, looking on—they were smart and, in that boyish way, graceful. Beyond, there were people on benches; I was able to tell the girls from the men only by their whitish crossed legs. It was one of those moist murky days past mid-August when one can already feel the fall, and as I dreamily made my toilet in the bathroom, I derived from the fields and dark trees, seen from the window through the haze-thickened air, a quiet enjoyment as I first caught the flavor of that rich lapsing of the long autumn which makes us taste a kind of freshness even in the beginnings of luxurious decay. There was no one in the dining-room when I at last went down, but I enjoyed having breakfast alone: the brightly sprig-flowered curtains and the light slender-runged chairs seemed pleasantly clean like my hands, which, I reflected, had not been so clean since I had gone up to camp for the summer. I noted the headline of the Boston paper: "Supreme Court Decides Sacco Appeal Today"—then I read the meager paragraphs which followed, and, as there seemed to be nothing else except syndicated comic features and advertizements, I turned to a copy of *Life,* which had a cover by John Held, Jr., in blue and red.

Afterwards, I idly lolled on a large dark porch enclosed in glass, and presently Ralph appeared with both the girls. "Do you feel testy this morning?" said Julia. "We're all feeling pretty testy." "Not a bit," I said. "Good-natured to a fault."

"That might get on my nerves this morning." "Well, you're *looking* extremely fresh." And so they always did—they were not Boston girls, but Californians and had the well-grown figures and strong color of the West. Julia wore white straw shoes with interwoven strands of red, light straw-colored stockings, a pretty straw-colored skirt flowered in blue and red, a close-fitting light blue jersey and a scarf of a pinkish violet which echoed and complemented both the red in her shoes and the blue of the jersey. I reflected that Julia and Lynn had a great gift of dressing attractively: they had also that amusing vocabulary, something entirely their own—such as their use of "testy" just now. "When I look at those white teeth," I said, "that clear skin—that clear tanned ruddy skin —and those brown eyes and wide eyebrows—I realize that you are two of the handsomest girls that this country has ever produced!" "That's just the inclemency of the weather," said Lynn. "It makes us come like bright rays." Julia and I laughed, but Ralph only smiled by stretching his mouth: his eyes behind his rimless spectacles were already more or less slits and could be little narrowed by laughter. The things that the girls said always seemed to be just beyond him: either such things as he wouldn't have thought worth saying or as he wouldn't have cared to hear said so quickly—at any rate, such things as made a kind of conversation in which he could not take a real part. Yet he evidently derived gratification from possessing a wife and a sister-in-law who pleased people as much and amused them as much as Lynn and Julia did. And he tried, in his way, to keep up with them. "Well, what shall we order?" propounded Lynn, who had just caught sight of a waiter. "Sarsaparilla with cream?—Four sarsaparillas with cream?" "I don't know whether I could stand that," I said. "It's nourishing," explained Julia. "You can dispense with luncheon entirely." "Yes," said Lynn. "It's not only nourishing, it makes the idea of food seem repulsive." "Oh, all right!" I yielded.

Ralph picked up the paper and read the headlines about Sacco and Vanzetti. I had tactfully refrained, the evening before, from mentioning this explosive subject. "Some of your friends were up here," he said. "Bill Morris came rushing over to Hoppner and Post to get us to cash a hundred-dollar check for him to bail the others out." "What do you think about it all?" I asked. "I think it's a shame," he said, "to arrest people like Powers Hapgood for speaking on Boston Common—he was making a perfectly law-abiding speech. The Common has been supposed to be a public forum ever since the Revolution." I thought he was going to draw some conclusion from this, but he did not pursue the subject. "What do you think about the merits of the case?" I inquired. "I think they ought to have a new trial," he answered, "but they haven't got a chance in the world. Fuller is a hard-boiled politician. They never had a prayer with that committee: Grant is *non compos mentis,* and of all the prejudiced people in Boston—and everybody in Boston is more or less prejudiced—Lowell is probably the most so. He's successful at raising endowments for Harvard—he has a wonderful way with millionaires—but it would be hard to find anyone less suitable for conducting an impartial investigation into something like this where the men accused are attackers of authority and property. I've given up saying anything about it, though—when I try to argue at the club, everybody jumps on my neck." The New Englanders did, after all, I noted, express themselves in a plain-spoken fashion. I had not myself assumed that the Governor's Committee was a farce: I had supposed that Lowell, Stratton and Grant were more or less intelligent men, and I had been imagining something like one of those plays by Galsworthy in which everyone does the wrong thing from the most conscientious motives. "I've been absolutely sure they were innocent," said Julia, "ever since I read how Vanzetti said, 'I am innocent of these two harms!' I'm sure that nobody who would say that could have done anything really bad—do you think so? 'I am innocent of these two harms.'"

The sarsaparilla and cream arrived. "They call things like this 'tonic' here," said Lynn. "It makes it sound bitter and bracing." But nothing could have been sweeter than this beverage—it did make me feel slightly sick. Then they began to debate what we should do. Lynn suggested going for dinner—we had had breakfast too late for lunch—to a place called

the Bass Point House; but Ralph disapproved of this—
though, it seemed, he had been in the habit of taking her
there before they were married. "As long as he's got to take
the seven-thirty train," he said, "—that is, eight-thirty day-
light-saving—we'd better have dinner in town." "Let's go to
the Squamscott Club!" said Lynn. "That takes a long time,
too," he objected. "Let's go to Mother's apartment and have
a regular lobster supper!" "Sea food," said Julia. "Shore dinner," said Lynn. They were being ironic in their Western
way, but Ralph was only partly aware of it. "I'll cook them
myself," he said. "I'll give you a superb dinner!" It occurred to
me that he might be afraid that, if he took us to the Squamscott Club, I might try to make a speech about Sacco and
Vanzetti. So we presently started off in the car: it was quite
a long ride to Boston. "Well," Lynn demanded, "where's
that snack?" "It's in that side pocket," said Ralph, who was
driving. She got out a ginger-ale bottle, which Ralph, in his
neat careful way, had wrapped up in newspaper and tied
with a string, and a set of paper cups. "We brought along a
little snack," she explained. It was alcohol and ginger ale.
"Well, it's a relief to have the ginger-ale famine over," I said.
"I hope that drink I concocted last night didn't make you ill."
When the ginger ale had given out, I had tried mixing lime
juice and alcohol. "What an awful drink that was," said
Lynn. "It tasted like turpentine!" "You did put a flower in it,
though," said Julia. "You put a snapdragon petal in each one
—so, while it may not have been a very good drink, it was
really awfully pretty. I'd like to have a dress like that," she
added. "Sort of a deep garnet on a sort of acidulous yellow—
I've never seen anything like it." "You'd have to have green
eyes to wear that color," said Lynn. "Green eyes and reddish
hair.—Do you smell the condemned clams?" A stench that
was rank and stagnant reached us from the mud of the shallow beach, where the water looked dull, thick and cold.
"What do you mean?" I inquired. "Are the clams here really
condemned?" "Yes," she said, "all the clams are condemned
between Nahant and Revere Beach. You can smell them."
"That smell hasn't got anything to do with the clams," said
Ralph. "It's just the way the water smells." "No," said Lynn.

"I'm sure it's the clams." "Well, you're absolutely crazy," said Ralph, in his insistent even-tempered way. "That smell has nothing to do with the clams. It's always smelt like that in summer." "There are two people clamming," said Lynn, indicating two distant figures: "Two condemned people clamming for condemned clams." "Only condemned people are allowed to go clamming here," supplemented Julia. We didn't, however, pursue this joke. "Well," said Ralph, "if you insist on having it that Revere Beach smells of condemned clams, you're at liberty to cherish that delusion. But it's silly to tell people that." We presently began to sing. The girls had been singing together all their lives, and I always found them delightful. They first gave us, "I can be happy, I can be glad, It all depends on you—"; and then, at my request, one of their most successful numbers, which they had learned on a cruise to the West Indies and which always reminded them, they said, of the wonderful nights on deck: "Forsaken—forsaken— forsaken I lie—Like a stone by the roadside, while men pass me by." This song did not move me with its pathos, but it brought before me the beauty of a southern night, the wide air of some white clean ship, and the voices of those young girls, with their dear American clearness, their American freedom and gaiety. Ralph sang *Flamin' Mamie, the Sure-Fire Vamp*, of which, as it were in competition with the girls, he had learned all the words, all the stanzas, and which he rendered with complacency but without expression. I followed with an old nonsense college song, so different from the modern kind that it had something of the strangeness of folk poetry. "Do you want to go past the prison where Sacco and Vanzetti are?" Julia asked me. "We can go around that way." "You can't go past," said Ralph. "The road is closed: they won't let cars go by."

We crossed the Charles and went up Beacon Hill. I looked out at the narrow old streets, with their British-looking chimney-pots and their walls of well-laid red bricks that now wore an impressive dinginess of antiquity; those silver-knobbed doorways of Bulfinch that melt on the eye like music: white panels and Ionic columns, under fanlights as clear as crystal and flanked by white-curtained panes. Then we turned off into less elegant streets, and Ralph apologized: "You may think I'm taking you slumming, but I know where to get the best lobsters." We stopped in front of a fish market, and while Ralph was inside, I bought a paper, but there was nothing about the case in it yet. "Be careful of that," said Ralph, handing Lynn in the back seat a paper-bag. "Oh, are those lobsters?" asked Lynn, taking it rather gingerly. "Those are lobsters," said Ralph. There were little holes for them to breathe through. She put them away on the floor of the car.

When we drew up at Ralph's mother's apartment, he produced from under a lap-robe one of those great glass gallon jugs in which they sell alcohol. "Great Scott!" I said. "Is that alcohol? I thought we drank that all up last night!" "It's a magic jug," said Ralph, his eyes narrowing with pleased satisfaction. "It's full again every morning." "The Hoppner wonder-jug," said Lynn. "The old oaken bucket," said Julia.

The apartment was old-fashioned and pleasant. Sitting on a couch, while Ralph mixed the drinks, among the bare floors and the shrouded furniture, I was glad to breathe the odor of an old city house. It made me think at first of New York, but then I took account of the fact that there was another American city in which the houses had that old-fashioned smell. That fragrance of the city interior, which I used to catch deliciously as a child when I came up from the country during the holidays to visit my New York relatives, now spoke to my mind through my nostrils in terms, not of odor, but of interest: it seemed to me that life was interesting where dark libraries and drawing rooms smelt like that; and I had, for the first time since my arrival, a vision of how interesting Boston had been. I remembered with something like a feeling of guilt how little I had been in touch with it—to the degree that when, the day before, I had got off the train at the South Station, I had not said to myself, "This is Boston!" but had thought more of the Santa Barbara which I was to find in Lynn and Julia than of the Boston I was to find in Ralph. There were an engraving from Raphael; some photographs of Italy; a painting of Roman ruins enveloped in that blue-green haze which seems so to preserve the atmos-

phere, at once romantic and stuffy, of the culture of the nineteenth century; and a picture of Apollo and the Muses. I had
once met Ralph's grandmother: she was a very old lady, with
a green eyeshade that concealed her eyes, and it had surprised
me that, in spite of the eyeshade, she should seem to be so
sharply aware of what was going on about her, or that so
dowdily dressed an old lady should talk with such style and
precision. She had known Sumner, Emerson, Lowell, and it
was said that she had had something like a flirtation with
Dickens when he had stayed with her family in Boston. Her
father had been Thomas Hoppner of Hoppner and Post, the
publishers, in whose office Ralph was now working. It
had, I thought, shown a great deal of courage for him to
marry an Irish girl—though, of course, her coming from California and her not being a Catholic made it somewhat different.

Ralph soon reappeared with a round of drinks and handed
them around unsmilingly, but with his usual self-satisfaction
—and we found ourselves grateful to get them. He presently
began to sing: "I can be happy, I can be glad, It all depends
on gin!"; and we gave him a smile on this. Then he unlocked
the glass doors of the bookcase and showed me some of the
first editions—they were mostly brownish yellow and had in-
scriptions in faded yellow ink—as well as a volume that recorded the proceedings of a Porcellian Club dinner, in which
the name of the elder Holmes appeared along with that of
Hoppner. "Well," suggested Lynn, "how about something
to eat?" "Yes: something to eat," said Julia. "Have the men
from Rumpelmayer's come? That's my prize line," she explained to me. "I got it out of an English novel." Ralph held
up the bag of lobsters: "Here they are, all alive!" he announced. "Would you like to see them? Would it whet your
appetite?" "Oh, no: don't!" said Lynn. "I hate them!" So
Ralph carried them off in the bag. "Well, I hate to do this,"
he said. "But I love to eat 'em!" "Do they boil them alive?"
asked Julia. "Yes: I guess so," I answered. "Oh, how awful!"
she said.

"Oh, I meant to ask you," I switched, following an association of shore dinners. "What's become of Lois and Ed? Did

you see them when you were in Santa Barbara?" "Oh, it's so
terrible!" she answered. "Lynn and I are so depressed about
it! She's in love with somebody else, and he doesn't want to
give her a divorce because he's still so in love with her. He
finally disappeared, you know, and went on a terrible bender
—he went up to San Francisco—and nobody knew where he
was—and Lois thought he'd killed himself. And then finally
he turned up, looking haggard and wan and as if he hadn't
changed his clothes for weeks—you know how spick and span
he always used to be! He just came into the house and asked
where the goldfish with the black tail was—they'd had a goldfish with a black tail that he'd been particularly fond of. And
the goldfish had been killed by the earthquake that had happened while he was away—but Lois said when she told him
she felt like a lying wretch, because it seemed so improbable
that one should have been killed and the rest be all right—
and she knew that he believed that his favorite had perished
through her neglect. And then afterwards he slammed a glass
door, you know, and it broke and cut her arm. And after
that, he was just in the depths, and they've both been sunk
ever since. Lynn and I have been brokenhearted over it—we
try not to talk about it! We can't think of anything to do.
They both write us letters separately. We've invited them to
come on and visit us separately—that's the only thing we can
think of to do." "And Ed's really such a nice fellow," I said.
Julia took up the tale: "When we remember how cute he
used to be—how he used to come cavorting into the house,
shouting, 'Hey! Hey! And how!' But Lois says he gets on her
nerves, and I can perfectly see how he would." Looking out
into the dim wet dusk, I reflected on how darling the girls
were: their humanity and generosity; they were scarcely even
jealous of one another!

Ralph summoned us into the dining-room for the supper
which he was proud to have prepared alone. He had produced tomato soup, canned succotash, and the lobsters with
melted butter. There were big thick slices of bread. We enjoyed it all very much. "Don't you want me to break that
claw?" he asked Lynn. "No, thanks: you eat it," she said.
"I will if you really don't want it." He took it into the

kitchen, and we heard him hammering. When he returned, he brought a gallon of alcohol, which he manipulated against his biceps, with his thumb in the little round hole in the handle. He had discovered a bottle of grenadine. "It's not as pretty as yours," Julia said to me. "I mean the drinks that you made last night." Ralph rather bored us by singing all the stanzas of "Oh, landlord, fill the flowing bowl Until it doth run over!" Before I reached the point of not caring, I was beginning to wonder whether college wasn't going on a little too long.

On the train, I read with cocktail-dazed eyes that the Massachusetts Supreme Court had refused, on technical grounds, to accept the appeal for Sacco and Vanzetti. The next day, when I had gone back to camp from Boston, two telegrams reached me. One—signed "Forsaken"—said, "Come back at once. The men from Rumpelmayer's are draining the old oaken bucket"; the other was from a friend connected with the Sacco-Vanzetti Defense Committee and told me that "picketers and speakers were needed for last protest." But I had used up my extra money, so I couldn't answer either summons.

September 28, 1927

JUDD GRAY AND MRS. SNYDER

JUDD GRAY and Mrs. Snyder have been electrocuted, with the result of arousing some qualms about the wisdom of capital punishment. In this case, there seems to be no question of the guilt of the persons punished, yet their fate has been horrifying. We take for granted the brutalities of the poor, the offenses of professional criminals, and when they are punished, we are rarely moved. But Judd Gray and Mrs. Snyder were "respectable": they seemed to have been living exactly like three quarters of the people in America. A corset salesman from East Orange, New Jersey, with a wife and a ten-year-old daughter; the wife of a middle-aged art editor of a motorboating magazine, also with one daughter, nine, residing in Queen's Village, Long Island—they arranged to murder her husband with a sashweight while he was sleeping, as a step toward the larger freedom, the fuller enjoyment of life, which is so much in the air of our period; and there is also our familiar motif of the ruthless ambitious woman who commands the submissive male. Ruth Snyder and Judd Gray thus become both tragic figures and dreadful examples, which fascinate the popular imagination. For they had dared to go all the way with a gamble that others must have dreamed of, must have tried on a smaller scale; and their deaths have been a purge for frustration, a petrifying warning to guilt, a substitute for baffled vengeance. The whole story has been deeply experienced by many a newspaper reader, and everything has been done by the press to make the executions vivid: the reporter of the *Daily News* even succeeded in getting into the death chamber with a camera strapped to his leg and took a picture of Mrs. Snyder in the chair. Gathered outside the prison, an enthusiastic crowd made holiday, as if for a medieval burning or a breaking on the wheel. To others the occasion was not so enjoyable: Elliott, the executioner, had a nervous collapse afterwards; and the warden, confessing that the case had been the most trying of his official career, announced with considerable feeling that he had ceased to believe in capital punishment. Whether or not one believed that the culprits deserved what the law was giving them, one could not help thinking of their children, their parents and Judd Gray's wife.

Who, indeed, will pretend that electrocution is not a method of inflicting death horrible out of all proportion to any possible deterrent effect? If we must have capital punishment at all, better the euthanasia of certain of our Western states. But what is the justification—even aside from the question of miscarriage of justice—of the physical destruction of first-degree murderers? Mass murderers, homicidal maniacs should certainly be put to sleep—as should probably all congenital idiots and hopeless maniacs of other kinds; but the judgments should be made on a basis of mental incapacity and harmfulness to society, not on a basis of retaliation or assumption of incurable turpitude, as is implied by our obsolescent legal code. Which of us is in a position to decide about the moral responsibility of Ruth Snyder or Judd Gray, or to take it into our hands to end their lives?

The day before the couple were executed, Thomas Hardy died. A survey has been made by Mr. Silas Bent of the relative amounts of space given to these two events by the five leading New York papers. These—counting total column inches: headlines, illustrations and text—turn out to be as follows:

	GRAY-SNYDER CASE	THOMAS HARDY
Herald Tribune	55.5	59
Times	63.5	31.5
World	78.5	20
American	116	5
Daily News	289	2

But even in the *Times* and the *Herald Tribune*, which gave a certain amount of space to Hardy, it did not occur to anyone to apply to the Gray-Snyder case the moral which a great man of letters had spent his life trying to impress on his age. If the personality of Tess of the D'Urbervilles may not seem to present an analogue to Ruth Snyder's, Thomas Hardy has left us a poem which is not inappropriate to this occasion:

On the Portrait of a Woman about to be Hanged

> *Comely and capable one of our race,*
> *Posing there in your gown of grace,*
>   *Plain yet becoming;*
>   *Could subtlest breast*
>   *Ever have guessed*
> *What was behind that innocent face,*
>   *Drumming, drumming!*
>
> *Would that your Causer, ere knoll your knell*
> *For this riot of passion, might deign to tell*
>   *Why, since It made you*
>   *Sound in the germ,*
>   *It sent a worm*
> *To madden Its handiwork, when It might well*
>   *Not have assayed you,*
>
> *Not have implanted, to your deep rue,*
> *The Clytaemnestra spirit in you,*
>   *And with purblind vision*
>   *Sowed a tare*
>   *In a field so fair,*
> *And a thing of symmetry, seemly to view,*
>   *Brought to derision!*

January 25, 1928

THE AGE OF PERICLES

An Expressionist Play

PERICLES, Prince of Athens
APHASIA, a shell-shocked hetaera
RABELAIS, a court jester
VOLTAIRE, a court philosopher
VELASQUEZ, a court photographer
PINO, a wine merchant
BINO, a pimp
LORNA ⎫
NORNA ⎬ FATES
PORNA ⎭
    LAFAYETTE AND CHORUS OF FROGS
    BALLET OF NYMPHS AND SADISTS

Music by Thersites and his Drunken Helots

The Grand Central Station in New York: the set shows both interior and exterior. An evening party in progress.

THE HOSTESS. Nine o'clock and nothing has come yet!

THE HOST. The bootlegger has changed his address. They say he's not at the old place any more!

THE HOSTESS. Have you asked the Information Desk?

THE HOST. No: I was afraid they wouldn't answer.

Mr. X, a guest, arrives. A porter checks his coat.

THE HOSTESS. We've just had a disappointment: our bootlegger has failed us!

Mr. X opens a suitcase full of Scotch.

THE HOST. A godsend!

THE HOSTESS. Can you spare it?

MR. X. Knowing how little you are making, Jack, I was afraid you couldn't afford the real thing.

Porters rush up with ice. They hastily brush everybody off,
and Mr. X and the Host tip them. Other guests arrive. They
tip the porters.

THE HOSTESS. I'm afraid there aren't enough chairs to go
round!

A GUEST. I don't see any chairs at all.

ANOTHER GUEST. Oh, well: we can always leave.

The party is broken up and scattered by an automobile con-
vention going back to their homes. Some are swept into west-
bound trains and carried rapidly to St. Louis, Detroit, Min-
neapolis, St. Paul, Cincinnati, Kansas City and Cleveland;
others are deposited on the lower level, where they get the
porters to bring them drinks and start a new party of their
own; others go to night clubs and movies. The Hostess meets
a man wearing horn-rimmed glasses who makes advances to
her and tries to lure her into a telephone booth. She hesitates
as to whether to yield, but finally decides in the negative.
The Host sees William Randolph Hearst, who is getting on
his special train and who makes him feel inferior.

A late guest from out of town encounters a beautiful
courtesan in the neighborhood of Fiftieth Street.

THE OUT-OF-TOWN GUEST. Can you tell me how to get
to the Grand Central?

She walks with him to the corner and shows him the way
to the station.

THE BEAUTIFUL COURTESAN. Now you must give me fifty
dollars.

He gives her a bad check.

THE HOSTESS (*running into the Host*). I see that you have
just met someone who has made you feel inferior.

THE HOST (*biting his nails*). Yes: William Randolph
Hearst.

A few of the party have reassembled, and have been joined
by some travelers waiting for trains.

A GUEST. Well, here's to Mr. X, who brought the drinks!

A victrola has been turned on, but is too far away to be
heard. Several couples begin to dance. A guest begins to fight
one of the travelers under the impression that he is a relative
whom he has always disliked. The man with the horn-

rimmed glasses makes an effort to blackmail the host. One of the ladies is robbed of a necklace of Tecla pearls, and another, who is jealous of her and knows her neurotic nature, tries to suggest to her the idea of suicide. One of the porters brings somebody a bill for the drinks brought by Mr. X. The Host, feeling inferior, throws the Hostess under a train.

A GUEST. The Hostess has been killed.

ANOTHER GUEST. Are you sure that it *is* really her and not somebody we do not know?

THE FIRST GUEST (*lying*). No: I am not at all sure.

THE SECOND GUEST. Then we don't need to bother about it.

A NOVELIST. You may perhaps be interested to know that I wrote my last book under the influence of aspirin, while running for the Lexington Avenue local. It came to me just as it is, and I couldn't change a word of it.

ANOTHER LITERARY MAN. Yes, indeed: I am very much interested, and I should like to write a book about you.

Several buildings in the neighborhood of the station sink into the ground by reason of their weight, and the people are suffocated. The guests buy morning papers and read about it. The Grand Central passes under a new management, and the permit to hold the party is no longer valid. One of the guests, who has a brother in the new administration, offers to take the matter up with him; but his brother is too busy to see him. This makes him feel inferior. He and the Host withdraw to a corner and attempt to raise each other's morale; they try to make friends with a porter, but he is busy protecting his interests. As the demolition begins, they are killed by falling beams. A new building, a block of offices, is erected on the Grand Central site; and Mr. X, whose company has moved there, turns up the next morning at nine o'clock sharp.

February 24, 1926

I I
THE EARTHQUAKE

October, 1930–October, 1931

DWIGHT MORROW IN NEW JERSEY

SINCE THE MIDDLE of October, Dwight Morrow has been campaigning in New Jersey. He is the Republican candidate for Senator in a state dominated by industrial interests, but is nevertheless receiving the support of New York's only liberal newspaper, the morning *World*. The great thing about Morrow, says the *World*, is that he is not a politician: he is that almost unheard-of phenomenon, a totally disinterested banker in public life, and he is a man of exceptional gifts. The *World* applauds his every utterance, goes into ecstasies over his courage and sagacity. It seems plain that it is backing him for President.

When we hear Morrow's speeches, however, we begin to wonder whether he is not overrated. It may be true that he is not a politician, but there are certainly politicians in the offing; and it is not clear how he would behave very differently if he were an old and shrewd hand at this line. If it is an act of great courage, as his supporters assert, for him to come out for the repeal of prohibition, it must be confessed that he could scarcely have picked a state more favorably disposed toward such a declaration. In New Jersey, the old cider mills are still barreling applejack and hard cider, the old beer saloons are still serving beer, the finest foreign wines and liquors are being unloaded along the coast, and the hot-dog stands on the motor roads sell gin. At least one enormously profitable experiment in distilling alcohol from a simple mash of garbage has given garbage-collecting a new dignity.

Mr. Morrow starts off his campaign, in his opening speech at Newark, with an idea which he is to propound many times. Of this idea, the *World* writes as follows: "The most notable quality of Mr. Morrow's first campaign speech was his ability to say what every intelligent person knows and no politician ever dares to utter. . . . It is all obviously true. In civilized society no one questions it. Yet how many candidates for office would admit it? . . . This is the language of intelligence. It is not, unhappily, the conventional language of politics. Indeed it seems to be Mr. Morrow's mission in American public life to demonstrate that to be simple, sincere, reasonable is not only pleasanter but is better politics than to be devious, calculating and strategical." What is this sincere, intelligent and non-political idea which moves the *World* to such admiration? Simply the conception that the nation's prosperity is not dependent on the accession to power of any particular political party. Now, it may be true that Mr. Morrow is neither devious, calculating nor strategical in making this particular statement at this particular time, but for us to be perfectly sure of this, we really ought to have heard him make it at a time when the Republicans were in and prosperity was booming or at a time when the Democrats were in and the country was going to the dogs.

For the rest, Mr. Morrow's speeches have been strikingly noncommittal and uninteresting. He has praised Mr. Hoover as a President and spoken with pride of the Naval Treaty, the product of "President Hoover's initiative and driving force," which has "eliminated, for the first time in the history of the world, competition in all classes of naval armament among the three leading naval nations of the world." Though he does not attribute the prosperity which we are supposed to have enjoyed under Coolidge to the beneficent influence of the Republican party, he is ready to accept the myth that such a distribution of wealth took place as piously as Senator Fess does: "A period of almost unparalleled prosperity began in 1923, a period in which the standard of living of the great majority of our people in all parts of the country was raised." But according to the calculations of the National Bureau of Economic Research, of the people gainfully employed in the United States in 1918, 85.9 per cent made less than $2,000 a year and 72 per cent made less than $1,500. So, in spite of the 20 per cent increase in income per person, it was still true, even at the peak of this period, that perhaps two thirds of the families in America were very badly off indeed, while a few of the rest were enormously rich. Mr. Morrow's was one of the ones that were rich, and Mr. Morrow is still a millionaire.

Mr. Morrow does admit, however, that an economic crisis now exists. He has a good deal to say about this and always the same thing. His message to the people of New Jersey on this subject is essentially the same as that recently sent out by the International Association of Lions' Clubs, who have been urging people to set aside the week of October 19 as Business Confidence Week. In his speeches, Mr. Morrow tells people that they have got to have confidence and that confidence will pull them through. He tells them that "every employer who has faith is doing something to end the depression" and that labor, by "avoiding strikes," can accomplish something, too. He is far from sure, as a matter of fact, that a little depression isn't a good thing: "There is something about too much prosperity that ruins the fiber of the people. The men and women that built this country, that founded it, were people that were reared in adversity." In the cold weather, it is reassuring to remind oneself that the men in the breadlines, the men and women beggars in the streets, and the children dependent on them, are all having their fiber hardened.

At Trenton, Mr. Morrow tells the people that "the resources of the United States are not going to help Trenton out of its difficulties. It will be accomplished by its people who have the courage of the men who built the city and by its industrial leaders who maintain their organizations until the turn comes." Well, it must have required at least dogged will to produce a city like Trenton, one of the most unrelievedly dreary of our major industrial towns—to choke up so many streets with factories and to make people work for you in them.

At any rate, Dwight Morrow is all for Trenton—and he is all for Asbury Park. He tells the Asbury Parkers that they have believed in their city of Asbury Park, that they have come there and worked and built it up because they did believe in it, and that they must now apply that mountain-mov-

ing belief to the United States as a whole. Now, it is true
that Asbury Park may be enjoyed, but what precisely does it
mean to believe in it? It is true that a certain number of people must have hoped to make a living out of the big Asbury
Park summer hotels, the boarding houses, the shore-dinner
restaurants, the merry-go-rounds, the roller coasters, the shooting galleries, the rubber surf-balls, the conch shells with pin-
cushions in them, the salt-water-taffy twisters and the hot-
buttered-popcorn machines, as other people have hoped to
make money out of the pottery factories of Trenton. But it
is hard to conceive of either as a community that can be
believed in by a statesmanlike imagination, and as soon as
you feel this difficulty about believing in Asbury Park or
Trenton, a belief which is evidently the first step in attaining
to a larger and higher belief in the United States as a whole,
you find yourself led to doubt whether the kind of faith in
the United States which Mr. Morrow desires to promote may
not be open to the same sort of objections as a belief in Asbury Park or Trenton.

Mr. Morrow is obviously an honest and well-intentioned
man. He seems both sincere and naïve, and—unlike most
politicians, to be sure—undoubtedly means every word he
says. And it is true that he is tactful and ingenious, that he
possesses great powers of concentration, that he is an admirable arbitrator, if arbitration is what you desire and you don't
care about the issues raised. He arbitrated between Church
and State, and between Mexican and American, as our "good
will ambassador" to Mexico. He did good work on the New
Jersey Prison Commission, he disentangled the Allied shipping during the War, and he presided, we have heard, ably
over the aviation inquiry. But Mr. Morrow, though no longer
a Morgan partner, has still the point of view of one.

As you approach Krueger Hall in Newark, where Mr.
Morrow is opening his campaign, you hear a gigantic mechanical voice, as bleak and unappealing as the Newark
streets, which does not sound in the least like a man talking
to other men but has the same impersonality as a factory
whistle. Even when you have gone inside and caught a
glimpse of the little man in eyeglasses almost hidden behind

the microphone, his earnest gestures and the movement of his lips still seem entirely unconnected with the great loud and hollow voice declaiming from the amplifiers on either side of the proscenium arch. What it declaims is a dull political speech, as padded and banal as any, and relying as much as any on meaningless catchwords and exhortations.

Dwight Morrow is a sound old-fashioned American. The son of a schoolmaster, brought up in the traditional plain living and high thinking, he has made his way to millions by the traditional American virtues of industry, shrewdness and thrift. But his ideas about the present economic chaos do not, apparently, transcend the conviction that there is still an opportunity in America for everybody to do as he has done and that, if everybody did, we should soon come round. And the giant ventriloquial voice which emanates from the nice little man is the voice of American capitalism.

POLITICAL HEADQUARTERS

THE HEADQUARTERS of the Republican Party are in an office building on Madison Avenue; they consist of an empty set of rooms separated from one another by ground-glass partitions. A few men in business suits are standing glumly around a radio, which is announcing the victory of the Democrats. A few not very smartly dressed girls with glasses and an anxious benumbed look are sitting along the wall in chairs; but most of the chairs are empty. Now and then somebody picks up a paper. Outside, the glass partitions are placarded with small posters of Tuttle's bull-terrier snout and Ruth Pratt's bright and practical smile.

————

The Democratic headquarters, on the other hand, are on the fourth floor of the Biltmore Hotel. Bright hotel corridors and rooms, done in white and light green; space to move in, white shirt-fronts, gaiety—pretty, smart and slender women in long evening gowns, young men full of kindness and charm, young men with droll turns of humor, who already hold public office and who tonight are getting elected to higher office; genial elderly men with gold spectacles, silver hair and pink, smooth, smiling faces. Al Smith in a beautifully tailored dress suit, short, pear-shaped, solid and sound, the most interesting Tammany face there. Plates with chicken croquettes and French peas left around on the desks and tables; bottles quietly and jovially slipped from hand to hand. The latest green edition of the *Graphic* provided in lavish piles, with Franklin Roosevelt's forcible-feeble gentlemanly face on the front page in thick black ink. A general atmosphere of warmth and good fellowship, like that of a college alumni banquet. Everybody knows everybody else and everybody is very happy; everybody feels his own dignity and importance in an entirely unaffected way. Some of the men have weak or common faces, but they are all pretty well turned out. No offices, no business apparatus, none of the harsh and dreary machinery of campaigning: the whole thing is a social occasion and an extremely amiable one. The doors are guarded by two big cops.

————

At the offices of *The New Leader* on East Fifteenth Street, the Socialists, who this year had had hopes, have already heard the worst. German Jews and their wives, ironic, respectable and serious-minded, mostly middle-aged, whose grandfathers no doubt came over in '48, crowd into a small room containing a French Socialist poster which represents Ramsay MacDonald weighing cruisers in the role of an heroic champion of peace, and an old bookcase imprisoning behind glass an old tight-packed encyclopaedia. They are listening in silence to Norman Thomas and Heywood Broun, who comment wittily and bitterly on the election. Norman Thomas is standing up and Heywood Broun is sitting down. It is evident that both have worked hard and taken the campaign very seriously. They would be incongruous figures in either of the headquarters uptown, and in a sense they are incongruous figures here: they are probably the only two non-Jewish middle-class intellectuals in New York who have gone out onto the platforms and the streets to protest against the economic system. Thomas, slightly tarnished from campaigning but with sparkling gun-metal eyes, cracks out machine-gun ridicule of his opponents; and as one listens to Heywood Broun, one realizes how much rankling rebellion his easy-going manner must always have masked. Where the Democrats had peas and croquettes, the Socialists have had thick white cups of coffee, sent up from the lunchroom below and now piled on a tray on the copy desk. One man says to another: "We did the best we could without an organization."

Another says: "What can you expect? They vote for the best Jew! Sirovich is a better Jew than Panken, so they vote for Sirovich!"

———

Rexobo (King of the Hoboes) Dan O'Brien has his headquarters in the back row of a double tenement near the corner of First Avenue and Sixteenth Street. As you cross the court from one building to the other, you see above you the white cloudland of clothes hung out between the houses to dry and, cutting the court in two, the little row of enclosed water closets. Dan O'Brien and his lieutenant, Red Shannon, keep house in two small rooms, where they have a stove, a sink and two beds. There is some ham fat hung in a corner. On the stove is a potato-and-onion stew. Dan O'Brien is a little old Irishman of sixty-eight, clean-shaven, with blue-gray eyes and a pink bald dome hedged behind with a semicircle of white hair. He has an easy Irish tongue and a good deal of humor and charm, and has acquired a certain reputation as a speaker on street corners and in labor temples on such subjects as "economics, psychology and sociology." He is a veteran of Coxey's Army and is engaged at the present time in organizing another such march. He plans to lead the unemployed to Washington, "to seek an interview with President Hoover," and "to call for work and wages, or else unemployment insurance."

Mr. O'Brien, like other political leaders, is perhaps a little vague as to how his aims are to be accomplished; but he says that he hopes to be able to muster at least 50,000 men from New York and to have them join at Philadelphia similar armies from other cities all the way to the Coast. Some will bum their way—others will have transportation provided. The army is receiving financial aid, but Mr. O'Brien will not reveal from whom, except that he emphatically wants it understood that the Communists and the Soviets have nothing to do with it. The army is to march under discipline, and he hopes that, when it reaches Washington, it will be possible to maintain it there; he believes that the great mistake in the case of Coxey's Army was that its leaders allowed it to disperse too soon.

Dan O'Brien was born on a farm in Tipperary, and, since the days of Coxey's Army, he has worked in mines, factories, lumber camps and harvest fields all over the United States; he has become a master hobo and recently succeeded in making the trip from New York to San Francisco—traveling only on the fastest trains—in a record time of eight days. He has clean stubby countryman's hands, and his color is pink and clear—he is very proud of his health at sixty-eight. He is a poet and has written for the hobo magazine, printed in Cincinnati—he contributed to it a damaging review of Jim Tulley's *Beggars Of Life,* which, he says, describes the lives of "yeggs" or "gay cats" and not of honest authentic hoboes. Last winter, he was in Washington, D.C., and started the first bread line ever known there; he began with fifteen cents, and two gallons of coffee and a dozen jelly doughnuts he had bummed. The Community Chest tried to discourage him, but the restaurants and bakeries helped him out, and he was soon taking care of three hundred people a day. One great difficulty in Washington, he found, was that people did not want blacks and whites mixed together even for purposes of charity—the race feeling there, he thought, was as bad as much further south.

So far as Dan is concerned, New York is not a bad place to live: it is the cultural center of the country and that makes it interesting. He knows that for many people it must be a lunatic asylum, but a hobo doesn't worry about that—you never heard of a hobo jumping out the window: they are the most optimistic people in the world. When reminded of Josiah Flint, he says that there must have been something organically wrong with him to make him so gloomy—like Schopenhauer. Dan O'Brien does not believe in altruism, he says that no one really wants to do things for other people—everybody is selfish, but if you could only make them see that the thing to do is to systematize their selfishness so that everybody can get as much as possible of what there is and enjoy it as safely as possible! That's a very simple idea, but that's just the trouble with it, it's too simple—if it was complicated, people might get it.

Dan campaigned for La Follette, and he has had a good many offers to do work for churches and missions which would have enabled him to make a great deal of money, but he refuses to serve any causes except those which, like his present one, aim to do something for the down-and-out. He disapproves of the Salvation Army because it tries to make a distinction between the "unworthy" and the "worthy" poor. He wanted to run in the last mayoral election as the candidate of the Hoboes' Party on a platform of Freedom and Beauty, but they wouldn't allow his name on the ballot.

FOSTER AND FISH

WILLIAM Z. FOSTER, the leader of the American Communists, is facing Hamilton Fish, the chairman of the House committee appointed to investigate Communism.

Hamilton Fish is a man of immense stature, wearing a dark blue suit and a very tall stiff white collar. He has coarse features, broad shoulders and a slightly finicking manner; he looks like a Hannibal turned tailor's dummy or a blank-eyed vacuous Bashan bull. Unlike most officials investigating radicals and unlike at least one of his colleagues, Mr. Fish has excellent manners and never bullies or insults the witnesses—though one notes a perceptible difference between his manner in thanking Roger Baldwin very much for his testimony and his manner in thanking the Communists very much. He is quiet, dignified and patient, but his hands tremble violently throughout the proceedings, and he is always rubbing his forehead. A smile which is meant to imply irony plays continually about his mouth, but it suggests rather simple nervousness.

Mr. Foster is nervous, too. Half-Irish and born in Massachusetts, he seems almost excessively sensitive at the same time that he is fortified and sustained by a Yankee tenacity and hardness. He has blue eyes, a bald crown, a finely modeled brow and nose, a small mobile Irish mouth and a plebeian Irish lantern jaw. He is rather an incongruous figure in the marble chambers of the Capitol, and his peculiar kind of eloquence is a new one to congressional committee rooms. At moments he seems an American workman with a grievance against his employer, attempting to defend his rights: he looks worried and harassed, his dropped hands with curled-up fingers make constrained ineffective gestures, his voice sinks to a whisper of pathos as if he were sighing to himself his hopelessness of ever being able to communicate with his opponents. He often smiles even more self-consciously when Mr. Fish asks him a question than Mr. Fish does when he hears the answer. Yet never once in the course of the three hours' grueling does his courage or his presence of mind fail him. Though he may falter for a moment before answering, he always picks himself up and meets the question; and as soon as he meets the question, he is the dominating figure in the room.

It is the regular procedure of Communists to make use of public appearances of all kinds as pretexts for propagandist speeches. There is a story that Charles Ruthenberg, for example, when commanded on the stand by the prosecutor to answer yes or no, would invariably reply: "The workers do not expect justice from capitalist courts!" This practice has its value: it enables the Communist to cut the ground out from under the assumptions on which the charges against him are based, to substitute his own version of the case for the version of the society which is trying him. But Foster on the present occasion follows this procedure almost a little too faithfully: one sometimes feels that he is doing it on principle and that his replies would be more effective if he merely answered the questions. Furthermore, an element appears in his language which is quite alien to anything which has hitherto been characteristic of even the militant American workman—it is the idiom of Russian communism. William Z. Foster today, the hero of the steel strike of 1919, always deals in "ideologies" instead of "ideas," and he talks about "liquidating" things. "Liquidating" something means getting rid of it. In Russia, they liquidated the kulaks, they liquidated the Church; and the Soviet prosecutor has recently demanded that the traitorous engineers be liquidated—in other words, shot. The House committee may well have been puzzled by Foster's continual talk of liquidation applied to everything from the collapse of capitalism to the dispersal of a recent Communist demonstration by the Capitol police. But all this is merely the platform of radical oratory to which Foster is obliged to lift himself in order to reach a vantage point from which he can face the policemen, the fat congressmen, the marble Capitol, the eagle and shield of the Republic, the high imposing gilt and white ceiling, the wilderness of documents on the big table, the female admirers of Mr. Fish and Mr. Fish's gentlemanly manners. Once safe on the plane of his faith, he can meet his opponents with a logic, an Irish readiness and a New England conviction which contrast in a startling way with the unsureness and incompetence of the committee.

Mr. Foster, after being sworn in as an atheist, first reads in a clear emphatic voice an uncompromising statement of the Communist position—dwelling scornfully on certain words: "The Fish committee is supposed to be investigating Communist activities in the United States. It is impossible to understand Communist activities unless one knows the conditions of the working class in this country, upon which these activities are based. Today more than nine million workers are unemployed and deprived of all means of living. There is nothing left for them except the bread lines and miserable charity crumbs. Thousands upon thousands of working-class families have been thrown out of their homes because they can no longer pay their rent. Those who are still employed are having their wages slashed and are being speeded up beyond the limit of human endurance. In the streets of every large city, workers are dropping, dying and dead from starvation and exposure. Every newspaper in the country constantly reports suicides of these workers, driven to desperation by unemployment and starvation. The Communist activities are the organized protest and struggle of the masses against these conditions.

"What is the cause of this starvation, misery and hardship of the millions of workers in the United States? Is it because some great national calamity has destroyed the food, clothing and shelter available for the people? No, on the contrary. Millions of workers must go hungry because there is too much wheat. Millions of workers must go without clothes because the warehouses are full to overflowing with everything that is needed. Millions of workers must freeze because there is too much coal. This is the logic of the capitalist system which the Fish committee is protecting against the protests of the workers."

He then goes on to recite the list of outrages against the workers: Centralia, Imperial Valley, Gastonia, Danville, Atlanta—and advises the Southern members of the committee to look into conditions in their own constituencies if they wish to understand the spread of Communism among the American Negroes. He describes the condition of the farmers—"hunger, poverty, wholesale bankruptcies, disposession of hundreds of thousands, the most tremendous overproduction of wealth and the consequent ruin and starvation of those who produce it." He declares that the American Federation of Labor has arrived at such a perfect understanding with the capitalists against whom it is supposed to be a defense that it has become to all intents and purposes a professional strike-breaking organization, as well as an ally of the underworld and a breeder of racketeers, themselves an inevitable product of the capitalist system of municipal government. Nor has the present economic crisis brought merely unemployment, wage-cuts, speeding-up and starvation for the masses—it has brought us also face to face with another war: "In spite of all the fake Kellogg peace pacts, disarmament conferences, etc., the imperialist governments, especially the United States and Great Britain, are arming themselves to the teeth against one another, preparing for a new world slaughter. Almost three fourths of the government income in the United States is spent for war purposes. . . .

"One of the root causes of the present crisis of capitalism is to be found in the Versailles Treaty, the war debts and indemnities, and especially the Young Plan of enslavement of the German people. In building and supporting this whole world structure of capitalist oppression, United States imperialism has played a leading role. More and more the workers are learning that the enslavement of the people under the Versailles Treaty, the exploitation of the masses of Europe by the war debts and the Young Plan, constitute one of the chief causes for their own misery and degradation. The activities of the Communist Party in the United States are winning more and more mass support because the Communist

Party leads and organizes the fight to smash the Versailles Treaty, to wipe out the war debts and reparations and to liberate the German masses from the yoke of the Young Plan. . . .

"The preparations for imperialist war are to-day concentrated against the Soviet Union. The enormous success of the Five Year Plan of Socialist Construction in the Soviet Union has filled the hearts of our capitalist rulers with fear and panic and desperate rage. The Soviet Union is revolutionizing the working class of the entire world by its very existence, and by the contrast which it presents to the conditions of workers under capitalism. While in the United States more than nine million workers are unemployed, in the Soviet Union unemployment has been completely abolished, and there is an acute shortage of labor. While in the United States wages of the working class are being slashed by eight billion dollars, in the Soviet Union the wages of the working class are steadily inceasing and are now 67 per cent above pre-War wages. While in the United States capitalist rationalization is destroying the health of the workers and throwing ever greater numbers into the ranks of the unemployed, in the Soviet Union every stage in industrial progress is raising the living standards of the workers. While in the United States even the eight-hour day has never been established except for a few privileged groups, the average hours of labor being around forty-nine per week, and large numbers of workers slave for ten, eleven and twelve hours per day, in the Soviet Union no one works more than eight hours, and the seven-hour day has already been established for half of the industrial workers. . . .

"While in the United States every worker lives under the lash of fear of being discharged at the arbitrary will of his boss, and is spied upon at every turn, in the Soviet Union the worker is the master of his job and the workers' organizations control the factories. . . .

"The Communist Party is leading and organizing the struggle against the imperialist war and for the defense of the Soviet Union. That is why the workers are turning towards the Communist Party and that is why the Fish committee is investigating Communism with a view to finding new measures to suppress the workers and the Communist Party, as a part of the preparations for war. . . .

"The Fish committee has spent many months trying to convince the public that the Communist Party is an organization of criminal violence, with the purpose of preparing the ground for the suppression of the Communist Party. This is nothing but hypocritical nonsense. If the theories of this committee were logically carried through, the committee would have to indict on the same accusation those who died on the battlefields of the American Revolution in the struggle to free the United States from the rule of the British landlords. . . . These revolutionists of capitalism, who freed America from feudal European rule, found out that the ruling class of Britain refused independence to the colonies in spite of the overwhelming desire of the people as expressed in the provincial legislatures. When the British ruling class met these demands for independence with armed force, these early revolutionists found that government is not a matter of majority votes, but the organized power which does not give way to the desires of the majority but only to a greater power. It was then that they decided that it was 'their right,' that it was 'their duty, to throw off such government and to provide new guards for their future security.'

"American history gives us another example of the same principle when, with the election of Lincoln, the overwhelming majority voted out of power in the United States government the Southern slaveholders, and those slaveholders took up arms to maintain their particular system of exploitation against the will of the majority. Only an armed struggle succeeded in eliminating the institution of chattel slavery. The same law of history will operate in the transition from capitalism to socialism. The bloody path that capitalism is traveling today over the lives of the workers is conclusive proof that when the workers, who are the majority, will become convinced by their own experience of the necessity of changing the capitalist order based upon private property and the enrichment of the few, into a society based upon common ownership of the means of production and the well-being of the masses, then the capitalists will use their last gun and their last dollar in defense of the only constitutional principle they ever really held sacred—that is, the unrestricted right to make profit out of the misery of the masses. . . . The Communist Party is preparing the working class for that day. . . . The Communist Party prepares the working class to carry out in the proletarian revolution that principle announced by the colonial revolutionists in the Declaration of Independence: 'it is the right, it is the duty,' of the working masses to throw off such government and to provide new guards for their future security. The only possible guard for the future security of the working class is the dictatorship of the proletariat and the establishment of a Soviet government."

When Foster has finished reading, the members of the committee cross-examine him—if one can apply the word cross-examination to an inquiry so aimless and diffuse. Representative Bachmann of West Virginia is the first to take the witness. Representative Bachmann of West Virginia is by way of being the caricaturist's ideal of the lower order of congressmen: he is pot-gutted and greasy-looking, with small black pig-eyes and a long pointed nose. He talks with a cigar in his mouth tilted up at a self-confident angle, and he questions Mr. Foster with a persistent and almost pathetic stupidity which he tries to conceal with a great air of cunning. He begins by asking whether Mr. Foster has prepared his statement himself. Mr. Foster says that he did. Representative Bachmann wants to know where he got his information to the effect that the Negroes are "disfranchised" in West Virginia—Representative Bachmann asserts that the Negroes in West Virginia have the franchise. Mr. Foster replies to this that they don't get to vote just the same, and adds that they are discriminated against by a general policy of Jim Crowism. Representative Bachmann denies this and says that there is a statute against it. Nonetheless, Mr. Foster insists, nobody pays attention to the statute—and, as a matter of fact, both whites and blacks in the South have been reduced to a condition of peonage—and particularly in West Virginia.

Representative Bachmann shifts to a different line of attack and accuses Mr. Foster of trying to take advantage of the unemployment situation to mislead the unemployed. Mr. Foster replies that, on the contrary, it is the capitalists who take advantage of the workers. Representative Bachmann wants to know how Mr. Foster proposes to prevent unemployment. "By socialism," says Mr. Foster. "So," says the Representative, "you would increase unemployment by insurance?" "I said relieve it, not increase it," says Foster. Representative Bachmann intimates that if the unemployed got insurance, they would never do any work at all. Then he shifts his ground again and asks sarcastically where the witness got his unemployment figures. Mr. Foster cites Dr. Steuart of the Census Bureau, who put the unemployed at 9,000,000—reminding Representative Bachmann that the Bureau was under suspicion of having falsified its earlier and lower estimates; the statement of the American Federation of Labor, which put the figure at 4,900,000, not counting office workers, agricultural workers and part-time workers that probably total another 4,000,000; and Ramsay MacDonald, who has said that if unemployment in the United States were estimated in the same way as in England, it would amount to from 10 to 12,000,000.

Mr. Bachmann makes no reply, but with a shrewd, humorous, skeptical look, changes the subject again: How many Communists are there in the United States? Ten to twelve thousand dues-paying members of the party.—And how many of these are foreigners? (Bringing out that many Communists are foreign-born is of course one of Mr. Bachmann's ways of discrediting them—though his own first name is Carl, and his mother's maiden name is given in *Who's Who* as Neuhardt.) About the same proportion as in American labor as a whole—from 60 to 70 per cent.—And how many of these are aliens? Foster doesn't know, but says that most of them are naturalized—the party always encourages its members to take out naturalization papers in order that they may vote—in the last election 75,000 people voted the Communist ticket.—How many Communist sympathizers are there—as many as 2,000,000?—Foster says that this question does not make sense, but that he regards the whole American working class as potentially Communist.—How many of the Communists are Negroes? About 10 per cent.—There ensues a long series of questions intended to elicit statistics as to the number of Communist votes in the various state elections, the membership of the Communist Trade Union Unity League, etc. Foster says that he has not brought these figures, but that he will gladly supply them to the committee.—Representative Bachmann, however, goes on and on asking his questions, written out on a sheet of paper, with his air of invincible slyness—receiving in every case the same reply from Foster: that he didn't bring the figures with him, but will gladly see that the committee gets them—he intimates that it would not have been difficult for them to have got this information themselves.

And indeed one of the most striking features of this congressional group which is supposed to have been investigating the Communists for six months is its apparent ignorance of everything connected with Communism. They do not seem to know even so much about Russia as one would suppose any ordinary newspaper-reader could hardly have helped picking up. They do not know what the Third International is, and have to have Foster explain it to them, and then they get very much mixed up when Foster goes on to refer to it as the Communist International—pounce on him as if he were trying to put something over on them by substituting one organization for another or as if he had let the cat out of the bag by admitting that the Third International had some connection with Communism. The committee does not seem even to have taken the trouble to provide itself with the Communist publications, sold openly on newsstands and in bookstores, in which they could have found the answers to most of their insidious questions. Mr. Fish even goes so far as to inquire whether the Communist newspaper, *The Daily Worker*, is published every day. And they not only ask Foster repeatedly what he understands by Communism, a question perhaps defensible—but want to know, also, what he means by capitalism, a word which seems honestly to puzzle them.

Representative Nelson of Maine takes up the inquiry after Representative Bachmann. He is a portly man with a white

waistcoat and a gay red carnation in his buttonhole. He asks
Mr. Foster whether he knows how many men there are in
the Red Army. Foster says he doesn't remember. Mr. Nelson
next severely demands how many men there are in the American Army. Mr. Foster, fresh from Bachmann's questionnaire,
replies that he has forgotten, but will gladly furnish the committee with this information, too. What Mr. Nelson is evidently getting at is that there are enough men in the Red
Army to make trifling with Russia dangerous. Mr. Nelson
goes on to inquire why the Communists should object to the
registration of aliens. Because, Mr. Foster says, it makes it
possible for the employers to blacklist them.—But the registration would be made by the federal government. The employers haven't access to the figures. The federal government has always known very well how to coöperate with the
local governments, and the local governments have always
known how to coöperate with the employers.—Does Foster
mean to say that the federal government will abet the local
governments in using the blacklist against alien workers?
The local governments have certainly been ready to coöperate with the federal government as represented by the Fish
committee, everywhere the Fish committee has gone, to help
it to check up on the activities of the workers.—Yet Mr. Nelson shows more decency and sense than any of the other
members of the committee and seems to some extent at odds
with the rest of them: he takes up little time himself, and he
makes several attempts to cut short the more obviously futile
maneuvers of the others—at one point he announces rather
sulkily that he objects, and has "objected from the beginning,
to these questions about the personal lives of the witnesses."

Mr. Fish follows Mr. Nelson. Mr. Fish has certain simple
objectives in view, based upon simple and fixed ideas. And
it is, in consequence, no part of his purpose to find out what
Mr. Foster's ideas are or why he thinks as he does—his sole
aim is to induce Mr. Foster to confirm his own, Fish's, pre-
conceptions. And in spite of his prolonged researches, it
seems plain that he has never yet succeeded in finding out
what Communism is. Mr. Fish has been accused of playing
to the gallery in order to advance political ambitions, but it is

evidently true that he is also an idealist. There is a tradition of public service in his family—his great-grandfather was a lieutenant-colonel in the army of the Revolution, his grandfather was Secretary of State under Grant, his uncle was ambassador to Belgium, and his father congressman from New York—and there can be no question that he differs essentially from the ordinary politician in honestly supposing himself to be defending the principles of the Republic. But his conception of the Republic at the present time derives rather from family tradition than from a grasp of the facts about it. And in consequence he never seems really to know what Foster is talking about. When Foster's replies fail to correspond with Mr. Fish's romantic notions, he patiently bides his time and presently asks the same question again.

Will Mr. Foster state the aims of the Communist Party? To organize the workers to defend their interests under the capitalist system and eventually to abolish the capitalist system and establish a workers' government.—Does this mean the confiscation of private property? It means the confiscation of the basic industries, the communization of the essentials of life—of private possessions, no.*—What is your attitude towards religion? I believe that religion is the opium of the people—as Karl Marx said.—Mr. Fish at this point tries to make the most of the anti-religious aspect of communism, and Foster lets him have the works; when Fish asks whether it is possible to belong to a church and be a Communist at the same time, Foster answers that this is possible, but that if a person doesn't cease to be religious very soon after joining the Communist Party, he will probably be a very poor Communist; and when Mr. Fish inquires whether a member of the Party can be married in church, Foster answers, that in his opinion any member of the Party who marries in church will be of little value to the Party. He would probably make a better impression on the committee if he sidestepped this religious question, but, on enemy ground though he is, he is

---

* Reported in the New York *Times* as follows: ". . . of private possessions *now*." This is only one instance of several in which the *Times* misrepresented Foster in such a way as to make him appear to have said the opposite of what he did say.

aware of the awful eye of the Third International upon him—itself a new secular church which rivals the sacred ones.

"Are the Communists opposed to our republican form of government?" "Surely: our government is controlled by those who own the industries. Gerard told the truth the other day when he gave his list of the men who rule the country." "Do the Communists in the United States take orders from the Third International?" "*Do the Communists in the United States take orders from the Third International?*" scornfully repeating the question. "That shows how far the capitalists are from the workers! The Communists in the United States *work out policies* with the Third International!" "Do you advocate a Soviet government in the United States?" "Capitalism must inevitably break down and be superseded." "Do the Communists regard the Soviet flag as their flag?" "The workers of the world have only one flag—the red flag." "Do you look forward to a Socialist revolution in the United States?" "I know that the capitalist system is bankrupt! You look all over the world and you see it in a state of collapse!" Mr. Fish returns again and again to the question of allegiance to Russia —not harshly, but with an air of polite William Gillette comedy: "And so you owe allegiance—er—to Russia—to the Soviet Republic?" But Mr. Foster who has been trying to explain the difference between the Third International and the Soviet government, simply refers him to the record, and Mr. Fish, still, one supposes, appalled by a vision of doom, in which he sees W. Z. Foster betraying the United States to an imperialistic Moscow and large estates on the Hudson ruthlessly expropriated, finally gives up the witness to Mr. Eslick of Tennessee.

Mr. Eslick's examination is brief but very noble. Mr. Eslick is rather an old gentleman: he wears an old-fashioned open congressional collar and a black ante-bellum bow tie, and he has been sitting all through the hearing with his arms hanging down beside his chair and his mouth gaping open as if he suffered from some difficulty of breathing or as if the muscles of his jaw were too weak to keep it closed. But when it devolves upon him to take up the inquiry, he is not found lacking in dignity: he demands in the round accents of Southern oratory whether the witness is advocating the overthrow of the government by "force *and* violence?" The controlling class, says Mr. Foster, never give up without a struggle.—And you owe loyalty not to your country but to Russia? I owe loyalty to the workers of the world. Russia is not the world. Mr. Eslick goes on immediately to the matter which evidently touches him most deeply—Foster's aspersions on the fair Southland: he takes exception to Mr. Foster's reflections on the administration of justice in Tennessee. Mr. Foster reminds Mr. Eslick that there have been a great many lynchings in Tennessee. We lynch, says Mr. Eslick magnificently, but we lynch the white man as well as the black—for *one* offense, we lynch a man, it doesn't make any difference whether he's white or black! Yes, says Mr. Foster, about a thousand blacks to one white.—So you make no distinction between the races? says Mr. Eslick. None, says Mr. Foster.—You believe in white people and black people marrying? I believe in people marrying whoever they want to.

Finally, the question of Russian gold is agitated, and Mr. Foster announces with some heat that, in spite of certain statements by Matthew Woll and others, the Communists in the United States are not lavishly endowed by Russia, that their salaries, when they get any, are paid out of contributions by the workers, and that he himself gets only twenty dollars a week—when times are hard, as at present, only ten dollars.

But though Foster can take a certain satisfaction in revealing that the American Communists are not lavishly subsidized, he evidently does not find it easy to deny that he owes anything to Russia. He several times seems on the verge of saying that he does not get a penny from Moscow, but always stops before he finishes his sentence and becomes involved in general explanations. "If you'd rather not answer," says Nelson, "you needn't. We want to be fair to you—" Foster here insists on making a speech of the Ruthenberg type. They do *not* want to be fair to him, he declares, and he doesn't expect them to be fair. He hasn't the slightest expectation of honesty and fairness on the part of representatives of a capitalist government towards the representatives of the workers.

—Won't he answer the question first? suggests Fish. "I'll answer the question," replies Foster. "You'll get it in the record plenty! But I want to say first that we have no expectation, in coming here, that you'll show us honesty and fairness," etc. At last, he comes back to the question and finally succeeds in saying, a little feebly, "No: I don't get a cent from Russia"—though the American Communist Party is certainly assisted by the Communist International, which is for the most part necessarily financed by Russia, and it must be that he is here sophistically taking advantage of some special feature of his present situation to evade a confession of Russian pay. As American as the lumber camps, trainyards and factories in which he spent his young-manhood and convinced with great difficulty, eight years ago, on the occasion of a visit to Russia, that he ought to subordinate himself to a movement of non-American origin, it is as if he were reluctant to admit this.

"That's all. Thank you very much."—A comrade congratulates him as he returns to his chair.

Israel Amter follows Foster. He is a dark, intense and fine-looking Jew, who answers the questions promptly, good-humoredly and firmly, with none of the querulousness or nervousness of Foster. Bill Foster is typically an organizer, but Amter is a sort of priest. He was formerly a professional violinist and has intelligent liquid black eyes. One becomes aware, as one watches him, even more than in Foster's case, that the Communists are at once the apostles of a religion and the captains of an army, sworn to industry, endurance and discipline, renouncing the common satisfactions of the society in which they live in order to fight for a conviction which runs counter to the values of that society and which can never win them anything but poverty, as it is unlikely to lead them anywhere but to jail. The Fish committee is far, to be sure, from representing our legislature at its best; but in the presence of the Communists today, these members of our government seem lacking in either moral force or intellectual dignity.

Fish asks about the Communists in the Poughkeepsie district, where Amter is at present operating—adding, "I'm par-

ticularly interested, because that's my district." "I'll take care
of it for you!" says Amter, with a quick humorous smile.
Roger Baldwin of the Civil Liberties Union is now summoned to the witness chair. One realizes, seeing him here,
what an anomalous and isolated figure he is, and what a
strain his singular career must cost him. Describing himself
as an anarchist and devoting his life to the defense of free
speech, he finds himself today between the Fish committee,
most of them men of his own class and tradition, who are
intent on doing everything in their power to abolish American civil liberties, and the Communists, from whom he is also
estranged by reason of his having lately made difficulties—
after the Gastonia prisoners jumped their bail—about putting
up any more bail for Communists. The Communists have
communism behind them, the committee have the American
Government; but Baldwin has only his truculent independence and his tense insistent will: he is a furious individualist,
defending the nonconformities of others—that is, what they
have most in common with himself. They ask him whether
he believes in God. "Not the kind of God," he replies, with
a wry defiant smile, "who punishes you if you don't tell the
truth!" So he "affirms" instead of swearing, and then, before
being questioned, insists upon reading to the committee, with
his screwed-up defiant smile, an indignant and forthright
statement double-damning them to their faces. They ask him
whether he approves of allowing people to propose overthrow-
ing the government by violence, and he answers that he does.
Does he approve of allowing people to advocate murder. Murder in general yes, but not murdering a particular person—
there is a law against that. "So you are in favor of allowing
people to advocate violence and murder?" "Certainly: it's the
old Hyde Park principle. If people are allowed to talk, they're
less likely to act."

In the midst of Mr. Baldwin's denunciation, Mr. Bachmann has insisted on interrupting and has protested that *he*
at least has not "prejudged the evidence," as Mr. Baldwin has
accused them of doing, "by announcing their remedies before
they have heard the testimony"; that he wants Mr. Baldwin
to understand that he has no personal feeling in the matter,

that he is sitting on the committee merely because he has been appointed to.

Last of all, one of the most untrustworthy-looking characters who have surely ever been called upon to testify—a pale-eyed, shifty-eyed, shaved-headed man, represented as an honest Russian farmer sent to prison for criticizing the Soviets —describes through an interpreter the horrors of forced labor in a Russian lumber camp.* This perceptibly makes them feel better. Mr. Fish for the first time today is able to drop his ironic smile.

The day after tomorrow will be Hamilton Fish's birthday, and on the big, shiny, mahogany table in the anteroom of the Foreign Affairs Committee there is already a whole florist's display of chrysanthemums in ornamental baskets, the tributes of the Union Club and other admirers.

Foster, Amter and a man from the *Daily Worker* are overtaken on their way out of the Capitol by the chief of the Capitol guard, an old, respectable and earnest policeman with gold spectacles and a square white mustache, who tells them that the building is closed and severely compels them to follow his escort down through Statuary Hall past the founders and heroes of the Republic, frozen in their marble waxworks, till he has seen them out at one of the underneath doors. They take a taxi together to the station and get the next train back to New York.

1957. The career of William Z. Foster has actually been a tragedy. As the leader of the great steel strike of 1919—about which he published a book—he seemed that rare thing in the United States: an effective and independent labor leader with a radical social philosophy. He went to Soviet Russia in the

---

* This represents a kind of thing that is to be sedulously avoided by honest reporters. On the strength of a physical impression and solely out of a sympathy toward the Soviet Union, about which at first hand I knew nothing, I assumed that this man was lying. His experience may well have intimidated him and turned his face gray, and he may well have been made uneasy by the presence of the American Communists. I leave my report of the incident as an example of the capacity of partisanship to fabricate favorable evidence.

early twenties and was there converted to Communism. Someone who was with him at the time has told me that this was accomplished only with the greatest difficulty: the representatives of the Party had had to struggle with him day after day. The instincts that must have prompted his resistance proved to be all too correct, for he has never since that time been anything but an obedient tool of the Kremlin. Though he had formerly been opposed to the ruinous policy of "dual unionism," he was now forced by the Communists to adopt it. In 1929, when Jay Lovestone had been elected secretary of the American party, this vote was overruled by Stalin, who did not approve Lovestone's policies, and Foster was made secretary instead. When Foster himself, however, showed signs of thinking for himself, he was replaced by Earl Browder as secretary and relegated to the role of "chairman." Browder, in turn, was dismissed in 1945, but Foster, now an invalid, is, at seventy-five, still chairman of the American party. As I write, he is justifying the Soviet suppression of the revolt against the Russians in Hungary on the ground that it is a "grim necessity" in view of "the acute threat of Fascism." The systematic coercion of the working class by a movement intended to liberate it, which has been governing in its name, is one of the great ironies of history. This has ended, in East Germany, Poland and Hungary, with the armed putting-down of strikes, demonstrations and workers' rebellions sometimes more merciless than anything done by the company police in our steel towns in the early years of the century. Then it was "the grim necessity of combating the menace of anarchy."

ALADDIN'S LECTURE PALACE

THE NEW SCHOOL for Social Research has just opened a new building on West Twelfth Street. It is a striking specimen of "functional" architecture. Bulging above the sidewalk, it makes a grim corrugated aggressive mask: square jaw set with stripes of clenched teeth that grin from ear to ear, and, above them, stripes of compound eyes. Between the old brick houses on either side, the New School has a look of bumptiousness, but it is a little too small to be bumptious.

The first floor of the New School is a theater: a gray oval igloo-like cave, with a vault of concentric ovals, from which a subdued lighting glows. On the floors above it are lecture rooms, blank and bare like offices or lofts, but the plain whites and grays of walls and floors are prettily varied with brighter tints—greens, buffs, blues, lemon-yellows, burnt oranges and chocolate-browns. The rooms have rows of silver-gray seats, continuous windows with rectangular panes, and, overhead, long straight boxes of lights dulled whitely by ground glass. There is also a circular picture gallery, with photographs of the New School, which make the ceilings look like segments of a dynamo and the façade like a factory front; and a library in white, black, gray, canary-yellow, hydrangea-purple and robin's-egg blue—with long reading tables like factory benches, gray chairs with the backs tilted forward as if to keep the readers studying, and a flat-topped triangular bookcase, containing books recommended by the lecturers, the two upper sides of the triangle formed by narrow black-railed factory staircases that come together above a clock. The whole place is a curious mixture of severity and frivolity, with frivolity rather predominating. It is a house for Harlequin turned industrial-adaptationist.

The aim of this functional architecture, which is becoming quite fashionable nowadays, is to make some distinguished use of the lines and shapes of office buildings and workshops in designing—without imitating traditional styles and without adventitious ornament—theaters, apartments and houses which shall be at the same time very comfortable. This may sound like a sensible idea when we remember, for example, the mansions built on Fifth Avenue by the Vanderbilts, which imitated French châteaux but turned out to resemble the Tombs. Yet there seems to be an inescapable fallacy at the bottom of the "functional" idea as applied to such a building as the New School. Industry and business have impoverished life. Institutions like the New School are supposed to enrich it. How can you arrive at enrichment by imitating that which is poor? And, on the other hand, these self-conscious efforts seem bound to miss such beauties as are possible for frankly commercial buildings: there is nothing in the New School, for example, so fine as the stripped vistas of glass partitions on certain floors of the Federal Reserve Bank—complex cages, demountable at need for any redistribution of space, in which, as in a non-reflecting hall of mirrors, the panes rule off the gray steel, the white ceilings and the creamy walls as an infinity of thin-lined rectangles like the compartments of the financial charts. The new architecture is quite correct in confessing the lack of meaning for man in the modern world of the more ornate or gracious styles; but the best it can do with its models provides a dismaying revelation of our helplessness under the industrial system. We have nothing left but bareness and straightness, and we are obliged to do what we can with it, even when we are making an effort to appeal to the aesthetic sense and to stimulate the imagination. When we try to doll it up a little, the result is what we get in the New School. Joseph Urban, the architect of the New School, is a brilliant theatrical designer—at least as far as the Ziegfeld Follies go. But when he tries to produce a functional lecture building, he gives us merely Ziegfeld settings which charmingly mimic offices and factories and among which we keep expecting to see bevies of pretty girls in blue, yellow and cinnamon dresses which will match the walls and the ceilings.

The most satisfactory features of the New School are the frescoes by Thomas Benton and the Mexican, José Clemente Orozco. Except for the price·of the materials, they were contributed by the artists free.

Benton's palette seems here, as so often, raw and rather ugly. The four sides of the room which he has decorated are congeries of squirming and striving shapes, as varied as a fisherman's haul: black niggers, their long arms knobbed with muscles; brawny burlesque girls shaking spotlighted fannies; lumberjacks, among straight gray sawn trunks, wielding gigantic green saws; scrawny city women with faces turned green by the light of a sentimental movie—a whole American panorama, the human bodies done in glaring blues, greens and pinks, and made to stand out in a hard and round, an almost stereoptican relief, amid the toils of a mechanical tackle of cranes, blast furnaces, airplanes, gas tanks, tractors, acetylene blowtorches, subway trains and automatic drills. The groups, thus packed in, partly merge but are partly fenced off from each other by an irregular silver framing which runs in broken lengths of arcs and angles like the tin ribbon you have to pry off from around the tops of caviar or tongue in glass. At the end of the room, and its culmination, is one of Benton's violent phallic locomotives, with headlong black body and stiff-standing smoke.

These pictures are tangled and jarring; they strain like the life that they represent, and their forms can never seem to rise from a matrix that is heavy and hard nor their color distil itself from a medium that is thick and dingy. Yet they are products of that life and true images.

The Orozco frescoes in a larger room are less crowded and more spacious. On one wall, Gandhi, sitting cross-legged in his glasses and white loincloth, confronts, with a pained, sidelong insect gaze, the bayonets and the hog-snouted gas masks; and on the opposite wall, the bald head of Lenin, with narrowed eyes and contemptuous nostrils, dominates the bayonets of the Red Guard and the solid embattled front of

Mongolians, Caucasians, Semites and blacks, with the hammers of the Soviets in their hands. All these walls are in clay-reds and earth-browns, against which the bayonets show livid and answer to the colorless head of Lenin. On the same wall with him, Felipe Carillo Puerto, the assassinated Socialist governor of Yucatan, rises in a prosaic gray business suit beside a livid truncated pyramid, while below him sit the blue-shawled Indian women, descendants of the Mayans, and the men, carrying guns, in sombreros and dark red cloaks; and on the opposite wall, livid naked slaves, in chains and iron collars, cower beneath a big Negro with a knife, while, on another plane above them, the yellow-faced white-collar workers choke in similar shackles, eyes rolled up and necks loose like hanged men. At one end of the hall, the races of the world, represented by varied types, from the fine-profiled silver-haired French philosopher to the amorphous and blue-brown, parrot-nosed African, sit about a square yellow table, on which lies an open book. On the front wall, two Mexican workers, with their picks over their shoulders, are coming home to their women and children, a big fire blazing on the hearth and plenty of food and some books on the table. There is a sickle over one of the doors, but where one looks for the hammer over the other, one finds that the space is blank, then discovers that the artist has got it in just outside, on the landing where workers are forging the rainbow.

These frescoes are broad and primitive, yet they are somehow overtense and disturbing. Among them we feel ourselves arrested at a moment of anxious expectation, of antagonisms protracted and taut, of conflicts too long waiting settlement. For all the earthiness and crudeness of the shapes, the morbidity of some vigil is upon them. The flat newspaper whites make a discord with the strong baked reds and browns. Even the members of the council of the races, who are supposed to be met in concord, seem sullen and taciturn: each stares into the air before him—as even the Mexican women, welcoming their men, look troubled.

The New School for Social Research was founded in 1919 by Thorstein Veblen, James Harvey Robinson and Charles

A. Beard, but Veblen is dead, and it is a long time now since the others have had anything to do with it. Nor has it ever undertaken any social research. It has become merely one of the organs of the "adult education" movement. This "adult education" in the case of the New School means simply miscellaneous lectures. At the New School, you can hear lectures on Dalcroze Eurythmics, The Intellectual Effects of Industrialism, The Abnormal Mind, Building a Modern Creed, The Advantages and Disadvantages of Capitalism, Behavior Problems in Children, Marx's Sociological Economics, Movies and Talkies, Recent Trends in Criminal Justice, Navalism and Security, Ethnology and Psychoanalysis, Modern Creative Prints, The Fugue Form from 1500 to 1750, The Ideal Element in Law, and Native Players on Their Own Instruments.

Some of these courses are given by very able and brilliant people, and the New School has made it possible—if one prefers going to lectures to reading books—to hear men who would probably not otherwise get a platform to expound their ideas. But the "adults" at the New School are being "educated" only to the extent to which it is possible to educate people by having them listen to lectures. Some of the branches of the "adult education" movement aim at workers' education, but the lectures at the New School are $1.50 apiece, $15 for a course of twelve, and comparatively few workers will be able to benefit by them, even to learn about Recent Trends in Criminal Justice or The Advantages and Disadvantages of Capitalism.

THE BANK OF UNITED STATES

A COMMITTEE representing the small depositors of the Bank of United States, which has recently failed, have come down to City Hall to see Mayor Walker. There are among the depositors about 35,000 people with savings averaging $400 who cannot afford the expenses of the Stockholders' and Depositors' Association organized to bring suit against the bank. The Mayor was to have received the committee at two-thirty. At three it is announced from his office that he won't be back till four-thirty, but that his assistant, Mr. Kerrigan, will see them. They are shown into a large colonial room, with fine high windows looking out on City Hall Park. White woodwork, slightly shabby blue hangings, festive glass chandeliers, portraits of the mayors of New York and the Marquis de Lafayette, and a big furled American flag stood up in a corner. The visitors continue to wait: they are mostly dark, stocky little Jews; they keep their overcoats on and move uneasily around the room, getting up and sitting down in the chairs and forming and reforming in little groups.

Finally Mr. Kerrigan comes in. He is a tall man with well-brushed light brown hair, a soft-fleshed pasty city face, a light brown suit and well-polished brown shoes. Mr. Kerrigan is a sort of understudy to Mayor Walker, and he has acquired the Mayor's mannerisms and methods. While M. D. Littman, the spokesman for the committee, is reading his statement to Mr. Kerrigan, the latter is continually raising his eyebrows, cocking his head to one side and looking down on M. D. Littman sideways with a mock-surprised almost humorous eye.

The statement read by M. D. Littman demands that the small depositors of the Bank of United States be paid first and in full; that the stockholders be taxed at the face value of their shares ($25,000,000), as the New York law provides, in case the bank funds are insufficient; that all the property of the stockholders and bank directors be immediately attached; that in the event of the bank's being unable to pay off the small depositors, the city or state float a loan for this purpose; that an immediate investigation be started into the criminal actions of the bank directors and officers, and that those found guilty of speculation with bank funds be prosecuted; that the small depositors be provided with halls for their meetings; and that a stop be put to the eviction of tenants who are out of work and who have lost their savings in the bank.

M. D. Littman goes on to request that the city arrange to have more branches opened for the depositors, who, as it is, are obliged to wait in line from six to eleven hours to get the loan of half their deposits at 5 per cent—the 5 per cent, it has been explained, provided out of consideration for the depositors, who will thus not be humiliated by the feeling that they are receiving "charity." In the event, however, of the money's having been deposited in trustee, it will not be given back even as a loan. M. D. Littman, who is young, self-respecting and determined, describes to Mr. Kerrigan how his wife caught cold standing in line and had to go home; how, when he himself had reached the window, they would not lend him the two hundred dollars which he had hoped to get back on the four hundred he had deposited, because he did not have his wife's signature; and how his wife has since come down with pneumonia. He also complains of the behavior of the police. He says that they took money to push people into places in the lines further forward than they belonged.

At the time of the original runs on the bank, though the police had at first tried persuasion, telling depositors they were perfectly safe and reassuringly remarking, "I only wish I had my money in that bank!"—as the hours of waiting had gone on and the crowd become impatient and indignant, the lines had been threatened by mounted cops. At the Freeman Street branch in the Bronx, on a day when it had been raining and some of the ruined depositors had organized a special line and announced their intention of going to the directors,

the police had beaten them up: one of the men in the committee had been knocked unconscious and a woman sixty
years old had been kicked and clubbed and finally arrested.
(The president of the Public National Bank and Trust Company had just sent the police a $500 tip "in appreciation of
police coöperation" in connection with "uneasy depositors.")

"I esk you," says M. D. Littman. "Here's a run on a bank
where not a single disorderly act is committed, not a window
is broken!—and while the stockholders and the big depositors
get Max Steuer, who is so good at defending criminals, to
protect their interests, us poor buggers get beaten up by the
police and called foreigners and Reds!"

The Tammany appointee has a special way of dealing with
people which is easier and more human than that of the
ordinary public official. You must never answer curtly the
humblest citizen or put a distance between yourself and him.
You may yourself be a man about town, you may be able to
afford a more expensive night-life than the Bronx furrier
or the Brooklyn cloak worker; but you must treat him with
geniality and sympathy—you are both citizens of the sidewalks of New York.

"I know," says Mr. Kerrigan frankly, with the tone of an
informal after-dinner speech, "that the Mayor has been very
seriously concerned about this—we've got one and a half millions in the bank ourselves. Of course, the difference is," he
concedes, "that we're not being evicted from our houses—and
we're not in a position where we can't pay our bills—but it's
just as much to our interest as yours to see that this is straightened out. As for the police beating people up, this is the first
complaint of that kind we've had. That'll be stopped." A
happy idea occurs to him. "We've heard of the police taking
people *out* of the line where they *didn't* belong and putting
them back where they did—and they did that because it was
—the right way to do—but we've never heard of this—other
thing."

Mr. Kerrigan scans the statement. "We can't do anything
about these first requests," he says. "The whole thing is up to
the state. As I say, the city's got money involved, too. I think
that Mr. Steuer can do more for you than we can. The city

can't float a loan. . . ." "If it was an earthquake or a flood,"
interrupts M. D. Littman, "the city would float a loan right
away—and isn't this as serious as an earthquake?—a million
people's lives affected by the failure of one bank!—a sixth of
the whole population of the city!" "But," Mr. Kerrigan replies, "an earthquake is an act of nature, whereas this"—After
a second's pause, he comes out with it candidly, informally,
in a low, grave, decisive voice—the custodian of their common
interests confessing to the people the worst he knows—"is
the act of a lot of crooks."

As for their holding meetings, however, that can be arranged. At one of their meetings, says M. D. Littman, somebody threw a stink bomb—"we don't want to say that anybody
had it done, but. . . ." "We had one down here the other
day," says Mr. Kerrigan amusingly, referring to a tear-gas
pistol which had gone off in a Chief Magistrate's pocket during a consultation with the Mayor. "It was an accident, but
it worked!" "We get called foreigners and Reds," persists
M. D. Littman, "because we try to get our money back, but
all the Nordics in the Stockholders' Association seem to want
theirs back just as much as we do." Mr. Kerrigan accepts
this as a little joke and tries to raise an amiable laugh by
turning aside to the company in Jimmy Walker's best after-
dinner manner, but his audience do not respond.

He brings the interview to an end: "I'll go now and send
you somebody from the Board of Education. He'll arrange so
that you can hold your meetings in a public school."

1957. I learned later that this committee had been inspired
and directed by the Communists. I had not yet seen enough
of them to recognize their hand in the framing of the depositors' demands. This does not, however, imply that the
hardships of these depositors had not been real or that their
protest was not in order.

THE METROPOLITAN OPERA HOUSE

THE OPERA is *La Bohème,* and the singers and the orchestra are doing their best, hemmed in by the forbidding neighbor-hood and with the opera house occupied by a bank, to liberate, at Broadway and Thirty-ninth Street, a little sweet Italian sentimentality, to recapture the gaiety and the heartache of a romantic 1840 Latin Quarter. When Mimi talks to Rodolfo in the snow and tells him that she cannot bear his jealousy and asks him to send her her belongings but to keep her bonnet to remember her by, we almost pass, for a moment, by way of the gray grilled gate, into the free, humane and chill air of France. In that country there are low-built towns and long-cultivated landscapes. Human emotions there are neither flippant nor raw. A café, on a winter's night, may be serious, cheerful and calm. But the brassy proscenium arch here rigidly clamps them in; the expensive disproportionate settings outbulk the sad little story. *La Bohème* at the Metropolitan neither derives from nor appeals to our imaginative life. It is simply a piece from Europe—that remote diamond mine of the fine arts—imported and guaranteed and sold to the opera subscribers.

You meet, between the acts, very tight, a friend to whom a subscriber has given his tickets. He was not able to find any-one to go with him, and he says he is alone, feeling miserable. It turns out that he has been thinking it was *Manon.*

COMMUNISTS AND COPS

THE COMMUNISTS have announced their intention of leading a "hunger march" on January 20. The city administration has agreed to receive a delegation at City Hall, but has not unreasonably refused a request to allow the Communists to make speeches from the steps.

In consequence, from ten o'clock on, a cordon of two hundred policemen are on guard around City Hall and the little park in front of it. You cannot get anywhere near the building without running the gauntlet of the cops and presenting unimpeachable credentials. It is like some scene on an old-fashioned German parade ground. The only human figures in the park are the immobile policemen, equestrian and on foot, with their blue coats and flat blue military caps, and the great snow-white booby Civic Virtue, with his thick trunk and sulky Irish face, trampling on confused female bodies.

At one o'clock promptly, the Communists arrive to the number of about 2,000, and the demonstration begins. The demonstrators deliver speeches and march around City Hall Park. A good many of them are Jews and some are Negroes—mostly small scrubby zealous people wearing red neckties, red hats or red dresses. A good many of the women have glasses. They have also succeeded in recruiting from the breadlines and employment agencies a considerable number of seedy men, to whom they have held out the hope that the authorities may be induced to provide unemployment insurance. They carry placards: "We Want No Charity," "No Evictions for the Unemployed," "We Demand Armories and Public Buildings for the Unemployed." They concentrate at the foot of the park opposite the Federal Building, and speakers get up on the iron dustbins. A crowd gathers—the newspaper photographers climb onto the roofs of the Coca-Cola and orange-drink stands and dominate the scene with their cameras.

The first speaker is a young Negro named Newton, the editor of the Communist Negro paper and secretary of the League of Struggle for Negro Rights, who was one of the Communists arrested last May in Atlanta for circulating radical leaflets. He was threatened with the death penalty under an ancient law which was originally intended as a weapon for dealing with rebellious slaves. Newton had never been in the South before: he is an educated Negro from Boston. Some years ago, while working in a hotel, he got a two-week vacation and arranged to go to a Y.M.C.A. camp; but when he arrived there, they wouldn't have him and gave him his money back. Later on, he met a Negro Communist, who told him that the Communists were working to abolish race discrimination, and he joined the Communist party. He is a good-looking fellow, with large sensitive dark eyes, skin closer to coffee than to mahogany and a thick but straight and rather unnegroid nose. He is joined almost immediately by other speakers, among them a Negro of a quite different type, blacker, with a round face and an old soft hat, whose voice sounds falsetto above the rest. Speaker after speaker leaps onto the dustbin till there is only a babel of yelling— then speechmaking is given up. The group on the dustbin begins rousing the crowd with methods like those of a college cheerleader—"We—want—*work*-or *wages!* We—want—*work*-or *wages!*" The harsh fanatical rhythm goes on and on—the people in the crowd get caught up into it and begin to shout with the leaders.

The street has become packed and impassable, and now the crowd is jamming the road. The taxis and the mail trucks cannot get by, and the police decide to break things up. Coming behind the speakers' stand, they push the people along the sidewalk. "Oh-oh!" exclaims a gaping bystander. "He's hittin' 'em on the head." From the road a mounted policeman starts out to ride into the crowd. As he does so, he screws up one side of his mouth: he is a clean-cut young fellow with his mind on holding in his horse. He scarcely does more than

turn its head in the direction of the overthronged sidewalk
and make a pretense of riding into it. "That's right!—go after
'em!" a young man among the bystanders eggs him on.
The crowd becomes liquefied and begins to move. A nice-
looking boy about ten in an old red-plaid Mackinaw—Comrade Charley, a Young Pioneer, who lives in Brighton
Beach—shouts from above people's heads with a voice that
sounds strangely fresh and live amid the systematic yelling
of the grown-ups. He is carried aloft on the shoulders of an
exceedingly tall Negro, another worker in the League of
Struggle for Negro Rights, who has recently served a sentence of three months for breaking up an anti-lynching meeting of the Pullman porters' association. The Pullman porters'
association are Socialists, but, according to the Negro Communists, keep on the right side of white respectability and
have been guilty of suppressing the evidence in connection
with the lynching of a porter in Georgia.

The demonstration pushes slowly around the park. "Aw
that's a lotta crap!" yells one of the spectators. "Oh, yeah?"
retorts a fierce little Communist. "What the hell do you know
about it?" "We want bread!" another shouts. "Try and get
it!" somebody answers. A shabby elderly Jew, who speaks
English very thickly, is handing out leaflets on unemployment insurance and repeating conscientiously again and
again: "Dis has got to become a law vedder de bosses like it
or not!"

The police watch behind iron posts that protect City Hall
from the traffic. Some are Negroes brought down from Harlem, who have almost the same Prussian stature, the same
square faces and mail-slot mouths as their white fellow officers. The policemen seem to fall into two classes: the husky
good-natured kind who accomplish their disciplinary duties
with conviction but without ferocity, and the stupid staring-
eyed type frankly hired as mobilizable brutes. Some of these
are evidently Jews, especially provided like the Negroes to
deal with agitators of their own race. In any case, the police
offer a curious contrast to everybody else present: if the Communists mostly look stunted, the office workers out for lunch
are hardly more prepossessing; and the policemen seem the

only healthy full-sized people and the only people decently dressed in these choked-up streets of milling human beings, bewildered or determined or half-scared or angry at being delayed, but all alike looking undersized, undernourished, dingy-featured, drearily dressed.

Only when the Communists sing one of their songs—*Solidarity Forever* or *The International*—does any note arise from among them of enthusiasm or human warmth.

It's the final conflict!
Let each stand in his place!
The International Soviet
Shall be the human race!

The bald words, the banal tune, by reason of all they have been coming to mean, do lift up the heart for a moment as the Communists raise their arms and wave them in time to the refrain.

All around them under the gray winter sky rise the high ugly walls of downtown New York, keeping the marchers, the crowd and the traffic crammed into the tight little space still left between the impregnably guarded park and the dense concentration of buildings: the men's wear shops, Schrafft's soda fountains, Liggett's drug-stores and cafeterias of Nassau Street and Broadway; the World Building with its rusty green dome, the red brick with green trimmings of the Sun Building, standing narrow and perpendicular like the fragments of some incomplete structure; a corner with cheap chop-suey signs over cheap investment-loan signs, a brick office building from whose flat cold red every suggestion of genuine color seems to have faded out past hope of revival by the sun; the somewhat handsomer high gray cliff of the Woolworth Building, eroded and lined like a giant butte and diminishing in tiers toward the top; the lower Federal Building, with its squashed-down, square-sided dome and its spotting of portholes like moles above a bulk of gray machine-made public dignity.

In this cramped and inhospitable area, the Communists produce simply confusion—a confusion which gets worse and worse. From the other side of the park, a woman's dreadful scream is heard.

In the meantime, at City Hall, to which it has been escorted by cops, a delegation is presenting demands. Mayor Walker is said to be ill—according to the Communists, afraid to face them—and they are received by the affable Mr. Kerrigan.

F. G. Biedenkapp, who acts as the spokesman, demands unemployment insurance; free gas, electricity and coal, no evictions for the unemployed, and free clothing and food for their children; reduced rents; the throwing open of vacant apartments and public buildings, and the use of schools and public halls for meeting places; the distribution of unemployment relief through a board composed entirely of workers and Communists, which shall also take over all the employment-agency work now being done by the State Labor Department, the Y.M.C.A. and all other organizations; no discrimination among workers on account of race, color, nationality or sex; and the immediate release of comrades who have been jailed in connection with previous demonstrations.

To this Mr. Kerrigan replies that "the city is constituted according to law, and a number of your demands would be illegal if carried out," that "if the city officials tried to carry them out they would be immediately removed," that the city officials are contributing out of their salaries for unemployment relief, that the city employment fund is to be increased, that the city is going to try to bring pressure to bear at Albany to amend the law in such a way as to make it possible to stop evictions, that the city has set up a free employment agency which will have the effect of suppressing private agencies and eliminating "the deception and dishonesty practised by some of them," that the Board of Education is already doing what it can to feed the children of the unemployed.

"I don't want to say," he concludes, "that if you don't like it here, you can go back to Russia, because many of you were born here—but I will say that I will pay the full fare, one way, of any ten of you who want to go there. That is about all we can do under the present system." F. G. Biedenkapp, in reply to this, declares the committee "entirely dissatisfied" with Mr. Kerrigan's "explanations and excuses"—and the Communists, under escort, withdraw.

Once outside, they make haste to climb onto the statue of Benjamin Franklin in front of the Sun Building. They shout that their demands have been refused: "We saw the acting mayor and told him our demands and he said that it was against the law to grant them. The unemployed workers must change the laws!"

This is a signal for the demonstration to swarm. They hang their placards all over the statue. Franklin stands with a discolored green bronze crown, one hand stretched out to the world as if in patriarchal blessing and at his feet some large funereal wreaths, presented by the Sons of the American Revolution. Comrade Charley, full of pep in his red Mackinaw, climbs up on the great bourgeois's shoulders and displays a placard: "Free Food for Our Children!" A crowd gathers on the opposite curbs. The statue is situated on a little lozenge of pavement between Nassau Street and Park Row, in such a way that any disturbance around it will cause a maximum jam of the traffic to and from Brooklyn Bridge: the Communists have picked a strategic point for obstructing the downtown life of the city. Taxis bawl and streetcars clang—curious office workers overflow the sidewalks, asking one another what is going on. Somebody in the Sun Building, from a high-up floor, drops a paper-bag full of water over the massed swarm around the statue. The bag comes apart in the air, and people watch the falling whirl of water.

The police decide at last to put an end to the demonstration. They force their way into the crowd and start pulling down the placards and speakers. An unintelligible mêlée ensues. The Communists flee before the police, and the bystanders get mixed up with them. One has a glimpse of a last indomitable speaker with a wild livid crazy face still vituperating alone on the statue—he has vanished a second later. People suddenly yell: "Look out!" Mounted cops begin galloping along the sidewalks, and everybody runs before them, demonstrators and innocent pedestrians alike. A Communist, grabbing apples from an unemployed apple-vendor, bombards the policemen with them and then crowns one of the

horses with the crate. Another seizes a horse by the tail—
a detective clutches him by the collar and beats him—two
women rush to his rescue and almost pull the policeman off
his horse. The traffic is impatient; the spectators dismayed;
the unemployed have scattered like leaves.

The Communists rally, shouting "Close up ranks!", and
rush up the entrance of the flat raised tunnel which leads to
the Brooklyn Bridge subway, completely taking possession of
the wide flight of steps and booing and hooting the police as
if from baseball bleachers. The police stretch a rope along the
back of the park and excitedly patrol the paths. At one stop,
quite remote from the disturbance, there is a shoe-shining
stand with a row of men peacefully sitting in the chairs and
reading the tabloids as they have their shoes shined—but at
the sudden appearance of the charging police, they all spring
out of their seats simultaneously and leap over the iron fence.
A gray flight of pigeons rises from the park, the only free
living things in sight.

Now the Communists are routed from the bridge entrance.
Some are chased under the monumental, the more than Roman, arches of the Municipal Building—they lurk there
awhile and then return. Others, retreating down Center
Street, return to the battle through Elm.

A patrol wagon and an ambulance arrive, a stretcher is
carried out of City Hall. You read the next morning in the
papers that the demonstrators have had their arms broken,
their skulls fractured, their teeth knocked out; an auditor
from the Comptroller's office has had his head cut open
against the Municipal Building; a policeman, who fell into
the hands of the demonstrators and got kicked in the stomach
by them, is in the hospital with internal injuries.

The Communists are shouting, "We want bread, not
horses' hoofs!" and trying to rally around speakers on the
curbs. But the speakers get dislodged, the groups dwindle.
Among the passers-by behind the park, a small plump sharp-
beaked Jewish woman in red—great wrath in a tiny body,
like one of Virgil's bees—is wandering by herself and scream-
ing, "Down with the police!"

At the corner of Center Street, a dingy little man who is

walking by, pauses as a spattering on the sidewalk turns out
to be too thick, too red and too profuse for spit. He says in a
foolish way to nobody in particular, with a mixture of surprise
and awe: "Blood!"

Now the streets are completely cleared—the great suction
pumps of downtown New York have pulled up their populations again. The people are coming out of the subway unimpeded, going up the steps to Brooklyn Bridge—the taxis are
on their way down to Wall Street, the trucks on their way to
the docks. The pretzel man with his basket and the roast-
chestnut man have come out again. The battle has been obliterated. No one passing has even heard of it. Many of the
people who witnessed it or in some way became involved in
it never even knew what it was about. They are neither sympathetic with the Communists nor particularly indignant
with them—they are not even particularly angry at having
been chased by the police. They feel no real stake in the city
in the sense of its being their community, and they conse-
quently take very little interest in abuses of administration
which do not vitally affect themselves. If they have jobs in
these hard times, they are glad enough to hang on to them,
without worrying about the unemployed. And they have all
long ago gone about their business.

DETROIT MOTORS

ON THE DREARY yellow Michigan waste with its gray stains of frozen water, the old cars wait like horses at the pound. Since the spring before last, Henry Ford has been buying them up at twenty dollars apiece, and people drive them in every day. Old, battered, muddy roadsters, sedans, limousines, touring cars and trucks—in strings of two or three they are dragged off to the disassembly building, following foolishly and gruesomely like corpses shaken up into life, hoods rickety and wheels turning backwards. Once inside, they are systematically and energetically dismantled: the flat road-ruined tires are stripped away; the rush-flare of an acetylene torch attacks the stems of the steering wheels; the motors are cleaned out like a bull's tripes and sent to make scrap iron for the blast furnace; the glass is taken out and kept to replace broken factory panes; the leather from the hoods and seats goes for aprons and handpads for the workers; the hair stuffing of the seats is sold again; even the bronze and babbitt metal are scraped out of the connecting rods and melted up to line new connecting rods. Then the picked and gutted carcass of the old car is shoved into a final death chamber—crushed flat by a five-ton press, which makes it scrunch like a stepped-on beetle.

The home of the open-hearth furnaces is a vast loud abode of giants: groans, a continual ringing, the falling of remote loads. The old automobiles sent in on little cars are like disemboweled horses at the bull-ring whose legs are buckling under them. A fiend in blue glasses who sits in a high throne on an enormous blue chariot or float causes it to move horizontally back and forth before the white-glowing mouths of the furnaces, feeding them the flattened cars like so many metallic soft-shell crabs—ramming each one in with a sudden charge, dropping it quickly with a twist. There are not many mouths big enough yet to accommodate a whole car at one gape, and, pending the completion of ten hundred-ton furnaces specially designed for the consumption of old cars—fifty thousand of which have been melted up since the April before last—they are being chopped up for the small-mouthed furnaces by a thousand-ton electric shear, which reduces chassis, springs, wheels, fenders and all to a junk-fodder of iron spines and bent tin shells, like horseshoe crabs cut up for pigs. When you put on blue glasses and gaze through the blinding hole in the furnace door, where the old cars are being digested with such condiments as limestone and pig iron, you see only a livid lake which vibrates with pale thickish bubbles. (The draft from the furnace heats a boiler—the boiler produces steam—the steam runs a turbine—the turbine turns the fan that makes the draft.)

Twice a day the old liquefied cars are poured out through the backside of the furnace into receptacles like huge iron buckets: a hot stink, a thunderous hissing, the voiding of a molten feces of gold burned beyond gold to a white ethereal yellow, a supreme incandescence, while a spray of snow-crystal sparks explodes like tiny rockets. In the arena below the gallery, during the pouring no human beings go. Giant cranes move along the ceiling and, picking up the caldrons of golden soup, lift them across the great barn and tip them into other vats, whence the liquid runs down through holes into cylindrical ingot molds. Eleven hundred tons of steel a day.

In the blooming mill's spacious gloom, ruby lights are sharp tiny watch gems under the clockwork of thin naked steel beams and the writhing of vermiform silver pipes. Hot breaths; a prolonged dull hooting; the acridity of pickling baths. A crane like a gigantic blue airplane comes sliding along the ceiling and from an elaborate suspended cab, which slides at right angles to the movement of the crane, it lifts, with great beetle-tweezers, the dark cooling ingots out of their molds, carries them across and lowers them into ovens —the soaking pits—where they soak in heat till, white-hot, they glow.

Silver pipes—a deafening clack-a-clack-clack—the spilling of metallic avalanches—the groaning barks of Cerbera in labor. Transmitters like the shells of red monstrous snails, fattened behind glass in white and spotless stalls, furnish underground power for the rollers. You look down from a narrow gallery at a runway of turning cylinders: the ingot, now cooling red-hot, lurches along it like a length of column roughly blunt-snouted and grooved. As it enters a mechanical grotto, the rollers above and below it crunch off the outer crust and a shear crops the bottom end, in which the impurities have settled, and drops it into a waiting receptacle from which it will be routed back to be melted up again.

Now the pigs have been bloomed into billets and are heated to be rolled in the rolling mill. Long strips of red-hot metal timber traveling along the rollers of the slides—squeezed out thinner and thinner, as they pass through the rollers of the stands, into longer and longer red worms, which a row of men, snapping the handles of black boxes in an upper gallery, cause to coast backwards and forwards or send spinning as they leave the wringers. Squared and cut in even lengths, they make at last a hangarful of piled steel stock.

Drop forges: a shattering whack-whack-whack, which, when, formerly, it whacked out crankshafts, could break down the mud-flat land and shake down the very building. But the crankshafts are now made at Highland Park. Here at Dearborn the big blacksmiths with bunged-up eyes, are stamping out connecting rods. By the steady steam-blown outflare of furnaces, with deliberate implacable bangs, the impacts of the dropping black trap, on anvil-die they bring hammer-die down, and out of red-hot lengths of tongs-held stock they cut cupcake-pans that still glow red-hot.

Machining: a finished connecting rod is the product of twenty-eight different processes. The rake-forks of the chain-conveyor wind zigzag in and out among benches and carry the connecting rods from one machine to the next. Each one of them must be toughened by a print heat-treat and softened by a draw heat-treat; rolled in a revolving tumbler, which rubs the scale away and turns the metal from dull to shining; straightened in swedge presses; drilled on revolving turrets;

rough-turned, finish-turned, chamfered and threaded; bored
with holes for the crankshaft and wristpin; the holes lined
with white babbitt metal and bronze, the babbitt and bronze
burnished smooth as satin; cleaned, oxidized, trimmed,
washed, oil-holes drilled and oil-pocket cut (a solid man in a
brown suit and round glasses has just invented a new machine for drilling all the holes at once, and he is supervising
its installation); oil-groove cut, oil-pocket broached; balanced
on a scale and corrected—the ones that weigh too much or
too little scrapped in thick-lipped iron buckets; holes in the
babbitt and bronze bored with a diamond drill; inspected in
constant-temperature greenhouses, lit blank violet by mercury tubes, and gauged to a millionth of an inch by a gauge
with a diamond point.

The part—the connecting rod—is now done with the production conveyor, and starts on another journey, along the
subassembly conveyor, in the course of which other parts are
added. The wristpins are now stuck in; the crankshaft and
the piston are fitted. The rod is important, it must be a sound
part: it has to withstand the wear and tear of a hundred
revolutions a minute. At last it is fixed in the motor-block.
The motor-block goes on its way and, piece by piece, becomes
fully equipped; it acquires a queer little muzzle and two pro-
truding eyes—takes on an animal aspect; and it finally crawls
up the conveyor track on its way to the assembly room like
an obedient tropical beetle.

In this assembly room, to the pointblank banging of hammers, the motor-block is seized and dropped down into an
empty still wheelless frame which, on a double-track conveyor, is passing beneath to receive it; and now there takes
shape on this track a kind of ichthyosaurus-shape that moves
slowly with sprawling paws and a single long knobbed snail-
eye which one recognizes soon as a gear-shaft. This shape,
as it moves along, picks up wheels, shiny fenders, shiny run-
ningboards. From above, the familiar body is dropped down
on the goggle-eyed frame: the thing is a motor car now, glossy
and fit to go, but still passive, still moved by another agency
as if it had not yet emerged from the womb. Now it gets its
last tests and touches: horns are made to speak, windshield

cleaners wiped around their arc, accidental scratches painted over. Black coupés; blue town sedans; maroon tudors; buff roadsters; green trucks—they leave the conveyor for good; are pushed out, self-possessed and gleaming, with their glass goggle eyes just opened, into their first electric-lighted show-room. They stand waiting to be driven away or to be taken to the dealers on trailers, over the long dreary Michigan waste.

————

"It's not human—I could just bust when I talk about it—break the spirit of an elephant, it 'ud. I'd starve before I'd go back! They don't give ye no warnin'. Pick up your tools and get a clearance, the boss says—then they inspect your toolbox to see you're not takin' any of the company's tools—then ye report to the employment office with your time card and they give ye a clearance that says they 'cahn't use ye to further advahntage'—then ye're done. I've been laid off since last July. Sometimes they leave ye your badge, and then ye can't get a job anywhere else, because if ye try to, they call up Ford's and they tell 'em ye're still on the payroll, though ye're not workin' and not gettin' a cent. Then they can say they've still got so many men on the payroll. He's a wonder at the publicity, is Ford.

"In England they do things more leisurely-like. I was an auto and tool worker in Manchester from fourteen years old. I got six shillin's a week for seven years—till the War, then I went into the Royal Air Force—but I failed in the nerve test—I was a second-clahss air mechanic durin' the War. An ahnt of mine had been in the States and had seen the pawssi-bilities, and when she came back, she said, 'Bert, you're wastin' your time!'—so I came over in September, '23. They're ridin' for a fall in England—they've got their back to the wall—the vital industries are bein' bled away from 'em, and they cahn't do away with the dole, but if they stop it, they've got to face the music. There's young chaps there that have grown up on the dole, and now you cahn't make 'em work—when they're given a job they get fired on purpose. The gov-

ernment's between the devil and the deep sea. Take the
bread away from the animals and they'll bite. The way they
do things in England, it's a miracle how they ever come
through!

"When I first came over, I worked at Fisher Bodies for three
months. I took a three-shift job on production at the start
rather than be walkin' around. But then I went to Ford's—
like everybody else, I'd 'eard about Ford's wages. And you do
get the wages. I got $5 a day for the first two months and $6
ahfter, for a year or so—then I ahsked for a raise and got forty
cents more a day for two and a hahlf years—I never saw this
$7 a day. But the wages are the only redeemin' feature. If
he cut wages, they'd walk out on 'im. Ye get the wages, but
ye sell your soul at Ford's—ye're worked like a slave all day,
and when ye get out ye're too tired to do anything—ye go to
sleep on the car comin' home. But as it is, once a Ford worker,
always a Ford worker. Ye get lackadaisical, as they say in
Lancashire—ye haven't got the guts to go. There's people who
come to Ford's from the country, thinkin' they're goin' to
make a little money—that they'll only work there a few years
and then go back and be independent. And then they stay
there forever—unless they get laid off. Ye've never got any
security in your job. Finally they moved us out to the Rouge
—we were the first people down there—we pioneered there
when the machinery wasn't hardly nailed down. But when
they began gettin' ready for Model A, production shut down
and we were out of a job. I'd tried to get transferred, but
they laid me off. Then I 'eard they were wantin' some die-
makers—I'd never worked at die-makin', but I said I'd 'ad
five years at it and got a job, and I was in that department
three years till I got laid off last July. I ahsked to be transferred and they laid me off. They'll lay ye off now for any
reason or no reason.

"It's worse than the army, I tell ye—ye're badgered and
victimized all the time. You get wise to the army after a
while, but at Ford's ye never know where ye're at. One day
ye can go down the aisle and the next day they'll tell ye to
get the hell out of it. In one department, they'll ahsk ye why
the hell ye haven't got gloves on and in another why the hell

ye're wearin' them. If ye're wearin' a clean apron, they'll throw oil on it, and if a machinist takes pride in 'is tools, they'll throw 'em on the floor while he's out. The bosses are thick as treacle and they're always on your neck, because the man above is on their neck and Sorenson's on the neck of the whole lot—he's the man that pours the boiling oil down that old Henry makes. There's a man born a hundred years too late, a regular slave driver—the men tremble when they see Sorenson comin'. He used to be very brutal—he'd come through and slug the men. One day when they were movin' the plant he came through and found a man sittin' workin' on a box. 'Get up!' says Sorenson. 'Don't ye know ye can't sit down in here?' The man never moved and Sorenson kicked the box out from under 'im—and the man got up and bashed Sorenson one in the jaw. 'Go to hell!' he says. 'I don't work here—I'm workin' for the Edison Company!'*

"Then ye only get fifteen minutes for lunch. The lunch wagon comes around—the ptomaine wagon, we call it. Ye pay fifteen cents for a damn big pile o' sawdust. And they let you buy some wonderful water that hasn't seen milk for a month. Sorenson owns stock in one of the lunch companies, I'm told. A man's food is in 'is neck when he starts workin'— it 'asn't got time to reach 'is stomach.

"A man checks 'is brains and 'is freedom at the door when he goes to work at Ford's. Some of those wops with their feet wet and no soles to their shoes are glad to get under a dry roof—but not for me! I'm tryin' to forget about it—it even makes me sick now every time I get on a car goin' west!"

————

This Englishman, whose name is Bert, lives with a man named Hendrickson, an American, who works for the Edison Company. Hendrickson gets thirty-five dollars a week for finding out what is wrong with dynamos and other machinery that doesn't work, but his interest in electricity does not stop with putting them back into running order. He has fitted up

* This story is a Detroit legend. I have heard it again and again.

a little laboratory and study in the house where Bert and he board—hardly more than a narrow closet off the sitting-room, but with space enough for a blackboard, on which Hendrickson can chalk up his problems; a considerable technical library, including Whitehead's *Introduction to Mathematics,* and one work of pure literature, Montaigne's *Essays;* blueprints of Detroit transformers: intricate structures of long taut lines—here and there threading series of blocks or clusters of truncated carets—of an abstraction almost mathematical and with the beauty of mathematical diagrams; a little wash-closet turned into a dark room, in which he is able to make these blueprints for a third of what he would have to pay a photographer; a pile of original papers dealing with various problems, neatly bound up in blue folders; and photographs of Tesla and Steinmetz.

Hendrickson is a great admirer of Steinmetz. He has two photographs of him and thinks one of them particularly good. He explains that it was hard to get a picture of him on account of his being a humpback—he wouldn't be able to get into the country if he was to come over now, he adds. Hendrickson never actually saw Steinmetz, but he can tell you about the way he used to lecture almost as if he had heard him. Steinmetz used to talk without notes and unless he was stopped, would go on forever, but he was always so interested in what he was saying and made everything so clear to his hearers that he carried them all along with him and you were willing to keep on listening as long as he talked. Bert declares that Hendrickson has the same gift.

In the next room, with its gray mottled wallpaper, its little prayer-meeting organ and its picture of Queen Victoria, the lady of the house, somewhat blowzy, is dozing among sheets of the Sunday paper, while her black-and-tan mongrel puppy disports itself on the carpet with a toilet-paper roll and a bone.

Bert has, in general, a great opinion of Hendrickson's abilities and feels that he is being exploited by his superiors. He claims that the experts of the Edison Company get the credit for learned scientific papers for which Hendrickson has furnished the material. In every organization, says Bert, one man owns the cart and another rides in it. But this doesn't seem to worry Hendrickson—he has no quarrel with the Edison Company. On the contrary, he takes a personal pride in the fact that Detroit can boast that it has more twenty-five-thousand-volt underground cables than any other city in the country. His face is permanently pocked and scarred with acid that was spilled on it some years ago, but this accident does not appear to have had any psychological effect on him. He is unceasingly preoccupied with the problems of electricity, and when for a few moments he has time on his hands, he sits down, no matter where he is, and immediately goes sound asleep.

It is plain that the British Bert is a maladjusted man not at home in America, unhappy between the middle and the working class; but Hendrickson seems to inhabit a world that is homogeneous, in which classes do not exist because everybody in it is consecrated to the progress of electricity.

Hendrickson is short on the practical side, and Bert on the theoretical. Hendrickson can figure anything out and provide the mathematics, but Bert has to build it for him.

————

"I wouldn't mind having my job at L———— back—I quit last November to get married.

"First I worked at R————; that's the worst place of all to work. The presses are awfully close together, and there are no stools, you have to stand. There's an awful ringing in your ears from the noise of the presses, but I used to hum tunes to the rhythm—I used to hum the *Miserere*.

"But I didn't stay there long—I got a job at L————, which is a much better place to work. They made interior parts—ash-receivers and dome-light rims and escutcheons—those are the little brass plates behind the doorknob that holds it in. You have a strip of brass and run it through the press—you step on a pedal, and the die comes down and cuts it out. We were working with small No. 4 presses and we were supposed to turn out 1,624 pieces an hour. Most of the girls couldn't make it, and if they couldn't enough times, they'd get their base rate lowered.

"For instance, if you were a dome-rim-maker, say, and couldn't do 512 pieces an hour, you'd be cut from thirty-two to twenty-eight cents. If you made a misstep on the pedal, you were liable to lose a finger—I always had some kind of a cut. When an accident happens nobody ever tells about it, and sometimes you don't know definitely till a week later—but I could always tell if something had happened as soon as I came into the room: the place always seems very clean and everybody's very quiet. Once when I was there, a girl lost her finger and gave a terrible shriek—and another time when the same thing happened to another girl, she just put a rag around her hand and quietly walked out. One day a girl got two fingers cut off, and they sent everybody home. A man in the hinge department lost three fingers once the same week. People often don't make use of the safety devices because they can work faster without them. Then your chest would get cut up from the trimmings—mine was all red. And the oil gives you an itch—your arms get itchy and you just about go crazy—they gave you some white stuff to put on it, but it didn't do any good.

"But I got so I had a certain amount of skill—I used to take satisfaction in turning out so many pieces a day, and I got to be known as a fast worker. I liked it better than the telegraph company. I liked the girls at L—— much better than the telegraph girls; the telegraph girls are always talking about the men who are going to take them out and how much money they spend on them. The girls at L—— were mostly married, and you could have a much better time with them. The telegraph girls are thin and nervous as a rule. They're always breaking down. The turnover is terribly high—it's supposed to be 100 per cent every three years. The machine that you punch out the messages on is speeded up to sixty words a minute—3,600 words an hour. No stenographer has to work that fast. And you've got the supervisor over you all the time. You have to join the company union—if you refuse, you're fired. Ever since the telephone and telegraph strike, the company has been scared of the C.T.U.

"I only make $75 a month now—less than at L——: I never earned less than $40 for two weeks when I was there.

And they're going to put in eighty-word-a-minute machines now, it seems—they've got them in Chicago already. When we get them here, I'm going to quit.

"There was a freedom at L————; you could go in a gingham dress. And I could bully the foreman and everybody. At the telegraph company, the supervisors aren't supposed to fraternize with the girls. And I enjoyed wearing a clean cap on Fridays—on Fridays we all wore a clean cap, and I used to get a kick out of it."

————

Fred Vogel is a man of fifty, who started in at twelve selling papers in New York, but has spent most of his mature life working in the Detroit motor factories. He was a superintendent for many years, but finding himself forced, at Briggs Bodies, to spend thirteen and a half hours a day at the plant with only about two hours' work, he has "shaved off his Simon Legrees," as he says, and taken a janitor's job.

Since then he has been attempting to organize an auto workers' union in a city where the manufacturers have in the past made organization impossible. He has spoken his mind about this in the following declaration:

"In recent statements handed to the press by several of the industrial Barons, that they were not going to reduce wages, they are rather vague as to what they are actually doing here in Dynamic Detroit, as it is termed throughout the United States.

"Here is a review of the true conditions. Mind you, gentle reader, these are not prehistoric figures, although I will grant you that they have a primitive color, but the writer stood in line three days in July to get a job. After I had passed the employment manager, I was passed on to the medical examiner, I was ushered into a small booth and told to strip, then entered another office in the nude, was weighed, eyes examined, and answered a few questions, and was then told to go to work.

"I started to work under the group piece-work system. For those of you that have never worked under this system, I will offer a brief outline of its workings. The individual worker loses his identification and becomes a part of a group. We will say anywhere from five to fifty or more are placed in these groups. The group that I was working in had twenty-six. There was nine different operations in the group. The completed part paid $1.09. The operation that I was working on paid 35¢ and the men would do from three to four every hour—it all depended on how fast the conveyor was running. Every operator took his turn if he was able, if not the group had to carry them along. The operation that I was on priced as bad as the rest, and when other operators would complain they were told not to worry, that they would make just as much as the rest, because the other operations would carry them through.

"How would you like to make from $1.05 to $1.40 per hour and be paid off anywhere from thirty-one cents to seventy-four cents per hour? Sometimes they will send an extra man in your group or loan a few men to another group and in that way it was hard to keep a record of production or hours. They used to keep a production sheet where one could glance at it, but not now. We could figure it out and know just what we were supposed to draw on pay day. Our day rate was seventy cents per hour, but that made no difference, if you complained, you were laid off, take it or leave it. We were told when they adopted this system that it was a much simpler method of keeping labor and production records.

"Another hijacking scheme is the group bonus. This system of banditry varies a little. You are paid a base rate, we will say of fifty cents per hour, you have an operation that the time study department has allowed you, we will say, two hours for and you make it in one hour. You have made 100 per cent efficiency and that gives you an extra twenty-five cents per hour, providing the rest of the group that you are working with are as fast as you and can keep the pace. If not, you just lose and make what the group makes. The other twenty-five cents you make—well, I don't know just who gets that. This group system enables the employer to take inexperienced help and put them in a group, and they are trained to be skilled workers at no cost to the manufacturer. Their training is paid for out of the group they are working with, so it is up to the worker to break in the inexperienced help as soon as possible. It never pays to complain about prices, they retime it and chop some more off. And don't forget that sweepers and stockmen, also repairmen, are paid off of the group. Group leaders and gang bosses get their split off of you, so you can readily see why the employer is in favor of the group—less overhead and bigger dividends. They have also installed the budget system. The time study department sends a budget sheet every month telling just how many you can have in your department according to their way of figuring. Should they make a mistake and the foreman has to put on some extra help, that's unfortunate, but they still have the old reliable group to fall back on and it is taken out of them.

"How would you like to start work at seven and work until ten or ten-thirty and receive as your stipend for the day and a half, $3.70, and work 134 hours for a two weeks' pay and receive $74? Figure it for yourself. This is not common labor, it used to be a trade, but since the advent of massed or messed production as is in vogue at the present writing, trades have lost identification, you're just an operator or otherwise termed, a skilled laborer.

"Henry Ford is belching forth like a volcanic eruption telling the world that in 1950 the industrial slaves will be paid at the rate of $35 per day. Well, half of that would go mighty nice right now and it would help a lot in solving the economic situation that the world is going through. When you announced your $1.00 per day increase, Henry Ford, the higher-priced men were laid off and replaced with cheaper help, so if you are sincere and intend to give the workers a little of the sunlight and this scheme is not another of your tricks to hog the front pages of the newspapers throughout the world, why send some of your expert investigators over to the Murray Cor'p of America and see for yourself the slavery conditions that exist there, where humans are building the bodies for your cars, where polishers work all day Sunday, eight hours to be exact, and receive the glorious sum of sixty-two cents for a Sabbath of slavery. Other skilled operators in the trimming department started an operation at

$1.40 and was cut 10¢ every week until they are doing the
same work for 90¢ and making 60¢ per hour when they work.

"While the worker has been cut from 70 to 150 per cent on
piece-work prices, the foremen have been reduced to hourly
rates and in numerous cases have been told to look for work
elsewhere, but dividends have not fallen off any. Dividends
paid investors in leading American enterprises for the year
1930 aggregate at least $8,200,000,000, or 8.3 per cent greater
than in 1929, according to reports gathered by the United
States Department of Commerce. So you executives that have
lost your position need not feel so bad, because these dividends just had to increase and you know the rest. When you
scions of wealth are rolling along the boulevard lolling in
the arms of luxury or maybe basking in the sunshine getting
your winter coat of tan, just stop and think of the blood
money that put you there. Some of the poor females that
was crowded out due to price cutting are walking the streets
offering their body for sale, so that they can get a meal and a
night's lodging, not that they care for this life but it is a
means of a livelihood."

"I came over from Glasgow in 1923, when I was sixteen—
they pretty near had a revolution over there in 1919 after
the War. My father had a barbershop—when he first came
over here, he was out of work for three months—our sole
piece of furniture was a trunk—we'd brought bedding from
the old country. My father finally went to worruk as a check-
strap-maker and got $8 a day. I went to high school—I won
a couple of prizes while I was there. I was on the debating
team, and I won a prize in an oratorical contest held by the
Better America Federation—that's a bunch of patriots in Los
Angeles. I was on the committee on the class-day program
the year that I graduated and I had a tiff with one of the
teachers: she said to me, 'James McRae, you'll either die on
the gallows or become a Socialist!'

"Then I went to City College. In the meantime, I carried
papers for the *Free Press*—then I checked accounts for a news

company. I also worruked in a department store for $5 a week
and as bookkeeper in a savings bank. One summer I worruked
at Packard. I was assistant treasurer at college—but we had
Weisbord and Scott Nearing come and speak under the
auspices of the YMCA, and as a result they kicked us out of
it. Then we forrumed a Liberal Club and became more
neurotic and radical than before. We got out a paper and we
asked an organizer of the Auto Worrukers' Union to speak
before our club, and as a result of that our club was forbidden to meet in the college. We had three sessions with
the Dean, and he finally threw us out of the office. He told
me to shut up or get kicked out. We were very nervous and
hysterical at that time. But then Forrest Bailey hearrud about
it and wrote it up in the Scripps-Howard papers, and the
Dean backed down and took me back as assistant treasurer.

"In the meantime, my father'd had an accident—he was
blown up in a shack where he was worruking and the company fought the case. My mother tried to go to worruk at
R————, but, what with the noise and the fear of losing a
finger, she collapsed after two days. There are more accidents
at R———— than anywhere else—they have no safety devices.
They used to say R———— supported the Checker cabs carrying people to the infirmary. Then the paint room blew up out
there in the spring of '27—the paint wasn't properly stored.
The papers said there were twenty-nine killed, but there were
a couple of hundred actually—lots of them were foreign-born
with families in the old country, and they just said nothing
about them. You couldn't get into the hospital that day for
stepping over bodies from the R———— blast.

"We lost our house because we couldn't keep up the pay-
ments—then the first big lay-off came, and they've been laying off ever since. I'd worruked at the Kelsey Wheel Company—I worruked twelve hours a night on the night shift
and got $30 a week. I carried rims from one section to an-
other section on the Chevrolet line. Then I got a job at Ford's
as a pushrod-grinder at $5 a day—I was raised to $6 at the end
of sixty days, and when the wage raise came in, I got seven
bucks—but by that time we were only worruking two days a
week, so I only got $14 a week. Finally I quit—I wanted to go

to Brookwood Labor College. I didn't mind factory worruk in itself—for two or three hours it used to stimulate my mind. But eight or ten hours of it deadens you—you're too tired to do much when you're through.

"I was disappointed in Brookwood. Muste asked me to be a delegate to the Conference for Progressive Labor Action, but I didn't have much faith in progressivism. I expect nothing from students and middle-class movements. When I used to go around and make speeches, I found the college audiences the worst of all.

"When I left Ford's, I was idle for three weeks, then I got a job as adding-machine operator in a bank. I stuck on by hook or by crook, till I was laid off the other day. I was laid off while I was eating lunch—they said, 'here's your pink slip—you're a fine worruker and so forth, but we've got to cut down expenses.' Now I'm looking for worruk. I'd like to go to Russia and worruk in a factory over there, if I could raise the transportation. At one time, I thought I wanted to be a college instructor—but when I saw the colleges and the teachers and the restrictions they were under, I gave up the idea—I'd rather be free.

"What we want here is a revolutionary movement geared into the peculiar needs of the American worrukers, and I'll say quite frankly that if it isn't the Communist party, I don't see any other elements in the country who will supply it. The Communists have done a lot—they've practically stopped evictions. When there's an eviction about to take place, the people notify the Unemployed Council and the Communists go around and wait till the sheriff has gone and then move all the furniture back into the house. Then the landlord has to notify the authorities again, and the sheriff has to get a new warrant, and the result is that they usually never get around to evicting the people again. They've got the landlords so buffaloed that the other day a woman called up the Unemployed Council and asked whether she could put her tenants out yet. The Unemployed Council said no.

"The Communists led the Flint strike last summer. It started as a spontaneous walk-out by the trimmers and was taken up by the Auto Worrukers' Union, where the Communists were dominant. They were striking against a wage-cut of 33⅓ per cent and certain foremen they didn't like and the speed-up and worruking conditions. The whole force of the state was mobilized against them. They broke up the strike meetings and the six leaders were taken out by dicks and beaten up in the woods. Finally they broke the strike by rounding up the leaders and locking them up—they couldn't get a lawyer in Flint to defend them. But the company took back the wage-cut and got rid of the foremen and granted their other demands. The union was wiped out, however. *The Auto Worrukers' News,* that had a circulation of twenty thousand, went out of existence after the strike.

"It's a weakness of the Communists just at present that they don't talk the language of the American worruker. Take the leaflets they pass out at these demonstrations—they're all stereotyped radical phrases. Your American worruker wants something concrete. I could wish, too, that they had more interest here in the discussion of their ideas. I went around one day with a book by Plekhanov on the philosophical problems of Marxism, a very illuminating book—but they wouldn't take any interest in it.

"There's a small IWW group, too—I went around there and tried to see them, but they're so suspicious that you can't get to them at all.

"What we need are democratic orrgans of education to educate the worrukers along Marxist lines."

————

Detroit is a simple homogeneous organism which has expanded to enormous size. The protoplasmic cells of Detroit are the same as fifteen years ago: drab yellow or red brick houses, sometimes with black rock-candy columns or a dash of crass Romanesque; tight, dreary, old, long-windowed mansions with fancy cupolas and jigsaw woodwork; little dull one-story frame houses of the Polak and Negro sections; apartment buildings, libraries and churches with gray wrinkled reptilian limestone skins which make them look like prisons;

obsolete brick garages and machine shops like the one in which Henry Ford worked on his first gas car.

All this, in the gray cold light and the slush of a February thaw—trimmed with the red ribbon-script and the blue borders of Neon signs that advertize brake service, Hudsons, Fords, candy and real estate—looks just as prosaic and provincial as it did fifteen years ago. But today the unattractive houses have spread on the flat lands, and they are dominated by other monuments. One remembers the Statler Hotel, the Penobscot office building, the giant stove from the Chicago World's Fair, which looms suddenly on Jefferson Avenue, the majestic old water-works. But the success of the motor industry has taken shape today as a herd of towering constructions that culminates in the new Fisher Building. This building has a vast arcade with a modernistic lighting through angular glazed-glass leaves; a kind of German mythological ceiling, the gold paint alone for which is said to have cost $100,000; and a theater archaeologically decorated in the style of a Mayan temple, to which the baby-voiced Helen Kane has this week brought her boop-boop-a-doop. The Fisher Building at night is illuminated with soda-fountain colors: orange above and peach below. There is also a new spectacular Masonic Temple, halfway between a palatial apartment house and a second-rate modern cathedral. And the streets, of course, are crawling with cars—can there ever have been so many in a city of comparable size? They are circulating around the boulevard with the swiftness and consistency of electric current, and they pack open spaces and side streets in regular long parked rows.

And yet, as a result of the depression, this flood of cars, it seems, has shrunk. In order to encourage car-owners not to get rid of their cars, the city, which cannot afford to have its gas stations go broke, is letting licenses run over till March so that they do not need to take out new ones. But so many, nevertheless, are selling them that secondhand cars are now being shipped away to keep prices from dropping to nothing.

In the region around Highland Park, which was left flat by Ford when he moved out to Dearborn, the houses and the stores are For Rent, For Rent, For Rent. Many of the automo-

bile plants are working only three or four days a week, and
some have closed down altogether. There have been universal
lay-offs and wage-cutting. Metal-finishers, for example, the
highest grade of skilled labor, who were formerly paid $1.10
an hour, get in some cases 15 cents now. The white-collar
class are losing their jobs as well as the factory workers: there
are probably as many as 66 per cent of the population either
entirely or partly out of work, and 45,000 families dependent
on the city Welfare Department. The banks have been
amalgamating and failing till there are comparatively few
left: thousands have lost all their savings. The employment
agencies and soup kitchens are crowded, and people without
jobs gloomily make their way from one factory gate to another
in the hope that somebody may be hiring again.

The employers are gloomy, too—it is beginning to be generally confessed that the normal demand for American cars
could be quite satisfactorily supplied with perhaps half the
present plant. The huge organism of Detroit, for all its
Middle Western vigor, is clogged with dead tissue now. You
can see here, as it is impossible to do in a more varied and
complex city, the whole structure of an industrial society; almost everybody who lives in Detroit is dependent on the
motor industry and in more or less obvious relation to everybody else who lives here. When the industry is crippled,
everybody is hit. "The cylinder-head has cracked!" says one
official of a large motor company, "and when the cylinder-
head is cracked, you have to get a new car. The system has
broken down!" But the minds of motor company officials have
not as yet been fertile in ideas for new systems.

As for Henry Ford himself, his reputation as a benefactor
of the American workingman has conspicuously declined.
His removal of his factories to Dearborn outside the city
limits, in order to escape city taxes, has relieved him from
contributing anything to the relief of the unemployed, a
third of whom, according to the city's calculations, have been
laid off from his own plant. Yet Ford is still the great personality, his career is the myth, as it were, on which the city
is founded; and if one wants to understand Detroit, one must

try to get at the realities that are partly concealed by this myth. Henry Ford, who has a great eye for publicity, has now been presented to the world through several official biographies, a so-called autobiography and several volumes of pronunciamentos written by Samuel Crowther. His legend has gone all over the world; he is one of the most famous Americans and one of the most favorably known, and has been, at one time or another, compared to Abraham Lincoln, Jesus Christ and Karl Marx (for this last analogy, see the March *Atlantic Monthly*). It has occasionally happened, however, that some one who has been in a position to study Henry Ford at close range, exasperated or worried by this legend, has attempted to reveal what he is really like. This was the case with the Reverend Samuel S. Marquis, who published in 1923 a book called *Henry Ford: An Interpretation*. Doctor Marquis had been Ford's pastor and afterwards ran his Welfare Department. It was also the case with Mr. E. G. Pipp, the original editor of the *Dearborn Independent* and the author of *Henry Ford: Both Sides of Him*. Even Mr. Allan L. Benson, the writer of one of the official biographies, *The New Henry Ford*, felt obliged, at the time when the Ford presidential boom was being got under way, to add to it a further chapter, unapproved by his subject, which warned people against taking Ford seriously as a candidate for the presidency. And this winter another former employee, Mr. W. M. Cunningham of the Ford publicity department, has published the harshest indictment of all, *"J 8," A Chronicle of the Neglected Truth about Henry Ford and the Ford Motor Co.*, which Ford's has been doing its best to suppress, as it suppressed Dr. Marquis's book. Most valuable, perhaps, of all because more detached and intelligent is Mr. Louis P. Lochner's book on the Peace Ship: *Henry Ford—America's Don Quixote*.

These books all agree in the main, and what one hears in Detroit confirms them. The account that follows here is an attempt to put a portrait together out of the testimony of a variety of witnesses—businessmen, newspapermen, Ford office men and Ford workers as well as the authors of the above-mentioned books.

Henry Ford is, of course, a remarkable man: he is a mechanical and industrial genius. It is true that he has made few important inventions, that he has usually been a mere exploiter of principles discovered by other people; yet the boy who ran away at night against his father's orders and swam across a creek in order to fix the engine of a neighbor's thresh-ing machine, whose hands, he says, "just itched to get hold of the throttle," who repaired his first watch with an old nail sharpened on a grindstone, who built a "farm locomotive" before he was twenty by mounting a steam engine on mowing-machine wheels—this boy exhibited already the ca-pacity for concentration and the instinctive affinity for a medium by which one recognizes the vocation of a master. From the improvised screw-driver and the farm locomotive, Henry Ford, in spite of formidable difficulties, has gone straight to the River Rouge plant, with all its sources of raw material and its auxiliaries, that self-sufficing industrial cos-mos, a masterpiece of ingenuity and efficiency. Few people in any field are capable of following their line with the in-tense singlemindedness of Ford; few people have a passion for their work of a kind that so completely shuts out other interests. ("I don't like to read books," says Ford. "They muss up my mind.") And it is a passion that has bred no ambition to do anything but satisfy itself. There is no evidence that Henry Ford has ever cared much about money. He has not applied himself systematically to acquiring a fortune for pleasure or show: his financial sense has been developed un-der the pressure of meeting emergencies. He needs money to expand his plant, and figuring in terms of the last fraction of a cent he has found to be one of the rules of the game he has set himself. This game is the direct expression of Henry Ford's personal character: to make cars which, though as homely as he is, shall be at once the cheapest, the most ener-getic and the most indestructible possible. When in 1921 the bankers almost had Ford on his back, he checkmated them by the unexpected and quite non-professional financial move of unloading all his stock on the dealers and making them pay him by borrowing from the banks (thus inaugurating, according to some, the era of high-pressure salesmanship).

Nor is there evidence that, except for a brief period, Henry Ford has ever cared very much about the welfare of the people who work for him. His immunity to social ambitions and to the luxuries of the rich has evidently been the result rather of an obstinate will to assert himself for what he is than of a feeling of solidarity with the common man. It has already been too difficult for Henry Ford to survive and to produce the Ford car and the River Rouge plant for him to worry about making things easy for other people, who, whatever disadvantages they may start with, can get along very well, he is certain, if they really have the stuff in them as he did. Has he not helped to create a new industry and made himself one of its masters—a boy from a Western farm, with no education or training, and in the teeth of general ridicule, merciless competition and diabolical conspiracies of bankers? Let others work as hard as he has. What right have the men in his factories to complain of the short eight hours that they are paid good money to spend there?

Yet to take good care of one's workers is a policy that saves money and that safeguards against rebellions, and a reputation for being humane is also good advertizing. In the volume called *My Life and Work,* Ford allows Samuel Crowther to write for him the following account of the establishment, at the beginning of 1914, of the eight-hour day, the six-day week and the five-dollar minimum wage. "It was to our way of thinking an act of social justice, and in the last analysis we did it for our own satisfaction of mind. There is a pleasure in feeling that you have made others happy—that you have lessened in some degree the burdens of your fellow men —that you have provided a margin out of which may be had pleasure and saving. Good will is one of the few really important assets of life. A determined man can will almost anything that he goes after, but unless, in his getting, he gains good will he has not profited much."

Here, however, is Mr. Pipp's account: "I . . . have heard of disputes as to who was responsible for the five-dollar wage. I have put the question directly to Ford, who said he worked many a night on it and concluded that machinery was playing such an important part in production that if men could be induced to speed up the machinery, there would be more profit at the high wage than at the low wage. He figured out a plan of doubling the wage of the lowest paid men and others accordingly, the wage to apply after they had been with the company six months and complied with other conditions. As I recall the figures he gave me, they were $4.84 a day for the lowest paid man of six months' standing. He said he put the figures up to Couzens, who said: 'Why not make it a straight five-dollar wage and it will be the greatest advertizement an automobile ever had,' or words to that effect. Couzens didn't have to say it twice to Ford. When the information came out, it was real news for the public and of high advertising value to the company, from which Ford still benefits."

One does not need to doubt that for Ford certain genuinely benevolent emotions were released by the unusual direction which the profit motive had taken. With so much imagination for machinery, he is not without imagination for life. Here is a third explanation of the $5 minimum, as made by Ford to Dr. Marquis: "I asked him why he had fixed upon $5 as the minimum pay for unskilled labor. His reply was, 'Because that is about the least a man with a family can live on in these days. We have been looking into the housing and home conditions of our employees, and we find that the skilled man is able to provide for his family, not only the necessities, but some of the luxuries of life. He is able to educate his children, to rear them in a decent home in a desirable neighborhood. But with the unskilled man it is different. He's not getting enough. He isn't getting all that's coming to him. And we must not forget that he is just as necessary to industry as the skilled man. Take the sweeper out of the shop and it would become in a short time an unfit place in which to work. We can't get along without him. And we have no right to take advantage of him because he must sell his labor in an open market. We must not pay him a wage on which he cannot possibly maintain himself and his family under proper physical and moral conditions, just because he is not in a position to demand more.'

" 'But suppose the earnings of a business are so small that

it cannot afford to pay that which, in your opinion, is a living wage; what then?' I asked.

" 'Then there is something wrong with the man who is trying to run the business. He may be honest. He may mean to do the square thing. But clearly he isn't competent to conduct a business for himself, for a man who cannot make a business pay a living wage to his employees has no right to be in business. He should be working for someone who knows how to do things. On the other hand, a man who can pay a living wage and refuses to do so is simply storing up trouble for himself and others. By underpaying men we are bringing on a generation of children undernourished and underdeveloped, morally as well as physically: we are breeding a generation of workingmen weak in body and in mind, and for that reason bound to prove inefficient when they come to take their places in industry. Industry will, therefore, pay the bill in the end. In my opinion it is better to pay as we go along and save the interest on the bill, to say nothing of being human in our industrial relations. For this reason we have arranged to distribute a fair portion of the profits of the company in such a way that the bulk of them will go to the man who needs them most.' "

But what actually happened was that, in spite of these benevolent intentions, between 1914 and 1927 the cost of living nearly doubled in Detroit, and although in 1919 Ford raised his minimum rate to $6, his workers were actually less well off getting $30 a week than they had been before the $5 minimum was established. In December, 1929, the rate was raised to $7. Ford announced this latter event, in a spectacular manner, at the White House, before an industrial conference called by Hoover after the first stock-market crash, and it produced the usual effect of reinforcing his reputation for boldness and generosity. Yet Ford was not only giving much less employment, he was distributing much less money than formerly, and he was saving on production. In 1925, he had been employing 200,000 men at $6, an aggregate of $300,-000,000, but by the fall of 1929, there were only about 145,000 men working at Ford's, who at $7 a day would get an aggregate of only $253,750,000. By December, 1929, then, when Ford was turning out more motorcars, he was employing many fewer men. This was due partly to the technological innovations which have been throwing people out of work ever since the Nottingham weavers broke their mechanical looms; but it meant also that the men still employed were considerably speeded up and that the fat bait of $7 a day made it possible for the manufacturer to recruit the quickest and most vigorous workers at the expense of the less able ones. Since the fall of 1929, the number of men employed at Ford's has shrunk from 145,000 to something like 25,000, and at the present time the plant is shut down for all but the first three days of the week.

In 1914, Henry Ford—still associated at that time with James Couzens, who later felt himself obliged to resign and has since become the liberal senator from Michigan—established a welfare department and brought in Dr. Marquis to run it. The Ford plant was decorated with placards reading "Help the Other Fellow," and, though Ford is implacably opposed to old age pensions, a special attempt was made to provide work for old men and cripples. At this time, also, Mr. E. G. Pipp received donations from Ford to help him take care of the situation created by the flooding into Detroit of workers attracted by the promise of high wages to whom Ford was unable to give jobs. The Welfare Department, however, went in for checking up on the home-life of the workers —Ford neither smokes nor drinks himself and is severe on the indulgences of others—and this was strongly resented by them. The Ford trade school, which has had much publicity, was soon converted in practice into a device for getting children to work in the shops—on the assumption, as has been said by Murray Godwin, that the mass production of radiators was the principal essential of a primary education.

Ford's pretensions to a solicitude about his men were rapidly and sweepingly abandoned. Dr. Marquis describes as follows the development of Ford's later policy: "I resigned from the Ford Motor Company in 1921. The old group of executives, who at times set justice and humanity above profits and production, were gone. . . . There came to the front men whose theory was that men are more profitable to an industry when driven than led, that fear is a greater incentive to work than loyalty. . . . The humane treatment of employees, according to these men, would lead to the weakening of the authority of the 'boss,' and to the breaking down of discipline in the shop. To them the sole end of industry was production and profits, and the one sure way of getting these things out of labor was to curse it, threaten it, drive it, insult it, humiliate it and discharge it on the slightest provocation; in short—to use a phrase much on the lips of such men, 'put the fear of God into labor.' And they were always thinking of themselves as the little gods who were to be feared." "I cannot say," says Mr. Pipp, "whether there was a marked change in Ford's attitude toward labor, or whether my close association with Ford and his organization resulted in my seeing things that I did not see before. But as time went on I would get one jolt after another, would learn of things in the Ford organization that I would have believed impossible in a civilized country. . . . I could see . . . in Ford an inclination to use the lash of his power more and more on those who resisted or opposed him. There grew, too, the desire to produce more and more at less and less cost, to get more out of the men and machinery than ever had been gotten out of them."

The idea that Ford is adored by his men has certainly never existed except outside Detroit. It is probably true that the lay-offs and speed-up due to the present depression have made them at this time particularly bitter; but one heard more or less the same story back in 1917, when the first flush of the high wages was beginning to fade. Today the Ford workers complain not only of being overworked, but also of being spied on by Ford's secret police and laid off on trumped-up pretexts. The Ford plant is infested with "spotters" looking for excuses to sack people. Mr. Cunningham tells of an old man who had been working for Ford seventeen years but who was discharged for wiping the grease off his arms a few seconds before the quitting bell, and of an office boy sent into the factory on an errand and fired for stopping off, on his way back, to buy a chocolate bar at a lunch wagon.

The most serious weakness of Ford, as an employer as well

as a public man, has been a certain instability, not in his mechanical purpose, but in his feelings and his ideas. It is not that he is hypocritical: he has in fact been far more realistic than many employers are in giving away from time to time the assumptions on which his policies rest. But his mind is illogical and volatile; his genius seems purely intuitive. It is as if he had been born with a special sense of materials and mechanical processes which enabled him to see instantly what could be done with them. But in other matters he seems to be naïve and capricious. It is possible to condone his wavering, at the time of his presidential ambitions, between the Democrats and the Republicans; but the inconsistencies of his attitude toward the War reveal an appalling unreliability. After returning from the adventure of the Peace Ship, he converted his plant into a munitions factory as soon as the United States became involved in the quarrel—though he had previously threatened, according to Mr. Lochner, to take down the American flag from it and fly an international flag instead. When Mr. Benson suggested to him in 1922, at a time when diplomatic relations between Turkey and Great Britain seemed strained, that he might "sound a warning against American participation in any more European wars— to my surprise, he did precisely the opposite. 'There is going to be another war,' he said, 'and the United States should get into it at the beginning and clean them all up.'" About the same time, however, he allowed Miss Bushnell to print the statement that he had been unwilling to make money out of the War and had turned his war profits all back to the government: "Henry Ford gave all his war profits—twenty-nine millions—to the government, with no hampering conditions. This vast amount was turned back to the Treasury to be used as the government saw fit. This was the act of a pacifist. If all the war advocates had done the same, the country's war debts would not be so staggering today and there would have been less talk of war profiteers." Several people have checked on this statement and have found that it is entirely untrue. Mr. Cunningham asked the Treasury Department about it in January, 1930, and received from Ogden Mills this reply: "Treasury records do not show the receipt of any donation from Mr. Henry Ford of his war profits." Of the end of the voyage of the Peace Ship, Mr. Lochner writes as follows: "That evening . . . Mr. Ford received various friends. To some he gave the impression that he was going right on with the Expedition; to others that he would remain behind. To me he said at 10 P.M. that he would come on to Stockholm; to Rosika Schwimmer, about midnight, that he was positively going home."

These sudden reversals are no doubt the result of an extreme sensitivity to suggestion and to the discords and discrepancies created by the coexistence in one personality of unusual gifts and rudimentary limitations. Dr. Marquis has described, in his book, the rises and falls of Ford's moods: one day he will seem "erect, lithe, agile, full of life, happy as a child. Out of his eyes there looks the soul of a genius, a dreamer, an idealist—a soul that is affable, gentle, kindly and generous to a fault." But the next day "he will have the appearance of a man shrunken by long illness. The shoulders droop, and there is a forward slant to the body when he walks as when a man is moving forward on his toes. His face is deeply lined, and the lines are not such as go to make up a kindly open countenance. The affable gentle manner has disappeared. There is a light in the eye that reveals a fire burning within altogether unlike that which burned there yesterday. He has the appearance of a man utterly wearied and exhausted, and yet driven on by a relentless and tireless spirit. Back of an apparent physical frailty there evidently lies concealed a boundless supply of nervous energy." "It is the boyish, smiling, youthful Ford that enters the office," Mr. Benson writes in his biography. "In ten seconds and for no apparent reason, the smile may flit from his face and you behold a man who, from his eyes up, seems as old as the pyramids. Many little wrinkles dart out sidewise from his eyes. The skin is stretched rather tightly over his brow, and on each temple is a little vein resembling a fine corkscrew." Mr. Lochner's account of Ford is slightly different but it fits in with these: "In no other person," he says, "have I observed so pronounced a dual nature as in my former chief. There seems to be a constant struggle for control on the part of these two natures. The natural Henry Ford is the warm, impulsive, idealistic 'Old Man.' . . . The other Henry Ford has been imposed by the artificialities of modern civilization, by his environment, his business associates, his responsibilities to the huge Ford interests."

Mr. Benson has testified, also, to the uncertainty of Ford's temper. At the time of his crank campaign against the Jews, Mr. Benson ventured to disagree with him, and Ford gave him bound volumes of articles from the *Dearborn Independent*. "One evening the subject came up again, and when I expressed the usual dissent, he asked me if I had read the books he gave me. I said that I had read most that they contained. 'Well, read them right away,' he continued, 'and then if you do not agree with me, don't ever come to see me again.' I was so astounded that he should try to bludgeon my opinion in this manner that he may have read my thoughts in my looks. At any rate, we continued talking, and in a few minutes he came over to me, placed his hand upon my shoulder and said: 'You can always come to see me any time you want to.'"

Though Ford never contributes to charity and has been outspoken and even violent in his disapproval of it, he sometimes performs erratic acts of kindness. He is said to have given a stove to an old hermit whom he found living in the woods near Dearborn and to have celebrated the birthday of another old man whose threshing machine he had fixed in his youth by sending one of his trimotor airplanes to take him out for a ride. And he has protected the birds on his place with a tenderness almost excessive, providing them with food in winter, building thousands of birdhouses for them and even on one occasion nailing his front door up so as not to disturb a robin that had nested over it. In his malevolent moods, on the other hand, he is capable of overturning his whole organization as if it were a house of blocks which a child pushes down in a rage because he thinks that the children with whom he is playing have taken the project out of his hands; and he is ready, on occasion, to dismiss his oldest and closest associates without a word of explanation or warning. People innocently come back to their offices to discover that their departments have been abolished and that they themselves are no longer supposed to exist; they have found, in certain cases, their desks smashed to bits with an axe.

"The upper part of Ford's face," Mr. Benson writes, "is distinctively feminine. I fancy that he has his mother's eyes. His head, from the eyes up, has the nobility and the poise that one associates with a noble woman; a woman who has suffered, endured and survived—such a woman as Whistler pictured in the etching [sic] of 'My Mother.' . . . He was always smiling as he approached, and his eyes were looking to the side and towards the floor." Henry Ford is apparently sensitive, evasive, fickle and rather vain. When there is anything unpleasant to be done, he invariably passes the buck to subordinates, blaming arbitrary dismissals on others and becoming completely invisible when it is a question of not keeping his promises—so that persons whom the day before he has received with geniality and enthusiasm may find themselves cooling their heels in the antechambers of his executive offices, with no explanation and no excuse. They never see or hear from him again.

The despot of River Rouge, for all the tenacity and boldness of his career as an inventor and industrialist, is full of suspicions and shrinkings. His crusade against the Jews was apparently inspired by the notion that Jewish bankers were conspiring against him; and when the United States entered the War, he is said to have explained his refusal to allow his son Edsel to enlist on the ground that sinister influences in Wall Street would be sure to have him shot in the back. One is told that, when motoring around Detroit, he refuses to use the toilets of garages for fear it will "put him under obligations" to their owners. His experience under cross-examination at the *Chicago Tribune* libel trial, when he confused Benedict Arnold with Arnold Bennett and asserted that the American Revolution took place in 1812, is said to have inspired him with a mortal terror of ever being called into court again; and his recent fanatical interest in early American monuments and relics is plausibly ascribed to a desperate desire to correct the impression produced on that occasion.

The result of all this is that Ford today is surrounded by

professional yes-men who live in terror of differing from him. But he is protected by a publicity department, one of whose principal duties is to prevent him from making a fool of himself in public. One gets the impression that Ford, spontaneous and full of original ideas, may be sometimes an agreeable companion; but he is a rambling and disjointed talker and, outside his special field, a very ignorant man, and he is always likely to embarrass his associates and get himself into trouble by issuing indiscreet or ridiculous statements. Today his publicity men, never forgetting the Peace Ship and the anti-Jewish campaign, sternly guard him from interviewers, censor his official statements and repudiate as unauthentic any interview which slips out by accident.

Ford's real first lieutenant is his general manager, that man of iron, Charles E. Sorenson, who has been with Henry Ford since his early days and who seems to carry the onus and the odium of his master's harshest policies. Mr. Lochner is no doubt right in assuming that it is mainly the logic of industrial relations themselves which has brought out the harsh side of Ford's character. Henry Ford at the time of the Peace Ship was a single unlettered idealist who, though enriched by the industrial system, had no idea of the fierce competitions which were involved in the gigantic war. When he wanted to run for president, he was not qualified in the least for the role of statesman. He was thus forced back to Detroit, to his triumphantly successful machine for more and more mass production, the only instrument of power he was sure of—in which, however, when business was bad and competition keener, he was forced to adopt the methods that his subordinates now carry out. When the market for his cars was booming and his payroll was at its thickest, he used often to drop into his factories and chat with his employees; he is said today never to visit them unaccompanied by a guard of twenty men.

The whole of the Ford plant seems stamped with its creator's qualities as few great industries are. You are aware of a queer combination of imaginative grandeur with cheapness, of meanness with magnificent will, of a North Western

plainness and bleakness with a serviceable kind of distinction
—the reflection of a personality that is itself a product of the
cold winds, flat banks and monotony of those northern straits.
The enormous motor plant which has overgrown the little
town of Dearborn where Henry Ford was born, truly original
creation though it is and wild dream though it would have
seemed to the earlier inhabitants of Michigan, has in certain
ways never transcended the primitive limitations of that crude
and meager American life. Beside the tight River Rouge, in
February mutton-jade and as dead and insignificant as ditch-
water, between its willow thickets and the dry yellow grass
of its banks, the office buildings of brick and concrete rise
block-shaped and monstrous before us, like the monuments
of some barbarian king approached after a journey in the
wilderness. But the taste of this king is the same as that of the
American five-and-ten-cent store, which is indulged here on
a scale almost stupefying. The platitudes over the doors about
industry and agriculture, though they are actually cut in
stone, give the impression of common cement.

Inside, the reception rooms—in which men that look like
police-court detectives check up grimly on everyone that
enters—are equipped with yellow gumwood panels and window sills of white-grained black marble. The offices themselves are furnished with rubber-black white-veined linoleum
and golden-oak furniture of flypaper yellow. Even the office
workers and attendants at Ford's seem to present certain
qualities in common, as if Ford had succeeded in developing
a special human race of his own. There is a masculine type
in Detroit which, though lumpish, is robust and dynamic,
with the genial hard-boiled bluffness of a Chicagoan. But the
subordinates at Ford's seem to run to an unappetizing pasti-
ness and baldness, an avoidance or a disregard of any kind
of smartness of dress. Some of them have sharp brown eyes,
others are gooseberry-eyed; but the preference seems to be for
pale keen blue eyes like Ford's, and like Ford, they part
their hair in the middle. The army of "servicemen" give the
impression of a last dilution of the lusterless middle-class
power which dominates the workers at Ford's. Openly jeered
at by these, upon whom they are set to spy, not particularly

beloved by the lower white-collars, whom they are supposed to have an eye on, too, they must keep to the right side of the middle-class line, and they prowl in the plant and the offices like sallow and hollow trolls, dreaming no doubt of executive desks.

Just outside the steel-and-concrete offices of Ford's engineering laboratory stands his early-American museum. This covers an immense area, and its main entrance—a complete reproduction of Independence Hall (according to Ford, an improvement on the original because it has the advantage of a concrete foundation)—is only a single façade in a whole series of colonial reproductions, which differ but little from one another and are limited to two or three types, very much like the sedans and tudors that one sees on the double-track conveyor, as if Ford had undertaken a mass production of Independence Halls. He likes to give old-fashioned balls, reviving the schottische and the polka, on a polished hardwood floor in these laboratories. The dancers disport themselves in a space between an antique collection of lusters and girandoles and a glossy gleaming row of new car models, and the host instructs the new generation of those older premotor families who twenty years ago, in Detroit, were still laughing at him as an upstart and a yokel.

One approaches the plant itself through the not yet salvaged materials of ancient discarded projects: a line of croquet-wickets that traces the now extinct electrified freight-line of the Detroit, Toledo and Ironton, a rusty junk-heap of still-tough steel vertebrae from old merchant-marine hulls bought by Ford from the government after the war. The water-covered thawing road lies before us a dull gray-blue, like Ford fenders beaten flat, like the eyes of Ford office workers. The buildings of the plant have a certain beauty, though still a little on the dime-store size: black-tipped silver cigarette chimneys rise above elongated factories of the dull green of pale pea soup, with large darker rows of little rectangular windows. The green cement has not been tinted, this is its natural color: it is a salvage from the blast-furnace slag. Beyond a level yellowish stretch, cinder-gritty on the hither side of tracks, where dark workmen's figures

move stolidly coming or going on the afternoon shift, there
looms a by-products plant, a set of black silo-shaped towers,
with white smoke pouring low in front of them, and a blast
furnace with silver cylinders and angular black cranes.

And there are parking-places densely packed with dingy
dirt-colored Ford cars. Ford workers are said to be more or less
blackmailed into buying these cars—whether they want them
or can afford them or not—in instalments stopped out of their
wages. When it was discovered a few years ago that a number of Ford workers had acquired cars of other makes, they
were ordered to park them outside so as not to cause a scandal
to the company; but then it was reported that the contraband
cars were exciting the derision of the passers-by, and their
owners were ordered to bring them in. It is doubtful whether
any Ford worker has ever dared to buy a Chevrolet: Henry
Ford—who once answered complacently, when asked what
color a new model should be, "I don't care what color you
make it so long as it's black!"—is being pressed hard by
Chevrolet, who have succeeded in producing a six-cylinder
car for a price almost as low as that of Ford's four-cylinder
car and with a smartness which Ford cars lack.

At any rate, these Fords that are waiting today inside the
Ford parking-yards have a dismal unalive look as if they were
under discipline and dumbly enduring the shift. The market
for Fords is poor, but these Fords have been driven here in
order that their owners may make more of them. There are
already far too many Ford cars, it would be well to cut down
their numbers: future Fords should be sure of good homes;
but the fate of their race was decided by a process of perpetual motion which was also supposed to accelerate. For
years they brought their masters to the plant in order that the
latter might earn money to buy more and more of the new
cars which their life was occupied in fabricating. And now
the old cars can feel it in their screws that the perpetual motion process, so far from accelerating, is rapidly running down
—that even after they themselves have been scrapped and
their bodies have been melted up to make crankshafts and
connecting rods for new cars, those new cars may find no one
to keep them. So, hitched, they wait here without hope.

For though Ford has fought the capitalist system according to his own lights, keeping out of the clutches of the bankers and refusing to issue inflated stock—standing out as best he could against all the attempts of big business to absorb or disintegrate his unique and intense personality, so inseparable from the thing it is making, he finds himself at last overwhelmed, helpless in the collapse of that system. Yet until we have succeeded, in the United States, in producing statesmen, organizers or engineers with the ability and the will to prevent the periodical impoverishment of the people who work for Ford and the wrecking of their energies in his factories, we cannot afford to be too critical of the old-fashioned self-made American so ignorant and short-sighted that he still believes that any poor boy in America can make good if he only has the gumption and, at a time when thousands of men, who have sometimes spent their last nickel to get there, are besieging his employment offices, can smugly assure the newspapers that "the average man won't really do a day's work unless he is caught and can't get out of it"—the man of genius so little dependable that he can break the careers of his closest associates with the petulance of a prima donna.

RED CROSS AND COUNTY AGENT

IN A STREET near the colonial capitol at Frankfort, there is a team of brown mules standing, and the last industrial plant to be seen as one pulls out on the train going east is the Kentucky Buggy and Harness Works. The meadows, rolling mildly and pleasantly, have now been washed by the winter rye a firm light green over brown, and the loose cow-manure-colored soil is miry with recent rain.

The rain is the first since last February. This morning the little streams are running for the first time in nearly a year with muddy water for the stock. In the pastures there are mules and fine horses, galloping or grazing—as well as red steers, black and white spotted hogs, flocks of fat-looking sheep with cunning little black-footed lambs. Stiff white sycamores stand in the meadows, with their delicate limbs and twigs, and mottled stems where the bark is peeling. Small farm houses, low and white, and a few old brick plantation houses with white-columned colonial entrances; sudden unexpected grandeur bulking sharply among the low hills of that sparse-grown and slow-paced country—with abandoned dwellings and barns, crazy-looking and with pinched-in roofs, like the things in Fontaine Fox's drawings.

The country becomes browner and more barren—more mountainous, mistletoe in the trees—gray unpainted cabins with outbuildings all leaning at different angles—houses without basements propped up on little supports of stones above the bare porous ground, "dog-run" houses with twin front doors that lead to the twin rooms inside, between which there is still sometimes found the little hallway for the hunting dogs which gives this style of architecture its name—the hills get higher and higher, and shaggy like the horses and cattle—a flattish range of mountains: the Cumberland.

————

It is court day in Clayville, Kentucky, and all the men have come in from the hills. Also, the Red Cross is giving out relief, and a man from the Department of Agriculture has come out to explain the Federal farm loans.

The courthouse is much the biggest thing in Clayville and completely dwarfs the two streets of houses which extend in front of it and behind it. The courthouse is built of brick and has white columns, like the plantation houses, and an iron fence around it.

All around this iron fence are mules, and in whichever direction you look, there are mules with a scattering of horses. Woolly-bellied and rabbit-eared, their tails knotted up in blobs, some buff or almost black or white, but mostly a standard brown that matches the mud and the mountains, they stand waiting, as if with brakes on, their heads held against the fences, absolutely moveless and mute, or shelved up along the steep slope of the dark poplar-bristling hill beneath the pale blue winter sky.

The owners of the mules, in their blue overalls or yellow coats and their mountaineers' wideawake hats, wander in and out of the courthouse, spewing tobacco-juice from the corners of their mouths. Some stop before a peddler with a truck selling cheap shoes, gaudy neckties and rainbow ribbons; some listen to a patent-medicine faker. Some pause for laconic negotiations with two thick-ankled and cotton-stockinged girls, whose coating of powder and rouge, moderate though it is, in broad daylight among the hills, amounts to provocation. These parleys seem usually to peter out, and the parties move away from one another. Rangy black-and-yellow pigs are out among the people on the streets, rooting around in the mud, colliding with the passers-by and breaking, from time to time, into sudden short gallops. At the back of the courthouse, outside the jail, the relatives and friends of the inmates are chatting with them through iron-barred windows.

A little red brick salesroom for Chevrolets, with a yellow-roofed porte-cochère and an announcement of "A Six in the Price Range of a Four," is the only up-to-date object in sight. There are a certain number of shabby cars, but they are far and away outnumbered by the mules.

Back of the courthouse they are trading mules and horses—the principal amusement in the hills. Men in long brown or blue overcoats that hang down on either side of the saddle are parading their dubious animals, specially cleaned and curried and with their rumps pulled in behind, back and forth along a sort of mud track. Others stand by and look on, betraying no interest by word or sign. Then suddenly some-one speaks up: "What d'ye want fer her?" The rider stops and gives a sales talk. The inquirer nine times out of ten shakes his head and falls back to the curb. Nonetheless, the mules and horses change masters fairly often: some of them must travel in their lifetimes through pretty much the whole county. You see people recognizing and hailing old animals they once owned.

Miss Dabney, the Red Cross worker, is a woman slightly over forty. Her face is lined and she is a little dry, but she has live black eyes behind her pince-nez and a really human and humorous smile. Miss Dabney, up to a certain point in her life, had spent all her time either living alone in a hotel in New York or visiting friends and relations in San Francisco; Litchfield, Connecticut; Morristown, New Jersey; Oxford and Florence. She has a tremendous admiration for Gilbert Murray, and it was once her ambition to know as much about Italian painting as Bernard Berenson. On one of her trips to Europe, she fell in love on the boat with an Italian doctor. In earlier days, she had a great deal of fun with intelligent little nephews and nieces, to whom her own intelligence appealed: she acted charades with them and taught them botany.

But the nephews and nieces grew up, and Miss Dabney got tired of visiting people. Since she had known the Italian doctor, she had never felt quite the same about museums. She went in for social work in New York and served on the staffs of foundations. But this turned out to be disappointing: she discovered that the foundation people drew fat salaries for sitting on committees and ultimately left the real work to underpaid college girls. One day when she saw a cartoon of an inflated and smug millionaire with a line of parasites trailing behind him, she mentally added the social worker along with the butler and the publicity man. So when the Mississippi flood occurred, Miss Dabney enlisted in the Red Cross and has been working for it ever since.

Miss Dabney, as a Red Cross worker, does not get so close to life as she hoped, because she has always felt that she made poor people shy and that they even on some occasions resented her, and this has made her shy, too. But her official duties at the present time are largely confined to going around among the local chapters and checking up on their work, and she is rather good at this because she has poise, common sense and a natural air of authority. The people in the local chapters need a good deal of keeping after: they get no pay for their work of raising money, investigating cases and distributing relief, and as they also have their own businesses and household duties to attend to, it is sometimes hard for them to get around to their work for the Red Cross. Moreover, though one would never expect it, they are capable of exploiting it for their own advantage. A certain merchant on one of Miss Dabney's committees was found to have been making deals with the applicants, promising to see that their requests were granted if they would ask to have their orders made out on his store. And sometimes the middle-class people from whom the committees have to be recruited seem to Miss Dabney so small-minded and indifferent that she gets rather cynical about the whole thing.

As for the mountain people themselves, they are really like nothing human. Their standard of living is so low that $3 a week for a family of five, $15 a month for a family of ten, is supposed to provide them with all their necessities, and they are so ignorant that the best they can usually do in the way of signing their names to applications is to touch one finger to the end of the pencil. Almost alone among the people of the United States, they manage, under ordinary conditions, to be quite self-sustaining and independent; but this is only because they are too ignorant and lazy to want anything beyond bare subsistence. They have never needed money for anything but clothes, and they don't wear very many of them. They live proverbially on meal, meat and molasses, which, before the drought set in, they raised for themselves. The meal was made out of corn, which they would get ground up at the crossroads mill, the molasses was extracted from sorghum, and the meat was always pork. In the course of the hog-killing season, Miss Dabney was invited to take part in fatty-pork-eating orgies, at which the conversation consisted of demands to "Gimme a rib!" or "Gimme a hunk off the jowl!" In other cases, however, they are most unfriendly and will tell the Red Cross to get out, no matter how badly off they are. Sometimes they insist upon eating the corn mixture which has been given them for their cows, even when they apparently don't need to. And though it is true that one sometimes nowadays finds them sleeping on corn husks, it is hard to be sure they haven't always done so.

Their morals turn out to be dreadful: they take as a matter of course certain practices which Miss Dabney knows to be statutory offenses. And the tradition of the mountain feud still makes coöperation difficult. In one of the wilder counties, Miss Dabney found that, on this account, she had to appoint several investigators, in order to get the factions taken care of. The original investigator, when told to find out what help was needed in a hostile community, indignantly replied: "He'p 'em! I wouldn't he'p 'em—I'd shoot 'em down!" And a problem has been created by an attempt to arrest a young moonshiner. He had been living in the house of his mother, a widow with eight children; and when the sheriff had come to the door, she had opened it and shot him dead. The brother of the sheriff, who was with him, had thereupon shot and killed her and the moonshiner and another of her sons. The other four sons had been jailed as witnesses, and two little girls, too young to be involved, had been left without family or home.

A good many of them, besides, have pellagra—they get listless and their skin dries up and they almost cease to eat. This is said to be caused by their diet, and the Red Cross gives them cans of tomato and salmon which are supposed to strengthen their gastric tubes. Miss Dabney has heard the legend that the ancestors of these people were Tories who took to the hills at the time of the Revolution, as well as the contrary legend that they descend from the indentured whites of the colonies. She has noticed some handsome old English names such as Montague, old English usages such as "holp" for "helped," and she has heard about, though not yet encountered, the old English ballads which the mountaineers have been so charming as to keep alive for folklore students at Harvard. At the same time, it sticks in her mind that a sociologist from one of the Kentucky colleges has assured her that, from his point of view, it would be a good deal better for society if all these poor whites of the mountains were allowed to die of the drought. And she vacillates between an uneasy feeling that $3 can't really be enough for a family of five to live on and the serious skepticism as to whether it may not be futile to try to equip people like that with durable gastric tubes.

At any rate, she has been out in these hills all winter with no other companionship than her only intermittent contacts with the other Red Cross worker in the region. She originally stayed in Booneville at a little model hotel run in connection with the college there, but the atmosphere of Christian Endeavor finally got on her nerves. She wasn't able to smoke in public or to buy cigarettes in the stores, and one Sunday morning the wife of the proprietor came up to her when she was reading the paper and said reproachfully, "You're not spending Sunday the way God means you to!" It seems that God meant her to teach a Bible class. She alternates, however, between this hotel and the only other possible tavern, where she is not bothered but has no comforts.

The Red Cross has been given headquarters in a witness room in the courthouse, which one reaches by way of a flight of stairs bespattered with tobacco-juice. Miss Dabney, when she arrives this morning, finds a good many vexatious questions to settle. The very respectful and conscientious school superintendent, with his Kentucky Indian face and his gold teeth, who in this county has given Miss Dabney much better assistance than she is in the habit of getting—has them ready to put before her. In the first place, another merchant has been misbehaving: he has succeeded in inducing a considerable number of people to sign a petition requesting the Red Cross to have their orders made out on his store. The trouble is that there are only two general stores in Clayville and that the man who got up the petition has already taken almost all his business away from the other man. He evidently wants to monopolize the trade, in which case the other storekeeper will go bankrupt. He is on the point of bankruptcy already, and unless the Red Cross buys something from him, will be a candidate for relief himself. Miss Dabney examines the petition. It is a very depressing document. Most of the signers can hardly write their names and a number of them have only made crosses. She wonders whether they know what they are doing and whether they really want to ruin the other storekeeper, and if so, why. Then there are the cases of people who live near the county-line and who have succeeded in collecting relief on both sides. These people will have to be checked up on and assigned to one county or the other, and their relief will be suspended for a while. Miss Dabney goes through the filled-out forms. The superintendent has done his best to keep down the applications granted to authentically needy cases; but out of the twelve hundred families in the county it has been estimated that at least eight hundred do seriously need relief. Miss Dabney, as she turns over the forms, reflects that, in spite of all the questions which the applicants have to answer about themselves and the pains which she tries to have taken to check up on them, it is hard to make out from these answers the actual situations of the applicants. You have to take into account their property, mortgages, debts and the number of people in the family. Where they are on record as owning more than one cow, the policy has been to disallow their applications on the theory that they ought to be able to sell the extra ones.

A new light is thrown on this assumption, however, by the arrival of an old man in gum-boots. This old man has been pestering the committee all morning, and they want to know if Miss Dabney won't deal with him. According to the rules, he is a dubious case, but they have found that it is impossible to put him off. He says he has a letter from President Hoover. The superintendent presents the old man to Miss Dabney, and he jerkily but vigorously shakes hands with her. He is tall, but bent forward from the waist; he has gray eyes, an obstinate intrusive nose, and a white mustache and beard, and he is wearing a long brown overcoat which has lost all of its buttons. Miss Dabney notes that he is pretty clean as the inhabitants of the county go, and she is struck by a resemblance to Bernard Shaw. She invites him to sit down.

"You've had help already, haven't you?" she asks. "I had two dollars and a half three weeks ago," he replies, very positively and promptly. "How many are there in your family?" "Four." "Who are they?" "My wife, my daughter, my daughter's boy and myself." "Have you any debts?" "No," says the old man, "but two dollars and a half don't last very long for a family of four!" "What are your initials, Mr. Davis?" Miss Dabney begins to look through the applications. "M.F. —Millard Fillmore. That's a president you may not know about, but they named me after him! Millard Fillmore— thirteenth president of the United States!" "But you have two cows, haven't you?" says Miss Dabney. "Couldn't you sell one of them?" "I could *give* it away," says the old man. "I don't know who I could sell it to!" Miss Dabney, after a moment's pause, inquires about his letter from the President. "I have it right here," says Mr. Davis. "I wrote to President Hoover when I couldn't get no he'p here two weeks ago." He produces a letter from an inside pocket, and Miss Dabney takes it and reads it. It turns out to have been written by the head of the Kentucky branch of the Red Cross, who refers Mr. Davis to the headquarters of his local chapter. Miss Dabney says, "Oh, yes." She folds the letter and hands it back. He puts it away in his pocket and continues to sit before her, his gumboots wide apart, his old cap held in both hands, his head thrown back and his beard stuck out, as who should say, "I've got a claim, and you know it!" He meets her with his bright gray eye. "Well," says Miss Dabney, "I'll give you an order, but I don't want you to tell anybody about it—please don't mention it to anybody." "I won't mention it to nary a soul!"

In the meantime, some other applicants have got in and taken seats on a bench beside the stove. Among them is a woman with a baby. Miss Dabney has the door locked and watched so that she can go on to deal with the paperwork as soon as she has disposed of these. There is a terrific amount of paperwork in connection with the Red Cross, and it is one of Miss Dabney's duties to see that it is kept in order.

Alone with her two assistants, the superintendent puts it up to her whether it would be a good plan to save postage on the granted applications, which have all been put into envelopes and addressed, by simply handing them out to the people, most of whom are right there at that moment milling around the courthouse. Miss Dabney says yes, why not. "The trouble is," explains the superintendent, "that the ones that don't get any relief are gonta make an awful lot o' fuss. I think we better spend the six dollars in postage and let 'em find out after they get home." Yes: that would perhaps be wiser.

An emphatic knocking is heard; the girl holds the door on a crack and talks to someone outside. The old man in gum-boots has come back and wants to know if his order is ready. She assures him they will mail it to him.

When Miss Dabney has finished with the paperwork at about four o'clock in the afternoon, she still has to wait for the accountant, who has come over with her that morning and is going back with her on the bus. He turns up extremely late—a cheery and active young man—and explains that he has been detained by a discrepancy of $700, due unquestionably not to dishonesty but to a simple lack of aptitude for figures; and that he will have to come back again next morning.

Outside, in front of the courthouse, they find the patent-medicine faker, still mounted on his motor truck and holding a considerable crowd. He is a big foursquare upstanding man with a new stiff-brimmed Stetson hat, a straight wide mouth and small greenish crafty eyes. Miss Dabney and the accountant stop and listen.

"Now I don't *have* to make these lectures!"—he pauses after

every sentence to make it possible for them to grasp its meaning—"When a minister comes to your church to preach a
sermon, he don't *have* to preach that sermon. And I don't do
this for my own good—I do it for *your* good!—You're deaf,
ain't ye?" he demands, turning to a man in the crowd. *"I say,
you're deaf, ain't ye?*—I thought ye were deaf from the
way ye held up your hand to your ear. Now just step up on
this platform a minute—I want to show ye something!" He
helps the man up on the truck: he is a little oldish hobo.
"What's your name? *I say, what's your name? Can ye hear me
now? I say, what's your name? Now I want to show ye something! Take a little of the liquid from this bottle—Dakota
Jack's Cherokee Snake Oil—and rub it behind both your ears
—rub it in good, like this!* Now some people [turning to the
crowd] can't hear. A husband usually can't hear when his
wife asks him for ten dollars. And when your mother-in-law's
in the house, ye wish ye *couldn't* hear! *That's right: rub it in
good—just behind the ear!* I knew an old woman who was so
deaf that she hadn't heard thunder in twenty years, and I
gave her a little of this oil and I had her rub it on her ears,
and then I said to her, 'Nancy, can ye hear me now!'—and she
said, 'Don't talk so loud—you'll deafen me!' *Keep rubbin' and
then leave it a little while to take effect!* I met a farmer once
and I ast him, 'Is stable manure good on potatoes?' 'Yes, if ye
like it,' he says, 'but down in Oklahoma we use ham gravy.'"
This brings a big laugh at the expense of Oklahoma. "Now
we're goin' to see how it works!" He turns to the old bum
and asks in his normal voice: "What's your name?" "Harry
Hill," the old man replies. "Now in the olden times they'd've
said that that was witchcraft! But today we know that it's
done with a medicine. You can buy it yourself for a dollar a
bottle. Dakota Jack's Cherokee Snake Oil—it took me seven
years to find out how this receipt was made, but finally the
old Indian who put it up told me the secret on his deathbed.
It's made out of sixteen different herbs, washed and powdered
at my mill in Deadwood, South Dakota. There isn't any snake
oil in it—that's jest the name that the Indians give it—so you
needn't hesitate to take it internally—it's made of clean
powdered herbs.

"Now I don't know if any of you ever wake up with a pain in the small o' your back—right here in the small o' your back! I don't know whether that's ever happened to any of ye. You may have had it and thought nothing of it—you may have thought it was jest a pain and would go away. But that pain will come back again and again—and there's nothing that can kill a man quicker than that pain in the small o' the back if it's not attended to in time. The right name o' that pain [portentously] is Hydronephrosis of the Kidney."

The crowd is momentarily scattered by the onrush of a runaway mule team.

Miss Dabney, looking around, sees a solemn line of men filing into the village drugstore and laying down their dollars for Dakota Jack's remedy. As she moves toward the bus, she reflects that it is certainly just as wise for the Red Cross to help these people with supplies rather than cash. Even so, it is perfectly possible that some of these victims of the faker may be sacrificing their last dollars to cure the deafness of members of their families, and so will soon land on the Red Cross's list.

Miss Dabney has heard a good deal about the benefits of the radio to the mountain people, but she has seen them in the store listening to Amos and Andy, and she wonders whether this sort of thing is doing much for them after all. She even can't help wondering at moments whether that professor of sociology wasn't perhaps right about them.

Nevertheless, she is there for the winter.

————

Brown dried-out fields and hills, with badly shaved beards of corn-stubble, forlorn dried-up plantings of corn that droop over like "Indian pipe"—orange signs advertising Nehi, a new competitor of Coca Cola, plastered along the roadside—dog-run cabins caving in, sag-roofed shacks on stone stems—chickens, mules and sheep—red infertile soil—the stream-beds running at last with their green and muddy drainage—little red-headed and tow-headed children in pink, blue and white of their Sunday best, playing around the church and the schoolhouse—a cement works, abandoned now, with the houses of a small company settlement—a couple of infinitesimal soft-coal mines, hardly more than black burrows in the clay—blackened chimneys left standing from fires.

The county agent stops his car just before the road crosses a creek, and he and Gillam, the head of the School Board, get out. The pathway, deep with mud, leads right into the hills and the wilderness. "The grocer over at Booneville found 'em," says the county agent. "He was fishin' for minnows in the creek and he happened to come across the cabin in the woods. He knew John Ingram's brother Fred. I reckon Fred's most as pore as John, ain't he?" "He's right pore," says Gillam —he speaks phlegmatically, with incredible slowness. "If it hadn't been for that rain," says the agent, "I reckon the fish would be dead in the streams like they are up in Ohio—they die and make a scum on top of the water up there, and it gives off a poisonous gas and the people come down sick from breathin' it." "I hear tell," says Gillam. He is a short man with a blank expression. He is typical of the dog-run people, but there is more in his head than in his face. He has ten children and several of them have distinguished themselves by winning prizes at school. The county agent is a big-boned blue-eyed red-faced rustic Kentuckian, who wears spectacles and a large tweed cap pulled down over his eyes. He was born in the next county—an agent must know his locality but cannot serve in his native county.

The disused road becomes an aimless clearing through thickets, under the brow of a hacked-down and rocky bank that has somewhat the aspect of a quarry. "The Devil musta dragged his apron-strings through here!" says the agent. "I don't see what anybody would want to clear it for!" The clearing widens and reveals a chimney, standing alone like a stump in the forest, from which every trace of the house has disappeared. The agent stamps on the ground. "You couldn't drive a railroad spike into it!" he says. "I reckon they found that out and moved the house away—it don't look like it had been burnt.—Say, that's a potato patch, ain't it? That's what it is! Somebody's planted a potato patch!" They gaze at the unpromising patch and pass on, and come out finally into a

miry field along the wide slope of a hill. As they slosh with
heavy shoes through the mud, they get nearer and nearer to
a log cabin, and when they are up to it, they look in. Inside
there is nothing at all: half the floor is even gone, and you
can see down through the cross-beams to the ground. "He
pulled the floor up and burnt it for kindling," says Gillam
in his impassive drawl. "Well," the agent remarks heartily,
"he moved out of it jest in time—it was jest about to fall in on
top of him!"

Where they are going turns out to be a long walk. "Did
you say this was only a mile?" demands the agent. They end
by having to climb the hill.

At last they see, looming above them, a little group of
shacks. As they approach it, a dog barks but mysteriously
remains invisible. One of the shacks has smoke coming out
of the chimney: it is a primitive backwoods log cabin, with
no windows and crude scale-like shingles such as the earliest
poorest settlers must have built.

They go to the door, which is open, but there is so much
smoke inside that they can hardly see. There are people
around a fire, and an old man, who, though he hardly comes
forward, seems the principal presence in the room. The agent
greets him with watering eyes: "Well, Ingram, we jest come
by to see how ye were gittin' along!—Ye able to keep warm
this weather?" "Yes: we keep the fire lit," says the old man.
"These your children?" The agent has made them out, gathered around the fire. "Yes," says the old man. "You want to
be careful this house don't burn down!" "Oh, we keep watch
on the fire," the old man replies, with simplicity and in a
rather dim and feeble voice, but with a dignity which declines to be submissive to the benevolent bullying of the
agent. "Well, you want to look out it don't catch fire some
day! I saw one burn down jest the other day, and the people
jest leaned against the fence and watched it burn." "I'm careful," says the old man, mildly and firmly.

"How're ye off for food?" asks the agent. "Have ye got
plenty of food?" "That's jest what we hain't got much of,"
says the old man, as if with quiet humor. He has a gentle
and rather sensitive face, with very pale blue eyes and a fron-

tiersman's drooping yellow mustache; his hair under his limp brown hat is so long that it comes down over his collar. He is small and thin and pale—so thin and pale that he gives the effect of having undergone some kind of purification. "Well," the agent demands, "how long d'ye think that what ye've got'll last ye?" "We've got 'bout two more messes o' meal— 'bout half a pound o' meat—a quart o' flour." The agent looks around: the flour is hung up in a sack immediately behind his shoulder under the low eaves of the sloping roof. That side of the cabin is filled by a dilapidated iron bedstead with most of the white paint scraped off and a frowzy mound of old quilts and mattresses. On the other side, to the left of the fire, is a table with dishes on it and firewood underneath it; and to the right, a blackened kettle on a stove, a chair and two wooden boxes. This is all there is in the cabin, and there is no room for anything more.

"Did ye git it from the Red Cross?" "Yes." "How many times did the Red Cross he'p ye?"—in talking to Ingram, he speaks his language. "Twice." "How much did ye git from 'em?" "Ten dollars." The agent is silent a moment, then he asks: "You make baskets, don't ye?" "I hain't been able to work lately—I've been sick." "What's been the matter with ye?—flu?" "I've had the fever." He is evidently not well yet— his eyes water, and he coughs continually. "Have ye seen a doctor?" "No: I hain't seen a doctor. I make myself some boneset tea. I take boneset for most complaints." He shows them a jar of stalks in water. "Does it he'p ye? Are ye gittin' better?" "Yes: I feel better."

The agent stares at the children. In the dim and smoky cabin, he is able to make out four. There are a baby; an oldish boy, evidently a cripple, crouched at one side of the fire, with his legs folded under him; a little girl almost hidden behind the stove; and a boy of about thirteen or fourteen sitting on a wooden box in front of it. "How old's that youngest child?" asks the agent. "She was 'bout three months old when my wife died—that was 'bout three years ago." Mr. Ingram takes up the baby and holds her in his arms as they go on talking —easily, with familiar tenderness, as women hold their children: the baby has a very dirty face. "How old's this boy?"

"I doan know—I've got it down here"—he nods vaguely. "How old's the little girl?" "I doan know"—he confesses it without embarrassment. "This other boy is crippled, is he?" "Yes; a boy threw a rock at him when he was small and hurt his back." The cripple, as they begin to talk about him, turns around toward the fire and holds a stiff withered arm to the blaze.

The agent still gazes at the children. "How old are ye, son?" he asks the other boy, a good-looking little blond fellow. "I doan know," the boy replies in a voice distinct and surprisingly deep, which contrasts with his father's faintness. "You'd ought to find out those children's ages, Ingram, and teach 'em to 'em!" the agent remonstrates with him. "I've got it all down here," says Ingram. "I cain't remember things since I've had the fever." It becomes evident that, in spite of his amiable manners, he is very dazed and vague—lightheaded, the agent imagines. One feels that he is slightly unreal, as if one were sharing his fever. But the resonant voice of the boy still vibrates and disconcerts them with the presence of normal life. "How many kids have ye got altogether?" the agent continues. "Five." "Where's the other one?" "I doan know: he's gone away somewhere." "How many children has your brother Fred got?" "I doan know: I never did count 'em."

"Now I'm goin' to ask ye a question," the agent emphatically announces, as if to impress on Ingram the seriousness of the subject he is broaching. "Did ye trade off some bedclothes the Red Cross gave ye?" "I traded the blankets for a heifer. I had to sell my two cows to pay the doctor when my wife was sick, and I had to sell the hawg because I couldn't feed him. The heifer kin graze this winter, and we'll git some milk." (God knows what she can graze on! thinks the agent.) "But it'll be nine months before she can have a calf, won't it?" "Yes," the old man assents. "An' where're ye goin' to git food when this gives out?" "I doan know," says the old man, with no trace of anxiety or pathos. "Well, you'd hadn't ought to traded that beddin'—you don't want to trade anything that the Red Cross gives ye! Is that why they wouldn't he'p ye any more? They found out ye'd traded the beddin'?" "That's what they said," says Ingram. "Well, you don't want to do anything like that again!" the agent speaks imperatively and loudly. "You needed those blankets to keep these children warm at night!" "We keep warm," says Ingram politely, but with the air of one who knows his own business. The agent looks again at the children: he is baffled and appalled by the Ingrams. All the time that he has been talking to their father, the children, never moving, have watched with a bright gaze that seems intelligent. Himself with goggled eyes and thick lips, a red, blunt-nosed, salmon-shaped visage, he recognizes in these clear oval faces, paled and refined by starvation, the pure type of that English race which, assimilated on the frontier to the Indians' hatchet profile and high cheekbones, inbred in Boston and Virginia, still haunts our American imagination as the norm from which our people has departed, the ideal towards which it ought to tend. "Why don't ye make 'em go to school?" "It's too fur and the children throw rocks at 'em." The agent has heard from the schoolteacher that the Ingrams, during their brief period of schoolgoing, seemed to be unusually smart. He addresses himself again to the children. "You better move away from that stove!" he admonishes the little girl. "You'll get too hot and catch cold." The little girl makes no reply, but partly draws in her head, so that only her bright eyes and blond hair are visible over the top. After a moment, the boy who spoke before makes a frustrated movement and sound as if to prompt his sister to obey, but he seems paralyzed in the visitors' presence and unable to break the spell: he can only sit silent and gaze. The agent persists, smiling: "You'll have to grow up, sis, and he'p your pappy keep house!" The little girl suddenly smiles—the first time that any of them has changed his expression—a lovely pleased and candid smile. "Yes," says the agent. "You'll have to grow up"—and he turns to Ingram: "Is the boy a he'p to ye? Has he learned to do things?" "Yes . . . he kin can blackberries pretty good."

"Well," the agent announces at last, "we'll have to be gittin' along!—I don't suppose you'll want to ask us to stay to supper!" "Won't ye stay to supper?" asks the old man. "No: I don't guess you want any friends to stop and take dinner with ye tonight!" "Won't ye stay?" repeats Ingram politely.

As they go out, the dog barks at them again, and this time they are able to locate him in a box beside the door. He is black and droops a flop-eared head on paws that hang out of the box. Though he goes through the forms of barking, he no longer lives up to his duty of flying out fiercely at strangers: he seems feeble and hopeless—hungry, too.

"I feel kind o' chilly," says Ingram, as he stands outside seeing them off; he begins to cough again. "Why don't ye go and live in that house down the hill? It's a better house'n yours, even though the floor's half tore up." "That's Peter Hunter's house," says Ingram. "Peter wouldn't want me to live in it."

"Now I'm goin' to talk to the Red Cross," says the agent, "and I want ye to go to 'em again, and I think they'll he'p ye. But I don't want ye to trade anything they give ye! Now remember that: don't trade anything they give ye!" "It don't matter what kind o' trade ye make," says Ingram, who, as it now appears, has completely misunderstood the objections to his behavior—"It don't matter what kind o' trade ye make, there's always folks that'll say ye made a bad trade—Gillam'll tell ye the same!" "Well," says the agent—it is all he can do—"the next time the Red Cross gives ye anything, you keep it!"

The boy has come to the door and is still guardedly peering out at the visitors with his disconcertingly intelligent face. "Wrap those children up warm," says the agent, "and don't let 'em catch your fever!"

It is getting dark as they go back down the hill. The agent feels kind of sad. His whole county is in a desperate way—half his work has been undone by the winter. He has spent years teaching the people what to raise and how to raise it, and in trying to get the children educated, and now, this last month, the local banks have failed through the speculations of some fool gambler in Louisville, and seventy-some members of his young people's club whom he had induced to start bank accounts have lost the whole of their savings at one blow. Two hundred and eighty thousand dollars amounts to a lot of money in a backwoods Kentucky county. And it needs more than farm loans and Red Cross relief to put the community on its feet.

The county agent's relation to the Red Cross is very much like Miss Dabney's relation to the New York social workers. He has observed in the Red Cross committees the phenomenon that discouraged Miss Dabney with the committees employed by the foundations: they leave the real work to somebody else. The little college town of Booneville is the center of civilization of the region, and the people there are good people, and they're fine Kiwanis—he recognizes that—but they won't take any responsibility: it always turns out that Mary hasn't had a chance to see John yet.

Now he's got to see the Red Cross about Ingram and try to get the cripple into an institution—his mother would never let him be sent to one, but they could probably persuade Ingram to give him up. And he might persuade local families to take in the two older children. As for Ingram, he will very possibly die, and although it's a sad thing to admit, it's probably the best thing he can do—he's such a sorry fellow. But then what could be done with the baby? People don't want strange babies.

"I don't think that story can be true," he remarks, after a time to Gillam, "about those children eating their fingers." "I don't see how it's possible," drawls Gillam. "They wouldn't eat their fingers," continues the agent. "I couldn't see any signs of it—I tried to make the little girl come out from behind the stove." But he remembers that she would not do so.

"This country is going wild," he says presently. "It's been going wild ever since the War. The people don't go to church any more—they listen to sermons on the radio. The highways have changed life altogether. The people used to help each other out, but they don't care about each other now any more than if they was stock!" "Down where I was born in Tennessee," says Gillam, "if a farmer's crop failed, a neighbor would lend him corn. They never gave each other notes—he'd pay it back the next year." "Nowadays," declares the agent, "people would shoot ye for a dollar! They don't mean to hurt ye, but they want the money!"

SENATOR AND ENGINEER

AT THE END of the Hotel Carlton ballroom, with its sumptuous crimson curtains, painted beams and imitation Renaissance chandeliers, Senator Norris, his face bright pink in the
light of a strong electric lamp, is addressing the Progressive
Conference, in front of a rich and dusky tapestry and behind
a shiny nickel-plated microphone. He is an old-fashioned political speaker, with hard Western r's and the rhetorical flowers of another age: the power trust is "the most gigantic, far-
reaching and comprehensive monopoly which has ever been
devised by the mind of man" and has "secretly enmeshed its
slimy fingers into the warp and woof of human life," but
before the "onward march" of public opinion, "the influences of monopoly, corruption and dishonesty" will "fade
away as the morning mist disappears before the rising sun."
   He is a short gray-haired man in a neat black suit, with a
white shirt, low collar and old-fashioned black bow tie, a
thin gold watch chain stretched from the top of a vest pocket
to a lower vest pocket on the same side, and trousers that
wrinkle over black polished shoes. His hair, brushed straight
back in a crest, shows a fine Western breeziness and defiance.
He has dark circumflex eyebrows, old eyes, a small mouth
with a gleam of gold teeth in one corner—a gentle sensitive
face, very stubborn, though beginning at last to break down
under age and unyielding opposition. But he is still unbent,
his carriage is straight; he lifts his head and raises his eyebrows with exhilarating haughtiness and disdain over a letter
from Senator Watson, the Republican leader of the Senate,
in which the latter tries to bait the Progressive Conference.
But there is no virulence in his sarcasm—even his denunciation of Watson reveals a nature essentially sweet. And his

gestures—old-time orator's gestures—show white hands with tapering fingers. But today, toward the end of a career which has included an obstinate effort to oppose our entering the war and which has recently had to struggle with attempts on the part of his own party machine to prevent his re-election by accusing him of cruelty to his children and of sybaritic living in a cottage built partly by his own hands, and even to rob him of part of his vote by putting a grocer with the same name on the ballot—Senator Norris's look of defiant pride sometimes approximates a look of pain.

He speaks at length about the power trust, which he has been fighting since Roosevelt's time and looking back for his inspiration to the Roosevelt of the trust-busting era. He shows that Buffalo, which depends on the power trust, has to pay more than twice as much for its electricity as Toronto, which owns its own power—though Toronto is obliged to transmit its current more than four times as far from the same river; that Rochester, with a population of more than 300,000, is charged four times as much as Ottawa, with a population of 120,000; that the power interests in Seattle have just succeeded, through their instrument the Mayor, in putting out a city lighting superintendent who had been on the point of persuading the city to vote for public ownership; and in Washington have caused the Power Commission to throw out one of the ablest of its experts, who had been trying to prevent the padding, to the tune of more than five million dollars, of the costs of the Clarion River dam.

"So, my friends, this power trust gets in its work. . . . What is the object of government, my friends? As I look at it and as our forefathers looked at it when they enunciated the Declaration of Independence, they said that the object of government was life, liberty and the pursuit of happiness! That is what we are here for. That is what the President ought to be there for. That is what you have your state governments for. That is what we ought to get out of government. . . . The object of government is human happiness. . . . Old Ben Adhem in the ancient days, that old soldier, was awakened one night from his slumber by an angel writing in a book. . . . Oh, my friends, we ought to lead our

political life and our religious life so that when the end comes
our names can be written upon that scroll, in eternity's language, that we are down as those that loved their fellow
men!"

————

The Taylor Society of scientific managers are giving a dinner for one of the American engineers who has been in Russia working for the Soviets. The dinner is not a very good
dinner: it is a wholesale New York production, planned
without taste or imagination and rather unappetizingly
cooked. But it makes no pretense to be anything else: the
Taylor Society is an organization of efficiency experts, and
the discussion of industrial efficiency is to be the main feature of the evening. From the point of view of scientific
management, the whole affair has been admirably arranged:
dinner is announced and served early, on the dot of 6:15, so
that there may be plenty of time for speeches afterwards,
and, on the other hand, the speeches themselves are to be
rigorously expedited and limited by a three-minute egg-
boiling glass planted conspicuously in sight of the speakers.

For the rest, there are certain amenities: the dinner takes
place in the Fraternity Club, under festively painted beams
of precisely the same kind as those in the ballroom of the
Washington hotel in which Senator Norris spoke; and one
can imagine in a vague fancy niche behind the speakers'
table an icon of Frederick Taylor, that great genius of Pennsylvania industry, engineer, factory-organizer and inventor of
labor-saving devices, the patron saint of scientific management. Over a handsome and convivial stone fireplace looms
the strangely incongruous motto: "*Dum vivimus vivamus.*"

Mr. H. J. Freyn is the president of the Freyn Engineering
Company of Chicago, and he has lived for four years in
Soviet Russia as an advisor on the construction of steel mills.
He is a shortish, solid, strong-looking man, all built in one
piece, with an exceptionally thick bull-neck, hair that bristles
straight up on his head and rather small greenish eyes behind
thick-lensed rimless glasses. He has kept a slight German ac-

cent, and speaks earnestly but with occasional irony. One somehow gets the impression that he is expecting, on the part of his audience, an attitude of opposition.

It is hard, he begins, to talk about Russia. A friend of his who has been there a good deal found out, when he came back from his first trip, that people who asked you about Russia always did one of two things: they either listened with interest when you told them what was taking place there or they froze up completely as soon as you began to talk about it and refused to hear a word you said. He had finally adopted this policy: when people wanted him to tell them about Russia, he always asked them first whether they wanted to hear good news or bad news.

Now the Taylor Society has invited him to talk to them about the management side of the Soviet Five-Year Plan. Well, they have sent him a bulletin explaining the Society's own aims. According to this prospectus, it is the Taylor Society's desire to promote "the full understanding and the adoption of the principles of administration and management which, intelligently applied to organized effort, are conducive to the gradual elimination of unnecessary labor and unduly burdensome toil in the accomplishment of the work of the world"; the Taylor Society is "inspired by the conviction that only those enterprises can sustain themselves which meet a genuine economic need, as ascertained by careful analysis of markets—those which conduct their operations through plans, schedules and methods that eliminate waste of human and material energies employed, and which maintain the spirit of working together toward a common end through harmonious personal relations." And he will attempt to analyze the Five-Year Plan from the point of view of the Taylor Society's program.

As he proceeds, it becomes apparent that the ideals conceived by the Soviets are precisely those of the Taylor Society, and that it is their aim to put them into practice on an unprecedented scale. From his observation of the steel and iron industry, he would say that "the principles of administration and management" are decidedly being "intelligently applied" —that the Soviets are "eliminating unnecessary labor and unduly burdensome toil" at a rate which will eventually make it possible "to replace hard labor by machines and the products of home industry by the mass production of factories. In this respect, the Soviet Union proposes to go much further than the so-called capitalistic countries. Whereas, elsewhere in the world, and notably in the United States, the trend of the times is towards the creation and organization of large and powerful corporations, towards consolidation of banks, manufactories, steel companies, railroads and power concerns, the Soviet government has frankly embarked upon a policy of complete state control, embracing practically every human activity." The worker and the small peasant are to be assured of "an existence of contentment and reasonable comfort"—and one of the means to this end has been the establishment of the seven-hour working day and the five-day continuous week. He asserts that "the Soviet state may readily be considered one huge industrial organization or economic enterprise 'designed to meet a genuine economic need'"—and leaves it to the members of the Taylor Society to assign it to the category of "those enterprises" as to which the Society is "inspired by the conviction" that they, and they only, "can sustain themselves." As for the "careful analysis of markets," he does not believe that this is necessary, "for the domestic market is virtually unlimited."

The members of the Taylor Society listen to Mr. Freyn impassibly—with the exception of one sharp-faced old man, who holds his hand behind his ear, takes notes and occasionally asks to have figures repeated, and a younger one, the full-blown type of the cheerful prosperity-promoter, florid-faced, with round bone glasses, a toothbrush mustache and a cigar, who begins by grinning at every statement which might suggest that the Soviets aren't so smart as they thought they were, but relapses, as it becomes more evident that the attitude of the speaker is enthusiastic, into a kind of dazed smirk.

There is only one item of the Society's program which Mr. Freyn does not explicitly take up: "the spirit of working toward a common end through harmonious personal relations." He does, however, try to explain what relations under the Soviets are like. He first reminds his audience that, in view of the fact that "the three most momentous historical events, the American and French Revolutions and the Protestant Reformation, passed over old imperial Russia without leaving any imprint upon the destinies of that vast country," it is "no wonder that the triumph of modern democracy could not be established" there. The Soviet government is frankly a dictatorship, but a dictatorship at the present stage is thought "essential for the welfare of the people." And it now appears that Mr. Freyn is far from regarding our kind of democracy as an ideally satisfactory arrangement: "a modern business enterprise can scarcely be operated or managed by applying the principles of democracy . . . on the contrary, the strong hand and mind of business executives are required, who know what they want and what is needed for the good of the enterprise." As a matter of fact, the Soviets are perhaps still a little too democratic: he has often wished "that more decisions might be made by responsible individuals rather than by committees and commissions."

He pays tribute to the unselfishness and integrity of the Soviet officials he has known, who live lives of Spartan austerity and are ready to work themselves to death; and insists that they make no attempt to suppress their mistakes and difficulties, but have a policy of publishing bad news and leave the people free to criticize the government—thus supplying the capitalist press with most of its ammunition against them. He denies that the trial of the engineers could possibly have been a put-up job, since technicians such as these were needed and could hardly have been sacrificed for a faked-up melodrama. He speaks of "the insidious schemes of these marplots," and tells the audience that he himself has had experience of their obstructive tactics.

In all this, he rarely mentions Communism, but as he goes on, one gets the impression that, from his engineer's point of view, he is as much sold on Soviet methods as, through the logic of Marxist doctrine, any Thirteenth Street party member. The outside world, he declares, speaking with a conviction and emphasis that have almost something of Soviet fervency, has been led to believe that if the Five-Year Plan fails, the Soviet government will fail. "Such ideas have no basis in fact. I believe that should the pressure become too great and lack of capital and credit too serious, the program will merely be slowed up and the time extended. I further believe that if the gigantic Five-Year Plan were completed by the end of 1933, even to only 75 per cent, a remarkable technical and managerial feat, unparalleled in the world's history, will have been achieved!"

So Mr. Freyn ends, and sits down. An economist from Brookings Institute gets up to open the discussion which follows: "Mr. Freyn, in his detailed, comprehensive and almost impartial account of the Five-Year Plan. . . ."

"STILL"—: MEDITATIONS OF A PROGRESSIVE*

THE BRIGHT DRAB glare of the airport grounds. As you get into the red-painted plane, they hand you a small oil-paper packet: two close little rows of seats in a narrow moth's body. Well, well, there's cotton and chiclets in the package—the cotton is to stick in your ears and the gum to steady your nerves. "Air-Sickness Containers Located under Each Seat"— that sounds ominous. I might as well use the gum and the cotton. The porter shuts the door—now we're off: faster, faster, faster, higher roaring pressure of speed of starting— great fun: now we've dropped the ground. The muddy flat Potomac; Washington a litter of brickyard fragments; the grayish Capitol, the white government buildings—like what? —like nothing but government buildings even from way up above, and not very handsome ones; the little aligned sub-urban houses. I don't like these elevator drops, when you feel your seat falling away. The March fields below; worn-out patches on an old nap-bare carpet that shows the warp and woof. The long straight roads with little black cars that travel straight and fast along them. The passengers are very quick, seem under a certain strain.

Still, all those people at the Progressive Conference did get to the point of getting together—and what a mixed as-sortment they were—curious to think about what being pro-gressive meant to the different ones! The senators at least had in common that they represented the agricultural West. Norris is an old-fashioned Western type who hates the in-dustrial people—preoccupied with the power question. Bob

---

* At that time the word "progressive" had not yet been taken over by the Communists.

La Follette has inherited the family radical tradition. Cutting
is so much of a New Yorker that one forgets he's Senator
from New Mexico. He's rather like an English liberal—like
some of the men in the Labor government—we've never, so
far as I know, had that type in the Senate before. He sounds
as if he were aiming at something like the English system,
the President and the Cabinet responsible to Congress, a congressional majority controlling policy. Would this really help
very much? All right no doubt for a Congress made up of
Cuttings and La Follettes, but there are only a few such men
—the rest are professional politicians.—Phelps Putnam, the
poet, with his black clothes and his monocle, hanging around
the conference—a little too much like Wyndham Lewis in his
menacing fascist make-up. Still, it shows that the literary guys
are taking public matters more seriously—God knows that
our belated bleeding-heart romanticism has run out even for
a writer like Phelps who is able to do something first-rate
with it.—I wonder what Hergesheimer was doing at a back
table in the Carlton dining room. Could he conceivably have
been interested in the conference or does he simply get a
kick out of a place like the Carlton? Those dreadful flavorless
expressionless mannequins that paraded back and forth in
Chanel and Patou gowns all the time we were having lunch
—dreadful flavorless lunch—the only time they looked at all
human was when they smiled at each other across the room.
—Costigan's quite a fine old type,* with his Spanish hatchet-
face and his dry yellow skin—his speech a little dry, too, but
it's clear he knows his stuff—I can never get the hang of the
tariff, but it is plain that, when these questions come up nobody sees very far beyond his own little racket—the man who
held up the Sears, Roebuck catalogue and said that there
were 30,000 articles listed in it and how was anybody ever
going to know enough about them to work out the tariff
properly—he pointed out that paint-brush handles were protected.—The Colorado beet-grower and the Filipino: the
Filipino, very tense and formal, in gold glasses and a dapper
cutaway, announced that if the United States would give

* Edward P. Costigan, Senator from Colorado, 1930–36.

the Philippines their freedom, they would willingly forego the free trade for their cocoanut oil and sugar. The beet-grower, a hearty loquacious fellow, rose to his feet to state that he was proud to be one of what people called the "wild jackasses of the West," that the wild jackasses never brayed unless there was some reason for it, that just now they were being ruined by free sugar imports from the Philippines, and that he hoped to God the Senate of the United States would have the decency and the brains to give the Filipinos their freedom! Another Filipino got up and declared that he sympathized with the American sugar interests, but that, after all, the United States had taken over the Philippines against their will and . . . "But honest, ain't ye glad now we did it?" the beet-grower interrupted. "Would ye want to be back with your swamps an' your bad roads an' no schools an'" . . . The Filipino said no, they were not glad. Those were the respective extents to which those two believed in progressivism.

The flat thick muddy branches of Chesapeake Bay like lung lobules on an anatomical chart—a few barges like beetles on the water, their noses turned toward Baltimore. Dull end of a March day—pale coldish sun now setting among faintly rusty clouds—on the horizon, dimness.—Hoover didn't look so unhealthy or so unattractive as one expected—grayish hair, pink face, smoke-blue eyes—the thing is that, since the depression, he's been becoming in people's minds a kind of great pulpy empty ectoplasm, an embodiment, hardly human, of the administration's stupidity and impotence. One hardly expected to find him a man. He muttered something about restriction in the oil industry. I wonder whether his rather sly smile, when he dismissed the reporters with "That's all for today," implied that they'd submitted to him questions about the Progressive Conference. He makes them write out all their questions beforehand and then refuses to answer most of them. Everybody at the conference was either denouncing Hoover or wondering why he behaved as he did—he does seem to be a case of political ambition completely devoid of ideals or ideas—I suppose he has the exaggerated respect for the rich which comes from having started poor—that's no doubt the real hole in the skimmer of the American

poor-boy-to-President idea—people who've had a hard time
to make money are likely to end by taking it too seriously.
—That plane in the airport below is fluttering around like a
moth that's just been burned in a lamp.—They wouldn't let
in old John Dewey on account of what they regard as his
merely loose talk about the need for a third party. Still, I
suppose that was the kind of thing that had to be pretty
rigorously limited—they were certainly quite right in keeping
out Prohibition. Ben Marsh of the People's Lobby, Dewey's
political manager, announced that he was going to come in
order to heckle the speakers. He claimed that the independent senators might have been able to force an extra session
and get some of these matters attended to, that Hoover would
have been glad of the excuse to call one. But he never made
good his threat.—Still, one would like to see them come out
and say, "Capitalism has got to go. It's just a question of time,
so we're trying to make the transition easy." If they're going
in for scaring the manufacturers, they might as well scare
them good and proper. I imagine that what they're afraid
of is scaring their constituents, too. But why are these American progressives so tongue-tied with inhibitions?—they're shy
of the whole language of real political thought. The surest
way to shake and embarrass an American political reformer,
the surest way to make him back down, has always been to
accuse him of socialism—that's what they did with Bryan,
and we ought to be beyond that stage. I suppose that we
still have a feeling that God is going to strike us dead if we
admit that our old-fashioned republic isn't the last word in
political science.

Big red bee-body of the motor always outside the window,
with its barb-armed behind and blunt head—springs quivering in the fierce jingle and continual beat of the rhythm—
what if that thick hoop that keeps them in place flew off.
—Leo Wolman's brother Sam met a man in the lavatory at
the Carlton who asked him what he thought of the conference—Sam said that he hadn't been to it. Well, the man said,
he had come all the way from Boston for it. What did he
think about it? asked Sam. "Well," said the man, "I don't see
what's the use of their planning what to do with industry

when industry's controlled by capital."—Leo Wolman's story about Lincoln Steffens—he met Steffens and found him beaming for the first time in history. "What's the matter? You look so cheerful," said Wolman. "I've been waiting for this moment for years—to see all you fellows together, up against a blank wall and not knowing what to do about it!"

Neutral brown land underneath, tree-bristling or mud-spongy—the water a dullish mirror. Those long roads that look like pipes, bent at moderate angles or curving only a little, with black cars traveling eternally along them. Well: this is a little dull—the time has come to read the *New Yorker*.

Long gray buildings—is this the Du Pont works?—gray colony of company houses. There's something solemn and grim about a great industry like that—it seems to weigh upon the executives as oppressively as it does on the workers—it's something like the weight of the army—but why the hell should it be?—I suppose that anything effective must come from the labor end. What can the progressives do but whip up a certain publicity and try to create a favorable atmosphere?—perhaps put through a little legislation.—Suppose Hillman got to be president of the AF of L—they had to ask William Green* to speak—he was hissed when he opposed the recognition of Russia. One of the labor experts was hopeful to a sensational degree—he thought that the AF of L would eventually throw out its leaders and would then, under enlightened leadership from one of the independent unions, embark on a whirlwind campaign—it would be easy to pick up the auto workers—if the Communists could go down South and get the textile workers, what couldn't a legitimate movement do?—Is this utopian? Somebody was telling me that he was talking to a representative of the Socialist Labor Party and asked him what he thought was going to happen. It was obvious, said the Socialist Laborite: capitalism was soon going to break down, and the Socialist Labor Party would step in and take over the government.

Philadelphia still seen by daylight, but with little yellow lamps on the bridges and along the notched streets—6:15,

* President of the American Federation of Labor.

exactly as scheduled.—I wonder whether Cutting has ever read Marx—he evidently reads a good deal—and has been to the Soviet Union, as few other Senators have. Still, those men in the British Labor government have unquestionably read Marx. I suppose that it is never possible for people to get to the point of taking any very drastic action till their interests are pretty seriously affected. A man who is badly off may take steps to better himself—but how can people with property go to the length of dispossessing themselves?—it seems to be true that a high standard of living, unless you're a saint or an eccentric, is something that you can't get away from—you can't help feeling more solidarity with other people with the same standard of living than with anybody else whatever, no matter how worthy or how badly off. It is only when people are far-sighted enough to see their standard of living threatened that they do anything more than talk. Borah denounced "the capitalists" for inflating General Motors and so forth, reminded us that 80 per cent of the money was owned by 4 per cent of the people, but then hastened to assure his audience—the big radio audience arranged for him rather than the one in the room—that he didn't propose to confiscate their money: "Let them keep it!" he thundered, with a blend of magnanimity and scorn. Somebody else had a plan for raising the standard of the poor without lowering the standard of the rich. The real trouble, no doubt, is that neither the politicians nor the intellectuals—the people who ought to supply the ideas—have been seriously hit by the depression—I've done unusually well this winter myself —I suppose that nobody at that conference was in anything but very comfortable circumstances—well-paid journalists, distinguished professors, grange and labor officials, idealistic manufacturers, political people with sound positions.—Well, there, with its gun-barrel chimneys, is a big public service plant, declaring itself in block electric letters, all alone on the Jersey mudbanks, somewhere in the neighborhood of Trenton—a few small boats resting on the river at evening—roaring red flames flaring from inside some factory—Trenton in the gathered darkness, a thickish ringworm rash of lights that twinkle in the haze, irregularly, as if in areas that grow successively sensitive but with a sort of steady rhythm—a red and dark sooty west, the looping streams.—It's probably unfortunate that Washington is detached from the rest of the country —a special city for political life, no wonder American politics has a way of not seeming serious—and literary New York's just as much cut off from the general life of the country— though it's the biggest industrial city, if you count Newark in—which we'll presently be coming to now.—The black countryside, a last glint of cold streams, roads in the dead black with the same little cars traveling, but now with their little lights on—unidentifiable lights of towns, embedded in the dark of distance—I can't even tell where Princeton is.

Another bigger rash of lights—that's Newark—an electric sign: a thick red arrow jerking back and forth, first points one way, then the other—thick wormwinding ribbons of water cut out on the black in clear gray. We're going into the big twinkling limitless light-bed, ruled strongly across with lines of light.—Up against a thing like that, there's not much that anybody can do, I suppose.—Still, you don't want to let it buffalo you.—Is there any real political consciousness coming to life down there?—that new independent union that Frank Vogel was trying to start in Detroit—that $8 that those Arkansas farmers sent in to the *Daily Worker*, vastly to the staff's surprise.—Could there be another farmer-labor movement? Could the white-collar workers be induced to support it? Could those progressive senators lead it?

A great criss-cross web of lights—signaling in the dark— field pricked out with green, yellow and red. This turning and milling in the air makes you a little sick—lists very far over to the left, encounters a pointer of light—down—gliding just above the ground—takes the opening neatly and cleanly in the enclosure picked out with green lights—a bump, taxiing in—the pilot gives her her head in a last snorting triumphing charge, tilted tail-down, to the port.

A BAD DAY IN BROOKLYN

ON WEDNESDAY, March 25, in Brooklyn, three people tried to kill themselves.

———

The Bay Ridge section of Brooklyn is inhabited chiefly by Scandinavians. Fifth Avenue from Leif Ericsson Square is an infinitely continuing suburban business street of drugstores, small department stores, five-and-ten-cent stores and phonograph and radio stores run by people whose names end in -sen. There are a good many cut-rate prices in the windows. The people on the streets are rather monotonously respectable, and they are not in too much of a hurry: tall blond Scandinavian men and girls and fat Scandinavian children. The Scandinavians become Americanized more rapidly than the immigrants from any other part of the world. The side streets consist of rows of little ugly brownstone houses, each with two stories of polygonal bay-windows, which go down the hill-like steps.

The German immigrant Otto Reich lives in a four-story building above a Beauty Shoppe, where the bright Scandinavian girl says she doesn't know anything about what happened, it was somewhere upstairs. The stairs are narrow and have green linoleum, a glue-yellow sticky-looking dado and a dispiriting backhouse smell.

Otto Reich is nineteen years old: he is a blond German boy with blue eyes, light hair smoothly slicked back, hanswurst nose, fleshy red mouth and very recessive chin. He was born in Berlin and trained to be a waiter—he used to work in the big Hotel Eden. But he wanted to see other places, and he wanted to get away from his family, with whom he had always lived. So he borrowed some money from his brother-in-law and a year ago came to the States. He wanted to be independent.

But when Otto first arrived in New York, the hard times had already set in, and he couldn't get a waiter's job. For eight or nine months he worked as bus-boy in various restaurants, clubs and hotels. A bus-boy works ten or twelve hours, with an hour off in the afternoon; his pay is about $40 a month, with practically no tips. Finally, Otto got a job at the St. Martin waiting on the hotel officials. He asked to be put on room service, and when a vacancy occurred, they had him fill it. He got $38 a month and about $12 a week in tips. Eating at the hotel, he was able to save almost the whole of his wages and was gradually sending back money to pay his brother-in-law.

But, as a result of the depression, the New York hotels have made a wage cut of 10 per cent and have been drastically reducing their staffs. When there is an increase of business over a holiday or a weekend, they make the room-service men help out after hours in the restaurant, with no extra pay but only tips. One Saturday night at the St. Martin, when Otto had been there four months, they told him to go to the restaurant. He was already working from seven in the morning till nine o'clock at night, which meant that, living out in Bay Ridge, he had to get up at 5:30 and didn't come home until after ten. If he worked after hours in the restaurant, he would not get home till after one and would have only four hours of sleep. In Germany everywhere, he says, you work only eight hours a day: the unions have fought it out with the hotels. (They have also the 10 per cent system, according to which a uniform tip was put on every check and every waiter got an equal share of the total.) At the Eden, he had worked from six to three, and then he had had his time to himself.

Besides, he didn't get along with the headwaiter in the St. Martin restaurant. This maître d'hôtel was an Italian, and Otto had a low opinion of Italian waiters. The German and French waiters were the only ones who understood "service."

He had been trained to give service in Germany in one of the best hotels. Service means wiping the knives and forks and polishing up the plates before they are set down on the table, removing the covers from the dishes and asking the guests whether they are satisfactory, and many other ceremonies and practical attentions. Otto had been authoritatively instructed in all this and knew exactly how these things should be done. But Italian waiters are quite untrained; they are imbeciles, and they are not clean—that is why, in even smart American hotels where they want to have good service, they can't get it. This Italian headwaiter at the St. Martin restaurant always used to be coming up behind Otto and nagging him and gabbling at him. He would keep telling him to do things differently, but the headwaiter was foolish —really he was foolish. He used to bawl Otto out in front of the people he was waiting on, and Otto always did what the Italian told him, but the Italian was wrong—always wrong. Tonight he felt he couldn't face it, he was much too nervous already—so he told them he was only hired to work from seven to nine, and he took the subway home to Bay Ridge. The next morning when he came to work, he found that his time-card was gone, and on inquiry learned that he was fired.

That was February 16. Every morning after that he went to the Geneva Association, the international waiters' organization, and every morning he found the same men there, waiting like him for jobs. He presently got so discouraged that he began applying at bakeries and factories, but things there were just as bad. The worst of it was that when he lost his job, he had only half paid back his brother-in-law. He had given him a note that bound him to pay him back in a year, and now the year was nearly over.

Every night he would go home to his room and brood. He had no friends that he cared about in Manhattan, so he had gone to live in Bay Ridge soon after he had come to New York, to be near a German couple who were the only people he liked. The wife had been a schoolmate of his sister's, and his sister had sent him her address. He had taken a room on the same floor at $5 a week and had furnished it in such style as he could manage. He bought a lavender sateen spread for the bed and lavender sateen cushions for the sofa and a cheap imitation tapestry to hang above the mantelpiece; and he decorated the wall with pennants of Bear Mountain, Palisades Park, Long Beach and the Statue of Liberty. He had a bottle of perfume standing exactly in the center of his dressing table, and on the wall on either side of it hung a pair of boxing gloves. He had always boxed regularly in Germany, and though he hadn't been able to since he came to the States, he continued to do boxing exercises every morning at 5:30 when he first got up. He never turned the heat on in winter and slept cold with all the windows open, since he believed that cold was good for the health. He had never gone out dancing when he had his job, though the other waiters had tried to get him to, but on his night off, once a week, had gone to the movies alone.

The German woman's husband, a coppersmith, was out of work, too—the best he could do was from time to time to put in a few days at the dry dock. He, too, would come home and brood, and he had finally bought a radio so as to make things a little bit gay in the evenings—it was the only thing that had kept him up. The German couple were very kind to Otto. He would go in every night and talk to them and listen to the radio and play with the kid. They had by this time told one another everything about themselves, and they were pretty well talked out: one of them got a letter from Germany, that was a big event—it gave them something new to talk about. They didn't know any of the Scandinavians.

But Otto was afraid to write home. Otto was an only son, and his parents counted on him, and he couldn't bear to let them know how badly he was doing in America. They were poor, and if they knew he was out of work, they would want to send him money. And he didn't want to admit to his brother-in-law that he wasn't able to pay him back. He got a letter from his mother, one day in March, telling him that his father was very ill.

Otto went on looking for work—he would have taken any kind of job—till he had only $4 left. The German family had been giving him meals. One night, about eight o'clock, he went out for a walk around Bay Ridge. The next thing he knew he was in his room, sitting up on the bed with his clothes off. His German neighbor was sitting beside him, and there was a man who had been working over him with a pulmotor. It seemed that there was also an ambulance and that he had tried to commit suicide. A man from upstairs had come down and found him lying unconscious in the corridor and the corridor full of gas. He had evidently turned on the gas and then, when he was partially asphyxiated, broken out of the room.

He couldn't remember anything about what had happened. He couldn't even remember deciding to kill himself. He thought he must have gone crazy for a while. And he wasn't able to sleep all the rest of the night after his friend had left him, worrying and blaming himself for having done such a thing.

———

The Brownsville section of Brooklyn is mostly Jewish. Only fifteen years ago, it was all country, and there was nothing there but little farms, but it has recently been built up on a real-estate boom, and today it is a paradise of brick. Everything is neat and new, and none of the buildings is very high: there are light-brown brick apartment houses; streets of brick double-houses, whose monotony has been carefully mitigated by the use of brick in different tints, red, yellow and orange, and by painting the woodwork, say, on one side green and on the other side yellow; apartment houses in red-brick cliffs, wired with identical green fire-escapes but slightly diversified by giving the individual façades somewhat unconventional curves at the top; little mansions of gingerbread brick with little brick and iron-grille walls enclosing their front yards, and, in their front windows, blue stained-glass fleurs-de-lis and the signs of Jewish doctors; then shabbier duocellular brick houses, all with green woodwork on red brick and each with a clothes-pole mast leaning askew at its summit; and on Livonia Avenue, under the El, fronts of even dingier brick.

Irma Meyer lives under the El in the first of a small solid

row of tarnished pink brick houses. Her parents are Polish
Jews. When she was sixteen, she married a truck-driver and
she has had two children by him. Now she is twenty-one,
and as a result of having the children, she is stouter and more
amorphous than any young woman wants to be, but she has
still an appealing little-girl-like face, with dark skin and slanting eyes and a Slavic-Jewish snub nose.

Jake Meyer turned out to be a loafer, and his sister, who
was well off, was eventually obliged to carry them. Jake's
sister was married to a custom tailor, who was in business
for himself, and she sent her sons to Duke University and
had two big white Russian wolfhounds. She helped Irma
out with money regularly—the Meyers, since their children
were born, hadn't had $10 of their own to spend on them—
and at one time Jake's sister had taken the whole family in
for two weeks.

But Jake didn't want to work. He had a little dinky $75
truck, and he was supposed to deliver orange drink in it and
get so much a case on commission, but some days he wouldn't
show up, and the company finally fired him. Irma went to
his boss and pled with him and told him about the children
and persuaded them to take him back. But then Irma found
he was going with other women and was driving them around
in his truck. Jake disappeared early this March and left Irma
without any money. The husband of Jake's sister, in the
meantime, had gone bankrupt on account of the depression,
and had now had to work for somebody else; the family had
had to sell all the nice things they had bought when they
were rich, and they couldn't give Irma any more help. It was
all they could do at the present time to pay for their own sons
at Duke. The only things they kept were the Russian wolfhounds. Irma couldn't go to work because she didn't have
anybody to take care of the children. She wasn't able to put
them in a nursery because the nurseries were closed on Saturdays, and any place there where you worked always did business on Saturdays. She couldn't take them and go to live
with her parents either, because her brother wouldn't let her.
Her father was a presser and since the slump had been making almost nothing: the pressers had been harder hit than

anybody, because the only time people got their clothes pressed now was just before the holidays, and he had only two seasons a year of about two weeks each. Her brother, who was doing better, had come to the rescue of their mother and father, but he said that he hadn't taken his mother out of that cold flat where she had been living and put her in C and D4 of a fine new apartment house to have her made a housemaid of.

Irma was behind with two months' rent, $32 a month, and she owed all the tradesmen money. She wasn't paid up on the bedroom set, and she expected to have it sent for any moment. For food, she had to go to the police station, where they gave her, once a week, some potatoes and onions and canned goods. The children were too young for this food—they needed milk; but they told her at the police station that she could feed them on boiled cabbage. She also appealed to the Jewish Aid Society, and they recommended her case to the Mayor's Committee, which gave her $15. At last she got a dispossess notice.

After two weeks, Jake turned up again. Irma got a warrant against him for abandonment and had him up in court, where the judge sentenced him to pay her $15 a week. Afterwards he followed her home, and she got a cop in to kick him out, but the cop said that Jake had a right to stay there. So he came home at night and flopped on the couch. He gave her a little money, but he wasn't doing well, and by the time he'd paid for gas and oil and the garage expenses for his truck, he only had a few dollars left. The bills kept piling up, and the apartment looked more and more of a mess, and it was nag-nag every night until finally they got disgusted and wouldn't talk to each other any more. Jake's sister used to come to see Irma and would leave one of the wolfhounds with her to keep the children amused. But nobody had any idea how low in her mind Irma was, because she kept up a good front and didn't talk about it.

One day she went out to the butcher's and saw Jake in his truck with another woman. When he came home, she refused to let him in, slammed the door in his face and locked it. That night, when she had put the two children to bed, she fastened some wrapping-paper over the place where a pane was out in the folding glass-doors between the sitting room and the bedroom. Then she closed all the windows and turned on the kitchen gas and sat down to wait. But as she sat there, she realized that if the gas was turned on the whole night, it might eventually leak through into the bedroom, and she decided she had better wait till it was close enough to the time for the milkman so that not too long after she was dead he would be sure to come and turn it off. So she wrote the milkman a note and put it outside in a milk bottle. Then she waited a good part of the night, and at last turned on all the burners of the stove and sat down in the kitchen to wait. She read a magazine called *Airplane Stories* to keep her mind off how long it was going to take. It wasn't bad, she found—she just gradually became unconscious.

But there wasn't any door to shut the sitting room off from the kitchen, and she hadn't allowed time for both rooms to get filled up. When the milkman arrived and found the note, she was still alive, and they brought her to.

Irma's attempt at suicide made no impression on Jake. He told her she had only done it to make people sorry for her, and he came back every night to flop without having anything to say to her.

————

Beaver Street, off Flushing Avenue, is a sort of Sicilian section. This part of Brooklyn is rather old, and most of the dwellings are clapboard affairs of a faded brownish-yellowish color. They run to wooden cornices with little fancy faded friezes, and their windows are ornamented with little peaked projecting hoods. There is also a sprinkling of new stucco houses in the Mediterranean taste, covered with pink, white and green scales like the tablets of peppermint and wintergreen in the old-fashioned glass jars of the cigar and candy store on the corner.

The Sicilian Dimicelis live in one of the clapboarded buildings above a grocery store. They had to move there from a better-class apartment when Mr. Dimiceli was earning so lit-

tle. They did not know many of the Italians in the neighborhood—they are not so friendly with everybody, because Mr.
Dimiceli is a respectable man who speaks not Sicilian dialect but good Italian and used to be in business for himself.
The tenements around them are inhabited by Italians of the
class that knife each other and live in squalor. The Dimicelis'
flat is extremely clean, and it is furnished with an unexpected
vividness that contrasts with the discolored streets of Flushing. The walls of every room are decorated with bright religious prints in green, blue and red—the Bleeding Heart and
the Holy Family, the Virgin with flowers in her arms that
presides above the bed in the bedroom, the Last Supper
over the kitchen table. The whole apartment, in fact, has the
brightness and the clear outlines of one of those simple
prints: bedroom walls in green, kitchen oilcloth in blue and
white squares, kitchen curtains in green and white, kitchen
table and sink smooth white, and three yellow canaries in
yellow cages.

The Dimicelis themselves are clear, vivid and handsome,
too. The mother and daughter have just been out to the
hospital, and they are wearing clean dresses in plain colors,
black stockings and polished shoes. The black-eyed daughter
is dressed in white, and the mother, with her black hair
smoked gray, in blue. Mrs. Dimiceli is a small woman with
a quick, attractive, fine-boned face, in which irony, sadness,
pride and calm succeed each other in swift responses.

Mr. Dimiceli himself is recognizable, not primarily as a
Sicilian, but as a type that, with the development of engineering, has become familiar all over the world. He is tall
and thin with strong dark eyes, which themselves give the
impression of lenses, behind the lenses of rimless spectacles,
strong black hair brushed back and parted in the middle, and
long efficient tool-like fingers.

When Mr. Dimiceli was still a young man, he left Sicily
and went to France, and he worked there for thirteen years
as a skilled machinist in automobile plants. Several years before the War, he came back to his native Palermo and went
into business as an electrical contractor. Electricity was at
that time still more or less of a novelty in Sicily, and Mr.

Dimiceli got a good many commissions wiring Sicilian towns. Then the War broke out, and he had to serve. He went through the whole four years and a half as sergeant of horse artillery. There is a picture of him with a kepi, a Caruso mustache and a whole rainbow of campaign ribbons. During the War, he had Mrs. Dimiceli sell all his electrical equipment so that the family would have something to live on in case anything happened to him.

When the War was over and he came home to Palermo, he could not get his business back: it had been captured during his absence by new electrical contractors. He decided that there were better opportunities in America than in Europe, so he brought the family over and found a job with a company on Long Island that made automobile parts. He got to be shop superintendent and worked there until the fall of '29, when the company sold the patent on a piston it had been making to another firm in Cleveland, and sent all its big machines out there. They laid off about three hundred men and among them Mr. Dimiceli: they gave him a recommendation which said that he was "a very reliable man, and only the fact we are reducing our production forces us to part with him." The few men they still kept on were the ones who had been with them longest. Mr. Dimiceli, however, got another job the next month with the Otis Elevator Company, but as the demand for elevators was also falling off, the Otis people, also, last spring, had to lay off their newest men.

After that, Mr. Dimiceli went out every day looking for work, but all he was able to find were odd jobs at the rate of one or two days a month. Sometimes the best he could do was to make a dollar a day driving a truck. At last Mrs. Dimiceli had to begin to look for work herself, and she succeeded from time to time in getting from $7 to $12 a week finishing dresses for a Brooklyn dressmaker. The youngest son also turned to working and earned $5 a week as a delivery boy. The eldest son was married and had a child and only made $20 a week as a presser, so that he couldn't help them out. The family had come down in the world, and as time went on, they couldn't see how they were even going to be able to stick where they were. They already owed three months' rent on their new and inferior apartment, and it was only the fact that the landlord was an Italian and a friend of theirs which made it possible for them to stay on there.

Mr. Dimiceli was a man in his fifties, who had once been a successful contractor in Palermo, whose career had been broken up by the War and who now spent every day going the rounds of the factories in Brooklyn and Jersey and not being able to get any of them to give him even the lowest-paid job. Wednesday night, when he came home, he was nervous and gloomy, but the family didn't notice it particularly because he was like that every night. He would come back and read the paper, and sometimes just lie down on the bed without talking. Nobody had any suspicion of what he was going to do. The family were down listening to the radio in the apartment of the woman below when the youngest boy, who was coming up, heard a shot from their own apartment. He found his father sitting in the kitchen with his head all covered with blood. He had turned on the gas in the stove, but had evidently been afraid that that wouldn't be quick enough. They took him at once to the hospital, and the doctors couldn't tell the family whether he was going to live or die; but now he is at home and recovering.

Mrs. Dimiceli says that the Italians who come to the United States and go in for racketeering have wonderful opportunities, but that it is no place for a skilled machinist.

MAY FIRST: THE EMPIRE STATE BUILDING; LIFE ON THE PASSAIC RIVER

THERE IS NO QUESTION that the new Empire State Building is the handsomest skyscraper in New York. The first five stories, with their gray façade, silver-framed windows and long rainlike lines in the stone, rise graceful and sheer from the street: one feels a sudden relief as one passes them— they do not crowd and overpower Fifth Avenue as most of the newer buildings do. And the successive tiers fall back, each just in time not to make too heavy and dull a wall— till the main towering shaft is reached. Seen close, the long lines of the nickel facings have the look of a silver inlay, and the whole pale and silver strip might be an inlay on the pale even blue of the sky. This towering shaft, though it is the tallest in the city, has almost always an effect of lightness. From far off, the gray observation tower looks as light as if it were built of shadows, its chromium cap, as it catches the sun, brittle and silver-bright like a Christmas-tree globe. In a warm afternoon glow, the building is rose-bisque with delicate nickel lines; the gray air of rainy weather makes a harmony with the brightish pale facings on their background of dull pale gray; a chilly late afternoon shows the mast like a burnished piece of silverware, an old saltcellar elegantly chased. And although in a rawer light the building looks somewhat less fine, it may still seem as insubstantial as a handful of straw-colored nabiscos stuck together and stood on end. In the cold dazing light of a winter morning, seen against a grayish-blue sky, the building has the beauty of a cake of ice, a bluish-gray block, half-translucent, with silvery gleaming edges. Only rarely, in glaring midday, does it appear hard, metallic and tool-like.

The Empire State Building is the tallest building in the

world: it is 1,250 feet high. There is a telescope in Madison Square Park for people to look at the tower through, just as they used to look at the moon. There are 86 stories, not counting the mast; 6,400 windows and 67 elevators. The building contains 10,000,000 bricks and weighs 600,000,000 pounds—distributed, however, so evenly that "the weight on any given square inch is no greater than that normally borne by a French heel." The plot on which it stands is only about 200 by 425 feet, but the building displaces in the air 36,-000,000 cubic feet. It is calculated that, if it were full, there would be 25,000 people working there and 40,000 more people going in and out every day.

In the immediate future, however, there will not be by any means that many, because business is extremely bad and even the office buildings already erected are full of untenanted space. Of the offices in the Empire State Building only a quarter so far have been rented, and, in moving into it, most of the tenants will merely be leaving more vacancies elsewhere. The Empire State Building was put up at top speed in less than a year, and forty-eight men were killed in the process. (One man, who lost his job, could not find work elsewhere and came back to be again turned away; he jumped off the seventy-second story and went through a one-inch tile on the sixth.) At one point they resorted to telephoto to get the right materials rushed from Cleveland. And now here the tall building is, planted right in the middle of the business district where nobody needs it in the least and where it is sure to make a good deal worse one of the worst traffic jams in town.

The people directly responsible for the Empire State Building, who contributed more than half the $52,000,000 required for it, are John J. Raskob of the Democratic National Committee, Pierre du Pont of the Du Pont powder company, and the presidents of the Nipissing Mines Company and the Chatham Phenix National Bank and Trust Company. Al Smith is the president of the owning company and is said to get $50,000 a year. Today, the first of May, the day of the formal opening, Al Smith, in his dark coat and black derby, with his official family around him, looks very compact, decent and well-satisfied. Al Smith's two little grandchildren perform the ceremony of opening the building by cutting a ribbon across the Fifth Avenue entrance. Then the lights are switched on by an electric button pressed by President Hoover in Washington. Then there are speeches on the eighty-sixth floor. Al Smith reads a telegram from President Hoover, which congratulates "every one who had any part in its conception and construction" on "one of the outstanding glories of a great city." Governor Roosevelt congratulates them on their "grasp of the needs of the future"— he asserts that the Empire State Building "is needed not only by the city, it is needed by the whole nation." There are two keynotes today, he says: one is the keynote of vision, the other is the keynote of faith. Mayor Walker, whose administration is under calamitous inquiry and whose impeachment has recently been demanded, congratulates the builders on having provided "a place higher, further removed than any in the world, where some public official might like to come and hide." Then the R.K.O. "Theater of the Air" broadcasts a radio program.

The entrance hall of the Empire State Building is four stories high and made of a strange specially imported marble with an effect of crushed strawberries smeared into gray. On the far cream of an illuminated ceiling shine suns, stars and circles of silver and gold—geometrical patterns supposed to be derived from snowflakes. At the end of the long hallway, a great flat steely plaque of the sun blazes on a flat steely plaque of the Empire State Building with a bombardment of rays like railroad tracks. The elevator doors are black, with somber silver lines: they suggest the doors of Egyptian tombs. The halls are full of uniformed guards, armed with guns in holsters.

The fifty-fifth floor is the show floor. Green marble and green doors: a great empty loft of bright white walls with black ends of wire sticking out of them and crumbs of plaster on the floor. Through the unwashed window streaked with dirt the windowed square-walled wilderness of buildings shows the same dreary yellow as the dirt-streaks. If you look down out of an open window, you can clearly see the water-tanks on top of other buildings; somebody's luxurious pent-house with steamer-chairs on the roof; an ad: "Buy Your Furs from Fox," painted in big letters on the roof of a build-ing and aimed at the occupants of the Empire State; and an American flag. Below, if you lean further out, you can see the straight streets of the city with the pedestrians and the motor-cars, very small, moving slowly along them. To the west, the steamboats and barges move slowly along the Hud-son; to the south, the narrowing wedge of the island is studded and pronged at the lower end with its own growth of monstrous buildings; to the east, the iron blue-gray East River is strung across with black skeleton bridges, a gray airplane moving above it; to the north, the Chrysler tower, now dwindled, a tinny-scaled armadillo-tail ending in a stiff sting-like drill, the white vertically-grooved and flat-headed Daily News Building, the Luna Park summits of the Amer-ican Radiator Company Building, like a chocolate cake with gooey gilt icing or a "castle" out of a goldfish bowl. Here the light of the setting sun strikes that scrambled mass of upright rectangles and broken-off graceless towers, bringing out in raw stone and drab brick their yellows without delicacy or brightness, their browns without depth or warmth. Brooklyn, Long Island City, Bronx, Englewood, Hoboken, Jersey City: rigid streets, square walls, crowded bulks, rows of rectangular windows—more than ten million people have been sucked into that vast ever-expanding barracks, which has scarcely a garden, scarcely a park, scarcely an open square and whose distances in all directions are blotted out in pale slate-gray. And here is the latest pile of stone, brick, nickel and steel, the latest shell of shafts and compartments, that outstacks and outmultiplies them all—that, most purposeless and su-perfluous of all, is advertized now as a triumph in the hour when the planless competitive society, the dehumanized ur-ban community, of which it makes the culmination, is bankrupt.

This big loft in which I am standing is at present abso-lutely empty, there is nothing to look at in it—with the ex-ception of one decoration: a crude mural drawn in pencil by one of the electricians or plasterers, which, all unknown to the management, confronts every visitor to the fifty-fifth floor. A towering masculine figure is seen fornicating, *Venere aversa*, with a stooping female figure, who has no arms but pendulous breasts. The man is exclaiming, "O man!" Further along is a gigantic vagina with its name in four large letters under it. One remembers that the Empire State Building is sometimes known as "Al Smith's Last Erection."

————

John Dravic came to Buchanan six years ago and got a job in the Semlin carshop. Before that he had been in Pennsylvania. He was born in Jugoslavia, and his wife was an Austrian. He was forty, and she was thirty. They had already two sons, five and six, and two years after they came to Buchanan, Mrs. Dravic gave birth to another son.

John Dravic bought a little house in Buchanan, on Broda Avenue—almost visible from the Empire State Building. There is more variety and more space on Broda Avenue than in most places in mill communities. The mill itself is a big low brick building, with a notched roof and a picket-fence, which is guarded like the Empire State Building by a man with a gun in a holster. But outside there are little gardens which have white flowers as well as green vegetables; a corner saloon equipped with Polish newspapers and billiard tables; stores with Italian names which have in the windows such relatively cheerful objects as vases of yellow flowers and a stuffed eagle spreading its wings; a backyard apple orchard with whitewashed trunks and branches just in bloom; and a small slimy and greenish but perceptibly alive stream in which lie a discarded baby-carriage and a rusty iron bedstead.

Across the street from John Dravic's house are several tiny bright-red brick mansions, with stone terraces built up from the street and thick clumps of creeping pinks, their color livid against the brick, oozing over the terraces. At the foot of the street is the Passaic River, fresh and gleaming below its falls and running eagerly past locust-green banks toward the freedom of the bay. The road that goes over the Passaic has on one side a splendid Tom Thumb golf-course, all garish in green and orange and with special little heart-shaped chairs, and on the other side a grisly dump for the old scrapped bodies of cars. Beyond the Passaic River, between a textile mill and a paper mill, is a factory-waste-blackened canal. And the whole landscape, even in May, coming to life though it is with spring, seems still irremediably infected with the disease that blights industrial settlements—so that what ought to be fields and green hillsides are everywhere wastes going bald of grass, and the finest country weather is made gassy and tainted with smoke.

John Dravic's own house is not fancy, as some Buchanan houses are—it has been painted a plain dark-green and has two stories, with a white double porch. He always let out the bottom floor and lived on the one above. There are four very small rooms and a kitchen and a bath on each.

About a year ago, an Italian woman with her family rented the bottom floor. She was a big tall strong woman from Bologna, with gray hair and gray eyes. Her first husband had been a butcher, but he has died of t.b. and left her with three tubercular children. Her second husband drank and left her. Both the girls, one nineteen and the other twenty-one, had to be sent to the free t.b. hospital. And when the boy, who was twenty-three and had worked in the dyeworks and supported his mother, came down with t.b., too, Mrs. Berelli had to go to work in the mill. When the slump came, she found herself earning only $15 or $20, working four days every other week. Pretty soon, she was laid off altogether. There had before that been two looms to a person, but now a single person was supposed to take on six looms. He had, however, to be a skilled machinist: there was no place for the old-fashioned weaver. They didn't want anybody over forty, and if you went to the factory gate, they'd chase you away like a dog. She had to sell her insurance and lost money on it: she had been paying thirty cents a week for thirteen years, and now she could only cash it in for $117. So that soon she had barely enough to live on. At this point, she got word that one of her girls, who had only had light symptoms, was being sent home from the hospital. Mrs. Berelli appealed to the city for relief, and the city agreed to pay her rent.

John Dravic was her landlord; and he wouldn't have put her out, but he was out of work himself. After five years in the Semlin car-shop, he had been laid off last January, and there was obviously now no hope of their taking anyone back. For a very short time after that he had had a job minding the furnace in a New York theater, but the play went off and the theater closed, and since then he had had nothing. He walked all over New York and Passaic and everywhere within walking distance (he had no longer any money for carfare), but he couldn't find anything to do.

The Dravics were quiet people and kept very much to themselves. They didn't know anybody well because they had only been in Buchanan six years, and in a community of mixed Germans, Poles, Hungarians, Italians and Jews, it takes longer than that to make friends—that's one reason they don't get together to organize. But Mrs. Berelli liked them, and they were nice to her. When Mrs. Berelli had just come back from the hospital after an operation, Mrs. Dravic, who was a delicate woman herself, had always come down every night, after Mrs. Berelli had got to bed, to see that she was all right. Every morning she would talk to John Dravic when he was starting out to look for work. He had become very gloomy about it. He would say, "You're the only one workin' in the house, and now you're not workin'!" She would try to cheer him up by saying: "Well, now that we're not workin', we might just as well not worry and go out in the backyard and take a sun bath!" That was what she used to do, though the truth was she didn't know which way to turn. But she always tried to keep the Dravics' spirits up, just as whenever she went to see her son in the hospital, she always said she was doing fine, so that he wouldn't worry about her.

Mr. Dravic, when he was home, used to work very hard over a little vegetable garden and a little strip of lawn beside the house. He had planted some sweet william, a lily-of-the-valley bed and a pinkish high-bush honeysuckle. He always kept himself busy. Another thing he liked to do was teach his two older boys music. He loved music and had two violins, a cello and a guitar. One of the boys learned the violin and the other the cello, and they would play trios almost every evening. Sometimes they would get other players in and organize an amateur orchestra.

John Dravic was extremely fond of his boys. Mrs. Berelli would see them all out walking together: Mr. Dravic was tall, and the four-year-old baby was tiny. The oldest boy went to high school, was bright. He used to build little airplanes and boats, and he had once made a dollar by writing for the interscholastic *World News* a digest of an article in *Popular Science* called "Is New Russia, Built by Americans, a World Menace?", which told about the American engineers in Russia and what the Soviet government was doing for the workers. Mrs. Berelli herself couldn't understand how the rich people could do such a thing as to let the millworkers starve. Buchanan, Passaic and Semlin and all the other neighboring mill towns were full of families out of work, and at the same time there were other families who had a good deal more work than they needed—four and five in a family working. Mrs. Berelli didn't know why that President in that White House didn't do something about it.

At last, a few weeks ago, John Dravic decided to go into business. He bought a little corner store which sold soft drinks, cigars and candies, across the river in Passaic. Somebody persuaded him it was a good investment, and he borrowed $300 to buy it. But it turned out that it wasn't such a good investment, because there was a much bigger and better store, also selling cigars and candy, only a few blocks away; and John Dravic knew nothing about storekeeping: he had never worked in anything but car-shops. He began to get discouraged when he came to realize how meager the stock he had was, that he had no money to buy any more and that he was $300 in debt. After a week of spending every day sitting alone in the shop and waiting for customers that didn't come, he got so that he hated to get up in the morning and go there. Mrs. Berelli would say to him when she saw him coming down the stairs so glum: "Look at me! *I* don't worry— and a man ought to be able to stand it if a woman can!" But he could never get to the point of doing anything about the slovenly-looking signs that said "Soft Drinks" and "Cigars," scrawled up in watery print on the insides of the store windows, and when the pile of "Between the Acts" boxes which was displayed in the window toppled over, he did not set it up again. He had done everything there was to be done to his garden, and the flowers had begun to bloom. Early in the morning of the first of May, sometime between one and two, Mrs. Berelli's daughter, who was home from the hospital now, came in and waked her up. She had just been waked up herself by an awful bang on the floor above. The next minute, Mrs. Dravic came running downstairs and said that her husband had shot himself. They rushed up and found John Dravic on the floor of the boys' bedroom: he was reaching out with his hands and straining the upper part of his body as if he were trying to grab something to pull himself up from the floor. Mrs. Dravic turned on the light, and Mrs. Berelli looked at the boys in bed, and there she saw one of them with his head all bloody and the bedclothes soaking in blood. She ran over and pulled down the covers, and there were the other two boys with blood running out of their heads.

Their father had shot them all in their sleep. A little while before doing this, he had lifted the baby from his crib in the room where Mrs. Dravic slept. She hadn't thought anything about it at the time, because he did that every night to carry the child to the bathroom. But tonight he had taken him in and put him into bed with the other two boys. Before he killed them, he had pulled the covers over them.

By six o'clock in the morning, all the children and John were dead, and poor Mrs. Dravic, who the day before had had a family that played trios in the evenings, was now left with four corpses. The cheap undertaker did his best to patch up the heads blown out with point-blank revolver shots. The only comfort was that the baby looked pretty good.

Mrs. Dravic still had her own family, who lived across the river in Passaic. They took her in, in a state of prostration. Her old Austrian mother kept sobbing, "*Es ist nicht gut! Es ist nicht gut!*" Her brother drank heavily every day until the funeral was over. He had been out of work a long time himself, had had only a day or two now and then; and both he and Mrs. Berelli, in their first reactions to what John had done, felt dismay, almost indignation, as if he had deserted his post, disgraced them. Hadn't they all of them been badly off, and had they had any reason to think that he was any worse off than they were.

But the tragedy in the apartment above, more and more, as the weeks went on, began to work on Mrs. Berelli's morale. Her other tubercular girl was sent back from the state hospital, and neither one of the girls seemed well. Mrs. Berelli got further into debt and was down to the last dollars of her insurance money. She couldn't even buy the girls any greens and had to feed them on soup and oranges. She herself lived on bread and coffee and often went without her meals, saying that she had eaten when she hadn't, so that the children would have enough.

One of her daughters was rather handsome: her beetle-browed gray-blue eyes glared strangely out of a very pale face, and she evidently had brains. She was much better educated than Mrs. Berelli and spoke and wrote excellent English. She had always wanted to go to high school. When she was younger, she had decorated a decanter with the colored paper from the insides of envelopes—this was almost the only ornament in the house.

Mrs. Berelli, at last, one day, got word from her son in the sanitarium that, although his lung was not yet cured, they had now kept him there as long as they were supposed to keep non-paying patients and that they were sending him back to the county hospital. Mrs. Berelli had stopped going to see him because she found it had become impossible to keep up a cheerful front—so that he didn't know how bad things were and wrote his mother that he didn't like the hospital and would rather come home to live. Mrs. Berelli had been told by the doctors that the climate in that part of the state—where the hospital also was—was damp and bad for t.b., and she wouldn't be able to give him the right things to eat—she could hardly give him anything. She wrote him to try to stay as long as he could, and the doctor gave him a reprieve.

She appealed again to the Mayor, and the Mayor said he would try to find work for her, but when she went round to his office again, she was told there was no work to be had.

She got lightheaded, couldn't sleep, found that she couldn't eat. When she lay down to rest, she got dreams, and that would make her get up again.

Mrs. Dravic's brother arrived, and packed up the Dravics' things and took them away; and Mrs. Berelli was left with the empty apartment upstairs.

She knows that *she* wouldn't be capable of doing anything like what John Dravic did.

TWO PROTESTS

BEN MARSH is the executive secretary of the People's Lobby in Washington. He is a tall stooping loose-jointed Westerner, with white hair, an aquiline Yankee beak and a genial and mobile bright black eye. In the nineties he was a YMCA worker and planned to go to South Africa, but he later became a radical and stayed at home.

The People's Lobby is an organization intended to accomplish for the public good what the other lobbies do for private interests. Its slogan is: "We fight for the people: we get and give the facts." Professor John Dewey, convinced of the necessity of his taking a more active part in politics, recently became president of the People's Lobby.

With John Dewey and Rabbi Wise as sponsors, Ben Marsh has got up a petition to request of President Hoover that he call an extra session of Congress. He has invited a group of professors, labor leaders and well-known Socialists to sign it and present it personally; and a certain rich lady has undertaken to pay the expenses of bringing them to Washington. The President's secretary has promised an appointment, but stipulated that the list of petitioners be submitted to be checked up on first.

We assemble in the dreary mezzanine of an old-fashioned Washington hotel: romantic prints in the hallways, brownish faded flowery carpets, red-plush valances muffling the windows. It is raining outside.

Among others, there have come for this purpose Mr. W. G. Bergman, the secretary of the Unemployment Committee of Mayor Frank Murphy of Detroit; Miss Elizabeth Gilman, the daughter of the late president of Johns Hopkins and the Socialist candidate for governor of Maryland; Harry Laidler, the Socialist president of the National Bureau of Economic Research; Frank Keeney, the president of the West Virginia Mine Workers' Union; Corliss Lamont, the son of Thomas Lamont, the J. P. Morgan partner—a professor of philosophy at Columbia; Miss Mary Winsor, of Philadelphia, one of the pioneers of the Woman's Party and now active in an organization which aims at the total disarmament of the United States; Professor Samuel Chiles Mitchell, a Southern professor of the old school, who has long taught history and classics at the University of Richmond; and A. J. Muste, that unique Dutch Reform minister, who left his church at the time of the war after an attempt to preach the gospel of peace; came to realize that peace and war were entangled with the social-economic situation; went in 1919 to preach to the Lawrence strikers and unexpectedly found himself made chairman of their executive committee and even more unexpectedly learned that he had won the strike for them just at the moment he was going to the station under the impression that their effort had failed. He is now dean of Brookwood Labor College, at which he trains labor organizers. A. J. Muste is a lean Netherlander who resembles a country schoolmaster and stands in the posture of a preacher, his hands clasped in front of him and his head tilted back, looking down his long nose through his spectacles with an expression at once dreamy and shrewd.

When everybody seems to be present, Ben Marsh calls up the President's secretary and is jolted to receive the news that, after all, Mr. Hoover will not see us. The secretary explains that he has written us a letter, and Ben Marsh goes around to get it.

We decide, however, to proceed with the memorial, which has already been tentatively drafted. Jerome Davis, a professor of sociology at Yale Theological Seminary, reads this document aloud for discussion.

It calls President Hoover's attention to the facts that, in the United States, during 1930, the loss of salaries and wages amounted to at least $9,000,000,000—one-fifth of the salaries and wages paid in 1928 to the 45,500,000 gainfully occupied persons getting less than $5,000 a year; that in the course of

1930, the payrolls in the manufacturing industries declined
34.3 per cent, and the number of workers 24 per cent; that
there are probably at the present time about 6,000,000 unemployed and almost as many only working part-time; that
there is every reason to believe that 1932 will be as bad as
1931; and that the relief supplied by charitable organizations, which has always been inadequate, is already beginning to give out at the same time that the state and local
governments are reaching the limits of their legal capacity
to borrow.

The undersigned persons, therefore, propose that the
President call an extra session of Congress in order to enable
the federal government to appropriate at least $3,000,000,000
for public works, for the extension of credit for measures
such as municipal housing programs; and at least $250,000,-
000 for subvention of state unemployment-insurance systems.

The money required for these measures, they point out,
could be provided by surtaxes on the higher brackets and by
higher taxes on estates. In 1929, according to the income-tax
reports, 14,701 people with incomes over $100,000 had an
aggregate income of $5,016,229,000—of which about 94 per
cent was derived from ownership or control of property—but
paid the federal government only about an eighth of it; and
in 1928 the federal government got only about a seventh of
the aggregate net taxable estate of $631,012,563 left by the
fifty-five people who died leaving estates over $40,000,000.

"To postpone until December the execution and even the
planning of these measures of relief is to ignore human
misery, and to court domestic disorders which, with one-fifth
of the working population unemployed or so irregularly employed as to make impossible even a health standard of existence, may be unprecedented in our history."

The discussion, as is usual on such occasions, reveals two
classes of opinion among the petitioners: one group wants
to word the memorial strongly, to give it the tone of a mani-
festo, while the other is in favor of tact, of framing the statement in such a way that it may not antagonize the recipient.
It is the latter school, in general, that prevails and determines
the final form. By the time we are done with the text, every

passage has been eliminated which could possibly be regarded as provocative—an assertion, for example, that "short of martial law, the federal government cannot compel profit-making corporations to do anything effective to meet the unemployment situation, and even by proclaiming martial law, cannot compel those with a deficit to help"; and another to the effect that, though "the American people will not readily submit to complete control over their private business," they "realize that the present tragic breakdown can only be relieved by. an immediate and drastic redistribution of the national income, and can only be remedied by a reorganization of industry."

Miss Mary Winsor, however, has an idea for a bolder opening.

The President, the day before, has delivered at Valley Forge a peculiarly annoying speech in which he compared the present plight of the American people to the sufferings of Washington's soldiers when that "little band of hungry and almost naked patriots kept alive the spark of liberty in the lowest hours of the Revolution." "It was a triumph of character and idealism and high intelligence," the President has told a well-to-do audience, "over the counsels of despair, of prudence and material comfort"—and "we are still fighting this war of independence. We must not be misled by the claim that the source of all wisdom is in the government. . . . Sirens still sing the song of the easy way for the moment of difficulty, but the common sense of the common man, the inherited tradition of an independent and self-reliant race, the historical memory of Americans who glory in Valley Forge even as they glory in Yorktown—all these tell us the truth for which our ancestors fought and suffered, the truth which echoes upward from this soil of blood and tears, that the way to the nation's greatness is the path of self-reliance, independence and steadfastness in times of trial and stress. . . . God grant that we may prove worthy of Washington and his men of Valley Forge!"

Miss Winsor's proposal is that we begin the petition by mentioning this speech and reminding the President that while Washington's troops were starving and freezing at Valley Forge, there were other Americans who found themselves quite comfortable: the wealthy American Tories. Somebody jokingly suggests that we might add "and their property was afterwards confiscated." Somebody else produces a newspaper cartoon which shows Hoover very fat, small and dismal in a cocked hat at Valley Forge, and suggests we put it into the memorial. But Miss Winsor is a serious and pungent person, and her proposal impresses itself: she has already made a draft of an opening paragraph incorporating her suggestion, and she gives it to the men who are to revise the memorial.

A. J. Muste has taken more responsibility than most of the persons present; he has followed with close attention the reading of the drafted memorial, and brought to bear on it a lucid intelligence, with a tincture of ironic humor, rather European than American. He withdraws with someone else to condense it and make the language more accurate. They equip it with Miss Winsor's opening.

Ben Marsh reappears, somewhat dampened. He reads the letter from the President's secretary.

This letter briefly explains that the President declines to see us, since he has already issued a statement on the calling of an extra session of Congress. A copy of the statement is enclosed: "I do not propose to call an extra session of Congress. I know of nothing that would so disturb the healing processes now undoubtedly going on in the economic situation. We cannot legislate ourselves out of a world depression; we can and will work ourselves out. A poll of the members of Congress would show that a large majority agree with me in opposing an extra session."

Ben Marsh is much disappointed but the President's secretary has promised to see us: we can at least leave the memorial at the White House. Miss Winsor proposes picketing the White House but her suggestion is received either laughingly as a joke or in silence as an impracticable idea.

We have lunch in the hotel grillroom, then set out for the White House in taxis. Since several of the party have melted away, two taxis are all that are needed.

At the White House, we are told by an attendant that the

President's secretary is busy. We sit and wait in the reception room.

We talk to the newspapermen and find them sympathetic. One of them tells us that Senator Kean of New Jersey has put himself on record as in favor of having no next session at all: "It will only upset the country," he has told the newspapermen. "If we could only just pass over this next session!"

After a time, Ben Marsh asks again whether the secretary is able to see us. Our appointment has been for 3. The doortender goes inside and comes back with a uniformed clerk, who explains that Mr. Richey is busy, that he will probably continue to be so for some time.

We give the memorial to the clerk and go home.

One of the members of the party has hired an umbrella at the hotel, and he amiably offers shelter to others.

———

Peter Romano comes from a little town in Sicily. For years he kept a large and prosperous fruit store under the Second Avenue elevated at the corner of Twenty-ninth Street. A few years ago, however, he got something the matter with his chest and wasn't able to work any more. He sold his business and put the money into Wall Street.

When the Wall Street crash came, Peter Romano lost almost everything. And by the time that Mrs. Romano had had a baby five months ago and had afterwards come down with pneumonia, he found he had only a few dollars left.

By June, he owed his landlord two months' rent, $52. The landlord, Antonio Copace, lived only a few blocks away on Lexington Avenue, in a house with a brownstone front and coarse white-lace curtains in the windows. The Romanos lived above the fruit store, on the same floor with a cheap dentist's office, in a little flat to which they had access up a dirty oilcloth-covered staircase and through a door with dirty-margined panes. The Romanos regarded Mr. Copace as a very rich man, but he, too, no doubt, had been having his losses.

At any rate, he was insistent about the rent. Peter Romano

had a married daughter, and her husband offered to help him out. He went to Mr. Copace with $26—one month's rent. But the old man refused it with fury and said that unless he got the whole sum right away, he would have the Romanos evicted. On June 11, he came himself to the Romanos and demanded the money again. He threatened to have the marshal in and put them out that very afternoon. Peter Romano tried to argue with him, and Mrs. Romano went out in a final desperate effort to get together $52.

When she came back empty-handed, she found a lot of people outside the house and, upstairs, the police in her flat. Peter had shot Mr. Copace and killed him, and was just being taken off to jail.

FRANK KEENEY'S COAL DIGGERS

THE PEOPLE WHO WORK at Ward, West Virginia, live in little flat yellow houses on stilts that look like chicken-houses. They seem mean and flimsy on the sides of the hills and at the bottom of the hollow, in contrast to the magnificent mountains, wooded now with the forests of mid-June. Between those round and rich-foliaged hills, through the middle of the mining settlement, runs a road which has, on one side of it, a long row of obsolete coal-cars, turned upside down and, on the other, a trickle of a creek, with bare yellow banks, half-dry yellow stones, yellowing rusty tin cans and the axles and wheels of old coal-cars. There are eight hundred or so families at Ward, two or three in most of the houses, and eight or ten children in most of the families. And these families are just as much prisoners, just as much at the mercy of the owners of their dwellings as if they did live in a chicken-yard with a high wire fence around it.

This settlement is situated in a long narrow valley which runs back among the West Virginia hills. The walls rise steep on either side, and the end of the hollow is a blind alley. The Kelley's Creek Colliery Company owns Ward, and the Paisley interests own Mammoth, another settlement further back in the hollow, where the houses are not even painted yellow and where the standard of living is lower than at Ward. The people who live in these houses mine coal from the surrounding hills. They work from eight to twelve hours a day, and they get from $2.60 to $3 for it. They are paid not in United States currency, but in chicken-feed specially coined by the companies—crude aluminum coins, thin and light and some of them with holes in the middle, like the debased French and German currency that was issued at the end of the war. Even Andrew Mellon, Secretary of the Treasury, who owns one of the mines in this field, pays his men in this imitation money. The company "scrip" is worth, on the average, about sixty cents on the dollar. The company forces the miners to trade at the company store—the only store, of course, on its property—and goods are sold there at so much higher prices than at the non-company stores only three miles away that the miners never come any nearer than 60 per cent to their money's worth. The local movie houses have established two prices for admission: one for regular money and one for company scrip. Compelling the miners to trade at the commissary is very important for the company: it is actually true at the present time that some of these West Virginia coal companies which are getting no profit from their mines are making a profit on the commissaries. So if a miner has the temerity to go to an outside store and cash in his company scrip at a loss, he finds himself immediately fired.

Nor are the people who work at Ward ever able to get ahead, to save up money and try to do better elsewhere. When they are paid at the end of every fortnight, it is not for the work of that fortnight, but only for the work of the fortnight before. From this pay—say $40—the company deducts its charges—say $6 for rent, $5 for gas, $1 for electricity, $1 as contribution to a compulsory funeral fund, $3 or more as compulsory fee for hospital and medical treatment (whether they need a doctor or not). This leaves only about $24, and the bill at the company store always turns out either to equal or a little to exceed the balance. It is only very rarely that the miner manages to come out fifty or sixty cents ahead. If he does, it is likely to be shown that, during the last two weeks, he has run behind, and the fifty or sixty cents is held back to make up the deficit; or it may be that his father or his son is in debt, and the gain is transferred to the other account. If, however, the company can find no pretext for withholding the fifty or sixty cents, the miner receives it in regular currency. This is the only regular currency he ever sees. Since he is only getting paid for his work of the fortnight before the last, he is always in debt to the company and must always be borrowing money to get through the fortnight ahead; and the money which the company advances him is always the company's imitation money.

When times are hard, as they are at present, and the coal business, which never does well, is doing particularly badly, the operators cut their rates and make up the difference to themselves and their stockholders by getting more work for less pay out of the miners. They put in mechanical cutters and loaders, and lay off as many men as they can. According to their practice, the first to go are the men over forty-five and the men who have been crippled in the mines (at Andrew Mellon's mine, they never keep a man who has been injured). And a medical examination weeds out other classes of workmen. If it is found, for example, that you are unable to read the bottom line of type on an oculist's chart—as comparatively few people can—you are likely to be eliminated. And the result is that the children at Ward sometimes go without food for days and that they have so little to wear that they are sometimes more or less naked and cannot even be sent to the union for clothes. Even at the time when their fathers were working, they had no shoes to go to school, had hardly ever eaten fresh meat or vegetables and had never known milk since they were weaned from their mothers. Their dish consists of sow belly, potatoes and pinto beans. If they had been living in certain of the other camps, they would probably already have died from drinking water polluted by the outhouse and so escaped the pains of starvation.

About a month ago,* a hundred and fifty miners, with their women and children, decided to appeal to the Governor. They set out to march to Charleston, more than twenty miles away. They camped at night on the road near a bridge on the outskirts of the city, and Governor Conley, hearing about them—in order to avoid a scandal—came out and met them there the next morning. The Governor received a delegation in front of a filling station, and a benevolent minister spoke for them. The minister told the Governor that the miners had had no work for weeks and now had nothing to eat. The Governor replied that he

* I was writing in June.

sympathized, that he had once been a miner himself—that he had even been a miner in the days when you still had to use a pick. "Whatever may be the shortcomings of our government," he said, "whatever conditions may be now, we have the best government on earth. We have eliminated all class distinctions, and any man, no matter how humble, may sometimes hold high office. It means something to live in a government like this, and your demeanor this morning shows"—the marches of striking miners had sometimes ended in shootings—"that you appreciate the advantages of our government." He went on to point out, however, that the mines were to reopen the next Monday: the company, becoming alarmed, had posted a notice to this effect after the marchers had left the camp. The miners wanted to know what they were going to live on in the meantime and how they were going to buy their powder (the miners have to pay for their own explosives), when they did start working again. The Governor then read them the Constitution and explained that it did not authorize him to do anything for them: the legislature had appropriated no funds for the purpose, and he was strictly forbidden by the law to divert funds from other purposes. He said that "the government was a business institution, and that its business had to be conducted along lines that safeguarded the interests of all citizens." "I am," he concluded in a munificent gesture, "turning over $10 of my own money to your presiding officers." The marchers went on to the courthouse, where they met with better success: the county raised some truckfuls of food.

The next Monday the mines did reopen, but not everybody was taken back. And, soon after, evictions began. Just at present, two dozen families are in process of being turned out at Ward. You can see the men from the company store dangling their legs from the back of the company truck, as they wait for the arrival of the constable who is to see that the families go; and one finds, a little further on, another evicted family, sitting on the ground by the road, in the inadequate shade of a small tree—the mother has an umbrella up—beside a pile of tables, bureaus, chairs and beds which has been very carefully stacked. They have been brought a safe distance from the settlement so that they cannot move back into their houses—as families have been known to do—as soon as the constable goes, or move into the house of a neighbor. In not only, thus, evicting its tenants but actually carrying them away, the company, as a matter of fact, has gone beyond its rights. The road is supposed to be public —it is supposed to belong to the county, and the company has no authority to drive other people's furniture off. Yesterday some of the younger men got sore and stopped the truck and brought a load of furniture back. It belonged to a young married man who had been one of the leaders of the hunger march and who had been laid off and turned out on that account.

This resistance frightened the constable: he was afraid something worse might happen. So he had a warrant served the next morning and arrested five of the miners, on the charge of interfering with an officer in the performance of his duty. They were sent to the Charleston jail, and their people are now angrier than before. Many of them have lived here all their lives, and they are dismayed at being treated like poultry to be casually dumped out of their coops. They know they are human beings. They have nailed possum-skins to their doors, trained pink and crimson ramblers over their houses, grown gray Columbia poplars in their yards. The women, in white slips, and with thin bare legs, sit in swings on the porches of their houses, like other women on hot afternoons. The girls put on fresh pink and yellow dresses and walk along the railroad track, which runs beside the road through the hollow and belongs to the company, too. They have learned, over their radios, the popular songs that all the other American girls have learned, and they amuse themselves by singing duets of *You—You're Drivin' Me Crazy!* and the ambitious *I Want to Be Bad!*

As for the men, they seem easygoing, good-humored and straightforward Southerners, so much in the old tradition of American backwoods independence that it is almost impossible to realize that they have actually been reduced to the condition of serfs. They themselves, in spite of much harsh experience, seem surprised at their position today. Some of them were Knights of Labor in the eighties of the last century, when labor had some reverberating victories. "I've lived in this hollow forty-two years," says one man, with wide serious eyes. "This country's gittin' corrupt! Under conditions, the President's agin' us and everybody!" "If it wasn't for conditions," says another—the young man who has been put out of his house—"Ward would be a right good place to live."

But they are not without leadership. Recently men who came originally from their own hollows and were trained in their strikes of ten years ago, have again become active among them. These leaders have had a good deal of difficulty in getting them organized: they are not allowed to hold meetings on the company property, and even the church is controlled by the company. So the organizers have had to go out to the blind-alley end of the hollow, where there is some land which is owned by an oil company. The oil company does not seem to care whether the coal workers organize or not. The miners have come out with enthusiasm to meet their old leaders in the midst of the oil derricks, to build bonfires and sign up for the union. Now they hold "speakin's" there every Sunday; but only in the afternoon, and, if possible—for fear of bullets from behind—with the speaker's truck backed up against something solid.

The coal miners have hailed these organizers as wrecked sailors would a ship. They are men, and the organizers are men. And the operators—who are they? They are corporations, holding companies, interests; vice-presidents, stockholders, boards of directors; a controversy with Pittsburgh, in the newspapers, over rates for freight to the Great Lakes, a franchise guaranteeing a monopoly of the Minneapolis docks; an office staff in a Charleston office building. The miners never see an operator—there is only a dubious legend that one of them once visited a mine on the occasion of a troublesome strike. But, in general, they merely send out orders from Pittsburgh or Chicago or Cleveland that wages have got to be cut, and they leave the rest to the superintendent (the superintendent at Ward is reputed to be a former detective). And since the operators have to make good with the stockholders, the superintendent tries to make good with the operators by paring down the payroll even further—if necessary, by shortweighting the men.

People hear that the operators are desperate. The coal industry is worse off than any other, because there is no future for coal as a fuel. The companies are all trying to undercut one another but, even at that, they can't sell their product. There are great mounds of coal lying around at Ward. According to the superintendent, there are now nearly 500 carloads of coal standing on the tracks unconsigned, and 400 carloads dumped on the ground. A few of the more intelligent operators want to stabilize prices and wages; but the competitive tradition is too strong for them. They keep on fighting one another and eventually going bankrupt.

Another organizer has come from New York—a young man trained at A. J. Muste's Brookwood—he holds night classes in the Negro schoolhouse—the only building which does not belong to the company. In Ward, the blacks and whites do not mix, but they live in neighboring houses, bathe side by side in the same creek, hold office together in the union and are now taking lessons in economics together. The speaker tonight is a Jewish girl from Vassar, an assistant to the Brookwood organizer, who seems to tower very tall in the low dimly gaslit room. The women sit at the desks with their babies; the men sit on the floor and stand up against the wall. The schoolchildren's cut-outs of flowers and figures make little ghosts on the windows.

The speaker explains to the miners that the reason they are now starving and being thrown out of their homes is that business is run for private profit. They are shy about answering questions, but they listen to her eagerly and with something like awe. One of the boys on a window-sill has heard a rumor that in Russia the government is run by the workin' people. The most loquacious person present is a round black Negro, who has thought the thing out with some intricacy and believes that the government "ought to be changed." At the end, the girl from Brookwood chalks up on the board the words of *Solidarity Forever* and has them sing it to the familiar tune that serves both for *John Brown's Body* and *The Battle Hymn of the Republic*.

An hour ago—as I saw from the train—along the beautiful
shores of the Kanawha and New Rivers, where paddlewheel
steamboats still ply, the small independent farmers were hoe-
ing their cabbage patches, while the sun brought out vivid
light green on the inside bank of a bend and the shadows
spread purple stains on the chocolate of the muddy water.
Here, at the end of the Southern day, a deliciously welcome coolness has welled up and filled the valley, and the
darkness seems richer than daytime. Large fireflies look big as
stars, floating among the mountains. And the miners, coming
home from work, with their lanterns strapped to their foreheads, look rather like fireflies, too. Outside, in the summer
dark, the boys are playing mandolins and singing ballads.
And, at the bottom of the black valley, in the little Negro
schoolhouse, the natives of the camp and the forest, not a roof
or a tree of which they own and where their only condition of
survival is to spend the hours of daylight grubbing in a hole
in the hill, are hoping to find out from the speaker why it is
they have to fight the constable, the Governor and even—as
we shall see—the President for the right to work and to live.

––––

The miners of the Kanawha Valley are men who will defend their rights. Before the coal-mining days, they were
primitive mountaineers who carried on implacable feuds. But
today the traditional hostility between the Hatfields and the
McCoys, for example, has been destroyed by a new kind of
antagonism. Today there are Hatfields and McCoys on both
sides of the economic line-up—both in the mines and among
the operators—and members of the same family are found
fighting each other as bitterly as the families fought each
other in the past.
The Kanawha miners were organized as long ago as 1920;
but the operators in the wild counties south of Charleston
were retaliating with strikebreakers and lockouts. Troops
were brought in to coerce them, and some 3,000 miners'
families spent the winter in tents. Then the United Mine
Workers' Union, under the leadership of John L. Lewis, who

had developed political ambitions and taken to making deals
with the operators, withdrew and left the miners flat. The
miners kept on striking just the same.

In May, while evictions were going on at Matewan, Mingo
County, a move was made by the operators to arrest the chief
of police, a Hatfield who had been a miner and who was
sympathetic with the strikers. The mayor, who was also sympathetic, attempted to interfere and was shot by a Baldwin-
Felts detective. In five minutes, Chief of Police Hatfield and
another man were summoned to appear in court. They went
unarmed and took their wives, and were shot on the courthouse steps by a gang of Baldwin-Felts men hidden behind
the courthouse pillars and led by a stoolpigeon who had been
working in the union.

Three weeks later, in August, the angry Kanawha miners,
7 or 8,000 strong, set out to march on the south. Their leaders
had been in the trenches; they were equipped with commissary and nurses, and proceeded in military formation.
They wore red handkerchiefs around their necks and blue
overalls. They cut the telegraph and telephone lines. Mother
Jones,* for all her natural militancy, came to them with
tears in her eyes and begged them not to go. But they told
her to get away. As they marched, they sang, "Hang Don
Chafin to a sour-apple tree!" Don Chafin was the local
sheriff. The Governor of West Virginia, who had refused
even to deal with the miners, appealed to President Harding
for help. The President sent a brigadier general, who protested to Frank Keeney, the district president of the miners,
threatening to bring in federal troops. Keeney said that he
would stop the march if the government would guarantee
the right—a constitutional right—of the miners to organize.
The government hastily agreed and sent out special trains
to bring the miners back; but, in the meantime, the Governor of West Virginia had sent the state police to arrest them.
Just as the miners were starting to go home, they heard that
three of their number had been shot. A battle ensued which
lasted nearly a week and in which fifty men were killed.

* A then well-known labor leader.

Hired gunmen, American Legion patriots, state militia and business men mobilized against the miners with rifles, machine guns and airplanes. The miners were just breaking through the line when the federal troops arrived. The march was stopped, and the union destroyed. Whole payrolls were indicted for treason, conspiracy and other offenses; and the first case was brought to trial in the same courtroom in Charlestown in which John Brown had been convicted of treason sixty years before.

John L. Lewis had become president of the United Mine Workers of America in the February of that year, 1920, and his slogan was "No Backward Step!" In 1929, the membership of the UMWA had shrunk from nearly 400,000 members to hardly 100,000. The only miners who derived any benefit from the UMWA were Mr. Lewis himself, who draws a salary of $12,000, and the officials of the Lewis machine.

When the hard times brought a crisis, there was need, in this situation, for a new union leadership. In March, 1930, the Illinois district held a national convention and tried to set up a reorganized union. In the meantime, the West Virginia union had completely petered out, and the prime movers of the 1920 days had settled down as ordinary citizens. Frank Keeney, the former district president and one of the heroes of the armed march, first ran an orange-drink stand and then speculated in gas and oil; Brant Scott became an automobile salesman. But when the Illinois convention was called, they attended it and came back to West Virginia to start their union over again. Keeney's services in this connection were promptly recognized: running behind in his rent, he found himself evicted from his house.

By March of the present year, the Illinois district officials had decided to go back to Lewis, the reorganized union was given up, and funds were cut off from West Virginia. Frank Keeney, however, went ahead alone. His union had been effective in preventing the operators from cutting wages and in securing a union checkweighman to keep the company from shortweighting the men. A. J. Muste sent him four trained organizers.

And while Keeney has been quietly organizing, the lid has been blowing off in the coal-fields both north and south. Since April, in Harlan County, Kentucky, where Andrew Mellon and Samuel Insull own mines, there have been evictions, looting of stores, dynamitings and wholesale burnings of miners' houses—culminating, on May 5, in a battle between miners who were trying to organize and mine-guards and deputy sheriffs who were trying to bring in scabs. Four men were killed and two wounded. District officials of the UMWA made an agreement with the Governor that state troops should be brought in to restore order, that the mine guards should be disarmed and that the miners should be allowed to join the union and hold meetings during the day.

The miners at first thought they were being protected, but they soon discovered that the state militia were as much the instruments of the operators as the guards at the mines themselves. These troops were kept in Evarts, near the scene of the recent battle, until twenty indictments had been brought on triple-murder charges and a hundred men had been put in jail, including a Baptist preacher, who, as a result of trying to speak for the miners, was charged with criminal syndicalism.

Now the whole county is under martial law. There have been walkouts, Negro strikebreakers fired on, mobs of miners besieging the jail, state cavalry, artillery and tanks. The local powers are desperate and ruthless. They have 45,000 miners against them, and they have been lately able to keep themselves in office only through a brazen disregard of the law. Judge Jones, who has jailed a hundred men and not one mine-guard or deputy sheriff, is said to have been defeated in the last election in spite of the fact that several thousand miners were coerced into voting for him at the point of a gun. But he remained on the bench, nonetheless. The miners' candidate for sheriff, though he is supposed to have been actually elected, was prevented from holding office, and has since been put in jail and denied bond.

More recently, the National Mine Workers, a Communist-organized union, has been taking the lead in a similar rebellion in Ohio and Pennsylvania. There resounds from the north, at the present time, to the workers in the Kanawha field, a wild uproar of picketings, jailings, shooting, bombings, troops called out, women and children arrested. The broadsides of class warfare crash. Even Governor Pinchot, in Pennsylvania, appealing to the operators to stop evictions and telling them that whether they have the right to evict is, in the present situation, "beside the question," has been met by a grim reprimand for "not properly maintaining law, peace and good order in the vicinity in which our mines are located." The Communists have even attacked Moundsville in the panhandle of West Virginia, one of the toughest nuts in the state to crack, a mining community with a guarded fence around it. And in the course of the last few days, persons who claim to be Communists have turned up in the Kanawha field—though nobody knows whether they are Communists or Department of Justice agents trying to pin Communism on Keeney and the Muste group from Brookwood College. Last of all, prodded into activity, the John L. Lewis organization has come to life and has been sending representatives to West Virginia to try to sign the miners up. By a characteristic stroke, it has made with some of the operators in the northern part of the state an agreement which calls for a wage rate six cents lower than the wage of thirty-six cents a ton which is the average in the Kanawha field. This agreement means that the operators everywhere in West Virginia will have to lower their rates, and this means that the Kanawha miners will have to strike.

Frank Keeney's independent union has a membership of 23,000. It stands today between the Communists, on the one hand, and the corrupt AF of L, on the other, as a spontaneous native labor movement. There is a gulf between the Keeneyites and the Communists which neither the admiration of the former for the Communists' undoubted guts nor the efforts on the part of the latter to convince the Keeneyites that their present course must lead them to Communism, has come anywhere near to bridging. The Communist point of view seems alien to the Keeneyites. The other day, the Communists in Pennsylvania requested a conference with Governor Pinchot and then denounced him as a tool of the operators—whereas the Keeneyites will tell you that Pinchot is "pretty good for old politics." As for the relations of the Keeneyites with the AF of L, they have been becoming tenser and tenser.

————

The United Mine Workers of America have announced an out-of-doors meeting, and the Keeneyites have decided to come to it. They have prepared a questionnaire, which they have had distributed in the streets and brought to the attention of the speakers. This questionnaire implies that the Lewis machine has sold out and wrecked the union. The man who has been passing it out has been told that he will be slugged if he attends the meeting. He had already been warned by his superintendent that if he should go, it would be held against him.

The atmosphere at the meeting is strained. Of the audience of about five hundred, about half are Keeney's men.

In the sweltering Sunday afternoon, they gather in the little ball park between the railroad and a small brick hospital. Immediately behind the hospital rise the green West Virginia hills—the upper half darkened with shadow—the white clouds and the limpid blue sky. A nurse in white cap and uniform, bright and sharply creased like white paper, passes from one building to another. In the window of a gray frame house, a girl rests bare arms on the sill, listens awhile to the speeches, then yawns and goes away. The miners listen standing, in blue overalls or gray Sunday pants, their blue or white Sunday shirts open at the throat. Some are Negroes and some are white. They are silent; there is little applause. The two factions are afraid of each other. On the platform sits a funny-paper creation: an immense bullfrog dressed in black, whose face, crowded up under the brim of his hat by a hypertrophied chin and jowl, fills a space which seems grotesquely small. He is a local businessman who has been asked to preside.

The first speaker is a tubby man, who looks as if he would melt into lard. He is a salesman: his light-brown hair is parted in the middle and brushed back; he might be a clerk in a Broadway shirt shop or a demonstrator in a department store. He tries to sell them the Lewis contract. "Some people will tell you," he says, "that this contract lowers wages. This contract raises wages—it raises them sixty cents a day! [Faint applause from a few who have not realized that the speaker is reckoning from the lowest known rate.] You'll get your eight-hour day—and you'll get a checkweighman—you *bet* you will! And you'll be able to trade at any store you want to! . . . People will talk to you about other unions—but there's only one union for a miner, and that's the United Mine Workers of America! [A faint voice: "Hurrah for John L. Lewis!"] . . . People will tell you about those *brave* men up in Ohio—especially at St. Clairsville [where the Communists have been active]—those *brave* men who don't fear the Devil himself—who aren't afraid to face tear-gas bombs and nightsticks! And those *brave* men are so *brave* that when they go up against those bombs, they put the women and children first! [This is actually a Communist practice.] . . .

"Now I see some fine colored folks here—and it reminds me of a story I heard about a colored man who was brought before the judge for beating his wife—I see you smile when I say that [bending down and speaking patronizingly and jovially to a Negro just below him]—I hope that you never did anything like that, because this fellah got into trouble! And the judge said, 'Looka here, Rastus, how come you're charged with beatin' your wife?' 'Well,' the colored man said, 'it's this way, Jedge—it seems like she's always askin' me for money—when Ah git up, it's "Gimme some money!," when Ah come back from work, it's "Gimme some money!" That's all Ah hear, money, money! from mawnin' till night!' 'Why,' says the Judge, 'she hadn't ought to do that. What makes her act that way?' 'Well, Jedge,' says Rastus, 'you see, Ah ain't never give her no money.' And I suppose that's probably the way you folks feel about the operators! Well, we've just made a contract with the operators that guarantees you money—the miners are entitled to a fair wage, and the operators are entitled to a fair profit on their investment. . . ."

(The Keeney men find they are being watched. One of

the leaders has kept his coat on and is suspected of carrying a gun.)

The second speaker is an older man, with wiry and grizzled hair, who looks as if he might play the roles of dignified bankers in second-rate stock: "This little union they talk about puts me in mind of two dudes from the city who went out to the country one day and saw a little hop-frawg. 'Look out!' says one of the dudes. 'You better kill it before it bites us!' 'You kill it,' says the other one. 'I'm scared!' 'Let's let it alone,' says the other one. 'If we let it alone, it'll beat its brains out!' And if you let that little union alone, it'll just beat its own brains out! . . .

"They say that we want to make money. Ha-ha! [throwing his head back in mirth] I don't do this for my salary! Mr. Van Bittner don't do it for his salary! We're doing it for you! [Compare with the patent-medicine faker on page 258.] We're doing it because we want you to have a fair wage! We're doing it for the mine workers of southern West Virginia! *Everything I do and everything I am*—[making a climax by leaning down and shaking his grizzled head at the crowd]—*is for the mine workers of southern West Virginia!*"

He is followed by the speaker of the afternoon: the man who made the contract, Van Bittner. He is wearing a neat blue suit, but when he takes off his new straw hat, he looks as if he had come out of jail: he is half-bald and his hair is cropped close; his eyes and eyebrows are a narrow slit, and his mouth makes another slit, grimly drawn down at the corners. Van Bittner, at one point, was thrown out of his own district, but Lewis has pulled him back into the machine.

"We're here to ask you to join the union!" he speaks more authoritatively than the others—"the union that was built with the blood of the miners!—and of their women!—and of their children!—the United Mine Workers of America! This other little union that's been misrepresenting and malinging [sic] the United Mine Workers of America—who's at the head of it? Who got it up? Short-haired women and long-haired men—Bolsheviks—crank professors who have come down here from New York—Professor Nutsky and Professor

Don't-Know-Nothin'-sky and Professor Never-Dug-a-Pound-of-Coal-in-His-Life-sky." . . .

(The "Musteites" in the meantime have been easily spotted. There is a Musteite type quite distinct from those of other radical groups. The Musteites differ from the Communists in maintaining the conventional dress, literate language and polite approach of intelligent middle-class people. They might be students or instructors from any college, and the influence of Muste himself has perhaps had the effect of making them a little like the students of a divinity school. On the other hand, they also differ from the truly academic radicals in possessing the conviction and the courage which carry them into industrial battles and make them do thankless work and venture into situations which few middle-class people care to face. And unminerlike and law-abiding though they appear with their berets and glasses, they are becoming aware at this meeting that they are the objects of growing suspicion. They realize that there are people watching them, circling around them like flies. One of them gets his back against a wall.)

"I've just been handed some questions signed by the miners in this field. I don't know whether they wrote them themselves. I'm glad to have the privilege of standing up here and answering these questions. They ask about this contract. They say that this contract calls for lower wages than non-union companies pay. They'll tell you that the Koppers Company, owned by Andrew Mellon, pays thirty-nine cents a ton. Now, you know that a ton when you dig it is a different thing from a ton on the tipple when there's no union checkweighman there.. And anybody who wants to go with a yellow-dog wage can go! Which would you rather go with—a man or a yellow dog? I'd rather go with a man any day! And yet some people will talk to you about the Koppers Company—because they're working with the operators to rob you! Now we want you to join the union and sign this contract that stabilizes wages. We want you to start in as a child and then grow up—a child crawls, and then it learns to walk—and then it grows up to be a boy—and then it grows up to be a man! We can't start in and be grown up right away! . . .

"I like to talk to miners—and I like to talk to operators. The operators aren't so bad—some of them are kind of dumb, that's all—they don't understand that the miner's got to have a fair wage if he wants to eat. You can't work if you don't eat, can you? And the operator's got to have a fair return on his investment. . . ."

(A silent disturbance: some men close in on one of the Keeney followers, who is standing against a parked car. They search him; a small group gathers.)

"Somebody's just handed me up a statement about this circular. I can't spend all day answering questions. If anybody wants to ask any questions, he can come round to the offices of the local any day, and we'll answer all his questions. . . . We want you to come back to the one union! Give up your little union! Give up your plaything—your hobbyhorse! We know you *will* come back, and when you come we'll stretch out our arms to welcome the prodigal son, and we'll give you the fatted calf to eat!—only you mustn't expect it to be *too* fat at first. Come back to the one miners' union: the United Mine Workers of America—the union that was built with the blood of children!—that was built with the blood of chi-i-il-dren!"

He works up three times to a climax, but the climax always misses: the first time the audience does not respond—the second time a train goes by—he comes to an end at last, but the swelling peroration has been sapped. It is received with inadequate applause. One of the UMWA people says that he has never heard Van Bittner do so badly.

The meeting breaks up, and both sides go away.

———

In the meantime, Frank Keeney himself has been holding a meeting in the hills. Men and women and children have turned out and shouted the songs and cheered for the speeches.

Frank Keeney is a short man, with a square face and stub-toed shoes. He has a straight black bang on his forehead, eyes like fragments of blue bottle-glass, a face as deep-seamed as if the battles of the miners had left their slashes there, and two solid-gold teeth. It has been said of him that he can talk to operators as if they were his own miners, and that he talks to miners like the captain of a ship. His right-hand man, Brant Scott, had his leg crushed in a mine accident years ago. They amputated it at the hospital and turned him out with no compensation, telling him that he would never be able to walk again. He has devised a cork leg, however, which is held on by an elaborate harness strapped around the upper part of his body.

Both Keeney and Scott are old Socialists, who became discouraged with Socialism after Debs was put in jail but who have held to their original principles. They took long chances as younger men in 1920, when the strikes became a real civil war, and now, eleven years later, they have left lives of middle-class security to take their chances again.

The miners have been called in the past the backbone of the American labor movement. Never yet broken in to the abject life of the workers in the industrial cities, they have still a tradition of resistance and a habit of joint action.

Frank Keeney's own grandfather at one time owned a good deal of the land in these hills which belong now to those operators who never go near them. And Keeney, by birth and by feeling, is a genuine leader of his people. He has the hypnotic influence of power. Even the passing of a union representative in one of the union cars brings a cry of "Frank Keeney!" from the streets and camps. And Frank Keeney, who was tried for murder after the shootings of the armed march, must now live or be crushed with his people.

TENNESSEE AGRARIANS

COUSIN CHARLES lives with his daughter in a high compact green-roofed house—a hundred years old—with iron curlicues and stars that show black against whitewashed brick. You are received in one of the equal-sized rectangular rooms on either side of the central hallway. A bright fire of big coal is burning in a wire-screened grate. The lady serves us rich fruitcake and clear thin agreeable wine.

Cousin Charles is a tobacco-planter and has fifty "niggers" on his place. He is lean, bald, distinguished and sallow, and exhibits the combined pride of the Southern plantation-owner, the man who is cleverer than his fellows and the accomplished classical scholar. When he laughs or makes a point, he creases his slanting eyes.

His feeling about the depression is that it serves the "industrialists" right. He pointed out in an article in a magazine seven years ago that the great present trouble with the country was that the cities were getting overgrown—Megalopolis, as Spengler calls it. Strange that it should have been left for a German to diagnose our American disease. But the effect of the depression should be salutary, because it ought to make the government get rid of the high tariff and send people back to the land. There's always a living on a farm—and he himself has been a dirt farmer, not a white-collar farmer!

Cousin Charles likes to argue with a clergyman brother over passages in Josephus and Origen. He has had a schoolhouse built on his place so that—for sheer love of French, Greek and Latin—he can instruct the neighbors' children in the humanities, and he once had a poor scholar from Nashville come and stay in his house all winter in order "to help him with his syntax."

He talks about Woodrow Wilson's father, a dignitary of the Southern Presbyterian Church, whom he had known when the latter lived in Nashville. Dr. Wilson had been very much of a clergyman—but he remembered his telling an amusing story about one of the women in his congregation, who had argued theology with him heatedly, saying: "You can take away the Redemption and you can take away Absolution—but you must leave me Total Depravity!" So one knew that, though a clergyman, he was human—like the Roman augurs in Cicero who couldn't look at each other without smiling. Woodrow Wilson was a good deal like Cicero—most eloquent as far as his words went, but ineffective when it came to action. He had been a very strange man—"I expect you would have to look for his complexes. . . . And yet his state papers were written in a more classical style than those of any other President." (As you listen to Cousin Charles, you realize that much of the antagonism which Wilson felt against big business must have been due to his coming from the agrarian South. He was vague about the industrial world no doubt because it was never quite real to him, as it never seems quite real to Southerners who have stuck, like Cousin Charles, to their land. Its evils were moral evils, and he believed he could preach them away. Cousin Charles—who is, of course, a Democrat—is of the opinion that Mr. Smith would have made a better President than Mr. Hoover—he had at least common sense. In his old-fashioned Southern way, which today seems a little naïve, he has always taken politics seriously. A citizen of the landowners' democracy, with a citizen's responsibilities, he expects to be represented—in spite of the Civil War—by the government of the United States; and, from time to time, writes to the papers long, elegant and well-reasoned letters.

Cousin Charles raises black tobacco, which, unlike the milder kind, has to be cured in a barn. Just inside the door of this barn, we find a "nigger wench" sitting on the floor: decently dressed in up-to-date clothes, she stares into the glowing red core of a writhen cypress log, not, perhaps, precisely sullen but paying no attention to us. Overhead, the big barn, dense with fragrance, loses itself among rich shadows of cross-rafters, from which brown wrinkled bunches hang. The Negroes are breaking off the stalks of the leaves and binding the stems of each bunch with a leaf. These look like unexpanded moth's wings, still shriveled inside the cocoon. A black boy shows you how resilient they are: if you bend one up, it bends right back—the livest plant there is.

Black tobacco is terribly strong and finds its market mostly in Italy. This market has been suffering from our recent high tariff: the Italians have been goaded to reprisals. Besides this, the tobacco planters are swindled by the outside buyers to whom, by immemorial custom, they auction their tobacco off. If it were possible for them to get together, they could protect themselves by fixing prices; but the planters have always been individualistic. It was their weakness in discipline and coördination, the younger generation will tell you, which kept them from winning the Civil War.

As you go, Cousin Charles makes apologies for having let himself run on at such length. "You know the saying, *Indulge pueris,*" he creases his slanting eyes as he closes the car door. "Perhaps we may make it, *Indulge senibus.*"

————

The younger generation of Nashville who share Cousin Charles's tastes are less firmly attached to the land. Brilliant poets and subtle philosophers—many of them the former pupils of John Crowe Ransom of Vanderbilt University, whom they still tend to gravitate around—they have gone off at one time or another to New York, to Oxford, to Paris. But, the offspring of a type of community more organic and homogeneous than anything to be found in the North, the products of a classical education, they come back to marry girls at home, to renovate family mansions, to do some farming with the aid of a sharecropper, to write books about the Civil War. They may, when they first tried to leave it, have felt a certain amount of impatience with that eighteenth-century world, forever feeding itself on its past. They were aware that the centers of activity had shifted away from the South, and they knew themselves entitled, by inheritance, to the freedom of a larger world. But after living in dark basements in Greenwich Village, floating with the drift of the Paris cafés, they have ended by finding these sojourns both expensive and unsatisfactory, and by forming unflattering opinions of the manners and the standards of the intelligentzia. They think tenderly of the South again; and they come, in the end, to blame all the ills of commercialized America on the defeat of the agrarian Confederacy by the money-grubbing merchants of New England. If only New Orleans, instead of New York, had become the chief port of the United States! They set themselves to writing biographies of the generals and the statesmen of the War, defending them against the slander or the belittlement of Union historians, attempting to explain their failures. If only General Bragg hadn't let the Confederates down, the merchants might never have triumphed! If Longstreet hadn't blundered at Gettysburg! And as lacking in a religion or a common ideal as their compatriots of New York or Paris, they try to find one in ancestor-worship. They revive the old myths of the family, brace themselves with the memory of their fathers' defiance. And they make a kind of common cause in agitation against the capitalists, largely Northern, who, taking advantage of low pay in the South and its lack of legislation for the protection of labor, have been bringing their industries south. These young people have published a symposium declaring their loyalty to "agrarianism," their repudiation of "industrialism"; and they have held a great conference at Richmond, which drew an attendance of thousands and at which was debated the question whether any further manufacturing should not be discouraged in the South.

Alas! they are locking the stable door long after the colt has bolted. The fierce battles of a new civil war—Gastonia, Elizabethton, Marion, Danville—are already being fought on their ground. They can no longer hope to exorcize it.

But, in the meantime, they can enjoy certain advantages. For the Northerner, the horror of slavery still poisons the memory of that feudal society. But, in a sense, perhaps, the Southern slaveholder was a somewhat more dignified figure than the contemporary beneficiary of capitalism. He might ignore the horrors of the slave trade. He might make a point of locating his slave quarters as far away as possible from his mansion in order that he and his family could not see or hear or smell them. But he could not help knowing very well what he was doing with the people who lived in them, and he did not often pretend to be doing anything else. He might flog his slaves or work them till they broke; but he could not evade accepting the plain implications of his acts— that was all that the blacks were good for.

The Northerner is sure to be shocked when the Southerner speaks frankly of the Negroes as creatures—an inferior race— for whom political or social equality is utterly and forever unthinkable. But the position of the Northerner himself depends upon human exploitation. He may, of course, be entirely unaware of it, not know who makes the clothes he wears, prepares the food he eats, digs the fuel that heats him or pours the steel for the building he lives in—he may not even know where the money comes from that enables him to buy all these things; but though his consciousness may be more innocent, he is none the better off for that. And the Southerner, on his side, becomes suspicious of the Northerner's pretensions—smelling hypocrisy in his humane anxieties, mania in his moral idealism, and in his eternal insistence on "service" an attempt to make up for, to palliate, the savageries of a mechanized society self-seeking and rapacious in the highest degree.

This is one of the things that rankle with the still unreconstructed Southerner, and is his instinct not partly correct? He feels that his tradition of living is somehow humanly right and that the modern industrial society which so flourished when his own was defeated is essentially inhuman and wrong. He resents the whole system of abstraction that constitutes the industrial world, and of which the complete divorce of the people who live on dividends from the people whose labor provides them is one of the inevitable features. This abstraction has its own kind of grandeur. It represents an astonishing triumph of certain of our human faculties; and we must still depend upon these faculties—the development of mechanical techniques, the rigorous ordering of activities—to get ourselves out of the mess in which this triumph has landed us. Engineers with the scientific imagination, statesmen possessed by principle, will be able to deal with problems that these jealous country squires of the South, loyal only to their little localities, have hardly been able to imagine. But who will pretend that perfection in the techniques of so many fields has resulted in human beings either amiable or appetizing? The deadening of feeling, the social insulation, which impoverish life in industrial communities have not yet struck their chill into the Southern agrarians. They are affected to some degree, like all of us, by the shiftings and collapses of modern society, but, in general, it may be said that among them the human relations have still a certain satisfactoriness that one misses in our mechanized system: they are more feudal yet more flexibly managed, more conventionalized yet warmer and closer, than ours are likely to be. Among them the men and women can still meet as men and women; kin, as they say, meet as kin; friends meet as friends; and master and servant are still master and servant. And those who still have gardens there to cultivate are not perhaps among the least lucky of us if they can succeed in getting a living out of them.

————

The countryside in Tennessee has a singular mildness and charm: now in summer, below the long mountains, darkish and bluish in the distance, the wheat-fields show a blond that glows under a delicate pale blue sky.

THE SCOTTSBORO FREIGHT-CAR CASE

CHATTANOOGA, TENNESSEE: old low sordid Southern brick buildings, among which a few hotels, insurance companies and banks have expanded into big modern bulks, as if by sporadic effort; business streets that suddenly lapse into nigger cabins; a surrounding wilderness of mills that manufacture some 1,500 different articles, from locomotives to coffins and snuff; and a vast smudge of nigger dwellings—almost a third of the population are Negroes. "Hell's Half-Acre" in the mill district is a place where people don't dare go at night: the saying is that among the niggers there is an average of a murder a day. In Chattanooga, the manufacturers, enslaving the Negro almost as completely as the planters did before the Civil War, have kept him in his African squalor and produced a new type of squalor: Southern slackness mixed with factory grime.

The night of last March 24, two white girls from Huntsville, Alabama, came into Chattanooga in a box-car—according to the testimony of one of them, in the company of several boys. Both had been workers in the old Huntsville cotton mills, and both had apparently from an early age been practicing prostitution to make a little money on the side. They are alleged to have lived indifferently among Negroes and whites, and one of them is said to have been arrested for "hugging" a Negro on the street. Victoria Price, the older girl, said she had been married twice; Ruby Bates, the younger one, said she had never been married. Both of them "dipped snuff."

According to the girls' story, they had spent that night in Chattanooga at the house of a woman they knew. They left the next morning at about 10:45 on a freight train bound for Memphis, traveling in a low roofless car of the kind that is known as a "gondola." The gondola was about two-thirds full of gravel. The girls had bobbed hair and wore overalls. Riding in the same car were about half a dozen white boys.

At Stevenson, Alabama, just across the state line, about twenty colored boys got in and scattered themselves through the train. They were a miscellaneous lot of hoboes—representing, like the white boys and girls, the bottom layer of that far-Southern society. Only one of the nine afterwards arrested was able even to write his name. Certain of these Negro boys said that they were on their way to Memphis to look for jobs on the docks. In some cases, they were friends who were traveling together; in others, they did not know one another.

What happened on the train is uncertain. But apparently one of the white boys, walking along the top of a box-car, stumbled over one of the Negroes and threatened to throw him off the train. At any rate, ill feeling was roused, and presently the colored boys came trooping down into the gondola. One of them had a gun and another a knife, and the white boys were outnumbered. Some kind of fight evidently took place, and the white boys either jumped off or were put off the train—all except one, who slipped down between the cars and was rescued by one of the Negroes.

The group who had been put off were furious, and one of them had a cut head. This boy went to the nearest railroad station and told the telegrapher there that the niggers had tried to murder them; and the telegrapher, very indignant, telephoned ahead along the line to have the Negroes taken off the train.

So when the train arrived at Paint Rock, it was boarded by the sheriff with his deputies, and nine of the boys were arrested. The others had disappeared. The Negroes supposed at first that they were being arrested for bumming a ride. One boy was found in an empty car, where he said he had been riding by himself ever since the train left Chattanooga. Four others had been traveling on an oil car and said that there had been a disturbance but they hadn't known what it was about. It seems reasonable to assume that, if violence had taken place, the responsible boys had escaped. The one with the pistol was never found; beyond the cut head of the boy who had complained, no evidence of foul play was discovered.

But there were the two white girls alone on the train with a gang of niggers. The authorities demanded of the girls whether the niggers hadn't attacked them. This the girls at first denied; but under pressure of repeated questioning, accompanied by a certain amount of prompting, they confessed that they had both been raped. The doctor who examined the girls found proof that they had been having sexual intercourse but no reason to conclude that they had been roughly handled, except for a small bruise on one of them which might well have been caused by riding on gravel.

The boys were put in jail at Paint Rock, but when a mob gathered and threatened to lynch them, they were removed to the town of Gadsden. In their cells, they went mad with fury—yelled wildly and beat on the doors and tore up their beds and bedding. They told their lawyers that they had been led from their cells at Gadsden by a lieutenant of the National Guard, then handcuffed together in pairs and systematically clubbed by people brought in from the streets. On April 6, they were put on trial at Scottsboro, Alabama, the county seat of Jackson County.

Scottsboro is a small town, and the people there have little excitement: it was a long time since anything had come their way so sensational as nine niggers accused of rape. The day of the trial was a festival: it happened also to be fair day and horse-trading day. Though the normal population of Scottsboro is only about 1,500, there were at least 10,000 people in town. The poor whites had come in with their guns, prepared to slaughter the boys then and there, and they might very well have done so if the Alabama branch of the Commission on Interracial Coöperation had not persuaded the Governor to send out the State Militia, who guarded the trials with fixed bayonets, machine-guns and tear-gas bombs. What with the bugle-music of changing guard, *The Star-Spangled Banner* and *Dixie* played by a band from the hoisery mill and a parade of twenty-eight Ford trucks, with a phonograph and amplifier, organized by an enterprising Ford agent who had taken advantage of the occasion to try to pick up his slackening sales, the town was in a delirium of gaiety.

In the meantime, inside the courthouse, Ruby Bates and Virginia Price were testifying that the colored boys had held them down in the gondola and raped them; each had been raped by exactly six. Ruby Bates could not identify her assailants; but Virginia Price rose to the occasion better. She turned out to enjoy the limelight, developed a sense of her role and—very much to Ruby's resentment—played the younger girl off the stage. Spurred on by the prosecutor's insistence, she got to the point, at one of the trials, of undertaking to identify the boys in the order in which they had attacked her. "Yonder he sits! Yonder he sits!" she would declare, as the State's attorney went through the half dozen—though at other times she admitted she wasn't sure. At any rate, the crowd roared: the hammering of the judge couldn't quiet them.

Three of the Negro boys testified that they had seen other Negroes attack the girls—though they afterwards told the lawyers that they had been induced to do this by the court officials, who had promised to shoot them in the courtroom if they didn't, but to have them let off if they did. The white boy who had remained on the train had testified before the Grand Jury that he had seen the Negro boys having intercourse with the girls, but was not called by the State at the trials because—as the prosecutor is said to have complained—he couldn't be persuaded to say that he had seen the girls "raped." The other white boys had either fled or been told to disappear: at any rate, they were never produced. The doctor in that Southern courtroom was asked whether the semen he had found in the girls had been that of a colored or a white man.

Eight of the boys were immediately found guilty and sentenced to death in the electric chair. At the announcement of the first two verdicts, the brass band struck up outside, and the crowd enthusiastically applauded: the jury had sat through the trials with the crowd in full view through the

windows. Only the youngest boy—fourteen (the oldest was
only twenty)—got off with a mistrial. The prosecutor, on account of his youth, had asked only for life imprisonment.
Yet, notwithstanding this clemency of the State, eight of
the jury, in this case, too, demanded electrocution. One of
the other boys had also said originally that he was only fourteen, but he later asserted he was nineteen. Pressure had been
brought to bear: it had been feared that he would get off
with the pentitentiary.

It had, of course, been exceedingly difficult to find anyone
to defend the boys. Each of the seven lawyers who composed
the Scottsboro bar had in turn been assigned to the defendants, and all except one had got out of it. One of these lawyers, attorney for the Alabama Power Company, is said to
have remarked that the Power Company had juice enough to
burn all nine of the defendants. The only man who was willing to take their case—even for formal decency—was Mr.
Milo C. Moody. Mr. Moody is, from all reports, by way of
being the town heretic. He has always made something of a
practice of taking up unpopular positions, but he is old now
and, in competition with the brass band and the Ford agent's
amplifier, was not able to do much for his clients.
    In the meantime, however, the Scottsboro case had been at-
tracting the attention of an intelligent Negro physician in
Chattanooga, Dr. P. A. Stephens. Dr. Stephens brought it to
the attention of the Interdenominational Alliance of Colored
Ministers, and they raised the inadequate sum of $50.08 and
appealed to Mr. Stephen R. Roddy, a Chattanooga attorney,
to undertake the defense of the boys. Mr. Roddy is young
and conventional; yet not so conventional that he would not
consent—for little remuneration—to make a trip down to
Scottsboro and see whether anything could be done. As soon
as he appeared in the courtroom, Judge Hawkins hastened
to announce that if Mr. Roddy would conduct the defense,
the Scottsboro bar would be released. Mr. Roddy replied,
however, that he had been merely sent to observe. Fresh from
getting through the crowd and the guard and with the music
of the brass band in his ears, he decided that there was no

hope for a postponement, and, a member of the Tennessee bar, he was unfamiliar with Alabama procedure. He asked to be associated with Mr. Moody; and he put on the stand, at the end of the trials, the commander of the National Guard and one of the court officials, and had them testify that the cheering of the crowd outside which followed the announcement of the first two verdicts had been so loud that the jurors could not have failed to hear it.

But Dr. Stephens and the colored ministers were not the only people interested in the Scottsboro case. The Communists had recently been active in Chattanooga, and on February 10, three of them had been arrested for an attempt to hold a street demonstration. They were tried during the last week of March and all found guilty of violating the Sedition Statute, a law which, dating originally from 1715, had never before been applied, construed or noticed during the whole hundred and thirty-six years of Tennessee's history. A motion for a new trial, however, was made, and on April 18, Judge Lusk of the criminal court, in an opinion which—though handed down in the state that had declared illegal the teaching of the theory of evolution—might serve as a model to other courts, set aside the verdict of the jury and granted the defendants a new trial. He pointed out that these latter had been arrested before they had had a chance to make any subversive speeches, and that in any case "membership in the Communist party and adherence to its principles" had been "recognized as lawful" by the admission of its candidates to the Tennessee ballots. "This case," Judge Lusk concluded, "has given the Court much concern. As a lover of the institutions of this state and nation, I look with deep concern upon the activities of subversive agitators of every sort. But, in meeting these movements, we must demonstrate our superiority to them by keeping, ourselves, within the law. The best way, in my judgment, to combat Communism, or any other movement inimical to our institutions, is to show, if we can, that the injustices which they charge against us are, in fact, non-existent."

In the meantime, the Communists in Chattanooga had heard about the arrest of the nine Negroes and had gone down to Scottsboro the day of the trial. One of their principal aims at the present time is to enlist the support of the Southern Negroes—to whom they have been preaching the doctrine, arrived at from analogy with the Ukraine and completely unrealistic in America, of "self-determination for the Black Belt."

The Communists assigned to Chattanooga, therefore, seized upon the Scottsboro case as an opening wedge for realizing this long-range program. Their first step was to have their defense organization, the International Labor Defense, send Judge Hawkins a telegram which amazed him and made him angry: this message described the cases against the Negroes as a "frame-up" and a "legal lynching" and said that the ILD would hold the Judge personally responsible. After the trial, Mr. Roddy says he was visited by ILD representatives and asked to conduct a spectacular defense. According to Mr. Roddy, they went through all the gestures of taking him up into a high place and showing him the kingdoms of the earth. They told him he had the chance to make a national reputation, to become a second Clarence Darrow—a dream, one gathers, entirely alien to Mr. Roddy's ambitions. He asked how they proposed to pay him. They explained that they would raise the money by holding meetings among the Negroes and getting them to contribute to a defense fund. This idea seemed distasteful to Mr. Roddy. He and the ILD did not inspire one another with confidence.

The ILD went next to the attorney who had so efficiently defended the arrested Communists. Mr. George W. Chamlee is quite a different type from Mr. Roddy. A shrewd lawyer and a clever man, humorous, worldly-wise, deep in the politics of the state and able to see every side of every question, he is by way of being a local character; he works by himself, forms his own opinions and pursues his own ends, and is not infrequently found in opposition to the conventional elements of the community. Some years ago, he made himself conspicuous by defending street-car strikers; and he has represented both Negroes and radicals in cases which it would perhaps have been impossible to get any other Chattanooga lawyer to take. It is true that, as a candidate for office, he has undoubtedly derived political support both from the Negroes and from organized labor. And, on the other hand, he once scored an equal triumph by getting off a group of Tennesseeans convicted of lynching, whose cases had been appealed to the Supreme Court. At the recent trial of the Communist agitators, when the prosecutor attempted to make much of the fact that the defendants were avowedly in favor of the overthrow of the government and had foresworn loyalty to the American flag, Mr. Chamlee reminded his opponent that both their grandfathers, when they had fought in the Civil War, had repudiated the federal government and professed allegiance to another flag.

Mr. Chamlee, at home and in the Communist press, is given the title of "General"; but this means merely that he once held the office of attorney general of Hamilton County. In the last Democratic primaries, he ran for renomination against Mr. Roddy, the Democratic county chairman. Both were defeated by a third candidate, but Mr. Roddy got more votes than Mr. Chamlee—and it may be that political rivalries have contributed to the antagonisms which have developed in the course of the Scottsboro case.

At any rate, the situation has been complicated by still another element. Dr. Stephens had been approached by the International Labor Defense, and at first he had coöperated with them. But their obvious tone of propaganda had strongly aroused his suspicions, and he and the colored ministers had broken off relations with them. Dr. Stephens had written for advice to the headquarters in New York of the National Association for the Advancement of Colored People, and the result was two defense campaigns not merely separate but mutually hostile.

Precisely what is the history of the split between the ILD and the NAACP is difficult to find out. But its underlying causes are plain. The National Association for the Advancement of Colored People is a non-political organization, which, under the leadership of Mr. Walter White, has in many cases been admirably successful in protecting the legal rights of Negroes. In the Arkansas riot cases of 1925, in which seventy-nine Negro sharecroppers and tenant farmers,

who had attempted to sue their landlords for money due
them, had been charged with insurrection and sentenced
either to long prison terms or to death, the NAACP fought
the verdicts and caused the Supreme Court to reverse its
decision (handed down in the Leo Frank case) and to hold
that if it could be shown that a trial had been dominated by
the fear of a mob, the conviction could be overruled. The
NAACP works quietly and by conventional methods. Its general tendency is to encourage the Negroes to approximate to
white respectability, in order that they may compete in the
same fields and claim the same rights as white citizens. The
aims of the Communists have been indicated. The rupture
between the two organizations was inevitable by their very
nature, as seems always to be the case when Communists and
bourgeois liberals attempt to work together. Whatever the
immediate occasion of the break, the result is that the liberals
end by accusing the Communists of disingenuous or Jesu-
itical tactics, of diverting money raised for special defense
funds to Communist propaganda, of prejudicing their particular causes by waving the red flag too openly and of being
willing and even eager to make martyrs for their atrocity-
mongering press, which aims to awake the class consciousness of its readers; while the Communists, on their side, accuse the liberals of insincerity or timidity, of sacrificing the
success of their causes by sticking too closely to the conventional machinery and trusting to the fair play of capitalist
courts, of being unwilling to deal with fundamentals for
fear of antagonizing the rich persons or foundations who sub-
sidize them and of attempting to mislead the proletariat as to
the latter's genuine interests in order to safeguard their own
bourgeois positions. In this particular case, the NAACP
pointed out that it was not the "bosses" but the white working
class who had forced the issue at Scottsboro, as it had been
not white bourgeois but workers who had lynched Negroes
in Alabama, persecuted Negro peons in Arkansas, stolen the
Negro school funds in South Carolina and in general excluded the Negroes from their unions, with the result that,
later on, at the time when white wages were being raised
and white working conditions bettered, the Negroes were

left out in the cold; whereas higher education for Negroes had been made possible only by the power trust and the steel trust, Standard Oil, the mail order chain stores and the capitalist Christian Church. To this the Communists retorted that the capitalists of these organizations did not give a damn about the Negroes; that what they were aiming at was to exploit them as strikebreakers and underpaid labor, and to make sure that the educated Negro leaders were conservatives who would stick on their side.

Walter White and William Pickens, the secretary of the NAACP went to Scottsboro and Chattanooga and took steps to engage new counsel. A ludicrous and pathetic contest began between the Communists and the NAACP to get the parents of the sentenced boys to endorse their respective organizations and to authorize their lawyers to defend them. The NAACP accused the Communists of having carried off certain members of the families of the defendants and of keeping them incommunicado; and the Communists charged the NAACP with having induced certain of the Negroes to sign statements which they could not read and which had never been read to them. Before the motion for a new trial had been made, the bewildered prisoners and their relatives had been persuaded to sign and repudiate a variety of documents. The Communists have had some success in exploiting the mothers of the boys, whom they produce at their money-raising meetings, and, according to the NAACP, have resorted to bogus mothers when they were not able to get the real ones. One of the genuine mothers, returning to Chattanooga, wrote as follows to her entertainers—I quote from the *Daily Worker*:

"Well I sure miss you all but I was just homesick. I'm sorry I was that way, but after all I love the Reds. I can't be treated any better than the Reds has treated me. And I am a Red too. I tell the white and I tell the black I am not getting back of nothing else. I mean to be with you all as long as I live. . . . Well, I am looking for you to come to see me like you said. You can't realize how highly I appreciate the kindness you all did for me. . . . I hope next time I be to see you all I will be less worried. I never stayed away from my family that long for I think my children don't get along without me. . . . Give all the Reds my love for I love them all. . . .

"From one of the Reds, Janie Patterson."

Another wrote as follows:

"My dear friend, organ of the League of Struggle for Negro Rights. This is Azie Powell's mother. I was away from home at the time those men was out to see me. I was out trying to collect some money what a man owes me to defend for my boy. . . .

"From birth I has work hard plowing, farming by myself for a living for my children. Have had no help supporting them. So sorry, deeply sorry to my heart that my boy was framed up in this. I am almost crazy, can't eat, can't sleep, just want to work all the time, so weak I don't see how I can stand much longer. Living on the will of the Lord. . . .

"Azie was raised on a farm, he was born on a farm, got one little girl, seven years of age already has heart trouble. Have two boys, two girls in all with no father assisting. Poor me, poor me, so burdened down with trouble, if I could only see my baby Azie once more. Lord have mercy on my poor boy in Birmingham. My boy is only fourteen, will be fifteen November 10.

"Poor me, worked hard every day of my life, can't make a living hardly to save my life. . . .

"From Josephine Powell, Atlanta, Ga.

"P.S.—Not knowing what to say or what to do for the best."

The Communists held parades and mass meetings, broke up meetings of the NAACP, themselves had a demonstration in Harlem broken up by the police, made indignant protests to the President, sent a hundred telegrams to the Governor and organized an "All-Southern Conference," at which the organizers were arrested.

Two parties appeared among the Negroes: those who were persuaded by the arguments of the Communists or were excited by Communism as a new form of revivalism (the meetings were often held in churches) and those who, from conservatism, caution or willingness to mind their place, were opposed to the agitation. In one case, a married woman named Bessy Ball attended a Communist meeting and was elected a delegate to the All-Southern Conference. Her husband had been listening to the counsels of the respectable Negro preachers, and when she got home, he beat her up. It was true she had gone to the meeting with the man who lived next door. When their daughter had Ball arrested, he was congratulated on his conduct by the judge, who advised him to use a shotgun on the Reds if they gave him any trouble. Bessy Ball was fined $10. The house next door was raided, and her friend and his mother were arrested, but eventually released. They went home and were immediately visited by their neighbor, Mr. Ball, who had been given carte blanche by the Court to wage a private war on the Reds. Finding a copy of the *Liberator,* the Negro Communist paper, he proceeded to tear it up; and when the Communist mother protested, he hit her on the head with a wooden block. Later, he shot at the son with the shotgun prescribed by the judge. Both he and the son were arrested on charges of assault with intent to kill. Mr. Ball was soon released, but the Communist was kept in jail.

The more docile Negroes were scared. It is reported that since the Scottsboro trials there have been practically no Negroes riding Southern freight trains, and at the time when feeling was running high, the white people in Scottsboro say they almost had to shake hands with their servants every morning to convince them that they meant them no harm. The white Southerners, of course, resented both the Communists and the NAACP as impertinent meddling from the North. On one occasion, the *Jackson County Sentinal* announced that it would "have no editorial this week on the 'Negro Trial' matter. We just couldn't do one without getting mad as hell." "The International Labor Defense of New Yawk and Rusha" had told them that they "must have Negro jurors on any jury trying the blacks if they were to get 'their rights.' A Negro juror in Jackson County would be a curiosity—and some curiosities are embalmed, you know." And the International Labor Defense received the following telegram from the Alabama Ku Klux Klan: "You Negroes are invited to

Alabama. We want your scalp along with the nine we already have. And we'll get you as well as any one else who is a party to the telegram sent South in behalf of the nine Negroes to burn. Read this to your entire body."

A change of venue to another county was first promised by the Court, then denied. A hearing on motions for new trials was set for June 5. Mr. Roddy, Mr. Chamlee and Mr. Joseph Brodsky, an ILD attorney, all appeared in court. Some of the jurors were cross-examined with a view to making them admit that they had been aware, during the trials, of the brass band and the demonstration, and Mr. Chamlee filed a motion for new trials, asserting that the indictments were vague and mentioned no exact facts or dates; that bias had been present in the case; that the defendants had had no chance to employ counsel; that the jury had been prejudiced and had included no Negroes; that the defense were in possession of newly discovered evidence; that it had been impossible at the trials to question Virginia Price as to whether or not she practiced prostitution; that the Negroes at the time they were arrested had displayed no consciousness of guilt; that the State had failed to produce the white boys; that there must have been on the train from fifteen to eighteen colored boys, and that if any crime had been committed, there was no certainty it had not been committed by the boys who got away; that the ride from Stevenson to Paint Rock could only have lasted forty or fifty minutes and that it would hardly have been possible for a fight and twelve rapes to have taken place within so short a time.

The hearing was the occasion in Scottsboro for another popular demonstration. Mr. Chamlee, when he went to the courthouse, brought a bodyguard along, and Mr. Brodsky was made to stay in the building till two or three hours after the hearing was over, by which time the crowd had gone home. Judge Hawkins, who, for reëlection, has to depend on the Jackson County voters, has denied the motions for new trials.

The defense will appeal the case to the Supreme Court of Alabama, and if they are unsuccessful there, will appeal it to the Supreme Court of the United States.

In the meantime, the Communists in Alabama have continued to work at their program. In the Southern states, the Negro sharecroppers are held in a state of peonage which differs little from their original state of slavery. The Communists have stimulated them to organize, and on July 16, under Communist tutelage, in a church at Camp Hill, a Sharecroppers' Union held a meeting of which one of the objects announced was to protest over the Scottsboro case. A white posse came to break it up, and as a result the sheriff was shot, a Negro picket was shot and killed, four Negroes disappeared—presumably lynched—and thirty-four Negroes were arrested.

THE ENCHANTED FOREST

THE PALE PRAIRIE with its dry light-green grass and its pale
blue sky above—darker dabs of rare trees—dabs of sage-grass
clumps—white dabs of clouds, light and lovely, spread along
like suds on the sky and intensifying a little its blue—tinny
windmills, rare farms with flat houses—a herd of small wild
red steers running together and raising a dust—a wrinkle of
land, queer, not like hills, that lifts itself in the flatness—
wild horses walking together, stopping to graze or stretching
up their heads—the dry pale clay, a scalloped eroded bank—
a sprinkling of orange black-eyed Susans—a boy with two
goats—a few fields under cultivation that show a slightly
richer brown—a dotting of sage-brush clumps show a little
darker.

And then two dim blue forms of mountains just outlined
on the sky, as if they had been washed in with water-colors
of faint heavier blues and light browns—now we have lost
them, they have slipped behind the prairie—the sage-grass
is gray now—now clear lodes of snow in the mountains beyond, which have suddenly loomed into view—all the way the
thin constant copper ray of the telegraph wire travels with us,
threading the brown hills, the blue sky, and paler against
the white clouds and redder against red and green banks—
square mud huts made out of pale clay, chunky reddish people living in them: Indians—a little spread of fresher green,
the clay dampened here, a water hole—riding now toward
rugous cindered grimmer hills—trees more frequent and
larger—a clay-colored settlement of houses up and down on
low rises of ground—now we are among hills and buildings—
a conspicuous clay-colored hill, stony and broken as a quarry,
with a sign up on top of it which says: "Trinidad."

Once engaged in those trails that climb and drop as well
as wind in every direction, you cannot see down—the trees are
so high—even from the mountainside into the valley.

The great pines that you pass at mid-length seem to rise
from the depths of the canyon and reach the heights of the
mountain-walls. Aspens, incredibly long, mingle with the
cigarbox-red of the pines or make groves of ivory-white on
the slopes of the green mythological valleys. When you come
close to them, they look like creamy flesh: the straight smooth
trunks of enormous white elephants or the throats and legs of
white antelopes. Some are blazed with the bold lettering of
Spanish names: Martinezes, Romeros, Bacas—a bungled
heart, an open hand; some of them, which seem to be planted
in ashes, are flecked about the base with gray characters that
look like Armenian or Sanskrit, the records of some prehistoric tongue. Or the trunks themselves become sentient tree-
beings, budding strangely with black animal nipples and
aware, through unpaired unfocused eyes whose expression
we never can fathom—laughter, gentleness, surprise, affright?
—and from whose pupils little branches may sprout, of some
non-human life of the forest, always present and very old,
which, passing through it, we can never know. Or in the
late light of afternoon, they are simply a cool iron-white, or
after rain a greenish-yellowish like glazed kid. Or their long
white boles are made black, high aloft where they rise against
white clouds; or they grow dim, dense and fine like grass—
where blue spruces blur them below, their tops seem a mere
whitish mist; or where the forest drops away into a hollow,
an exhalation from underground of vapor. The little branches
of their fallen limbs twist as light as the long yellow ashes
that pour crookedly out of the pills of Fourth of July "snakes."
But the taller pines, stretched on their sides, have the aspect
of gigantic picked fish-spines, of the naked-ribbed carcasses
of cows, of huge centipedes grown rigid in petrifaction.
Some, decayed to a red woody powder, are obliterating themselves in the mold.

Or, riding down into one of the high vivid bottoms, soft
and greased with green like the palm of the canyon's hand,
where the skull of a steer lies white, you gallop through New

Mexico sunflowers that, orange and wild, with disheveled petals, are gold-rusting the wide sudden green. A log house with vacant door, abandoned—a red cow with her head out the window. And high up, straight up the trail, the grass of the hill-brow is sprinkled with the tiny hair-hung bells of the beardtongue, mixing the green with vermilion, and hummingbirds—tobacco-leaf brown, necks a metallic red—swoop past your ear with a whir so loud that you can mistake it for the motor of an airplane or the roar of a distant bull, and speed away as if snapped on elastics across the green abyss. A hobbled sorrel horse limps and tinkles on the opposite hillside, above a screen of aspen stems, smooth and flat like white brush-strokes on a canvas. And from here you can look away to uplands that rise even higher and sunlit celestial pastures, where little round white clouds in the sunlit blue have come almost to poise on the grass. Looking behind you, you see a dark cover that is sliding over the bowl of the hills, about to unburden rain. Yet a few minutes later, in the queer variable weather, the gray cover has withdrawn again: the sun has grown too hot, strains the eyes—then a quick breeze chills you a little—then the dark clouds shove in again, this time from a new direction—but no brightness now, no more breeze —you go home in a late quiet light. The great aspen trunks now are gray in the shadow of the forest: as you travel in mid-air along the trail, where the mountain shuts off the sun, they fall past you in a downpour of rods, a dumb unearthly enormous rain.

Or on another day, a different trail—as the forest grows darker and cooler—you can look up the long nude stalks toward the rustling that stirs above them, and see tree tips abruptly bright, their little leaves fine and distinct, and always, as it were, itching, on a background of afternoon sun as white and clean as the aspen. You are riding on a level with this sun as it drops behind the next dark ridge. An invisible bull bellows loudly—another prolongs a blast that might come from a bull of bronze. Cooler and darker. A birdnote, high up, is a frail vibration of the ringing of a shaken silver sheet, which balances against towering tree-trunks with the same curious disproportion that makes the little stars and clusters and tufts and bells of the flowers, blue and mauve and maroon and red—and even the half-liquid yellow prim-roses with their tails of Prince Rupert's drops, the white flimsy blossoms of the mallow looking perishable where they grow in the moister ground—seem designed for a different scale from the vastness and violence of the canyon which, darkly feathered with spruce-peaks, yawns like the trough of a wave.

Darker and cooler still. Then suddenly sunlight—the after-noon has made a green return—as we cross a clear way to the west. And then, even more surprisingly, a bright felicity of morning hovering in the tops of the trees—remote hills, faint, exquisite, iridescent—pink and yellow and blue and pale green like some tropical fish seen through water—with above them the faint blue of sky and the clouds that seem stained with the yellow of the desert. And as you rip through thorny locust, pink pea-blossoms, those clouds beyond the pink and brown pine-trunks, beyond the pink clay of the trail them-selves turn from yellow to a claylike pink—till at last they make a flat queer formation which seems actually more solid than the mountains when you saw them a moment ago.

Or you come out into a great wide green valley which the mountains lift up into the sky. When you look down into it from high on the hillside, where the pine forests begin, you see flocks of sheep below you that appear the same size as the mushrooms which are growing in clumps in your path, and the cattle in clusters of specks that unpleasantly recall the bugs in the bed of the Mexican farmer who once put you up for the night. The clouds look painted in white on the sides of a blue clay jar: they are hard, neither cottonlike nor smokelike; and their shadows, as slow-moving oblong blots, are swallowed up by the enormous basin. Far below a human figure is moving: you can only just make it out. You ride down towards it; it shows small and clear: an old man with two little gray burros. When you come close, you see that one of the burros is laden with wooden casks, and that the old man, bending over and dipping with a tin cup, is pa-tiently filling the casks at a spring which gushes out from

under a boulder and runs down to where it reaches the cattle
in the velvety plain below.

At evening, in those high mountain bowls, the sun has
dropped down out of sight long before it has set. To the
east, you see the upper pinewoods either gilded or ruled off
with shade and, to the west, the light gray clouds, also gilded,
in the soft thinning blue of the day—leaving only such a
narrow layer of the lower liquid gold and white as reminds
you of the furnaces of summer blazing over the lowlands
and the ocean, so many trails to descend, so many roads to
travel below. Up here the clouds are now smoke-blue—or
rather they are exactly the color of those biscuits resembling wasps'-nests that the Indians make of blue cornmeal
spread out on a heated stone. They are tinged underneath
with red-gold from the eruption of the sunken sun.

Or draperies mantle the west with a strange brilliant
grape-juice purple, which quickly turns deepest black—while
a moon of congealed solid brightness rises free from the pine-
notched ridge. Obscured by a bank of clouds, it makes them
seem whitely luminous—all about them the sky shows blue,
but with the stars vividly pricking and, in that blue heaven
of night, both beautiful and rather queer. To the west, the
far meadows of the mountains, high as the moon itself, show
silvery blue, milky white, a kind of mother-of-pearl. You can
hear the little river Jemez hurrying down through the valley
like a person, and when you reach it, see it live and quivering,
like all these small watercourses which give to this giant landscape its surprising volatile spirit—running where the bed
widens, crawling over the cluttering stones—on its way to the
sterile plateau.

————

The great valley—five miles by nine, where 55,000 head
of cattle graze—was once a volcanic crater, which, millions
of years ago, boiled over and smothered the country in an
ocean of lava and ashes. Whatever had lived there was killed,
and life had to begin anew.

A race of people came from no one knows where and

wandered, disunited at first, among the mesas and the mountains, building themselves little huts of brush. Then they dug
houses in the ground and roofed them over. Then they found
it more practical to live together. The ash-deposit had turned
to tufa, as porous as a sponge, and the people moved into the
holes. They built houses of piñon-beams, mud and stones in
terraces up the sides of the cliffs, and farmed the land along
the little streams at the bottoms of the canyons. The houses
were community houses, and everybody had the same kind of
quarters. They all ate the same kind of food and they all
had to work to get it—with the exception of the cacique, the
high priest, who was the real ruler of the community and
was given leisure for higher things. But the cacique could
not inherit his rank. Nobody could inherit rank or position,
and nobody could claim exemption. There were no orphans
and no poor.

Today you ride for many miles along the spine of a high
narrow mesa, through forests so dense that you cannot even
see into the canyons on either side. Then suddenly you find
yourself on the brink of an immense gash between reddish
cliffs. The opposite wall is honeycombed with holes, especially toward the base, and you can see tree-tops and little
roofs as if at the bottom of a deep lake. For half an hour you
follow a trail that zigzags along in the sheer wall—and now
you can see the innumerable holes are the oven-like rooms of
the cliff dwellers. They run far back along the canyon and a
good way up the side of the cliff. There must once have been
hundreds of people living in them.

When you crawl into them, you find walls painted red and
the ceilings blackened with smoke—and there are vents for
the smoke to escape through. Crude pictures have been
scratched over the doors: the plumed serpent that figured the
lightning, concentric circles that symbolized the sun. The
big round cellars in the ground were temples; and so high up
the side of the cliff that you have to reach it by a series of
ladders is a sacrificial cave, which itself contains a round ex-
cavation. These are supposed to be survivals from a period
when these peoples had lived in dugouts instead of in caves.
They had had a cult of the earth, believed they had got

their life from it, liked to feel they were keeping in touch with it. The very sunken sanctuaries had holes in the floors which went further down still. They thought that all mankind had once lived underground.

In the caves, of the implements they used, there are only the metates left—the big stones on which they ground their meal. Other instruments and fragments of pottery have all been taken away to the museums. But in one of the largest caves, which you climb to by steps in the rock, you find a Borden's condensed-milk can, a red pasteboard Supreme Biscuit package, a hatbox with a label "Aux Modes de Paris," and a glass peanut-butter jar.

———

And you find also dead or dying settlements of the later civilization.

Down at the bottom of Bellamy canyon, underneath the perforated cliffs, there are today only eight people left in a town that had once six hundred. During the nineties there was a gold boom in Bellamy; but apparently the mines didn't pay. People say that the company that worked them must have put as much as a million and a half into Bellamy and couldn't have got more than half a million out. In the end, they closed down altogether. For one thing, they had been using a cyanide process and draining the cyanide into the creek: the cattle had drunk the water and died, and the ranchers around had protested. But the company could not afford to instal a different kind of process. So today, in Bellamy canyon, there is thousands of dollars' worth of abandoned equipment: great rusted leaching-tanks, a power plant that burns wood and is obsolete, a weighing platform stove-in, a trestle across a gully and a toppled-over scale.

The houses left are mostly raw-timber shacks. Inside you see the tin cans and papers that were thrown on the floor when the people moved out—one shack has a copy of *The Angelus* still nailed to the wall. Some have been taken apart by people who needed the boards. One has keeled over backwards so that it looks like the mask of a house; another is a roofless stone shell with grass growing inside; others are merely cellars, bushed with purple mint.

There are only three decent-looking buildings in Bellamy: the postmaster's house, the hotel and a house that belongs to the company, which is closed and the shades pulled down. The postmaster is a stout lethargic man from Michigan, who used to be a forest ranger, but is now able to draw a pension as a result of having hurt his back in the service. People say that he is just lazy, that his wife does all the work at the post office, that he sometimes forgets his injury and lifts up heavy boxes or takes part in local dances, and that he has never told a straight story as to whether it was a bucking horse that did it or falling out of a tree. He has collected an almost complete set of the government's ethnological reports and a library of scientific sex books. One of his favorite pastimes is going through bookdealers' catalogues, and his principal ambition now is to compile a comprehensive index of the literature about the Indians.

The postmaster is philosophical. He loves living in New Mexico and hated the raw Michigan winters, where, he remembers, if there happened to be just one bright day, everybody was crazy with joy. And modern Detroit is a terrible place—if you think there are other things in life besides just working yourself to death and making money. He is not a socialist, he tells you, as he sits musing with his feet on the rail—but he thinks there is something wrong with a country in which it is possible for six million men to be out of work. He doesn't believe that people ought to be made to work, but he thinks that if they want to work, they ought to be given a chance to.

The old hotel, a narrow box of raw pine planks, has lately been opened up, rather for a home than as an enterprise, by a little wiry man with bone spectacles who used to run a curio shop in Carlsbad. But, since the depression, there are fewer tourists and keeping accounts was too much for him anyway: it used to worry him so that his wife thought it just wasn't worth while to have him so nervous all the time. So he has bought the old Bellamy hotel and brought his family here to live in it, and, on the whole, they have been much happier.

Just beside the hotel is a pit filled with junk. This used to be the main saloon, and for years it stood there just as it had been, with its roulette table and its bar stocked with empty bottles. But somebody carried off the roulette table, and then the building was wrecked for its timber. A rusty tinny safe is lying on its side in the pit, and there are old rosette-shaped iron cuspidors among the yellow-flowering weeds. The brother-in-law of the man at the hotel believes that he can sell these spittoons to Fred Harvey for $25 apiece. Fred Harvey is the restaurant proprietor who has opened up the romance of the old Southwest, providing luxury buses, fancy Spanish-style railroad stations and comfortable modern hotels.

There are also two old prospectors still left in Bellamy canyon. The postmaster says they are better than most, the best he has ever seen—most of them are plumb nutty.

Art and Ed have been living in Bellamy for thirty-seven years and have witnessed the whole rise and fall of the town. Art is tall and lean and wears spectacles and a short pointed beard on a receding Swinburnian chin. Art was born in Brooklyn, and his father was a prominent attorney in the early days in Santa Fe. People declare it's a shame that a man of Art's brains and education should hang around a place like Bellamy. You couldn't find a greater student of the dictionary than old Art is anywhere. He has Funk and Wagnall's Unabridged in his shack, and he is always disputing with you about the meaning of a word.

Art has a sharp shrewd eye, but the gray gaze of his partner is limpid and mild. Ed is shorter and chunkier than Art. He has a ranch beyond the canyon and used to live there part of the time—but he lost so many cattle that he finally gave it up: it was the Mexicans that stole them, but he never knew it. Now he spends all his time in Bellamy. He sits all day in his one-room shack, reading and smoking a pipe and spitting into a cuspidor beside his chair. The cuspidor is full of used matches. Ed's bedclothes are extremely dirty, but he always seems to be wearing a clean and freshly ironed shirt. Ed has

the expressionless visage and the laconic impassive speech of
the traditional Western prospector, which contrasts with
Art's Eastern edge. Ed comes from the Middle West. One
thing he will never talk about is his early life and his family,
and people think he hasn't any relations.

Art and Ed have a good time together. They sit and kid
each other for hours about one another's watches and phonographs. Their watches never agree. Art will say to Ed: "That
snort you took at Peña Blanca must have speeded up your
time!" Periodically they get drunk together, and their toots
last a week or more. They like to sit and drink and play
their phonographs for days on end. They bought a Ford together some years ago, but use it so little that it still looks
like new. Once when they were off on a spree, they drove
as far as Peña Blanca in first. A sheepherder, who saw them,
got on the running-board and showed them how to shift into
high; but as soon as the man got off, they put it in low again.

Ed is seventy-seven, and Art not much younger. The postmaster never gets over his amazement at Ed's superb constitution. "There's a man," he will say, "who defies every rule
of health—you'd think he would have been dead long ago,
but he seems to thrive on it! He drinks—he don't eat anything but ham and eggs—in the winter he seals himself up
in that shack so he doesn't get a breath of air! He violates
all the rules of hygiene. There isn't a tooth in his head that
a dentist wouldn't say ought to be extracted—they're all worn
down to the gums!"

Art and Ed still have their claims, and they still assume
that the company will come back and work the mines. The
real reason for the company's withdrawal remains more or less
of a mystery in Bellamy. The last manager got cirrhosis of
the liver—"hobnails, we used to call it—from drinkin'," Ed
scornfully says—and went out to Los Angeles for his health.
There's plenty of gold and silver still here—Art and Ed know
that very well: there's gold lyin' uncovered up the canyon.

For there is gold-dust here still in the air. Even the postmaster and the hotel proprietor are not men who have simply retired but speculators who are hoping to win. An in-

quiry about the value of land will at once release a glimpse
of the visions which shimmer inside their minds.

Ed says confidently that the only thing for Bellamy is for
somebody like Phelps-Dodge or Rockefeller to take the whole
thing over.

————

Not far from Bellamy canyon, the lumber mill has closed
down. But Pete Ferguson, who owns it, is keeping his crew
on. He hopes to be able to start up again, and he doesn't
want them to be getting into their heads any IWW ideas. In
Albuquerque, there's fifty out of work for one that's got a
job, and people are goin' around wantin' to shoot somebody—
they don't know who, but they want to kill somebody. Pete
thinks that the government could be improved, but he
wouldn't want to see things changed like the Bolsheviks. He
has liberal ideas, however: he figures there'll be a third man
at the next election. Everybody knew Hoover was a so-and-
so: that came out during the War; but there was nobody else
to vote for (Al Smith, for the West, never really existed). Pete
believes that his crew will be better off in the camp than
goin' out and gettin' in trouble—dabblin' in bootleg whisky
or stealin' somebody's milk-cow.

Pete claims to be feeding nearly 400 people. He has the
reputation of being a great blowhard. People say that if he
had done all the things he says he has, he would have to be a
hundred and fifty years old. He likes to pose as a big lum-
berman, but his mill has never been much of a success. Pete
has a tough cunning face, in which a defiant stare serves
to mask a great lack of integrity. He likes to pose as a pa-
ternalistic employer: unlike the real captains of industry, he
is obliged to live among his men and cannot use his superintendent as a buffer. He knows that the lumber-camp is dull:
the mountains are all right for a while, but then they get
monotonous—"lots of people come out here to build up their
health, but we have our health when we come." So he gives
dances every Saturday night in a room over the commissary

—and the price of the fiddler and the refreshments is taken out of his employees' pay.

The employees, who live in unpainted crates, are, of course, always in debt to the commissary. When they have first started in and have used up all their money trading at the nearest town, it always turns out that Pete can't pay them their first wages because he hasn't got cash on hand. He will give them credit at the commissary. The commissary has a tentacle of credit glued to every family in the camp.

Among the employees of Pete Ferguson the highest social position is held by the trucker and his wife. Fred Casey has only been here a month; he used to be a trucking contractor in the oil-fields, but there is nothing doing now in the oil-fields, and he has had to take a humbler job. This is the first time that he and his wife have ever lived in a house that wasn't modern. Fred Casey is proud of his wife: she plays the piano like a professional, and his sister-in-law is a professional violinist, who plays sometimes over the radio. Fred is very proud of her, too. They have brought the piano with them—though actually there is hardly space for it in the little one-room house, where Fred and his wife are compelled to sleep in the bed with the two children.

Pete Ferguson treats Fred as an equal, takes him into his confidence freely and obtains his coöperation. Fred dresses conspicuously and consciously better than any of the rest of the crew—he blows himself to beer on Saturday nights and gets hearty and watery-eyed. He also gets rather high-hat and expresses contempt for the "Mexicans,"* whom he regards as inferior to "Americans." But when the Mexicans are having a dance and have invited the lumber-mill people, he and his family are always sent over by Pete so that the Mexicans won't be sore at nobody else's going.

Fred Casey likes to talk a good deal and has told everybody how well he is doing—he says that he is making $90 a week. But people remember what happened to the truckers who were there before Fred. A man and his son, for example, who had been working in Pete Ferguson's mill till they

* In the Southwest, a Mexican is a Spanish-speaking American.

thought they had earned about $1,000, found at the end of that time, that they could collect only $75. It turned out that they were in debt to the store for all kinds of unexpected items, from new overalls at $2 apiece to equipment which they had never used or heard of. And Fred hasn't seen his commissary bill yet.

————

The white people in the United States have reached a stage somewhat similar to that at which the Indians decided to come up out of the separate holes in which they had been living and to combine in an organized society: better ventilated, more sociable, safer. We have already achieved interdependence; the whole country is bound together by our railroads, our shiplines and our telephones; and the enterprising individual can no longer escape even to the West to win riches and find independence. Lumber, mining and cattle-grazing all today fail the private adventurer. All are controlled by remote combinations. Yet these overall combinations are, in a large way, quite independent and unaccountable to a higher authority. They have hardly emerged from their cellars. The very beauty and wonder of the forest would unquestionably long ago have been turned into planks by the sausage machine of Pete Ferguson's sawmill if Roosevelt, by an act of socialism, had not shut it off as a national preserve; the very record of the past it contains might already have been destroyed if Woodrow Wilson, by another act of socialism, had not found the money to have it protected.

As for the Indians, their small communal cities have survived all the pressure from alien races, the four centuries since the advent of the Spanish. They are narrow, unbusinesslike, incurious, illiterate, unhygienic, unscientific; but as one old-timer of the Rio Grande says from long experience with both Indians and whites: "The Indian's religion and government are the same thing, and they fit him like a glove —whereas our laws don't fit us anywhere—nor our religion either!"

INDIAN CORN DANCE

CAL CLAY, the Crooning Cowboy, rides in a purple roadster with his signature in gold on both doors. People say that he has never been on a horse—that he used to work in a Denver hotel. But he always wears enormous chaps and a silver-studded sombrero. He has appeared in movies, vaudeville and night clubs all over the country, and he has made popular phonograph records. He whines to a guitar about the prairie, the coyotes and the old Chisholm Trail. Lately, however, his General Motors stock has shrunk to almost nothing, and it is harder for him to get engagements, so he has thought seriously of putting on a tent-show at the Indian ritual dances, and he has come to take it up with the Indians.

Muna Gibbs has had some losses, too, but is still in a very sound financial condition, since her father was a Morgan partner. The great passion of her life has been the Indians. She spent years persuading Navahos and Hopis to make sacred sand-paintings in her patio so that she could frame them under glass, and she ended by going to live in a pueblo, where she tried to look as dumpy as a squaw. The Indians, however, who, though they do not prize chastity, disapprove of wanton promiscuity, decreed at last that Muna must leave. She still dresses like a squaw and continually smokes cigarettes.

Dirk Macdougal, from Albuquerque, is an old real-estate man, who set out a few years ago to run a dude ranch de luxe —$150 a week, with a bathroom and radio in every cabin, a guide on every ride and all you wanted to drink. For a while he was fairly successful, and the Santa Teresa Valley was full of bellowing millionaires. But the overhead turned out to be high—especially for liquor and crippled horses—and there were no longer so many millionaires. Dirk has had to cut down his rates and now charges his patrons for drinks and for taking them to the Indian dances. The party he has brought over today are behaving very sourly, because they don't think they are getting their money's worth.

Gus Fay and Luella Lamb have just arrived from Hollywood. Mr. Fay is going to direct Miss Lamb in a picture which will show the struggle between a white man and a Navaho Indian for the love of a covered-wagon girl, so they have come in a big blue Pierce-Arrow to get the spirit of a pueblo dance. Mr. Fay has bone-rimmed spectacles, marcelled hair and a green whipcord riding-suit with polished puttees, and he has brought the little one-legged portable stool that he carries around on the lot. He watches the dance through field-glasses. Miss Lamb is also dressed in riding-costume; she is a doughy-looking blonde. When they first arrived in the pueblo, the Indians were engaged in their cruel sport of snatching a rooster from horseback, and Miss Lamb assumed that the antics and yells were a demonstration in her honor.

Bill Peck is a well-meaning fellow. He started to go to Yale, but was always having awful hangovers and not showing up at his classes, and on trains he would get into card games with people who won all his money. So his father, a wealthy drug-manufacturer, sent him out West to a ranch. At the ranch, Bill read books about lost gold mines and the buried treasures of the Spanish; his allowance had by that time been cut down, and he decided to go out and search for them. He wears a pistol slung under his arm and an old hat slouched over his eyes, and he goes for long walks in the woods with a pickaxe over his shoulder. One day he came back much excited and said that he had got into a cave which was all frozen full of ice and that in the ice were two American soldiers in a perfect state of preservation. But when people went out with him to look for the cave, he couldn't find the way again, and he never succeeded in getting back there.

Jo Romero runs the peanut-and-pop stand and shortchanges the women and children. He has even mastered a trick which makes it possible for him to let people see that he has the right amount of money in his hand and then hold part of it back in his palm. He always overcharges for the pop, making everybody return the bottles and then not giving them their nickel rebate.

Lobo Baily is an old Roosevelt Rough Rider, who draws a small pension and has been drunk ever since the Spanish War. He used to live in Texas, but was recently convicted of killing a man who had said to him, "You think you're tough, don't you?" Lobo shot the man full of holes, and when he came out of jail after serving his sentence, he was met by a group of his townsmen, who ran him out of the state. Nobody likes him in New Mexico either, but people take a certain satisfaction in hearing him swear at Jo Romero. Lobo has been refusing to give the pop-bottles back, and as Jo keeps on demanding them, he slings one of them into Jo's stand with a parting high-pitched spew of bad language, and knocks over all the crackerjack boxes.

Ella Davis and Sam Furstman are married, though Miss Davis keeps her maiden name. She comes from Kansas and paints flat lengths of landscape, diversified only by sagebrush or cactus, and with darkish mountains rising in the background. Today she is wearing neat boots, a fancy pink sombrero and a green silk scarf at the neck of her blouse; she has spectacles with yellow rims, because, with her feeling for color, she wants them to harmonize with her hair. Sam Furstman is a writer, and they live mostly on what he makes: he has been quite successful in a moderate way with an Indian-lore series for boys and is now doing a set of magazine articles for grownups called *The Golden Legend of the Rio Grande*. In conversation, he has psychoanalytic theories about Geronimo, Kit Carson, Archbishop Lamy, Montezuma and Billy the Kid.

Father Rafaele is the priest and, unlike most of the priests in the country parishes, he is serious and even fanatical. The Indians are nominally Catholics, having been baptized centuries ago by the Spaniards—so their dances are always inaugurated by a ceremony in honor of the local saint, after which the rain-invocation proceeds as in the days before the Christian medicine had been added to the native ones. Father

Rafaele is a Spanish-speaking New Mexican, and he has been profoundly disturbed by the news of the Spanish revolution. Just outside the pueblo stands a little white adobe church, which has been decorated partly by the Indians; for reasons never quite understood, they painted on the façade, many years ago, not only two brightly colored angels, but some butterflies and two horses, one spotted and one red, and both with saddles on—perhaps to carry the saved to Heaven. The day after Father Rafaele had read about the burning of the convents in Madrid, he went around to the pueblo and had the butterflies and horses painted out.

Clifford Leadgood comes from Rockport, Massachusetts, and did postgraduate work at Harvard in the Italian lyric before Dante. Then he came down with t.b. and was sent out to Santa Fe. He is cured now, but still stays on—he has a very small income from an interest in the Lawrence textile mills. Ever since he came to New Mexico, Clifford has been fascinated by the Penitentes, the Franciscan sect of flagellants which has survived in old Mexico and here. On Good Fridays, the Penitentes go out at night and flagellate themselves in the hills. They also, on this occasion, have a rite of crucifixion; one of their number is fastened to a cross, and the others first whip him fiercely, then, with cactus-spikes clasped in their armpits, kneel down before him and worship him. Clifford has been cultivating the Penitentes, and they have admitted him to their windowless chapels. He will not tell you what he has seen there, but he will assert with quiet casual Harvard assurance that the Penitentes are one of the only really great things left in the world today. He has long thought of trying to join them, and the dream which he nurses in secret, and which he has intimated to a very few friends, is of offering himself as the crucified. The government some years ago put a stop to their nailing people up the way they used to do; they are only supposed to tie them up now, and Clifford is by no means certain that this isn't a degradation of the cult. Yet they tie you terribly tight and leave you a long time and lay it onto you with whips and cactus; three years ago a man died. Clifford wonders whether they really do have a doctor—as the government has tried to require—to check up on your pulse at intervals and be sure you're taken down in time.

It is thus that the white race is represented at such of the Indian dances as the public are allowed to see. In the case of the Hopi snake dance—which Lawrence has done so much to advertize—the Indians are said to feel that the attendance of curious whites has caused it to lose its virtue, with the result they now have two dances, one to deceive the whites and one in a sacred place. Some of the dances have always been secret; but people have done their best to get into them. It is as if they felt that the Indians were in possession of some sacred key, some integrity, some harmony with nature, which they, the white Americans, lacked. And as they watch, they imagine the dancers experiencing some profound satisfaction, renewing themselves with some draft of the ecstasy of religion or poetry which they themselves do not know.

FOURTH OF JULY CELEBRATION

TILL COMPARATIVELY RECENT YEARS nobody had paid much attention to the big cave at Carlsbad, New Mexico. There was a great flock of bats that flew out of it like a streamer of black smoke at sunset, and a shaft was sunk to get their guano. But no one had had the nerve to explore it till an old cowboy named Jim White went in with guiding strings and a wire ladder. For years he spent all his spare time in the cave —getting further and further inside it: it seemed to go on indefinitely. It turned out to be the largest cave known: twenty-seven miles of it have already been discovered, and there is a theory that it connects with the Grand Canyon. At last, in 1925, the government took it over and put a superintendent in charge. It got to be a thing for tourists. At first, Jim White was employed as a guide, but the superintendent did not like him—it was true that Jim drank a good deal—and finally succeeded in having him fired. The government paid him something, and he relinquished his claims to the cave. Electric light was installed, and an elevator was projected.

The cave brought a boom to Carlsbad. There are estimated to be 3,000,000 bats in the cave, and 100,000 tons of their guano have been removed and sold for fertilizer; and it has been possible during 1930 alone, for the Carlsbaders to levy tribute on 80,000 tourists. Their rapacity has known no bounds.

There is only one bank in Carlsbad, and the tradesmen and hotelkeepers have coöperated with the bank to keep other business enterprise out. It got to be such a scandal that one departing motorist, who had been brought there by the roadside publicity urging people to "See the Carlsbad Cave," hung a sign on the back of his car with the warning, "See the Carlsbad Cave, but Keep Away from Carlsbad!"

One of the great drawing events at Carlsbad has been the Fourth of July celebration. The town is on the Pecos River, and the fireworks are set off over it, so that the reflection makes a brilliant effect. This year, however, something went wrong. Nine thousand people had gathered, prepared to enjoy the display, when suddenly, for reasons not known, about half the fireworks went off at once. Bombs exploded, geysers spouted, giant Catherine wheels made buzz-saws of light, rockets like Gadarene swine dived headlong into the water, uncontrollable Roman candles emitted innumerable tangled balls. The banging and cracking were terrific. The municipal bathing-beach trembled, and heavy waves beat on the shore. The weeds along the Pecos caught fire. Everybody fled for his life.

But the most unfortunate thing was that the big American flag, the set-piece which had been meant for a finale, got touched off and blazed forth prematurely in the midst of the misdirected rockets, the irrelevant flower-pot poppings and the ghastly glare of red and green light. Some who were not too scared patriotically stopped and cheered.

1957. It is now known that the bats in the Carlsbad cave have been infected with rabies. Hundreds died of an epidemic in 1956. The Sante Fe *New Mexican* has, however, asserted that no human being, visiting the cave, has been known to have been bitten by a bat, and the tourist trade is still encouraged.

HOOVER DAM

BLACK CANYON, in which tunnels are now being cut to divert the Colorado River and leave a dry stretch of bed for the building of Boulder Dam, is a steep narrow gap between two immense burnt-out cinders. In summer, the heat of these cinders suggests that they may still be smoldering from the primeval volcanic disturbance which has left the whole landscape an infernal desert: hard blue and black hills, full of metal, that look as if you could ring them with a hammer, seem to lie with their heads down in the plain like monstrous pre-human animals; sunken mirage-like marshes in which it is impossible to tell from a distance whether the dried-blood red is water or earth. The walls of Black Canyon become so hot that you cannot put your hand on them, and the very wind that blows through it is like a furnace-breath.

On the side of one of these huge brownish coals, where the porous lava has crumbled down and made a slope at the base of the cliff, a camp for the dam workers has been constructed. The buildings are crude dormitories like army barracks in which the men sleep close together and in which the disinfectant for the water-closets pervades the stupefying air.

These quarters were supposed to be temporary. It was a gesture of Mr. Hoover, wishing to seem to do something about unemployment, to start work on Boulder Dam at once and before any proper facilities had yet been provided for living there. Boulder City, nine miles away, was supposed to be a model camp, but it would take a long time to complete it. In the meantime, the main part of the crew were to do the best they could in the desert. The married men had wretched shacks in what came to be known as Rag City; the single ones the river camp.

The Reclamation Service engineers had been there before the men. They had been there when there was nothing, and they remember it as a "hell-hole," where you "got goofy with the heat." But though these engineers have their own complaints against the government as an employer, they are at least in the service of the government, and as one of them now declares, "It's having a little responsibility that makes all the difference." Boulder Dam, with all its hardships and dangers, makes a challenge one can take pride in meeting: it is the biggest project of the kind that the United States has ever undertaken. And the men felt this pride, too, at first. The government had stipulated in its contract with the companies that ex-service men should be given the preference, and when the men who have been working there started in, they evidently had something of the army spirit. The trouble was that as time went on, they found out that they were not really working for the United States, but for a group of construction companies.

The situation at Boulder Dam is peculiar. The idea originally was that the government should put through the whole project; but it was later, characteristically, decided by Mr. Hoover's administration that it should be handed over to private business, the government only regaining control at the end of a construction job which is supposed to take at least six years. Secretary Wilbur* signed a contract with a combination of six Western companies, associated as "Six Companies, Incorporated," who had offered a bid of $49,-890,995—$5,000,000 less than that of any of their competitors. He had Boulder Dam rechristened Hoover Dam, which nobody can remember to call it.

Mr. Wilbur, by an unfortunate chance, arranged this contract just eight days before the going into effect of the Davis bill, which was to regulate wages on government projects. The companies were all non-union, and the only stipulations in regard to labor that Mr. Wilbur was able to make, beyond the clause about ex-service men, were that Mongolians should not be employed; and that 80 per cent of the men

* Ray Lyman Wilbur, Secretary of the Interior under Hoover.

should be housed in Boulder City—and the latter of these was suspended when it was decided to start operations before Boulder City was built. The result was that there was nothing to restrain the companies from resorting automatically and immediately to that systematic skimping, petty swindling and frank indifference to the fate of their employees which are necessary to provide officers with salaries and stockholders with profits. In the first place, the men at the river camp had no means of refreshing themselves: spending all day in the tunnel with shovels and drills, so hot that they always work naked, they could not even get a shower or a cold drink. The only water they had for drinking or washing was the water of the Colorado River, which, full of silt from the decomposing tufa, is always an opaque yellow like coffee with too much cream; and this, with no water-coolers, would get tepid or hot in the tanks. As the weather became hotter and hotter, the water began making people sick. Nor were there any facilities for cooling the barracks. The nights were so suffocating and uncomfortable that one welcomed the diversion of work. And for the shift that got its rest in the daytime, with the sun glaring through the windows and heating the shack like an oven, sleep, if they managed to get any, became a heavy sweating coma. When they got up to go to work, they would find their drills so hot that they had to cool them off before they could take them in their hands.

At Black Canyon, during the last days of July, the thermometer had never dropped below 79, and at times it had been 128 in the shade. The lowest maximum was 104, and thereafter it got steadily worse: it was always at least 100 at night.

The work on the dam is dangerous. The casualty company which is insuring the Six Companies has estimated at 200 the number of lives that is likely to be lost during the course of the first year; and the companies seemed to have done very little in the way of safety precautions. According to the government's own report, there have already been twenty-six men killed since May—including two drowned, two hit by falling rocks, three blown up in explosions and thirteen who died from the heat. When a man would collapse from the

heat, the other men—half-stunned by the sun themselves
and with no way of giving him relief—could only stand
around him and watch him gasp out his life. For till lately
they have had nothing at the river camp but a small first-aid
station, and there was bound to be a long delay in getting
an ambulance from Boulder City. The government has declared that the laws of the state are not valid on the reservation which has been set aside for the dam, and it is evident
that the Six Companies have taken advantage of this to ignore
the safety laws of Nevada. They had, for example, been sending men back into the tunnels fifteen or twenty minutes after
the blasts, though it is usual to allow an hour for the nitro-
glycerin fumes to evaporate. The Nevada laws insist upon
ventilation in tunnels, safety men at the headings and change-
rooms where the men can dry themselves before going out
into the air, but none of these has been supplied. The river
camp itself is precariously propped on the broken-stone talus
at the bottom of the cliff, where freshly loosened boulders
sometimes come hurtling through the mess-room window;
and the men have been looking forward rather anxiously to
the beginning of the cloudburst season, which they fear may
undermine and upset the wooden stilts on which the dormitories are perched, and send the whole outfit down into the
river.

And since the companies, in order to make good on that
bid that undercut their competitors, have to concentrate on
squeezing out nickels between the men and the government,
so the subcontractors must grind out pennies between the
men and the companies. It is a difficult undertaking to
supply decent meals at Black Canyon. The cooks, working
over the stoves, are sometimes prostrated after two or three
days; the pork goes bad and poisons the men. And the board-
and-supply company which has to make good on *its* contract
with the Six Companies and provide *its* profits at the same
time is in no position to do this problem justice. One of its
ways of skimping has been to recruit its help from transient
unemployed who have had no experience in the kitchen but
who are willing to work for their meals. And the pay that
the dam worker actually gets is reduced by the usual devices

of charging him huge prices for board and supplies and de-
ducting this from his wages. Common labor at Boulder Dam
is supposed to get $3.50 a day.

Not long after the work had begun a succession of disturbing rumors reached the International Brotherhood of Electrical Workers, and they sent an investigator, who brought back
a very bad report. The news also came to the IWW's* who,
dormant of recent years, seem lately to be coming to life.
They soon picked out Hoover Dam as a strategical objective.

In the middle of July, eleven men—some, if not all, of
them, dam workers—were arrested as IWW's. The leader, a
man named Frank Anderson, admitted that he was a professional organizer, and, when asked what he would do if released, replied that he would go on organizing until he was
arrested again, when he would make it a test case of the
Nevada laws. The prisoners were all released for insufficient
evidence. As a result of this incident, the government seems
to have brought a certain amount of pressure to bear, for,
soon after, some reforms were made: the powder house was
moved from where it had formerly been, next door to the
blacksmith's shop, to the other side of the river, and a frigi-
daire water-cooler, which had been promised in the original
plans, was at last installed in the cookhouse. This water-
cooler, however, had only one electric coil, and the demands
upon it were so constant that it did very little cooling. In
the meantime, the hot weather went on.

At last, at three o'clock in the afternoon of Friday, August
7, a notice of a wage-cut was handed to the foremen. According to the subsequent statement of the companies, this was
merely an announcement that thirty of the men, who had
been displaced by new mucking machines (mucking is
cleaning out the tunnel after the blast), were to be transferred to work outside the tunnel at a dollar less a day. The
workers, however, claim that the wage-cut affected a number
of groups, including pipefitters, muckers and shift-bosses,
inside as well as outside the tunnel. These mucking machines
had already been installed a month, and, in any case, though

* International Workers of the World; also referred to as Wobblies.

they did far more work, required as many men to run them. The men assert that the companies were trying to take advantage of the limitless supply of labor which had been pouring into Las Vegas as a result of the news of the dam: if the men of the present crew wouldn't work on their jobs for the lower pay, there were plenty of others eager to get them. Las Vegas at one time became so thronged with wanderers looking for work that the town had to have them deported, and at present the open space in front of the station is so full of sleeping men at night that it looks like a battlefield.

At any rate, the Wobbly leaders came out on the bridge across the river and called the men out of the tunnels. The whole shift of 125 walked out, and the majority of their foremen went with them. The whole 14,000 workers struck. They had heard of the President's exhortations against wage-reductions by employers, and they trusted him to ward off a scandal in connection with a government project which had just been given his name. What happened, however, was that, when they stated their demands to the companies: ice water, first-aid service, a minimum wage of $5 a day, a flat board-rate of $1.50 a day, the inclusion in the eight-hour working day of the time that it took to travel the nine miles from Boulder City to Black Canyon and the reëmployment of the whole crew with no discrimination against the strike leaders —they were told to pack their things and get out.

In the meantime, trucks had arrived, with guards armed with sawed-off shotguns, to drive the strikers out of the camp. The men had been about to obey when the strike committee came back and told them not to go. The leaders were still hoping for the support of the government. They sent a telegram to Secretary Doak:* "As American citizens, we ask protection on Hoover Dam in case of deportation. Strike called in protest against wage-cuts."

The government had so far acted with convincing impartiality. The United States marshal searched both parties to the dispute and everybody who entered the reservation. The sawed-off shotguns and tear-gas guns were taken away from

* William N. Doak, Secretary of Labor under Hoover.

the companies. Some sticks of dynamite were found on two unknown men who tried to enter the reservation as prospectors.

Some of the strikers drew their pay-checks and left; others stayed on in the camp. It becomes known, on Tuesday night, that the government itself the next morning is sending officials to put them off the reservation.

That night at the river camp is full of unease and suspense. The Wobbly core of the strike is there, but they seem doubtful as to how far they can go. Driving back late at night in a car, the Wobblies at the boundary of the reservation make an attempt to kid the marshal who holds them up to search them: "Well, have you got that case of beer for us?" "I guess you fellows'll be goin' out of here in the morning," he replies, "and I guess you won't be sorry, and we won't be either!" When they are out on the dark desert, which looks more than ever like the floor of Hell, they stop the car and search each other—they mustn't be found with guns. The chief organizer, Frank Anderson, is a short strong-knit man with a dark glaring purposeful eye; but these are younger fellows who seem to run to a slim blue-eyed blond type, and they cultivate the Wobbly jauntiness: open collars, rakish soft hats. They show a spirit and a humor quite different from the solemn determination of the Communists: "Some people," says one of them, "wouldn't believe that a fellow can get a kick out of this kind of work. But you get a kick out of pulling off a strike—get sent to San Quentin and get a kick out of it!"

One of them gives me his views on the general situation. American labor, he says, is the worst-exploited in the world, but then, they have the highest standards of living—and the trouble about American capital, from the revolutionist's point of view, is that it's always smart enough to make concessions. . . . Then, the difficulty of getting the farmers to feel any solidarity with the industrial workers. He was talking to a farmer the other day and said, "When the battle comes, I'll at least know which side I'm on, but you won't know whether to side with labor or with the banker who holds a mortgage on your farm." . . . Nevertheless, the final line-up has got

to come some time now—they used to be able to send people
West when they got discontented with labor conditions in
the East—'Go West, young man!'—but what's the good of
telling *me* to go West? I *am* West already! . . . The trouble
with the Communists is that they don't know how to deal
with American conditions—they get all their ideas from Russia, and those ideas don't apply over here. Their campaign
with the niggers in the South, for instance—it's impractical
—they don't understand what they're up against." He can
accept race equality in theory, but when he actually goes
down South, he can't stomach it. . . . The Wobblies have
never forgiven Foster for going over to the Communists.
. . . As for the liberals, he always says that it's like holy
water: it probably doesn't do any good, but then it doesn't
do any harm. . . . When the showdown finally comes,
they're likely to act the way they acted in Russia—but then
maybe he's doing the same thing that he accused the Communists of doing—drawing conclusions about America from
Russia, when things aren't really the same. . . . There's one
liberal he doesn't think would ever sell out: that's Roger
Baldwin.

At the river camp, the pickets appear in the illumination
of the headlights, stripped to the waist in the heat. It is after
three in the morning, and the strike leaders have had very
little sleep. They invade the "bosses' " dormitory—"Don't you
know that's leez majesty?"—"What the hell is that?"—They
find a small water-cooler; ironic comment; they try it: "That
water's old and gray!" They flop in their clothes and debate
whether the government has the right to put them out—they
wish they had the advice of a lawyer. But when somebody's
already done something to you, one of the Wobblies points
out, there's no use saying "You can't do that!" Some talk as if
they meant to resist.

The windows are utterly black: the opposite wall of the
canyon blocks them. That waste without vegetation is as silent as if it were a splash of slag just shot off from the whirl-
ing sun, now hardened but still very hot. Not far away, I
remember, is a cave full of the bones of giant sloths—you
can see where they rubbed themselves against the wall. Today another race of creatures is attempting to dig themselves

in. One man exclaims aloud: "Well, next week I'll be on Frisco Bay!" The pickets have come down from the slippery cliffs; there are only two watching the road. The mice in the inhuman quiet make noises like people marauding. They are a kind of wild jumping mice that astonish me by hopping on the cots and running over the faces of the sleeping men, who are so used to them that they brush them away like flies.

The next morning is overcast and cooler—which proves to him, one man says, that "there's somebody up above, after all!" They get up early and wait in uncertainty. They have chipped in and bought a few eggs, and they boil some coffee over and over until everybody has had a cup. A little runty Scotchman takes an unenthusiastic view: he was one of the shift that walked out, but he knows they'll never get what they ahsk for. A man with a wife and children cahn't let his family starve. The psychological moment to have struck would have been when the heat was at its worst. The Wobblies always overdo things. In Butte, he says, they've never even been able to have a union since the Wobblies blew up the meeting hall.

At last, about eight o'clock, the government cars arrive. Mr. Walter R. Young of the Reclamation Bureau, the engineer in charge, drives his own car, with the marshal in it. Mr. Young is a small thin man, with leather puttees, a long birdbeak and a cap pulled down over his spectacles. He has that clean-shaven discipline-and-efficiency look which has to be worn in the government service. But he is pale, as if worried by the strike. The marshal, with a shoe-string tie, is a mild elderly man.

The strike committee bawls out with bravado that the marshal and Mr. Young are to come up on the porch of the shack. It is raining now, and all gather under the shelter of the roof behind the mess-hall.

Mr. Young gets up on a bench. Both he and the marshal are applauded by the strikers and generally treated with respect. Mr. Young begins by telling them that he appreciates the orderly manner in which they have conducted the strike, and that he hopes their behavior will continue to be as good —that he and the marshal have come alone and have brought two trucks and a bus to take them off the reservation—that the bus is carrying the plate of the government—and that the reservation is now to be cleared not only of the striking workers but of everybody on it, except the men who are in the hospital—"I don't think you boys want them put out, do you?" Voices: "No, no."

And if they refuse to move, the government will use force, will it?—"We ask you to go," says Mr. Young, "and we depend upon you to go. There's been no question at all of force."—"But if we don't go, you'll make us?"—"Yes," Mr. Young admits, "if you should refuse to go, we'll—make you." —"Have you got a warrant to put us out?" someone breaks out angrily. "Mr. Fulmer," says Mr. Young, after a moment's hesitation, nodding toward the marshal, "is taking care of that end of it."

In the middle of this discussion, several large rocks, either loosened by the rain or launched by a strategic hand, come bowling down the cliff toward the porch. There is a cry of, "Look out! Look out!"—a stampede to get away. Mr. Young and the marshal retreat. Then everybody comes back to the porch, and Mr. Young mounts his bench again.

Several speakers protest with bitterness that the companies only want to get them out so that they can bring in a crew of scabs. One of them uses obscene language and is hushed. Mr. Young makes an ambiguous statement to the effect that the thing to do is to clear the camp completely and then to "make a clean start"—mentioning at the same time that he "hates to call any man a scab."—If they get out, can they picket against scabs?—What they do when they get out is up to them: they will have to take their chances with the law. He isn't there to investigate labor conditions, but to see that the work goes on.

Another belligerent voice: They want conditions investigated by the government. "I can't do that," says Mr. Young, "you'll have to ask for that yourselves. Apply to Secretary Doak."—Does Mr. Young approve of conditions in the river camp?—"Our job is not to approve or disapprove—the company submits plans to us, and we OK them."—"Did you OK these conditions here?"—"No, we did not," he admits, for the first time a little lamely: "We've OK'd Boulder City, and that's all."

The conference is brought to an end by one of the leaders of the strike—apparently not a Wobbly—a powerfully built red-haired man, who has been interrupted in shaving and has not removed the patches of soap from his face. He delivers himself of a brief piece of oratory, in which he exhorts the men to go quietly and show they don't intend any violence but merely want their rights. And the men, who on the whole trust the government, who cannot bring themselves to challenge or resist it, assent and climb into the trucks, and are removed to a place on the desert halfway between Boulder City and Las Vegas, where they have been given permission to camp.

By this time the rain is a cloudburst, and it makes the government drivers feel uncomfortable. They say how sorry they are to be forced to move the boys in the rain.

The strikers trust the government, and the government people sympathize with the boys. The upshot of the strike is this. The leaders and their adherents camp out—about two hundred of them. But most of the strikers go back to work at the reduced rates of pay. The camp comes to be known as "Camp Despair," and the strike is then given up.

Filters and water-coolers are put in at the river camp; Boulder City is rushed along; the companies make an announcement that they are guaranteeing the present wage scale. The government takes a more active hand—arranges to have the hiring done in future by a man from the Labor Department. And Boulder City gets a new police, with every member a deputy U.S. marshal. This police force is designed to purge the reservation of booze-sellers and tinhorn gamblers, whom the easy laws of Nevada encourage and who were one of the principal reasons for the government's insisting that the reservation should be outside Nevada jurisdiction. But a further duty of this federal police is to keep out labor-organizers. The new chief is the former deputy who ordered the arrest of the Wobblies, and he is looking out for Wobbly cards. Today you need a special permit even to get into the reservation, and afterwards when you have been admitted, you have to have your permit OK'd at the police station in Boulder City.

THE CITY OF OUR LADY
THE QUEEN OF THE ANGELS

FROM THE HEART of thriving Los Angeles rise the grooves
of gorgeous business cathedrals: the blue Avocado Building,
bawdy as the peacock's tail, with its frieze of cute little
kewpids; the golden Lubrication Building, one of the glories
of Southern California, which has just failed for $50,000,-
000; the regal and greenish Citrus Building, made throughout of the purest lime candy, which has gone a little sugary
from the heat.

And there is Aimee McPherson's wonderful temple, where
good-natured but thrilling native angels guard the big red
radio-tower love-wand and see to it that not a tittle or vibration of their mistress's kind warm voice goes astray as it speeds
to you in your sitting-room and tells you how sweet Jesus
has been to her and all the marvelous things she has found
in Him. There is Syd Grauman's Babylonian Garage, where
Purr-Pull and Violet Ray gasolines ensure a maximum of
road comfort and soothe the eye with a pretty color. There
are little black-silver sandwich bars, functional *à la moderne*
and fit to make Frank Lloyd Wright's heart go pit-a-pat in his
boots. Nuestro Pueblo de Nuestra Señora la Reina de Los
Angeles has more lovely girls serving peach-freezes and appetizing sandwich specials with little pieces of sweet pickle
on the side than any other city in the world.

Now we motor agreeably and speedily through the beautiful residential boulevards. The residential people of Los Angeles are cultivated enervated people, lovers of mixturesque
beauty—and they like to express their emotivation in homes
that imaginatively symphonize their favorite historical films,
their best-beloved movie actresses, their luckiest numerologi-

cal combinations or their previous incarnations in old Greece, romantic Egypt, quaint Sussex or among the high priestesses of love in amoristic old India.

Here you will find a Pekinese pagoda made of fresh and crackly peanut brittle—there a snow-white marshmallow igloo—there a toothsome pink nougat in the Florentine manner, rich with embedded pecans. There rears a pocket-size replica of heraldic Warwick Castle—and there drowses a nausey old nance. A wee wonderful Swiss shilly-shally snuggles up beneath a bountiful bougainvillea which is by no means artificially colored; and a hot little hacienda, a regular *enchilada con queso,* with a roof made of rich red tomato sauce, hardly lifts her long-lashed lavender shades on the soul of old Spanish days.

Here and there handsome old flat houses of the early California frame-dwellers, or more imposing patrician mansions with scrolleries, cupolas and gigolos, give a conservative reminder of former fashions—while a big red brick Methodist church strikes a croak of coarse decorum. Yet not all the places of worship are sober—many cheery little odd-boxes, god-boxes, offer you a thousand assorted faiths and a thousand assorted flavors, from Theophistry to Christian Sirens. And in that rose garden, rapt in a trance, sits Buddha-like a roguey old Yogi, while pink clematis or purple clitoris rises or droops in rhythm to the movement of the mystic's fingers.

Those tall palms with their stiff tousled wigs are like Topsy, they just growed. And here we are in beautiful Beverley Hills—all flats, it is true, but what flats!—classy homes of real French filmsy-flamsy, coffee, toffee, chalky, cream, crome and bluff. Can't you just imagine Greta Garbo, lovely, alluring, aloof, slinking down the luxurious portico of that gay Riviera villa on the arm of a Mediterranean count! And hot little Clara Bow, who can romp with sailor boys like a *gamine,* serves tea with the grace of a *grande dame* in her chintzy classical palace which she has christened the Baths of Claraclara!

Leaving Hollywood itself behind, a bewilderment of fabricated features amazes us on either side: a blue will-o'-the-whimsy windmill and a trapper's cabin of plaster pine-logs that sells lime and lemon dope-flavored pop, a statue in papier-mâché of a woman in an old-fashioned sun-bonnet milking a cow with bright nickel teats, an ice-cream freezer in papier-mâché that deliciously glorifies ice cream and a big papier-mâché orange that seems to have gone bankrupt.

And you must visit the Hollywood zoo in its excitingly simulated bamboo-brake—where you can see a plaster lion, a rubber cobra, a mechanical crocodile, a gorilla with a colored boy inside and a new model of ball-bearing dinosaur that stands only eighteen inches high.

Surely that pretty little pink peppermint cabaña must be the home of dear Mickey and Minnie! And ye olde halffe-timberedde Pigglie Wigglie and ye Olde Gooffie Boofulle Shoppe—what fairy-tales these wonder-folks make true!

Here you may find real bargains in beach-lots of sand that is white as snow and lovebirds that will set you cooing—you can buy a swanky snooty chow puppy or a sunny walnut farm for a song! For a theme song, a Moorish sinagogue, a dream of dreams, a pitti-pitti palace, with bathrooms done in onyx Napoleonics and pornographic Pompeian red, with coverlimps in emerald and mauve sateen on the die-away divans for didoes, and a private slipping pool filled with green fountain-pen ink—a little bit blushful perhaps at selling itself to the pictures for $20,000 a year but happy as a real bribe and with all its prollems slobbed! And the Be-Happy-with-a-Home Realty Company is just a brokenne-downe olde picturesque cobwebby comfy shacke recalling the quaint olde toy-makers of Nuremberg who would plan you a little gingerbread cottage that the oil-trailers pass at high speed on their way up the macadam highway for about $9,000, including Paris-green blinds, a roof oh so lovingly poked in in spots, a weathervane shaped like a frolicsome seal and a view that takes in both the blue-blue sea where every little floozy wave croons, "Sunkist Caliphonia, here I come!" and the brown papier-mâché hills where every prospect appeases and the goofs hang like ripe fruit.

The Reverend Bob Shuler was born in a log cabin in the Blue Ridge. His people were mountain whites, all poor and most of them illiterate. As a boy, he worked with oxen in the fields. His clothes were made on a spinning-wheel by his mother out of flax grown behind the barn.

Bob's father had never got beyond the Second Reader, but he had always wanted to be a minister, and at thirty he studied for a degree at the Elm Creek Academy, while Mrs. Shuler took in boarders and Bob sold papers on the campus. They papered their new house, a two-room shack that had belonged to the Negro blacksmith, with the copies of the *Toledo Blade* and the *Cincinnati Post* that Bob hadn't been able to sell; and Bob read them all on the walls. He wanted to be a circuit-rider, too.

He tramped the railroads hunting jobs, cut wood behind back-doors for handouts, hoed corn, peddled stereoscopic views, worked at logging camps and finally taught in country schools. He worked his way through a Methodist college, and at seventeen he was licensed to preach.

He preached the Methodist gospel in the coal-mining towns of Virginia and Tennessee. At twenty-five, he married the only daughter of a family that had a big brick house with a big wheat plantation that was one of the show-places of the county. The next year he was transferred to Texas to take charge of a small circuit of churches and was paid a dollar a day, but the second year he was earning a thousand dollars.

He got to be more and more popular in Texas, but he was so fierce against the saloons and antagonized the liquor interests and the drinkers so that the bishop didn't know what to do with him. The people he attacked in his sermons used to get him into fist-fights outside, and somebody prosecuted him for libel. Then he was called to Trinity Church in Los Angeles.

Trinity Church, when Bob Shuler arrived, had only 900 members and was $70,000 in debt, and Bob Shuler has always believed that the bishop meant him to go down with the ship. But thirty days after he started in, the new pastor had raised $20,000. And in ten years the membership of Trinity had grown to 42,000, and the minister, through his genius for publicity, his evangelistic zeal and his passion for politics, had become one of the most powerful persons in Los Angeles.

Bob Shuler first made the front page with a sermon directed against some high-school girls who were reported to have had themselves photographed naked. This stimulated pious people to think about nude high-school girls and at once increased his following. Not long afterwards, he went to a charity bazaar; he won a ham in a raffle, and then took a chance on a wheel of fortune and had the man who ran it arrested for conducting a gambling game. Tipped off that if he would wait on a certain night at the door of a certain night club, he would see something that the public ought to know about, he caught the Los Angeles Chief of Police coming out with the wife and sister of a Mexican who was wanted for a crime.

All this went very big in Los Angeles, which has a solid Middle-Western foundation. Of the three million population of Southern California, at least half come from the Middle-Western farming states: Iowa leads with 400,000, but Illinois and Missouri are not far behind with 350,000 and 300,000. And Bob Shuler's appeal was perfectly gauged for these retired farmers and their families, who, finding themselves, after the War, unexpectedly rich from their wheat and corn, had come out to live in California bungalows and to bask in the monotonous sun, but for whom listening to sermons was one of their principal pastimes. Side by side with sporting oil-millionaires, an exotic California underworld and the celluloid romances of Hollywood, they were glad to get an intimate peek into the debauched goings-on of their neighbors, and at the same time be made to feel their own superior righteousness, and even—what was probably most gratifying of all—to have a hand in bringing the wicked to judgment.

Bob Shuler himself seemed one of them: he persisted in remaining rural. With his round head, humorous eyes and brown hair brushed boyishly across his forehead, his thick-set figure and cylindrical-looking arms that moved dynamically, as if all in one piece and with no trace of theatricality, his sudden alternations between rousing religious eloquence and the crackerbox vernacular of the backwoods, he seemed outspoken, homely and earnest, as well as exhilaratingly resourceful, indefatigable, engaging, magnetic. And he lived out at El Monte like a farmer, raising his own stock and vegetables. People who called him up on the phone might be greeted by Mrs. Shuler with, "You'll never guess what we've been doing! We've just killed a pig, and you ought to see my hands!"

"I came from the poorest of the poor," he would say. "I have been an underdog all my life, and my sympathies and efforts will always be on the side of the common people. . . . I must be forgiven for wanting this city run in the interests of the common people for the benefit of those who need protection and defense." He did not believe that "an honest officer would be active in enforcing the law against the defenseless and friendless while he closed his eyes to the lawlessness of the rich and powerful"; and he was "against the third degree, against special assessment of the poor, against confiscation of humble homes for public improvements." "I've found very few millionaires," he would say, "who didn't get their money in a manner that I doubted if God could own or bless." He was indignant in his intimations that his Baptist rival, Aimee McPherson, had diverted the money she raised on the pretext of pious purposes to her own luxurious living. When she had elicited, on one occasion, contributions for a monument for her husband's grave, Bob Shuler, several months afterwards, had photographs of the grave taken and would display them to his congregation, showing that there was nothing there but the original ignoble headstone.

It was true that he defended the power interests and was in the habit of going yachting with one of the big public-utility men; but he assured his congregation that this particular millionaire was "right with God."

Furthermore, he was a firm fundamentalist. Some years ago he fought a stout battle with a Congregational minister in Los Angeles, who accused Shuler of trying to "throttle progressivism" and attempted to dislodge him from the presidency of the ministerial union. Shuler stood fast: "If the old-time religion is not genuine," he declared, "then Christianity is bunk of the first water. No need to try to revamp it, to doctor and mend it, to repair and fix it up. If Jehovah is not God, then away with Christianity forever! It is unworthy of ordinary respect. It is a lie, a humbug, a cheat, a fraud! . . . For I am as certain as I live that either the old-time religion is genuine and worth a hundred cents on the dollar or else it is the very quintessence of rottenness and falsehood!" He triumphed; and Trinity Church "took her place as God's messenger and Christ's ambassador in a wicked city."

In Shuler's crusade against local corruption, his public lent him active support. First, an anonymous admirer in Pasadena supplied him with a private detective, who made it possible for him to delegate part of his labors of digging up scandals about public men; and then, when this assistant was mysteriously withdrawn, a big auto-supply man rallied to the pastor's rescue and set him up to a whole corps of spies.

But the climax of Bob Shuler's success came on Christmas, 1926. A woman called him up on the phone and said that she wanted to see him—she invited him to meet her in the Santa Monica Hotel. "Lady," was his immediate reply, "it would be as much as my life was worth to do it!" Since he had taken to exposing people, he had become apprehensive of being framed. But he checked on her and satisfied himself of her perfect respectability, discovered that she was a devout spinster, a Miss Glide who had made money in oil. He at last arranged to see her in the hotel lobby, with a male chaperon present. It turned out that she wanted to give him a Christmas present of a private radio station. He accepted; and thereafter his audience was multiplied to such an extent that he was able to play for Southern California the part of a veritable voice of God. Starting with 200,000 new hearers, he is said to have acquired 100,000 more every year—one of the largest religious audiences in the world.

KGEF was dedicated, in Shuler's own words, to "spreading the gospel and advancing civic betterment, and no modernist or evolutionist shall be allowed to speak over it." Two nights a week were consecrated to the advancement of civic betterment, and these soon came to outshine in public notice the purely religious part of the program. Bob Shuler was able to break a district attorney, a city prosecutor and another chief of police. The politicians began to play up to him—the newspapers and the juries came to fear him. No public official now was so powerful that the preacher had to respect him— no sin was too unseemly or too intimate for Shuler to search it out and to make it known to his public. He would reveal the rendezvous of Hollywood actors and actresses, the bootlegging of high-school students and public officials, the selling of birth-control devices by drug-stores, the attempts of the colored schoolteachers to flirt with the female white ones and the seduction of stenographers by millionaires. On one occasion, when a male schoolteacher had been hit and killed by a trolley while walking with a woman schoolteacher, he painted for his hungry audience the passion of their probable embraces, and suggested that the woman be tried for manslaughter for leading a married man to his death. It got to a point in Los Angeles where Bob Shuler's mere suspicions and hints were able to make courtrooms tremble: "Now I don't want to say anything against Judge Smith!" was his formula—"Judge Smith's sittin' up thar on that bench tryin' to be as fair as he can—but I will say that if I was Judge Smith, I wouldn't want people to think that a guilty man's money had saved him!"

It was impossible for the people the pastor attacked to retaliate by getting anything on him. "I have paid the price in clean living," he would say, "to be able to go on fighting the enemies I have made or may make in the future. One group of men did try to find something in my past life that they could use to stop me from fighting, but the investigator they sent on my trail came back and reported that he couldn't find a bug under any single chip in my past life. They can't find a scratch on my name if they hunt back to the cradle. I have never fooled with liquor, gambling, a woman or a dishonest deal. And they're never going to catch me in the situation Jacobson was found in because I never go to any woman's house in the course of my work as pastor of Trinity Church without taking a man along." Jacobson, a pious city-councilman who had obstructed the smooth functioning of the local machine, had, as everyone knew, been framed: a blonde had called at his office ostensibly to protest like Bob Shuler against the "special assessment of the poor," and had been found with him in her house under allegedly compromising circumstances by a party of detectives, reporters and simple amusement-seekers who had been summoned for the fun beforehand.

And that vast body of Middle-Western sentiment, marshaled and directed through the air, became one of the most formidable forces in Los Angeles. When the group known as the Julian oil swindlers did some 40,000 investors out of some twenty million dollars, Bob Shuler was able not merely to arouse popular opinion against the promoters and to facilitate the conviction of the District Attorney for conspiracy to take a bribe by accusing him of participation in drinking parties and improper intimacy with the female defendants, but even to cause the dismissal of a city prosecutor, the morning after the latter had denounced Shuler over the radio for the use of inflammatory language; and, when a crazed old man who had lost his money shot a banker involved in the scandal and was found to be carrying a copy of one of Shuler's pamphlets on the "Julian Thieves," he immediately obtained the dismissal of the policeman who had told a reporter about it and raised an outcry in his own vindication which caused the shooting to be forgotten.

There have been several attempts to "get" Shuler, but they have so far proved ineffective. Twice he has been tried for criminal libel: once for suggesting that the Mayor had acquired more money in office than his salary accounted for, and once by the Knights of Columbus, since he has always made war on the Catholics and has written against them a pamphlet called *The Rise of Beastism*. And at the time of the Pantages trials—when Mr. and Mrs. Pantages, the theatrical magnates, had, by an unlucky coincidence, been indicted at the same time for the crimes of, respectively, rape and killing a man through drunken driving—Bob Shuler so hampered the impaneling of the jury by charges that the Pantages' money was being used to fix it that the Los Angeles Bar Association finally had him up for constructive contempt of court. He was fined and given fifteen days in jail; but this only had the effect of stimulating the loyalty of his followers. When released, he was enthusiastically welcomed both by the new Mayor, his own man, whose election he had engineered, and by the District Attorney; and he was met outside by a cheering throng who escorted him in triumph to his home. In the meantime, they had raised the money to pay off the mortgage on his church.

Some pressure has lately been brought on the Federal Radio Commission to refuse him a new license, and, pending its final decision, he has been forced to be a little more discreet. But in the meantime, he has his own mayor and is for a season the real boss of Los Angeles. At the election two years ago, he is said to have ruined by vilification the chances of a dozen other possible candidates and to have caused his adherents to vote for the present mayor, John C. Porter, a dealer in secondhand automobile parts, an active worker for the lay Church Brotherhood and a former member of the Ku Klux Klan—whose principles Shuler has endorsed. Mayor Porter has flabby hands and a long pale morose face. Though undoubtedly a godly man, he is entirely uneducated and, except for once having served as foreman of a grand jury, devoid of executive experience. Since taking office as mayor, he has achieved international notoriety by telegraphing King Alphonso of Spain, ousted by the revolution, to come to the Los Angeles fiesta and "forget his troubles" there.

In Trinity Church, at any rate, radio license or no radio license, an air of calm confidence reigns. They continue to fill the pews, those dowdy and dry-faced women, those dowdy and pasty girls, those old men with thin necks and sparse hairs, drooping forward their small bald foreheads, drawing in their recessive chins—while the Reverend Bob Shuler, with an American flag hanging down from over his head, amid gargantuan baskets of chrysanthemums which scent the Sunday-morning chill and underneath a dome painted years ago with a cloudscape, now indistinct, in which, however, one bright electric bulb is intended to symbolize the Savior—the Reverend Bob Shuler can still hold them with his every word.

In his loose brown suit, his flapping mottled tie and his greenish-yellowish bone-rimmed glasses, he shifts from one gear to another with an easy and expert hand. How tellingly, by a quite sudden change of tone, he can come down face to face with his hearers—a coarse-spoken and hearty old hillbilly talking frankly to neighbors about everyday things! His sermon is a blast against make-up, and he is explaining that, nevertheless, it is not the case that everything artificial is bad: "I have a couple o' false teeth myself, and they make me a lot o' trouble—I wish I didn't have to wear 'em! I have to take 'em out at night and put 'em back in again in the morning. But I've got to wear 'em to chew—I wouldn't know what to do without 'em!" And then, still candid and straight, with what seems a welling-up of real feeling, he rises to dignity and eloquence: "When the spirit of Christ enters in you, you don't need any false embellishment! Your friends will see without that what's happened to ye—they won't need to be told about it, they'll know by themselves about it, they won't have any doubt about it—maybe ye won't say very much about it!"

It is Communion Sunday. The sermon over, the pastor announces that for those who stay there will be "a very beautiful service." He steps down from off the platform, and a young man in the orchestra comes forward and turns the microphone down to catch his words. He takes the sacrament first himself: "This is the body of Our Lord. . . ."

————

Dr. Gustav A. Briegleb, Bob Shuler's former lieutenant and present rival, is a graduate of Yale and a Presbyterian, and his congregation is recruited from a "better class" of people than Shuler's. Also evidently of Iowa and Missouri stock, they are better dressed and have fresher complexions. And Dr. Briegleb's fine new church, with its white walls and rough-hewn rafters, its furled American flag with a gleaming gold spike at the top, its choir in white gowns and only one basket of flowers on the platform, is a very much smarter affair than Bob Shuler's rather shabby temple.

Dr. Briegleb himself wears white flannel trousers and a semi-formal blue coat, with a handkerchief sticking out of the pocket. He does not pretend to be a man of the people like Shuler; and though, when active in the Ministerial Union at the time that Shuler was president, they battled side by side against "progressivism," and though, at the time of the Pantages' trials, Dr. Briegleb—for contempt of court—was fined twenty-five dollars when Shuler was fined seventy-five, he was often criticized by Shuler, even before their split, for his willingness to play up to the rich. When Dr. Briegleb had lent his support to the rich man's candidate for mayor rather than to the God-fearing Porter, Bob Shuler expressed himself as follows: "Dr. Briegleb thinks I'm stubborn and contrary, and that I constitutionally hate rich men and refuse even to go right if they want me to. On the other hand, I think Briegleb is one of the best fighters for the right who ever buckled on a sword. As I see it, his trouble is that the 'big boys' can feed him stuff."

Dr. Briegleb is, besides, a quite different type of man from the mountaineer Methodist preacher. With his stocky build, his grizzled hair and his frowning arrogant face, which is marked off by heavy lines in solidly molded sections, he suggests some Germanic divine of the days of the Reformation. When he reads the lesson and announces the hymns, his broad a's and rolling r's impose themselves as if with the authority of some sound theological seminary.

The first hymn on this Sunday evening is allowed to run its modest course. Reverent Sunday voices invoke the divine calm:

> *Peace, peace, sweet peace,*
> *Wonderful peace from above!*
> *Peace, peace, sweet peace,*
> *Wonderful gift of God's love!*

But at the end of the first stanza of the second hymn, with its lustier refrain of "Who could it be but Jesus?" their two-fisted pastor cracks down on them: "How many of you have never sung that hymn before? Those that have never sung it hold up their hands!" A certain number obey. "Those that have, hold up their hands!"—"Why I've sung that hymn at Christian Endeavor ever since I was a boy!" In a voice quite different from his seminary voice, a voice domineering and brutal and appropriate to somebody's idea of a powerful and hard-boiled business man, he tells them that they have got to do better. But, in commanding them, he does not fail to temper his severity with humor: "It reminds me of the story about the churches on the Yale campus. Over on one side of the campus, they were singing, 'Will there be any stars in my crown?' and over on the other side they were singing, 'No, not one!'" He makes the women do a stanza by themselves, the men do a stanza by themselves, and then both do a stanza together—and he tries to get them into the spirit of the thing by a minstrel joke about men and women. A strange thing happens to Dr. Briegleb's face every time he tells a joke: his mouth, which is habitually tight and grim, partly opens in a constrained gape. He is pausing for a laugh and trying to smile. But the Doctor, though he has evidently applied himself to acquiring the folksy technique of modern evangelism, will never be able to make people laugh. The responses to his sallies are meager. Nevertheless, before starting his sermon, Dr. Briegleb speaks highly of cheerfulness: he says that cheerfulness will help cure the depression.

But the sermon itself deals with a matter much closer to the Doctor's heart. Last May, just before the municipal elections, a young politician named Clark, who was a candidate for municipal judge, shot and killed two other men in what was supposed to be a real-estate office on Sunset Boulevard. One of the men was a former saloonkeeper, who had risen to be boss of the Los Angeles underworld; the other, the owner of a local magazine, had evidently been one of his henchmen. When Clark was tried in August, he offered a plea of self-defense: he said that, in his campaign for the bench, he had pledged himself, if elected, to clean up Los Angeles, and that Crawford and Spencer had tried to kill him. Spencer had already talked to him over the telephone and warned him to lay off or "you will drive into your driveway some night and you will not get out of your car!" In the story told by Clark at the trial, Dr. Briegleb played a curious role. The pastor of St. Paul's Presbyterian Church had been on the friendliest terms with the murdered underworld boss. Crawford had come to the service one Sunday and had dropped a diamond ring, said to be worth $3,500, into the contribution box, and he had thereafter had himself baptized by Dr. Briegleb and had made further donations to the Faith, which had enabled Dr. Briegleb to build his new beautiful church, with its device, "A Church Where Sinners Are Welcome." This church contained a soundproof room, which was designed for a private radio station. With a radio station of his own, Dr. Briegleb was to achieve equality with his former colleague and captain, Bob Shuler. But at this point—before the station had actually been installed—Boss Crawford was shot by Clark.

Clark testified on the stand that he had approached Crawford before the election as to whether there was any chance of getting the influential Briegleb's support. Crawford had explained the situation as follows: "I have talked to Dr. Briegleb, but there is something big going to happen. Dr. Briegleb is going to have a radio, and I am back in the saddle, and next year is going to be the Olympic Games, one of the biggest years Los Angeles has ever seen, and I am going to run things the way they have never been run before." "And he had the sample ballots there," Clark went on to tell the court, "pink and blue sample ballots, and he said that Miss Fisher was going to typewrite a thousand of those, and that he would deliver those to friends of his and people he knew, and that each ballot that was delivered would guarantee from ten to fifty votes—also a clipping from one of the newspapers with a list of prospective grand jurors." Crawford had figured that about half the grand jury would be made up of his friends, and that, with these and the 75,000 or 100,000 votes that Briegleb was sure to bring him, he ought to be pretty safe. Clark had asked, "What about the district attorney's office?" Crawford had replied: "I was indicted for bribery, for bribing the Corporation Commissioner, and Buron Fitts dismissed it." "He said, 'Don't ask me any more questions about that. He won't say anything.'"

The boss had then, according to Clark, proposed that he

should help them in a frame-up of Chief of Police Steckel at a Santa Monica hotel. Clark, at this, had denounced them as follows: "You dirty lowdown skunks!—you were indicted for framing Councilman Jacobson some time ago, and now you join the church and profess to be a Christian, and you throw a big diamond in the plate! You dirty skunk, I am going out and I am going to tell the people from every platform that I get on and from every radio what happened in this room. You are two rats!" "With that, he [Crawford] said, 'No ———— has ever talked to me that way!' and he pulled a gun out of his belt." The other man had pulled on Clark, too, but Clark had been quicker and had shot them both.

Clark's story was not generally believed by people who knew the personalities involved. It was assumed that the boss must have attempted to blackmail him: "There were three racketeers in that room!" it was said. But Clark was good-looking and young, and the jury, half of them women, would have acquitted him on the spot if it had not been for one stubborn old man, who—in defiance of his fair fellow jurymen, even with tears in their eyes—persisted in disbelieving the defendant's story. The forewoman, announcing mistrial, put on record the following statement: "I think he [Clark] is one of our noblest Americans. We believed every bit of his story of self-defense. We considered him a fine upstanding young man who told a straightforward story." (The old man who had disagreed later found a bomb under his house.)

Dr. Briegleb, who was Crawford's pastor and who was present at the boss's deathbed, takes, naturally, a different view, and he has spared no effort to make it prevail. One of the jurors originally chosen had turned out to be a trustee of St. Paul's Presbyterian Church, and he had had to be excused from duty when he admitted that he had been strongly influenced by his pastor's opinion of the case. Dr. Briegleb appeared at the trial, but he was never called as a witness, and on this account he is openly furious. He announced last week his intention of preaching about the trial, since he was not allowed to testify at it, and tonight there are reporters in the congregation.

The text is from Acts V, 1–4, the fate of Ananias and Sapphira, and the application is that Clark was a liar.

When Dr. Briegleb gets on to the Clark defense, he entirely loses touch with that excellent seminary. He casts doubt upon the honesty of Clark's counsel, who, he says, had Clark's revolver cleaned before the trial; makes a damaging attack on Clark's character—if he was one of the noblest Americans, why was he kicked out of Annapolis?; insists that he himself was not trying to run away when, immediately after the shooting, he had gone up to his summer camp, but was merely in search of a little rest from a distressing experience and arduous labors; acts the rôle of a broken old man as he depicts the terrible grief of the godly parents of Clark, disgraced by the evil behavior—more especially by the *lies*—of their son. He denies that he had ever promised to deliver Crawford any votes, points out the absurdity of the accusation, remarks to the congregation that he supposes a good many of them don't vote at all—several members of his own family don't vote—declares that there was never any question of the radio's being installed to guarantee 100,000 votes for Crawford: it was for spreading the gospel of Jesus Christ. He wrings the hearts of his audience with an account of Crawford's deathbed and his late repentance, and insists that, though cartridges were found in Crawford's desk, he was positively not carrying a gun. He points out that he himself, Briegleb, had got Chief of Police Steckel his job, so how under Heaven could Crawford have wanted to frame Steckel? He strives to bring home to his audience the horror of telling and living a lie; and pounding the pulpit with his fist, he demands, "If religion isn't for sinners, what in God's name is it for?" Some of the women in the congregation are weeping.

Now and then in his sermon, Dr. Briegleb resorts to devices which surprise you even after you have become accustomed to his transitions from pompous to brutal. He occasionally resorts to a trick which is peculiar to singing evangelists' talks in the streets of Western towns and which is calculated to put a spell upon persons of simple intelligence: "And Peter said to Ananias—ah, 'Why hath Satan filled thine heart—ah, to lie to the Holy Ghost—ah?'" And, with an effect even more incongruous, he sometimes tries an imitation of Bob Shuler's folksy humor: "I called up the District Attorney from Arrowhead Lake and I told him how I felt about it—Ah wish Ah had muh money back!—it cost me $2.80, and Ah wish Ah had it back!" And from his frequent references to Shuler, his anxiety to associate himself with him and to show that they are both of the same mind, one can see how much he still looks instinctively to the authority of his old chief.

Poor Dr. Briegleb! When he accepted Crawford's diamond ring and was promised a private station and received his new underworld convert into the Presbyterian Church, Bob Shuler publicly declared that he would "as soon baptize a skunk as Charley Crawford!" and let Briegleb go his own way. And now Charley Crawford is dead, and Dr. Briegleb has still no station. He will never be quite clever enough to satisfy the whole of his ambition. He makes a point of being present on all public occasions, and he gives out long public statements to malign reporters who lead him on and then do not print what he says, while Bob Shuler can make the front page every time without putting himself out to go anywhere. Poor Dr. Briegleb! Some basic Germanic simplicity, Puritanical inflexibility, professional respectability, will always, one fears, prevent him from appealing to the public of Los Angeles as Aimee McPherson and Bob Shuler do. Shuler can still charm every heart with a whiff of the cow-manure from his heels. Aimee, in her jolly gaudy temple, enchants her enormous audience by her beaming inexhaustible sunshine and her friendly erotic voice. She writes them operas in which ancient oratorios and modern Italian opera are mingled with popular songs and tunes from musical comedies. She warms the hearts of the lonely by urging them, before they leave, to shake hands, in the auditorium, with at least three people whom they do not know. And she has recently excited them especially by her glamorous marriage in a plane to the young man who sings Pharaoh in her current opera and by subsequently having broadcast from the bridal chamber the kisses and cooings of the happy pair. They adore her and hand her their money. They feel good about their neighbor and themselves.

But poor Briegleb will never do this. However much he may labor to be racy like the Reverend Bob, to cultivate the tone of a sales manager giving pep-talks to tepid salesmen, though he may study the incantations of the humble Come-to-Christer and announce that "the worst harlot in this town can come to this church and be received!" —he will always be handicapped by his education and by his Calvinist conviction that religion is authoritative, rigorous and grim!

EISENSTEIN IN HOLLYWOOD

SERGEI EISENSTEIN, the director of *Potemkin* and of *Ten Days that Shook the World,* arrived in Hollywood in the spring of 1930. In Paris he had signed a contract with Jesse M. Lasky to work for Paramount at $3,000 a week.

The first subject proposed to the Russian was the adventures of the early Jesuit fathers among the Indians of the Southwest—a subject which did not appeal to him. He did find, however, in California history an episode that aroused his imagination—the story of Sutter's gold. His idea was to show the trader building up his pioneer settlement, his stronghold of civilization, among the Mexicans and Indians of the West; and then when gold was discovered on his land, immediately deserted by his men, robbed of his property and stripped of his prestige. Eisenstein prepared a scenario which is said by those who have seen it to have had brilliant possibilities; but the movie people did not like his moral, and he was obliged to find another theme.

Dreiser's *An American Tragedy* was next brought to Eisenstein's attention. This interested him very much: he understood it as Dreiser had certainly meant it—as a tragedy of bourgeois ideals. But the scenario he made from Dreiser did not please the movie producers either. And there seem to be, for artists in Hollywood, only two possible choices: either—like Jannings, Chevalier, John Barrymore and Ernst Lubitsch—to give in to the stereotypes or to stand out against them and get the gate. And the Russians from the Soviet Union are in a particularly unfortunate position. Boris Pilnyak, the novelist, brought out this year to Hollywood by MGM, found that they wanted him to work on a film in which an American engineer was to get into trouble with the Soviets and be forced to make an escape from Russia; and when he explained that in Soviet Russia American engineers occupied a highly privileged position and were invariably sent home in state, he was told that, nevertheless, that was the way they would have to have it, and was allowed to return to New York. And, in the same way, the kind of thing that they tried to get Eisenstein to give them he stubbornly refused to supply. He, furthermore, refused to work with the high-salaried performers they offered him and insisted on casting the *Tragedy* with authentic non-professional types as he had been in the habit of doing in Russia: he wanted to look for his Roberta Alden among the Los Angeles shopgirls and for his Clyde Griffiths among the young employees of hotels and filling stations. The producers came to doubt his ability to make a commercial American film. In the meantime, besides, he is said to have aroused the jealousy of the directors and the cameramen, who, having learned to subdue their abilities to the demands of the Hollywood tripe-merchants, were now apprehensive lest Eisenstein should be given a real chance.

It was inevitable, also, of course, that Eisenstein should soon be attacked by the professional California patriots. A certain Major Frank Pease, who is supposed to be in the pay of the Better America Federation, started a vehement campaign against him. He telegraphed congressmen and senators; he circularized the whole community. He characterized Eisenstein as a "Red Dog" and made him responsible for all the crimes alleged to have been committed by the Soviets since the November Revolution. He demanded to know whether Californians were going to sit idly by and let this Bolshevik murderer and robber insinuate his poison through American films. The result of this agitation was that the people at the head of Paramount disagreed over Eisenstein, and that the group who were against him won out. He was not allowed even to start work on a picture, and at the end of the six months of his contract, he was told that they had no further use for him. The producers were so anxious to get rid of him that they bought him his ticket back to Russia for the moment when his contract ran out. His passport would expire with the contract.

Eisenstein, thus rejected, applied to Upton Sinclair, who lived not far away in Pasadena. He could not bear to return to Russia with nothing to show for his trip and admitting that Hollywood had beaten him; and he wanted to go to Mexico—since he was compelled to leave the United States —and make there a film of his own. Sinclair undertook to raise money for this. He got Eisenstein's passport extended, and he appealed to some of the radical millionaires, who, with the rising flood of Iowans around them, flourish so oddly in that part of the world. Eisenstein made a trip to New York, where he bought the Russian rights for *Once in a Lifetime,* George Kaufman's satire on Hollywood; and then, in December, he got off to Mexico with his camera and scenario men.

When Eisenstein was out of Hollywood, a film of *An American Tragedy* was made by an American director, Von Sternberg. Dreiser had been much disappointed at not having Eisenstein to direct the picture, and when he saw what had been done with it, he was furious. He issued a public protest and sued Paramount for having violated the terms of the contract by misrepresenting his whole meaning. This suit Dreiser lost; and, as a result of the fuss he had made, certain things in the picture were changed. And his protest had its moral effect: its reverberations in Hollywood can still be heard. The writers of the movie columns are still spitting and hissing at Dreiser, and the more intelligent people seem embarrassed about the episode. The truth is that Hollywood at present is very much like a mill-town. The writers, shut up by day in small cells in large buildings, which, like mills, have armed guards at the doors, compelled to collaborate in twos just as a pair of weavers is given so many looms and reporting like schoolchildren to supervisors who commend or suppress or censor, display, even outside the studios, a psychology of mill-hands or children. They have no choice about the nature of their subjects and no influence on the quality of their products; and, once having foregone the right to express their own tastes and beliefs, they are disturbed at seeing anybody fight for it.

Dreiser, in his public statement, had called on American

writers to stand up for their work when it is bought for the films. He reminded them that the national imagination got most of its food from the movies; and that at a time when the country, in its crisis, was in need of realistic criticism, the movies were still giving it nothing but sentimental falsifications; and he issued a warning that the film of the *Tragedy* did not say the same thing as his novel. People hastened to object to this that if you took the producers' money, you ought to know what was in store for you and be willing to kiss your creation good-by. But the truth was that Dreiser had upset them by taking the movies seriously—something which was not being done. It was too awful to allow oneself to think that anything important depended on what Hollywood fed to its audiences. The movies had been one of the features of the big prosperity wallow, and everybody had wallowed in them more or less.

Yet Von Sternberg's *American Tragedy* is a kind of product at second hand of Eisenstein's sojourn in Hollywood. It is not exactly bad, but half-baked. It has pretensions to artistic sincerity, but it is basically unsatisfactory. Some of the characters are happily cast, and there are some well-directed scenes of realism; but it is true that the picture betrays the intention of the novel itself. What is left out is Clyde Griffiths' own point of view, which alone can give the story significance. Lacking this, it becomes simply a melodrama of more or less conventional seduction, with the formula varied only a little by making the villain weak as well as mean. In the original Hollywood version, Clyde's early life was left out altogether. Dreiser forced them to put some of it in; but what was added is quite inadequate. The white-collar motif is not used at all—though Dreiser, by having his hero work in a collar factory, supplied the director with an excellent symbol. As for the trial, it has much the effect of any trial in a detective picture; and we do not see Clyde in the death-house —though Dreiser tried to make them include this. At the end—no doubt in deference to the author—Clyde's poor old mother is introduced and made to explain that it really isn't his fault, since his parents had never paid proper attention to him; but this is the first we have seen of them. The Holly-

wood make-ups—the pale powdered faces and the lipstick
that seems painted on—the hollow-looking "flats" of the sets,
never let us get far from the studios. The result is an inept
performance which is neither one thing nor the other—neither a *bona fide* serious film nor an effective popular melodrama.

Eisenstein in Mexico, in the meantime, was having a free
hand for the first time in his life. True, his development as
a master director could have been made possible only by
Communism. A non-profit-making enterprise, it had freed
him from commercial considerations; a church, it had given
him a framework of dogma, a definite and responsible point
of view; a program of efficiency and economy, it had spurred
him to technical discovery and at the same time ruled out
waste or display; a cult of the most rigorous realism, it compelled him to seek drama and beauty in ordinary men and
events. But efficiency may hurry an artist, and an insistence
on economy may cramp him; and a rigid political creed
which is always demanding fables to point its morals may
have its irksome side. Eisenstein, entranced with the Mexican scenery, so different from the bleak Gulf of Finland or
the flat expanses of collective farms, seems to have been carried away by an ambition to produce a perfect film, which
should excel as both photography and drama. And he was
fortunate in interesting in his project the owner of a large
hacienda, on the road between Mexico City and Vera Cruz,
who put the whole place and its personnel at Eisenstein's
disposal.

Eisenstein has now been in Mexico nine months, and he
has sent back 110,000 feet of film. He wants to make 160,-
000 feet. He is working under peculiarly difficult conditions
since he has no way of seeing his "rushes" and never knows
how his shots have come out, and since he will not, when
he sees them in Hollywood, be able to correct by retaking.
He now sends up these rushes in batches, and they are cen-
sored by the Mexican consul and inspected, for the producers, by film reviewers who do not know what to make of
them. As you watch, in the darkened silence of the little

projection room, the jumbled successions of shots, each one so beautifully composed and each sequence possessing as a whole the fluid design of a passage in music; the bursts of light or shade, clear shapes or obscure masses, balancing against one another; the retaking a dozen or more times of a scene or a look or a gesture, with all sorts of variations of tempo, perspective and motivation; the hardly varying long stretches of landscape or of the pose of some object or figure, from which the significant single glimpse must eventually be selected—as you watch, you get a new idea of the plasticity of the films as a medium, and you are ready to believe that Eisenstein is indeed in process of creating the, to date, supreme masterpiece of the moving pictures. For this Russian is able to work with the raw materials of life, and he succeeds in absorbing these—people, landscapes, plants, animals, tools, furniture, clothing and buildings—into his artist's imagination in a way that no Hollywood director has ever been able to do with the actors and animals trained for him or with the costumes and sets of studios.

This Mexican film is designed as a suite of three separate episodes,* each with a different set of characters, but illuminating one another and making a single composition. The first is a tragedy supposed to take place during the regime of Porfirio Diaz; the second—in this period, also—a romance of the master class; and the third, the story of a camp follower in the army of the Revolution. From a day's showing of rushes, I was able more or less to disengage·the latter part of the first of these episodes. A peon boy has killed his sweetheart, who has been raped by the master of the hacienda, and he has fled with two companions. He has been shown, in an earlier sequence, with his profile alongside the profile of the statue of an Aztec king, which it is seen to resemble closely. Now the boy must be hunted down.

White sunlight: a white sky, with, against it, a shifting abstract pattern of whiteness, created by a parody bull made of paper stretched on a frame and carried by one of the peon boys; the great white round sombreros of the boys making

* From the biography of Eisenstein by Marie Seton it appears that there were to have been four.

ellipses against the dark background: one of them is summoned by a guard, sullenly he comes forward; a bull hopping
about in a bull ring, the spectators—who swim and tilt dizzily
—are seen from the point of view of the toreador; the tangled
crabfeet of the cactus jungle; the pursuers come through on
horseback, the boys in sombreros hide under the cactus;
white light and black shadow in the arcade of the hacienda,
an architectural drama from an angle above the roofs: the
guards pace along the arcade, the boys follow them on the
roof and watch them; a blurred forest, gray blurrings of moss
—the first light, a mountain stream quick and quivering
where all else is numb—it grows brighter, men lie asleep—
they wake, one rouses the others—at once with swift simple
movements, they take up their guns and go; a brightly
white round sombrero in relief against duller rounded cloud-
masses: a dark face with white teeth and amiable eyes is
made to smile and smile again; now he is shooting among
the cactus—he has made a good shot, he smiles—then you see
his hand gone suddenly limp and the cartridges rolling out
of it; the daughter of the hacienda in a riding costume of
the nineties, tremulous and feminine, caricatured; crouching
beneath a cactus, she gets in the way of one of the hunters
and is hit by a bullet from the hunted; she lies dead amid
Catholic trappings; open door of the corral in the morning,
beyond it the wide valley and the mountains: the burros go
out, the sheep follow; the goats, the herds and the dogs; the
cattle crowd the door with their backs; finally a cowboy
emerges, a moment after the rest, dashing after them and
flourishing his lariat (this last surely one of the most beautiful scenes ever managed by a movie camera); the sullen
bronze visage of one of the boys standing among his captors;
his sweetheart, unmoving and dumb, with her shawled head
and Indian face, looking on from the arcade; a portrait of
President Diaz hung above a small table, on which are a
vase of peacock feathers and a Pekinese that looks like the
President; a strange dance of three men on fine horses, bucking and rearing on the crest of a hill, against a white white-
clouded sky, like angular kaleidoscope fragments that cannot
be shaken out of their triple pattern; we see, through the

eyes of the peon watcher, far off but distinct and ominous in the bright Mexican sun, a little group of men, who are rapidly digging in a bank; now we are close: on the crest of the hill, a man on horseback against the white sky, with a single sharp gesture and word, bids the boy go down into the hole; the spurred foot and the long lean boot stamping the ground down about the boy's neck, he turns his face to avoid the spur; left alone in their living graves, the peon boys wait, flies crawl across their faces, their heads begin to droop; later they convulsively gape, the shadow of a buzzard passes; the girl with the Indian face comes over the crest of the hill, is suddenly down among them; she kneels beside the head of her lover, with a quick desperate movement turns away; a broad landscape with small grazing cattle and snow-whitened Popocatepetl in the distance, under a wide-washed cloudy sky, in the foreground a strip of river moving sensitively and swiftly while the landscape broods and sleeps; a dark sharp sheaf of cactus lizard-tails standing out against a blank white background in fierce and rigid relief.

1957. The end of this potentially great picture was an ironic and tragic fiasco. The whole story of *Que Viva Mexico!*—as Eisenstein was going to call it—may be read in *Sergei M. Eisenstein: A Biography* by Marie Seton—though some aspects of it remain rather obscure. It is, however, clear that Sinclair became worried when the Russian, who had agreed to complete the film within three or four months, continued to stay in Mexico for more than a year. Sinclair had to raise $53,000 and even mortgage his house. At last he shut down on funds and insisted that Eisenstein return. He says that he had received in the meantime a cablegram from Stalin in which Eisenstein was characterized as "a deserter." Though thirty-five miles of film had been shot, the last episode had not been made. Eisenstein was forced to go back to Russia, and Sinclair had promised to send him the whole of the film for cutting. But relations between him and Eisenstein had by this time become embittered. A brother of Mrs. Sinclair had gone along on the expedition and had not got on with the Russian. He came back before Eisenstein and gave the Sinclairs most unpleasant reports on Eisenstein's frivolity, his sexual life and his failure to make progress on his film. This conventional Mississippian had been persuaded by Eisenstein to play the role of the sadistic horseman—type of the master class—who dances on the skulls of the buried boys, and I had the impression—though I have not seen this mentioned in any of the controversies about the film—that, unmistakably not a Mexican, he was unwittingly made to figure as an odious grasping Yankee equally guilty with the Mexican landowner of exploiting the Mexican peasants. When I hinted this to Upton Sinclair—not knowing that the actor was his brother-in-law—he assured me that Eisenstein had promised not to bring the United States into it. But Eisenstein had also promised not to criticize the Mexican government, and he had met President Obregon and General Calles and had photographed them in all their pomp of office; yet we know from his subsequent statements that he had meant to use the pictures in such a way as to show these republican officials in a cruelly satiric light. He was cheating on his American backers in the interest of the Marxist line, to which, with whatever guile, his position as a spokesman for the Soviet Union compelled him to remain loyal. Yet one can well believe Upton Sinclair when he suggests that the liberated Russian was enjoying himself so much in Mexico and was so little eager to return to Russia that he purposely prolonged his work. Miss Seton makes it clear that the fourteen months that Eisenstein spent in Mexico were the happiest time of his life; and since cynicism toward bourgeois socialists and capitalistic liberals was a part of the Marxist-Leninist code, it would not have troubled his conscience to exploit Sinclair and his friends.

But he was to fare equally badly at home. Sinclair had reported to the Soviet authorities what he regarded as the director's misbehavior in Mexico, and seems to have given later a similar reprobatory account to the head of the Soviet film trust, when the latter was visiting Hollywood. This man already hated Eisenstein, and, for three years after the director's return, rejected all his projects for films. They told Eisenstein at home that the line had changed. His dramas of group life and mass action, in which the characters were simply types, were not what was wanted now. The time had come, not precisely for an emphasis on the individual, but for the official recognition of "the laughter and romance" of human life. I am glad to learn from Miss Seton that Eisenstein declined to make the film *Merry Fellows,* which was supposed to promote laughter and which culminates in the wholesale wrecking of the furnishings of a bourgeois mansion by an invasion of cattle, pigs and other farmyard animals. Eisenstein was reprimanded later—in 1935—and instructed in his future duties, at a conference called by the film industry. He was lectured for four hours by Sergei Dynamov, who represented the Central Committee. Dynamov was the head of VOKS, the bureau that handled relations with the visiting writers and artists from foreign countries, and I saw him a number of times when I was in Moscow in 1935, not long after this conference occurred. He was what I should be tempted to call a hick but what is more accurately described by the Russian word *poshlyák,* which does not exclude intellectual pretensions. He had a mouthful of gold teeth, but not enough intelligence or artistic sensibility to have qualified as Eisenstein's secretary. He had, furthermore—as Eisenstein pointed out—no experience whatever of film-making. Yet Eisenstein was not merely scolded by the cultural greeter of VOKS; he was officially degraded and put on the spot to emerge from his solitary studies—any sort of independent research was suspect in the Soviet Union—and produce a true Soviet film. In response to this summons, accordingly, he devoted two years to a picture which was supposed to invest with an heroic prestige the collectivization of the land. He combined with *Bezhin Meadow,* one of Turgenev's *A Sportsman's Sketches,* a true contemporary story of a kulak who had murdered his Communist son. But though Eisenstein had never allowed himself to falter in his loyalty to the Revolution or to admit of any question of the firmness of his Marxist principles, he had developed other interests which proved to be incompatible with "socialist realism," the theory—then official in Russia—that imaginative literature should consist of stories and plays which, however melodramatic, stuck close to the common life and illustrated socialist morals. Eisenstein, half-Jewish and brought up in the Orthodox Church, had a strong religious streak. He was forced, by his Bolshevik position, to caricature the Church, but he read about religion voraciously, and he studied it in connection with philosophy, psychology and anthropology. He was preoccupied with certain symbols—especially that of the Trinity—and certain typical situations. He had begun in his Mexican picture to embody in his compositions—perhaps the most powerful ever filmed—these pregnant recurrent symbols; and a ritual crucifixion by the Mexican Penitentes was, it seems, to be intercut with the punishment of the three peon boys. In *Bezhin Meadow*, he could not restrain himself from expanding his Soviet fable into something more universal and more psychologically interesting: he put into the situation of the kulak and his Communist son something of Abraham and Isaac—with the result that he was directed by his supervisors, at a relatively early stage, to remake the whole picture in such a way as to exclude from it everything not directly relevant to the class struggle. He did his best to comply with this order; but when the two years of work on the picture were finished, it was suppressed by the head of the film trust, and Eisenstein was officially disgraced. He was compelled to make a public apology, in which he explained his failure to keep up with the progress of Soviet society, and—a master of imaginative art, widely traveled and read, intrepid explorer of modern thought in science as well as in art, and perhaps the only first-rate genius that the Soviets ever recruited—to acknowledge his grievous error in departing from the morality of the Young Pioneers.

In the meantime, the complicated filmings for the symphonic *Que Viva Mexico!* had never been forwarded to Eisenstein, and he learned in 1932 that Upton Sinclair had turned them over to Hollywood for the purpose of having Sol Lesser get out of them, under his own supervision, something that could be shown to an American audience. Sinclair had at one time, he says, offered the material to the Soviet government, in return for a guarantee of $50,000, which would enable him to repay the film's backers; but the Russians would not meet these terms, and, in view of what has just been said about the attitude toward Eisenstein in Russia, there is no reason to believe that the film trust were anxious to have the film completed. The news of the making of the American film had a shattering effect on Eisenstein. "For three weeks," his biographer writes, he "behaved like a man going out of his mind. Long periods of anguished silence behind his locked door gave way to storms of despair. It no longer mattered to him what anybody thought [in Russia], since no further harm could be done to him." The picture produced in this way—called *Thunder Over Mexico*—exploited only the peon boy episode and was thoroughly unsatisfactory. It seemed to me to have little or nothing of the brilliance and bite of the rushes. A Hollywood preview took place in May, 1933, and partly, at any rate, it seems, as a result of receiving an account of this, poor Eisenstein, eclipsed at home and now faced with the mutilation of his most ambitious project, went into a sanitarium. Though his personal relations with Upton Sinclair had by now become extremely strained, Eisenstein appealed to him through Louis Fischer over and over again to let him have a print of the film when he had got out of it what he could for America. But Sinclair, a Puritan, a moralist and something of a prig, had become so embittered by Eisenstein's duplicity, his failure to keep his promises, and a practical joke he had played on him by sending him to get through the customs a trunk containing pornographic photographs, that he could not be induced to relinquish the film. The last straw in Sinclair's disillusion—though it is a little bit difficult, from his own account, to understand exactly why—was the betrayal of an agreement with the Russians (made, apparently, before their refusal to give a guarantee for the film) to ship the material to Russia and have Eisenstein cut it there. The director did not go straight home but managed to stay in New York, where he succeeded in getting Artkino to allow him to intercept the film. One can easily understand why he should have wanted to cut it here. But Sinclair, hearing of this, had the film taken away and sent back to him. "Of course," Sinclair writes Miss Seton, "that was the end of both Eisenstein and Russia for us. We never had any idea of shipping him a print or anything else after that. We'd as soon have shipped it to the devil." He later allowed Sol Lesser to extract from it a two-reel travelogue called *Death Day,* out of shots that had been meant for an epilogue. In the years that followed this disappointment, Eisenstein proposed two more projects: a film on the Spanish Civil War and a film on the creation of the Red Army—neither of which he was allowed to do. But in 1937 he was permitted to begin a picture on the thirteenth-century hero Prince Alexander Nevsky, who defeated the Teutonic Knights. Eisenstein's notes for the film are full of references to *Paradise Lost,* for he wanted to recall in the rout of the Knights the downfall of Satan's army; but he was given a co-director to keep him within the bounds of propaganda. And he was now, for the principal roles, compelled to use regular actors instead of people from ordinary life that he picked up wherever he found them. The result was a general coarsening: the film is melodramatic and overdone. The patriotic analogy, of course, was with the menace of Hitler's Germany, but, nine months after the film was completed, the Soviets signed their pact with Hitler, and the picture had to be suppressed. The half-Jewish Eisenstein, who was known to speak fluent German, was now, furthermore, directed by the government to deliver a broadcast to Germany, in which he declared that the pact should make the basis for a cultural alliance "between the two great peoples." In the meantime, Marie Seton, who was a friend of Eisenstein's, had discovered that what was left of the Mexican film after the making of *Thunder Over Mexico* and *Death Day* was still stored in a Hollywood vault. It had been the intention of Upton Sinclair to hand it over to Hollywood for travelogues, but Miss Seton, with limited resources, succeeded in buying part of it up and took a two-year option on the rest. Neither Miss Seton nor Eisenstein could get Artkino to do anything about it. Nor could Miss Seton get anyone in America to rescue it—not even the Museum of Modern Art. The second World War had begun, and this had made everything more difficult. She herself pieced out a film, which she called *Time In the Sun,* from the footage she had succeeded in purchasing, and Sinclair had the rest ground up into half a dozen one- or two-reel documentaries intended for use in schools. But Eisenstein, now occupied with *Alexander Nevsky*, was, in any case, forced to recognize that he would never be allowed to make anything which embodied the aesthetic principles he had been forced to abandon after *Bezhin Meadow*. He was hopelessly committed now to the crudities of his present technique, which were already, under official direction, approaching the popular quality of American detective strips.

These crudities were carried still further in the two films on Ivan the Terrible made between 1941 and 1946. Here the whole of Eisenstein's cast is made up of professional actors, whose bellowings and hammy grimacings become horrific and comic. And yet even this film has its moments. It is the proof of Eisenstein's genius that, in spite of all the handicaps imposed on him, it was impossible for this artist to subdue himself to the demands of the propagandist: he cannot keep out of his work the truth about the world he is living in and the expression of his own emotions. Ivan was supposed to have been glorified as an imperial prototype of Stalin, ruthless toward those who betray him yet the far-sighted builder of his nation. But the picture is politically ambiguous. I have been able to see only Part I, in which Ivan is constantly betrayed and loses a beloved wife. Yet it ends on a disquieting note. The Tsar, discouraged by treason, has been urged by a confidential adviser to surround himself with new supporters "who have foresworn all ties of family and home in order to know only the Tsar," and, leaving Moscow, he has made the announcement that he has decided to abdicate the throne until, "by the people's summons, I shall acquire unlimited power and, reanointed, complete a great task without mercy." He is seen, in a remarkable shot, lurking within an archway—suspicious, malignant, sinister—while a procession with banners and icons comes winding through the snow to recall him. There had originally, it seems, been a prologue—which was never publicly shown—in which Ivan, as a boy of seven, is present at the death of his mother, who has been poisoned by the party of the boyars. Eisenstein himself, at the age of twelve, had been shockingly abandoned by his mother, who had gone off without warning to Paris, almost denuding the house of its furniture, and left him to a Russian nurse and an uncongenial father. He did not see her again till he was twenty-four, and this terrible early desertion had so shaken his confidence in women, set up such a barrier between him and them, that it was impossible for him to the end of his life to have intimate relations with them. Though he seems to have valued affection and to have depended much on certain associates, he had a reputation for inhuman coldness and for lack of consideration for others; and his close friends believed they could recognize in the psychology attributed to Ivan a projection of his own personality. But he was also dealing with Stalin, and in Part II the Christian religion, which had always been important for Eisenstein, emerges, in the person of the Metropolitan Philip, to try to bring Ivan to book for his crimes. It is impossible to know how this was treated without having seen the picture; but it would seem from Eisenstein's scenario that he was aiming to condemn the recent murders of Stalin while at the same time exalting him as a statesman. He also never lets it appear that either Ivan or his enemies is supposed to be on the right side. Ivan is denounced by the Church, but the Church is represented as in alliance with his opponents the boyars, and this results in a massacre of boyars, in which Ivan is seen at his worst. Yet the Church's arraignment continues: "Like Nebuchadnezzar, Ivan, you burn your nearest in the fire. But an angel with a sword will come down to them and rescue them from the depths." And later Ivan is seen prostrate under a fresco of the Last Judgment, explaining to the "Tsar of Heaven" that he has committed his murders for reasons of state. The Tsar of Heaven is silent. "And around him the hierarchy of angels are also silent. The sinners are silent, writhing in eternal fire. On the ground Ivan groans. His soul is on fire. . . . He rises from his knees, Ivan stumbles through the cathedral: 'I go to confess.' . . . 'Who calls to God?' 'The unworthy slave Ivan.' " This was followed by a few brief scenes in which the statesmanship of Ivan abroad is scoring its first suc-

cesses; and Eisenstein had planned a third film, which was
to deal with Ivan the warrior and show him defeating the
Germans. But Part III was never made because Part II was
never released. The reasons for this will be plain. One of the
objections was that Eisenstein had shown Ivan's bodyguard
as too much "like the Ku Klux Klan." He had again to make
a public apology. It was reported at the time in the newspapers that he had expressed his humble regrets at "having
been misled through historical accuracy," but the document
Miss Seton prints contains nothing so insolent as this. Eisenstein merely speaks of the tradition of the terribleness of Ivan
as he had read about it, in his youth, in benighted tsarist
Russia, and of the testimony against Ivan of his enemies, and
concedes that he ought not to have trusted such testimony
and such a tradition.

Just before he had finished Part II of *Ivan*—in 1948—he
at last received from the United States prints of *Thunder
Over Mexico* and *Time in the Sun*. He had never seen any
of this material since the spring of 1932, when he had had
run it off in New York. In a letter to a French film critic,
he wrote, *"Ce qu'ils en ont fait comme montage est navrant."*
He still wanted to take these pictures apart and try to make
something of them; but just after he had finished *Ivan*,
while attending an evening party, he fell down with a heart
attack, and he died two years later, at fifty, without having
attempted this. He had in the meantime been awarded the
privilege of doing a trilogy on the life of Stalin.

This story is, I think, worth telling as a sequel to the
chapter above. But what is the moral of it? It is obvious that
the film director is in a position of special difficulty as compared with other artists, since, in order to do anything at all,
he is obliged to induce some producer, some group of millionaires or some government to put at his disposal large sums
of money. No artist of the first rank save Chaplin has beaten
the Hollywood game, and Chaplin has ended up in exile.
The resilient genius of Eisenstein is in evidence in every film
he made; but how shattered in the Mexican fragments! how
vulgarized in the subsequent Soviet films! Not, of course, that

he would have been better off if he had been a musician or a writer. One thinks of Shostakovich and Pasternak—fortunate even to be still alive. At the time I wrote *Eisenstein in Hollywood,* I was already well aware of the dangers for the artist in Russia—less paralyzing then than they later became; but I hoped that the Soviet Union might eventually produce a culture more satisfactory than what I regarded as our capitalistic one. I could not forsee the lengths to which the tyranny of Stalin would go, but I ought to have foreseen the effect on the once brilliant Russian arts of a hardly literate public. The level of taste in the United States—a democracy with public schools—should have shown me that the taste of Russia was bound to be even worse.

THE JUMPING-OFF PLACE

THE CORONADO BEACH HOTEL was built by the California millionaire John Spreckels and opened in 1887. Spreckels had made his money in Hawaiian sugar, and in 1887 the United States signed a treaty with the Hawaiian king—a treaty which guaranteed to the Americans the exclusive use of the harbor at Honolulu.

In the same year, the first vestibule train was put on the tracks by George Pullman, and the revolt of the Apaches under the formidable Geronimo, the last attempt of the Indians to assert their independence, had been put down by the government and the Apaches penned up in a reservation; the American Federation of Labor had just been founded, Kansas and Nebraska were parching with a drought, and Henry George had just run for mayor of New York and had been beaten only with difficulty by a coalition against him of the other parties; Grover Cleveland was in the middle of his first term of office and threw the capitalists into consternation by denouncing the protective tariff, and an Interstate Commerce Act designed to curb the rapacity of the railroads was in process of being put through by the small businessmen and farmers; inquiries into the practices of the trusts were being got under way in Congress, while the Standard Oil Company, entering the drilling and pumping field, was already well embarked on the final stage of its progress; and Edward Bellamy had a huge and unexpected success with his socialist novel, *Looking Backward,* which prefigures an industrial utopia.

The Coronado Beach Hotel must represent the ultimate triumph of the dreams of the architects of the eighties. It is

the most magnificent specimen extant of the American sea-
side hotel as it flourished on both coasts in that era; and it
still has its real beauty as well as its immense magnificence.
Snowy white and ornate as a wedding cake, clean, polished
and trim as a ship, it is a monument by no means unworthy
to dominate this last blue concave dent in the shoreline of
the United States before it gives way to Mexico.

The bottom layer of an enormous rotunda is slit all around
with long windows that remind one of those old-fashioned
spinning toys that made strips of silhouettes seem to move,
and surmounted, somewhat muffled, almost smothered by a
sort of tremendous bonnet. This bonnet involves a red roof,
a second layer of smaller windows and an elaborate broad
red cone that resembles an inverted peg-top and itself includes two little rows of blinking dormer windows and an
observation tower with a white railing around it, capped in
turn by a red cone of its own, from which, on a tall white
flagpole, flies an American flag. Behind this amusing rotunda
extends the main body of the great hotel: a delirium, a
lovely delirium, of superb red conical cupolas, of red roofs
with white-lace crenellations, of a fine clothlike texture of
shingles, of little steep flights of stairs that run up the outside
of the building and little outside galleries with pillars that
drip like wedding-cake icing, and of a wealth of felicitous
dormers, irregular and protrusive, that seem organic like the
budding of a sea-hydra. In the pavement of the principal
entrance have been inlaid brass compass-points, and brass
edges mark the broad white stairs which, between turned
banister-rungs, lead up to the white doors of bedrooms embellished with bright brass knobs.

The whole building surrounds a large quadrangle, admirably planted and gardened. The grass is kept vivid and
tender by slowly revolving sprays, and against it blooms a
well-conceived harmony of the magenta and vermilion and
crimson of begonia and salvia and coxcomb, bouquet-like
bushes of rose-red hibiscus and immense clumps of purple
bougainvillea that climbs on the stems of palms, tall-grown
and carefully trimmed, in mounds of green fern or myrtle.
The trees are all labeled with Latin names, as in a botanical

garden. In the middle stands a low polygonal summerhouse, vine-embowered and covered with bark, inside which a boy is chalking up on a blackboard the latest stock-market quotations, while interested male guests sit and watch them in silence.

This courtyard has real dignity and brilliance. With its five tiers of white-railinged porches like decks, its long steep flights of steps like companionways, its red ladders and brass-tipped fire hose kept on hand on red-wheeled carts around corners, the slight endearing list of its warped floors and the thin wooden pillars that rise, at the bottom, from flagstones flush with the ground, it manages to suggest both an ocean liner and the portico of a colonial mansion. As you look out from one of the higher galleries at the tops of the exotic tame palms and at the little red ventilators spinning in the sun, you feel that you can still enjoy here a taste of the last luscious moment just before the power of American money, swollen with sudden growth, had turned its back altogether on the more human comforts and ornaments of the old non-mechanical world.

In the lobby, you walk as on turf across carpeting of the thickest and softest. There are wicker chairs; soft plush couches; panels of greenish-bluish tapestries on which ladies with round pulpy faces take their pleasance in Elysian boskage; sheets of stock-market quotations on hooks at the head of the stairs going down to the barbershop; and a masterpiece of interior decorating, elaborate and not easily named, but combining a set of mirrors covered with yellow curlicues, yellow-varnished rows of banister-rungs and an ambitious stained-glass window representing red poinsettias.

In the spacious, round and many-windowed dining room, where yellow-shaded candles light white tables, old respectable ladies and gentlemen eat interminable American-plan meals. After dinner, they sit on couches and talk quietly or quietly play cards in the card room.

You can wander through long suites of apartments—passing from time to time through darkish in-between chambers, made unlivable by closed-up grates, glossy mahogany mantels and sometimes a pair of twin vases cold as funeral urns.

Eventually reaching the rotunda, you come upon a swarming convention of the California Federation of Business and Professional Women's Clubs. (The General Federation of Women's Clubs was organized about two years after the opening of the Coronado Beach Hotel.) The business and professional women are fussing on the outskirts of the ballroom: "I've just seen Mildred, and she hasn't done anything about the corsages yet! Do you think we ought to give them to all the officers or just to the incoming ones?" And in a conclave under hanging electric lamps in the shape of enormous coronets, they are solemnly reading aloud and debating, one by one, the amendments proposed to their innumerable by-laws.

From time to time the chambers of the vast hotel resound to a chorus of feminine voices, deliberate, school-girlish, insipid. They have composed an anthem of their own, to the tune of *John Brown's Body,* in connection with a fund they are trying to raise:

> *Twenty thousand dollars by nineteen thirty-four!*
> *Twenty thousand dollars by nineteen thirty-four!*
> *Twenty thousand dollars by nineteen thirty-four!*
>   *Our fund is marching on!*
> *Glory, Glory, Hallelujah!*
> *Glory, Glory, Hallelujah!*
> *Glory, Glory, Hallelujah!*
>   *Our fund is marching on!*

These business and professional women are not altogether sure about what they are going to do with this money after they have succeeded in raising it; but they have arranged for a speaking contest at which a speaker from each district will be given three minutes to offer suggestions on "How can the income of $20,000 be used to the greatest advantage of the Federation?"

————

The new hotel at Agua Caliente across the border, where people go to see the Mexican races, has taken a good deal of the trade away from the Coronado Beach Hotel; but people still come from all over the country to San Diego across the bay.

The Americans still tend to move westward, and many drift southward toward the sun. San Diego is situated in the extreme southwestern corner of the United States; and since our real westward expansion has come to a standstill, it has become a kind of jumping-off place. On the West coast today, the suicide rate is twice that of the Middle-Atlantic coast, and the suicide rate of San Diego has become since 1911 the highest in the United States. Between January, 1911, and January, 1927, over five hundred people have killed themselves here. The population in 1930 was only about 148,000, having doubled since 1920.

For one thing, a great many sick people come to live in San Diego. The rate of illness in San Diego is 24 per cent of the population, whereas for the population of the United States the sick rate is only 6 per cent. The climate of Southern California, so widely advertised by Chambers of Commerce and Southern California Clubs, but probably rather unhealthy with its tepid enervating days and its nights that get suddenly chill, brings invalids to San Diego by the thousand. If they have money to move about and have failed to improve in the other health centers, the doctors, as a last resort, send them to San Diego, and it is not uncommon for patients to die just after being unloaded from the train. In the case of "ideational" diseases like asthma—diseases which are partly psychological—the sufferers have a tendency to keep moving away from places, under the illusion that they are leaving the disease behind. And when they have moved to San Diego, they find they are finally cornered, there is nowhere farther to go. According to the psychoanalysts, the idea of the setting sun suggests the idea of death. At any rate, of the five-hundred-odd suicides during the period of fifteen years mentioned above, 70 per cent were put down to "despondency and depression over chronic ill health."

But there are also the individuals who do not fit in in the conventional communities from which they come and who have heard that life in San Diego is freer and more relaxed. There at last their psychological bents or their peculiar sexual

tastes will be recognized, allowed some latitude. It is certain
that many such people find here what they are seeking; but
if they fail to, if they feel themselves too different from other
people and are unable to accept life on the same terms, they
may get discouraged and decide to resign. And then there
are the people who are fleeing from something in their pasts
they are ashamed of or something which would disgrace them
in the eyes of their friends in the places where they previously lived. San Diego is not quite big enough so that the
members of the middle-class groups do not all know one another and follow one another's doings with the most attentive
interest. If your scandal overtakes you and breaks, your whole
circle will hear about it; and if you are sensitive, you may
prefer death. And then there are settlers in San Diego who
are actually wanted by the law. This September the city is
being searched for a gangster escaped from New York, who,
in a beer-war, turned a machine-gun on some children. California has been a hideaway for gangsters in trouble elsewhere
ever since Al Capone came here. And there are also the people with slender means who have been told that San Diego
is cheap, but who find that it is less cheap than they thought;
and the girls (married young in this part of the world) deserted by husbands or lovers; and the sailors and naval officers
who have had enough of the service.

Since the depression, the rate has increased. In 1926, there
were fifty-seven suicides in San Diego. During nine months
of 1930, there were seventy-one; and between the beginning
of January and the end of July of 1931, there have already been thirty-six. Three of these latter are set down in
the coroner's record as due to "no work or money"; two to
"no work"; one to "ill health, family troubles and no work";
two to "despondency over financial worries"; one to "financial
worry and illness"; one to "health and failure to collect"; and
one to "rent due him from tenants." The doctors say that some
of the old people who were sent out to San Diego by their
relatives but whose income has been recently cut off, have
been killing themselves from pride rather than go to the poorhouse.

These coroner's records in San Diego are melancholy reading, indeed. You seem to see the last futile effervescence of the burst of the American adventure. Here our people, so long told to "go West" to escape from ill health and poverty, maladjustment and industrial oppression, are discovering that, having come West, their problems and diseases remain and that the ocean bars further flight. Among the sand-colored hotels and power plants, the naval outfitters and waterside cafés, the old spread-roofed California houses with their fine grain of gray or yellow clapboards—they come to the end of their resources in the empty California sun. In San Diego, brokers and bankers, architects and citrus ranchers, farmers, housewives, building contractors, salesmen of groceries and real estate, proprietors of poolrooms and music stores, marines and supply-corps lieutenants, machinists, auto mechanics, oil-well drillers, molders, tailors, carpenters, cooks and barbers, soft-drink merchants, teamsters, stage-drivers, longshoremen, laborers—mostly Anglo-Saxon whites, though with a certain number of Danes, Swedes and Germans and a sprinkling of Chinese, Japanese, Mexicans, Negroes, Indians and Filipinos—ill, retired or down on their luck—they stuff up the cracks of their doors and quietly turn on the gas; they go into their back sheds or back kitchens and eat ant-paste or swallow Lysol; they drive their cars into dark alleys, get into the back seat and shoot themselves; they hang themselves in hotel bedrooms, take overdoses of sulphonal or barbital; they slip off to the municipal golf-links and there stab themselves with carving-knives; or they throw themselves into the bay, blue and placid, where gray battleships and cruisers guard the limits of their broad-belting nation—already reaching out in the eighties for the sugar plantations of Honolulu·

BACK EAST: OCTOBER AGAIN: A STRIKE IN LAWRENCE, MASS.

THE WAGE-CUTS have begun with the winter; and the streets of Lawrence this October are as bleak as those of Newark were last October when Dwight Morrow was running for senator.

Since then, Mr. Morrow has gone to the Senate and voted against government control of Muscle Shoals, against fighting the dismissal from the Power Commission of the commissioners opposed to the power trust, against relief for unemployed and drought sufferers, and in favor of granting the War Department appropriation for military training in schools and colleges. Mr. Morrow has just died in his sleep of cerebral hemorrhage, perhaps as a result of the effort to reconcile his belief in individual initiative and non-interference by government in business with the present condition of the country. Dwight Morrow was an honest, public-spirited and serious-minded man. He must have worried a good deal about the depression, and anything that worried him obsessed him: that was the cause of his legendary absent-mindedness. His allegiance to his chief, the President, must have set up an extreme strain; and it may well have been this strain which killed him. At the time when the Power Commission question was being debated in the Senate, he is said to have admitted privately that his sympathies were on the opposite side from his vote, and he is known to have congratulated Senator Borah on an eloquent speech in favor of the drought relief he was denying.

And since last winter the liberal newspaper that had been supporting Dwight Morrow, the only liberal newspaper in

New York, has discontinued publication; a lay-off at the big Ford plant has been the occasion for rioting and breaking of machinery; and the West Virginia miners have been out on strike and have been starved back again, the operators refusing to meet the union and evicting so many families that there is now quite a large miners' colony sheltering in tents along the road, living on black coffee and pinto beans and watching their children die of typhus and malnutrition.

————

It is drizzling and dark at six in the morning: the sad New England dawn. The motors have to keep their lights on; the faded yellow of trees that one glimpses along the side streets is the only kind of color that tints the gray. The gray houses, their fronts bulging out in two stories of longish bay-windows, with white curtains looped up on opposite sides, look like long-jawed cross-eyed skulls.

From the grayness, the still half-sleepy street, breaks a gruesome booing and groaning. A vague crowd about the doors of the Arlington Mill. This mill, with its square knobbed turrets, stands silent and dark like a fortress. But occasionally a man goes in: he threads his way between the strikers very quickly, pretending not to notice them. They howl, but he goes through the door: the police are there to see that they do not stop him. Then the pickets—dismal, persistent—go on parading in an endless belt.

Some of them have been out since three. A few are wearing raincoats; a few raise umbrellas. There is a fresh-faced, cheeky, pretty, round-shouldered girl who marches in high heels. The captain of the line is hatless and has his collar around his ears. Between booings, he leads them in song:

> *I bought a scab for half a cent—*
> *Parley-voo!*
> *I bought a scab for half a cent*
> *And the son of a gun jumped over the fence!*
> *Hinky dinky parley-voo!*

And,

> *When a scab he dies, he goes to Hell,*
> *Where the rats and skunks and weasels dwell!*

A Negro, coming to work with booze on his breath, stops at the sight of the pickets and vehemently addresses a by-stander: "Don't you think them folks is right?—I think everybody ought to be with 'em!—all the workin' people in the United States ought to be with 'em!" He works now in a private home, but he used to work in the mills. The police make the bystanders move on.

Behind this early morning picket-line is gathered the whole force of the Lawrence strike—23,000 people who have quit work. And on the outcome of the Lawrence strike depends to some extent, unquestionably, the fate of all the textile workers this winter.

The spring, for the workers in the mills, is a relatively cheerful season. Life is easier, and they have more self-confidence. If a wage-cut were declared in the spring, they would presumably be better able to fight it. So the manufacturers wait till the edge of winter, when the cold and the dark days have just begun. The big textile companies of Lawrence waited till the beginning of October and announced a general wage-cut of 10 per cent, and now the other companies are watching to see whether they are going to be able to get away with it. Both the woolen mills and the print works at Lawrence are the biggest in the world.

Now, the textile business, as industries go nowadays, is apparently pretty well off. According to the Borsodi Analytical Bureau, the index of textile production during July "marked a new high in the present recovery." It is true that neither the Pacific Mills nor the American Woolen Company has paid any dividends for several years; but that they are both in sound financial condition is shown by the fact that the ratio of the current assets of the latter to its current liabilities is about ten to one, that of the former about twenty to one. The woolen and worsted industry seems this autumn to have taken a definite upturn.

So the workers in Lawrence have decided to fight, cold

weather or no cold weather. They have a long tradition of successful strikes—a tradition going back to 1912. The difficulties that formerly existed of organizing all together the groups of different races—Anglo-Saxons, French Canadians, Italians, Russians and Poles—have with time largely disappeared. The new English-speaking generation has been brought up in the strike tradition. And it is said that all you need in Lawrence in order to bring the workers out is a picket-line around a mill. Fifteen thousand of the strikers turned out at a recent demonstration—one of the largest ever held in this country. So organized labor in general is watching the result of this wage-cut.

The textile workers, it seems, are the worst paid industrial group in the country. In 1929, the average cost of living for a family of from three to five was $1,594.95 a year, but the average earnings of a textile worker were $1,013, and this had declined during the "prosperity" era, when, except in the case of the leather workers, the earnings of the other groups had been increasing.

In Lawrence, before this wage-cut—which deprives them of 10 per cent—about 80 per cent of the mill workers got less than $20 a week. The rent for a family tenement, unfurnished, with "nothing but the bare walls," seems to average about $6—which the workers in Lawrence are particularly unfortunate in being obliged to pay weekly. The poverty of their homes is wretched. The women often make all the clothes and do all the housework and cooking, including baking the bread. They never get a chance to leave the house. The children who are old enough for school often cannot go for lack of shoes. If each child has a pair of his own—usually handed down from the next oldest one—the parents consider themselves lucky. Some of the families buy stale bread in bags. Some try to count on steak once a week and look forward to a chicken for New Year's; some are surprised if you ask them about meat, they get it so very seldom. They borrow money on their furniture and on the Morris Plan, and then when the payment comes due, they cannot pay their other bills. They try to hang on to a family ornament or two —a big crucifix or a statue of the Three Graces. The children go to work as soon as they are old enough, if they are able to find any work.

The standard of living of the Lawrence workers had been reduced since 1929 even before the recent wage-cut—which in fact was only the climax of a long process of stretching out work and shaving down pay. You can find men in some of the mills who had been working 60 hours a week for about $22. The looms had been speeded up till they were getting smashed right and left—the management had figured that the saving effected through the tax on the weavers' nerves more than compensated for the cost of the breakages. The rates for piecework had gradually been lowered by a series of petty deductions, which is said to have been initiated by the Washington Mills, when it abandoned extra payment for certain complications in fancy weaving. It is curious to listen to the loom-fixers explaining the devices for accomplishing this. Petty, intricate and technical to a layman, they are the relentless campaign—"pick" by "pick," cent by cent—of the men and women who own the mills against the men and women who keep them running. The power behind those square miles of great brick blocks that rise above the houses on every side and bar the city from the outside world, like some overgrowth of fortification, is driving, little by little, the people inside the city to their last bag of stale bread, to their last heelless pair of shoes—to their last fresh flicker of strength when the coffee and the morning sun are still able to reanimate their faith in life. You forget that the people who run the mills have authentic faces, too—from here you cannot see their faces any more than they can see the faces here. In spite of weak and ailing children, in spite of foolish broken-spirited men and slatternly-looking stringy-haired women, you find here, on the wrong side of the social wall, much strong and rich human material: handsome well-formed Portuguese girls, who look worried; pretty and plump French-Canadian women with civilized black eyes, who don't know now how they are going to take care of all the children their beauty has brought them; German and Polish men, self-confident, accurate and energetic, who know as much about the factories as their masters.

The strike has been on a month. The strikers are still picketing the mills, and the companies have sprung a whole repertoire of tricks to discourage them or to scare them back.

One day it is announced in the newspapers that the American Woolen Company is moving its machinery to Utica— several truckloads have already left town. But the story gets round among the strikers that the looms that have been taken away are old ones which have been superseded by new. The next day the papers shout in headlines that a neighboring mill at North Andover is permanently suspending work: "The first industrial casualty growing out of the Greater Lawrence textile strike," etc. The truth of this is that the North Andover workers have walked out, too.

This is followed by more drastic methods. "Red Mike" Shulman, a young Socialist organizer, who has come in from the outside and been one of the most spirited of the strike leaders, is kidnapped on his way back from a picket-line. Red Mike had been picketing the Shawsheen Mills, where the workers had not come out with the same alacrity as elsewhere.

The owner of the Shawsheen Mills, William M. Wood (a Portuguese, born Silva), of the American Woolen Company, felt compunction after the 1925 strike and used a million and a half of a surplus of something like six million to build a model village for his employees. His son had shared his sympathies and had been in charge of the welfare department; but the younger Wood had died, and the heart had gone out of the project. The model village was never completed; Mr. Wood committed suicide in Florida.

Yet since the beginning of the strike, a number of the inhabitants of the village, still trusting to the benevolence of the management, have continued to work at the mill, and even those who have struck have been reluctant to picket. The strike leaders have had to call a special meeting to haul the Shawsheen workers over the coals. Red Mike, who leads their picket-line, has tried to ignite them with some of his fire: if you won't picket, he told them, it means only one of two things—either you're too damn lazy or you're afraid! Are they scared of not getting their jobs back because they've been seen in the picket-line?

The next day Red Mike disappears: a strange car picks him up as he is leaving the line to go back to the evening meeting, and he isn't seen again. During the meeting, some-one outside throws a large paving-stone through the window. The owner of the car is identified as one of the Shawsheen mill guards. A gang of strikers go round to his house, de-mand Red Mike, get arrested, are immediately haled into court and each sentenced to a year or so in jail. Some anony-mous person calls up the head organizer and threatens to blow his brains out. Red Mike turns up the next day: he had been slugged and shut up in a shack. The picketing is fiercer than ever: Red Mike leads the Lawrence strikers over to picket the Andover mill. The girls at a mill in Maynard refuse to work on material which they know has been sent from Lawrence because it "looks scabby" to them, and the company closes down the mill.

The Lawrence Citizens' Committee announces that it will conduct a secret ballot enabling the workers to vote on whether or not they are willing to come back. The next night a huge crowd of strikers join the pickets at the Arlington Mill, filling the streets for four blocks. They have learned that two hundred people—mainly the office staff—have now gone back to work, and when they come out, the crowd starts to mob them. The police make a flying wedge and rescue them—they arrest eleven strikers. More riots and more arrests. Mrs. Glendower Evans comes up from Boston, goes to the strike meeting at the Labor Temple and tells the strik-ers that, although she owns stock in the mills, she wants them to win out. She donates $100. She is accompanied by some champions of free speech.

The companies, in spite of their sob-stories about their desperate financial condition, refuse to open their books to any investigating committee whatever.

There are three different unions involved in the Lawrence strikes. When the combers in the Pacific Mills struck last March—against the plan of the efficiency experts to make two combers take care of eight frames instead of each man's hav-ing two—the Communists came in and organized the Pacific.

But by the time the strike was over, the Pacific workers were leery of the Communists. When the organizers, in their speeches, would begin attacking the government, the audience would protest; and the Pacific workers knew that the employers would not deal with known Communists. They dissociated themselves, then, from the Communists and organized their own union, which controlled the Pacific Mills and had a considerable membership in the others: the American Textile Workers. They seem amazed and shocked at the Communists. Their own point of view is simply that they want certain grievances removed and a decent standard of living assured, whereas the Communists, they say, "thrive on" agitation, hurl themselves into the hands of the law with an impulse which seems to the mill workers as mysterious as that which impels the lemmings to throw themselves into the sea. The Communists now collaborate in picketing with the members of the other unions; but the captains of the picket-lines complain that the former jeer at them as "labor fakers" and deliberately confuse their maneuvers by swinging the line in the wrong direction.

When the present strike was started, however, the AF of L appeared. Its organizers here are the usual type, resounding professional orators, each with his platform personality, each with his bag of tricks. They are suspect to the rank and file, who have concluded from past experience that, drawing regular salaries as the AF of L officials do, getting a commission as they are supposed to do on every member signed up for the union and sending 85 cents on every dollar to the AF of L headquarters in Washington, these AF of L representatives, though prompt to arrive on the scene, have no particular interest in winning strikes.

The AF of L has, however, succeeded in signing up some 7,000 members in their United Textile Workers' Union. (The American Textile Workers have from 4 to 5,000 members; the Communists claim 1,000.) The AF of L organizers are thus the official heads of the strike. But they are assisted by Red Mike, a Socialist, and by Sam Bakely, a product of Brookwood.

Red Mike and Sam Bakely both are young and poor and

deeply in earnest—they share a room, live on nothing at all and work themselves thin and blue. Red Mike makes a point of talking tough, but quotes Anatole France to the strikers. His passionate speeches have a quite different ring from the eloquence of the AF of L men. Sam Bakely is from Philadelphia—as a kid, he worked on a newspaper, then he was a pocketbook worker at a time when there was a pocketbook workers' strike. He went to Philadelphia Labor College, then Brookwood. He was happy at Brookwood, he says—if you want to see what life would be like under socialism, he believes you can see at Brookwood. He admired Muste tremendously, and when just after he had finished his course, the Lawrence strike broke out, he was crazy to go up there. He had a special feeling about Lawrence because Muste had won his first fight there. So he scraped together $15 and came.

The AF of L people may not make any important decisions without the consent of the new local union, the American Textile Workers. These latter are the most interesting element in the strike. Like the West Virginia Miners' Union, they are an example of the kind of independent group made inevitable by the deterioration of the American Federation of Labor. They stand, as they say themselves, between the AF of L and the Communists—disinterested and determined as the AF of L is not but not aiming at the destruction of capitalism.

It is worth while, in this connection, to tell the story of the plan for employee representation initiated by the management of the Pacific Mills after the 1925 strike.

This scheme provided for a shop committee made up of representatives of all the departments of the company's four mills; for a plant committee consisting of a representative from each of the mills and of four representatives of the employers; and for a board of arbitration to be composed of one representative of the employers, one of the employees and a neutral party to be agreed on by both. The Pacific at that time advertized widely its spirit of coöperation and fairness, and went on the air with speeches that strongly endorsed the Golden Rule.

The plan worked all right for small matters: a personal grievance, for example, or the application of a worker who had invented some technical improvement to be compensated for the money he had saved. But the machinery broke down last May when the girls in the curtain department went on strike against a wage-cut of 25 per cent. Any intention of cutting wages, according to the above agreement, was to have been announced first to the shop committee. But the committee had been ignored. It met now, however, and demanded that the plant committee meet. The employers then announced that they would abolish the curtain department and give the girls jobs in other departments. But the next thing the employees knew, the curtain department had been moved to a mill belonging to a different company in the comparatively remote town of Malden, where the management of the Pacific Mills was continuing to operate it at the reduced wages.

Then the general wage-cut of 10 per cent was suddenly decreed by the company, also without notice to the shop committee. They protested. Mr. Southworth, the company's agent, told them that he had no authority to make recommendations or promises. They insisted on talking to someone who had and got the treasurer to come to Lawrence. The treasurer gave them no satisfaction: he told them that if they had been cut 25 instead of 10 per cent, they would still be better off than the other textile workers. But the Pacific people knew better: they had learned that they were less well paid than the textile workers in Rhode Island or New Hampshire.

They insisted on a meeting of the plant committee. The four representatives of the employers came; Mr. Southworth was the principal spokesman. The employees had rather liked Mr. Southworth: he was young, quiet, good-natured, well-mannered, had been to Amherst, seemed to them a gentleman. The union leaders were the pick of the personnel—young men with sound minds and strong wills: some of them spectacled like students, avid for technical education, taking night-school courses after hours; others with intent direct eyes, and, though wearing the pallor of the mills, hard-cast

and positive-acting like the machines among which they
lived.

The committee put it up to Mr. Southworth about employee representation and the board of arbitration which was
supposed to have been intended for just such situations as
this. The employers said how could they be sure that even
if the board were set up, the employees would accept its
decision? The employees replied to this that they were taking
the same chance on them. The employers suggested a board
of which one man should represent the employers and one
the employees, and a third should be chosen by the employers
from among the employees. The employees protested that this
had not been the idea.

Mr. Southworth cut the discussion short. He gave them
shortly but definitely to understand that the wage-cut was
going through: "Gentlemen," he concluded, "I move that the
meeting be adjourned." And he abruptly left the room. They
were speechless. The conference had lasted only about five
minutes.

It had been all the union leaders were able to do to keep
the workers inside the mill that morning. But even after the
conference at noon, they wanted them to stay on the rest of
the day. They were afraid some of the radicals would break
machinery, and they wanted to announce the strike overnight. But when the workers heard about the conference,
it was impossible to hold them in any longer: they all got
up and walked out.

MR. AND MRS. X

MR. SOUTHWORTH, whom the union leaders had always liked, left the room and left them blank.

It is not hard to imagine Mr. Southworth—let us call him Mr. X, since the following picture is purely imaginary: I want merely to describe a type. You can see him as one of those decent, pleasant, well-pressed and well-barbered people who may be seen around country clubs. He represents "the better element." Though his satisfactions are more bound up than he realizes with things that money can buy him, he never spends money ostentatiously; and he has a conscience about civic affairs, giving to charitable causes and being opposed to political corruption, especially as practised by low politicians who have never been to Amherst. His wife feels this even more strongly; she was opposed to Al Smith in the White House on the ground of his dreadful commonness. She dresses extremely well, and she usually notices in a Pullman that she is the only really smart woman there. Mr. X plays a pretty good game of something—probably tennis or golf. He may collect first editions or etchings. He gets his liquor from the same high-class bootlegger who serves the *very* rich, but he never drinks to excess.

Yet Mr. X's conviction of his intrinsic importance has very little basis in fact. He is as helpless, he occupies just as cramped a position between the upper and nether millstones of society, as the old West Virginia detective who, as superintendent at Ward, has to shortweight the miners at the tipple, or as "Hurry Up" Crowe at Boulder Dam. Mr. X had to explain to the shop committee when they came to protest the wage-cut that he could make "no promises or recommendations." And because he has no real authority, the culture and the distinction of Mr. and Mrs. X, all that Mr. and Mrs. X regard as the foundation of their social position, have no solid or durable value. Such pretensions can only be valid in the case of a real governing class. And Mr. X does not govern. He gets his orders from officials higher up, and these may very well get their orders from the bankers from whom they borrow. Yet neither bankers nor higher officials constitute a governing class: they are all merely people of various origins, various ideals and capacities, who come and go in lucrative positions. The system they belong to governs, but they are only individuals on the make. They take no collective responsibility, and their power is not hereditary; they have none of the special training which permanent position requires and which may dignify a well-established owning class.

Yet Mr. and Mrs. X are firmly convinced of their superiority. Let us see what this superiority consists of. If Mr. X is descended from some family who have already been property-holders for a generation or two during the simpler days of the Republic, he will attach himself to the memory of family habits as if they were in fact the characteristics of such an established class—a higher civilization from whose standards the present is a lamentable lapse. If, say, Mr. X is a Southerner, he will like to talk about the Civil War, will cherish family photographs of the Civil War generation, will dream of retiring from industry and going to live in the country, where he will be able to keep hunting dogs and perhaps a stable. If a Bostonian, he may still live in a family house, square and solid but rather bleak and Spartan, in the taste of his fathers who built it, and decorated with copies of paintings and old brown photographs of Italy brought back from abroad by his mother. If a New Yorker or a Philadelphian, the glamor of his ancestral memories will gleam from an expensive social life, polo and yachting, champagne and brandy, and historical research or civic reform. If Mr. X, on the other hand, is a Middle Westerner, he will have the pride of affluence hard-won, of virtue and distinction maintained amidst the deprivations of the wilderness. If Mr. X is a Californian, he will look back to the days when food and drink were so plentiful and cheap out there, when people were so hearty and gay, when life was so easy, so free. In any case, he will respect his college as the stronghold of good-fellowship and learning, guard his club as the temple of manners and honor, and in his business and domestic relations he will scrupulously observe the old-fashioned rules of integrity among equals.

This is Mr. X's morality, and in this way he manages to live, for a part of the time at least, in a world which does not really exist, which has never except briefly and locally existed. The actual conditions of Mr. X's life are being determined by quite other public standards, which have been crowding or modifying his private ones more and more every day. For the society that Mr. X lives in is not a society of planters or ranchers or pioneers, nor of gentlemanly bankers and businessmen who have built up their own houses: it is an enormous machine for money-making which has long ago rendered impossible the advantages once enjoyed by communities that were simpler and had more independence. In America, in the period that followed the war, our life had become a stampede to produce and sell all sorts of commodities —the question was not whether people really needed or wanted these things but whether by any means they could be induced to buy them. Hence American advertizing—one of the most fantastic features of capitalist society. Advertizing, as we have it in the United States, is a sheer waste of money and brains; but if you allow competitive business for private profit, you have to have a whole corps of poets, artists, preachers, blackmailers and flatterers to compete in selling its wares. It is a formidable undertaking to persuade people to invest at high prices in valueless breakfast foods and toothpastes; in cosmetics that poison the face, lubricants that corrode your car, insecticides that kill your trees; in health-builders made of cheese, fat-reducers containing cascara, coffee made of dried peas, gelatine made of glue, olive oil made of cottonseed, straw hats composed of wood shavings, sterling silver that is lead and cement, woolen blankets, silk stockings and linen sheets all actually woven of cotton, sealskin coats that are really muskrat, mink and sable that are really woodchuck, mahogany furniture of gumwood that will splinter into bits under use; in foods that do not nourish, disinfectants that do not disinfect, shock-absorbers that cause you to ride more roughly and gas-logs for the fireplace that asphyxiate—all articles which have lately been put over with more or less success. Even when the article offered is of genuinely good quality and what it pretends to be, it has to have its ballyhoo, also, to outshout or underinsinuate other products in the same field. And the result of all this publicity is that the Americans have come at last to accept an ideal of success based solely on the possession of things: cars, clothes, toilet accessories, electrical appliances; and a conception of patriotism that glorifies the United States as an inexhaustible market.

And Mr. and Mrs. X, though they may treat this advertizing with a certain irony, must end by being "sold" like everybody else. Mr. X's textile company, for example, will find the market glutted for ordinary sheets and towels, and it will call upon its sales department to invent some new way of stimulating a demand. The sales department will propose making colored sheets and towels to harmonize with the colors of people's rooms; and Mr. X will find himself involved in the production of green, pink, purple, yellow and blue sheets and towels, and committed to the excitation of an unnatural appetite for them through mendacious and hypnotic methods which disfigure the rural roadsides, interrupt stories in the magazines and razzle-dazzle people with jumpy signs on the streets. If Mr. X wants his daughters to go to dances at the country club, if he wants to send his sons to old Amherst or Harvard or Yale or Princeton, he is obliged to turn out green and purple towels. If he is the agent for a bathroom-fixture company, he will have to turn out green and purple bathtubs. If he is the agent for a paper mill, he will have to turn out green and purple toilet-paper. And he will be forced to view with complaisance the publication of absurd and repulsive advertizements threatening the reader with horrible diseases and immediate loss of social prestige unless he uses this particular product. Finally, poor Mr. X, who has begun by imposing on the simple-minded in order to obtain the means of remaining superior to them, will end by becoming simple-minded himself. He and his wife will grow more and more to resemble the men and women depicted in the advertizements, insipid, fatuously cheerful, two-dimensional, spic and span—more and more identified with smart new cars, clean shaves, exclusive face lotions, unrippable silk stockings and Louis Quatorze radio sets. They will try to own all the things that people are supposed to own; and Mr. X, in the long run, must fall victim to his own blackmail: the X's will install in their bathrooms the green and purple toilet-paper. Without being conscious of it, they will already have become partly dependent for their assurance of superiority on their patronage of this article of luxury. They will, in short, finally come to be patronized by the imperial paper itself.

But no one, of course, can do more than approximate to some degree to the ideal of two-dimensional happiness invented by the advertizements; if he is more or less serious-minded, as I have been imagining him to be, to the degree that he falls short of attaining it, Mr. X can only find his life confusing. He cannot but feel the lack of harmony between what he regards as his principles and the society of which he is part. If he has an inquiring mind, his commerce with political and social ideas must be largely confined to books. In the society Mr. X frequents, the present economic system has come to play for his generation very much the role that religion did for his grandfathers' generation: it is something that must not be discussed. Private enterprise and private profit have taken the place of the book of Genesis and the divinity of Jesus Christ—with the Soviets in the role of Darwin, Huxley, Robert Ingersoll, Renan and Strauss. The newspapers will not deal with this subject; even the philosophers try to get around it; and if, in Mr. X's circles, you bring it into a conversation, you are guilty of an act of bad taste comparable to joking about Scripture in the presence of a devout old lady. The result is that, although by the time our society has found out how to deal with its present problems, certain of Mr. X's assumptions will inevitably have been knocked sky-high, it is probable that he will still remain dim as to what has been going on. He believes himself to be free-minded and free to express what he thinks; yet he lends himself to a general conspiracy not to mention, not even to recognize, the implications of what has happened. He has tried in the past to be satisfied with making money and owning things; but now he can no longer even make money, and it is not permitted seriously to ask what is wrong.

If, however, Mr. X is gay and likes people who are sophisticated and funny, they will talk about the things they drink, play records of Cole Porter and Gershwin, laugh about the jokes in the *New Yorker* and the imbecilities in Mencken's *Americana,* go to first nights of Philip Barry and read the novels of S. S. Van Dine. They will be knowing about Lesbians and fairies; meet each other in France in the summer; furnish their apartments and houses with silver-glass tulips and chairs on bent pipes. They will suffer a good deal from unreciprocated love, will go abroad to get away or get nearer; they will spend years with unfaithful mates, and their friends will be made to know that liquor, travel and entertaining are a poor consolation for unhappiness. And they will try to find in sterile affairs which involve no responsibility, which serve only an ideal of desperate pleasure, the passion, the romance, the power which their other pursuits do not offer. The women, with good brains and strong wills, still cling to the privileges and comforts which they have been brought up as ladies to claim, and do not care to be either conventional wives or independent economic producers. The men, with their skill and their energy exploited by the capitalist enterprises out of which they can get nothing but money, have lost the force of male authority. Or—provided with an income for which they do not work and with no real relation to its source—though they may start out with certain abilities, they have not even use to keep them bright and can only try to find their way back into life through snobbery or sport or debauchery or dilettante art or collecting till, baffled by their idleness and boredom, they end up as hypochondriacs who can do nothing but nurse themselves, or as tuberculars or alcoholics.

A good many kill themselves. The suicides of workers in

these pages ought—to make the picture complete—to be supplemented by examples of the suicides of the owning class. The machine has been running down, and its momentum no longer carries us. We exhaust the excitements and the pleasures of a life which aims at nothing beyond itself, which is a part of no general human effort; and we quit out of sheer futility. Or people find themselves, at a stroke, despoiled of the small or large fortunes which they have been at great pains to acquire and which are the only things they have acquired. Brokers find their livelihood gone, and do not know now what to do with themselves. Bankers are compelled to realize that they have caused to vanish like smoke the savings of thousands of depositors, and that they are not only ruined themselves but, in the eyes of their victims, swindlers. Artists who have been unsuccessful in supplying the capitalist market or unhappy in spite of success find that they do not possess enough originality or self-confidence to put through first-rate work of their own under conditions which make not merely unremunerative but also lonely and hard the individual restating of experience of which the first-rate artist is capable. And to very well-off people the lowering of a standard of living which to people less well-off seems luxurious may appear just as catastrophic as the loss by the poor of their means of subsistence and eviction from their only shelter. An attorney for the Pennsylvania Railroad, who had formerly been a millionaire, was recently driven to suicide when he found that his income had dwindled to $25,000 a year. He could not bear to face the privation.

In the meantime, Mr. X and his associates are all repeating the same banalities. They say that we have now got to learn new uses for surplus leisure; that we have got to go back and live as our fathers lived (and presumably, if we are workers out of work, to die as our fathers died); that prices are coming down so that money buys more than it did before and that "equilibrium" (a magic word) has got to be established again through an "adjustment" (another magic word) of wages— that is, that wages have got to be cut; that American labor has been badly spoiled, that the working people in other countries have known very well how to get along by dint of hard

work and thrift, and that the American workers can very well
stand to do without their radios and cars until "business" has
a chance to "recover"; that the American Federation of Labor
—regarded as a radical organization—has got to back down
and moderate its demands; that taxation of the big industries
would cripple them, and that the burden must be distributed
more evenly; that we must leave relief to voluntary charity,
since otherwise it would be eaten up by graft; that the dole
has ruined England; that your guess is as good as mine as
to what is going to happen now. Or if they are the younger
and cleverer kind, they will talk about pulling out for a distant island or enjoying the last twenty-four hours of capitalism; or they will say that, after all, the only practical kind
of government is a monarchy; or they will even declare—
archly—that they have a red flag in the attic.

At any rate, poor Mr. X, who had supposed he was a
kindly and agreeable man coöperating with his employees,
has found out that when the machine stops running, he is
forced to play a quite different role: that of an arrogant master. Not, however, that he really understands the consequences of what he is doing. Mr. X really does not know
about the hunger and cold and fatigue and hopelessness of
Lawrence this October; he does not know about the hatred
and suspicion and fear that the efficiency experts and the
company's spies bring into the lives of the workers; he does
not know that Lawrence just now is a festering disgrace to
humanity—with decent people turned into outlaws and sent
to jail for demanding a living, and with other people essentially no different set on to beat them up, to take their jobs
away from them, to kidnap their leaders and break up their
meetings. Mr. X does not really see this, let alone see the
part that he plays in it. So he and the union leaders do not
yet confront each other like Foster and Fish—the champions
of two hostile classes.

But in the meantime the strike goes from bad to worse.
Two days after the Arlington riot, Sam Bakely holds a meeting on the Common, sets out to lead a mob of 15,000 strikers
in a march on the Monomac Mills, where several hundred

have gone back to work. A line of police halts them, and a police captain reads them the riot act—the strikers refuse to disperse. The police then charge them with clubs—people trampled on, strikers arrested. Sam Bakely is arrested, too. But Sam Bakely has Muste for a hero and the morality of socialism for a guide—he is neither surprised nor saddened to find he has landed in jail; while the amiable Mr. X, who does not have any leader or any morality based on anything real, is probably not a little dismayed to find himself behind the policemen's clubs.

In any case, the strike is broken, and even after the other mills have reopened, the Pacific—in punishment for their insolence—makes a point of keeping its workers locked out.

A MAN IN THE STREET

HE IS A TALL MAN with square shoulders—looks able-bodied and self-dependent. A pure Nordic type, he has straight brows and a long straight nose. But his color is pale, he seems soiled, as if his quarters and his food were poor; and though his face is not demoralized, he has a curious dazed expression, as if he were not really a part of the world in which he is walking, as if his life had come under a shadow from which he can see no way of escaping and for which he has no means of accounting. His overcoat is dark brown, old; his flat-topped straight-brimmed hat is too small for him. You cannot tell whether he is a skilled mechanic or a former auto-dealer or a department-store manager or a bank cashier—he might even have been a provincial lawyer. But he wanders along West Fifty-eighth Street—out of place there, but where is his place?—past the restaurants with smart French names and the big apartment houses, half-empty, where the liveried doormen stand.

III
DAWN OF THE
NEW DEAL

1932–1934

ELECTION NIGHT

As you enter the little restaurant, you hear a loud and distinct voice making what sounds like a public speech. It is a middle-aged man, all alone in the room, sitting on one side of a long table.

"Swine! scavengers!" he declares. "Walker or O'Brien—O'Brien or Walker! Turn the bums out—put more bums in! Who cares? It's just too bad! The woman ahead of me in the polling booth wanted to write McKee's name in on the ballot, and the cop tried to interfere—told her to get out, she'd been in the booth long enough. And then he tried to do the same thing to me! They're scavengers!—swine!"

His skin is absolutely sallow, unflushed by any animal warmth; his face, with that salient Anglo-Saxon nose which marks a positive mind, shows a certain cultivation and dignity; but his eyes are blind and dead, as if the spirit had departed from behind them. Hunched down in his chair, his chin on his chest, he talks straight ahead at the wall, as diners and drinkers come and go, pick up the cues of his rhetorical questions and feed him a little while, then get bored and withdraw their attention. As he talks, he repeatedly strikes his forehead with the palm of a stiffened hand, whose fingers stick out and bend back like the prongs of a dying starfish.

"Hoover or Roosevelt—who cares? There's no difference, is there? Of course not! I've just spent six years in the Argentine, and I come back, and this is what I find! We're at the mercy of these scavengers, aren't we? Of course we are! And what are we going to do about it? Elect Roosevelt! Reëlect Hoover! The only good thing Andy Mellon ever did was make Old Overholt whisky! Turn the bums out—put more bums in! It's just too bad!"

"You say you've been in the Argentine?"

"Si, signor!" he replies to prove it.

"How are things down there?"

"Terrible! The first day I arrived there, the papers were all full of those two scavengers Sacco and Vanzetti. They were all over the front page, and everybody was asking me about it. I told them that people in the States didn't pay any attention to it—at home it would have had just a couple of sticks somewhere on an inside page. The streetcar motormen went on strike on account of Sacco and Vanzetti, and if you wanted to get any place, you had to walk!"

"You think Sacco and Vanzetti were guilty, do you?"

"Of course they were guilty!—they were Sicilians—fiends! And these scavengers kept them six years before they executed them! They had all the evidence in the world!—they found the cap that one of them wore! They were Sicilians—scavengers—swine!"

From time to time, with much bitterness, he complains that he has been abandoned by the lady who came there with him. "In the kitchen!" he announces. "Always in the kitchen! Give 'em a kitchen, and they're perfectly happy! And that's the right place for 'em—that's where they belong! Give 'em a kitchen and they're happy!"

But, as a matter of fact, the girl-friend is not in the kitchen at all. She has gone into a little back room, where she and another woman are swigging down brandy and soda, absorbed in their own conversation.

November, 1932

HULL–HOUSE IN 1932

THE LANDSCAPE has turned gray: the snow-fields gray like newspaper, the sky gray like pasteboard—then darkness; just a crack of gray, distinct as a break in a boiler, that separates darkening clouds—a black fortress with one smokestack: the Northern Indiana Public Utility Company—darkness, with light at long intervals—a sudden street with lighted stores and streetcars—then the darkness again: dim front of a frame house, dim signboards—a red electric globe on a barber's pole —bridges in the blackness, a shore?—black factories—long streets, with rows of lights that stretch away into darkness— a large blunt tower embroidered in coarse beadwork of red, green and gold lights—then the endless succession of cars speeding along the dark lake-front, with the lights at shorter intervals now—then a thing like a red-hot electric toaster as big as an office building, which turns out to be one of the features of next summer's World Fair.

But mostly black midland darkness. Chicago is one of the darkest of great cities. In the morning, the winter sun does not seem to give any light: it leaves the streets dull. It is more like a forge which has just been started up, with its fires just burning red, in an atmosphere darkened by coal-fumes. All the world seems made of gray fog—gray fog and white smoke—the great square white-and-gray buildings seem to have been pressed out of the saturated atmosphere. The smooth asphalt of the lake-side road seems solidified polished smoke. The lake itself, in the dawn, is of a strange stagnant substance like pearl that is becoming faintly liquid and luminous—opaque like everything else but more sensitive than asphalt or stone. The Merchandise Mart—the *biggest* building in the world, as the Empire State Building is the *highest*

—is no tower, in the fog, but a mountain, to brood upon whose cubic content is to be amazed, desolated, stunned. The Chicago River, dull green, itself a work of engineering, runs backward along its original course, buckled with black iron bridges, which unclose, one after the other, each in two short fragments, as a tug drags car-barges under them, like the peristaltic movement of the stomach pushing a tough piece of food along. The sun for a time half-reveals these scenes, but its energies are only brief. The afternoon has scarcely established itself as an identifiable phenomenon when light succumbs to dullness, and the day lapses back into dark. The buildings seem mounds of soft darkness caked and carved out of swamp-mud and rubber-stamped here and there with red neon signs. A good many of the streets, one finds, aside from the thoroughfares, are dimly lighted or not at all; and even those that are adequately lighted lose themselves in blurred vistas of coal-smoke.

————

In that dull air, among those long low straight streets—the deadened civilization of industry, where people are kept just alive enough to see that the machines are running—the almost neutral brick walls of Hull-House have themselves an industrial plainness. The old big square high-windowed mansion of earlier family grandeur, embedded in the dormitories, eating halls, gymnasiums, nurseries and laundries that today pack a city block, has been chastened as well as expanded: it has something of both the monastery and the factory. The high Victorian rooms that open into one another through enormous arched and corniced doorways, though they still contain mahogany tables, sofas and faded Turkish rugs, are in general scantily and serviceably furnished. The white woodwork and the marble fireplace have been painted a sort of neutral drab green, so that the use of the house may not soil them. In the little polygon room, in which one imagines hanging pots of ferns and a comfortable window-seat, one sees a typewriter and a set of colored charts showing the shift of nationalities around Hull-House. Yet one finds also

traces of a cult of art: copies of paintings and statues, a frag-
ment of a Greek frieze. Behind the glass doors of bookcases
are nineteenth-century sets of Ruskin and Augustus Hare's
Walks in Rome. The hallway is lined with photographs of
residents and friends of the house; and on the walls of the
polygon room hang the patron saints and heroes of Hull-
House: Kropotkin and Catherine Breshkovsky, Arnold Toyn-
bee and Jacob Riis—and Jane Addams's father. Over the desk
by the front door is a picture of Jane Addams herself, in a
big-sleeved and high-collared gown of the nineties, a young
woman, slender and winning and almost like an illustration
for some old serial by William Dean Howells or Mrs. Burton
Harrison in the *Century Magazine*.

A little girl with curvature of the spine, whose mother
had died when she was a baby, she abjectly admired her
father, a man of consequence in frontier Illinois, a friend of
Lincoln and a member of the state legislature, who had a flour
mill and a lumber mill on his place. Whenever there were
strangers at Sunday school, she would try to walk out with
her uncle so that her father should not be disgraced by people's knowing that such a fine man had a daughter with a
crooked spine. When he took her one day to a mill which
was surrounded by horrid little houses and explained to her,
in answer to her questions, that the reason people lived in
such houses was that they couldn't afford anything better,
she told her father that, when she grew up, she should herself continue to live in a big house but that it should stand
among the houses of poor people.
    At college, in the late seventies, she belonged to a group
of girls who vowed before they parted for their summer vacation that each would have read the whole of Gibbon before
they met again in the fall. In a Greek oration she delivered,
Bellerophon figured as the Idealism which alone could slay
the Chimera of Social Evils; and for her graduation essay she
chose Cassandra, doomed "always to be in the right and always disbelieved and rejected." She heard rumors of the doc-
trines of Darwin and borrowed scientific books from a
brother-in-law who had studied medicine in Germany; and

she resisted with invincible stubbornness the pressure brought to bear by her teachers to make her go into the missionary field. The year that she graduated from college, she inherited a part of her father's estate and gave the college a thousand dollars to spend on a scientific library.

She herself went to medical school; but her spinal trouble got worse, and she had to stop. She spent six months strapped to a bed. This gave her a lot of time for reading, with no uncomfortable feeling that she ought to be doing something else, and she was very glad to have it; but when she was able to get about again, she felt dreadfully fatigued and depressed. She tried Europe; but one day, in London, she went out for a bus-ride in the East End. As she looked down on the misery and squalor, she remembered De Quincey's *Vision of Sudden Death:* how, when confronted with a pair of lovers about to be run over by the mail coach in which he was traveling, he had found himself powerless to warn them till he had remembered the exact lines in the *Iliad* which describe the shout of Achilles; and she was suddenly filled with disgust for the artificial middle-class culture upon which she had been trying to nourish herself and which had equipped her to meet this horror with nothing but a literary allusion, and that derived from an opium-eater as far removed from life as herself.

What was the good of enjoying German operas and the pictures in Italian galleries? In the interval between two trips to Europe, she visited a Western farm on which she held a mortgage—it was one of the American investments which made her traveling possible. She found there a woman and her children almost starved by the drought and attempting to raise money on a promissory note for which she could offer as collateral nothing but a penful of pigs. The pigs were starved, too, and horrible: one was being eaten by the others, all hunched up and crowded together.

She gave the mortgages up and went back to Europe again, and there she saw some striking match-girls suffering from phossy jaw. She decided to return to Chicago and to found a settlement house—there had never yet been one in America. The "subjective necessity" for settlement work she analyzes as follows: "first, the desire to interpret democracy in social terms; secondly, the impulse beating at the very source of our lives, urging us to aid in the race progress; and thirdly, the Christian movement toward humanitarianism." But she did not exclude "the desire for a new form of social success due to the nicety of imagination, which refuses worldly pleasures unmixed with the joys of self-sacrifice" and "a love of approbation so vast that it is not content with the treble clapping of delicate hands, but wishes also to hear the bass notes from toughened palms." Her father had impressed upon her early that scrupulous mental integrity, the unwillingness to make pretenses which one knew inside one did not live up to, was practically the whole of morality.

In South Halsted Street in Chicago, where there were Italians, Germans, Russians and Jews, she tried to help relieve their difficulties; to teach English to those who had immigrated as well as to give the young generation some idea of the European tradition from which they had been cut off. But this led to looking into their living conditions; and the problems of their living conditions led to the industrial system. When it was a question of children of four spending their whole day indoors pulling out basting threads or pasting labels on boxes, she found that she felt it her duty to get some labor legislation put through. She got one of the Hull-House residents appointed factory inspector.

At the time of the Pullman strike in 1894, Miss Addams was surprised and dismayed to find Chicago split up into two fiercely antagonistic camps. She had known Mr. Pullman and had been impressed by the excellence of his intentions in building a model town for his employees. She tried to maintain relations with both camps; but by the time the strike was over, it turned out that she and Pullman were on different sides of the fence, and that he was highly indignant with her. The Socialists and other radicals tried to convince her that she ought to be one of them; but, though she carefully looked up socialism, she resisted them as she had the teachers who had tried to make her be a missionary. She could not bind herself to parties and principles: what she did had to be done independently, on a basis of day-by-day experience. And she had still so vivid an impression of the classless democracy of the Western frontier that it was difficult for her to imagine a general class conflict in the United States.

Yet the winter after the World's Fair Chicago was full of people left stranded with no employment; and she was assailed by a new sense of shame at being comfortable in the midst of misery. The activities carried on at Hull-House now began to seem to her futile; its philanthropy a specious way of reconciling one's own conscience to the social injustice from which one profited. She remembered that the effect on Tolstoy of a similar period of suffering in Moscow had been to make him degrade his own standard of living to that of the poor themselves. She was again incapacitated by a serious illness, but got well and decided to travel to Russia and discuss the problem with Tolstoy himself.

Miss Addams found the great moralist working in the hayfields with the peasants and eating their black bread and porridge, while the Countess with her children and their governess had a regular upper-class dinner. He pulled out one of Miss Addams' big sleeves and said that there was enough material in it to make a frock for a little girl; and he asked whether she did not find "such a dress" a "barrier to the people." She tried to explain that, since big sleeves were the fashion, the working girls in Chicago were wearing even bigger ones than hers, and that you could hardly dress like a peasant on South Halsted Street, since the peasants there wore middle-class clothes. But she was abashed when he asked her who "fed" her and how she got her "shelter," and she had to confess that her income was derived from a large farm a hundred miles away from Chicago. "So you are an absentee landlord?" he said scathingly. "Do you think you will help the people more by adding yourself to the crowded city than you would by tilling your own soil?"

She went away feeling humbled, and, before she arrived at Bayreuth and could allow herself to enjoy the *Ring*, she resolved that when she got back to Hull House, she would spend two hours every day in the bakery. Yet as soon as she was actually at home again and found the piles of correspondence and the people waiting to see her, she decided that this and not baking was the proper work of her life, and she forgot her Tolstoyan scruples.

Her efforts for labor legislation embittered the manufacturers against her; her attempts to get garbage and dead animals that had been left in the street removed embroiled her with the political machine: garbage-collecting was a racket, and the rackets seemed to go right on up. She was astonished to find that her opposition to reëlecting a corrupt alderman roused both pulpit and press against her. When Czolgosz assassinated McKinley, the editor of an anarchist paper was arrested and held incommunicado, not allowed to see even a lawyer. She protested, with the result that Hull House was denounced as a hotbed of anarchy. When the agents of the Tsar succeeded in making Gorky a pariah in America by circulating the news that he and his companion were not properly married, she asked a Chicago paper to print an article in his defense and found that she was at once accused of being an immoral woman herself by interests that wanted to get her off the school board.

At last, when, in 1900, she saw the Passion Play at Oberammergau, it struck her for the first time that the real enemy of Jesus was the money power. The young agitator had antagonized the merchants by interfering with their trade in the temple, and hence the Pharisees, whose racket depended on the temple, too. Church and State had stood solid with the Pharisees; and the money power had bribed Judas to betray him.

When she advocated peace at the time of the war, she found that President Wilson bowed her out and that she was presently being trailed by detectives. And then, when the war was over, people were more intolerant than ever.

Hull-House had always stood for tolerance: all the parties and all the faiths had found asylum there and lived pretty harmoniously together. And it still stands planted with a proud irrelevance in the midst of those long dark streets—where its residents occasionally get beaten and robbed—only a few blocks from a corner made famous by a succession of gang murders. With its strong walls, its enclosed staircased courts, and a power plant of its own, it stands like a medieval château protected by a moat and portcullis.

Inside it there is peace and a sort of sanctity. Jane Addams at seventy-two still dominates her big house among the little ones—though she is supposed to have been forbidden by the doctors to spend more than four hours a day there—with her singular combination of the authority of a great lady and the humility of a saint. In the large refectory-like dining room with its copper and brass and bare brick, the quick glances of the "seeing eye" which fascinated young women in the nineties and excited them to go in for settlement work—that glance at once penetrating and shy—still lights its responses around her table. Through her vitality, Hull-House still lives —the expression of both pride and humility: the pride of a moral vision which cannot accept as its habitat any one of the little worlds of social and intellectual groupings; the humility of a spirit which, seeing so far, sees beyond itself, too, and feels itself lost amid the same uncertainties, thwarted by the same cross-purposes, as all of those struggling others.

————

All around the social workers of Hull House there today stretche. a sea of misery more appalling even than that which discouraged Miss Addams in the nineties. This winter even those families who had managed to hang on by their savings and earnings have been forced to apply for relief.

A relief worker's cross-section of an industrial suburb shows the sinking of the standard of living. The people here are mostly Poles. Every pressure has been brought to bear on them to induce them to spend their money on motor-cars, radios, overstuffed furniture and other unattractive luxuries; and they are caught now between two worlds, with no way of living comfortably in either. The most urgent problem, however, is how to be sure of living at all.

In one house, a girl of seventeen is interpreter for her mother, in whom the girl's stocky figure has expanded to enormous amorphous bulk, and she changes not only her language but her expression and gestures, her personality, in passing from English to Polish. She had till lately, at $2 a week, been doing all the housework for a real-estate man; but she decided he was imposing on her and quit. She is handsome and evidently high-spirited—Americanized during the whoopee period. Her brother had had a job on the conveyer at a bookbindery; but, due to a mechanical improvement, this job no longer exists: the boy has been laid off, with no prospect of reëmployment. The girl takes us up from the downstairs kitchen, where the family mostly live, and shows you the little-used floor above, which is papered with big blue, pink and magenta blossoms and furnished with all the things that the salesmen of the boom have sold them: a victrola and wadded chairs and couches, spotted with a pattern of oranges, which nobody seems ever to have sat in. On the walls, as in all these houses, exhibited in ornate gold frames, hang Slavic saints and Madonnas, bristling with spiky gold crowns, Byzantine embroidery and Polish inscriptions.

Elsewhere an old man is dying of a tumor, with no heat in the house, on a cold day. His pale bones of arms lie crooked like bent pins; nothing is heard in the house but his gasping. His old wife, her sharp Polish nose sticking out from under a bonnet-like cap, stands beside him, as silent as a ghost. Their granddaughter, who is married and wears well-fitting American street-clothes—an American middle-class woman, but today as badly off as they are—has just been to the relief station for coal.

In another place, a family of five have three small rooms in a basement, and they have sunk below any standard: the father grinningly and glaringly drunk in the middle of the morning, the mother stunned and discouraged by her struggle against poverty and filth. They live around the stove with their small dirty children, in the close sweetish sickish smell of cooking and boiling clothes. Where they sleep on two narrow cots, the bedclothes are old twisted gray rags that have not even been smoothed out flat. They do not know very much English, and they cannot explain to the relief worker what they have done about relief and insurance; they do not understand, themselves. All they know is that they are living in that dirty hole, from which they have not yet been expelled, and where the man, with a little liquor in him, can imagine himself the shrewd and sound father of a family, with the situation well under control. In another basement, however, the young husband has carpentered and painted the big cellar room which, with a tiny bedroom, is all they have, so that it almost resembles a human dwelling. He used to work for the Fruit-Growers' Express, but has been laid off a long time. The stout blond girl to whom he is married has had to be on her feet all day and, from the strain on her heart, has just had a collapse. They do not have any children, but they keep a canary in a cage. The young wife in another household has put kewpie dolls around in an otherwise bare apartment, and has made blue curtains for the cot in which her two children sleep. She and her husband are very fond of one another and very fond of the children. They are the kind of people who do not like to ask for relief, and they have put it off as long as they could, with the result that, though goodlooking and youthful, they are now pale and thin with undernourishment.

A pink clear-eyed innocent-eyed woman, alone in an immaculately kept kitchen, all white oilcloth and green-and-white linoleum and with the latest thing in big gleaming gas-ranges, flushes at the relief worker's questions. She is going to have a baby and has applied for money to pay the midwife. The relief worker offers her a doctor but she is used to having the midwife. An elderly couple from Zürich are living in an apartment equally immaculate, though far less completely equipped, amid blue-and-green chromolithographs of Swiss waterfalls and mountains and lakes. The woman is cooking a few slivers of onions on a tiny coal-stove, which was intended primarily for heat. The husband is out on the railroad tracks picking up pieces of coal in order to keep it going. The woman suddenly begins to cry as she is answering the relief worker's queries, then as suddenly stops. The husband, a little smiling man with Kaiser Wilhelm mustaches, comes back with a few pieces of coal: the railroad detectives have chased him away. He was formerly an industrial chemist and has recently turned his ingenuity to inventing little gambling toys. One of them, he says, he has a fair prospect of selling: you shoot a marble which drops into a hole and knocks up a little tin flap; "Swiss Navy" counts lowest and "America" a hundred per cent. In another place, the bookbinder who has lost his job through a technological improvement has a fellow in the musical field—a young violinist whose profession has been partly abolished by the talkies.

Above the straight criss-cross streets the small houses of brick and gray boards, the newer little two-story Noah's Arks, prick the sharp Roman Catholic spire and the bulbs of the Orthodox Church.

The single men are driven to flophouses. During the last year—September 30, 1931-September 30, 1932—50,000 have registered at the clearing house. Those who are not residents of Chicago are ordered to leave the city: if they got there by paying their fare, they are given a half-fare which will take them home. Others are sent to the asylum, the poorhouse, the veterans' home; referred to the blind pension, the juvenile court. About 500 men a month are disposed of in this way. The Oak Forest poorhouse, called "the Graveyard," has people sleeping in the corridors and turned 19,000 away last year. The rest are directed to the shelters, where they get two meals a day and a bed.

Among the high whitewashed walls of an obsolete furniture factory, the soiled yellow plaster and the scrawled and punctured blackboards of an old public school, the scraped-out offices and pompous paneling of a ghastly old disused courthouse; on the floors befouled with spittle, in the peppery-sweetish stink of food cooking, sulphur fumigations, bug exterminators, rank urinals doctored with creosote—ingredients of the general fetor that more or less prominently figure as one goes from floor to floor, from room to room, but all fuse in the predominant odor of stagnant and huddled humanity—these men eat their chicken-feed and slum amid the deafening clanking of trays and dump the slops in g.i. cans; wait for prize-fights or movies of Tarzan (provided to keep them out of the hands of the Communists or from holding meetings themselves) in so-called "recreation halls," on the walls of which they have chalked up "Hoover's Hotel"—big bare chambers smothered with smoke, strewn with newspapers like vacant lots, smeared like the pavements with phlegm. Here they sit in the lecture seats, squat on the steps of the platform, stretch out on the floor on old papers. In one room a great wall-legend reminds them: "The Blood of God Can Make the Vilest Clean," and they get routed to mess through a prayer meeting. When they come back to the recreation hall, they discover that a cheerful waltz has served merely as a bait to draw them to the harangue by an old Cicero policeman who says that he has been saved. They are obliged to send their clothes to be fumigated, and, if they are wet with the winter rain, ruined. They herd into steaming showers, the young men still building some flesh on straight frames, the old with flat chests, skinny arms and round sagging bellies; and they flop at last on the army cots or in the bunks in double tiers, where the windows which are shut to keep out the cold keep in the sour smell—men in slit union suits and holey socks, men tattooed with fancy pictures or the emblems of some service they have left—resting their bunioned feet taken out of flattened shoes or flat arches wound around with adhesive tape—lying with newspapers for pillows, their arms behind their heads or with a sheet pulled over their faces or wrapped up in blankets, rigid on their backs, their skin stretched tight over their jawbones so that these look like the jaws of the dead.

There is a clinic which does what it can to head off the venereal diseases. There is also a great deal of t.b., to which the Negroes have a fatal susceptibility; and in one shelter spinal meningitis got out of hand for a while and broke nine backs on its rack. Another common complaint of the flophouses is the poisoning that results from drinking a dilution of wood alcohol which the inmates buy for fifteen cents a pint, which looks and tastes, as somebody says, like a mixture of benzine, kerosene and milk, and which usually lands them in the infirmary or the psychopathic ward. And yet one man, given his choice between his bottle and admission to the shelter, refused to give up the bottle: he preferred to spend

the night in the cold rather than surrender his only support
in a life so aimless and hopeless. In the Salvation Army shelter, they will not take in steady drinkers, but the others do
the best they can with them. In one, there is a hobbling
cripple who comes in drunk every night. "I wouldn't be surprised," says the manager, "if a hearse drove up and a dead
man got up and walked out and asked for a flop." One man
turned up "lousy as a pet coon—so lousy nobody would go
near-um and they put-um in the stable with the horse for the
night, and the horse tried to get away. The next morning
they gave-um a shower and scrubbed-um with a long-han-
dled brush." But most of the cases in the infirmaries—from
exhaustion to bad kidneys and body sores—come down to
the same basic disease: starvation.

Razor-slashings and shootings bring in other patients—
though the prospect of a day of work a week, with its brief
liberation from the shelters, is said to have diminished these.
The bad characters are sent to the bull-pens in the basement,
where, crowded together, in fetid air, they sleep on hard
benches with their coats under their heads. Newcomers for
whom there is no room have to be dumped down among
them.

Yet Chicago has apparently been particularly efficient in
providing and running these shelters. At best, it is not unlike
the life of barracks—but without the common work and purpose which give a certain momentum to even a dull campaign. In the shelters, there is nothing to coöperate on and
nothing to look forward to, no developments, no chance of
success. The old man is ending his life without a home
and with no hope of one; the wage-earner who has hitherto
been self-dependent now finds himself dropped down among
casuals and gradually acquires their attitude; the young man
who comes to maturity during the workless period of the
depression never learns the habit of work. (There are few
actual hoboes here: the hobo can do better by begging or
stealing.)

In so far as they are unable to adapt themselves, they must
live under a continual oppression of fear or guilt or despair.
One sees among them faces that are shocking in their con-

trast to their environment here: men who look as if they had never had a day's ill health or done a day's careless work in their lives. Now they jump at the opportunity of spending a day a week clearing the rubbish off vacant lots or cleaning the streets underneath the Loop tracks. This is the only thing that stands between them and that complete loss of independence which can obliterate personality itself—which degrades them to the primal dismal undifferentiated city grayness, depriving them even of the glow of life that has formerly set them off from the fog and the pavements and the sodden old newspapers, rubbing them down to nothing, forcing them out of life.

Yet none of these single-men's shelters produces such an impression of horror as the Angelus Building on South Wabash Avenue, where families of homeless Negroes have taken refuge. This neighborhood was once fairly well-to-do; but at the present time, left behind by the city's growth in other directions, it presents a desolation that is worse than the slums. When the snow in the darkening afternoon has come to seem as dingy as the dusk and the sky as cold and tangible as the snow—as if the neutral general medium of the city were condensing in such a way as to make it hard to move and exist—the houses, interminably scattered along the straight miles of the street, monotonous without being uniform, awkward or cheap attempts at various types of respectable architecture in gray limestone, colorless boards or red brick, all seem—whether inhabited or not—equally abandoned now. The windowless slots of one open into a hollow shell: it has been gutted of even its partitions; the Romanesque prongs of another make it look like a blackened pulled tooth; on the brownstone façade of a third, some distance above the ground, is stuck a pretentious doorway, from under which, like a lower jaw, the flight of front steps has been knocked. And, as a suitable climax to this, the Angelus Building looms blackly on the corner of its block: seven stories, thick with dark windows, caged in a dingy mesh of fire-escapes like mattress-springs on a junk-heap, hunched up, hunchback-proportioned, jam-crammed in its dumbness and darkness with miserable wriggling life.

It was built in 1892 and was once the Ozark Hotel, popular at the time of the old World's Fair. In the dim little entrance hall, the smudged and roughened mosaic, the plaster pattern of molding, the fancy black grill of the elevator, most of it broken off, do not recall former splendor—they are abject, mere chips and shreds of the finery of a section now dead, trodden down into the waste where they lie. There is darkness in the hundred cells: the tenants cannot pay for light; and cold: the heating system no longer works. It is a firetrap which has burned several times—the last time several people were burned to death. And, now, since it is not good for anything else, its owner has turned it over to the Negroes, who flock into the tight-packed apartments and get along there as best they can on such money as they collect from the charities.

There are former domestic servants and porters, former mill-hands and stockyard workers; there are prostitutes and hoodlums next door to respectable former laundresses and Baptist preachers. One veteran of the war, once foreman of the Sunkist Pie Company, now lives in cold and darkness with his widowed mother, even the furniture which he had been buying for $285 the outfit and on which he had paid all but the last installment of $50.20, taken away by the furniture company. For light, they burn kerosene lamps, and for warmth, small coal-stoves and charcoal buckets. The water-closets do not flush, and the water stands in the bathtubs.

The children go to play in the dark halls or along the narrow iron galleries of an abysmal central shaft, which, lighted faintly through glass at the top, is foggy and stifling with coal-smoke like a nightmare of jail or Hell. In the silence of this dreadful shaft, sudden breakages and bangs occur—then all is deathly still again. The two top floors have been stripped by fire and by the tenants' tearing things out to burn or sell: apartments have lost their doors and plumbing pipes lie uncovered. These two floors have been condemned and deserted. Relief workers who have visited the Angelus Building have come away so overwhelmed with horror that they have made efforts to have the whole place condemned—to the piteous distress of the occupants, who consider it an all-right-enough place when you've got nowhere else to go. And where to send these sixty-seven Negro families? Brought to America in the holds of slave-ships and afterwards released from their slavery with the chance of improving their lot, they are now being driven back into the black cavern of the Angelus Building, where differing standards of living, won sometimes by the hard work of generations, are all being reduced to zero.

Those who want to keep clear of the jail-like shelters get along as they can in the streets and huddle at night under the Loop or build shacks on empty lots. On whatever waste-places they are permitted to live, the scabby-looking barnacles appear, knocked together from old tar-paper and tin, old car-bodies, old packing boxes, with old stovepipes leaning askew, amid the blackened weeds in the snow and the bones of old rubbish piles. One "Hooverville" on Harrison Street flies a tattered black rag like the flag of despair.

The inhabitants of these wretched settlements chiefly forage from the city dumps, as do many of those whom charity will not help or who for one reason or another will not go to it or for whom the relief they get is inadequate. There is not a garbage-dump in Chicago which is not diligently haunted by the hungry. Last summer in the hot weather, when the smell was sickening and the flies were thick, there were a hundred people a day coming to one of the dumps, falling on the heap of refuse as soon as the truck had pulled out and digging in it with sticks and hands. They would devour all the pulp that was left on the old slices of watermelon and cantelope till the rinds were as thin as paper; and they would take away and wash and cook discarded turnips, onions and potatoes. Meat is a more difficult matter, but they salvage a good deal of that, too. The best is the butcher's meat which has been frozen and has not spoiled. If they can find only meat that is spoiled, they can sometimes cut out the worst parts, or they scald it and sprinkle it with soda to neutralize the taste and the smell. Fish spoils too quickly, so it is likely to be impossible—though some people have made fish-head soup. Soup has also been made out of chicken claws.

A private incinerator at Thirty-fifth and La Salle Streets which disposes of the garbage from restaurants and hotels, has been regularly visited by people, in groups of as many as twenty at a time, who pounce upon anything that looks edible before it is thrown into the furnace. The women complained to investigators that the men took an unfair advantage by jumping on the truck before it was unloaded; but a code was eventually established which provided that different sets of people should come at different times every day, so that everybody would be given a chance. Another dump at Thirty-first Street and Cicero Avenue has been the center of a Hooverville of three hundred people.

The family of a laid-off dishwasher lived on food from the dump for two years. They had to cook it on the gas of the people downstairs, since their own had been shut off. Their little girl got ptomaine poisoning. Two veterans of the war, who had been expelled from Washington with the bonus army and made their homes in the fireboxes of an old kiln, were dependent on the dump for some time, though a buddy of theirs found he could do better by panhandling at people's doors. One widow with a child of nine, who had formerly made $18 a week in a factory and who has since been living on $4 a week relief and two or three hours' work a day at fifty cents an hour, has tried to get along without garbage but has had to fall back on it frequently during a period of three years. Another widow, who used to do housework and laundry but who was finally left without any work, fed herself and her fourteen-year-old son on garbage. Before she picked up the meat, she would always take off her glasses so that she would not be able to see the maggots; but it sometimes made the boy so sick to look at this offal and smell it that he could not bring himself to eat. He weighed only eighty-two pounds.

Many people in the Hooverville on Cicero Avenue have been poisoned from eating the garbage. One man ate a can of bad crab-meat thrown away by a chain store, and was later found putrefying.

On the endlessly stretching latitude of West Congress Street—lit only on one side at long intervals by livid low-power lamps—along which huge cubes of buildings are infrequently belted by lighted-up floors and where black and blind ranks of trucks stand posted in front of dark factories, some anonymous hand has chalked up on a wall: "VOTE RED. THE PEOPLE ARE GOOFY."

ILLINOIS HOUSEHOLD

A PICTURE OF LINCOLN, a desk, a dictionary on a stand. The countryside of central Illinois is large and flat and calm and covered with snow.

WIFE. Why, the Battle of Mulkeytown, as they call it, is going to get to be like the *Mayflower* for the miners—people being able to say they took part in it! They say there were eighteen hundred cars and trucks gathering strength all the way—the march was thirty or forty miles long. They were orderly—there wasn't any traffic trouble—they'd decided not to carry arms, and they didn't expect any violence——

HUSBAND. A star reporter from Chicago rode along with 'em, with a cane and a chow dog!

WIFE. They were going to Dowell, where the people were friendly. They had a camp all ready for them there, and the people were carrying in food for them, and the city officials were going to receive them. But when they got to Duquoin, the police shuffled them around so that the ones who knew the way were behind—and they'd changed the signs on the road! They'd put the signs that said "To Dowell" on the road to Mulkeytown!——

HUSBAND. They had machine guns across the road so that they couldn't go that way anyway!

WIFE. They had machine guns across the fork of the road that went to Dowell, and they told them to go on, that the other fork went to Dowell—and so they went on to where the businessmen were lined up waiting for them in the gullies beside the road—they say they were along the road for two miles. The businessmen had been drilling for weeks— regular military drill! The fire whistles would blow, and they'd all run out of their offices and stores and go to the drill-grounds and drill. They had baseball bats and billiard cues and clubs! They smashed the headlights and the windshields, and they'd reach in and club people's arms. The people left the cars and ran to the farmhouses—and they turned the machine-guns on the fields to keep them back. They could see the machine-gun fire mowing down the corn, and there was a panic. The people in the houses just about went insane—they were afraid to go out. They just sat inside and heard it over the radio! Some of the men got shotguns and wanted to go out to fight, but they couldn't get enough courage to go up against the machine-guns. People couldn't eat for a week, they were so sick. There was blood all over the concrete—and food all alongside of the road!—loaves of bread hanging on the fenceposts!—those crazy hoodlums had come down there and stamped on the tomatoes and things! There was only one doctor in town who'd take care of the people who were hurt—and the gas stations wouldn't give them any gas! Some of them have never got their cars back! They wouldn't pick up the people who'd been hurt. There was a woman with a baby in her arms who'd been shot, and they took her into the hospital—but nobody else! There was a man out all night with a broken arm. After that, the people were boiling——

Husband. That was when they organized the Progressives.

Boy (*eleven*). Progressive Miners of America!

Wife. The UMW officials had stolen the tally sheets, you know, when the members voted against the $5 wage scale. Then when the locals voted to strike, the Lewis men started shooting and beating up people in Franklin County. The chairman of the local union down there presides with a gun instead of a gavel—his brother's a deputy, and he's deputized himself. That's where the Orient Mine is—it's supposed to be the biggest mine in the world. They've got a great huge factory—it used to employ two thousand before they got the machines. They murder people brutally down there! The people are scared to come to their doors—when anybody knocks at night they turn out the lights real quick and come to the door with a gun. Last August they called Joe Colbert aside and shot him when he was out picking mushrooms. His wife heard the shots, and she thought somebody had shot a dog—then she saw some men in a car, and she went out and found him dead. They say the sheriff was sitting in his car around the corner all the time.

BOY. They killed Lauranti on the picket-line!

WIFE. His body had sixteen shots in it. As a woman was picking him up, a man crazy drunk swung with a bat and broke his neck. The gun-thugs are drunk all the time—they give them a lot of liquor.

HUSBAND. They're full of whisky and dope. The sheriff comes around screwing up his mouth and twitching his arm like this. Don't tell me! I know what's the matter with him! And there's a circuit judge that's a hophead, too. A gun-thug'll start out with a head full of snow and think he's a hell of a fellow when he drives the women around with a baseball bat!

WIFE. I never thought such things could happen in Illinois!

HUSBAND. It's the pressure of the Insull receivers, I suppose.* The Peabody Coal Company is one of the Insull interests, and they'd just got a couple of railroad contracts.

WIFE. I just came back from down there. They say they ran me out. I'm the president of the Women's Auxiliary—that includes wives of the UMW members as well as Progressives. We're trying to unite the north and the south that way——

HUSBAND. They're all with us even in Franklin County—the only way they're able to enforce the UMW contracts is through intimidation. The UMW locals are sending the Progressives money for relief.

WIFE. We got our first auxiliary out of Franklin County—and they're all joining. They wanted to call it the Ladies'

* Samuel Insull of Chicago had built up an enormous utilities corporation, which supplied nearly an eighth of the electrical power of the United States—a complex structure of holding companies, investment companies and affiliates, which had just completely collapsed, leaving its stock worth nothing.

Auxiliary—they didn't know why coal-miners' wives couldn't be ladies—but I said we ought to call ourselves women. —They told us it was no use going down—that the Law said there never would be a Progressives' meeting held in Franklin County—but we held about six meetings with the gunmen right across the street. We had meetings in people's houses with miners on guard outside and in UMW halls—it's against the Lewis* constitution to let anybody else speak there, you know, but they let me. I taught school five years in the next county, and all my family worked in the mines, and the people know me down there. And I'd come at the psychological moment—they were mad about the special assessment. I'd say to them, "They're assessing you men to shoot people up in Taylorville!—There are six hundred deputies and gun-thugs in Taylorville alone!—they've even got a thug up there who was mixed up in the Kincaid robbery—a man who killed his own brother and stuck him in the straw-stack!—and that's what they're assessing you men to pay for!" And I said that I'd heard that some of them from down there had gone up to Taylorville to scab. That's what I can't understand—their being so shameless about scabbing! I told them that the boys were saying that any miners that went up to Taylorville were gonta come back in boxes! They say they sent one man back with an S branded on his cheek. At one of the meetings there was a Lewis man there, and he got up and tried to oppose me—and then somebody pulled out a razor and said, "You're not going to insult a woman here!" And then the Lewis man tried to stop me on a point of order—he said I was going beyond the five-minute limit, and so they took a vote on whether I was to have all the time I wanted, and everybody got up except the Lewis man.—The whole thing has got the women up in arms! When the women were coming from Mt. Olive to go on the Taylorville picket-line and a bunch of young National Guardsmen met them and threw tear-gas bombs at them, those women said things men wouldn't say! There was one woman, I never heard anything like it—a mother of Boy Scouts!

* John L. Lewis, then president of the United Mine Workers of America. See *Frank Keeney's Coal Diggers*.

But the second week we went down to West Frankfort. They told us that Lewis would never let us speak there—that's where Orient No. 2 is. But we went down anyway—we said, "Those women expect us, and we're going!" We'd written to the State's attorney, and he'd promised that we could hold a meeting—he said he'd give us an escort out of the county if we had any reason to believe we were in danger. Well, when I went to go to the meeting, the street was full of people and the hall was dark. The sheriff and the gang had been after me in people's houses, but they hadn't found me—and I walked down the street in plain view with a roll of charters under my arm. But when I got to the hall, the women said, "Come here quick!—the sheriff's gonta kill you!" I said, "That's hot—the sheriff's gonta kill me!" They said, "They're walking up and down the street—they're drunk—you better get away!—you can't go up against the Law!" But I waited for the meeting of the trustees. The trustees of the building were having a meeting about it, and they were willing to have me speak—they said: "We own the building, and these women pay us for the building." But the sheriff stood over them, and he raved and he threatened, and he told them, "If you try to have her speak, you got no more card, you got no more job! I'll bar that door, and if she tries to speak, her life ain't worth a damn!" They used clubs to drive out the women—there were about a thousand there. One woman who was there with her daughter tried to go to a movie to meet another woman, and a deputy chased her and hit her on the back of the head and knocked her down—and the girl tried to scream, and he slapped her—but she screamed, "Oh, my God! don't kill my mother!" And another gunman who wasn't quite as crazy came up and prevented him. Then the sheriff came in, and he said that I'd have to get out of town right away—and what do you think he had in his hand to identify me? He had the letter the state's attorney had written me promising to give me protection!

HUSBAND. If you go to the Peabody offices in Chicago, you can see a special kind of hickory club they've got there. They've got them right there in the office!—so a man who was in there the other day told me. And tear-gas in tanks!

WIFE. If you could only find out what it is between Lewis and the operators! There ought to be a congressional investigation!

HUSBAND. They want to hang on to their salaries and their graft—and the officials have got so much on each other they're scared to rebel against the organization.

WIFE. They say Lewis owns Insull stock.

HUSBAND. We've still got to reckon with Lewis.

BOY. Gotta fight John L. Lewis's gun-thugs!

WIFE. He's the Mussolini type!

HUSBAND. People go to see him and come away as if they'd had a dose of hop. He never had that effect on me, but he does on lots of people. He's sort of squat and wears his hair long and talks without moving his mouth. He walks up and down the floor and pours forth a torrent of eloquence.

WIFE. The operators and Lewis and the authorities are all together against us. They've threatened to kill us if we go back down there.

BOY. While you're down in Franklin County, Ma, you're not doin' anything for Taylorville!

1933

1957. I learned later from the *Progressive Miner,* a newspaper published by this union, of further shootings and beatings, one murder and thirty bombings, in the war of the operators against the miners. Here is an item that deals with the Wife of the above dialogue: "Agnes Burns Wieck provoked Lewis into a rage when she told the conference of a miner's wife dying with a new-born baby in the strike-torn village of Kincaid. As she lay on her lingering deathbed, dying from lack of food, Mrs. Wieck said, her last words were curses for Lewis. The beetle brows of the tyrant frowned and suddenly he was on his feet, lunging towards the head of the Women's Auxiliary." But the Progressives held out for years. Saul Alinsky, in his *John L. Lewis: An Unauthorized Biography,* published in 1949, writes about them as follows: "This union has survived every attack made upon it by Lewis, and today it still numbers approximately 10,000 members. Its unifying force is hatred for Lewis. The bitterness of its members is so deep that they instinctively oppose any position that Lewis adopts. When he supported Roosevelt, they bitterly attacked the President. When he supported the Guffey Coal Act and the Wagner Labor Act, the Progressive Miners condemned both of these laws. Today the ranks of the Progressive Miners are thinning out to extinction."

Yet, in the meantime, John L. Lewis had resigned from the American Federation of Labor, with its old-fashioned craft unionism, and had organized the gigantic CIO (Congress of Industrial Organizations), which recruited entire industries, unskilled as well as skilled labor. The kind of independent union—I have described several examples above—which the pressure of extreme hardship and the apathy of the AF of L were forcing the workers to organize and which, in the mining field, John L. Lewis had tried to suppress, had mostly been absorbed by the CIO, and their members had become loyal to Lewis. Even John Brophy and Powers Hapgood, whom Lewis had had beaten up when they tried to form an independent union as early as 1930, were to ask for readmittance to the UMWA; the latter became, under Lewis, the National Director of the CIO. "We're about to go into a campaign," said Lewis to Hapgood on this occasion, according to a statement by Hapgood included in Mr. Alinsky's book, "that I do not feel at liberty to discuss here [the CIO] but let me just tell you, Powers, that it will be everything you dreamed about and everything you've talked about. We're going out to fight for those things, and we're going to get them. You see, Powers, I've never really opposed those things. I just never felt that the time was ripe and that trying to do those things back in the days when we had our violent arguments would have been suicide for organized labor and would have resulted in complete failure. But now the time is ripe; and now the time to do those things is here. Let us do them." "Lewis stopped talking," adds Hapgood, "and I can't tell you how I felt. It was just as if everything I dreamed of had finally come to pass." I spent an evening, in the summer of 1939, with leaders and former leaders of the Progressive Miners' Union, one of whom had narrowly escaped with his life in the days when Lewis's gunners were hunting him, and it was curious to hear them tell stories of his grandiose eloquence on the platform, his blasting retorts to opponents, his terrible scenes with the operators. They felt in him a kind of pride of which I was later to be reminded in connection with the attitude of white émigré Russians when, at the time of the defense of Leningrad, they would regale me with the crushing remarks attributed to Batyushka Stalin.

In the case of the rather remarkable family whose conversation is reported above, it should be mentioned that the Husband, Mr. Edward A. Wieck, has been working in the Department of Industrial Studies of the Russell Sage Foundation and has published a series of monographs on the history of miners' associations and the prevention of fatal explosions in coal mines; and that his son David Wieck, the Boy of eleven, went to jail as a conscientious objector at the time of the second War. He afterwards collaborated with Lowell Naeve, another conscientious objector, with whom Wieck had been confined, on an interesting book, called *A Field of Broken Stones,* which deals with their experiences in prison.

A GREAT DREAM COME TRUE

THE EMPIRE STATE BUILDING was the largest building in the world. The Radio City Music Hall in New York City is the largest theater in the world. It contains 6,200 seats, has a stage 144 feet wide and 80 feet deep, and cost $7,000,000. The Music Hall and its fellow, the RKO Roxy Theater, represented for Samuel L. Rothafel "the fulfillment of the aspirations of a lifetime, a great dream come true." He had already had a notable failure with one monster amusement palace; but, applying to the Rockefellers, under the sponsorship of Mr. Owen D. Young, that large-visioned electrical magnate, he was able to persuade these capitalists to back him in a second attempt on an even more tremendous scale. One of the features of the original Roxy's had been a bust of Napoleon in the lobby.

And in less than two years' time, over 11,000 tons of steel, over 9,600 tons of brick, had been assembled into two gigantic theaters and a limestone-and-aluminum skyscraper, which makes against the pale New York sky what seems a sheer shaft of packed sand.

Outside, a long aluminum-gray strip winks "Radio City" vertically in rose-red neon letters. The lobby is paved with mats in subdued colors, brown and gray, and from the ceiling shine round light-reflectors with black-blobbed bulbs in the centers, like the eyes of enormous Mickey Mice.

Inside, the Grand Foyer has a majesty which might be described as imperial if it were not entirely meaningless. Against walls of henna-red, with wainscots of dried-blood-red marble, rise mirror-lengths, framed in long gray curtains and with cylindrical lusters embedded in them, to the height of the highest mezzanine; but if one looks up past the chandeliers—two immense cylinder-shaped crystal tassels—one finds that the distant ceiling, a reddish cartridge-copper and studded with unpunctured cartridge-tops, contracts the vertiginous hall to the shape of a straight tin canteen. The doors that swing into the auditorium are bossed with bronze plaques by Paul Manship, on which, interposing the Orient between Roxy and his vaudeville art, he has managed to reduce the idea of a song-and-dance team, a trained-seal act, a wild-animal act, etc., to his conventionalized smoothness and roundness. And what has become of the still-lifes of Picasso, Léger, and Braque?—they lie like autumn leaves underfoot, their banjos and guitars, their broken surfaces, uniformly brown and gray now, trodden into the pattern of the carpet, which stretches away and away. It extends up a giant staircase, which mounts to a greenish-and-brownish mural: "the upward march of mankind," in dim unconvincing figures and pale decorative colors.

The Grand Lounge installed in the basement is suggestive of a cave of mystery at some amusement park. Large bright gray diamonds in the ceiling are made to shed a sort of indoor twilight on dim gray diamonds on the floor. Diamond-shaped pillars, black and polished, reflect the lounge as a maze of lozenges. On a background of pale crinkled curtains, zigzagged with zebra-stripes, a number of big round frameless mirrors take the pillars as polished black streaks. A dancer by Zorach, dull silver, a giantess with legs like thick lead pipes and a rounded wad of hair like a lead sinker, kneels stiffly and stiff-neckedly turns her head.

The auditorium itself—from the point of view of comfort, quite perfect—rather gives one the impression of being inside a telescopic drinking-cup. Under magnificent looped-up portières—revealed by another curtain that opens and closes like a camera shutter and needs thirteen electric motors to work it—and to the music of a gigantic orchestra that rises on an elevator, a veritable grandstandful of girls, in green and red Indian headdresses and equipped with tambourines and fans, sing *My Old Kentucky Home, Dixie* and other beloved Southern melodies, with a vast heart-shaped lace valentine for background.

In the center sits poor old DeWolf Hopper keeping time with one foot. It is about the only thing he can do. You feel melancholy as you see him and Weber and Fields, ineffective in the enormous theater, abjectly delivering lines about the greatness of Rockefeller Center. First—as these remind you —there was Weber and Fields, a show that people visited like a household; then there were the "extravaganzas," the equivalent of English pantomimes, with favorite funny men and fairy-tale stories—*Bluebeard, The Wizard of Oz, Babes in Toyland,* etc.—usually framed among the blue and green peacocks of the pre-Ziegfeld New Amsterdam Theater; then, later, there were the Hippodrome shows, which, though too big for personalities—with the exception of the great Spanish clown Marceline—though lacking in human interest, had something of the excitement of a circus; then there were the Ziegfeld Follies, which, framed richly by their gold proscenium, caught the speed, the intensity, the savagery, the luxury, the dazzle of the city. And now there is the Radio City Music Hall, the most elaborate theater ever built—a theater not merely too huge for personality, story, intensity, but actually too big for a show.

The performance with which the Music Hall opened scarcely survived even the first night. On such a stage, the frame, although gorgeous, is so far beyond and away from the actor that it can no longer focus interest on him: he might as well be trying to hold an audience in the grand concourse of the Pennsylvania Station. Even the girls cannot make much impression except by appearing in quantity and executing "precision" dances that suggest setting-up exercises. One can almost believe them controlled by a photo-electric cell. The comedians and the singers have actually been partly electrified: though their faces may go for nothing, their voices have been swollen by loud-speakers—fifty—till they devour the whole house. And they also talk into microphones for the benefit of radio audiences—with an effect rather disconcerting on the audience in the theater who have paid. The theater is, thus, no longer really a theater, but rather a source of canalized entertainment; the performance is no longer for you, but something that is also directed at thousands of scattered old ladies sitting around in mortgaged farmhouses, at thousands of stocking-footed men reading the paper in Statler hotels.

As for the program, there was a tabloid version of *Carmen*, which resembled one of those fifteen-minute film prologues but which in this case had the added demerit of not leading up to a film. And, at one point, an army of toe-dancers burst out of surprise entrances in the audience, grouped itself as a great white wedding cake, and enacted the death of a Long Island swan farm on a slowly revolving turntable. A serious German dancer, whose inclusion seems to have been due— like the works by Manship and Zorach—to Roxy's imperial desire to have a little of the best of everything—this unfortunate German dancer had apparently missed fire so badly in the first two or three performances with a ballet called *The Angel of Death* that he was provided with a humorous announcer who gave a kidding account of the scenario and caused some to think it was meant to be funny.

Nor was the spectacle confined to the stage. It was contrived that the immense auditorium itself should change color, with every new number, like the inside of a chameleon watermelon. This was supposed to represent "a stylized sunset, an idea conceived by Roxy while standing on a ship's deck at dawn." The half-circle of the stage is the sun, and the watermelon stripes are rays, which run through a gamut of lavender on green, red on green, red on red, etc. There are no less than two hundred spotlights, each capable of forty changes. Two strong-lunged cathedral organs play *Leave the Dishes in the Sink*.

And Roxy himself, the Sun King, has quarters befitting his rank. He has had installed, above the Music Hall, an apartment of which the equipment and furnishings—charged to the Rockefellers as part of the opening expenses—cost $250,-000. There is a dining room nineteen feet high, with a separate solid silver service for each of the three meals, and there is a dining staff which includes a chef, a pastry cook, a headwaiter and two other waiters. These are supposed to be in constant readiness to serve up, at short notice, a dinner for as many as thirty people. The pots and pans in the kitchen alone cost $2,200.

But Roxy was unable to do the honors. Though the Rockefellers, Owen D. Young, Will Hays and Nicholas Murray Butler all loyally attended his openings, the auspices were already ominous. Roxy himself had fallen ill, and, the night of the second opening, was removed from the theater on a stretcher. It was decided that the Radio City Music Hall, though a flop on an unheard-of scale, was unmistakably, irretrievably a flop, and that it would have to be turned into a cinema.

When Roxy had got well enough to be interviewed, he was invited to make a statement on the present depression. "All you can do," he said, "is spread your feet a little wider and stand it. Don't ever sell this country short. We'll all be proud of this country some day. Proud of America like an Englishman is proud of England after he has gone to see *Cavalcade!*"

I remember him as I saw him once some fifteen years ago, with his little round head and straight talk, in a discussion with other men of the movies. I remember how his energy and assurance seemed to contrast with the qualities of the rest, and I regret that he should have been encouraged to make such a fool of himself. There are people who have never recovered from the fantastic ambitions and imaginings engendered by the boom of the twenties.

Apparently the only person who has been pleased by the opening of the Music Hall is a veteran financier who was at one time roughly handled by Rockefeller. "Think of that son of a bitch Rockefeller," he is said to have exclaimed with jubilation, "losing $100,000 a week!"

1934

1957. Radio City Music Hall has prospered as a movie theater and makes use of its stage facilities with an elaborate spectacle that precedes the film.

WASHINGTON: INAUGURAL PARADE

EVERYTHING IS gray today. From a distance, the dome of the Capitol looks like gray polished granite, and against this bleak sky of March, it has a sort of steel-engraving distinction. Seen close to, in this weather, it seems a replica of itself in white rubber; clouds in colorless light are threatening snow or rain. An aluminum blimp hangs below them.

The people seem dreary, even apathetic. The Washington banks have closed, the banks throughout the country are closing; and, though the newspapers are trying to conceal the news that New York and Illinois have given up, there creeps over us, through all the activity and pomp, a numbness of life running out. The prosperity of America has vanished; even the banks do not know where the money is; even the banks say they have not got it; so they are simply shutting up, no more checks cashed; general dismay and blankness. And—what somehow seems of special bad omen—the most popular member of the Cabinet, Thomas Walsh, on the eve of taking office, has suddenly died.

The crowd waits in front of the Capitol. "What are those things that look like little cages?" "Machine-guns," says a woman with a giggle. They wait until Roosevelt's figure appears dimly on the platform on the Capitol steps, till they dimly hear the accents of his voice—then the crowd rapidly thins.

But even when one reads them later, the phrases of this speech seem shadowy—the echoes of Woodrow Wilson's eloquence without Wilson's exaltation behind them. The old unctuousness, the old pulpit vagueness: "in every dark hour of our national life," "and yet our distress comes from no failure of substance—we are stricken by no plague of locusts," "where there is no vision the people perish," "the money-changers have fled from their high seats in the temple of our civilization," "our true destiny is not to be ministered unto but to minister to ourselves and to our fellow men." The old Wilsonian professions of plain-speaking followed by the old abstractions: "I am certain that on this day my fellow Americans expect that . . . I will address them with a candor and a decision which the present situation of our people impels. This is preëminently the time to speak the truth, the whole truth, frankly and boldly," etc. What then? In finance, he tells us, we must "restore to the ancient truths" the temple from which the money-changers have fled; and in the field of foreign affairs, he "would dedicate this nation to the policy of the good neighbor."

There is a suggestion, itself rather vague, of a possible dictatorship.

The first part of the parade is respectable.

Preceded by well-drilled motorcycles and a squadron of khaki cavalry, leaning forward as they briskly canter with their sabers against their shoulders, the silk hats and the admiral's gold-braided bicorne roll along in open cars on their way from the Capitol to the White House. The new President smiles his smug public smile, doffing his high hat and calling back to greetings from the crowd. "He looks like Wilson, doesn't he?" says a woman. "The glasses and pointed nose look like Wilson." "He looks so aristocratic, I think!" another woman says to her neighbor, as she shows her a picture of Roosevelt graciously receiving Hoover. Mrs. Roosevelt sits beside her husband, looking small, dark and unpretentious, smiling, her little round black hat tilted fashionably over one ear.

An interim of waiting; the weather grows colder. The parade proper now begins. The branches of the service pass first. Chief of Staff, General Douglas MacArthur, who drove the veterans out of Washington last summer; the flare of flags of the First Division; the ranks of Knickerbocker Cadets, tall and rigid and gray; marines in clean white caps and gaiters, with a red and yellow rattlesnake flag; bluejackets; Negroes in khaki, always with a white officer at their head; khaki trucks, khaki anti-aircraft guns; a new kind of short black machine-gun as shiny and perfect as the little screw-out pencils that people used to wear on watch-chains; stretchers; a drum-major in a white shako; the blue Richmond Blues, the gray Richmond Grays, and the red and gray Richmond Howitzers, all with white plumes and pre-Civil-War uniforms. It is inspiriting to hear *The West Point Cadets' March* and *The Stars and Stripes Forever*—they bring back the America of boyhood: the imperial Roosevelt, the Spanish War. And the airplanes against the dark sky, flying in groups of nine and moving as they reach the reviewing stand into exact little patterns like jackstones, awaken a moment's pride in American technical precision.

But from this early point on—and there are something like three hours of it still to pass—the procession degenerates crazily. It first recalls those college reunions for which the classes dress in fancy costumes, but then proceeds to lengths of absurdity that make the carnival at Nice look decorous.

It is the militarizing girls from the provinces who introduce the musical-comedy element. The delegation from Atlanta Tech High is headed by a pretty girl in a red coat and white pants, with a white overseas cap and a white Sam Browne belt. Another in high heels leads a company of girls in gray and blue. The John Marshall Cadet Corps from Richmond are handsome in long gray coats and red cloaks.

Now the governors of the states are coming, sandwiched in between bands. Delaware Post Number One have shiny steel trench helmets, sky-blue coats, white breeches and black puttees. Gifford Pinchot, in an open car, bows and takes off his hat in response to the cheers that follow him, with gestures willowy and courtly like the White Knight turned politician. But the next sound we hear is a breeze of laughter. One of the bands has a funny drum-major, whose specialty is hip-wiggling and mincing: he puts one hand to his waist, holds it out marking the time with wrist limp and little finger extended, turns sideways and, with a rumba-dancer's rhythm, pretends to make billiard-shots with a naughtily phallic baton. And the effect of the pansy drum-major is to impart to the features that come after a circus-parade effect of clowning. He is followed immediately by Governor Ritchie, who looks like a silk-hatted Mr. Woodchuck out of the Bedtime Stories of Thornton Burgess; he shakes howdy with one gloved paw, and you expect to see the automobile go off with a blaze and a bang, and the silk hats tumbling in the sawdust.

There follows a strange little closed car, which displays, on the radiator, the blue Lone Star of Texas. It has the streamlines of a small goblin army tank; and the spectators murmur as it passes that it cost ten thousand, thirty thousand dollars. The Green Trojans of Greensburg, Pennsylvania, are frog-green with bersaglieri's feathered bonnets. The Veterans of the Indian Wars are old men in a big green bus.

And as the weather grows darker and more ominous, the parade becomes more fantastic. The American Legion Posts, which dominate the later sections, startle, trouble and shock. Are these the implacable guardians of an Americanism tempered by battle? There are legionnaires with bright blue coats and trench helmets of canary yellow; legionnaires as hussars in orange; legionnaire drum-and-bugle corps, weaving fancy evolutions as they march. A great many women among them. One detachment of patriotic ladies wears red cloaks and blue and white plumes. The circus illusion is heightened by a cute-kid cowboy on a donkey and by a man who walks all alone made up as Abraham Lincoln and whom you expect to see stop for some comic trick—puff smoke, perhaps, out of his stovepipe hat.

Now the spectacle grows phantasmagoric. Comic lodges and marching clubs pass. Men appear in curled-up shoes and fezzes, dressed in hideous greens, purples and reds. Indians, terribly fat, with terribly made-up squaws. A very large loose old Negro in a purple fez and yellow-edged cloak, carrying the prong of an antler as if it were the Golden Bough. The airplanes overhead have at the present stage been replaced by an insect-like autogyro, which trails a big advertising banner: "Re-Tire with Lee's Tires." The Negro lady-hussars wear gorgeous bright purple stockings. The Spirit of '76 are evidently more or less cockeyed: one of the trio is always getting behind and then running to catch up with the others.

Real Cherokees in white-fringed suits and headdresses of pink-tipped feathers; one rides a horse, bareback, and sends a murmur through the crowd, who remark that he is practically naked.

A passage of real dignity and gravity ensues. The cornets of the New York Police Band, who march in a dense blue formation and announce they "fear no music written," make an attention-compelling impact for the solid ranks of silk hats of Tammany, which go on and on like an army. No fantasy and no frivolity: each marches in a dark coat and with a white carnation in his buttonhole. Al Smith, with a red face, is in the front line with John F. Curry, and gives rise to a high wave of cheering. They are followed by a comic Dutchman wheeling a red, white and blue keg, and Miss Columbia leading the Queens County donkey.

But a mutter of expectation now agitates the crowd. Al Smith has had his ovation; but he is now to be eclipsed by Tom Mix.* Not even the President is so popular. They catch sight of his white suit and sombrero while he is still several blocks away, and they go wild with delight as he passes by, making his beautiful little pony—jet-black in its silver harness—dance. He has come on as a part of the publicity for a new film called 42nd Street—arriving in a royally appointed and electric-bulb-studded train, "The Better Times Gold and Silver Leaf Special," with an assortment of Hollywood beauties.

These beauties are presented on a "Better Times Float," which resembles a merry-go-round. As it is pulled along, it revolves, exhibiting the waving girls, who—in front of a background of giant tulips and under a canopy of yellow and red—are posing on wicker couches as summery as Beverly Hills.

But Hollywood is nothing to the marching clubs. A faint uncanny music now tickles the ear, and ambiguous figures loom, out of Little Nemo's Adventures in Slumberland. Some seem half-Indian, half-angel, with feather headdresses that sweep to the ground; others—who get great applause—wear

* A favorite moving-picture actor.

hoods with spiky dorsal fins, like Martians in the barbershop weeklies; and all are clad in pale flowing female robes, tinted with celestial pinks and blues and making an effect of unpleasant iridescence such as sweat sometimes leaves on white shirts. As they move, they tease mosquito-buzzing dance music out of xylophones, banjos, violins and guitars. Interspersed are the Loew's Theaters Cadet Band; a drummajor who can juggle two batons; and a drunk with Leon Errol rubber legs, who ricochets back and forth and shakes hands with the people on the sidelines.

A small group from the Virgin Islands, soberly uniformed and quietly behaved, and a float of chilly-looking trained nurses incongruously end the procession.

If the parade went on any longer, it would be too dark to see, too cold to stay out. And you are glad when it is over, anyway. The America it represented has burst with the bursting of the boom, and you realized, as you watched the marchers, how abysmally silly it was. This delirium is the ghost it has given up.

March, 1933

SUNSHINE CHARLEY

A YOUNG COLLEGE MAN, according to a legend of the boom, went to work at the National City Bank. One day Charles E. Mitchell, then its president, came through on a tour of inspection. "Mr. Mitchell," said the young man in a low voice, "may I speak to you for a moment?" The great banker and bond salesman scowled: "What is it?" he demanded. The young man politely pressed him to step aside out of earshot of the others present. Still scowling, Mitchell complied. Said the young man in a gentle whisper: "Your trousers are un-buttoned, sir." "You're fired!" flashed the great financier.

In those days the trousers of Charles E. Mitchell could no more be unbuttoned than Louis XIV's grammar could be at fault. He was the banker of bankers, the salesman of sales-men, the genius of the New Economic Era.* He was the man who had taken the National City Company, that subsidiary of the National City Bank—established, according to the practice of the New Economic Era, as an institution legally distinct but actually identical with the bank, for the purpose of marketing securities which the bank was prohibited from selling—and had transformed it in six years' time from a room with a stenographer, a boy and a clerk into an organi-zation with a staff of fourteen hundred and branch offices all over the country, which sold a billion and a half dollars' worth of securities a year—the largest corporation in the country. At its summit, like an emperor, sat Mitchell, dy-namic, optimistic and insolent, sending out salesmen in all directions as he preached to them, bullied them, bribed them; had them clerking in security shops, on the street level of

* The New Economic Era was the name that the Republicans gave to the period of "prosperity" that preceded the depression.

every provincial city, from which they disposed of bonds
like groceries in A and P stores; had them knocking at the
doors of rural houses like men with vacuum cleaners or Fuller
brushes; had them vying with each other in bond-selling
contests; had them hypnotized, intoxicated, drugged and always fearful of losing their jobs if they failed to sell more
and more bonds—"You cannot stand still in this business!
—you fellows are not *Self-Starters!*"—till they resorted to
faking orders in order to inflate their figures, and invested
their own salaries in the National City Bank's securities,
about whose value they knew as little as the people they
were selling them to.

The days of the highly respectable banker who gave young
people and widows advice were over. The public had the
salesmen after them; and the salesmen had always behind
them the megaphone voice, the indomitable jaw, the intimi-
dating telegrams of Mitchell. He sold the American public,
in the course of ten years, over fifteen billion dollars' worth
of securities. He sold them the stock of motor-car companies
that were presently to dissolve into water; he sold them the
bonds of South American republics on the verge of insol-
vency and revolution; he sold them the stock of his own
bank, which dropped in the course of three weeks, after
October, 1929, from $572 to $220, and which was recently
worth $20. In the minds of the public, of his minions, of
himself, Charles E. Mitchell had reached an apotheosis. In
his days of greatness, it was boasted, he always traveled by
special train. One of his salesmen, who was afterwards ruined
by his investments in the Mitchell securities, described his
master's brains as "spinning like a great wheel in a power
house" and spoke almost with trembling of the terror he inspired. Bruce Barton was taken by Mitchell to the top of the
Bankers' Club and shown the kingdoms of the world from
the window. When bond salesmen came to him, said Mitchell, complaining that they were unable to find buyers, he
always took them up into the Bankers' Club and said to
them: "Look down there! There are six million people with
incomes that aggregate thousands of millions of dollars. They
are just waiting for someone to come and tell them what

to do with their savings. Take a good look, eat a good lunch, and then go down and tell them! If there is nothing in that picture which stirs a man's imagination, he doesn't belong in New York!" Bruce Barton prostrated himself in the pages of the *American Magazine,* and since his father had been a minister, soon announced that Jesus Christ's true mission had been that of the Supreme Salesman. Charley Mitchell thus blazed like the great central source of the energy and heat of Prosperity: his colleagues called him "Sunshine Charley."

Today that sunshine has faded. Charley Mitchell looks cheap in court. Through long sessions of the muggy June weather, while the reporters go to sleep at their table and the judge invites the jury to take off their coats; among the pallid creatures of the courtroom, whose skins never know any light save that from the soapy globes of the overhead chandeliers, whose fat legs seem to have taken no exercise save stalking the courtroom floor, he sits behind the wooden railing that separates the spectators from the trial, broad-shouldered but short-legged, his grizzled hair growing down his neck and forehead, his long nose with its blunt end no longer driving salesmen out but bent humbly toward the table before him. In contrast to the neutral complexions and the tasteless clothes of the courtroom, he is conspicuous by reason of his ruddy face and of the high stiff white collar, the blue serge suit, the white handkerchief sticking out of the pocket, of the big downtown days of the boom. Behind him, ledgers, suitcases, crammed briefcases are all that is left of those days—those dizzying profits, those mammoth transactions, the millennial boasts of the bankers, the round-eyed hopes of the public, now nothing but a tableful of papers which has to be produced in court.

Sitting quiet, looking often toward the clock, he listens to the witnesses called to testify as to whether or not his sale to his wife of certain shares of National City Bank stock, his sale of certain other shares of Anaconda Copper stock, and his failure to report $666,666.67 from the management fund of the National City Bank, were devices to evade the income tax. Max Steuer, Mitchell's lawyer, has called him a "big-fish victim of mob hysteria"; and the idea of big fish haunted me as I watched the officials of J. P. Morgan and of the National City Bank trying not to get their bosses into trouble. The boom produced its own human type, with its own peculiar characteristics, physical and psychological: a more overblown and softer-headed species of the traditional American business man. Enormous, with no necks, they give the impression of hooked helpless frogs, or of fat bass or logy groupers hauled suddenly out of the water and landed on the witness stand gasping. They pant, they twitch in the chair, they make gestures finlike and feeble—one can imagine behind their jowls great gills that are vainly straining to respire the alien air. One of them, with a hideous exactitude, reminds one of those goblinlike monsters that have been dragged up by William Beebe from the depths of the South Seas: the same head that seems bigger than the body, the same gaping mouth of long sharp teeth, the same nose flattened down to nothing to give scope to the undershot jaw. The only thing lacking in this financier is the natural rod with its luminous bait which grows out of the forehead of the "anglers" and entices the prey within range of their mouths, but the imagination can fill this in. The National City Bank in its time performed some of the biggest mergers on record; and it is reported that certain fish of this species can swallow a fish five and a half times their length. Beebe says he found seven wild ducks in one of them.

Mitchell himself is a man of more character, but he, too, is out of his element on the witness-stand. The great salesman of salesmen is himself washed up, and the two Jewish lawyers fight over him. Steuer speaks so gently, works so quietly—shrunken, round-shouldered, round-headed, bald, with a shrewd old Semitic face—that all the spectators can catch of his case is a faint continual lisp. With mouse-ears that stick out from his head, he mouses between witness, judge and jury, keeping the whole thing profoundly discreet. George Medalie has weight and solidity, and far from hushing down his questions, he launches them very distinctly in tones of metallic sarcasm and moves back to make the witness speak louder when he wants to bring an answer out. Poor Mitchell seems almost as uncomfortable with the one as with the other. Deliberately but very haltingly, at the *sotto voce* prompting of Steuer, he tells about the sale of the stock. The sales were genuine sales, his wife really wanted to buy the stock, he had the very best legal advice to guarantee their legality, etc. When, at the time of the first market crash, he pledged his personal resources to help the bank buy its own stock, he had not hoped to get anything out of it, he had merely been trying to save the bank. Yet Mrs. Mitchell, Medalie shows, had not had enough income even to pay the interest on the loan from J. P. Morgan which would have been necessary for her to carry this stock; there had been no transfer stamps attached to the letter recording the sale; and afterwards Mitchell had bought back the stock at exactly the same price. He had bought back the other stock, too; and the $666,666.67 which is asserted by the defense to have been a loan, had, according to the prosecution, been written off the books of the bank as if it had been a bonus.

On the stand, Mitchell's prestige evaporates. He is no longer the perfect type of the powerful business executive of the success course and cigarette ads. Confronting the lawyers with his formal blue suit, his robust torso, his grizzled crest, with his scowling brows and his self-assertive nose joined by a pair of coarse lines to a wide and common mouth, he throws out his hands in stock gestures of frankness and exposition, making things clear weakly; tries to put over points with a finger that no longer carries conviction; breaks down in the middle of sentences, frowning helplessly, his mouth hanging open. In reply to his attorney's questions, "I did!" "I certainly did!" he declares with the emphasis of a movie actor playing a big executive. And there is a suggestion of the race-track about him—yes, he used to take bets on securities. It has always been a mannerism of Mitchell's to hitch up one of his eyebrows and pull the other down, thus producing a portentous effect of squinting into the mysteries of high finance which the ordinary man couldn't penetrate but which to him revealed golden visions. Year after year, as the depression deepened, still did his prophecies never fail. But today the shaggily squinted eye seems shying at awkward questions.

One should not take out on individuals one's resentment at general abuses. Charley Mitchell, the investment superman, could never have been created, of course, without the

mania of the public to believe in him. It was the climate and
soil of the boom which made of the ambitious young man
who had worked his way through Amherst by giving courses
in public speaking, the smart clerk at Western Electric who
paid out part of his weekly $10 in order to take business
courses at night school—it was the climate and soil of the
boom which nurtured this being and his fellows. So the eyes
of the fishes of the dark ocean-depths eventually become
atrophied and blind, so they learn to excrete their luminous
mucus; so, dwelling below the level where a diet of plants
is possible, they develop their valise-like carnivorous jaws.
And it is cruel to expose the discomfiture of a man enduring
such humiliation. But all the prosperity-writers have been la-
boring these many years to build up the man we see here as a
respectable public figure. And even today they are at it: the
newspaper reporters at the trial have worked hard to provide
Mitchell with a firmness of front which he certainly did not
show when I saw him. One financial journal, in particular,
has grown emotional and almost poetic in describing the effect of his testimony. The auditors, it says, as they heard him,
relived the great days of expansion—for a moment the pulse
throbbed, the spirit lifted, as they caught again that lost hope
and faith—and how could they refuse to imagine themselves
in the place of their tragically mistaken leader, how could
they find it in their hearts to condemn him? Well, it is time
that we ceased to allow the newspaper writers on finance to
determine our impressions and moods. Charley Mitchell has
been arrested at the orders of the President of the United
States, and while we have got him before us, we might as
well take a good look at him. Here is the head of a financial
house which was for many years the largest in the United
States, whose arrogance was lately so great that it was reputed
to constitute *lèse-majesté* to tell him his pants were unbuttoned, and who did not even consider it necessary to go
through the barest formalities of covering up his frauds. He
is a man with a full-fleshed face and a fierce unconvincing
eye—a man of a low order, caught in suspicious circumstances
and hard put to it to talk himself out.

1933

BERNARD SHAW AT THE METROPOLITAN

It was with feelings uncomfortably mixed that one listened to Bernard Shaw at the Metropolitan Opera House.

The most effective way to present the scene would be to use modern movie technique. First show the figure of Shaw in all its distinction and beauty. Slim and straight, in a double-breasted black coat buttoned up high under the collar with an austere effect almost clerical, so that it sets off the whiteness of his beard, as his eyebrows against his pink skin look like cotton on a department-store Santa Claus—he walks on and off the platform in his shiny black shoes with the lithe step, all but prancing, of a cavalier; clasps his long tapering hands around his knee, as he leans forward to talk to someone, with a self-consciousness of grace almost feminine; and diversifies his long speech with movements and gestures self-conscious and precise like an actor's. And there are also the old Irishman's reddish nose, the squared shoulders, with arms folded, of the schoolmaster, the rare moments of silliness or shyness of the young man who learned to face the public "like an officer afflicted with cowardice, who takes every opportunity of going under fire to get over it and learn his business." All these are accommodated to an artistic creation of which Bernard Shaw's voice is the supreme expression. This voice has the fine qualities of his prose: with an accent, half-English, half-Irish—what the Irish call a Rathmines accent after the fashionable quarter of Dublin, an accent which says "expawts" when his voice rises, "exporrts" when it deepens, with a style from eighteenth-century Dublin in which phrases of the most commonplace modern slang start into vulgar relief, and in a tone of old-fashioned courtesy which varies between the sarcastic and the kindly, he caresses and enchants the auditor with the music of a master of speech, enmeshing him—though somewhat less surely than he does by the written sentence—in the strands of a skein of ideas of which he reels out the endless thread.

Here in this black arrowy figure, this lovely cultivated voice, is the spirit which for those of us who were young when Shaw had reached the height of his power, permeated our minds for a time, stirring new intellectual appetites, exciting our sense of moral issues, sharpening the focus of our vision on the social relations of our world till we could see it as a vividly lit stage full of small, distinct, intensely conceived characters explaining their positions to one another. It was an explanation that burned like a poem. And here is the poet still burning.

Now widen the scope of the camera, and take in the double row of dignitaries on the platform behind the speaker. Trustees of the Academy of Political Science, under whose auspices Shaw is appearing: a bank president and a Morgan partner; Archibald Henderson; Walter Lippmann; odd liberal ladies and editors of second-rate magazines—the kind of committee that one might expect for a lecture by John Drinkwater or Norman Angell.

Now widen the scope again: pull the camera back and swing it up toward the ceiling of the theater. The straight black figure diminishes: it stands at the bottom of a gulf—the vast canyon of the Metropolitan, with its ugly and stale decorations: the heavy tarnished gold of the proscenium arch, the gilt boxes lined with red plush and embellished with electric bulbs which themselves have a red-plushy aspect. Tier upon tier of boxes; balcony after balcony. The tall slim figure behind the pulpit is all but drowned at the bottom. All about him gapes a huge dumb audience—thousands and thousands of people who have bought seats for a show at the Met with a much-advertized performer.

In the orchestra, one recognizes a type not unlike the regular opera-goer: old ladies and old gentlemen in evening clothes—the members, presumably, of the Academy. But who are all the rest?—who knows? We know them but we cannot name them. They are the eerie half-human attendants at anything that is new on Broadway—the dead-pans of the Theater Guild openings. They never laugh and they never applaud; they never seem to know what the play is about; if they ever seem to react at all, it is only to grumble a little. They have turned out tonight to see Bernard Shaw with the same simple phototropic instinct which draws them to those other entertainments by which they never seem to be entertained. They arrive at the theater, they take their seats; the curtain goes up and reveals a set, and for a moment the bright-lighted scene appears to command their attention; but then they are confronted with situations that have to be attentively followed, long passages of dialogue to be sat through, emotions to be entered into, developments of ideas to be grasped, and—though, in deference to this Manhattan audience, our drama has been lately growing thinner and thinner—they still don't understand it, don't like it; they just sit there—wondering? sullen? Again, one cannot say, one cannot know how they respond to these stimuli.

Before this dull tribunal of trolls, then, more dismaying because they never pass sentence—poor Bernard Shaw appeared. During the earlier part of his speech, he was driven to comment on the silence that followed his most emphatic points. It was not till about halfway through that he evoked any spontaneous enthusiasm, and this was only from a special quarter. When, after dealing with economic issues in rather a gingerly fashion, he reminded us that the sole argument by which capitalism was able to justify itself had been that, despite inequalities in the distribution of wealth, it could guarantee the working class a living wage, and declared that a crisis like this which left millions of them unemployed amounted to a breakdown of the system—a vigorous burst of clapping was heard from the highest balcony. Shaw looked up in surprise. "I confess," he said, "the splendor of this building had blinded me to the fact that the majority of my audience apparently belong to the unemployed!"

But it was not the majority of his audience: it was only some radicals in the dollar seats. They broke into applause again when he said that, in financing the war, America had got "pretty fair value for her money from the political point

of view," because she had "achieved the salvation of Russia"
—and now and then at similar statements; but when one
looked down into the shirt-fronts of the orchestra, where the
seats were five dollars apiece, one could not see a pair of hands
stirring. One man in the next-to-top gallery remarked, after
two or three of these salvos: "The gallery seem to be having
a good time!" as if he had no idea what Shaw was saying nor
why the people should clap him nor why he himself should
have come; and this man gave the tone of the house.

The speaker himself seemed to feel it. From the breakdown of capitalism and the salvation of Russia, he picked
his way through detours highly circumspect. He achieved
one effective satiric stroke in telling us that we ought to be
pleased to have helped, by taking part in the war, to turn
Russia into a Communist state, since otherwise we should
have had to contend with another great imperialist power,
and that we should hope for the same reasons for a Communist China. But he leaned a little too far backwards in
praising Stalin's 100 per cent nationalism and telling his audience not to "bother so much about Karl Marx."

This injunction, which he delivered toward the end of his
speech and just before acknowledging his debt to Henry
George—which also pleased the top balcony, but left everybody else blank—pointed up the incongruities of the whole
affair. Most of the people whom Shaw was addressing had
never bothered about Marx at all; that they were not in the
least likely to bother about him too much, he had recognized
in kidding them about Russia, when he said, "If you do not
like to establish communism among yourselves, if you cannot
appreciate communism," etc. It was only the people at the
top of the house who had bothered about Marx at all. And
would Shaw have given any such warning to the radicals at
the top of the house, insisted in just that way on the nationalism of Stalin, if he had been addressing no one else?
At the beginning, he had not, I think, known quite what
sort of audience he was facing; and when he began to feel it
out, his line became somewhat confused by the necessity of
addressing himself to two different and irreconcilable elements: what he evidently imagined, on the one hand, to be

a regular after-dinner speaker's audience of conventional after-dinner dodos, and, on the other, a certain number of leftists. Thus tacking between the two, he navigated his course with difficulty—baffled, no doubt, even further by the fog of the radio audience which was dense all about him outside, an audience even more mixed, which sent in several hundred complaints while the speech was still going on.

Yet the curious ambiguity of the whole occasion was due to the ambiguity of Shaw himself. Why could he not have spoken under the auspices of some Socialist organization, to whom he could have talked directly and who would have met him with a positive response? The truth is that Bernard Shaw has allowed himself, with less justification, to suffer the fate of Mark Twain: he has become a favorite public character. Though, of course, it is his dramatist's gift, making it inevitable that he should dramatize himself, which has delivered him into the hands of publicity, the effect is, nonetheless, somewhat compromising. After all, why, at seventy-seven, should Shaw be making public speeches in which he has to handle like hot potatoes convictions which were once incandescent and with which he once dazzled our minds? His training as a public speaker has been valuable in giving Shaw what acting on the stage gave Shakespeare, Molière and Ibsen: first-hand knowledge of the reactions of an audience. But why should he persist so in his public appearances? and to audiences on such a scale? He can write so much better than he speaks. In his speaking, those elaborations which in his books would be assigned to subordinate clauses give the effect of halting digressions; and in order to convert his ideas into after-dinner jokes he is obliged to disguise them, to blur them. If Bernard Shaw never talked to reporters at all, they would never misrepresent him. But his relation to the press and its public has become today a vital part of him. If the poet still keeps his insight into the larger life of mankind, the entertainer of the bourgeoisie is getting gaga with the bourgeois themselves. Today, as appeared in his New York address, the Spenglerian vision of doom bulks as large as the socialist hope.

Shaw carries his own paradoxes within him; yet it is still

his poet's distinction that he can study and explain himself, that through the arguing characters of his plays he can give his own conflicts expression. And even in his public character, less authentic though it is than his literary one, he can thrill us from time to time when he is able to make the timbre of challenge, the old piercing intellectual clarity, ring out amid the banalities of the lecturer. Even in this pompous auditorium and before this dead bourgeois audience, which Shaw himself has let himself in for, he continues to stand for something which enables us to see audience and theater—and Bernard Shaw himself—as we have never quite seen them before.

April, 19 ̄3

1957. I did not, of course, foresee that the Soviet Union was itself to become what Shaw said it was not: "another great imperialist power." But I partly misunderstood Shaw's line in praising the nationalism of Stalin. It was not till five years later, when I came to write an essay on Shaw, that I was forced to take account of the natural affinity with dictators, the admiration for a strong hand in government, which made him so uncritically loyal to Stalin, Mussolini and Hitler and so firmly unsympathetic toward the victims of their persecutions. As for "great imperialist powers," he had criticized them only sparingly. He was far from being an Irish patriot, and at the time of the Boer War had supported the British against the Boers. Would he have even disapproved, one wonders, of what Stalin and the heirs of Stalin have been doing to their subject peoples?

THE OLD STONE HOUSE

As I GO NORTH for the first time in years, in the slow, the constantly stopping, milk train—which carries passengers only in the back part of the hind car and has an old stove to heat it in winter—I look out through the dirt-yellowed double pane and remember how once, as a child, I used to feel thwarted in summer till I had got the windows open and there was nothing between me and the widening pastures, the great boulders, the black and white cattle, the rivers, stony and thin, the lone elms like feather-dusters, the high air which sharpens all outlines, makes all colors so breathtakingly vivid, in the clear light of late afternoon.

The little stations again: Barnevald, Stittville, Steuben— a tribute to the Prussian general who helped drill our troops for the Revolution. The woman behind me in the train talks to the conductor with a German accent. They came over here for land and freedom.

Boonville: that pale boxlike building, smooth gray, with three floors of slots that look in on darkness and a roof like a flat overlapping lid—cold dark clear air, fresh water. Like nothing else but upstate New York. Rivers that run quick among stones, or, deeper, stained dark with dead leaves. I used to love to follow them—should still. A fresh breath of water off the Black River, where the blue closed gentians grow. Those forests, those boulder-strewn pastures, those fabulous distant falls!

There was never any train to Talcottville. Our house was the center of the town. It is strange to get back to this now: it seems not quite like anything else that I have ever known.

But is this merely the apparent uniqueness of places associated with childhood?

The settlers of this part of New York were a first westward migration from New England. At the end of the eighteenth century, they drove ox-teams from Connecticut and Massachusetts over into the wild northern country below Lake Ontario and the St. Lawrence River, and they established here an extension of New England.

Yet an extension that was already something new. I happened last week to be in Ipswich, Mass., the town from which one branch of my family came; and, for all the New England pride of white houses and green blinds, I was oppressed by the ancient crampedness. Even the House of the Seven Gables, which stimulated the imagination of Hawthorne, though it is grim perhaps, is not romantic. It, too, has the tightness and the self-sufficiency of that little provincial merchant society, which at its best produced an intense little culture, quite English in its concreteness and practicality—as the block letters of the signs along the docks make Boston look like Liverpool. But life must have hit its head on those close and low-ceilinged coops. That narrowness, that meagerness, that stinginess, still grips New England today: the drab summer cottages along the shore seem almost as slit-windowed and pinched as the gray twin-houses of a mill town like Lawrence or Fall River. I can feel the relief myself of coming away from Boston to these first uplands of the Adirondacks, where, discarding the New England religion but still speaking the language of New England, the settlers found limitless space. They were a part of the new America, now forever for a century on the move; and they were to move on themselves before they would be able to build here anything comparable to the New England civilization. The country, magnificent and vast, has never really been humanized as New England has: the landscape still overwhelms the people. But this house, one of the few of its kind among later wooden houses and towns, was an attempt to found a civilization. It blends in a peculiar fashion the amenities of the eastern seaboard with the rudeness and toughness of the new frontier.

It was built at the end of the eighteenth century: the first event recorded in connection with it is a memorial service for General Washington. It took four or five years in the building. The stone had to be quarried and brought out of the river. The walls are a foot and a half thick, and the plaster was applied to the stone without any intervening lattice. The beams were secured by enormous nails, made by hand and some of them eighteen inches long. Solid and simple as a fortress, the place has also the charm of something which has been made to order. There is a front porch with white wooden columns which support a white wooden balcony that runs along the second floor. The roof comes down close over the balcony, and the balcony and the porch are draped with vines. Large ferns grow along the porch, and there are stone hitching-posts and curious stone ornaments, cut out of the quarry like the house: on one side, a round-bottomed bowl in which red geraniums bloom, and on the other, an unnamable object, crudely sculptured and vaguely pagoda-like. The front door is especially handsome: the door itself is dark green and equipped with a brass knocker, and the woodwork which frames it is white; it is crowned with a wide fanlight and flanked by two narrow panes of glass, in which a white filigree of ironwork makes a webbing like ice over winter ponds. On one of the broad sides of the building, where the mortar has come off the stone, there is a dappling of dark gray under pale gray like the dappling of light in shallow water, and the feathers of the elms make dapplings of sun among their shadows of large lace on the grass.

The lawn is ungraded and uneven like the pastures, and it merges eventually with the fields. Behind, there are great clotted masses of myrtle-beds, lilac-bushes, clumps of pink phlox and other things I cannot identify; pink and white hollyhocks, some of them leaning, fine blue and purple dye of larkspur; a considerable vegetable garden, with long rows of ripe gooseberries and currants, a patch of yellow pumpkin flowers, and bushes of raspberries, both white and red—among which are sprinkled like confetti the little flimsy California poppies, pink, orange, white and red. In an old dark red barn behind, where the hayloft is almost collapsing, I find spinning-wheels, a carder, candle-molds, a patent boot-jack, obsolete implements of carpentry, little clusters of baskets for berry-picking and a gigantic pair of scales such as is nowadays only seen in the hands of allegorical figures.

The house was built by the Talcotts, after whom the town was named. They owned the large farm in front of the house, which stretches down to the river and beyond. They also had a profitable grist mill, but—I learn from the county history—were thought to have "adopted a policy adverse to the building up of the village at the point where natural advantages greatly favored," since they "refused to sell village lots to mechanics, and retained the water power on Sugar River, although parties offered to invest liberally in manufactures." In time, there were only two Talcotts left, an old maid and her widowed sister. My great-grandfather, Thomas Baker, who lived across the street and had been left by the death of his wife with a son and eight daughters, paid court to Miss Talcott and married her. She was kind to the children, and they remembered her with affection. My great-grandfather acquired in this way the house, the farm and the quarry.

All but two of my great-grandfather's daughters, of whom my grandmother was one—"six of them beauties," I understand—got married and went away. Only one of them was left in the house at the time when I first remember Talcottville: my great-aunt Rosalind, a more or less professional invalid and a figure of romantic melancholy, whose fiancé had been lost at sea. When I knew her, she was very old. It was impressive and rather frightening to call on her—you did it only by special arrangement, since she had to prepare herself to be seen. She would be beautifully dressed in a lace cap, a lavender dress and a white crocheted shawl, but she had become so bloodless and shrunken as dreadfully to resemble a mummy and reminded one uncomfortably of Miss Haversham in Dickens's *Great Expectations*. She had a certain high and formal coquetry and was the only person I ever knew who really talked like the characters in old novels. When she had been able to get about, she had habitually treated the townspeople with a condescension almost baronial. According to the family legend, the great-grandmother of great-grandmother Baker had been a daughter of one of the Earls of Essex, who had eloped with a gardener to America.

Another of my Baker great-aunts, who was one of my favorite relatives, had married and lived in the town and had suffered tragic disappointments. Only her strong intellectual interests and a mind capable of philosophic pessimism had maintained her through the wreck of her domestic life. She used to tell me how, a young married woman, she had taught herself French by the dictionary and grammar, sitting up at night alone by the stove through one of their cold and dark winters. She had read a great deal of French, subscribed to French magazines, without ever having learned to pronounce it. She had rejected revealed religion and did not believe in immortality; and when she felt that she had been relieved of the last of her family obligations—though her hair was now turning gray—she came on to New York City and lived there alone for years, occupying herself with the theater, reading, visits to her nephews and nieces—with whom she was extremely popular—and all the spectacle and news of the larger world which she had always loved so much but from which she had spent most of her life removed.

When she died, only the youngest of the family was left, the sole brother, my great-uncle Tom. His mother must have been worn out with childbearing—she died after the birth of this ninth child—and he had not turned out so well as the others. He had been born with no roof to his mouth and was obliged to wear a false gold palate, and it was difficult to understand him. He was not really simple-minded—he had held a small political job under Cleveland, and he usually beat me at checkers—but he was childlike and ill-equipped to deal with life in any very effective way. He sold the farm to a German and the quarry to the town. Then he died, and the house was empty, except when my mother and father would come here to open it up for two or three months in the summer.

I have not been back here in years, and I have never before

examined the place carefully. It has become for me something like a remembered dream—unearthly with the powerful impressions of childhood. Even now that I am here again, I find I have to shake off the dream. I keep walking from room to room, inside and outside, upstairs and down, with uneasy sensations of complacency that are always falling through to depression.

These rooms are very well proportioned; the white mantelpieces are elegant and chaste, and the carving on each one is different. The larger of the two living rooms now seems a little bare because the various members of the family have claimed and taken away so many things; and there are some disagreeable curtains and carpets, for which the wife of my great-uncle Tom is to blame. But here are all the things, I take note, that are nowadays sold in antique stores: red Bohemian-glass decanters; a rusty silver snuff-box; a mirror with the American eagle painted at the top of the glass. Little mahogany tables with slim legs; a set of curly-maple furniture, deep seasoned yellow like satin; a yellow comb-backed rocker, with a design of green conch-shells that look like snails. A small bust of Dante with the nose chipped, left behind as defective by one of my cousins when its companion piece, Beethoven, was taken away; a little mahogany melodeon on which my Aunt "Lin" once played. Large engravings of the family of Washington and of the "Reformers Presenting Their Famous Protest before the Diet of Spires"; a later engraving of Dickens. Old tongs and poker, impossibly heavy. A brown mahogany desk inlaid with yellow birdwood, which contains a pair of steel-rimmed spectacles and a thing for shaking sand on wet ink. Daguerrotypes in fancy cases: they seem to last much better than photographs—my grandmother looks fresh and cunning—I remember that I used to hear that the first time my grandfather saw her, she was riding on a load of hay—he came back up here to marry her as soon as he had got out of medical school. An old wooden flute—originally brought over from New England, I remember my great-uncle's telling me, at the time when they traveled by ox-team—he used to get a lonely piping out of it—I try it but cannot make a sound. Two big oval paintings, in tarnished gilt frames, of landscapes romantic and mountainous: they came from the Utica house of my great-grandfather Baker's brother—he married a rich wife and invented excelsior—made out of the northern lumber—and was presented with a solid-silver table service by the grateful city of Utica.

Wallpaper molded by the damp from the stone; uninviting old black haircloth furniture. A bowl of those enormous up-country sweet peas, incredibly fragrant and bright—they used to awe and trouble me—why?

In the dining room, a mahogany china closet, which originally—in the days when letters were few and great-grandfather Baker was postmaster—was the whole of the village post office. My grandmother's pewter tea-service, with its design of oak-leaves and acorns, which I remember from her house in New Jersey. Black iron cranes, pipkins and kettles for cooking in the fireplace; a kind of flat iron pitchfork for lifting the bread in and out, when they baked at the back of the hearth. On the sideboard, a glass decanter with a gilt black-letter label: "J. Rum." If there were only some rum in the decanter!—if the life of the house were not now all past! —the kitchens that trail out behind are almost too old-smelling, too long deserted, to make them agreeable to visit—in spite of the delightful brown crocks with long-tailed blue birds painted on them, a different kind of bird on each crock.

In the ample hall with its staircase, two large colored pictures of trout, one rising to bait, one leaping. Upstairs, a wooden pestle and mortar; a perforated tin box for hot coals to keep the feet warm in church or on sleigh-rides; a stuffed heron; a horrible bust of my cousin Dorothy Read in her girlhood, which her mother had done of her in Germany. The hair-ribbon and the ruffles are faithfully reproduced in marble, and the eyes have engraved pupils. It stands on a high pedestal, and it used to be possible, by pressing a button, to make it turn around. My Cousin Grace, Dorothy's mother, used to show it off and invite comparison with the original, especially calling attention to the nose; but what her mother had never known was that Dorothy had injured her nose in some rather disgraceful row with her sister. One day when the family were making an excursion, Dorothy pleaded indisposition and bribed a man with a truck to take the bust away and drop it into a pond. But Uncle Tom got this out of the man, dredged the statue up and replaced it on its pedestal. An ugly chair with a round rag back; an ugly bed with the head of Columbus sticking out above the pillows like a figurehead. Charming old bedquilts, with patterns of rhomboids in softened browns, greens and pinks, or of blue polka-dotted hearts that ray out on stiff phallic stalks. A footstool covered in white, which, however, when you step on a tab at the side, opens up into a cuspidor—some relic, no doubt, of the times when the house was used for local meetings. (There used to be a musical chair, also brought back from Germany, but it seems to have disappeared.) A jar of hardly odorous dried rose-leaves, and a jar of little pebbles and shells that keep their bright colors in alcohol.

The original old panes up here have wavy lines in the glass. There are cobweb-filthy books, which I try to examine: many religious works, the annals of the state legislature, a book called *The Young Wife, or Duties of Women in the Marriage Relation,* published in Boston in 1838 and containing a warning against tea and coffee, which "loosen the tongue, fire the eye, produce mirth and wit, excite the animal passions, and lead to remarks about ourselves and others, that we should not have made in other circumstances, and which it were better for us and the world, never to have made." But there is also, I noticed downstairs, Grant Allan's *The Woman Who Did* from 1893.

I come upon the *History of Lewis County* and read it with a certain pride. I am glad to say to myself that it is a creditable piece of work—admirably full in its information on geology, flora and fauna, on history and local politics; diversified with anecdotes and biographies never overflattering and often pungent; and written in a sound English style. Could anyone in the county today, I wonder, command such a sound English style? I note with gratification that the bone of a prehistoric cuttlefish, discovered in one of the limestone caves, is the largest of its kind on record, and that a flock of

wild swans was seen here in 1821. In the eighties, there
were still wolves and panthers. There are still bears and deer
today.

I also look into the proceedings of the New York State
Assembly. My great-grandfather Thomas Baker was primarily a politician and at that time a member of the Assembly.
I have heard that he was a Jacksonian Democrat, and that he
made a furious scene when my grandmother came back from
New Jersey and announced that she had become a Republican: it "spoiled her whole visit." There is a photograph of
great-grandfather Baker in an oval gilt frame, with his hair
sticking out in three spikes and a wide and declamatory
mouth. I look through the Assembly record to see what sort
of role he played. It is the forties; the Democrats are still
angry over the Bank of United States. But when I look up
Thomas Baker in the index, it turns out that he figures solely
as either not being present or as requesting leave of absence.
They tell me he used to go West to buy cattle.

That sealed-up space on the second floor which my father
had knocked out—who did they tell me was hidden in it? I
have just learned from one of the new road-signs which explain historical associations that there are caves somewhere
here in which slaves were hidden. Could this have been a
part of the underground route for smuggling Negroes over
the border into Canada? Is the attic, the "kitchen chamber,"
which is always so suffocating in summer, still full of those
carpetbags and crinolines and bonnets and beaver-hats that
we used to get out of the old cowhide trunks and use to
dress up for charades?

It was the custom for the married Baker daughters to bring
their children back in the summer; and their children in
time brought their children. In those days, how I loved coming up here! It was a reunion with cousins from Boston and
New York, Ohio and Wisconsin, as well as with the Talcottville and Utica ones: we fished and swam in the rivers, had
all sorts of excursions and games. Later on, I got to dislike
it: the older generation died, the younger did not much
come. I wanted to be elsewhere, too. The very fullness with
life of the past, the memory of those many families of cousins

and uncles and aunts, made the emptiness of the present more oppressive. Isn't it still?—didn't my gloom come from that, the night of my first arrival? Wasn't it the dread of that that kept me away? I am aware, as I walk through the rooms, of the amplitude and completeness of the place—the home of a big old-fashioned family that had to be a city in itself. And not merely did it house a clan: the whole life of the community passed through it. And now for five sixths of the year it is nothing but an unheated shell, a storehouse of unused antiques, with no intimate relation to the county.

The community itself today is somewhat smaller than the community of those days, and its condition has very much changed. It must seem to the summer traveler merely one of the clusters of houses that he shoots through along the state highway; and there may presently be little left save our house confronting, across the road, the hot-dog stand and the gasoline station.*

For years I have had a recurrent dream. I take a road that runs toward the west. It is summer; I pass by a strange summer forest, in which there are mysterious beings, though I know that, on the whole, they are shy and benign. If I am fortunate and find the way, I arrive at a wonderful river, which runs among boulders, with rapids, between alders and high spread trees, through a countryside fresh, green and wide. We go in swimming; it is miles away from anywhere. We plunge in the smooth flowing pools. We make our way to the middle of the stream and climb up on the pale round gray stones and sit naked in the sun and the air, while the river glides away below us. And I know that it is the place for which I have always longed, the place of wildness and freedom, to find which is the height of what one may hope for—the place of unalloyed delight.

As I walk about Talcottville now, I discover that the being-

* This description may seem inconsistent with my account of our Talcottville location in another book, *A Piece of My Mind,* but the main highway was later shifted, put through along another road, and my mother had succeeded, in the meantime, in getting rid of the hot-dog stand by buying back the lot across the street.

haunted forest is a big grove which even in daytime used to
be lonely and dark and where great white Canadian violets
used to grow out of the deep black leaf-mold. Today it is no
longer dark, because half the trees have been cut down. The
river of my dream, I see, is simply an idealized version of
the farther and less frequented and more adventurous bank
of Sugar River, which had to be reached by wading. Both
river and forest are west of the road that runs through the
village, which accounts for my always taking that direction
in my dream. I remember how Sugar River—out of the stone
of which our house is built—used, in my boyhood, so to fascinate me that I had an enlargement made of one of the
photographs I had taken of it—a view of "the Big Falls"—
and kept it in my room all winter. Today the nearer bank has
been largely blasted away to get stone for the new state highway, and what we used to call "the Little Falls" is gone.

I visit the house of my favorite great-aunt, and my gloom
returns and overwhelms me. The huge root of an elm has
split the thick slabs of the pavement so that you have to walk
over a hump; and one of the big square stone fence-posts is
toppling. Her flowers, with no one to tend them, go on rag-
gedly blooming in their seasons. There has been nobody in
her house since she died. It is all too appropriate to her pessimism—that dead end she always foresaw. As I walk around
the house, I remember how, once on the back porch there,
she sang me old English ballads, including that gruesome
one, "Oh, where have you been, Randall, my son?"—about
the man who had gone to Pretty Peggy's house and been
given snakes to eat:

> *"What had you for supper, Randall, my son?"*
> *"Fresh fish fried in butter. Oh, make my bed soon!*
> *For I'm sick at my heart and I fain would lie down!"*

She was old then—round-shouldered and dumpy—after the
years when she had looked so handsome, straight-backed and
with the fashionable aigrette in her hair. And the song she
sang seemed to have been drawn out of such barbarous
reaches of the past, out of something so surprisingly different
from the college-women's hotels in New York in which I
had always known her as living: that England to which, far

though she had come from it, she was yet so much nearer than I—that queer troubling world of legend which I knew from Percy's *Reliques* but with which she had maintained a real contact through centuries of women's voices—for she sang it without a smile, completely possessed by its spirit— that it made my flesh creep, disconcerted me.

My great-aunt is dead, and all her generation are dead— and the new generations of the family have long ago left Talcottville behind and have turned into something quite different. They were already headed for the cities by the middle of the last century, as can be seen by the rapid dispersal of great-grandfather Baker's daughters. Yet there were still, in my childhood, a few who stayed on in this country as farmers. They were very impressive people, the survivors of a sovereign race who had owned their own pastures and fields and governed their own community. Today the descendants of these are performing mainly minor functions in a machine which they do not control. They have most of them become thoroughly urbanized, and they are farther from great-grand- father Baker than my grandmother, his daughter, was when she came back from New Jersey a Republican. One of her children, a retired importer in New York, was complaining to me the other day that the outrageous demands of the farm- ers were making business recovery impossible, and protesting that if the advocates of the income tax had their way, the best people would no longer be able to live up to their social positions. A cousin, who bears the name of one of his Ips- wich ancestors, a mining engineer on the Coast and a class- mate and admirer of Hoover, invested and has lost heavily in Mexican real estate and the industrial speculations of the boom. Another, with another of the old local names, is now at the head of an organization whose frankly avowed purpose is to rescue the New York manufacturers from taxation and social legislation. He has seen his native city of Utica decline as a textile center through the removal of its mills to the South, where taxes are lighter and labor is cheaper; and he is honestly convinced that his efforts are directed toward civic betterment.

Thus the family has come imperceptibly to identify its interests with those of what my great-grandfather Baker would have called the "money power." They work for it and acquiesce in it—they are no longer the sovereign race of the first settlers of Lewis County, and in the cities they have achieved no sovereignty. They are much too scrupulous and decent, and their tastes are too comparatively simple for them ever to have rolled up great fortunes during the years of expansion and plunder. They have still the frank accent and the friendly eye of the older American world, and they seem rather taken aback by the turn that things have been taking.

And what about me? As I come back in the train, I find that—other causes contributing—my depression of Talcottville deepens. I did not find the river and the forest of my dream—I did not find the magic of the past. I have been too close to the past: there in that house, in that remote little town which has never known industrial progress since the Talcotts first obstructed the development of the water power of Sugar River, you can see exactly how rural Americans were living a century and a half ago. And who would go back to it? Not I. Let people who have never known country life complain that the farmer has been spoiled by his radio and his Ford. Along with the memory of exaltation at the immensity and freedom of that countryside, I have memories of horror at its loneliness: houses burning down at night, sometimes with people in them, where there was no fire department to save them, and husbands or wives left alone by death—the dark nights and the prisoning winters. I do not grudge the sacrifice of the Sugar River falls for the building of the new state highway, and I do not resent the hot-dog stand. I am at first a little shocked at the sight of a transformer on the road between Talcottville and Boonville, but when I get to the Talcottville house, I am obliged to be thankful for it—no more oil-lamps in the evenings! And I would not go back to that old life if I could: that civilization of northern New York—why should I idealize it?—was too lonely, too poor, too provincial.

I look out across the Hudson and see Newburgh: with the neat-windowed cubes of its dwellings and docks, distinct as if cut by a burin, built so densely up the slope of the bank and pierced by an occasional steeple, undwarfed by tall modern buildings and with only the little old-fashioned ferry to connect it with the opposite bank, it might still be an eighteenth-century city. My father's mother came from there. She was the granddaughter of a carpet-importer from Rotterdam. From him came the thick Spanish coins which the children of my father's family were supposed to cut their teeth on. The business, which had been a considerable one, declined as the sea trade of the Hudson became concentrated in New York. My father and mother went once—a good many years ago—to visit the old store by the docks, and were amazed to find a solitary old clerk still scratching up orders and sales on a slate that hung behind the counter.

And the slate and the Spanish coins, though they symbolize a kind of life somewhat different from that evoked by Talcottville, associate themselves in my mind with such things as the old post office turned china closet. And as I happen to be reading Herndon's *Life of Lincoln,* that, too, goes to flood out the vision with its extension still further west, still further from the civilized seaboard, of the life of the early frontier. Through Herndon's extraordinary memoir, one of the few really great American books of its kind, which America has never accepted, preferring to it the sentimentalities of Sandburg and the ladies who write Christmas stories —the past confronts me even more plainly than through the bootjacks and daguerreotypes of Talcottville, and makes me even more uneasy. Here you are back again amid the crudeness and the poverty of the American frontier, and here is a man of genius coming out of it and perfecting himself. The story is not merely moving, it becomes almost agonizing. The ungainly boorish boy from the settler's clearing, with nobody and nothing behind him, hoping that his grandfather had been a planter as my great-aunt Rosalind hoped that she was a descendant of the Earls of Essex, the morbid young man looking passionately toward the refinement and the training of the East but unable to bring himself to marry the women who represented it for him—rejoining across days in country stores, nights in godforsaken hotels, rejoining by heroic self-discipline the creative intelligence of the race, to find himself the conscious focus of its terrible unconscious parturition—his miseries burden his grandeur. At least they do for me at this moment.

> *Old Abe Lincoln came out of the wilderness,*
> *Out of the wilderness, out of the wilderness—*

The echo of the song in my mind inspires me with a kind of awe—I can hardly bear the thought of Lincoln.

Great-grandfather Baker's politics and the Talcottville general store, in which people sat around and talked before the new chain store took its place—Lincoln's school was not so very much different. And I would not go back to that.

Yet as I walk up the steps of my house in New York, I am forced to recognize, with a sinking, that I have never been able to leave it. This old wooden booth I have taken between First and Second Avenues—what is it but the same old provincial America? And as I open the door with its loose knob and breathe in the musty smell of the stair-carpet, it seems to me that I have not merely stuck in the world where my fathers lived but have actually, in some ways, lost ground in it. This gray paintless clapboarded front, these lumpy and rubbed yellow walls—they were probably once respectable, but they must always have been commonplace. They have never had even the dignity of the house in Lewis County. But I have rented them because, in my youth, I had been used to living in houses and have grown to loathe city apartments.

So here, it seems, is where I must live: in an old cramped and sour frame-house—having failed even worse than my relatives at getting out of the American big-business era the luxuries and the prestige that I unquestionably should very much have enjoyed. Here is where I end by living—among the worst instead of the best of this city that took the trade away from Newburgh—the sordid and unhealthy children of my sordid and unhealthy neighbors, who howl outside my windows night and day. It is this, in the last analysis —there is no doubt about it now!—which has been rankling and causing my gloom: to have left that early world behind yet never to have really succeeded in what was till yesterday the new.

1933

THE SECOND BATTLE OF ORISKANY

IT WAS ONLY a few days after this—after my return from Talcottville to New York—that I began to read in the papers of a milk strike that was going on in the region from which I had just come. I had been there so short a time and had been so much preoccupied with the past that I knew nothing of what was happening to the farmers; and I immediately went back to find out.

In Talcottville, I was invited by a Talcottville farmer to attend a strikers' meeting in Boonville, and—on account of my city clothes—was at first mistaken for a stool pigeon in the pay of the dairy interests. They were going to put me out, but the man who had invited me intervened and explained to them who I was.

I had read in the New York City papers about the ruffianly bands of marauders—not natives nor even farmers and, according to Hamilton Fish, under the leadership of Communist agitators—who were prowling about the country dumping milk, poisoning wells and destroying property. What I found were simply the Lewis County farmers whom I had known all my life, and who, though they certainly railed against "the capitalists," were indignant at being called Communists. They were, however, extremely aroused. I have never seen such furious feeling in any industrial strike. The industrial workers of the towns are accustomed to having their standards of living cut away, and then, when they try to rebel, having the police called out to suppress them. They have evolved their organization and their strategy; they are not surprised by bullets or clubs. But the farmers of upstate New York have never been clubbed before.

They have, however, struck before, in 1920, but there was no violence and they won their demands. Lately, their condition has become unbearable. With heavy debts and mortgaged farms, they have been dragging on year after year, unable to produce a profit and compelled to live on their savings. They have recently—rightly or wrongly—been seething at having their herds, as the result of the new tuberculosis tests, condemned and taken away. And they now find themselves getting less for their milk than the upkeep of their cows costs them.

They had hoped for relief from the Pitcher Bill, framed by a man from upstate; but they say that by the time it was passed, the Legislature, under pressure from the milk-distributors, had rendered it ineffective. A milk board, to be sure, was set up; but it very soon lost its prestige because the farmers believed it to be dominated by their enemies, the distributors. It immediately rejected the farmers' demand for a minimum price for milk at the farm, and fixed, instead, a price at the milk stations for cream and fluid milk only, with the "surplus"—that is to say, the milk in excess of the fluid demand—to be paid for at lower prices. This surplus is about half the farmer's output. It is made into butter, cheese, powdered milk and ice cream. The farmers claim that they have been swindled on this surplus—that they have no means of checking up on how much milk the distributors actually sell as fluid and how much they put into the secondary products. They believe that the distributors make a practice of paying them for their milk at the lower prices and selling it to the consumer at the higher, and that the classification of the different kinds of milk destined for different purposes has intentionally been made very complicated in order to prevent the farmers from finding out what is being done. The milk board had announced that it was depending on the inspectors and on the force of public opinion to keep the milk companies from cheating the farmers—to see that when the price to the consumer was raised, the farmer got his share of the increase. But the price to the consumer went up, and the farmer was as poor as ever.

The inspectors having apparently failed, it was time for public opinion. The prolonged drought this summer, which has burned the pastures brown, came as a last straw. The farmers' savings had all been used up; there were families who were already starving. A meeting was called at Utica, and representatives of some 50,000 farmers voted to strike simultaneously on the morning of August 1, refusing to deliver their milk to the dealers. They demanded for the farmer forty-five cents on the consumer's dollar.

The strike was put into effect, and the farmers not only kept their milk at home but picketed the milk plants and dumped the milk of farmers who tried to deliver. Oneida County was at the core of the strike, and the farmers in the neighborhood of the little city of Boonville had been among the most active. The authorities apparently decided to make an example of Boonville, and state troopers were sent there last Monday night. About 10:30 on Tuesday morning, a crowd of some three hundred farmers and spectators gathered along the road outside the town, waiting for a truck that was headed for Sheffield's. They had a long board with spikes ready to lay across the road. The troopers came out in their cars and marched down between the lines of the crowd, who, never having done any picketing before, did not hesitate to make fun of the troopers. The troopers, encountering this spirit, marched back again to their cars and, to the continued amusement of the crowd, proceeded to put on gas masks and steel helmets and to arm themselves with submachine-guns, gas bombs and riot sticks. The people had never seen submachine-guns and did not know what to call them. The troopers have asserted since that they ordered the pickets to disperse, that no movement was made to obey, and that somebody threw a stone; but it was impossible to find among the Boonville people anyone who would corroborate this. At any rate, the troopers assaulted the crowd, shooting gas bombs at them and clubbing them: men and women, old and young, alike.

They chased people into fields and woodsheds, rushed up and beat them over the head when they got stuck in the barbed-wire fence. I saw many broken heads and bruises. There was one man who had had a gas bomb fired point-blank into his back, injuring him severely and setting his clothes afire. The troopers yelled at the farmers that they were sons of bitches, rats, Reds; the people thought they must be drunk. That the crowd was unarmed is proved by the fact that they ran away and that the troopers were not hurt.

I have never seen a whole community so shaken by horror and anger. Nothing like this, in New York State history, had ever happened to the dairy farmers, and the result was precisely the opposite of what the authorities had contemplated. "They thought they'd teach 'em a lesson," said someone, "but they only made 'em fierce!" Four days after the Boonville incident, the troopers were acting as escort to another truck just outside the town of Oriskany. They were led by their commander, a Captain McGrath, who was asserted by the Boonville people to have been present at the previous attack, but who denied this, declaring, when questioned, that he did not know who had led the state troopers that day. This time the farmer-pickets were prepared for them: they had ax-helves, pick-handles and stones. Though they came away with wounds of their own, they succeeded in stoning the troopers so effectively that five of them had to be taken to the hospital, including Captain McGrath. Captain McGrath had been the officer in command when the prison revolt at Auburn was suppressed, and the farmers passed around the saying, "This is no prison revolt!" Oriskany had already been made famous by a battle between the revolutionary army and the Tories and Indians in 1777, and people got to referring to the encounter with the troopers as the "Battle of Oriskany." A correspondent in the Rome *Sentinel* began talking about Lexington and Concord.

In this region, unlike certain of the Western communities, there is no split between the town and the country. The merchants, dependent on the farmers' trade, are 100 per cent with the strikers. Here is a protest to Governor Lehman signed by a "Committee of Boonville Business Men": "We, the business and professional men of Boonville, having witnessed the medieval atrocities perpetrated today by your brutal state troopers against the best citizenry of America, do protest and demand that you take immediate steps to remove these brutes from our midst and rectify a condition that should never have existed in connection with the milk holi-

day." The Kiwanis signed a similar protest. It was strange
to find the local paper, the *Boonville Herald and Adirondack
Tourist,* which, with its immemorial idyllic cut of a stag's
head, a creel and a rifle, has never, in all the years I have
known it, chronicled anything but the most pastoral happen-
ings, coming out with denunciations of "Cossacks" and
"half-crazed thugs," and bulletins on local battles.

The editor and other leading citizens, unable to believe
that the behavior of the troopers could be known to or backed
by the authorities, went down to Albany themselves and appealed to the Governor for an inquiry. The Governor sent
Major Warner, the chief of the state police. Major Warner,
they told me, arrived in town without allowing his presence
to be known, entered the hotel by the back door—there was a
crowd standing around the front door—and interviewed his
own troopers. When the citizens insisted on his seeing one
of the farmers who had been beaten up, he listened to what
the man had to say and then grimly replied that if they
hadn't enough troopers, he would send them forty or fifty
more—which he did. He arranged for an investigation, but
appointed to conduct it the same Captain McGrath who had
asserted that he did not know who had led the charge at
Boonville and who had afterwards been sent to the hospital
by the rocks of Oriskany Falls. The citizens demanded of
the Governor that Major Warner be suspended from office
and that some person not injured in the battle be appointed
to conduct the inquiry. The bitterness was increased when
the announcement came that not only would the inquiry be
conducted by McGrath but that it would take place behind
closed doors instead of—as had been first said—in public, and
that not even the New York press would be allowed to report it.

In the meantime, the situation between the state troopers
and the farmers had been growing tenser and tenser. The
farmers went on picketing and dumping. I saw one man who
had been up five nights; he had been picketing a plant
where the troopers had finally scalded the pickets with a hose
of boiling hot water, and he was literally foaming at the
mouth—the first time I have ever seen this phenomenon. One

old man who had been chased by the troopers took his stand on the railroad track and shouted that he owned stock in the railroad and that the troopers couldn't touch him on his own property. The farmers had been ambushing the big milk tanks that were being sent down from the north: they punctured the tires with rifle balls. They also fired on the cans in the milk trains. They put irresistible pressure on farmers who refused to join the "holiday," dynamiting their milk houses and pouring kerosene in their milk; and in the case of one fancy farmer who owned a herd of prize cattle and who by reason of his attempts to discourage the strike was suspected of being in the pay of the enemy, they drove his cattle away and, according to rumor, cut off their tails.

This last was a great joke at the strikers' meetings, which were held out of doors every afternoon. Their leaders would speak from a truck. It was not in the least like an industrial strike: there was no professional eloquence and no one sent in from outside. There was a more desperate rage underneath and a more jocular and easygoing surface. No gaze can look so fierce as the clear and steady eye of a farmer. I remember the fixed warlike grin of one boy who was trying to salvage his truck, which had been used in the picketing the night before: the troopers had smashed the windshield, broken the steering wheel and systematically put out of commission all the more important parts inside. The troopers were carrying guns where the farmers had only clubs, and were able to drive the farmers off. The women had been churning their milk into butter with electric washing-machines, and they sometimes took part in the battles with such weapons as pop bottles and bricks.

The Governor, reluctant to call out the militia—which would certainly have been a signal for civil war—instructed the sheriffs to appoint their own deputies. But the sheriff of Oneida County pointed out that, in an attempt to eliminate jobs, it had been ruled in Oneida County that the sheriff should pay deputies out of his own pocket; and the Ways and Means Committee of the Board of Supervisors refused to appropriate funds for this purpose. "I wonder," said one of them, "what the farmers would say if we spent the money they pay in taxes for deputies to fight them with." It had made the farmers particularly mad to reflect that the troopers, maintained by their own money, were really "the farmers' hired men." The Governor had to make haste to get a bill through the New York State Legislature in order to provide the funds to pay deputies in Oneida County.

Governor Lehman also made an attempt to have the Legislature investigate the milk board; but the Republicans passed the buck back to him and told him to deal with the matter himself. Then the rotogravure supplements of the Sunday papers published a picture of the Governor calling on the President at Hyde Park—Roosevelt looking up at the camera with his usual alert affability and Lehman bending forward toward the President in an attitude of gratified compliance. And though the Governor would not treat with the farmers till the strike had been definitely called off, some kind of assurance from the top had evidently been received, for the strike leaders gave the signal for the dairymen to begin delivering milk again.

Yet I came away gloomy from the milk strike. Governor Lehman is supposed to own stock in Borden's; and the chimerical smile of Roosevelt hovers very far away on the horizon. What the farmers are immediately faced with is the countenance of Captain McGrath—that ominous phenomenon, the military policeman, who has come to play such a role in American life since the war—sitting down behind closed doors, in the midst of their own community, to pass judgment on himself and his underlings.

1933

SAVING THE RIGHT PEOPLE AND THEIR BUTLERS

CHRIST, THE SPEAKER TELLS US, has come to the Akron, Ohio, tire factories: You've heard about the non-skid tires they make out there. Well, now they're making non-skid lives! And the salmon fisheries in British Columbia. There had been a strike called up there which would have stopped work in the whole salmon-fishing industry in British Columbia. But the boss got together with the radical leader, and he shared Christ with him, and the strike was called off. And again, in the Ford hospital in Dearborn, the doctor there shares Christ with the Ford workers that come to him as patients. And so labor and capital get together, and they coöperate in the spirit of God, and that's the only way they *can* get together!

The speaker is one of those colorless, amorphous, outlineless, expressionless Americans who seem never to have grown up and never to have acquired a personality. He is probably a man of middle age. All the front part of his head is smooth of hair, but his face is as blank as a baby's. He is wearing a dinner jacket with a remarkably wide bow tie, which stretches from lapel to lapel.

This lackluster figure is framed in an immense and splendid setting: the ballroom of the Plaza Hotel. All is diamond, cream and gold. There are gold moldings and gold-trimmed Ionic columns, medallions of dainty cupids outlined on apple-green backgrounds, and big dazzling chandeliers made of clusters of tiny bulbs as dense as incandescent chain mail. In red-curtained boxes so spacious that each seems a small proscenium, each lighted by a lesser chandelier which dangles like a bright diamond pendant, sit ladies in evening gowns, very unprovocative evening gowns, and gentlemen

in dinner jackets, with white handkerchiefs sticking out of
their pockets.

It is a meeting of the First Century Christian Fellowship,
otherwise known as the Oxford Group—the evangelical
movement led by Frank Buchman and formerly called Buch-
manism. The occasion is a rally preparatory to Buchman's arrival in New York.

But the man who has just been speaking and who believes
that Christ has come to the salmon fisheries has a more positive force behind him. A rotund and fleshy chairman in bone
spectacles, evidently one of Buchman's lieutenants, picks up
the high pressure of the meeting with an emphatic voice and
hearty Southern accent. "What you've just heard," he declares, "is news, not views! Events, not theories! We do a lot
of talking about what *might* happen—well, what you've just
heard about is what *has* happened!"

The next speaker is a middle-aged lady in black, gentle-
voiced, touchingly sincere, and with little of the exhibition-
ism of the convert, who explains that going to church had
ceased really to mean anything to her and that the Oxford
Group had finally awakened her to the truths of religion
again. She is followed by a long-legged blond boy, who has
the innocently smirking self-consciousness of a freshman who
has just made the glee club. He had gone to a church school,
he tells us, and so he ought to have learned better, but he
had thought only of having a good time and had failed to
consider other people. The result was that he became "a periodical drunkard." He had tried being psychoanalyzed and
that had lasted about two weeks; then he had tried religion,
but it wasn't presented to him in the right way. Finally, he
had found friends in the Oxford Group who were willing to
lay down their lives with him, who wanted to share with
him and help him. "And they certainly have!" he ends rather
abruptly, and sits down and goes on innocently smirking
through most of the rest of the meeting. A second boy from
college announces that he went to prep at Hotchkiss, "which
is a very good school," and afterwards to Princeton, "which
is usually considered a pretty good college." At college, he
had "learned to behave like a gentleman" and he had "broad-

ened his intellectual horizon," but he had never had any direction. It was the Oxford Group that had given him direction. At school he had always been afraid that people would think he was queer because he had come from China, but the Oxford Group had brought him such true happiness as he had not believed possible.

The chairman now puts it to us whether it isn't true that these big social movements—these big social movements that spread so wide!—aren't the result of first one person being changed and then changing other people.

So far, I am a little disappointed. I seem to be back in prep school at a YMCA meeting. I had expected something more sensational. Some years ago, I remember, Frank Buchman became so objectionable to the authorities at Princeton that they forbade him to come on the campus, and since then I have heard colorful reports of the movement's triumphal progress. I have observed during the last few years, in the industrial Middle-Western cities, that the success of the tours of the Oxford Group among the propertied classes seems to have been proceeding at equal pace with the increasing acuteness of the crisis. I have heard about the Buchmanite house parties which begin with an atmosphere of well-bred cheerfulness and white handerchiefs sticking out of dinner jackets, but end with sin-spilling and hysterics; and I am let down by these infantile jokes, these woolly schoolboy opinions, this audience of giggling and better-class-dressed and half-baked-looking people. It is not even up to an AF of L meeting or a Rotary Club dinner. The faiths of the respectable churches must now be burning low indeed if this is the hottest flare that their firebrands have to offer.

The chairman himself, I admit, compares favorably with any Rotary Club pep-talker or AF of L orator. He has mastered a technique very similar to theirs, and the similarity of his ideas is surprising. "Some people," he remarks with sarcasm, "will tell you that religion is something so *private*, so *personal*, that you can't speak about it to other people! Well, the Communists don't feel that way! *They* don't hesitate to speak out! *They* let people know about what they think! And if we don't want the Communists and the radicals to get control of the whole world, we'll have to speak out, too!"

But as I look at this chairman and hear him, a gradual realization astounds me. The chairman is an old friend of mine, whom I have not seen for many years. I knew that he was one of Buchman's disciples, and I had wondered whether I should find him here. I had fancied I had had a glimpse of him at one moment when I first came in, standing up with his back turned toward me—the tall, stooped, ungainly, earnest youth whom I had known and liked at college. He was already headed then for the Episcopal Church, and he was the only man I knew at that time who had an unmistakable religious vocation. We used to call him "The Bishop," and predict for him a sybaritic future of fine chasubles and gossipy tea-drinking in a well-to-do parish. Well, our friend has certainly fooled us, though I was always aware in him of something serious, something which would not allow him to become the typical snobbish rector. It was this, with his genuine appreciation of cathedrals and classical music, which used to make me find him good company. And, once I have recognized him now, I can still see the seriousness in him, totally metamorphosed though he otherwise seems; and my old liking for him now causes me to follow the developments of the meeting with a certain sympathetic interest which I have not felt up to now.

A new speaker at this point does something to make me understand my friend's transformation. He is a nice funny little Episcopal clergyman, the rector of a church on Long Island—with a round, pink, bald, boyish head so shiny that it might be buttered, and his silver cross dangling distinctly against the black expanse of his waistcoat—who stands as if on tiptoe, with his arms held out from his sides, like the Bishop of Rum-Ti-Foo in the *Bab Ballads*. This buoyant little rector tells us that he had been preaching sermons for many years and that he was never able to see that they had any effect on people. He preached a sermon one Sunday on the Seventh Commandment, and a man came up to him afterwards and said, "That was a magnificent sermon!" And then, just a few months later, that same man ran away with somebody's wife. Then the rector's own wife had come home one day and told him that she had been talking to the Oxford Group, and that, for the first time in her life, they had made religion seem real to her. He had been a little taken aback to realize that, living with him all these years, she had never been able to take religion seriously. So he had looked into the Oxford movement, and the effect on his sermons had been electric. One of his parishioners had come to him one Sunday and asked him, "What did you say in your sermon this morning? Alice came back all upset. She's been crying ever since." Another of his congregation complained that she didn't know what had got into him, he had used to preach decent, sensible, reasonable sermons, and now he preached like a Methodist!

Well, suppose, the outsider puts it to himself, you found yourself an Episcopal clergyman these days: would you be content with the duties of your parish, such good works as you find the occasion for through the offices and forms of the Church, such dignity as one may derive from an ancient and distinguished tradition? Suppose you were not ambitious in Bishop Manning's way—suppose you really wanted to reach people's souls? Suppose you wanted to make people aware of the deeper moral realities which the conventional world covers up? It would hardly be possible to accomplish this through the regular Protestant churches: they are none of them alive enough. Among Protestants, the only religion which still seems to take hold of its communicants is the outlawed religion of the evangelists, of the Aimee McPhersons and the Buchmans. And, given the vocation of saving souls, I should certainly agree with my friend that all the cathedrals and Bach in the world cannot compensate for the deadness of the churches—which will build no more real cathedrals nor commission any more great masses.

But as the proceedings of the evening go on, my sympathies become terribly dampened.

Somebody, the chairman tells us, asked him lately whether there was anybody in the Oxford group who was not more or less rich; and a slight titter is heard from the assembly, which seems to me a little self-conscious. It is a fact that the leaders of the Oxford Group have always frankly gone out for the "socially prominent," the theory of its leader being that, for purposes of general conversion, such persons are the key men and women in any college or other community. The soul of a boy in the very best club, of a lady who lives in the East Eighties, is particularly pleasing to God, because He knows that their example will be followed by the members of more humble clubs, the dwellers at less splendid addresses. The ballroom and the dinner jackets of the Oxford Group really belong to the realm of class advertizing, with the pictures of social leaders, posing in expensive interiors, that are used to sell onion soup and mentholated cigarettes. And so does calling it the Oxford Group instead of, as formerly, Buchman-ism—though it has, of course, no connection with Oxford or the Oxford movement. The "Oxford," with its suggestion of Old World correctitude, takes off the curse of vulgar evange-lism, and the happy invention, "First Century Christian Fel-lowship," disarms any imputation of snobbishness which may be roused by the idea of Oxford.

But the chairman, at the present moment, wants to em-phasize the latter of these aspects; and, after pointing out the importance of kindness to servants, he produces a reformed butler. This butler, says the chairman, was down and out, and then he came to work at Calvary Mission, and then they got him a job with a lady who was a member of the Oxford Group, and he will tell you now all that it had meant to him to work for a family who has been "changed."

The butler is a bald little Irishman, who explains that for many years he had led a life of drunkenness and sin. Drink had been his god; he had rolled in the gutter drunk, and once he had lain in a speakeasy for five days and five nights without ever changing his clothes. He had been in the alco-holic ward at Bellevue Hospital five times with delirium tre-mens, once for six weeks at a stretch. When he had first taken the job with the B————s, he had had to mix cocktails for them, and he hadn't been sure at first whether he could stand it, but he had held up and now he has the keys to the cellar—and, he adds, with obvious pride, "Mrs. B———— has quite a cellar!" The other night, when the nurse had been out, he had been asked to go upstairs and stay with the little daughter. She was kneeling down and saying her prayers, and this is what he had heard her say: "God bless my Mummy and God help my Mummy to win my Daddy to Christ!"

The members of the First Century Christian Fellowship are vaguely troubled by the events of the twentieth. The world crisis is always present as a remote but uncomfortable background which persists in making itself felt even after one has succeeded in easing one's own discontent. One lady points out that "Europe seems to be on the verge of chaos" and that "it seems as if we might not be far behind." She has thought about it a little more seriously than the others; and, in general, the women of the Oxford Group seem more serious and genuine than the men. They tell how they had formerly tried social work, charities, acting, teaching, raising money for cathedrals, and how none of these activities was satisfactory. The effect on the businessmen is curious. One young man from a well-known rubber company says that people had warned him that you couldn't mix religion with business, but they had tried mixing everything else with business, and look at business now! He himself had had a hard time to bring himself to go to all the customers he had deceived and confess to them how they had been cheated, but he had done it and, instead of their resenting it, he had found that it had brought him and them closer together.

The concluding exhibit of the evening is a couple from Great Neck, Long Island. The wife is presented first and explains that she had been married to an intellectual and unable to share his interests, and that this had made her very unhappy till she had discovered the Oxford Group. At this point the husband appears—a white-faced man in glasses, with a round forehead that dwarfs his chin—and turns out to be simply an advertizing man who has just written a book. He had protested, when he first talked with the Oxford Group, that you couldn't be honest in the advertizing business, and they had replied that you could if you'd take the loss. So he had tried, he had tried to be all the three things that the Oxford Group said you ought to be: *pure, unselfish,* and *loving.* It was hard enough, he found, to be pure. In his advertizing copy in the past he had depended a good deal on suggestiveness, on the sensual appeal; he had, for example, written advertizements for a perfume which he had named after a famous prima donna, and these had brought letters from women who wanted to know whether it would really bring back their lost lovers. He had had to cut all that out. And it was hard, he found, to be unselfish, to sacrifice profitable contracts because you couldn't conscientiously supply the copy. But the hardest thing of all was to be loving. He had always formerly hated his competitors, especially when they were successful at his expense, and he now found it very difficult to love them. But he had succeeded, and now when anybody beat him out, his attitude toward them remained loving: instead of cursing them, he would wish them good luck, hope that their success might continue and their lives be full of happiness. Besides this, he had been able to be much nicer with his family at the time when he had been working on his book; he had ceased to be so cross at the dinner table. And finally he had taken the step of putting the book "under guidance," had "asked God to write it for him." The chairman stands up with a copy of it and announces that it is soon to be published.

The whole occasion makes an impression infinitely sad and insipid. I have seen these people before: these people whom their work does not satisfy, these people who are coming to realize that their functions in society are not serious and to seek anxiously for something to hang on to which will give them an anchor outside it all. If they were a little more uncomfortably neurotic, they would be going to psychoanalysts; if they were sillier, they would be nudists; if they were cleverer, Gurdjieff would get them. But the house parties, the butlers and the ballrooms of the First Century Christian Fellowship seem to be just what is needed for these particular cases. It has been the great achievement of Frank Buchman to put patent-leather pumps on the Christ of the missions and get him into a dinner jacket, and to give him for Mary Magdalene a refined Anglo-Saxon lady, chastely but expensively gowned. They have invested him with the fatuous cheerfulness of the people in the American advertizements and of the salesmen who try to sell you what they advertize. One of the characteristic features of the Oxford Group is the continual chuckling and bubbling, the grinning and twinkling and beaming which goes on among its members, and which makes an outsider feel quite morose.

It is ominously symptomatic of the condition of the propertied classes that it is possible now to make them accept the old shouting confession-forcing God of the camp meeting and the Salvation Army shelter. I noticed some Salvation Army people among the Buchmanites, watching, I did not doubt, with a keen professional eye. Are they envious of Buchman as they realize that nowadays it is not only the poor who need to be reconciled to their lot?

1934

WHAT TO DO TILL THE DOCTOR COMES

From the Diary of a Drinker-Out

It was good to be clear-headed again: the night before now seemed inconceivable. There the three of us had sat getting tight and raking up that old three-cornered disgrace, in the Oyster Bar of the Grand Central. Now my mind seemed as limpid and perfect as the big round biological cell in the center of the Diego Rivera mural which the Rockefellers so stupidly destroyed.

I could summon the address with distinguished ease, and I could remember the names of the people who had asked me. I had decided not to drink at this party at all; and it would be interesting to find out more about them—not to drink, and then to see Sally, and to drink only a little with her. I noticed a marble cupid choking a dolphin in the entry, and I thought it looked like something I might have seen if I had got off to Italy this spring.

My nerves, however, shied a little as I broke into the hub-bub of the party. I hadn't run into Arthur Fern for years, and I am always glad to see him. I wondered why I never look him up. He seemed clammy and a little ascetic as if he had been reading André Gide—as I do not doubt that he had. He told me that he was on the wagon and that he was afraid he shouldn't enjoy the party; and we shook hands on it and swore to stand by one another. Joe Peranza came up: I was glad to see him—he had always been my favorite press agent. He was very funny about the shows—though I think there might have been the makings of a really good theatrical season if only the new plays had been any good and if only there had been somebody to take a real interest in staging and directing the revivals. We had one of their purple cock-tails. I was glad to see Elsie Flinders, though she is certainly

not physically attractive; and we all began laughing like
hyenas.

There is a girl I always see at these parties, and I never
know who she is, but this time it turned out she was married
to Joe. When I meet her, I always forget that she is capable
of being funny, so have long dragging conversations with
her, and then when she begins to be funny, it is too late:
someone else comes up. On this occasion, thanks to my sobriety, I remembered and immediately encouraged her to
make cracks about the other guests. The second set of cocktails carried us high. She told me that she and Joe had got
horribly on one another's nerves. At first, they had worked
together, returning each other's nifties; but then she found
she couldn't help scoring off him in a way he couldn't cope
with and resented, and now they worked against one another. It is true, I suppose, that Joe is essentially a wit of the
nineties—a more debased form of that.

There is a princess who is always at these parties, and it is
a part of her performance to talk about art, and it is hard
to do anything about it. Luckily, Lou Flagg and her husband
came out of the cactus collection. Lou is really nice in her
loud loose way, though no longer particularly attractive. She
and Will are one couple, at any rate, who seem to be satisfactorily married. They really give each other something:
what she lacks in taste and tact he makes up for by those
overelaborate dinners, and for his queer deficiency in human
feeling she compensates by her hearty howl. An advanced
round of cocktails reached us. Arthur Fern and I explained
that we were on the wagon. The purple was wearing thin
and the alcohol base so strong that it made them rather hard
to get down.

I realized that I ought to go, because I had to meet Sally
for dinner. It was just that exhilarating moment of the second real evening of a love affair when neither knows the
other well and you are so eager to find out more about one
another. I looked forward to her slightly slanting eyes, which
seemed to me to compare very favorably with anything I
could see at the party. I finally identified the blond little
hostess, who seemed to be more or less of a guest, since the

apartment, it seemed, really belonged to other and taller people.

When I got home, I found a phone message from Sally saying she couldn't come, so I went back to the party again to see if I could get somebody for dinner.

I met Lou coming down the stairs. She said that Will had already left and that she had nothing to do for dinner. In the cab, we fell into one another's arms. We worked up quite a convincing little passion, and all on the strength of the way in which she used to wear one of those big floppy hats in the summer of 1926, her respect for my intellectual integrity and my former interest in her younger sister. We talked about what had happened to Al Jolson and thought we should prefer the Hopi snake dance, which neither of us had seen. The night traffic and neon lights were beginning to seem exciting, and we hoped we might be able to think later that there was a movie or something we'd like to see. We went to the Brangwyn Grill.

There we found Rollo Furstman and Phil Beatty. It was jolly to hear Rollo's stories through those big thick Old-Fashioned tumblers, with pieces of yellow and red fruit salad in them. The only trouble about him is that if you try to tell him a story yourself, he is likely to burst out laughing and say "Marvelous!" when you are still only halfway through, and immediately start one of his own.

We went around afterwards to Phil's apartment, and there we found a big burly fattish fellow with a kind of brown Victorian beard, and a little schoolteacher-like woman who seemed bright enough behind her eyeglasses and who was putting down drinks as unobtrusively as if she had been crocheting. The man had a burly *blagueur* line which seemed slightly to throw Phil off—Phil's manners are rather old-fashioned, scrupulously ceremonious.

It turned out that the man was a fanatical hunter. He had had the idea of going to Komodo after the man-eating dinosaur lizards long before Douglas Burden, but Burden had beaten him to it, and bungled it, according to him; and he told us that nobody really knew how far down in the water Will Beebe went, since a confederate kept track of the cable.

He assured us that leopards and tigers were nothing, and that rhinoceroses, though tricky, were yellow; and he told about fighting an ounce, which he says is the gamest of all wild animals.

The ounce came out of the corner just behind Phil's big victrola and slunk along the top of the bookcase past a series of Lachaises the size of meteors—they are all right, of course, but you can have too many of them. Then it sprang and knocked over the cognac, breaking several glasses. Phil Beatty, with his easy urbanity, paid no attention to this and wouldn't allow anybody even to pick up the bottle, which luckily had the cork in it. The man with the beard dodged quickly aside, and the animal landed on the carpet only about three feet away from him. Before he could shoot, it sprang again, and he had to stave it off with his gun-barrel. The doorbell rang, and a little man came in who looked as if he had been boiled to make him softer—he was an intelligent and well-read accountant, whose job, he said, was systematically falsifying the balance-sheets of big corporations. He explained the Communist line and pointed out the importance of not deviating from it. It was pleasant to watch the good breeding with which Phil, who is a consummate Tory himself and even favors the restoration of monarchy, listened with perfect attention, refrained from engaging in argument and hardly even put forward his own views. Lou told him that what she had against the Communists was that they wanted to do away with pure beauty and pour Mozart's symphonies down the drain. The accountant replied that, though he personally would be sorry, this was something that might have to be done.

A young Englishman came in with Arthur Fern. He told us that he was going back to Persia, because Persia was old, quiet and corrupt. He couldn't go back to Oxford because people like Spender and Auden would have made the place impossible for him. He liked Cambridge, Mass., better, because there wasn't so much ferment going on there. But Persia was really the best of all. He thought that the whole course of Western civilization had suffered a decisive setback when the Greeks kept the Persians out.

We decided to go over to Baracci's, where I found Sally dining with Jake. She came over and explained to me that Jake had had one of his nervous spells when he couldn't stop retching, and that she hadn't wanted to leave him.

They kept serving rounds of champagne cocktails, which we drank but which nobody wanted. The bearded man got back to his hunting: it seems that an ounce is the same as a lynx. I asked the woman with the schoolteacher's glasses, who was evidently the hunter's wife, if she knew a lot about animals, too. She replied that the only wild animal she had known was a sick chipmunk she had once had at Westport. The man with the beard, overhearing her, stopped short in the middle of his story and looked as if he were going to burst into tears. "So I'm a sick chipmunk!" he said sourly. "Not you," said the woman. "A real chipmunk—I had one in Westport years ago." "I should say," put in Phil with his usual tact, though not understanding the conversation, "that in comparison with many at Westport, Jack presents a perfect specimen of *mens sana in corpore sano.*" "I guess Gauguin wasn't neurotic!" said the hunter, getting up and glaring at Phil. "I didn't say you were neurotic, my dear fellow," said Phil. "Don't dear-fellow me, you damned art-taster! You damned phonograph-record gloater!" said the hunter, getting burly again. "All right!" shouted Phil unexpectedly in a coarse and raucous voice. "If you like to fight ounces so much, here's a hundred and ninety pounds!" and he suddenly leapt upon the man with the beard and knocked him over backwards. The proprietor rushed in and picked them up. Rollo Furstman made Phil go home; and the woman with the glasses took her husband away. Arthur Fern told me afterwards that he had known her at Westport, too, and that he had thought at first she meant him. I had to pay most of the check for the cocktails, which apparently nobody had ordered.

The little soft-boiled accountant insisted on having Lou and me come up to his apartment in the Guilford, promising us magnificent entertainment. But he found there was no liquor and had to go out to get some, and Lou and I, before he came back, had half an hour or more together among the bogus Buddhas and the equally bogus Americana. I was impressed by the size and beauty of her breasts, which her stringy neck and awkward figure had given me no idea of. We agreed that we had been nice together when we had been talking about our past in the cab. I struck a completely false note by remembering and repeating a line from Swinburne: "If ever I leave off to honor thee, I were the worst churl born!"

When our host at last came back, he had beer in pasteboard containers—he said it was all that he could get at that hour. He called up a great many people but couldn't induce anybody to come. Lou suggested that we might ask some of our friends, and we succeeded in getting Laura Frink and Fanny Murdock's brother, whom we had never seen before but who had answered the phone at Fanny's. In the meantime, before they got there, two tough little numbers turned up, sordid friends of the Communist accountant—one a platinum blonde, with the eyebrows she had plucked showing through; the other a brunette, who was more or less plastered and pretending a foreign accent. Lou afterwards said she had forgotten how drunken and *déclassée* Laura Frink always made her feel—she said that Laura didn't drink herself but loved to have other people drinking; she liked to think that everybody was going to pieces and would tell about us, after she got home, with ironic surprise and sorrow, to that smug little broker she is married to. The accountant's two fallen girl friends were a regular godsend for Laura: they enabled her to get snootier and snootier in a nicer and nicer way. It turned out that Fanny Murdock's brother was a young mining engineer who believed in getting oil out of shale. The girl with the phony accent evidently wanted to take him home, but he only wanted to talk to her about shale. Lou finally came back at Laura and told her that virtue was making her haggard and that the brokers would soon be wiped out; Laura retaliated by intimating that all of us people had been morally wiped out already. Fanny Murdock's brother insisted that we oughtn't to be discouraged, on account of the vast possibilities of shale.

Phil Beatty now reappeared, walking stiffly and speaking

remotely, like one who has risen from the dead. He said that he had gone to sleep and then waked up feeling terribly. Lou told him that his dual personality made Jekyll and Hyde look like a sister act; and he immediately started off—always the raconteur but with too much self-justification—on a long rather tiresome story about his relations with the bearded man, which, it seemed, went back to the time when they had been at school together and Jack had put dead birds in Phil's bed.

What sounded like the voice of another tart called the accountant up on the phone. Laura Frink at this point left with offensive sobriety, and Lou and I decided to go. In the taxi, we swore that in future we must see one another often. There was a sudden shattering crash, and great glass splinters fell out of the window. We saw a group of men milling around in the road, and somebody stopped the cab. It was the taxi strike. They made us get out. Lou gave them a piece of her mind, and we found another cab round the corner.

We were running down and rather glum, so we tried a little downtown bar that had funny blue lights in the window. Lou told me that Will had a mistress and that he hadn't lived at home for four years, and that the mistress had been a friend of the children's nurse, and that she didn't think he even liked the mistress, and that every time he decided to kill himself she had to go and quiet him down, and that the children had got to loathe him, and that she was getting cross with the children, and that she had never taken a lover because the only man she could really go for was married and lived in Seattle. She wept in the most horrible way.

When I had left her, I called up Sally, and she said that Jake was still there and retching again, that I could hear him over the phone. Then I called up Rollo Furstman, and by some diabolical chance Alys Ludovici was there, so I said I couldn't go around, but had to talk to her and promise to see her, and it brought up that whole hideous business.

And the most damnable thing of all was that, after I got home and was going to bed, I broke both my watch and my glasses.

1934

WASHINGTON: GLIMPSES OF THE NEW DEAL

1. Japanese Cherry Blossoms

EVERYWHERE YOU GO in Washington, there are signs that direct you to the Cherry Blossoms. The Board of Trade and the Greater National Capital Committee have got up a big Cherry Blossom Festival, which has brought five hundred thousand people to Washington and caused them to spend five million dollars. There are firework displays, bands, the cherry blossoms lighted up at night and the coronation of one of the young Roosevelt girls as Queen of the Cherry Blossoms.

The cherry blossoms are Japanese cherry blossoms; and every spring, when they bloom, the Japanese ambassador and his family have to have their pictures taken with them for the rotogravure sections of the Sunday papers. This year an anti-war lobby, the Women's International League for Peace and Freedom, has attempted to persuade the chairman of the Cherry Blossom Parade Committee to take advantage of the opportunity to make a gesture of good will toward Japan. The idea was to have a float showing American and Japanese children together and the slogans "Blossoms not Bullets" and "The Pacific Is a Highway not a Barrier." But the chairman of the Parade Committee and the leader of the parade itself was a certain Major General Fries, formerly head of the Chemical Warfare Bureau. He told the lady from the League for Peace and Freedom that such a float could not be admitted: it would amount to propaganda for peace. And when the cherry blossom parade took place, it included, among the chiffon and the pretty faces, thirty-four units of horse-drawn artillery, thirty-six units of motor-drawn artillery, a battalion from the Third Cavalry and small detachments of men from every other military unit in Washington. Among the floats, there was one that presented Commodore Perry arriving with his gunboats in Uraga Bay and another that showed the development of the rifle.

2. The Old Brick and Marble Shell

THAT CURIOUS CITY, half languid with the South, geometrically designed by a Frenchman but rather incompletely filled in as a maze of broad streets and brick houses, where one misses those dense high blocks that make of the business section the climax of the ordinary American city, where the avenues with their pretty little parks, their spirited equestrian statues, converge, but disappointingly, on the Capitol—that city which, after other American cities, seems at first such a relief, so agreeable, turns out, when one has stayed there for any time, to have little personality of its own and to come to taste rather flat. The distinction of Washington is all official: the handsome façades of the embassies, the white shaft of the Washington obelisk mirrored in its long straight lake, the White House with its fine open American lawn and its cloudy little pincushion fountain, frilled with daffodils, embedded in greenery. But, apart from this, the life of the town itself is singularly without flavor. The food, for example, for a city only a little way from Baltimore and just over the river from Virginia, is almost everywhere incredibly unappetizing. These inhabitants who cannot vote, who have no part in any commonwealth, seem to follow current events with a humility close to apathy. They have traces of a Southern accent but they are not exactly Southerners. And the other constant element in Washington, a race of government clerks who come mostly from the Middle West, pervade and have the effect of denaturing the place as those other Iowans and Kansans do Los Angeles, which in some respects Washington oddly resembles. For the rest, the people in Washington are in one way or another transients: office-seekers, lobbyists, sightseers, people who have come here for committees or hearings. Even those who hold office are transients. The city is a great brick and marble shell which—provided by the early

Republic in what was to become, with the growth of the country, a very non-central location—harbors one administration after the other.

Just now it is more entertaining than I have ever known it before, and more lively than at any time since the war. The last administration weighed on Washington, as it did on the entire country, like a darkness, like an oppressive bad dream, in which one could neither speak nor act; and the talk and animation in Washington today are a relief like waking up from a dream. The social life has been much enlivened by the arrival of young college graduates. The bright boys of the Eastern universities, instead of being obliged to choose, as they were twenty years ago, between business, the bond-selling game and the field of foreign missions, can come on and get jobs in Washington—with the result that, as one lady said to me, the place is like a Yale-Harvard-Princeton reunion. Then there are the New York "intelligentzia." It is equally true that, for a graduate of the school of New York liberalism, it is Old Home Week today in Washington. Everywhere in the streets and offices you run into old acquaintances: the editors and writers of the liberal press, the "progressive" young instructors from the colleges, the intelligent foundation workers, the practical idealists of settlement houses, the radicals who are not too radical not to conceive that there may be just a chance of turning the old order inside out and the Marxists who enjoy looking on and seeing how the half-baked liberals are falling victims to their inherent bourgeois contradictions.

For these last, the Franklin Roosevelt Washington is providing a rich field. For all the fermentation and the hopeful discussion, a confusion of purpose is evident—and especially at this moment when the recalcitrance of Congress, the outburst of Dr. Wirt and the stalemates with industry of the NRA are putting brakes on the Administration.* Will the Wirt incident undermine the brain trust? Will the President get his agenda through Congress? Will the NRA get its injunction against the Weirton Company? Will it favor

* These matters are dealt with below.

big business or little business? Will the President bear to the Right or the Left? One hears from the camp of the Rights outraged talk about socialism and communism; from that of the Lefts, dark forebodings of fascism. In the office of one of the brain-trusters, a liberal, I ran into another liberal who was merely a passing visitor. A couple of years ago, I should certainly have assumed that these men were of the same political complexion; yet I observed, in talking to the second, that he seemed now to take little interest in the policies for which the first was one of the chief spokesmen. He was wondering about the left-wing parties. "Dr. Wirt is all wrong," he said. "The trouble with the Administration is that it hasn't got a brain trust and needs one."* A lady who has had a close view of a good deal that has been going on since Roosevelt came to Washington says that it has all been a wonderful show, which has stimulated, thrilled and diverted, but that it is now getting to be like a show which has been on the road too long, so that the costumes are beginning to look stale and the scenery is somewhat shaky. The work which the New Deal is attempting—the stocktaking of the country's resources, the inquiry into the condition of the people and the development of some equitable plan for enabling the people at large to get the benefit of these resources —if it is not completed now by the Roosevelt administration, must eventually be carried through. But, in the meantime, one feels this spring that if Roosevelt's movement forward should suddenly go into reverse, the whole of the nesting brain trust might be swept out of the capital overnight, leaving not an idea behind. The voteless inhabitants would not care; the substratum of government clerks would remain; the Washington and Lincoln monuments would look at each other across the lake. The old shell would forget its new inmates as it already has the death of Jess Smith and the squalor

---

* It was this attitude which led certain liberals into secretly joining the Communist Party, and, as a consequence, working for the Soviet Union. There was evidently, though I did not know it, at least one Communist cell in a government department. It did not, however, consist of the persons denounced by Dr. Wirt.

of the house on H Street in which the Harding gang used to make whoopee.

3. *Miss Barrows and Dr. Wirt*

DR. WILLIAM A. WIRT and Miss Alice Barrows had for twenty years been friends and allies in the field of advanced education.

Dr. Wirt is the inventor of the school system which he prefers to have called the work-study-play plan but which is more commonly known as the Gary system. After experimenting with it first in 1902 in his native town of Bluffton, Indiana, he went on as school superintendent to Gary. Gary was then simply a tract of land which had recently been bought by the Steel Corporation and named after its honored chairman, and where there were only three hundred people.

Dr. Wirt had been inspired and influenced by John Dewey and William Morris. He wanted schools where the children would have a chance at an all-around cultural development and where they would be free to cultivate special aptitudes. He was opposed to routine teaching, to regimentation and to the kind of vocational training in which Henry Ford has taken such interest and which is designed to break in young people to factory work before they have left their schoolhouses. He thus found himself in opposition to the policies of the United States Steel Corporation, which believed that the children of workers should not be allowed to learn too much, that, in fact, the non-tendentious rudiments of reading, writing and arithmetic were about all they could be trusted with. When Dr. Wirt tried to purchase a plot of land in order to put up a new kind of school building which would enable him to carry out his ideas, the steel company refused to sell it to him, and one day he found that the plans for it had mysteriously disappeared from his files.

But the doctor's work-study-play system had the advantage, from the point of view of efficiency, that, applying, as it did, systematically the balanced-load principle of industry, it increased the capacity of the students by 33 per cent. And William A. Wirt at that time was a young strong-willed and

dynamic man possessed by his vision of education. He succeeded in getting his fine new schoolhouse, and he gave his
pupils such excellent training that a remarkably large number went on to college. The music teaching was particularly
good, and several of the graduates of the Gary school distinguished themselves as musicians. The steel people, who
by 1918 were in rather bad odor with the public and who
were uneasy over the discontent of their workers, began to
take an interest and a pride in Dr. Wirt's educational gift
to Gary. The doctor had provided for the children even
tennis-courts, gardens and ponies.

And the Gary system spread through the country. By 1933,
it had been adopted by schools in five hundred cities. Miss
Barrows, who was an educational specialist, became interested in the work-study-play plan, and in 1917, when Dr.
Wirt came to New York to instal it there, she worked with
him as his secretary. Their political views had little in common: Dr. Wirt was an old-fashioned individualist, and Miss
Barrows believed in a planned economy. But they both believed in the work-study-play plan, and, in the field of education, they were both radicals. In New York, they had to
fight together the officials and the conservative educators.
When Tammany at last won out and Dr. Wirt went back to
Gary, he and Miss Barrows remained close friends: Miss Barrows visited Gary every year.

When the depression came, Gary was hard hit: 90 per
cent of the people were out of work, and the mill superintendent was serving as watchman. Dr. Wirt, whose prime
preoccupation for years had been the welfare of the children
of Gary, had the crisis before his eyes and on his mind night
and day. He arranged to have the children make clothes for
themselves through the domestic science department of his
school; and he established a record for public schools by giving them breakfast and dinner for four cents a day. And he
thought up a scheme to end the depression. This scheme was
to send up prices and at the same time devalue the dollar.
He became—at the age of sixty—more or less of a crank on
this subject; and he looked with extreme disfavor on many of
the policies of the administration. He himself had had to fight

for an original idea, and he believed that, since he had been able to put it over in Gary, he had been given a fair field. The brain-trust government, it seemed to him, were trying to dictate to people, to regiment them, to interfere with the free play of forces. And Dr. Wirt became a member of that active organization, consecrated to American individualism and "alarmed over the dangerous trends in business," called the Committee for the Nation. He made use of the Committee for the Nation to publicize his scheme for devaluing the dollar; and they evidently made use of him.

When Dr. Wirt came on to Washington in connection with the business of the Committee, he would usually look up Miss Barrows, who had now for fourteen years been a school-building specialist in the educational office of the Department of the Interior. Last fall, Mr. Robert Kohn, the director of the housing division of the PWA, wanted someone to help with education in connection with the subsistence homesteads. Miss Barrows suggested Wirt; but they did not find him favorably disposed. To put people in subsistence homesteads meant reducing the population of cities, and without the large modern cities, it was impossible to get the equipment that was needed for work-study-play schools; and, besides, the whole thing smacked of socialism. But Miss Barrows invited Dr. Wirt to dinner to meet some of the liberals in the administration. She hoped to interest him in the kind of thing they were doing.

The other guests were Miss Hildegarde Kneeland, an economist in the Department of Agriculture, appointed during the Coolidge administration; Miss Mary Taylor, the editor of the consumers' guide of the AAA (Agricultural Adjustment Administration); Mr. Robert Bruère, the director of the NRA (National Recovery Administration) Industrial Relations Board of the textile industry; Mr. David C. Coyle, a consulting engineer and a specialist in wind resistance, a member of the Technical Board of Review of the PWA (Public Works Administration); and Mr. Laurence Todd, the American representative of the Soviet news agency, Tass.

Dr. Wirt began by talking about education, but soon got

off on his money theory, and though efforts were made by Miss Barrows to get back to education, he went on expounding his theory for four solid hours. He reviewed for them the history of currency from the earliest times to the present day and demonstrated that what he proposed was logically inescapable. The audience began by being rather impressed but ended by becoming exhausted. Miss Kneeland, who had been chafing to debate with him, was able to interrupt him only once—when he spoke of his great objective of bringing the country back to the conditions of 1926—by asking him why he should want to; but he brushed her aside and swept on. A lady who was ill upstairs testifies to having heard from her bedroom the interminable drone of the doctor, and to the piteous complaints of the other ladies when they got away for a moment.

Everybody wondered at Dr. Wirt; Mr. Coyle, after the doctor's departure, was congratulated on his fortunate equipment as an expert in wind resistance. The doctor expressed to Miss Barrows, when he saw her the next day, a fear that he might perhaps have talked too much. Miss Barrows and Dr. Wirt continued to see each other as before.

What happened then, however, was astounding. The president of the Remington-Rand Typewriter Company read before a Senate committee certain statements made by Dr. Wirt in one of his currency leaflets, which was circulated by the Committee for the Nation. Wirt claimed to have definite evidence that there was a Red plot on foot in Washington: radicals concealed in the Administration were planning to shanghai the President and to impose a Communist dictatorship on the country.

The Democrats demanded at once that these charges be investigated and summoned Dr. Wirt to Washington. A few days before he came, he wrote Miss Barrows a letter:

"I have hesitated to write you because I did not want to inadvertently mix you up with the present controversy. However, since the press notices have come to me concerning the dinner party in Virginia . . . I am quite sure that I will be asked about the dinner at the hearing. . . . In order to remove what may be a serious strain upon you I want to state very definitely, and support it with copies of my letters to you concerning my visits, that my relationship with you and everyone in the Department of Education was purely on educational matters. . . . I shall state . . . that I asked to see Mr. Coyle because I was interested in discussing with him his argument in a publication concerning the 'present era' of plenty and the necessity of increasing the service-occupations activities. . . . I shall emphasize that, so far as Mr. Coyle is concerned, he did not directly or indirectly refer to the general social or economic program of the New Dealers. As to Robert Bruère, I shall make very clear that he was constantly objecting to the diversion of the conversation from the subject of schools. . . . I merely want to advise you of the situation so that you and Dr. Zook and other persons in the Department of Education will understand my attitude. The only thing that I remember about you and government is the statement that you made to me that you were working on schools and leaving saving the country to the other fellow.

"With best wishes, and kindest regards to Dr. Zook, I am
Cordially yours,
William Wirt."

Miss Barrows had not been worrying, and she continued to remain quite untroubled till she turned on her radio the morning of the hearing and heard Dr. Wirt testifying that Miss Taylor, Miss Kneeland and Mr. Todd had told him at her dinner in so many words that Franklin Roosevelt was the Kerensky of a revolution for which they would presently find the Stalin; that though the President appeared to be making his own decisions, the truth was that they had him now in the middle of a swift stream in which he could not turn back; and that—Miss Kneeland was supposed to have quoted this from Rexford G. Tugwell*—the ultimate aim of these radicals was to do away with private business and to set up a new social order.

---

* Rexford G. Tugwell, a professor of economics at Columbia University, had been one of Franklin Roosevelt's advisers at the time of his campaign for the Presidency, and was afterwards—from 1934 to 1937 —Assistant Secretary of Agriculture.

Now, Miss Kneeland had never met Tugwell nor had she ever read any of his books, nor could anybody at Miss Barrows' dinner remember that anyone had said anything about Roosevelt, Kerensky or Stalin. Dr. Wirt had himself introduced into a statement for the Senate committee a number of passages from Tugwell, and it has been thought that he may have got Kerensky from the last paragraph of the new book by Ernest Lindley called *The Roosevelt Revolution.* Perhaps he had intended to concentrate attention on the published opinions of the brain-trusters and to leave Miss Barrows' dinner out of it. Or he may have confused in his mind what he had read with what he had heard. But the fact is that, under examination, he charged the guests at the dinner with having recited long passages out of Tugwell. And the fact is that he delivered them all into the hands of the Republican opposition, already snapping and yapping and only too eager to rag the Reds. Had not Robert Bruère, during the war, defended the IWW? Had not Frederick C. Howe—now in the AAA—once attempted, as Commissioner of Immigration, to save anarchists from being deported? At this signal, the reactionary press, which had been recently becoming restive, burst into full cry. It was the first fierce and full-throated outbreak against the new administration.

Dr. Wirt must have got more than he bargained for. He protested at one point rather pathetically: "I am not a Bourbon. I believe in social reform." Nor need one necessarily assume that he had been acting as the tool of the Steel Corporation. But, although Dr. Wirt in the past has had to fight the steel people in the interests of his schools, he is at bottom more completely at one with them than, in his earlier years, he may have supposed. He has always been anti-union. He destroyed several years ago the Gary local of the teachers' union. And now, lined up with the other anti-union forces, he finds himself in incongruous company. One of the principal figures in the Committee for the Nation and apparently the chief guiding spirit behind Dr. Wirt's strange performance has been an anti-union hosiery manufacturer. And among the Committee for the Nation are men who represent the cotton interests, the warship interests and the aviation interests; one of the Committee's directors is the president of the Dairymen's League, regarded by the New York farmers as the agency chiefly responsible for the milk racket against which they are now in rebellion. And one of the Committee's chief objects has been to block the Copeland Pure Food and Drugs Bill, inspired by the Bolshevik Tugwell.

You can see the kind of thing which is hoping to profit by the defeat of the Pure Food and Drugs Bill in the "Chamber of Horrors" exhibition collected in the Chemical Building. Here are hair dyes that make people bald, beauty lotions that cause the teeth to fall out and give rise to necrosis of the jaw, aniline "lash lures" that cause blindness; inflated and adulterated ice creams, boxes for cheese and candy with false bottoms that cheat on the content, malted milk that is faked out of sucrose, faked egg noodles containing no egg; horse liniment which has been sold as a cure for tuberculosis and which destroys the victim more quickly than the tuberculosis germ itself, remedies for diabetes derived from the horsetail weed, which are shown with testimonials on one side and death certificates on the other.

Dr. Wirt, the educational reformer, the disciple of William Morris, cuts a curious figure today as he appears before that background of catarrh remedies, kidney elixirs, female tonics, rheumatic compounds, liver aids—inexterminable witnesses, while capitalism lasts, of the drawbacks of that economic system which the doctor is exerting himself to rescue.

And Miss Barrows, who for twenty years admired and worked with Wirt—she, too, finds herself being driven into a position which she had never thought inevitable. Miss Barrows has been brought to the conclusion that a new deal in education is impossible without a new society.

4. Reinstating the Red Man

IN THE SENATE committee's hearings on the Indian Bill the brain trust is seen in dramatic contrast up against the conventional politicians.

John Collier, the new Commissioner of Indian Affairs, is

one of the few intellectuals in the new administration who know precisely what they want to do and precisely how they mean to do it. The pure type of reformer-idealist, tending even toward mysticism, he has, in his practical activity, proved amazingly effective in getting his aims accomplished. Since he cares nothing about making money and has no interest in his personal advancement, he is free to concentrate on his cause, and it is hard for mere officeholders to stop him.

In 1924, John Collier, then the executive secretary of the Indian Defense Association, succeeded in defeating the Bursum Bill, which would have legalized the encroachments of squatters on the pueblo agricultural lands and irrigation ditches, when this bill had already gone through the Senate and was then in the hands of the House. The Indians had never up to this time been able to make any concerted resistance; they had only assailed the Indian agents with endless individual complaints. John Collier performed the heroic feat of going to each of the pueblos in turn and persuading the Indians to authorize him to obtain legislation in their interest. He is eloquent, and the Indians like eloquence, even when the meaning of what the speaker says has to be transmitted to them through an interpreter. He drafted and explained to the Indians with an inexhaustible patience the highly technical and complicated Pueblo Lands Bill; and then he went on to Washington and, in the teeth of bitter opposition, succeeded in getting it made into law.

When the Roosevelt administration came in, Secretary of the Interior Ickes, who has always taken a great interest in the Indians, appointed Collier Indian Commissioner; and Collier immediately addressed himself to repealing the espionage acts, dating from the Indian wars, which had given the Indian Bureau the power to suppress among Indian communities free press, association and speech; to getting money from the PWA for new Indian hospitals and schools; to rescuing the "Five Civilized Tribes" from the very much reduced plane of civilization to which they were being brought in Oklahoma; and to putting through an epoch-making bill designed to give the Indians land and self-government. At this moment, just before the adjournment of Congress, he is facing the hostile cross-fire of Democratic and Republican senators.

John Collier is certainly not the political type. Standing up and leaning over, his hands on the long table, he looks scholarly, small, rather frail, with his stooped shoulders and his lifted eyebrows, almost plaintive as if from long anxiety, his rimless spectacles, his light hair which is parted in the middle with some straight wisps that hang down his forehead, his blue eyes benevolent and visionary, his sensitive mouth with its underdrawn lower lip drooping now under the strain of days of struggle, and his long bony demonstrative finger. An incongruous figure among senators: he cares nothing about making a personal impression, he is incapable of asserting an ego—he receives the bristling resistance—"There's more Collier than truth in that statement!" Senator Wheeler at one point remarks—with the utmost gentleness and tact. But he cares more deeply, more intensely, about saving the American Indians than the senators have probably ever cared about anything, and he has succeeded in getting them into this committee room, and they will eventually have to do what he wants.

Senator Thomas of Oklahoma is a trim oldish man with a sharp nose and a pale steely shrewd-looking eye. Representing the state in which the Five Civilized Tribes have been lately at the mercy of the oil interests, and as the author of the Thomas Silver Bill, which the White House is finding unacceptable, he is opposed to the Indian Bill, which the White House is known to favor and which aims to restore to the Five Civilized Tribes the property that originally belonged to them. The interests opposed to the bill have not failed to follow the course of Dr. William A. Wirt and denounce it as "communistic." Senator Wheeler of Montana, the chairman of the committee, as a rule maintains technical politeness but he conducts the proceedings with acidity and a distinct though restrained impatience. There is a considerable pressure to defeat the bill on the part of the Montana cattle interests. Senator Frazier of North Dakota, with his solid and blunt-featured face, an old Farmer-Labor man, gives the bill his weight of silent support. Once, when it is objected by one of the others that Congress will never be willing to vote the two-million-dollar-a-year appropriation with which it is proposed to buy back the Indian lands, he says that he believes it is true that Congress will be reluctant to consent, because this is one appropriation that cannot be spent by the politicians.

In the background and surrounding the long table are the experts of the Indian Bureau; the Indian racketeers, who for years have been collecting money from the Indians on the promise of getting back for them vast areas which they once possessed, and who resemble patent-medicine men; a white-haired Catholic priest with a finely modeled old Western profile and a long white old Western beard with which a long white mustache merges—he has long been anxious to get something done for a dispossessed tribe in Oregon who have come wretchedly to shelter about his parish; the missionaries who oppose the bill for the reason that, by leaving the Indians to themselves, it will, they believe, tend to "paganize" them; and representatives of various Indian tribes, some of them witnesses for the Indian Bureau and others instructed dummies for the interests against the bill. One of these latter, who had stalled at the beginning of his speech after uttering the words "I come here . . . ," was obliged to prompt himself from a paper produced from his pocket in order to continue with "uninfluenced." These faces, stout and knobby or dark and gaunt, all equally unresponsive and solemn, look strange above blue suits, soft collars, striped ties and gold stickpins. Cigarettes smoke from motionless fingers. One Indian who wears his black horsehair mane braided tight over his shoulders in pigtails sits stonily, gazing straight before him through black goggles like death's-head orbits, which seem to engulf the proceedings.

On a rack near the head of the table, the maps of remote states are unrolled: Minnesota and Arizona—with the Indian reservations in yellow and the national forests in green. That irreducible old wild America, that inexpugnable primitive life, still at home among the canyons, the mesas, the plains, the rivers and woods of the West!—why should they come up as a problem now more acutely than at any time since fifty years ago, firing the imagination of some of the men in this room, stirring the rancor of others? The Indian Bill, to be sure, is a relatively minor feature of the Administration's liberal program; but there is a special and profoundly significant issue at the bottom of the antagonisms here. John Collier is the first Indian Commissioner in the history of the Indian Bureau who has valued the Indian's civilization so highly as to want him to remain an Indian. The Dawes Bill of 1887, though it was backed by humanitarian feeling, was based on the assumption that the thing to do for him was to enable him to become a white man, and, in response to the demands of the land-grabbers, it broke up the old reservations and gave the Indians scattered allotments; and when the Indians themselves, through their innocence or through the corruption of the Indian agents, had allowed two-thirds of the 138,000,000 acres which they were supposed to possess in 1887 to pass into the hands of white lumbermen and grazers, they found themselves now for the most part scattered miserably among the whites, inhabitants of neither world. The new bill attempts to reintegrate them by enabling them to live on large tracts of land held in common by the tribe and inalienable, where they will be left free to make their own laws, to administer their own justice and to cultivate their own arts and religions, instead of being exploited by the cattleman, governed by the Indian Bureau, punished without jury by the Indian agent and evangelized by the Protestant and the priest. They are not to be compelled to proceed in this way, merely given the opportunity to do so; but in a series of tribal councils, in which the Indian Bureau people say that the question has been debated with remarkable sagacity, a considerable percentage of the Indians affected have expressed their approval of the scheme. The effect on the Indians of John Collier—whom, in his role of Indian Commissioner, they at first received with coolness and suspicion, has been to revive their morale and to inspire them with genuine enthusiasm for perhaps the first time since it was possible for them still to hope to exterminate the white man. Where they could formerly only drive their white guardians mad with their miseries, their accusations, their complaints, they seem now to be getting together and preparing to settle down on their land and organize their own society.

But, in the course of these hearings, the sharp opposition between, on the one hand, the philosophy of John Collier and, on the other, that of the committee, is repeatedly and strikingly shown. It is plain that both Thomas and Wheeler are impatient of Indians as Indians, and that they desire to see them absorbed by the whites. Senator Thomas, in that traditional language, with its inflation and its touch of poetry, which is spoken even by senators with the keenest noses and the shrewdest crow's-feet at the corners of their eyes, declares that the policy of the government with the Indians has always been "to disseminate 'em, to disintegrate 'em—so that this problem may melt away like the mist," whereas the purpose of the new bill is nothing less than "to perpetuate tribal ways, to put 'em back on the reservation and reverse the trend of a hundred years!" And Senator Wheeler enlarges with feeling on the injustice implied for the half-breeds. The half-breeds are as good as white men; we ought not to be casting them back to the hogan, the tepee and the blanket. What a scandal that a former vice-president, Mr. Curtis,* should, by reason of his Indian blood, have remained technically a ward of the government! But the Senator betrays his real point of view, when, even in defending the half-breeds, he refers to the Indians as "which."

Finally, the Senator turns to the chairman of the Blackfeet Tribal Council, a man named Joe Brown, with a great slash through one side of his face which has sliced his ear in two, cut a deep seam along his cheek and put out his right eye. The Blackfeet reside in the Senator's state, and the Senator knows Joe Brown: he addresses him familiarly as "Joe," and Joe addresses the Senator as "sir." Though Joe Brown bears the marks of savage strife, his voice, unexpectedly, is soft, his poise is perfect and his accent almost as cultivated as the Senator's. The Senator explains to Joe Brown that the new

* Charles Curtis of Shawnee County, Kansas—vice-president under President Hoover.

bill would only hurt the Blackfeet. How can they hope to better themselves by it? Don't they sit, as it is, on the school board? Don't they sit in the legislature? Don't they practically run the community? If the Indians are thrown in on themselves, they will lose all the advantages of the white community—won't they be worse off than they are at present? Joe Brown, with great gentleness and a certain charm, a hardly perceptible smile—recalling, no doubt, that the Indians who practically ran the community had been run by the Indian Bureau—replies that, since they would then be doing everything themselves, they are willing to take a chance. But suppose they make laws for themselves which conflict with the laws of the community? Joe Brown believes that this can be handled. The Senator reminds him firmly that a conflict of this kind might arise and that it is not to be taken lightly. With that thought Joe Brown is dismissed.

What John Collier has here to contend with is the mentality of white imperialism; and what he represents himself is a point of view which makes the senators' seem obsolete, for the new Indian Bureau Commissioner no longer thinks in terms of dominant cultures and divinely appointed races, but is aware that the human spirit is at home in a variety of dwellings, and that none of us has the right to compel our neighbor to live in ours. He finds himself, also, here up against an even narrower provinciality, that of the self-sufficient American. Whenever one of the people from the Indian Office attempts to throw light on the subject by referring to the methods by which Mexico or Canada has dealt with its Indian problem, the senators visibly freeze. The government of the United States needs no instruction from foreign peoples.

On Thursday, the going seems heavy; the obstruction of the committee is stubborn. Senator Thomas and Mr. Collier become engaged in what seems to be a hopeless argument as to whether or not the Indian is "competent." The bill, asserts Senator Thomas, confers on the Indian rights to which he is not entitled because he has not the requisite competence. But it is precisely the purpose of the bill, the Commissioner firmly retorts, to declare that the Indian *is* competent. But that can't be done, says the Senator, because, from the very beginning, our legislation has declared him incompetent. But this is a new piece of legislation designed to make a new departure. The Indian, says the Senator, is incompetent.

The proponents of the Indian Bill have been doubting whether they could put it through this session. After all, it has not been listed among the measures which President Roosevelt has insisted on having attended to before the adjournment of Congress. But Monday the atmosphere changes. At the opening of this hearing, Senator Wheeler begins by explaining that he has just had a letter from the President requesting him to put the bill through. He murmurs that they must "try to get something out of it."

5. The Delegates from Duquesne

THERE ARRIVE in Washington, on the first day of May, two workers from the Duquesne plant of the Pittsburgh Carnegie Steel Company. One is a large heavy man with graying hair, a small and gentle mouth and a gray and gentle eye; the other, a younger man, is a typical dark compact Pittsburgher, who talks the emphatic Pittsburgh tongue and whose black eye lights up with gaiety when he uncorks a Pittsburgh wisecrack. The older man works on the open-hearth furnace; the other manipulates the levers which control the red-hot ingots in the blooming mill.

They have just come from a convention in Pittsburgh of the Amalgamated Steel, Iron and Tin Workers. This convention will have to decide some extremely critical matters. Since the steel strike of 1919, the Amalgamated, affiliated with the AF of L, has been hardly even a skeleton. Essentially a skilled workers' union which felt little real solidarity with its less accomplished fellows, it had at that time weakened the morale of the strike by attempting to make separate agreements with the companies. Its achievements since then have been summarized in a pamphlet passed around at the convention which bears on the cover the title, *What the Amal-*

gamated Officials Have Done for the Steel Workers, and which inside consists of blank pages. The convention is dominated by Mike Tighe and other reactionary Amalgamated officials. The "old union" delegates represent less than five thousand steel workers, mostly from independent mills not in the grasp of the colossal U. S. Steel Corporation, which, wherever it reigns, with its Cossacks and its spies, is able to keep track of its employees, whether at work or in their homes, and sometimes even to prevent outside organizers from getting off a train at the station. And these older officials of the Amalgamated are too prudent, too much cowed by the steel company, really to want action. But today, with the promises of the NRA* and the continued impoverishment of the steel workers, new elements have appeared to press their claims. There are new delegates at this spring's convention representing perhaps 150,000 steel workers, many of whom work for U. S. Steel itself, and these delegates demand to hold elections and to organize in earnest. The convention has not wanted to admit them, but has finally been forced to seat one delegate for each of the new lodges. The older group denounce them as "Reds," a name which has been very much resented by the two who have come on to Washington. These men have come to ask the Labor Board to arrange for a free election in order that the steel workers may choose between their union and the company union for the purpose of bargaining collectively with the steel company, a right which Section 7a of the National Recovery Act is supposed to have guaranteed them.

But in a steel town dominated by the steel company, Section 7a cuts no ice—it is, in fact, as much as your job is worth to mention it. A steel worker who leaves the convention and comes to Washington to ask the government to help the steel workers hold free elections is assuming a serious responsibility. The younger man's brother, a foreman, reasoned with

* The National Industrial Recovery Act. President Roosevelt attempted to regulate industry through a set of some seven hundred and fifty codes, which were to establish minimum wages and maximum hours and other conditions of work. It was declared unconstitutional by the United States Supreme Court in May, 1935.

him and tried to dissuade him: "You may be going to your funeral!" he told him. But the lever-manipulator, a "correspondent representative" of his lodge, felt that he had to go just the same when the president of the lodge sent a man into the mill after him, and he got off, after his 3 to 11 shift, together with the president, on the midnight train. The president's father is also a foreman, but years ago he took part in the Homestead strike, and the son never forgets that Duquesne, which is just up the Monongahela from Homestead, was one of the mills that kept running and made it possible to break the strike. Duquesne has a stain to wipe out.

They have not come at a very propitious time from the point of view of the Administration. The government is still trying to prove that it is able to insist on unimpeded elections in the case of the Weirton Steel Company, which is only a subsidiary of National Steel, a mere "independent." Mr. Ernest T. Weir of the Weirton Company has not hesitated to break an agreement which he had made with the Labor Board. When the Labor Board men went to Pittsburgh to arrange for having the elections supervised, the Weirton Company ran them out as promptly as if they had been Amalgamated organizers. And at this moment, the Attorney General is trying to get an injunction against the Weirton Company to prevent them from behaving in this way. The case is being argued in Wilmington, and the Deputy Attorney General is adducing affidavits to the effect that the Weirton Company had not only used violence and threats for the purpose of inducing its employees to vote for the company union but had even gone so far as to try to work upon the women employees by inviting them to the employer-class country club, giving them too much to drink and teaching them to shout in unison little verses, called "cheers," such as the following:

> If you want your bread and butter every day,
> Vote, vote the right way!

But, at the present time, the members of the Labor Board who have forced the case into court in order that it might be demonstrated one way or the other whether the government has really the authority to carry out its promises to labor and have done so in opposition to those members of the Labor Board who, in the fear that the government might be defeated, were reluctant to have Section 7a brought to the test —these Labor Board people are gloomily reflecting that counsel for the Weirton Company may perfectly well be able to enmesh the case in legal technicalities and prevent its being decided before the summer of 1935, when the NRA is due to expire.

And in Harriman, Tennessee, where the management of the hosiery mills has also balked, refusing to sign an agreement with its employees, the withdrawal of the Blue Eagle by General Johnson,* instead of resulting, as contemplated, in the ignominy of the employers, has caused the merchants and professional men of Harriman to divest themselves of their own Blue Eagles in sympathy with the hosiery manufacturers. The NRA Compliance Board, after sending investigators, has just announced that it is not possible to settle the matter without "more or less protracted negotiations." In the coal country of western Kentucky, the coal operators themselves are attempting to get an injunction which will prevent the enforcement of the coal code. This aims to secure for bituminous coal miners a wage of at least $4.60 a day.

The NRA is in a dubious phase: no one can be sure whether it is coming or going. The big threatened strike of the automobile workers in Detroit has been averted by the intervention, first of the Labor Board, then of the President himself; but the workers are not solid enough, the government not sufficiently self-confident, to win for the automobile industry the unequivocal right to organize. On the labor side, the AF of L is weak, it is so long since it has tried to act in earnest; the representatives of the radical groups, who are opposed to the AF of L, are creating further confusion by also fighting each other. The big strike has been averted, but separate bodies of workers have been calling independent

---

* General Hugh S. Johnson was Administrator of the National Recovery Act. The Blue Eagle was a label supposed to be attached to their products by manufacturers who had met its requirements.

strikes, and, in spite of the "settlement," they go on striking. The problem has not really been solved; the first impetus of the NRA is flagging; and General Johnson is now under open attack by the business men and manufacturers, who demand lower pay, longer hours and the sanctification of company unions. It is true that the Labor Board has just repudiated the principle of compromise embodied by the automobile settlement—that is, it is backing labor against the company unions; but, on the other hand, young Averell Harriman, the ranking assistant to General Johnson, has just made, with apparently equal authority, a speech before an association of business executives in which he has asserted emphatically that it is not the purpose of the NRA to bring any coercion to bear on business.

But the men from Duquesne can still hope. When the Weirton Company had defied the government, the matter had been shelved for a month and a half in the Attorney General's office, but the Weirton workers were able to get action by sending delegates directly to the White House. And the insurgent representatives of the Amalgamated, though they have by this time come to distrust a good many people, do still hope for justice from the President, whom they refer to as "the old man." On March 10, they appealed to the Labor Board for an election in accordance with the President's order of February 1; and later, getting no satisfaction from the Board, they sent a telegram to the President asking whether they had to go on strike in order to get his order carried out. The President never replied; but his office referred the telegram to the Labor Board, which, after further appeals from the steel workers, has finally summoned them to Washington.

The two delegates from Duquesne request a conference with Senator Wagner, and the Senator, after promising them one and making them wait for hours, finally sends them Bill Green instead. He arranges for them to hold a conference with members of the Labor Board. The men ask to have an election outside the company plant and a ballot with a choice between the two unions, instead of a choice between individuals, the device by which the Weirton workers were led to favor the company union. They are equipped with large sheets of figures which show the incomes of over a hundred Duquesne steel workers. At a recent hearing on the Wagner Bill,* the steel company sent company union men to assure the senators that the steel workers disapproved of this measure and did not need any other organization, since they were making $20 a day. But the figures of the delegates show that at least 139 steel workers in Duquesne are earning on the average between $200 and $500 a year. The young man himself, a skilled worker, has his card with him, and this shows that in the course of the last year he has earned only $430.85. He has to supplement his eight-hour shifts by another job on the outside.

But the National Labor Board turns out to be almost as deeply troubled at the prospect of standing up to the Steel Corporation as the conservative officials of the Amalgamated. When the danger began to loom last winter of the government's taking serious steps to bring the question of collective bargaining to an issue, the steel company summoned to protect itself the renowned company-union wizard, Mr. Arthur H. Young. Mr. Young has made a brilliantly successful career out of promoting company unions. He worked formerly for the International Harvester Company, then ten years for the Rockefellers. Last February, United States Steel took him over from the Rockefellers, made him vice-president of the corporation and set him to contriving company unions which should be admissible by the legal provisions of Section 7a and thereby evade its intention. They paid him $75,000 a year, a figure which rankles with the steel workers, who cannot help feeling that the company might just as well have spent the money to lift them a little above the poverty

* Senator Robert F. Wagner of New York drafted and introduced a bill which was designed to set up a National Labor Relations Board that would guarantee the rights of workers to organize and hold elections without influence on the part of the employers. This was defeated in 1934 but went through in June 1935, just after the NRA had been declared unconstitutional by the Supreme Court. Its legality was also challenged, and its activities were considerably hampered till its legality was upheld by the Supreme Court in April, 1957.

and misery into which the NRA has not been able to prevent them from sinking. Mr. Young has lately appeared before the Senate committee and characterized the Wagner Bill
as "vicious," for the reason that it "assumes the regimentation
of each side into a warring camp" and "refers to the intercourse between the two in terms of permanent struggle." And
Mr. Young keeps in such close touch with the Labor Board
and brings to bear upon it such anxious pressure, that the
Board hardly knows now which way to look when a delegation of steel workers comes to it and asks it to give them
support against Mr. Young's company unions.

Shocking as it must seem to persons who wish to believe
in the Labor Board's impartiality, the first thing it does is to
recommend that the members of the Amalgamated abandon
their union, an AF of L organization of some forty years
standing, and yield to the company unions. They send the
petitioners away to think over this recommendation; but it
does not take these long to decide. The president of the Duquesne lodge exclaims that if he were to "let the Labor Board
shove company representation down his neck, and if he were
to go back and try to shove it down his men's necks, he might
just as well commit suicide!" They tell the Board they can't
accept. One of the more sympathetic members asks them
whether they cannot arrange to join the company union and
then manage to capture it later—he wants to know whether
Sidney Hillman in their place wouldn't be able to do that.
Somebody on the steel workers' side goes so far as to express
the opinion that Sidney Hillman, Mussolini and St. Paul,
all working together, wouldn't be able to capture the steel
company's union. The president of the Duquesne lodge turns
to the AF of L members of the Labor Board: "You don't mean
to say you want us to go back and bust up your own AF of L!"

Bill Green cannot admit that he does want this, and he
promises that they shall have their election. Outside the
plant? Yes. With the choice between two unions? Yes. But
when they are handed the little typed release of the Labor
Board's decision, they find that it promises only that "an election shall be granted, the form, method and procedure of
the election to be determined and announced later." And,

in the meantime, they have heard from the convention that the old leadership has made a decision which may involve them in a strike in the middle of June—when the peak of steel production will be past and, since the company will not need the labor, it is likely to prove a failure—instead of in the middle of May, when the insurgents had hoped to have it. The Labor Board has taken the attitude that, in advising the Amalgamated insurgents to accept the company unions, they were saving them from a ruinous strike. But this state of mind on the part of the Board involves a vicious circle. The position of labor is weak partly because the Board does not back it. It is in reality the Board itself which has rendered the prospect unhopeful by accepting Mr. Arthur Young.

The president of the Duquesne lodge and the young man from the rolling mill, taking the train back to Pittsburgh that evening—after warmly thanking everyone who has helped them, after thanking and complimenting the room clerk for his excellent accommodations and after the wisecracking younger man, who has been put to wait in an official's chair, has declared that nobody could ever say that he hadn't sat behind a desk in Washington!—the two steel workers now find themselves, returning, confronted with an exceedingly serious problem. Strike in June and lose? Split the union? Suppose the little carbon with its five typed lines that one of them has in his pocket doesn't secure them the election, after all? If the Labor Board isn't really behind them and they still have combined against them the old machine of the union, the Cossacks and the spies of the steel company and the resourceful Mr. Arthur Young who has $75,000 a year to gain by preventing their organization. . . .

They remember that the company is reported to have said that it was necessary to crack down on the steel workers about every fifteen years—and the last big strike was in 1919. Before that, in 1892, at Homestead, the company, after cutting wages, surrounded the steel plant with a barbed-wire wall, brought in Pinkerton thugs and militia, repulsed a bloody siege and, at the end of a strike of four months, made the strikers go back to work. In 1909, it cut wages again, fought the union for fourteen months and finally wiped it out. In 1919, new resistance on the part of the steel workers was stimulated by the higher cost of living, the comparative scarcity of labor and the obvious war profits of the steel company, which opposed this resistance, from September till the beginning of the following year, with every sort of brutality and violence, including raids on struck towns by the company's mounted police which were suggestive of pogroms in eastern Europe, and eventually drove the strikers back to their twelve-hour day and their under-subsistence wage, with no gains and heavy losses. The photograph is still on record, without seriously embarrassing the steel company, of the smashed skull of a woman organizer, who had been slugged and shot and dragged by the heels by drunken deputy sheriffs. Labor leaders for forty years have been breaking their backs against steel. The government tried vainly for seven years to win a suit for dissolution against the Steel Corporation. Woodrow Wilson exerted in vain all his moral force and all his eloquence to induce the Steel Corporation to arbitrate the 1919 strike. And the Roosevelt administration, from the beginning of the NRA, has had no coöperation from the steel people: they walked out last summer on a conference at which William Green was to be present and so flustered General Johnson that he declared—what was not the case—that Green had not been invited; and they did their best to prevent Frances Perkins, the Secretary of Labor, from speaking to the steel workers at Homestead, driving her out of a hall into a park, and out of the park into a post office, where she made a stand on federal property as yet uncontrolled by the Steel Corporation.

But on the other side the working class pressure behind the men from Duquesne is mounting. At one mill in a recent election, when three hundred voted for the Communists and three hundred for the company union, five hundred voted for the Amalgamated when the Amalgamated had nobody there.

Now soon, the delegates reflect—though you would never find it out from the press, though not even the Pittsburgh papers will give their convention anything but a paragraph hidden on a back page, making a sensation of "some old mur-

der instead of something that means something to humanity"
—a critical issue is to be decided. It must come to a definite
showdown "whether the United States Steel Corporation is
bigger than the United States government." And they begin
to weigh their wives and children against other considerations.

6. Madam Secretary

THE REPORTERS come out grumbling. "She doesn't understand," they complain of the Secretary of Labor, "the ma-
jority-minority question!" "I could have asked her"—But he
hasn't asked her. Madam Secretary has the press intimidated.
Frances Perkins' position in Washington is peculiar but
nevertheless characteristic of the New Deal. Miss Perkins,
though she was once a social worker, is not at all the settle-
ment-house type; nor is she the type of fighting woman labor-
leader, nor of formidable woman statistician. She is an attractive lady from Boston, who dresses with considerable
elegance. She has always hated personal publicity and, even
as Secretary of Labor, she sees to it that reporters keep their
distance. Reporters and everyone else. Miss Perkins is so
much a woman and so much a fine-grained person that she
inspires universal deference, and as a result she has been almost immune from criticism.

It may be that the clever Mr. Roosevelt, who, in New
York, made Miss Perkins Commissioner of Labor, has
counted on her present appointment to disarm reactionary
sentiment and to induce the hard-boiled employers to treat
the Labor Department politely. But what has been gained
in this way in politeness has probably been lost in force. Miss
Perkins has had to take many affronts. I have told how, in
Homestead last year, the steel company would not let her
speak and drove her to take sanctuary in the post office.
Would it have been possible to behave in this way toward
a male Secretary of Labor?

The point is, however, that Miss Perkins is an appropriate
Secretary of Labor for the Roosevelt administration. She has

never been close to labor, and her disadvantages in dealing with it are great. She has never been an industrial worker; she is a graduate of Mt. Holyoke and Hull-House. Her interest in improving the conditions of labor dates from the Triangle fire, which started her on her career as a specialist in factory legislation. But she knows little about labor politics, and in this she sets the tone for the whole labor side of the Roosevelt administration. It is hard to find anybody in it who, even from a journalist's experience, knows anything of the way that the American world looks and feels to labor. (The representatives of the AF of L do, of course, know something about this, but they now make a social group of their own which does not really belong to the working class.) For the Roosevelt administration, labor has tended to figure as something called "consuming power"—that is, as an abstraction invoked from the farmer's and the manufacturer's points of view and not from its own point of view, the point of view of human beings who want to eat, keep dry and warm, give their children some education and have some chance to enjoy their lives—in a word, of American citizens who want ordinary American rights. But food, shelter and education and all the other things are dependent on the right to organize, and this the Roosevelt administration has never yet been able to guarantee. Neither William Green nor General Johnson nor Miss Perkins, though all of them backed by the President, has ever yet been able to make industry recognize the right of its employees to bargain collectively with it—the denial of which on industry's part implies nothing less than the assumption that these employees are not citizens at all.

This is not written without appreciation of what Miss Perkins has been able to do nor without sympathy for the difficulties of her office. But her appointment seems one of those strokes of tact by which the adroit Roosevelt is able to get over rough places with a minimum of awkwardness or friction but which leave things much as they were. Does not he himself disarm criticism in very much the same way as Miss Perkins? He is a gentleman, he is so charming, he works so hard, he croons so beautifully over the radio, he has suffered so severe a disability. And he has behind him an energetic, sincere and conscientious woman, who gives body to his ambiguity. Mrs. Roosevelt gets about where the President cannot go, appears in all sorts of places as the President's vicarious presence. The President and Mrs. Roosevelt have come to compose together an impressive and amiable human unit, to whom nobody wants to be disobliging, to whom nobody could bear to be rude, but whose actual authority, nevertheless, falls short of its benevolent intention.

And General Johnson, that drillmaster of industry, that thundering, foursquare, two-fisted, table-banging titan, set up to prove the government's purpose of bringing capital and labor into line—General Johnson, according to report, has largely been taken over by his secretary, Miss Frances Robinson. One can believe it as one watches him at a press conference, bracing himself back behind his big desk and waiting for the questions like pistol-shots. Having started the NRA so emphatically, it is hard for him now to have to hedge. But in a corner, at a little desk, sharp-eyed and quick, sits "Robbie," not embarrassed at all, since she is sure of her woman's function, which is managing General Johnson. And one leaves sympathetic with the General, who is evidently a very likable if not a brilliant person, who has made a terrific effort and is having a difficult time and who is being so loyally guarded by the shrewd and resourceful Miss Robinson. One leaves almost with a feeling of chivalry.

1957. The Roosevelt administration differed from any before it by reason of the important part played in it by women and by social workers. Eleanor Roosevelt had brought them both in, and it was only after Roosevelt's death, when I read her two remarkable books—*This Is My Story* and *This I Remember*—so sure and firm in their judgments yet so dry and restrained in expression—that I realized how strong a rôle she must have played in her husband's administration. As for the relation of Miss Perkins to labor, my impression of it was partly based on a conversation at which I was present between her and one of the members of the Labor Advisory Board who was the government representative on the Automobile Board, an extremely able expert in the financial department of one of the most successful of the clothing-makers' unions. She had just come back from Detroit, where she had been struggling with the first stifled efforts of the automobile workers to get their grievances heard, and I felt that she was still very much on the periphery of the labor world. My friend from the clothing workers astonished me by expressing skepticism about the spying which he had just been told went on at Ford's and which was said to make organizing impossible. Yet I knew from my own experience that the Ford espionage apparatus was one of the most striking features of Dearborn. It is interesting, then, to find Miss Perkins—in her book *The Roosevelt I Knew*—explaining that "there were many things about trade unions that Roosevelt never fully understood. I doubt that he understood what solidarity really means in the trade-union movement. He tended to think of trade unions as voluntary associations of citizens to promote their own interests in the field of wages, hours and working conditions. He did not altogether grasp that sense of their being a solid bloc of people united to one another by unbreakable bonds which gave them power and status to deal with their employers' terms."

It was Lewis who was to put over Section 7a of the National Recovery Act—which he is also said to have invented —by forcing the President's hand and who considerably stretched the truth, at the time that it at last became law, by announcing to the miners: "The President wants you to join the union." It was he who, through the sitdown strike of 1937—one of the great battles of industrial history—brought a teeth-grinding General Motors to accept collective bargaining and who thus breached the walls of Detroit, which, when I visited it in 1931, had appeared among the most impregnable. He was then in so strong a position that he was able to make the terrible steel company come to terms with but little resistance. And, in order to gain his ends, he did not hesitate to be rude to the President, to confront him with his evasions and duplicities. He was the masculine principle in the New Deal without whom, in the labor field, it would have been able to accomplish little. Franklin Roosevelt, with his instinct for pleasing and for getting around people, with his entourage his entourage of social workers and women, had himself a good deal of the feminine.

7. The Zero Hour

YES: IT IS the zero hour in Washington. The first splendor of the New Deal has faded, and the next development of policy has not yet clearly dawned. The clear and ringing call to play the game with which the President was able at the beginning to inebriate his supporters, to overwhelm and silence his opponents, no longer vibrates in people's ears. The emergency measures which revived our morale have not achieved all that they promised; the Republicans are becoming insulting; Congress is becoming recalcitrant, is reverting to its natural condition of responding to the pressure of special interests; the tough fundamental problems of the industrial situation are embarrassing the NRA.

There is a good deal of intelligent talk and a good deal of stimulating activity. All about, in auditoriums, in hotel rooms, in offices, the hearings on the NRA codes are being argued every day: all the actual little-known phenomena of the functioning of the great American plant, all the anomalies and antagonisms and scandals—from the special problems of pretzel-benders and maraschino-cherry pitters to the conflicts in the big basic industries, from the problem of the overgrazing of the goats of the Navahos to the ramifications of the milk racket—are for the first time being dragged to the surface. For the first time it is becoming possible to fill in the whole American picture. Yet this is not being done in any coördinated fashion. The different departments know different facts, and they propose to deal with them in different ways—different people in the same department propose to deal with the same facts in different ways. There is no real over-all policy for reassembling the broken-down competitive mechanism. The opponents of the President do not know quite what to do; and his liberal supporters are baffled. And then there is the group of Progressives, the President's liberal opponents. At the moment, the needle of a compass seems to

quiver between the opposite attractions of reaction and further reform. Dr. Wirt rouses opinion against Tugwell; Tugwell is at pains to make a speech disavowing socialistic intentions; the President promotes Tugwell; the Senate refuses
to pass the promotion; Tugwell says he will resign if it does
not go through.

And the President himself is still handling things so
suavely, still showing himself so accomplished a politician,
that it is hard to tell how firmly he grasps the problems involved in the experimentation which constitutes the New
Deal. One of the liberals in the government said to me:
"Now that there are signs of recovery and the businessmen
are trying to throw off the controls of the New Deal, the
President is adopting the policy of paying out to them
enough rope to hang themselves—he is going to let them
speculate and then crash again, and then he is going to bring
down the controls in earnest and nobody will have the nerve
to oppose him." Yet this liberal had an anxious look, and he
added after a moment, dropping his eyes: "Unless he really
doesn't understand what is happening and has no far-sighted
policy at all." In the meantime, behind all the activity and
talk, there is fundamental confusion in Washington; and in
the meantime, Congress will soon be adjourning, and the
Washington summer will come, with its hot and enervating
weather.

April–May, 1934

POSTSCRIPT OF 1957

1957. The domestic reforms of Roosevelt were sidetracked when we entered the second war. In December, 1943, the New Deal was officially abandoned. The threat of the belligerent Cherry Blossom Parade of the spring of 1934 turned out to have been all too serious.

Charles A. Beard, in his two valuable books on American foreign policy—*American Foreign Policy in the Making, 1932–41* and *President Roosevelt and the Coming of the War, 1941*–has shown how, after promising peace through the election of 1940 and declaring himself against intervention in the current European war, the President did in fact bring us into this war not much more than a year later. He had, in the meantime, after putting through Lend-Lease in March of 1941, sent convoys to accompany our shipments to Europe and attempted, by calling it "patrolling," to camouflage this warlike procedure, which, since Congress had not declared war, was clearly unconstitutional. He had met Churchill at the Atlantic Conference of August, 1941, and had given him secret assurances of collaboration with Britain in the event of her being attacked by Japan and of the occupation of the Azores by American troops to prevent their being occupied by Germany, and had afterwards lied about this to the press; and, together with the British Prime Minister but without consulting American opinion, had drawn up an "Atlantic Charter," in which, though in rather ambiguous language, both nations seemed to pledge themselves to the "destruction of the Nazi tyranny." When our so-called "patrols," as was inevitable, began battling with the Germans on the sea, he deliberately misrepresented the incidents of the *Greer* and the *Kearny*, in September and October of the same year, in such a way as to make it appear that these vessels had been gratuitously torpedoed by the Germans when actually, in company with the British, we had ourselves been pursuing or firing on the submarines before any torpedo was shot. Beard, furthermore, believes that the President, also without taking the public into his confidence, put the Japanese into a position where there was nothing for them to do but attack us. He points to an entry in the diary of Secretary of War Stimson of November 25: "The question [at a White House conference] was how we should maneuver them into the position of firing the first shot without allowing too much danger to ourselves." Five days before this, the Japanese had presented to our government proposals of a decidedly conciliatory kind, and, the day after Stimson's entry—against the advice of the Army and Navy and the Far Eastern Division of the State Department—these were flatly rejected. The Government called upon Japan to withdraw all her forces from China and Indo-China, to recognize only the Chungking government and to respect the Open Door—that policy by which the United States, together with other powers, had maintained its own trade with China by preventing her from raising her tariff and in other ways kept her so weak that she fell an easy prey to the Japanese. This rebuff was made so provocative that no Japanese cabinet could have accepted it without being overthrown; but the American people were not told of it till after Pearl Harbor had been attacked. Beard also seems to imply that at Pearl Harbor the Army and Navy were intentionally left in ignorance of the moves of the Japanese, so that they could not avoid this attack, which our government knew was coming. Even if this was not actually the case, their exposure to the Japanese bombs must have been due to incredible shortsightedness. Admiral Kimmel and General Short were, in any case, made the scapegoats and compelled to take all the obloquy without ever being brought into court and allowed to defend themselves. In Russia, they would have been forced to confess and shot. In America, the Republican opposition demanded an investigation and cleared them of the charges against them. Yet the whole thing was very unpleasant, and since key official papers were sometimes withheld at the time of the investigation, we still do not know what had really happened.

Beard seems also to suggest that the whole train of action

—the intention of President Roosevelt to bring us into the war—was started by the second financial crash of the autumn of 1937 and the resulting recrudescence of labor trouble. This had followed a defeat for the President: Congress had blocked his attempt, in the interests of New Deal legislation, to add new judges to the Supreme Court's nine. His first move toward intervention—the "quarantine speech" in Chicago—occurred on October 5. Beard has made of this chain of events what is really a horror story almost comparable to *The Turn of the Screw*, if we assume that in the latter the narrator has herself imagined the ghosts and is herself the tormentor of the children. The narrative of Beard has a similar twist: the gay Hudson River squire, the champion of the "Four Freedoms," the benefactor of the "common man," surreptitiously and unconstitutionally, imposes on his people conscription, sends them abroad to die and to inflict death by methods as cruel as any in use by the Nazis, and leaves it to his successor to go the Nazis one better by destroying whole Japanese towns—killing or crippling for life all ages and sexes of noncombatants—through the effects of radioactivity. Charles Beard made a useful contribution to our understanding of recent events when he presented the story in this way. Yet the picture is not a complete one. His mind was incisive and clear, but tended to be rather two-dimensional. Too purposive and flint-like himself to understand the basic porousness of Roosevelt, he does not see that, in the early stages, at any rate, the President was responding to pressures. He resisted the pressure of Stimson to bring us into the war at once; he seems even to have made some effort to resist the pressure of Churchill; but he did, in the long run, decide to push us into the general mess and he did pretend to the public that he had not made such a decision. Why did he behave in this way? Inability to resist England? The fact that the Navy was his favorite toy? A real fear of domination by Hitler? And how did he persuade people to follow him? How did he get us committed, trapped in the Army again, without our ever having consented to anything? There had been strong opposition in Congress, and under the leadership of John L. Lewis, a large bloc of labor had op-

posed intervention. There had seemed to exist in all classes
and localities an overwhelming sentiment against it. Did
Roosevelt overcome this by his tact and his sense of timing?
By his plausible propaganda? By appealing to our own ap-
prehensions of Hitler—which were to cause us to ally ourselves with another tyrant equally atrocious. I doubt it: both
Roosevelt and the country at large were moved mainly by
the irresistible instinct of power to expand itself, of well-
organized human aggregations to absorb or impose themselves on other groups. If it had not been for this instinct—
a propulsion we rarely confess and which proceeds, as a matter of fact, from a domain far below our rational minds—we
should never, for all Hitler's crimes, have sent our soldiers to
Europe at all; nor should we ever, for all our desire to have a
free hand in exploiting China, have provoked a war with
Japan, any more than the zeal of the Abolitionists to see the
Negroes freed plus the desire of the commercial North to
protect its manufactures could by themselves have started the
Civil War. We thought we were liberating Europe and fend-
ing off the imperialism of feudal Japan, but we turned up
after the war occupying or controlling foreign countries all
over America, Europe, Asia and the Middle East, and sometimes as unwelcome as the French in Algeria, the British in
Cyprus or the Russians in Central Europe. After years of being shocked by the imperialism of others, we are developing
a new kind of our own, and we find ourselves scowling at
the Soviet Union and spending billions for weapons against
it—and weapons even the testing of which is dangerous to
our own population—without any real provocation and for the
simple sub-rational reason that we are challenging the Soviet
Russians for domination of large sections of the world. Is
there no progressive element in these conquests—of the South
by the North in the Civil War, of Germany by the Allies?
It is futile, at this time of day, to approach such situations
in these terms. We know that superior civilizations have
fallen before barbarous ones, which were simply more savage
and more ravenous, and that great "ideological" conflicts such
as the wars between Christians and Mohammedans and between Catholics and Protestants have ended with stabilized

stalemates, in which the two irreconcilable faiths settled down to live side by side. The only thing of which we can be sure is that the impulse to widen the scope of the territory ruled by one's will appears to be universal save in isolated places like the South Sea Islands where there is little opportunity for it, and that there is something about the spectacle of a nation throwing out its chest and indulging in warlike behavior which leads other nations, however remote, to behave in the same way. But in the interests of world peace and world civilization there is nothing at all to be gained—although, of course, such pretenses are necessary in inducing populations to go to war—by adopting self-righteous attitudes toward the people we propose to subdue, or by whom we have been subdued. The Nazis smothered people in gas-ovens but we burned them alive with flame-throwers, and, bomb for bomb, we did worse than the Nazis with their long-distance buzz-bombs and rockets. We justify the horrors we have perpetrated on the ground of military necessity and condemn the slaughter of the Jews as gratuitous, inhuman and horrible. Yet the Nazis, absurd though we think them and suicidal though this policy proved, imagined, as everybody else did, that they were acting in the interests of national defence. The important thing today to realize is that, though this primitive animal instinct to challenge, to subdue and, if possible, to exploit other groupings of human beings may be more or less unattractively exercised—to the man on the receiving end it is bound to be unattractive—it springs always from the same hidden sources, and that it is foolish, not recognizing this, to formulate high-minded "war aims" or to fabricate, after the conflict, retrospective justifications.

When Stimson and the Chinese lobby and Churchill and the British propagandists and the other pro-interventionist elements had finally had their way with the President, and he had gradually worked up the public, and then thrown on the switch with Pearl Harbor, all the usual passions of wartime were at once released. The desire to believe in a bad bad nation which consists entirely of barbarians, or in a wicked wicked man who has put himself outside humanity, always asserts itself on these occasions. One meets it often on a lesser scale in the attitude of some little country town toward some almost identical town only a few miles off down the road. We most of us know very well that we are not nearly so good as we should like to be, and the creation of a ripsnorting bugaboo stimulates our sense of virtue and enables us to be perfectly sure we are fighting on the side of the right, with, invariably, God behind us. Hitler *was* certainly bad enough to justify real fear and hatred, but, crazily idealistic, he was less of a villain than Stalin, who was supposed to be on our side; and, at the time of the earlier war, we had behaved, to a lesser degree, in the same way about the Kaiser, with whom, only a few years before, our ex-President Theodore Roosevelt had been hobnobbing as emperor with emperor. Once the United States had entered the war, we decided— very much like the Germans in relation to the Poles and the Jews—that Germany, adored by Americans all through the nineteenth century, had never been genuinely civilized; and that the Japs, whom we had beamingly applauded at the time of the Russo-Japanese War as "a wonderful little people," became hideous hissing insects which to kill was a moral duty.

This fury—so distorting in its view of the world, so degrading in its effect on ourselves—broke out also, at the time of the war, against an able and courageous man who was regarded as obstructing the "war effort." This was John L. Lewis, the president of the United Mine Workers. He had organized whole industries in the CIO, which, by the end of 1937, had over four million members, and, though Lewis had resigned from it the year before, he had remained the great power in the labor world. Not believing that Franklin Roosevelt would run for a third term, he had attempted to incorporate in the CIO the Works Progress Administration, which created federal jobs for the unemployed, and had ambitions either to run for Vice-President on the Democratic ticket or to found a new political party of which he should be the leader. When Roosevelt was reëlected, John Lewis began to attack him, and there ensued a duel to the death between Roosevelt and Lewis, which will provide one of the most dramatic chapters for the historian of this period. That Lewis won this duel with Roosevelt—though he was afterwards defeated under Truman—has been somewhat obscured by the fact that two of his decisive victories occurred at moments when public events diverted attention from them. In the strike of the steel industry's "captive mines"—when there had been talk of bringing in troops —Lewis compelled the President to appoint an arbitration board through which it at last became possible to secure for them a union shop. But this occurred the same day as Pearl Harbor. Though Lewis had opposed our intervention in the war, he supported it after this; but the Government had frozen wages at a level where they were quite insufficient to meet the increased cost of living, and, despite the loud cries of disloyalty, he did not hesitate to have his miners continue to strike. These strikes were strategic, sporadic; and Lewis had always made certain that there was enough coal available for war needs; but he was soon declared a public enemy and bitterly denounced by the operators, the press and the armed forces. This did not, however, daunt him, and he managed in 1945 to wrest from the masters of the coal industry a more nearly adequate wage for the miners. But the next day the President died.

Knowing something of Lewis's methods in dealing with the independent miners' unions in the cases described above, during the days before labor was encouraged by the Government, I was not under the least illusion that John Lewis was any less unscrupulous than F.D.R. himself. I had written in *Inaugural Parade* of "the suggestion of a possible dictatorship," but in this I was mainly following the contemporary line of Marxism, according to which the dictatorship of Stalin was the beneficent dictatorship of the working class while the dictatorship of anyone else meant the maleficent dictatorship of fascism. I was later at least partly won over by the early policies of the New Deal, and it took me some time to see that not merely Hitler and Stalin but Roosevelt and Lewis, too, had all certain tendencies in common—that they all, under differing conditions and to very different degrees, represented a general development in the direction of one-man power. All the radicals of that time like myself who were impressed by the efforts of the Soviet Union without any first-hand experience of Russia were bemused by a certain utopianism, against which—in spite of the ridicule that Marx and Engels had poured on their utopian predecessors—we had not been put on our guard by these two "scientific" socialists because Marx's own Hebraic vision of the future of human society was utopian to the point of apocalypse. When, in *Senator and Engineer,* I wrote about Mr. H. J. Freyn's returning from Soviet Russia full of enthusiasm for the Five-Year Plan and intimating this enthusiasm to the efficiency experts of the Taylor Society, it did not occur to me that such a message communicated to such an audience might, in the long run, have onerous consequences; when, in *Tennessee Agrarians,* I intrepidly announced that the only way to rescue our industrial society was through "the development of mechanical technique" and "the rigorous ordering of activities," I did not suspect that these methods, applied by a national government, might impose a stern regimentation not much different from what I disliked in the old kind of industrial community. I could never have foreseen at that time that the dissatisfied but stream-lined type of minor career executive that I was describing in *Mr. and Mrs. X* would, in some cases, a few years later—when the Kremlin had turned bureaucratic—be capable of splitting his allegiance between his own and the Soviet government, regarding the latter now as potentially the great super-industrial-machine, the great over-all super-bureaucracy: For me and for others like me, the Kremlin meant the Third International, and this meant the organization of the "workers of the world" to vindicate their human rights against everything we hated in contemporary society.

Charles A. Beard, in the final chapter of the second of these volumes on our foreign policy, has shown how the American public submitted with an ominous readiness to Roosevelt's devious methods and were led by his mesmeric influence to enter a foreign war which they had formerly wished to avoid. I did not realize that mechanized man was everywhere in process of surrendering his rights—his ideas, his desires, his freedom of movement, his organic personality itself—to the requirements of the great machines, built of human as well as of inorganic matter, which were everywhere taking over. Nor do these governments today, at the point we have reached, seem even to need a director; the people continue to obey them without even a top man to idealize.

So I cannot repress a foolish nostalgia, after reviewing the pages above—in these days of an administration which is as nearly as possible faceless and which seems to keep blindly going without anyone in particular directing it—for the prophets and fighters of those days, those desperate days when nothing worked: the Mustes, the Wiecks, the Frank Keeneys (poor fellow, he reverted to drink), along with how many others with whom I then came into contact but whom I have not revived in this volume. Of course, such nostalgia *is* foolish. In our Martin Luther Kings and Thurgood Marshalls today, facing the enemies of Negro rights, in Walter Reuther, who has organized the auto workers, the American tradition of political courage still stubbornly and toughly lives; and in how many others, no doubt, that, no longer a practicing journalist, I have not been able to see in action. A. J. Muste, at seventy-two, is the leader of a civil disobedience group protesting by Gandhian methods against war and nuclear weapons, who have been getting themselves arrested for trespassing on a Nevada bomb site when an explosion was about to take place and who have even been sentenced to jail in New York for refusing to comply last summer with the Civil Defence regulations at the time of the mock raid. But these incidents were hardly reported in the press. It has recently been asserted by the FBI, in connection with an American Forum for Socialist Education, that Muste has "long fronted for Communists," and something of this, with the denial of Muste, reached the columns of the New York *Times*. But the activities of this veteran of labor, this astute and courageous idealist, have otherwise attracted no attention. He is not even to be found in *Who's Who*. At the moment the prospect is dismal. The papers, with King Saud and Suez, the bomb tests, the crushing of Hungary, the colossal corruption of certain of the unions, the monotonous *gaffes* of Dulles and the President's invalidism, are likely to poison one's breakfast, to unsettle one's morale for work.

In the meantime, when I revisited Washington in the spring of 1953, it did not make upon me at all the impression of "a litter of brickyard fragments" or of an "old brick and marble shell"; nor was the Capitol so much a cynosure that its effect of being made of "white rubber" seemed to dominate the Washington scene. The city had changed very much since I had seen it last, before the war. I realized—and with some surprise—that Washington was now a world capital. Our recent expansion had made it so. The new National Gallery of Art had given it an artistic importance that the city had hitherto lacked; the older Washington galleries, as it were, now clustered about it and—together with the Library of Congress, the Folger Library and the Smithsonian Institute —seemed to coagulate as a cultural store that one had hardly before been aware of. The Federal Bureau of Investigation, with its exhibits of fingerprinting and demonstrations of marksmanship, had become a great sight for tourists. The young man who took us around told us that he worked in the fingerprint department, but that employees were made to conduct these tours in order to give them practice in talking to people and—it was the era of the McCarthyan denunciations—in "controlling nervousness." He did seem under a certain strain, and he was given an opportunity to exercise his power to control it when he encountered two girls who had made the mistake of climbing the stairs by themselves. He had them go back to the bottom floor and come up by the elevator. I had been informed by visitors from Europe—invited by the State Department, subdivision International Information Exchange of Persons—that they had been subjected in Washington to a certain amount of Sovietesque indoctrination, had been given a schedule of lectures and films on American town government, maternity hospitals, etc., which, however, despite cordial pressures, they were not actually compelled to attend. An Italian friend from Rome had told me that an official greeter had explained to him that a little stream which now flows under

the city had originally been called the Tiber, expecting, as
the Italian annoyedly thought, that he would take up the
proffered cue and reply that Washington was the new Rome.
Quite Roman, in any case, was the enormous new marble
building—provided since I had last been in Washington—
in which the Supreme Court sits. It made an overpowering
contrast to the Court's former quarters in the Capitol, and
I reflected that, if anything in Washington deserved such
imperial housing, it was now the United States Supreme
Court, which has become more and more important as the
arbitrator of our complicated problems and as the guardian
of our citizens' rights. Enduring through the ups and downs
of the varying administrations, the alternations of parties in
power—though it has had, of course, its own vicissitudes—
it has survived to become today perhaps the most morally impressive of our original institutions.